The Research Experience

Sara Miller McCune founded SAGE Publishing in 1965 to support the dissemination of usable knowledge and educate a global community. SAGE publishes more than 1000 journals and over 800 new books each year, spanning a wide range of subject areas. Our growing selection of library products includes archives, data, case studies, and video. SAGE remains majority owned by our founder and after her lifetime will become owned by a charitable trust that secures the company's continued independence.

Los Angeles | London | New Delhi | Singapore | Washington DC | Melbourne

The Research Experience

Planning, Conducting, and Reporting Research

Ann Sloan Devlin

Connecticut College

Los Angeles | London | New Delhi
Singapore | Washington DC | Melbourne

FOR INFORMATION:

SAGE Publications, Inc.

2455 Teller Road

Thousand Oaks, California 91320

E-mail: order@sagepub.com

SAGE Publications Ltd.

1 Oliver's Yard

55 City Road

London EC1Y 1SP

United Kingdom

SAGE Publications India Pvt. Ltd.

B 1/I 1 Mohan Cooperative Industrial Area

Mathura Road, New Delhi 110 044

India

SAGE Publications Asia-Pacific Pte. Ltd.

3 Church Street

#10–04 Samsung Hub

Singapore 049483

Acquisitions Editor: Leah Fargotstein

Developmental Editor: Eve Oettinger

Editorial Assistant: Yvonne McDuffee

Production Editor: Veronica Stapleton Hooper

Copy Editor: Sheree Van Vreede

Typesetter: C&M Digitals (P) Ltd.

Proofreader: Lawrence Baker

Indexer: Sheila Bodell

Cover Designer: Karine Hovsepian

Marketing Manager: Susannah Goldes

eLearning Editor: Laura Kirkhuff

Copyright © 2018 by SAGE Publications, Inc.

All trademarks depicted within this book, including trademarks appearing as part of a screenshot, figure, or other image, are included solely for the purpose of illustration and are the property of their respective holders. The use of the trademarks in no way indicates any relationship with, or endorsement by, the holders of said trademarks. Qualtrics is a registered trademark of the Qualtrics software company, Provo, Utah. Google Glass, Google Scholar, and Google Docs are registered trademarks of Google Inc., Mountain View, California. Skype, Microsoft Word, Excel, and PowerPoint are registered trademarks of the Microsoft Corporation, Redmond, Washington. PsycARTICLES, PsycINFO, and PsycTESTS are registered trademarks of the American Psychological Association, Chicago, Illinois. ILLiad is a registered trademark of OCLC Online Computer Library Center, Inc., Columbus, Ohio. AmazonMTurk is a registered trademark of Amazon.com, Inc., Seattle, Washington. SurveyMonkey is a registered trademark of SurveyMonkey.com, Palo Alto, California. SPSS is a registered trademark of International Business Machines (IBM) Corporation, Armonk, New York. Uber is a registered trademark of Uber Technologies Inc., San Francisco, California. Myers-Briggs is a registered trademark of Consulting Psychologist's Press, Sunnyvale, California. The Multiple Affect Adjective Checklist-Revised (MAACL-R) is a registered trademark of Educational and Industrial Testing Service (EdITS), San Diego, California. MMPI is a registered trademark of Psychological Corporation, San Antonio, Texas. The University Residence Environment Scale, Bem Sex Role Inventory, State-Trait Anxiety Inventory for Adults, and Moos Family Environment Scale (FES) are registered trademarks of Mind Garden, Inc., Menlo Park, California. SAT is a registered trademark of College Board, New York, New York. ACT is a registered trademark of ACT, Iowa City, Iowa. NEO-PI-3 is a registered trademark of PAR, Inc., Lutz, Florida. SurveyGizmo is a registered trademark of SurveyGizmo, Boulder, Colorado. QuestionPro is a registered trademark of QuestionPro Inc., San Francisco, California. Palm is a registered trademark of TCL Corporation, Huizhou, Guangdong, China. DOTT is a registered trademark of BBH Design, Pittsburgh, Pennsylvania. NVivo is a registered trademark of QSR International, Doncaster, Victoria, Australia. MAXQDA is a registered trademark of VERBI GmbH, Berlin, Germany. Adobe Photoshop is a registered trademark of Adobe Systems, San Jose, California. iTunes, GarageBand, Mac, and Keynote are registered trademarks of Apple, Inc., Cupertino, California. Facebook is a registered trademark of Facebook, Inc., Menlo Park, California. YouTube is a registered trademark of YouTube LLC, San Bruno, California. Sona Systems is a registered trademark of Sona Systems, Ltd., Tallinn, Spain. Operation is a registered trademark of Hasbro, Inc., Pawtucket, Rhode Island. Dropbox is a registered trademark of Dropbox, Inc., San Francisco, California. Wordle is a trademark of Jonathan Feinberg. SAS is a registered trademark of the SAS Institute, Cary, North Carolina. Stata is a registered trademark of StataCorp, College Station, Texas. MPlus is a registered trademark of Muthen & Muthen, Los Angeles, California. Prezi is a registered trademark of Prezi Inc., Budapest, Hungary. Beck Depression Inventory-II is a registered trademark of the Beck Institute for Cognitive Behavior Therapy, Bala Cynwyd, Pennsylvania. The Profile of Mood States 2nd edition is a trademark of MultiHealth Systems (MHS), North Tonawanda, New York. The Sixteen Personality Factor Questionnaire is a trademark of Pearson, San Antonio, Texas. Eating Disorder Inventory-3 is a registered trademark of PAR: Psychological Assessment Resources, Inc., Lutz, Florida.

Printed in the United States of America

Library of Congress Cataloging-in-Publication Data

Names: Devlin, Ann Sloan, 1948- author.

Title: The research experience : planning, conducting, and reporting research / Ann Sloan Devlin, Connecticut College.

Description: Thousand Oaks, California : Sage, [2018] | Includes bibliographical references and index.

Identifiers: LCCN 2016040974 | ISBN 9781506325125 (pbk. : alk. paper)

Subjects: LCSH: Social sciences—Research—Methodology. | Psychology—Research—Methodology.

Classification: LCC H62 .D49549 2018 | DDC 001.4/2—dc23 LC record available at https://lccn.loc.gov/2016040974

This book is printed on acid-free paper.

17 18 19 20 21 10 9 8 7 6 5 4 3 2 1

BRIEF CONTENTS

DETAILED CONTENTS

PREFACE

Instructors of research methods courses face a major challenge: how to cover the necessary theoretical foundations adequately and provide enough practical help to guide students through a research project. This book is designed to accomplish both goals. The foundations of research design and methods are covered (e.g., how the nature of the research question determines the research design that is used; correlational, experimental, and qualitative designs), but there is a good deal of attention to the practical issues involved in research: finding measures, writing questionnaire items, and using online survey software such as Qualtrics®; obtaining participants and ethical review; statistical analysis; and ultimately writing a report of the research based on the format of the American Psychological Association (i.e., in APA style). Research is increasingly influenced by the availability of the Internet to conduct studies, and this book covers not only online survey software but also crowdsourcing platforms like Amazon Mechanical Turk® as a source of participants. Many research methods books overlook the practical aspects of doing research. The information in this book will enable students to conduct a research methods project in a single semester.

This book can be used in a variety of social and behavioral science departments, from Psychology and Behavioral Neuroscience to Human Development, Education, and Social Work; Sociology, Criminology, and Political Science; Environmental Studies; and Communication. In addition, because research is increasingly a part of the practice of architecture, the book could be used in architecture studio courses where research is discussed. The book could be used in research methods courses taught in one or two semesters. Although statistics are covered in the book, the text is better suited for courses taught after an introductory statistics course.

The practical emphasis in the book is a major feature, and several appendices provide easily understandable summaries of fundamental issues: (a) research approaches, scale types, and associated statistical analyses; (b) a decision tree for statistical analyses (i.e., which test for which research situation); (c) commonly used "analyze" functions in SPSS Statistics®; and (d) sample informed consent and debriefing documents.

Each chapter contains several pedagogical aids to promote understanding and retention of information. For example, three kinds of questions are included in each chapter: **REVISIT and RESPOND**; **Try This Now**; and **Build Your Skills**. The **REVISIT and RESPOND** questions are considered review questions; the **Try This Now** questions push you to expand your understanding of the information just presented in the chapter; and the **Build Your Skills** questions at the end of the chapter are typically more activity-based and invite you to practice some skill introduced in the chapter (e.g., write your own survey questions). The book also contains glossary definitions in the chapter margins when a term is introduced in the text.

ACKNOWLEDGMENTS

First, I would like to acknowledge the work of Vicki Knight, my former editor at SAGE (now retired), who encouraged me to write this text. Without her expression of interest in the project, this book would not have come to fruition. Next, I would like to thank the wonderful team at SAGE: Eve Oettinger, Leah Fargotstein, and Yvonne McDuffee. Upon Vicki's retirement soon after the project was launched, the team took charge and provided excellent counsel about ways to improve the text. They identified reviewers, summarized feedback, provided benchmarks, and were always available to answer questions. In addition, during the production process, Veronica Stapleton Hooper and Sheree Van Vreede kept me on schedule and made sure the final product was visually appealing.

Several people at Connecticut College where I teach deserve special mention. Emily Aylward of the Interlibrary Loan staff processed my request for articles; Ashley Hanson, the library's liaison to the Psychology Department, provided a perspective on the kinds of questions students ask about library materials used in research; and Michael Dreimiller in the Advanced Technology Lab taught me how to prepare high-resolution graphics.

I would also like to thank my research methods students at Connecticut College. The material in this book is the foundation of my research methods class, and the students' sense of accomplishment when they present their research projects at the end of the semester motivated me to share this material with others. Repeatedly students tell me how much they learned in the class and how often they refer to the material provided in the book. After the research methods course, the book continues to be a resource for upper level individual study, honors thesis, and graduate level study.

I would also like to acknowledge the thoughtful, thorough, and constructive feedback from my wonderful reviewers: Charles Baker, Delaware County Community College; Jerry L. Cook, California State University, Sacramento; Douglas P. Cooper, Johnson C. Smith University; Mark W. Dewalt, Winthrop University; Kerri Modry-Mandell, Tufts University; Stephanie Rahill, Georgian Court University; Michael J. Rovito, University of Central Florida; Pauline S. Sawyers, Oakwood University; Jill K. Schurr, Austin College; Christina S. Sinisi, Charleston Southern University; Jeannine Callea Stamatakis, Lincoln University; Angela L. Walker, Quinnipiac University; Deidre L. Wheaton, Jackson State University; and Tina M. Zottoli, Montclair State University.

PUBLISHER'S ACKNOWLEDGEMENTS

SAGE wishes to acknowledge the valuable contributions of the following reviewers.

Charles Baker, Delaware County Community College
Jerry L. Cook, California State University, Sacramento
Douglas P. Cooper, Johnson C. Smith University
Mark W. Dewalt, Winthrop University
Kerri Modry-Mandell, Tufts University
Stephanie Rahill, Georgian Court University
Michael J. Rovito, University of Central Florida
Pauline S. Sawyers, Oakwood University
Jill K. Schurr, Austin College
Christina S. Sinisi, Charleston Southern University
Jeannine Callea Stamatakis, Lincoln University
Angela L. Walker, Quinnipiac University
Deidre L. Wheaton, Jackson State University
Tina M. Zottoli, Montclair State University

INSTRUCTOR TEACHING SITE

SAGE edge for instructors supports teaching by making it easy to integrate quality content and create a rich learning environment for students.

These resources include an extensive test bank, chapter- specific PowerPoint presentations, discussion questions, SAGE journal articles with accompanying review questions, video links, and web resources.

STUDENT STUDY SITE

SAGE edge for students provides a personalized approach to help students accomplish their coursework goals in an easy-to-use learning environment.

This site includes mobile-friendly eFlashcards and web quizzes, SAGE journal articles with accompanying review questions, video links, and web resources.

ABOUT THE AUTHOR

Ann Sloan Devlin teaches at Connecticut College in New London, Connecticut, where she is the May Buckley Sadowski '19 Professor of Psychology. She is a published author with more than three decades of academic and research experience in the area of environmental psychology with a particular focus on health-care environments in recent work. She is currently the editor-in-chief of the journal *Environment and Behavior,* one of two premier journals devoted to the area of environment-behavior studies. She has published four other books, including *Transforming the Doctor's Office: Principles from Evidence-based Design* (2015, Routledge); *What Americans Build and Why: Psychological Perspectives* (2010, Cambridge); *Research Methods: Planning Conducting, and Presenting Research* (2006, Wadsworth/Thomson); and *Mind and Maze: Spatial Cognition and Environmental Behavior* (2001, Praeger). In addition, she has published numerous research articles in such journals as *Environment and Behavior, Journal of Environmental Psychology, Journal of Applied Social Psychology, Professional Psychology: Research & Practice,* and *Journal of Counseling Psychology.* She is a former Environmental Design Research Association board member and secretary. At Connecticut College, she has received the John S. King Faculty Teaching Award and the Helen Brooks Regan Faculty Leadership award. She is also a fellow of Division 34 of the American Psychological Association.

INTRODUCTION

Research. Many professors view research as the foundation of their discipline, the most important part of what they do. I agree. This book is written with the goal of exciting you about the research process. Many of us believe Research Methods is the most important course in the social and behavioral sciences, outweighing statistics, which might be viewed as a support system. Statistics are important, but their real value lies in their use to answer research questions.

Despite whether you plan to conduct research as part of a career, knowing the core values of the research process is important for you. Knowing the fundamentals of research design and analysis will not only help you in your education, but it will also make you a more sophisticated consumer of information in your personal and professional life.

Before taking a course in research methods, students provide interesting answers to the question "What is research?" Some students think doing a Web search constitutes "research" (i.e., looking for articles by a given author); others think writing a literature review is "doing research" (i.e., presenting the existing research). In this book, we take the position that doing research involves (a) the formation of a hypothesis (or statement of purpose in exploratory investigations); (b) the acquisition of data to test that hypothesis or explore relationships (there are many approaches to such data acquisition); (c) evaluation of data or information, typically using inferential statistics; and (d) presentation of a conclusion or summary of findings based on the evidence.

One major hurdle in conducting sound research is avoiding the biases and faulty assumptions that are characteristic of human thought. That is why this book begins with an examination of such biases in thinking. Throughout the book, we will return to this theme of how the way we think influences the choices we make about the research process.

By working through the chapters in this book, you will learn how to:

1. Recognize how biases in thinking are active during the research process

2. Select an area of interest and search the literature to see the published research on that topic

3. Formulate one or more hypotheses based on this literature

4. Design a study based on recommended approaches

5. Select valid and reliable scales to measure your variables of interest

6. Prepare a survey or other instrument to collect your data (using online survey software or a paper-based document)

7. Write a proposal to be evaluated by an ethics board [typically called the Human Subjects Institutional Review Board (IRB)]

8. Collect data (using a campus subject pool, a source off campus, or an online source)

9. Create a data file or download your data from survey software

10. Analyze your data using a statistical package such as SPSS Statistics®

11. Understand what your data mean and how to report your results

12. Discuss your findings in the context of your hypotheses and the broader literature

13. Identify the limitations of your research, and propose directions for future research

Finally, you will learn how to write up this research following the guidelines of *The Publication Manual of the American Psychological Association* (APA, 2010b) and avoid common mistakes in writing and style. In addition, you will learn how to prepare your article for publication and decide where to submit it if that is a goal. At the end of this book, you should have the skills to produce a well-executed project and a well-written research report or manuscript.

The skills you have acquired in the process of conducting research will enable you to compete successfully for internships and jobs. Students who have mastered the research process know how to locate measures, how to use survey software such as Qualtrics®, how to analyze data using SPSS, and perhaps even how to collect data using a crowdsourcing online tool such as AmazonMTurk®. With these skills, you are well positioned to compete effectively for a variety of jobs.

Each chapter contains three kinds of questions to promote learning: **REVISIT and RESPOND; Try This Now;** and **Build Your Skills. REVISIT and RESPOND** items generally ask directly about the information in the chapter (e.g., explain why or list 2 examples of . . .) and would be considered review questions. **Try This Now** questions ask you to pause and stretch a bit to go beyond the information given at the moment (e.g., after reading the list, come up with three additional settings where you think ethnographic research could be conducted, Chapter 6). **Build Your Skills** items at the end of the chapter are either questions or activities that ask you to apply what you have learned to some of the major issues in the chapter. For example, you might be asked to make a case for having institutional review board (IRB) review (see Chapter 4) even for projects with no more than minimal risk or to create an account to try out a free version of an online survey software (see Chapter 5).

RESEARCH, BIASES IN THINKING, AND THE ROLE OF THEORIES

CHAPTER HIGHLIGHTS

- Why research matters
- Humans as limited information processors
- Heuristics (representativeness and availability)
- Shermer's (1997) categories of how thinking goes wrong:
  - Problems in scientific thinking
  - Problems in pseudoscientific thinking
  - Logical problems in thinking
  - Psychological problems in thinking
- The role of commonsense in posing research questions
- The difference between a law, a theory, and a hypothesis
- What makes something a good research question?

WHY RESEARCH MATTERS

In the movie *The Big Short*, which depicted the implosion of the housing market and the collapse of the financial system in the United States, hedge-fund manager Mark Baum (the character played by actor Steve Carell) and his team go out in the field to collect data on the "health" of the housing market. Rather than accepting someone else's conclusion that the housing market was a "bubble" about to burst, they collect their own data by consulting a real estate agent, several mortgage brokers, and even an exotic dancer (who has adjustable rate mortgages on five houses, as it turns out). Social scientists might not consider this credible research, but at least Baum and his team were willing to look at some evidence. As you will learn later in this book, there were some problems with their approach, although their conclusion was correct (it wouldn't have made a good story, otherwise). As we will see in Chapter 9, their sampling strategy was flawed because they looked at only one housing market in the United States (Miami); they needed a random sample of housing markets across the United States to be more certain about the housing bubble.

Every day you see behavior that triggers questions ranging from the mundane—"What do people think of students who wear pajamas to class?"—to the more important—"Do people disclose less information to their health-care providers when a 'medical scribe' (i.e., someone taking notes for the physician) is in the room?" How do we evaluate the research in terms of its credibility? That is, what makes research believable or convincing? What criteria should we use in evaluating the findings of a research study? Courses in research methods provide the tools to evaluate research. Students may take research methods because it is required, but the information will serve them far beyond the course. Learning how to evaluate research may help students make more informed and potentially life-altering decisions in the future (e.g., whether to take a particular medication to treat a condition or how much to pay for a particular home).

Research can help you answer a variety of questions, some of them very important. Being able to evaluate research gives you a powerful set of tools to solve problems, especially because the body of knowledge is expanding exponentially. To ask and answer good questions, it is helpful to understand how humans think because we humans have cognitive capacities that both help (category formation; commonsense; flexibility; creativity) and hurt (stereotypes; **heuristics**, that is shortcuts in thinking) the research process. In fact, the same cognitive capacity can be adaptive in some situations and maladaptive in others. For example, using speed to make a decision under duress might save your life, but it might make you an unreliable eyewitness. Recognizing these cognitive characteristics in yourself will help you maximize the positive aspects and minimize the negative aspects in the research process. In this chapter, you will learn about the kinds of heuristics or shortcuts we use in thinking and how these may shape our approach to research. Armed with this information, you will be better prepared to both evaluate the research that others conduct and carry out your own research.

In this chapter, four categories of how thinking "goes wrong" from a list generated by Michael Shermer (1997) will be highlighted. We will also look at some adaptive

Heuristics: mental shortcuts (e.g., estimations and commonsense) that often guide thinking and problem solving.

characteristics humans have, most notably, commonsense. The chapter also introduces you to the distinctions between law, theory, and **hypothesis** (a proposed explanation for the relationship between variables that must be tested) and explores how a good research question is connected to theory.

THE RESEARCH PROCESS: HUMANS MAKE PREDICTIONS

Humans are limited information processors; what this characteristic means is that we cannot process all incoming information at once. As a consequence, we learn to focus on the most important features of an object (or situation). An important consequence of this limitation is that we are forced to make predictions. Predictions are the essence of research: we make hypotheses (proposed explanations about the relationships of variables we want to test). If you see traffic lined up along an artery where traffic usually flows smoothly, you likely conclude there is some kind of traffic tie-up.

This limited ability to process information has some important effects on how we organize material (and think about research). To manage the overload of information around us, humans evolved to chunk or categorize information into groupings or clusters. This kind of organization leads us to form overarching categories; we have words that designate those categories, like vegetable or sports or furniture. A term that is often used to describe such mental representations of knowledge is a **schema.** If we have a schema for something, we understand its gist or essence; a schema serves as a generalized description of the core characteristics of a given role, object, or event. We might have a schema for a role (e.g., father), for an object (e.g., a chair), or for an event (e.g., going to a restaurant). The benefit of having a schema is that it provides a condensed version of the information that is available about an entity in the world and it helps us make predictions.

Our ability to compartmentalize by categories minimizes the cognitive load and leaves our brains available to respond to incoming information that may have implications for survival (a car speeding toward us; a loud noise). That's the upside. The downside is that such compartmentalization leads to stereotypes and overgeneralizations, which can interfere with thinking objectively about research. Redheads are tempestuous, people who live in Detroit drive American-made cars, New Yorkers like to wear black, and so on. Our propensity for categorization may lead us to minimize the differences across dimensions and to categorize stimuli as similar when, in fact, there may be important differences.

Hypothesis: "a testable proposition based on theory, stating an expected empirical outcome resulting from specific observable conditions" (Corsini, 2002, p. 463).

Schema: mental representation of a category that can be a role, an object, or an event (e.g., parent, table, or going to the dentist, respectively).

HEURISTICS AND THE WORK OF KAHNEMAN AND TVERSKY

We have discussed some advantages and disadvantages to the formation of schemas. Let's talk about some other cognitive characteristics of humans and how they interact with the research process. In particular, we will focus on what are known as cognitive heuristics or mental shortcuts and how they both shape research questions and the answers participants provide.

The researchers Daniel Kahneman and Amos Tversky (see, for example, Kahneman & Tversky, 1972, 1973, 1979; Tversky & Kahneman, 1971, 1973, 1974) studied these predictive tendencies (heuristics) or shortcuts in thinking. Kahneman received the Nobel Prize in Economics (psychologists like to claim him as one of their own) for the work he and Tversky did on these cognitive biases. (Nobel prizes are awarded only to living recipients, and Tversky had died by the time the work was honored.)

We can comprehend the evolutionary value in being an animal that operates on incomplete information and the ability to use schemas for prediction. The work of Kahneman and Tversky focuses on these heuristics or shortcuts and illustrates how these shortcuts may lead us to incorrect decisions. Before you become discouraged about human capabilities, it's useful to remember that the work of Kahneman and Tversky applies to particular kinds of decision-making problems, not to all problems. A good deal of their work focuses on the idea of representativeness (e.g., Kahneman & Tversky, 1972) and **availability** (e.g., Tversky & Kahneman, 1973), *both of which have applications to the research process.* Here the idea of representativeness is its frequency of occurrence in a population. It can also mean the extent to which an array of events or objects or people reflects the characteristics of its parent population (discussed in terms of sampling). Availability involves using examples that come easily to mind (e.g., because you just read an article on that topic).

Availability: one of the heuristics talked about by Kahneman and Tversky (1972) in which we use examples that easily come to mind.

The Representativeness Heuristic in Research

In one of Kahneman and Tversky's classic examples, participants were presented with the following: "All families of six children in a city were surveyed. In 72 families the exact order of births of boys and girls was GBGBBG. What is your estimate of the number of families surveyed in which the exact order of births was BGBBBB?" (Kahneman & Tversky, 1972, p. 432). Not surprisingly, a significant number of the respondents (75 of 92) said the second option was less likely to occur because, as Kahneman and Tversky argued, it seems less representative of the population. When the question is posed in terms of the frequency with which two birth sequences occur (BBBGGG vs. GBBGBG), the same participants pick the second sequence. The first looks "fixed" or nonrandom to us (and them). How representative something looks is one heuristic or bias that may influence the research process. We might select a stimulus (e.g., photograph) as representative of a population of interest (e.g., recreational areas with camp sites) without knowing the full range of existing

FIGURE 1.1 Forest Landscape

©iStockphoto.com/Arsty

sites (compare Figure 1.1 and Figure 1.2), particularly in different geographical regions. If we try to generalize from a limited range of pictures to say something definitive about people's evaluations of such settings, we might be overstating the results.

Although the work of Kahneman and Tversky focuses on the cognitive decision-making process (i.e., about the decisions we make, for example, about stimuli), the idea of representativeness emerges in other ways in research. You may be familiar with such phrases as "a representative sample" or "a randomly selected sample" (the example from *The Big Short* earlier in this chapter raised the issue of sampling; see Chapter 9 for a fuller discussion of sampling).

One central question in every research project is who the participants are and to what extent the results of the study are therefore "representative" of the population of interest. If we do research using a participant pool that consists of students enrolled in an introductory psychology course, we can ask several questions about who participates, starting with the degree to which people who take an introductory course in psychology are representative of that student body as a whole (by gender, race, income, and many other qualities). Every decision we make about securing participants (e.g., the time of day we run the study) is likely to influence the representativeness of our sample and, in turn, of our results.

The Availability Heuristic in Research

Let's now turn to the availability heuristic, the second heuristic from Kahneman and Tversky to be discussed. The availability heuristic suggests that we make decisions to some extent based on how easy it is for us to think of examples from that domain. One well-known example of Kahneman and Tversky's work on availability involves the judgment of word frequency (Tversky & Kahneman, 1973). Take the letter K. Question:

FIGURE 1.2 Desert Landscape

©iStockphoto.com/ SmithMade

In words with three or more letters in English text, does the letter K appear more frequently in the first or third position?

When we hear this question about the letter K, what happens? We start to generate words that BEGIN with the letter K because it is *available* to us. That seems easier to do than to think of words with K in the third position. But, after you've run out of key, knife, knight, and knit, you begin to realize that, well, bake, cake, fake, lake, make, rake, take, bike, hike, like, mike, . . . (k in the third position) generates far more possibilities; in fact, two times as many in a typical text (Tversky & Kahneman, 1973).

The availability heuristic emerges in research in many ways. For example, if we develop a questionnaire that first asks people to rate a list of items, for example, what they like about their university (e.g., food, school spirit, academics, career counseling, cost, and residence halls), and then we ask them an open-ended question about advantages and disadvantages of attending that university, the items from that initial list will be AVAILABLE in memory and will likely influence what people say in the open-ended question. If we had asked the open-ended question first, we might get a different set of responses. Thus, the order in which information is presented to participants may influence their responses and is related to the availability heuristic. Chapter 8 discusses one way to address this problem of availability by doing what is known as **counterbalancing** the order of presentation of materials. In complete counterbalancing, all possible orders of presenting the materials are included in the research approach.

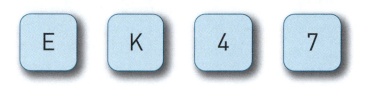

FIGURE 1.3 Example of Wason Selection Task

E K 4 7

Humans Want to Confirm Hypotheses

What we have available in memory influences us in other important ways, specifically when we think about ways to confirm our hypotheses rather than when we think of ways to disconfirm them. Figure 1.3 shows a well-known example of our preference for thinking about information in terms of the way it is presented: the **Wason Selection Task** (1966, 1968). This task involves making decisions about two-sided cards. This task has many variations, but in one version (Figure 1.3), people are told the following: These cards have two sides: a letter of the alphabet on one side and a number on the other. Then people are told a "rule," and their job is to make sure the rule is being followed. Here is the rule: If there's a vowel on one side, there's an even number on the other.

Then they are asked:

Which card or cards do you have to turn over to make sure the rule is being followed?

> ⏩ **Try This Now**
>
> Before You Read Further, what card(s) did you select? People usually select E and frequently E in combination with K and 4; they hardly ever select 7.

Why? One reason is that people heard the statement, "If there's a vowel. . . . ," and so what do they see? They see a vowel (E). They have a vowel available (think availability heuristic), and it seems logical to investigate the other side of that card. And they are correct, at least to that point; they should turn over the E. But they must also turn over the 7 to make sure that there is no vowel on the other side of that card. People don't do that; they don't think to disconfirm the rule.

The Wason Selection Task demonstrates an important part of thinking related to research. Humans have a much easier time thinking of ways to confirm information (think hypotheses) than to disconfirm it. What comes far less easily is taking a disconfirmational strategy to the hypothesis or the theory by seeking to disconfirm it. In research,

Counterbalancing: presenting orders of the treatment to control for the influence of extraneous variables in an experiment.

Wason Selection Task: logic problem in which you have to determine which of four two-sided cards need to be turned over to evaluate the stated hypothesis (e.g., if there is a vowel on one side and there is an even number on the other).

Confirmation bias: tendency to look for information that confirms our hypotheses.

we seem far more willing to seek to confirm rather than to disconfirm. We tend to exhibit what is known as **confirmation bias** in that we look for information that confirms our hypotheses. We also need to ask ourselves the question, what situation(s) would be a good test to show that the hypothesis is *incorrect*?

In the research findings of Kahneman and Tversky, we have already discussed that our cognitive processes are susceptible to a wide range of influences and biases. Even such respected researchers as Kahneman and Tversky may have been susceptible to the biases they studied. In the article "Voodoo Correlations Are Everywhere—Not Only in Neuroscience," Klaus Fiedler (2011) showed that the use of the letter K (discussed earlier in this chapter) for Tversky and Kahneman's (1973) demonstration of the availability heuristic may have used an unrepresentative letter (K). Because this finding has not been replicated with many other letters of the alphabet [as Fiedler reported, citing the work of Sedlmeier, Hertwig, and Gigerenzer (1998)], using K may not have been a good test of Tversky and Kahneman's hypothesis. In selecting their stimulus (K) intuitively, Fiedler explained, Tversky and Kahneman were fallible human beings: "Such an intuitive selection process will typically favor those stimuli that happen to bring about the expected phenomenon, making mental simulation an omnipresent source of bias in behavioral research" (Fiedler, 2011, p. 165).

In other words, Fiedler (2011) argued that the authors (consciously or otherwise) selected a stimulus that was likely to prove their point. The larger message of this research example provides a cautionary tale: As researchers and cognitive animals, we want to validate our hypotheses; by reinforcing what the Wason Selection Task shows, we seek to prove, not to disprove, and we are likely to select stimuli that support our hypotheses rather than stimuli that challenge or refute them.

How can we guard against this common "affirming" behavior? Being aware that we are likely to make these errors is the first step. Asking how we might disprove or refute the hypothesis is another step. Imagining the conditions under which a prediction would not hold is as important as identifying the conditions under which the prediction is likely to hold. In other words, we need to ask ourselves what evidence would counter the hypothesis.

REVIST AND RESPOND

At this point, you should be able to:

- Explain what it means to say humans are limited information processors
- Describe the concept of a schema and its adaptive and maladaptive implications for research
- Define heuristics and give examples of representativeness and availability
- Explain the Wason Selection Task and what it shows about the difference between confirming and disconfirming hypotheses

TABLE 1.1 ■ Twenty-Five Fallacies That Derail Thinking

"Problems in scientific thinking" (pp. 46–48)

1. Theory influences observations
2. The observer changes the observed
3. Equipment constructs results

"Problems in pseudoscientific thinking" (pp. 48–55)

4. Anecdotes do not make a science (stories recounted in support of a claim)
5. Scientific language does not make a science (watch out for jargon)
6. Bold statements do not make claims true
7. Heresy does not equal correctness (belief/opinion contrary to religious doctrine)
8. Burden of proof—convince others of validity of evidence (not of mere existence of evidence)
9. Rumors do not equal reality
10. Unexplained is not inexplicable
11. Failures are rationalized (**pay attention to negative findings**)
12. After-the-fact reasoning (correlations do not mean causation)
13. Coincidence (gambler's fallacy)
14. Representativeness (base rate)

"Logical Problems in Thinking" (pp. 55–58)

15. Emotive words and false analogies (not proof; merely tools of rhetoric)
16. *Ad ignorantiam*—an appeal to ignorance; belief should come from positive evidence in support of a claim, not from lack of evidence for or against a claim
17. *Ad hominen* (to the man) and *tu quoque* (you also)—watch that you focus on the content, not on the character of the person making the argument or on the consistency of the behavior of the person relative to the argument the person is making
18. Hasty generalization—prejudice/improper induction; conclusions before facts warrant it
19. Overreliance on authorities (false positive: accept results just because supported by someone admired; false negative: reject results just because supported by someone you disrespect)
20. Either-or—fallacy of negation or the false dilemma (creation vs. evolution); dichotomizing the world, such that if you reject one position, you are forced to accept the other
21. Circular reasoning—begging the question; tautology
22. *Reductio ad absurdum* and the slippery slope—refutation of an argument by carrying the argument to its logical end and so reducing it to an absurd conclusion

"Psychological Problems in Thinking" (pp. 58–61)

23. Effort inadequacies and the need for certainty, control, and simplicity (have to practice thinking logically and clearly; thinking is skilled work)
24. Problem-solving inadequacies—we don't seek evidence to disprove
25. Ideological immunity, or the Planck problem—we all resist paradigm change; opponents have to die out gradually; we build up immunity against new ideas; the higher the IQ, the greater the potential for ideological immunity

Source: Adapted from Shermer, 1997, pp. 44–61.

OTHER PROBLEMS IN THINKING

We have discussed several problems in thinking; let's discuss a few more and in the process reinforce some of the information we have covered. In Shermer's (1997) *Why People Believe Weird Things,* Chapter 3 is titled "How Thinking Goes Wrong: Twenty-Five Fallacies That Lead Us to Believe Weird Things." In that chapter, Shermer discussed four major categories of difficulties in how we think about evidence and data (Table 1.1). To illustrate the categories and the problems they present for our research, we will focus on examples (see shading) in each category.

Problems in Scientific Thinking: Theory Influences Observations

As part of the category "Problems in Scientific Thinking," Shermer listed "Theory influences observations" (1997, p. 46). What this statement means for us is that theory in some sense directs, shapes, or may even limit the kinds of observations we make. Again, we see that we might limit ourselves because we look for a particular kind of behavior rather than being open to any kind of activity in the environment. Most people have never heard a peacock's scream and would never guess that the sound they hear when visiting a suburb outside Los Angeles comes from that bird. Why? Because most of us think peacocks are birds that reside in captivity. But peacocks have roamed wild in some places (like Rolling Hills on the Palos Verdes Peninsula in California) for more than 100 years. We limit our choices to the most likely suspects. As Shermer stated, "[O]ur perceptions of reality are influenced by the theories framing our examination of it" (p. 46).

Problems in Pseudoscientific Thinking: Scientific Language Does Not Make a Science

Pseudoscientific thinking: involves reference to a theory or method that is without scientific support.

Pseudoscientific thinking involves reference to a theory or method that is without scientific support. What we are thinking about may be called science, but it may have no scientific basis, and it is not based on the scientific method. Shermer notes, "Scientific language does not make a science" (p. 49). It is tempting to use words that sound impressive and appear in a discipline, even when no convincing explanation of their meaning or importance is provided. What's better than coming up with a new term, especially with your name linked to it? Social science is replete with such terms. The use of scientific terms is not necessarily incorrect, but what is a problem is the use of terms without an explanation of their meaning in everyday language.

Furthermore, using such words without supporting evidence and confirmation is an example of pseudoscientific thinking. In the area of health-care research, for example, many architects now use the term *evidence-based design* to describe their work. Without a clear understanding of what that terms means, and what qualifies as credible evidence (e.g., subjective measures such as patients' self-reports? Objective measures such as vital signs, levels of pain medication, and recovery time?), simply using that phrase makes designers sound more authoritative than they actually are. The use of a term in a discipline without an explanation of its meaning or clear indication of how the term is operationalized (i.e., how it is being measured) creates misunderstanding.

COINCIDENCE (GAMBLER'S FALLACY) AND REPRESENTATIVENESS (BASE RATE) Two other important aspects of this category "Problems in Pseudoscientific Thinking" according to Shermer (1997) are **coincidence (gambler's fallacy)** (pp. 53–54) and **representativeness (base rate)** (pp. 54–55). These two aspects frequently appear when we make assumptions in the research process. In the gambler's fallacy, we commit a logical fallacy and lose sight of the facts of probability; we think an event is less likely to occur if it has just occurred or that it is likely to occur if it hasn't for a while. When we toss a coin, we have a 50–50 chance of heads. Each toss of the coin is an independent event. Yet if we have seen three heads in a row, we may be very likely to predict that the next toss will yield tails when, in fact, the odds of a tail (or head) appearing on the next coin toss is still 50–50.

A related idea is the mistaken belief that correlation (for example, of two co-occurring events) is causation. Superstitions are an example of this erroneous thought process. Athletes are notorious for superstitions (Vyse, 1997). For example, if you win two games in a row in which you tie your left shoelace first as you prepared for the game, you may believe that tying that left shoe first influenced the victories. These two events (left shoe tying and game victory) are correlated, that is, when one event happened the other also happened, but shoe tying did not achieve the victory. We are pattern seekers because we are limited information processors. We look for causal relationships that may not exist; we see patterns (a series of coins coming up heads) and predict that the next coin toss will produce a tail. We make this prediction because such an outcome would be more representative of the occurrence of events as we know them. This is an aspect of representativeness (which we discussed earlier in the chapter).

In representativeness, we are on the lookout for events in the world that match or resemble the frequency of occurrence of those events in our experience. When we encounter a situation that does not look representative, we are likely to ignore, disregard, or mistrust it. As we have already discussed in this chapter, Kahneman and Tversky's work is full of examples of problems in thinking related to representativeness. The base rate is the frequency with which an event (e.g., twins, a hole in one, or perfect SATs) occurs in a population. We may have little knowledge of the actual base rate of events in a population, and we often overestimate the occurrence of events (e.g., likelihood of a plane crash or

Coincidence (gambler's fallacy): thinking that an event is less likely to occur if it has just occurred or that it is likely to occur if it hasn't occurred for some time (e.g., assuming a slot machine will pay off because it hasn't for the past few hours).

Representativeness (base rate): one of the heuristics talked about by Kahneman and Tversky (1972) in which we make decisions based on how representative or characteristic of a particular pattern of events data are (e.g., people think the birth order BGBBGG is more representative of a sequence of births than is BBBGGG).

likelihood of winning the lottery). Our overestimation of the base rate may be influenced by the availability heuristic (discussed earlier in the chapter). If we have read or heard about a recent plane crash, for example, we are more likely to overestimate the occurrence of a plane crash for our upcoming trip.

The odds of dying from a motor vehicle accident are far greater than the odds of dying from a commercial airline accident. Likewise, we are far, far more likely to die from heart disease than we are from homicide (Kluger, 2006). In other words, we are not logic machines, and we don't carry around statistics in our heads; instead we carry estimates of events based on the frequency with which we have encountered them, and exposure to media typically elevates our estimates of the base rate, or the frequency with which events actually occur.

These errors in understanding the base rate underscore the importance in research of assessing the degree to which participants in your study may have familiarity with the topics under investigation. For example, if you were evaluating patients' reactions to hospitalization, you would certainly want to ask a question about the number of prior hospitalizations. You want to ask yourself what aspects of a participant's background might have relevance and possibly influence your research. As another example, if you were investigating students' satisfaction with their educational institution, it might be helpful to know if the college they attend was their first choice.

> **» Try This Now**
>
> What kinds of background variables and experiences might influence students' satisfaction with their educational institution, aside from qualities of the institution itself?

Logical Problems in Thinking: Hasty Generalization and Overreliance on Authorities

Hasty generalization: reaching decisions before evidence warrants, or faulty induction.

Faulty induction: reasoning from the premises to a conclusion that is not warranted.

Among the logical problems in thinking that Shermer lists, he gives us "**hasty generalization**" (p. 56)—reaching conclusions before the evidence warrants—or **faulty induction**. Induction is reasoning from premises to a probable conclusion. In faulty induction, the conclusion is not warranted. People also describe this kind of thinking as stereotyping. As but one example, when we take a limited range of evidence about an individual and ascribe those qualities to the group of which the person is a member, we are stereotyping. A popular television show,[1] *The Big Bang Theory*, has characters that embody stereotypes, whether

---

[1]Ranked seventh in prime broadcast network television shows in the United States the week of June 1, 2015, according to Nielsen (**http://www.nielsen.com/us/en/top10s.html**).

Sheldon Cooper, the brilliant but interpersonally less skilled theoretical physicist, or Amy Farrah Fowler, his "girlfriend" (those who faithfully watch the show will recall that initially Sheldon describes Amy as a "girl" and his "friend" but not his "girlfriend" in the traditional meaning of the term). For long-term watchers of the show, the staying power of the series comes through the evolution of these characters over time as they become less true to the stereotype they represent. But many individuals argue that the portrayal of these characters reinforces unfortunate and hurtful stereotypes about scientists and gender (Egan, 2015).

Hasty generalizations are a problem in many steps of the research process. We can consider the problem of hasty generalization when we talk about how much data are needed before conclusions are warranted. We can also include hasty generalization when we talk about sampling (see Chapter 9). Because humans are limited information processers and pattern seekers, we are eager to take information and package or categorize it; this process makes the information more manageable for us, but it may lead to errors in thinking.

A second kind of logical problem in thinking that Shermer lists is "**overreliance on authorities**" (pp. 56–57). In many cases, we accept the word or evidence provided by someone we admire without carefully examining the data. In the domain of research, we may have an overreliance on the published word; that is, we assume that when we read a published article, we should unquestioningly accept its data. Unfortunately, as we increasingly observe in academia, we should be far more skeptical about what has been published. Instances of fraud are numerous. Consider the relatively recent case of fraud involving a graduate student, Michael LaCour (and Donald Green, the apparently unknowing faculty mentor), who published work in *Science* (LaCour & Green, 2014) showing that people's opinions about same-sex marriage could be changed by brief conversations (**http://retractionwatch .com/2015/05/20/author-retracts-study-of-changing-minds-on-same-sex-marriage-after-colleague-admits-data-were-faked/**). LaCour apparently fabricated the data that were the basis of his article, and the story of how this came to light reinforces the idea that findings must be reproducible. Two graduate students at the University of California–Berkeley are responsible for identifying the anomalies in LaCour's data, which were revealed when these students from Berkeley tried to replicate the study. This revelation quickly led to the identification of other inconsistencies (e.g., the survey research firm that was supposed to have collected the data had not; no **Qualtrics**® file of the data was ever created).

The broader issue of reproducibility has been in the news recently with what is known as the **Reproducibility Project** (**https://osf.io/ezcuj/**), in which scientists are trying to reproduce the findings of 100 experimental and correlational articles in psychology published in three journals. The results (Open Science Collaboration, 2015) have been less than encouraging as many replications produced weaker findings than the original studies did. The authors emphasize that science needs both tradition (here reproducibility) as well as innovation to advance and "verify whether we know what we think we know."

Overreliance on authorities: trusting authorities without examining the evidence.

Qualtrics®: online platform for survey research.

Reproducibility Project: project in which researchers are trying to reproduce the findings of 100 experimental and correlational articles in psychology.

Simply because an article has been published does not make it good science. Even well-known researchers publish articles that contribute little to the literature. In Chapter 2, we will see that we also need to take into account the standards of particular journals (e.g., their acceptance rates, scope of research they publish, and rigor of methodology) rather than treating the work in all journals as equal. Relying on authority without questioning the evidence leads to mistakes in repeating what might have been weak methodology, for example. As Julian Meltzoff (1998) stated in his useful book about critical thinking in reading research, we should approach the written (here published) word with skepticism and always ask, "show me." Meltzoff went on to say, "Critical reading requires a mental set of a particular kind," and he believed this mental set can be "taught, encouraged, and nurtured" (p. 8). The value of a particular argument has to be demonstrated with evidence that stands up to rigorous questioning. In regard to the research process, being willing to challenge authority by asking questions is an essential skill.

Psychological Problems in Thinking: Problem-Solving Inadequacy

Problem-solving inadequacy: when we do not seek to disprove hypotheses, only to confirm them.

The last category Shermer offered is "Psychological Problems in Thinking." Among the problems identified is the idea that we exhibit "**problem-solving inadequacy**" (1997, p. 59) when we don't seek evidence to disprove, only to prove. We discussed this issue earlier in the context of the Wason Selection Task where people rarely thought that turning over the 7 was necessary. We invariably turn over the E (that is, look for evidence to confirm the hypothesis).

Consider the sobering evidence that "most doctors quickly come up with two or three possible diagnoses from the outset of meeting a patient. . . . All develop their hypotheses from a very incomplete body of information. To do this, doctors use shortcuts. These are called heuristics" (Groopman, 2007, p. 35). The word *heuristics* is familiar to us from material covered earlier in this chapter and, unfortunately, in the current context! Once we develop our hypotheses, we tend to stick with them; relinquishing them is difficult.

DOING SCIENCE AS TRADITION AND INNOVATION

When we think about how science advances, we can talk about the social and behavioral sciences broadly as a combination of tradition and innovation. As the work of Kahneman and Tversky (and others cited here) has shown, tradition is easier than innovation. It is much easier to operate within an existing framework and harder to figure out how to head in new directions. Most of the time we hope to master the tradition through a review of the literature, and then we take a small step toward innovation by figuring out how we can advance the discipline with this small step. We have to write a literature review or

FIGURE 1.4 Examples of Representational Images of Nature

Photo © Ann Devlin

summary of the work in the field that shows our knowledge of past work; at the same time, we have to propose research that goes beyond the existing literature in some way. We should be able to answer the question, "What's new here?" If views to everyday nature enhance recovery for surgical patients (Ulrich, 1984), why not see whether substitutes for nature such as representational paintings of nature have beneficial effects such as pain reduction. That use of "manufactured nature" would be a step forward. Researchers have done this work, and such representational paintings of nature do in fact reduce stress (Hathorn & Nanda, 2008; see Figure 1.4).

In your work, the problem of being governed by a **paradigm** or way of thinking about a research topic directly affects the kinds of research questions you are willing to ask. Some of the major changes in science have come from young researchers who perhaps were not fully wedded to a single theory or methodology (that hypothesis itself might be testable). As but one example, George Sperling's (1960) doctoral thesis at Harvard University transformed the way we think about the storage capacity of short-term visual memory by introducing the partial report technique. Prior to that time, using the whole report technique, participants in research in visual memory storage had to call out or recall everything that they had just seen in a brief exposure to visual stimuli. Sperling's breakthrough was to have participants call out information presented on only one row in the visual array of three rows (Figure 1.5).

Paradigm: in science, an overarching approach to a field of inquiry that frames the questions to be asked and how research is conducted.

FIGURE 1.5 Example of Sperling's (1960) Partial Report Technique

"7 1 V F
X L 5 3
B 4 W 7"

Source: Adapted from Sperling, 1960, p. 3.

Sperling (1960) argued that to recall the information successfully from this *one row*, participants must have had *ALL of the rows available* at the time the particular row in question was cued. The cue was presented through an auditory tone (high, medium, or low) to correspond to the position of the rows of information on the page. This approach is a masterful example of tradition and innovation.

REVISIT AND RESPOND

At this point, you should be able to:

- Give an example from each one of Shermer's (1997) categories:
  - Problems in scientific thinking
  - Problems in pseudoscientific thinking
  - Logical problems in thinking
  - Psychological problems in thinking
- Explain why science is a combination of tradition and innovation

RESEARCH AND THE VALUE OF COMMON SENSE

You might be a bit discouraged about how limitations in thinking affect the research process. There is reason for concern; on the other hand, humans have some remarkable cognitive assets.

In 1995, Marvin Minsky gave an address at Connecticut College at the dedication of its new interdisciplinary science center, funded by the Olin Foundation. His address was as wide ranging and stimulating as his research. Minsky is considered a founder of artificial intelligence, and one of his corporate affiliations was as a fellow of Walt Disney Imagineering (http://web.media.mit.edu/~minsky/minskybiog.html). Minsky died in 2016. Imagineers, as the name suggests, were part of a research and development think tank and worked on imagining ideas that might result in possibilities for entertainment (Remnick, 1997). In David Remnick's article describing Disney Corporation's view of amusement in the future, Minsky was reported to have accepted the offer to be an Imagineer because it "reminded him of the early days at the Artificial Intelligence Lab" (Remnick, 1997, p. 222). In describing his view of the future, Minsky said: "I'm telling you: all the money and the energy in this country will eventually be devoted to doing things with your mind and your time" (p. 222). Speaking about what he thought future amusements might have in store, he said, "you'll put on a suit and a special pair of glasses, and you'll become involved in an experiential form of entertainment" (p. 222). Virtual reality and Google Glass®? This article was published almost 20 years ago.

Minsky was obsessed (not too strong a word) with the workings of the mind. Among Minsky's many contributions, his book *The Society of Mind* (1985), written for a general audience, stands out because it provides a perspective on what makes the human mind amazing and distinctive. The book is presented as a series of short topics and reflects Minsky's wide-ranging approach to discourse. Researchers often focus exclusively on the errors we make (Kahneman, 1991); in this book, Minsky also points out some of our cognitive assets, in particular, commonsense.

Discussing all of the processes that must be involved when making something with children's blocks, Minsky stated, "In science, one can learn the most by studying what seems the least" (1985, p. 20). Furthermore, "What people vaguely call common sense is actually more intricate than most of the technical expertise we admire" (1985, p. 72). Minsky argued it is easier to represent expertise than commonsense because with expertise you are dealing with a limited domain of knowledge; humans, on the other hand, bring to bear many different kinds of expert systems in solving the simplest of everyday problems. Hence, commonsense is anything but common, according to Minsky.

Much of what Minsky said can be applied to the research process. Research does not have to be sophisticated to be powerful; in fact, you could argue that the most powerful research is simple and elegant [think of Sperling's (1960) partial report technique described earlier in this chapter]. People often complain that results in the social sciences are obvious, that is, we just demonstrate what everyone already knows—the we-knew-it-all-along effect, which is also called **hindsight bias**. But many such findings are not obvious until after you conduct the research. Commonsense may lead us to ask questions that have been overlooked. Don't be afraid to ask questions that others would view as "obvious," that is, as commonsensical. After research emerged showing that patients have positive judgments of therapists whose offices are neat but also personalized (Nasar & Devlin, 2011), a therapist is reported to have commented, "Isn't that obvious?" If it were obvious, then why did so many therapists' offices used in this series of studies fail to conform to these criteria?

Hindsight bias: after an event has occurred, we have the tendency to claim that it could have been easily predicted.

FLEXIBILITY IN THINKING

Research is essentially about problem solving, and humans are very good problem solvers. In addition to commonsense, we can imagine objects used in a variety of ways. In essence, seeing potential or flexibility is a form of creativity. This kind of problem-solving creativity we have as humans was described by Hubert Dreyfus (1972) when he said that humans don't necessarily see the function of an object as fixed. Consider using a turkey baster to fill a sports car running low on transmission fluid or a door as a desk surface. The artist Marcel Duchamp used found objects, called *readymades*, as art; his bicycle wheel mounted upside down on a stool from 1913 is a well-known example. Nevertheless, we shouldn't take this flexibility for granted, for either objects or processes. For example, we may apply the same process (procedure) when it is no longer appropriate to solve a problem. This is essentially a problem-solving set effect, meaning that we approach a problem using an established (repeated) procedure. In other words, we don't recognize that there might be a more efficient way of solving the problem. This repeated procedural approach is a problem for researchers because we might settle in on a particular approach to evaluate a hypothesis because that is what other researchers have done (the tradition). We need to stop and ask ourselves *how else* we might go about investigating that particular issue. Can we improve on the tradition?

In the case of work on bias and discrimination, for example, researchers have been limited by using scales that directly ask questions about beliefs and attitudes. For example, an item from the Modern Sexism Scale is "It is rare to see women treated in a sexist manner on television" (Swim, Aikin, Hall, & Hunter, 1995). Participants who see such scale items are likely to self-monitor and answer with **social desirability**, presenting themselves in a good light (see Chapter 5 on measures).

Social desirability: responding to experimental stimuli and/or scales in a way that presents the respondent in a positive (socially appropriate) light.

A procedural breakthrough in addressing these kinds of problems with self-report measures has come in the form of Implicit Association Tests (IATs; Greenwald, Nosek, & Banaji, 2003), which use reaction time to measure people's associations to topics (e.g., race, sex, obesity, and age) where your explicit response might be different than your implicit response (see **https://implicit.harvard.edu/implicit/takeatest.html** if you want to try out an IAT for yourself). If the pairing of "fat people" with the adjective "good" takes longer to react to than the pairing of "thin people" with the adjective "good," then we, as well as the individual taking the IAT, have learned about whether the individual's biases are congruent with the explicit positions that person expresses about weight. In all likelihood, if we had only explicitly asked about people's attitudes toward people who are thin versus heavy, we would not see differences. Generally, people do not want to appear biased, in this case, against those in a particular weight category.

The challenge of research is to appreciate what previous studies have shown us (tradition) without becoming limited by them in the questions we can ask (innovation). But with experience, our thought processes become routinized, regularized, and less likely to see the new in the old, to think outside the box. All too soon we are unwilling to break out of the box. Are you up to the challenge?!

THEORIES: WHAT THEY ARE AND WHY THEY MATTER

We have spent a considerable amount of time talking about how information can be packaged in manageable ways to support the research process. There are three important terms that reflect different kinds of "packaging:" hypotheses, theories, and laws. In *The Dictionary of Psychology* (Corsini, 2002) a hypothesis is defined as "a testable proposition based on theory, stating an expected empirical outcome resulting from specific observable conditions" (p. 463). This dictionary defines a **theory** as "a body of interrelated principles and hypotheses that explain or predict a group of phenomena and have been largely verified by facts or data" (p. 994). A **law** is defined in this dictionary as "a theory accepted as correct, that has no significant rivals in accounting for the facts within its domain" (p. 536). Thus, a theory is the pivotal link between hypotheses, which are generated from theories at the least verified end of the spectrum, and laws, on the other end of the spectrum, which emerge when a theory is viewed as having been consistently verified and operates without challenge (Figure 1.6).

From a cognitive standpoint, theories are a way to organize and package information; they are a kind of compacting. Theories have superordinate points of view that allow predictions to be made; these are a kind of generalization from which specific predictions (hypotheses) emerge. These points of view need to be overarching, demonstrating their elasticity or applicability.

A question you might ask is whether the social and behavioral sciences have any laws. Three-and-a-half pages of laws are listed in Corsini's (2002) dictionary, including the law of association, the law of belongingness, the law of common fate, the law of effect, the law of mass action, the law of proximity, and the law of vividness (pp. 537–540). These "laws" may conform to the idea of a theory being accepted as correct and lacking significant rivals, but many social scientists might have some difficulty easily coming up with an example of a "law" in their discipline. In contrast, we could all probably think of some of the laws of thermodynamics from high school; at the very least, we would know that there were laws of thermodynamics. Many of us think of laws as those referred to as natural laws, a "phenomenon of nature that has been proven to invariably occur whenever certain conditions exist or are met" (**http://dictionary.reference.com/browse/scientific+law**).

As is evident in that definition, one challenge in the social and behavioral sciences is that human behavior doesn't conform to this idea of invariable occurrence. As a result, in research, we spend most of our time testing hypotheses; if we are fortunate, these hypotheses are generated within the context of a theory. Thus, hypotheses and theories and their interrelationships are important to understand.

Theory: "a body of interrelated principles and hypotheses that explain or predict a group of phenomena and have been largely verified by facts or data" (Corsini, 2002, p. 994).

Law: "a theory accepted as correct, that has no significant rivals in accounting for the facts within its domain" (Corsini, 2002, p. 536).

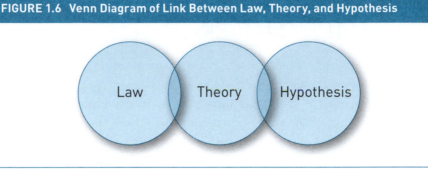

FIGURE 1.6 Venn Diagram of Link Between Law, Theory, and Hypothesis

A theory, this pivotal concept, can be described as a set of principles or as an explanatory framework. In the social and behavioral sciences, theories use interrelated concepts to describe and predict behaviors (events) by making clear the relationships among variables. In Ulrich's (1991) theory of supportive design, his explanatory framework, he offers three dimensions predicted to enhance patients' well-being in health-care settings. These dimensions are (1) positive distraction, (2) social support, and (3) perceived control. Having (1) positive aspects of the environment (e.g., artwork, a view to nature, or music) to distract us from our worries; (2) the social contact of others, either in person (accommodated by seating) or by phone, e-mail, or Skype®; and (3) the ability to control aspects of the environment around us, for example, by using the remote control or adjusting the temperature, is theorized to lead to greater well-being. These three constructs have in common their focus on the physical environment, on the one hand, and their predicted effect on human well-being, on the other. Could we imagine generating hypotheses within this theoretical framework? Before answering that question, let's revisit the concept of a hypothesis, which is based on a theory, is testable, and states an expected empirical outcome based on observable data.

>> **Try This Now**

Come up with two hypotheses based on Ulrich's (1991) theory of supportive design.

Theories are important because they help to organize and structure information and provide a way to think about ideas. Theories provide a structured foundation that should support the generation of hypotheses. At the same time, in returning to one of the themes of this chapter, it is important to recognize that biases may be embedded in theories. Shermer (1997, p. 46) quoted the physicist and Nobel laureate Werner Heisenberg who stated, "'What we observe is not nature itself but nature exposed to our method of questioning.'" In the case of Ulrich's (1991) theory, for example, we may stop thinking of other dimensions of supportive design if we accept his three-factor model. You can see that research questions are shaped by theory, and it is always a good idea to question whether the theory is limiting how you might think about the topic. In the case of Ulrich's model, you might ask whether other aspects of design could be supportive beyond the three dimensions he identifies. For example, perhaps maintenance and upkeep need to be considered.

One other aspect of theories to appreciate is that they are powerful; in some instances, theories may become self-fulfilling (Ferraro, Pfeffer, & Sutton, 2009). In their commentary about why theories matter, Fabrizio Ferraro et al. cited the work of Carol Dweck (2006), who showed that people's beliefs about intelligence (whether fixed vs. mutable/changeable) can shape their behavior. In particular, those who believed that intelligence was fixed behaved differently (e.g., avoided tasks where they thought they would fail) than did those who believed that intelligence was mutable. Dweck's research also showed that these beliefs about intelligence can be changed through social influence. In every situation, we need to ask research questions about the tenets or principles that theories propose.

MAKING A CONNECTION BETWEEN A THEORY AND A GOOD RESEARCH QUESTION

Often the way research questions are posed limits their scope and potential generalizability; that is, questions are asked in a way that limits them to a particular situation. As an example, you might be interested in the size of artwork displayed in a doctor's waiting room and the effect of that displayed artwork on patients' satisfaction with their time spent in the waiting room. Notice that the statement did not say patients' satisfaction with the entire visit. Here is an important observation. When we think about variables we might manipulate or vary, such as the size of artwork, and the outcomes that might be affected, we need to think about the "distance" between these manipulated variables (such as artwork) and the outcome variables (such as satisfaction). Why would we expect the size of artwork in the *waiting room* to affect satisfaction with the entire visit? Wouldn't we want to limit our test to a more reasonable relationship—satisfaction with the time spent in the waiting room?

Now when we return to the idea of the size of the artwork, we need to pose this question in a way that avoids a restrictive and narrow focus. If we try to answer this question only for one particular size of art at two different distances, won't we have to repeat the study with many other sizes and distances? Thus, it would help to see our research question in terms of a larger framework, something like the psychophysics of size, where we could answer the question in terms of the ratio of the size of the art displayed relative to the viewing distance in terms of the effect on satisfaction. For an example of this

**Weber–
Fechner law:**
when the
magnitude
of a physical
stimulus is
increased/
decreased
by a constant
ratio, people's
reactions to it
also increase/
decrease
by equal
increments.

kind of study, see the work of Jack Nasar and Arthur Stamps (2009) on what are called infill McMansions ("too big" houses constructed in existing smaller scale neighborhoods). Basing their research on the **Weber–Fechner law** (proposing a relationship between the magnitude of a physical stimulus and the intensity of people's responses), Nasar and Stamps showed that what bothers people is not the actual size of the infill house but the relative size of the house (i.e., how the house fits into the neighborhood). Furthermore, in terms of style, large discrepancies in the height of the infill houses relative to neighbors' houses were more disliked than were large discrepancies in width. This study uses computer-generated houses as stimuli (a very effective means of experimental control) and demonstrates how the order of presentation can be counterbalanced (Chapter 8) to make sure it is the stimuli themselves, and not the order in which they are seen, that influences our responses. In our example of the research on size and distance of art, we would need to test our hypothesis with carefully selected sizes and distances, following the Weber–Fechner law, to reach a conclusion about the ratio of size to distance that produces the most positive outcome. We want to take a specific research question and ask it in a way that has more generalizability (i.e., greater reach)—but not so much that we wouldn't expect to see any impact (see Chapter 2 for more discussion of the research "gap").

REVISIT AND RESPOND

At this point, you should be able to:

- Explain the value of commonsense in posing research questions
- Explain the difference between a law, a theory, and a hypothesis
- Describe what makes something a good research question

Summary

We have considered in depth the qualities of thinking that both may help (schema development; commonsense) and hurt (stereotypes; heuristics) our approach to the research process. You have observed the kinds of cognitive shortcuts or heuristics that characterize some decision-making situations and can recognize when those biases may come into play. Exposure to Shermer's (1997) list of how thinking goes wrong should have made you more attentive to the decisions you will make in your own research. But as researchers likely at the start of your investigative career, you are in a good position to think innovatively because you are less likely than some of your professors to be constrained by a particular way of doing research. You understand the different levels of predictability and generalizability related to laws, theories, and hypotheses. You are ready to begin your journey to combine tradition and innovation.

If you have not had time to consider them earlier, here is the list of **REVISIT and RESPOND** questions from this chapter.

- Explain what it means to say humans are limited information processors
- Describe the concept of a schema and its adaptive and maladaptive implications for research
- Define heuristics and give examples of representativeness and availability
- Explain the Wason Selection Task and what it shows about the difference between confirming and disconfirming hypotheses
- Give an example from each one of Shermer's (1997) categories:
  - Problems in scientific thinking
  - Problems in pseudoscientific thinking
  - Logical problems in thinking
  - Psychological problems in thinking
- Explain why science is a combination of tradition and innovation
- Explain the value of commonsense in posing research questions
- Explain the difference between a law, a theory, and a hypothesis
- Describe what makes something a good research question

BUILD YOUR SKILLS

1. Think of a situation in your life where you reached an incorrect conclusion, and explain how "your thinking went wrong."

2. *The Atlantic* is a monthly magazine that has a section called "Study of Studies" featuring research findings. Locate the magazine online and the "Study of Studies" section for April 2016. For that month, the focus is "Brag better: How to boast without seeming to." From the descriptions, select a study you think falls into the category of "commonsense" and one that does not. Explain your answers.

$SAGE edge™

edge.sagepub.com/devlin

Sharpen your skills with SAGE edge!

SAGE edge for students provides a personalized approach to help you accomplish your coursework goals in an easy-to-use learning environment. You'll find action plans, mobile-friendly eFlashcards, and quizzes, as well as videos, web resources, and links to SAGE journal articles to support and expand on the concepts presented in this chapter.

GENERATING AND SHAPING IDEAS

Tradition and Innovation

CHAPTER HIGHLIGHTS

- Overview
- Sources of ideas
- Using library resources
  - Reference materials, Library of Congress classification system
  - Keywords—what they are and how to use them
  - Using PsycINFO (truncation, subject headings, times cited)
  - Google Scholar versus the Web
- Kinds of useful articles (primary vs. secondary sources; reviews, meta-analyses)
- How journals differ in quality (including Beall's List)
  - Journal publication practices
  - File drawer effect
- How to obtain an article physically
- Reading an article: What to note in the Introduction, Method, Results, and Discussion

- Research questions and the role of third variables; closing the gap
- Suggested semester timeline
- Academic fraud

OVERVIEW

As indicated in Chapter 1, research in science acknowledges the past as it looks to the future. These two views, one back and one forward, take the form of reviewing the literature (looking back) and then generating hypotheses that advance literature (looking forward). The research should enable us to answer the question, "What's new and noteworthy here?" Thus, research combines tradition and innovation.

In building on a theme of Chapter 1, it is useful to try to generate some ideas before you consult the literature. Why? Because once you look at what other people have done, that information may influence how you think about a particular topic. In other words, consulting the literature as your first step may limit the range of ideas you consider. After you have generated possible research areas, consulting the literature is next.

This chapter will emphasize the "looking back" part of the process by discussing sources of ideas, techniques for tracking down articles about your ideas, and approaches to reading that literature once you obtain it (that is, how to identify what's important). A significant portion of the chapter focuses on library resources and using them to locate and obtain articles.

The chapter will look forward by including examples of research questions that are broad versus narrow, considering the role of what are called *third variables,* that is, variables that are unmeasured and can undermine the relationships we seek to measure. A recommended timeline for conducting research in a single semester is provided. The chapter will conclude with a definition and discussion of academic fraud. Plagiarism, a particular kind of academic fraud, is covered in Chapter 11 in the context of writing up research.

Sources of Ideas

Generating a workable idea is one of the most difficult parts of doing a research project. This chapter will give you suggestions for sources of ideas, including yourself and extended sphere of activity, the media, the literature (journals, books, abstracts from professional meetings) and other sources (department resources, courses). The suggested timeline for research will help keep you on track.

Ideas: The Student Sphere of Activity

In Chapter 1, we spent time talking about the kinds of biases in thinking and limitations humans have, as well as about some of our strengths, such as commonsense. A major source of ideas starts with you and the people and activities in your life. Instructors who teach writing often tell students: "Write about what you know." The same advice could be directed at researchers: "Study what you know." You are probably knowledgeable about many spheres of activity that are less familiar to your instructors, whether social media, technology more broadly, or interpersonal relationship protocol among teenagers and young adults. Making a list of ideas or topics that are important in your life and in the lives of your friends is a good way to generate a research topic. This approach also makes sense because the participants in your research may be students your age (from your institution) who may be interested in participating in a project about a topic that interests them as well.

In recent semesters in my research methods courses, students have submitted papers on a range of topics including social media use, paranormal beliefs, child-rearing styles, stereotypes surrounding athletes, academic dishonesty, and use of mental health services by college students. Here are some examples of project titles:

(1) Parental Involvement and Student Academic Achievement

(1) Personality and Attachment Style as Correlates of Facebook Use and the Need to Belong

(2) Relationships Between Birth Order, Gender, Anxiety, and Perceived Parental Control

(3) Race and Long Distance Dating: Effects on Perceived Relationship Success

(3) College Students' Attitudes Toward Individuals With Seen and Unseen Disabilities

(3) Think Before You Speak: Perceived Authority of Women's Voices in the Workplace

(3) Gender Perceptions in Hiring: Effects of Hair Color on Predicted Capabilities of Female Job Applicants

(3) Perceived Femininity of Women Weightlifters

(4) Mental Health of First and Fourth Year Students

These titles are examples of projects done by students taking a course in research methods—for most their first research project. These projects have been divided into four categories (see the numbers in parentheses by the project title; Figure 2.1). These categories will be topics in future chapters. Projects in Category 1 represent what are called *correlational projects* (there is no manipulation of variables and results are about the sample as a whole; a common correlational statistic is Pearson's *r;* see Chapters 3 and 6). Projects in Category 2 are also called correlational in the sense that there is no manipulation of variables, but these projects differ from those in Category 1 in that they include a consideration of group differences. Statistics are typically a *t* test, analysis of variance, or multivariate analysis of variance, depending on how many groups and outcomes there are (see Chapters 3 and 6). Projects in Category 3 are true experiments. In these projects, variables are manipulated (e.g., the hair color of female job applicants). Statistics are typically a *t* test, analysis of variance, or multivariate analysis of variance, again depending on how many groups and outcomes there are. Note that the statistics in Categories 2 and 3 are the same, but only in Category 3 are there true experiments (see Chapter 7). In Category 4, we have a special case of the group difference approach in correlational approach: cross-sectional design. In cross-sectional design, the researcher is typically looking at people (here students) who represent different points of development or maturation, but the data are collected at one point in time because there is no possibility to follow student development over a long period of time in a semester-length project. Cross-sectional research approximates this developmental progression at a single point in time by contrasting students of different class years, for example (see Chapter 8). The end of the book (see Appendix A) includes a more complete statistical decision tree if you want a refresher on which statistical test is appropriate for several common research approaches.

FIGURE 2.1 Diagram of Common Research Approaches

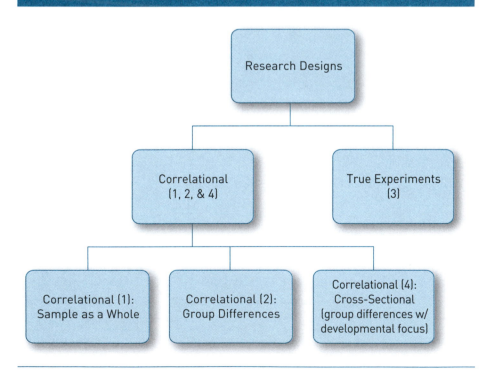

Common Student Research Themes

What themes do you see in these projects? It makes sense for students to pick topics related to some aspect of their experience—media, gender, race, achievement, sports, relationships (with peers, with parents, with siblings), substance use, and health. On occasion students undertake topics related to some medical or emotional problem familiar to them, for example, a relative or acquaintance with a seen or unseen disability. Doing such research is possible, although it involves great care and sensitivity. There is a difference between asking people about their attitudes toward sensitive topics, such as those with seen and unseen challenges, and asking people *with* those challenges to participate in the research. In general, projects that study sensitive topics (e.g., individuals who are taking medication for Parkinson's Disease) and/or vulnerable populations (e.g., individuals with autism or children) require a series of permissions from "gatekeepers," a process that involves a full meeting of your institution's **institutional review board** (IRB; a committee that evaluates the risks and benefits and ethical issues involved in research done with **human subjects**; see Chapter 4). Such involved projects are better suited to courses longer than a semester, such as a two-semester senior honors study or graduate thesis.

Research ideas often emerge in situations where people are trying to solve a practical problem, such as those who work in your institution's offices of dining services, buildings and grounds, campus safety, or housing. For example, offices connected to student life are interested in the amount of money spent to maintain the facilities that students use. Investigations of graffiti, litter, breakage, and other concerns may produce useful and meaningful research projects. People who work in these offices are important sources of information (and ideas).

One distinction made in types of research is whether the research is applied or basic. In **applied research**, the focus is on solving a particular real-world problem (e.g., reducing graffiti in residence halls), with a particular set of conditions or circumstances. The scope may be narrow. In **basic research**, the aim is to test fundamental principles or theories, with an expectation that the knowledge would be generalizable beyond a particular set of circumstances. Even when the research is applied, it can still be framed in the context of a theory. For example, applied research on residence hall design may be framed in the context of theories of crowding.

Finally, simply observing what goes on around you can produce good ideas for research. Some investigators find it helpful to carry a small notebook (or use a smartphone) to jot down ideas that occur to them in the course of daily life, whether it is the length of time it takes you to find a specific product when the grocery store changes its organization of products by aisle or the clientele of a particular bar or restaurant and its associated ambiance. A particular restaurant in town went out of business within a year of opening, and some patrons attributed this closure to the negative reviews of the restaurant's

Institutional review board (IRB): deliberate body that evaluates research with human subjects; required where institutions received federal funds for research.

Human subjects: with regard to the federal definition (45 CFR 46), involves living individuals from whom the researcher obtains data through an interaction or intervention, or about whom the research obtains personally identifiable information.

Applied research: research designed to answer practical questions; typically contrasted with basic research.

Basic research: research that focuses on testing fundamental theories or principles, with the goal of generalization.

FIGURE 2.2 Sources: The Student Sphere

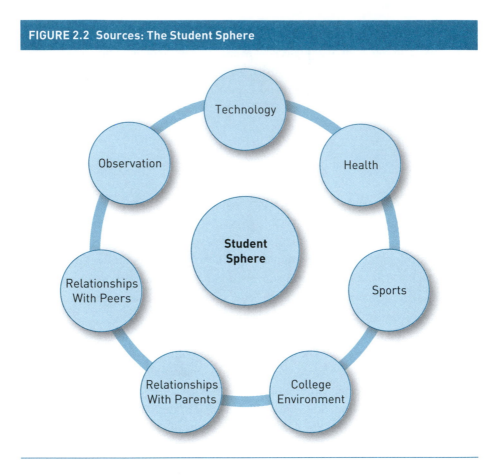

service posted on Yelp.com. Investigating people's belief in the validity of such reviews (and whether they had ever written a review themselves) and more broadly in the validity of information on social media might make an interesting research project. What these examples indicate is that ideas for research surround us. Some very good research projects come from observations of daily life.

Ideas: Academia and Media

COURSES Before starting a course in research methods, students may have taken one or two introductory survey courses and possibly one or two more advanced content courses (i.e., courses that focus on a defined domain within a particular discipline). If students are majoring in psychology, such content courses might be in personality, social, or health psychology. In human development, these courses might focus on individual differences or social development. In sociology, possibilities might be courses dealing with sex, gender, and society; social movements; or ethic and race relations. A colleague of mine teaches a course called "Race, Ethnicity, and Baseball in the US," which includes the role of baseball in the assimilation of immigrants. Courses are a great source of ideas, from the topics covered and theories presented to the research approaches used.

THESES, RESEARCH GROUPS, AND DEPARTMENTAL PUBLICATIONS Other possibilities for research ideas include past honors theses or even masters' theses in your department. Unpublished honors theses and published research are similar in that they typically include a section dealing with limitations of the study or directions for future research. These theses are also a useful source of measures and scales (see Chapter 5) because such projects typically require that appendices include all items in the measures, which is not common in published research.

Your department may have research groups run by professors. Attending these groups is beneficial—in particular, hearing about other people's research and the suggestions made to improve it. Because being part of such a group reflects initiative, this experience is useful in graduate school applications. Research experience is highly valued in evaluating candidates for graduate school. Aside from graduate study, potential employers are impressed by this initiative as well; it may set you apart.

CONFERENCES AND UNDERGRADUATE JOURNALS At conferences, many poster presentations (see also Chapter 11) are from students or the collaborative work of students and professors. Abstracts from the local, regional, national, or international association meetings in a discipline (e.g., psychology, neuroscience, sociology, environmental design, and anthropology) provide sources of ideas for research. As an example, here is a title of a poster from the 2013 annual meeting of the Environmental Design Research Association (EDRA). In the poster, the lead author was an undergraduate student when the work was conducted (and his poster appears in Figure 2.3):

Jeremic, B., & Devlin, A. S. (2013). *Reading performance, memory, and mood in different classroom lighting conditions.* Poster presented at the 44th annual meeting of the Environmental Design Research Association, Providence, RI.

During poster sessions, a condensed version of the research paper is posted on a bulletin board. Student researchers stand near their posters, ready to answer questions from conference attendees.

Guidelines for how to create a successful poster are discussed in Chapter 11. Even if you do not attend such conferences, your professors can share the online program with

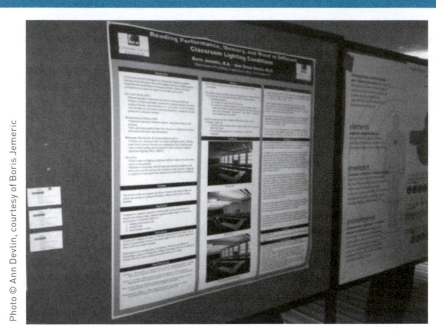

FIGURE 2.3 Poster Presentation Example

Photo © Ann Devlin, courtesy of Boris Jemeric

you as a way to search the presentation topics. Many conferences are moving away from distributing a paper program (as a result of sustainability and other cost concerns), and online programs are easily searchable.

In addition, many colleges and universities publish journals of undergraduate student work (**see http://www.cur.org/resources/students/undergraduate_journals/**), and some national journals publish student work (e.g., *American Journal of Undergraduate Research*). Psi Chi, the International Honor Society in Psychology, also publishes a journal of psychological research. Not only do these publications provide resources for generating a research idea, but also they serve as possible publication outlets for completed student projects.

MEDIA The media are excellent sources of ideas, from *The New York Times* and *The Wall Street Journal* to *The National Enquirer* and TMZ.com. In all likelihood, you will access media from a variety of platforms. One drawback to some online news sources is what is called the **digital paywall**, which limits Internet users' access to the publication without a paid subscription. For that reason, accessing these publications through your library's databases (the institution pays the subscription) is recommended.

Digital paywall: limits Internet users' access to the publication without a paid subscription.

In 2014, a survey of how Americans get their news reported that most Americans had consulted four different platforms for news in the previous week and that the most frequently consulted devices were "television (87 percent), laptops/computers (69 percent), radio (65 percent), and print newspapers or magazines (61 percent)" (American Press Institute, 2014, para. 4). Sources of news vary tremendously in their point of view (liberal to conservative), their perceived credibility, and the news stories they emphasize (you might already be thinking about a research project that investigates the news publications and platforms consulted by students in different majors, for example).

Wall Street Journal

The Wall Street Journal (WSJ) is an excellent source of ideas, especially for technology in the workplace, career strategies, or employment trends. The WSJ has columns and blogs devoted to many of these topics. The digital version is useful in that the dropdown menus (e.g., for Business) list all the industries covered. Technology is a particular strength of the publication.

FIGURE 2.4 Sources: Academia and Media

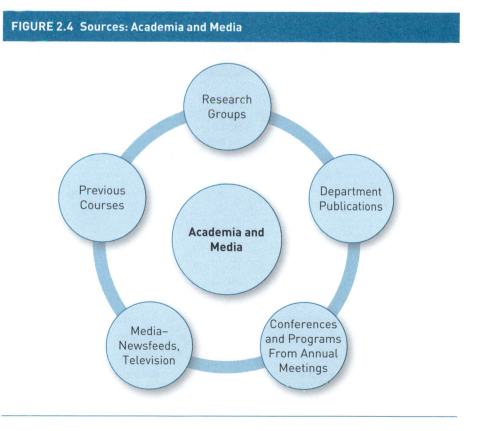

Chronicle of Higher Education

If your interest is education, *The Chronicle of Higher Education* is a comprehensive place to start. Articles in *The Chronicle* may focus on curricular issues in higher education (e.g., student evaluation of instruction or core requirements), personnel issues (e.g., Title IX and sexual harassment, including romantic relationships between professors and students), or student culture (e.g., the Greek system or the role of athletics). In print, the publication is weekly; online, it is published daily. This publication has sections on a range of topics, including technology (Wired Campus; the latest on tech and education). For example, a recent article in Wired Campus talked about banning smartphones during final exams (McIntire, 2015).

Television

Regarding television, Nielsen ratings of viewers' habits are a good source of ideas (**http://www.nielsen.com/us/en/solutions/measurement/television.html**). Nielsen measures far more than television viewing; it also assesses music, retail, and food sales (e.g., top-selling brands for a particular week), which are accessible to some degree through its "top 10s" ratings.

REVISIT AND RESPOND

- Why might it make sense to think of some ideas before consulting the literature? What advantages are there to using your personal experience to develop research ideas? Write down two potential research ideas that come out of your personal experience and two that come from the Internet.

IDEAS: INFORMATION SERVICES, AKA THE LIBRARY

When recently speaking to a librarian about student use of the resources in the library, her perspective was that students often want to use the sources that are expedient (e.g., full text) and exhibit occasional impatience in cases where resources must be ordered. In addition, she stated that students often don't know what to do with an article once they obtain it—that is, they don't know what is worth spending time on. Another issue she raised was students' lack of awareness of what could be found in a book chapter versus a journal article. In this chapter, we will try to provide you with the tools to change her mind about students!

For library users, materials can be accessed in a variety of ways, which this chapter will cover. Libraries own a collection of current and bound journals, books, newspapers, magazines, visual media, and government documents available to you. What they don't own can be accessed through electronic databases or loans from the collections of other institutions.

IDEAS: SEARCHING EFFECTIVELY IN THE LIBRARY

To search for materials effectively, it is helpful to know how collections in the library are organized. Some aspects of libraries are essentially the same across institutions, independent of size. Libraries in the United States use the Library of Congress Classification System for the call numbers of books. To get a better idea of what topics are covered under which letter classifications of the Library of Congress classification outline, try **http://www.loc.gov/catdir/cpso/lcco/**. Then you can click on the hyperlinked letter (e.g., B), which will take you to the subclass (B, BC, BD . . . BX). If you want, you can then examine a subclass in more detail. As an example, B is linked to Philosophy, Psychology, and Religion.

Library Holdings

A useful starting strategy is to look at your library's holdings through its electronic catalogue. You will need to use some search terms or **keywords** you have thought of or identified (e.g., by looking at the relevant thesaurus in your discipline, such as the *Thesaurus of Psychological Index Terms* [11th ed., revised] for psychology). As an example, in a recent search looking up the keyword "personal space" in my institution's library catalogue, 528 entries cover a wide range of topics, from art to medicine, which are in some way related to the topic of personal space. Expanding the search to include the consortium of libraries (2 others) in which my institution participates (to expand its range of holdings), the number of listings for personal space jumps to 3,199.

Keywords: search terms for information retrieval.

Reference Section: Encyclopedias and Handbooks

The reference section has many useful handbooks and encyclopedias to obtain and refine ideas. Because each institution will be different, this next section will provide examples using psychology as the discipline rather than a comprehensive listing.

PSYCHOLOGY AND OTHER SOCIAL SCIENCES The Psychology section under the Library of Congress heading "BF" has a variety of reference materials related to psychology, including encyclopedias of psychology and handbooks that include specialized topics (e.g., alternative reality). You will also find dictionaries or handbooks on fundamental topics such as emotion, stress, intelligence, and health. A small sample of the reference volumes you might typically find under the heading "BF" is as follows:

Encyclopedia of Psychology, Volumes 1–8 (Kazdin, 2000)

Encyclopedia of Perception, Volumes 1–2 (Goldstein, 2010)

Encyclopedia of Human Intelligence, Volumes 1–2 (Sternberg, 1994)

APA Dictionary of Psychology (2nd ed.) (VandenBos, 2015)

The Dictionary of Psychology (Corsini, 2002)

Handbook of Child Psychology (4 vol., 6th ed.) (Damon & Lerner, 2006)

The Reference section is also a good place to find sourcebooks of research measures and test critiques, a topic we will cover in more detail in Chapter 5:

Measures for Clinical Practice, Volumes 1 and 2 (Corcoran & Fischer, 2013)

Under "H" in the Library of Congress headings, you are likely to find more general coverage of the social sciences (e.g., *Dictionary of the Social Sciences;* Calhoun, 2002) and coverage of topics traditionally found in sociology. For example, HM-HQ includes important sources of attitudes such as the *Gallup Poll Cumulative Index: Public Opinion 1998–2007* (Gallup & Newport, 2008). Other topics indexed under this heading include sexuality, women's issues, and criminal behavior.

Under "L" in the Library of Congress heading are topics in education. Particularly useful are sources about research in education, and there are many volumes related to the work of the Educational Testing Service.

Material related to medicine is found under "R" in the Library of Congress heading. Examples include *Handbook of Community Psychiatry* (McQuistion, Sowers, Ranz, & Feldman, 2012) and *The SAGE Handbook of Health Psychology* (Sutton, Baum, & Johnston, 2004).

❯❯ Try This Now

Physically go to the library at your institution, identify the Library of Congress call numbers in your area of interest, and see what reference books are on the shelf.

Reference Materials: Style Guides and Thesauruses

In addition to handbooks and encyclopedias, the Reference section also typically includes style handbooks such as the *Publication Manual of the American Psychological Association* (APA, 2010b); the *MLA Handbook for Writers of Research Papers* (Gibaldi, 2009); *The Chicago Manual of Style* (University of Chicago Press, 2010), used by the American Anthropological Association, which also has its own downloadable style guide; and the *ASA Style Guide* (2010), used by the American Sociological Association.

The reference section also includes an array of thesauruses, such as the *Thesaurus of Psychological Index Terms* (Tuleya, 2007), which can be helpful when you begin database searches for articles (see later section in this chapter on "Thesaurus of Psychological Index Terms"). Electronic databases such as **PsycINFO**® also include a parallel thesaurus function that is updated periodically. PsycINFO is a database managed by the American Psychological Association; it includes article citations, summaries, and bibliographic material.

PsycINFO®: electronic database of citations and summaries from the American Psychological Association (APA) with almost 4 million records.

Online Reference Resources: Dictionaries and Encyclopedias

In addition to bound volumes, colleges may also offer online dictionaries and encyclopedias, which are useful for general overviews of topic areas (the encyclopedias) or for looking up the derivation of words in the case of a source like the *Oxford English Dictionary.* Common sources for a library to offer online are the *Encyclopedia Britannica* and the *Oxford English Dictionary.* Often these online sources will be available under a heading like "Reference Tools" or "Online Reference Sources," which may be accessible from the library's home page.

BibMe: free bibliographic tool that automatically fills in the citation information; useful for a variety of citations styles, including American Psychological Association (APA).

Subject and Research Guides

Colleges and universities may also develop their own list of subject and research guides, which offer specific kinds of help to students including the proper form of citations. Typical offerings are links to citation generators such as **BibMe** (that will autofill information about a source you have located); links to **RefWorks** (a Web-based bibliographic and database manager); links to APA resources; to MLA resources; to Chicago resources; to Turabian (a style guide named after the original author); and links to instructions about how to cite government documents.

RefWorks: bibliographic management tool.

REVIST AND RESPOND

- What is the Library of Congress classification system? What is a keyword? What kinds of resources would you expect to find in the Reference Section? In what ways can librarians help with your research project?

ELECTRONIC RESOURCES AND KEYWORDS

Electronic database: electronic searchable collection of materials; useful in research.

Beyond the print and online reference sources and bound volumes, libraries offer a range of **electronic databases**, both general and discipline specific. Most of your search for materials will use these electronic databases.

KEYWORDS: THE "KEY" TO SUCCESS

Before proceeding, a fuller discussion of keywords is in order. Whatever the stage of your search (beginning or further along), and whether you target journals, books, or other sources of materials, your search will be more effective if you choose appropriate keywords. As mentioned, keywords are search terms for information retrieval. In most journals, for example, authors are asked to provide five to six keywords (words or phrases) for their article that represent the focus of the work. In the case of journals that follow APA style, these items are listed right under the Abstract (Figure 2.5, illustration from Nier, Bajaj, McLean, & Schwartz, 2013).

FIGURE 2.5 Example of an Abstract With Keywords Listed

Abstract

The Stereotype Content Model proposes that competence (or alternatively, agency) is a fundamental dimension of stereotypes. According to this model, beliefs about agency are partially due to the status relations between groups, such that high status groups are perceived to possess agency, whereas low status groups are perceived to lack agentic characteristics. Despite the considerable support for this model, the psychological processes that produce these stereotypes have not been fully explored. In the current studies, we examined whether the correspondence bias may be partially responsible for the stereotype that members of low status groups lack agentic characteristics, relative to those who belong to high status groups. Across both studies, a measure of the correspondence bias predicted such stereotypical beliefs, even after accounting for variables that are known to be associated with beliefs about high and low status groups. This effect was observed when beliefs about the status of groups were experimentally manipulated, and when we measured stereotypical beliefs about two sets of actual high and low status groups.

attribution   correspondence bias   stereotype content model   stereotypes

---

Source: Nier, Bajaj, McLean, & Schwarz (2013). Group status, perceptions of agency, and the correspondence bias: Attributional processes in the formation of stereotypes about high and low status groups. *Group Processes & Inter group Relations, 16,* 476–487.

Keywords are important for both authors and users because keywords link the search terms you use in a database to articles that use those keywords. In a recent article looking at the stress patients feel in hospital rooms (Andrade & Devlin, 2015), the authors evaluated Roger Ulrich's (1991) theory of supportive design (a theory that predicts what types of elements in design will reduce patients' stress). The authors selected the following keywords: hospital rooms, design, patients' stress, and Ulrich's theory of supportive design.

> **⟫ Try This Now**
>
> Are some of those terms more effective than others, in your view? Which ones? Why?

PsycINFO

Because it is so heavily used in research in the social and behavioral sciences, we will emphasize PsycINFO in this book. As mentioned, PsycINFO is a database of citations and summaries offered by the American Psychological Association.[1] The database covers journals, books, technical reports, and dissertations in psychology and psychology-related disciplines such as psychiatry, medicine, nursing, education, sociology, anthropology, and linguistics. In 2015, the number of records offered in PsycINFO was "nearly 4 million:" (**http://www.apa.org/pubs/databases/psycinfo/index.aspx**). In PsycINFO, when you enter a keyword and click on the "Suggest Subject Terms" option, related terms appear, which might give you other ways to search for a topic of interest. For example, if you enter the search term "environmental psychology" and click on "Suggest Subject Terms," pages of terms appear, presented in order of relevancy. Beneath the term "environmental psychology," the next most relevant term is "ecological psychology" (see Figure 2.6).

Thesaurus of Psychological Index Terms

A thesaurus of index terms can be useful to students in selecting the most effective keyword to search the literature on a given topic. The thesaurus is usually arranged in such a way that if you look up a particular term, you will see terms that are both broader and

---

[1]For purposes of illustration here, PsycINFO is being accessed through EBSCO*host*, an online reference database system. Your institution may use EBSCOhost or one of the other online reference database systems, such as OVID. The web interface may have a different graphical presentation in these different database systems than the examples used here.

FIGURE 2.6 Screenshot of Suggested Subject Terms in PsycINFO

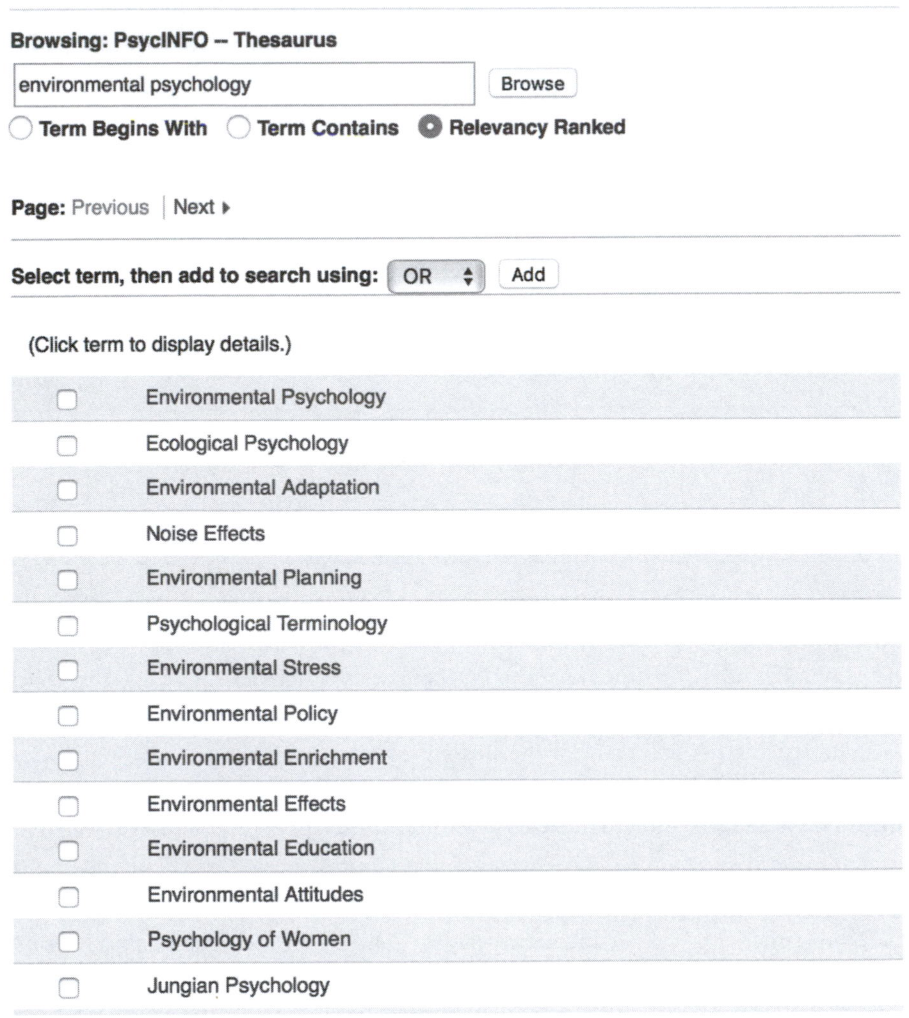

Browsing: PsycINFO -- Thesaurus

environmental psychology		Browse

○ **Term Begins With**   ○ **Term Contains**   ● **Relevancy Ranked**

Page: Previous │ Next ▶

Select term, then add to search using: OR ▲▼   Add

(Click term to display details.)

☐	Environmental Psychology
☐	Ecological Psychology
☐	Environmental Adaptation
☐	Noise Effects
☐	Environmental Planning
☐	Psychological Terminology
☐	Environmental Stress
☐	Environmental Policy
☐	Environmental Enrichment
☐	Environmental Effects
☐	Environmental Education
☐	Environmental Attitudes
☐	Psychology of Women
☐	Jungian Psychology

Source: PsycINFO®

narrower. Often students initially enter keyword terms that either lead to "zero" hits or 1,000 hits; that is, the search leads to no or few relevant articles or so many that it would be overwhelming to sort through them. If you look up the keyword "terrorism" in the PsycINFO database, for example, you will get more than 7,000 hits. A recent search consulting the thesaurus function of PsycINFO under "terrorism" showed the year the term was introduced to the tracking citation system (1982), a definition (Scope note), two broader terms "antisocial behavior" and "violent crime," a narrower term "bioterrorism," and a list of nine related terms in alphabetical order. Entering one of these terms, "Radical Movements," into the PsycINFO keyword search function, produced 376 hits, which is a more manageable place to start (if this is the direction you are heading).

Another way to manage the number of "hits" you have is to use the "Subject: Major Heading" listing. After you have entered "terrorism" as a search term, look over at the left-hand column of PsycINFO, which is labeled "Refine Results" and you will see several headings including "Limit to," "Source Types," and "Major Heading." Under Subject: Major Heading, I saw *terrorism, violence, war, emotional trauma, posttraumatic stress disorder,* and *disasters,* each with the number of articles associated with that term. You may be interested in *emotional trauma,* which has far fewer references, by a factor of 10, than does *terrorism.* This kind of information is helpful in managing your search to avoid becoming overwhelmed. To become more adept at doing searches, you might want to work through a search exercise with a reference librarian.

At the very least, an indexing thesaurus or its online equivalent will give you other keywords to test out. Using the appropriate keyword is critical to accessing the published work in a given area. That is why becoming familiar with the Thesaurus function of the electronic database you are using is essential.

Other Techniques in Searching: Truncation and Times Cited

Scheduling a session with a staff member in your library can help you learn the tools that will maximize your search efforts. Useful terms to understand are *truncation, advanced searching, cited by,* and *analyze search results.* In a database, a truncation tool, often an asterisk (*), may be added to the root of a word to capture multiple endings of the word. This approach will help you broaden your search to capture closely related words. MIT has a useful guide to using truncation (**http://libguides.mit.edu/c.php?g=175963&p=1158679**), and its website on this topic shows that using a truncation approach with the word "child*" could also produce *childs, children, childrens,* and *childhood,* all of which might be useful. An asterisk (*) is the truncation tool in PsycINFO. In Advanced Search (staying with PsycINFO as our platform), you have the opportunity to refine or limit your results. You could do so with many different parameters, including age groups, publication type, whether peer reviewed, methodology (you might be interested only in empirical studies), supplemental materials (e.g., 3-D modeling images), and so on.

A very useful function is the "times cited in this database" option (in PsycINFO) or "cited by" (in Scopus, another useful database). This option tells you what other published research (in that database) has cited the particular article you selected. This information is very helpful if you pick an article that may have been written 10 or more years ago and you want to see who has referenced it (and possibly does related work on it) recently. Scopus also has the nice feature of showing you the publication pattern in a particular topic, that is, how many articles dealing with a particular topic were published in a given year. In that way, you can see the ebb and flow of interest in a topic. For example, if we enter the search term "residence hall*" in Scopus, we see 834 documents (in June 2016). If we click on the option "analyze search results," it will produce a graphic representation as well as a frequency count of the number of articles published on that topic (in this case, from 1855 to the present) (see Figure 2.7).

You can see that there was some interest through the 1970s and 1980s (related to the beginning interest in environment-behavior research), but that there has been a fairly steady increase in publication on the topic since the late 1990s. In 2014, 44 articles on this topic were published, but this was down from 57 in 2013. It will be interesting to see whether this area is declining in interest. In contrast, if we put in the search term "student anxiety" (June 2016), we get 16,558 "hits." When we analyze the search results, we learn that 1,265 articles on the topic were published in 2014, with a dramatic increase of interest in the topic starting around the year 2000. Graphically, such information from Scopus shows the number of published resources that are available and the level of interest in the topic.

FIGURE 2.7 Graph in Scopus Showing Number of Documents Related to Search Term "Residence Hall" by Year

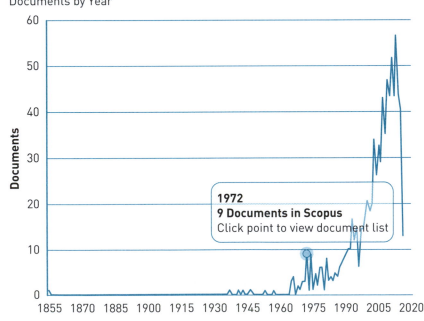

Documents by Year

OTHER DATABASES AND INDEXES IN THE SOCIAL SCIENCES

Beyond PsycINFO, it is important to be familiar with other commonly used databases. Some of the most common databases and indexes in the social sciences are Academic OneFile, Web of Science, PsycINFO, Scopus, SocINDEX, Anthropology Plus, AnthroSource, and Science Direct. Often, under the heading Databases and Indexes, there is the option to access the list alphabetically or by subject. For example, in many library systems, if you click on "listed by subject" under Databases and Indexes (to find journal articles), a list of subject areas appears alphabetically (e.g., from Africana Studies to VAST: Academic Video Online). You can click on the subject area of interest (e.g., education, psychology, or sociology) and a list of the databases in that subject area appears. The other option is an alphabetical list of databases and indexes, for example, from A and ABI/Inform to W and WorldCat. If you don't know the names of the databases typically used in your field, then the subject listing is a better starting point.

Google Scholar® is a search engine that searches academic resources. The results of a search in Google Scholar should not be confused with the results of a search you would get from a general Google search (more on that soon), which would include public Web content. We have a link to Google Scholar on the Databases page of my institution's electronic library resources, reflecting the fact that we think Google Scholar is an acceptable tool for scholarly work. There is some research suggesting that the results of a Google Scholar search produce citations as scholarly as those from an equivalent database search (Howland, 2010). Is Google Scholar recommended *over* a database such as PsycINFO? Although there is overlap, Google Scholar may not provide as much access to full text links as traditional library databases do, increasing the number of steps you need to take to obtain those full texts.

General Databases

In the social sciences, broad and commonly used databases and indexes are Academic OneFile (covering more than 8,000 journals); ERIC (Education Resources Information Center), which is funded by the U.S. Department of Education and covers education and related issues; and **JSTOR** (short for "journal storage"), which is full text for more than 1,500 scholarly issues. What distinguishes JSTOR, as its name suggests, is that it provides back issues of journals, usually 3–5 years (described as a moving wall) behind the most current issue of a particular journal. **Project Muse** is an electronic source *for current journals* (greater than 300 scholarly journals in the social sciences, humanities, and arts).

Google Scholar®: search engine for academic resources.

JSTOR: electronic database that provides access to articles usually 3–5 years (the moving wall) behind the current issue.

Project Muse: electronic database of current articles that includes 300 scholarly journals in the social sciences, humanities, and arts.

LexisNexis: electronic database, which is almost always full text and covers almost 6,000 sources of news, business, legal, medical, and reference publications.

LexisNexis is almost always full text and covers approximately 6,000 sources of news, business, legal, medical, and reference publications. Incorporating information from newspapers or other current periodicals may supplement academic sources. Statistics from newspapers or other sources may catch readers' interest, but always question the accuracy of the information and the credentials of the author. If possible, confirm the accuracy of the information by checking it against primary and/or academic sources. A **primary source** is a source presenting original material (e.g., journal article), whereas a **secondary source** provides descriptions, summaries, analysis, commentary, perspectives, evaluation, or conclusions about the primary source material. A textbook is considered a secondary source.

Primary sources: original sources (e.g., data collected for the project or existing sources such as census data) that were created during a particular time period and are used to draw conclusions based on that research.

THE WEB AND PEER REVIEW

Remember that a general Google search is an avenue to explore research topics and keywords, but there is no **peer review** *requirement* for the material you find on the Web. Across disciplines, most published journal articles undergo a peer review. In this process, a manuscript submitted for publication without its identifying information (e.g., no author's name or affiliation) is evaluated by other academics (i.e., reviewers) selected because they are knowledgeable about the topic. This process is supposed to lead to an unbiased evaluation of the article and ultimately to the publication of articles that are sound methodologically and contribute to the discipline. There is no "peer review" on the Web. For that reason, you have only your assessment of the work, which may not be sufficient to judge its quality. The topic of peer review is discussed in more depth later in the chapter.

Secondary sources: sources that analyze or critique the primary sources. Textbooks, magazine articles or blogs summarizing research, systematic review articles, or handbooks on a topic are common secondary sources.

PARTICULAR KINDS OF ARTICLES

Various types of research articles may be found. Review articles and meta-analyses are the two most common.

Review Articles

Review articles provide an overview and brief history of the topic and current challenges. For that reason, such articles are useful as you begin to develop a research question. Often these articles are labeled "Annual Review of _____." Good sources of overview articles in psychology are *Psychological Bulletin* and the *Annual Review of Psychology*. Ask your reference librarian for publications that offer review articles in other areas of social science, such as sociology, human development, and anthropology.

Meta-analyses: Their Special Value

A **meta-analysis** is sometimes referred to as a study of other people's studies or "an analysis of analyses" (Glass, 1976, p. 3). Another definition is the "Integration of the findings of several research studies by means of statistical techniques focusing on the same research question leading to meaningful quantitative data" (Corsini, 2002, p. 588). Results of meta-analyses combine the data from studies that are asking the same research question to produce a result that tells you how strong the impact of the variable of interest is. The result is reported as an **effect size.** An effect size is a quantitative indicator of the strength of a particular occurrence. For example, you might be interested in having onsite parking at work and whether having an onsite parking garage is associated with lower absenteeism than having an offsite parking garage that requires using a shuttle bus to get to the office. If you were to conduct a meta-analysis on this issue, you would use appropriate search terms, in a comprehensive list of databases, to find research where onsite versus offsite parking was examined and one of the outcomes was a measurement of absenteeism. There are specific steps you would then take to combine the results of the studies you found numerically to determine the effect size.

One value of a meta-analysis is that it includes a systematic review of the relevant research by the authors. The research studies that were included to calculate the effect size are included in the published meta-analysis, giving you a solid list of references. When you look at a meta-analysis, you get a pretty good idea of the research conducted on this topic. But it is wise to remember another saying sometimes associated with meta-analyses: "garbage in-garbage out," a phrase that appears to have originated in the computing world (**http://www.worldwidewords.org/qa/qa-gar1.htm**). What that phrase means is that the scientific rigor of the studies included in the meta-analysis is important. If the studies are not of high quality, then the outcome of the meta-analysis is questionable.

HOW JOURNALS DIFFER: ISSUES RELATED TO QUALITY

Journals differ from each other in many ways, from the number of issues they publish each year to their standards of acceptance and their **impact factor**, which is a number that reflects the average number of times articles from a specific journal have been cited over a particular period of time (e.g., 2 years or 5 years). This impact measure is considered by some to be a proxy for the importance of the journal. You can usually find the impact factor for a given journal on its home page. The *Journal Citation Reports (JCR)*, published by Thomson Reuters, list journals and their

Peer review: used in the context of academic work to indicate that a submitted work has been reviewed (usually anonymously) by experts knowledgeable in the field.

Review article: provides an overview and brief history of a topic and its challenges.

Meta-analysis: meta-analysis is a "study of studies" that uses a statistical approach to synthesize the findings on a particular topic and to report the impact of a given intervention. That impact is reported as an effect size.

Effect size: quantitative indication of the strength of a particular occurrence.

Impact factor: number that reflects the average number of times articles from a particular journal have been cited over a particular period of time (e.g., 2 years).

associated impact factor. Access to this report requires a subscription, which your institution may have.

To understand better the differences in journal quality you might encounter, it might be helpful to contrast the scope and depth of the articles in such journals as *The Journal of College and University Student Housing* with those in such periodicals as the *Journal of Personality and Social Psychology (JPSP)* or the *Journal of Applied Psychology*. Arguably these journals differ with regard to the sophistication and complexity of work each publishes. *JPSP* and the *Journal of Applied Psychology* are among the premier journals in psychology in terms of the quality of the articles, with high rejection rates, which some interpret as an indicator of quality. An article on the operation of journals published by the American Psychological Association listed the rejection rate for the *Journal of Applied Psychology* at 91%, which was one of the highest for any of the APA journals listed (**http://www.apa.org/pubs/journals/fe atures/2013-statistics.pdf**).

The articles in *JPSP* and the *Journal of Applied Psychology* often contain a series of experiments, many participants, advanced kinds of analyses, and extramural funding. In contrast, *The Journal of College and University Student Housing* (published twice a year) typically contains research of more modest proportions, in terms of scope. The articles are often single studies of narrow scope with less advanced statistical analyses. A paper from the second issue of the 2015 publication of *The Journal of College and University Student Housing* illustrates these characterizations. "Is Three a Crowd? Exploring the Development and Satisfaction of Students in Triples" (Long & Kujawa, 2015) was conducted at one institution, focused on a fairly narrow topic, and used analysis of variance and chi square as the primary statistical approaches. In contrast, a paper by Mann and Ferguson (2014), "Can We Undo Our First Impressions? The Role of Reinterpretation in Reversing Implicit Evaluations," published in *JPSP*, presented seven experiments and was funded by grants from the National Institutes of Health (NIH) and a National Science Foundation (NSF) Graduate Research Fellowship award. The research used meditational analyses, as well as a mixed design (both between- and within-subjects factors; see Chapter 8).

Journals differ in the criteria used to determine research that is likely to be (a) accepted for review and (b) published in a particular journal. Nevertheless, it is worth remembering that journal impact is not synonymous with journal quality. Remembering Meltzoff's (1998) comments about the importance of critical reading, mentioned in Chapter 1, every journal article needs to be approached with the attitude "show me." We should not exhibit an overreliance on authorities, one of the logical problems in thinking (Shermer, 1997) discussed in Chapter 1, and assume that a high rejection rate = high quality.

> **» Try This Now**
>
> Check out articles in a current journal in your discipline. Note differences in number of experiments, who the participants were, kinds of statistical analyses, sample size, and indication of grant support. In your discipline, what might be the equivalents of the *Journal of College and University Student Housing* and *JPSP?*

OPEN ACCESS AND PREDATORY PUBLISHERS

Several journals you may come across are called **open-access journals**. Open Access publishing refers to "unrestricted access and unrestricted reuse" according to the definition on the PLOS website (**https://www.plos.org/open-access/**). PLOS publishes several highly respected open access journals primarily in the sciences, but there are open access journals in every scholarly discipline; for example, *Ergo,* is an open access journal in philosophy. In the summer of 2015, there were more than 10,000 open access journals listed in the Directory of Open Access Journals (**https://doaj.org**). In principle, the movement toward open access should provide numerous benefits, including faster publication of articles and availability of information. Many (but not all) open access articles follow a rigorous peer-review procedure, which means there is a kind of gate-keeping to try to ensure the quality of the publication. These journals are free to the reader, but there may be costs associated with the publication of these journals, many passed on to authors.

Open-access journals: journals that offer free access to the published articles.

Not all open access journals are created equal. Jeffrey Beall, a tenured librarian at the University of Colorado, Denver, established a website titled Scholarly Open Access (**http://scholarlyoa.com/about/**), which provides an evaluation of open-access publishing. On this site, he maintains a list of what he calls Potential, Possible, or Probable Predatory Open-Access Publishers, often referred to as **Beall's List**. Criteria for identifying predatory open-access publishers are also provided on Beall's website (**https://scholarlyoa.files.wordpress.com/2015/01/criteria-2015.pdf**) and include such characteristics as evidence "showing that the editor and/or review board members do not possess academic expertise to reasonably qualify them to be publication gatekeepers in the journal's field." Frequently there are fees charged to authors to publish in these journals (called the *author-pays model*); at one time, book publishers that charged authors to publish their books were called *vanity publishers.*

Beall's List: list evaluating open-access publications in terms of their standards; named after the originator of the list, Jeffrey Beall.

Null hypothesis: hypothesis that there are no group differences or relationships between variables.

Null hypothesis significance testing procedure (NHSTP): using statistical inference, a procedure for evaluating whether the null hypothesis should be rejected.

Alpha level: probability (usually set at .05) of incorrectly rejecting the null hypothesis.

p value: probability value based on the characteristics of the observed data used for hypothesis testing.

Confidence interval: shows range of values that you can be sure contains the population mean a certain percentage of the time (e.g., 95%).

In 2011, Beall's list of Potential, Possible, or Probable Predatory Open-Access Publishers included 18 such publishers; in 2016, that number had reached 923. Beall recently started two new lists: one that includes journals whose metrics (regarding calculation of impact factors) are suspect, the other identifying what he calls hijacked journals, where the name of a legitimate journal has been hijacked by a counterfeit one.

It is probably prudent to stick with Google Scholar or one of your institution's databases, to decrease the probability that you will end up with an article from a journal on Beall's List. A useful overview of the problems surrounding open access publishing and the pressure to publish is an essay titled "Anarchy and Commercialism" by Altbach and Rapple (2012, March 8) from Inside HigherEd (**https://www.insidehighered.com/views/2012/03/08/essay-problems-state-journal-publishing**).

PUBLICATION PRACTICES OF JOURNALS

Most journals share criteria used in evaluating the merit of articles, including significance levels and the intellectual contribution of the article. Such criteria may be shared across journals, but journals obviously differ in the content of articles they publish; even within a given journal, editors-in-chief (who usually serve a specific length of time) may be interested in promoting a particular focus within the discipline. Furthermore, specialized journals are being added to address emerging fields, especially in technology.

Significance Levels

In most research that uses inferential statistics (and most research in the social and behavioral sciences does), the aim of the project is to be able to reject the **null hypothesis** of no difference between sampled populations. This process is sometimes called the **null hypothesis significance testing procedure (NHSTP)**. As a scientific community, researchers therefore need a decision rule about when differences exist (that is, when to reject the null hypothesis represented by the data). Most members of the scientific community accept the standard of a statistical outcome with a probability value of .05 (5 / 100) or less frequent. The value .05, called the **alpha level**, represents the likelihood that in only 5 of 100 cases would the outcome occur by chance. This number is stated (acknowledged) before the analyses are conducted. This **p value** (or probability value) of .05 is the standard used by most journals for having significant results. In addition to the p value, some journals also request that **confidence intervals** be provided. For example, a 95% confidence interval shows the range of values within which you can be sure the population mean is contained 95 out of 100 times.

It should be noted that at least one journal (*Basic and Applied Social Psychology*) has banned the use of NHSTP in papers submitted to the journal. In its place, the journal editors call for:

> [S]trong descriptive statistics, including effect sizes. We also encourage the presentation of frequency or distributional data when this is feasible. Finally, we encourage the use of larger sample sizes than is typical in much psychology research, because as the sample size increases, descriptive statistics become increasingly stable and sampling error is less of a problem. (Trafimow & Marks, 2015, p. 1)

Most journals are interested in publishing results that advance the literature in some way. For that reason, research in which the null hypothesis is accepted (i.e., not rejected) is unlikely to be published.

Reviewer Selection

When a journal states that it is a peer-reviewed journal, what that means is that people knowledgeable about the topic in question have been invited by the journal editor to evaluate the quality of the paper. Usually a journal specifies particular categories for comment, including the currency and coverage of the literature, as represented in the introduction, the theoretical grounding, the scope of the research question, methodological issues (e.g., sample size and adequacy of measures), appropriateness of statistical approach, significance of findings, and contribution of the study to the literature (answering the "what's new and noteworthy here?" question).

Journals editors are increasingly aware that fraud occurs in the reviewer process (e.g., authors create false e-mail addresses for reviewers and suggest these fictitious reviewers provide a review—essentially generating the reviews for their own manuscripts). In one instance, a reputable journal retracted 60 published articles after it was determined that there was author and reviewer fraud (**https://www.sagepub.com/en-us/nam/press/ sage-statement-on-journal-of-vibration-and-control**). Many journals subscribe to the **Committee on Publication Ethics (COPE)** for reviewers. The guidelines are available on the COPE website: **http://publicationethics.org/resources/guidelines**.

In addition to what one would normally expect of a reviewer (e.g., expertise in the subject area and agreement to keep the manuscript and review details confidential), providing fair reviews involves degrees of separation. The reviewer should not have collaborated with

Committee on Publication Ethics (COPE): sets standards for reviewers who evaluate research.

the author (usually there is a time frame, for example, 3 years), be at the author's institution, or in other ways be familiar with the manuscript that is being reviewed.

Intellectual Contribution of the Article

Large numbers of manuscripts are submitted for publication, and few can be accepted for publication (e.g., the rejection rate for the *Journal of Personality and Social Psychology* was 89% in 2013). The statistics provided by the APA indicated that 988 manuscripts were submitted to that journal in 2013. For that reason, research must be more than methodologically sound and well written; research must make a contribution and advance the state of knowledge in a meaningful way. The extent of the contribution and whether the research is of sufficient scope or merit is a subjective decision, which is why the expertise and fair-mindedness of the peer reviewers is important.

With the recent work of the *Reproducibility Project* (see Chapter 1), which is determining whether the published findings of 100 correlational and experimental studies in psychology are reproducible, journals may be more welcoming of replications than in the past. Because replications (for the most part) have not been judged to advance the field, there has been a bias against publishing replications to this point.

Editorial Policy

As suggested in their titles, journals are interested in publishing work about a specific area of interest (e.g., *Health Environments Research & Design Journal, Cultural Sociology,* and *Attachment and Human Development*). Editors generally serve for a particular period of time (e.g., 3 years) and may have a specific focus they want to emphasize during their tenure. For example, Ronald Brown, editor of *Professional Psychology: Research and Practice,* is "focused on publishing research that could increase access to mental health treatments" (**http://www.apa.org/pubs/journals/pro/**).

Specialized Journals

As knowledge expands, new journals are introduced to provide a home for those topics, whether related to technology (e.g., *Digital Applications in Archaeology and Cultural Heritage,* begun in 2014); mental health (*Spirituality in Clinical Practice,* begun in 2013); or demographic groups that have been underrepresented in the literature (e.g., *Asian American Journal of Psychology,* begun in 2009).

When you are considering where to submit research for publication, it is important to select a journal that is a good "fit" for your research. Often you can make an informed judgment by looking at your references and assessing where most of the research you cite has been published. It makes sense to submit your manuscript to a journal you have cited!

Editors will often "desk reject" a manuscript they judge to be a poor fit for their journal (e.g., as evidenced by a lack of citations to that journal). A desk reject means that the manuscript is not sent out for review.

File Drawer Phenomenon

Earlier we talked about the difficulty in having an article accepted for publication, with one of the basic criteria being research where the null hypothesis has been rejected. Not all research works out, and then it may be "filed away." This problem with nonsignificant results being filed away contributes to what is known as the **file drawer phenomenon or effect**, a term introduced by Robert Rosenthal in 1979 in his article "The 'File Drawer Problem' and Tolerance for Null Results." This problem is a form of publication bias, in which nonsignificant results do not contribute to the body of knowledge about a particular issue and are therefore not published. When this happens, particular findings appear to be more robust or reliable than in fact they are, given the unpublished data that remain "in the drawer," so to speak.

At the other end of the file drawer spectrum, a problem may occur when data produce significant results *unwanted* by the researcher (e.g., supporting the work of another theorist). If this researcher then decides to "file" the data, the case is problematic. Not only do we have less information about a research topic, but there is also a kind of academic dishonesty in not sharing significant findings inconsistent with one's predictions or theoretical model.

> **File drawer phenomenon or effect:** form of publication bias in which research appears more reliable than it is because articles on the topic that have not rejected the null hypothesis have not been published.

JOURNAL ARTICLES VERSUS BOOK CHAPTERS

Overall, the primary mode of advancing knowledge in the social and behavioral sciences is the journal article, and in particular the peer-reviewed journal article, as was discussed earlier. Journal articles have the advantage of a short "time-to-market" because it takes much less time to publish an article than a book; this is even more likely to be the case with the availability of electronic journals. Furthermore, although books may be peer-reviewed, that is less likely the case than for journal articles. In addition, even though books may present original research (i.e., be considered *primary source* material), they are more likely to synthesize existing research (i.e., be considered *secondary source* material), especially in the case of edited volumes. For those reasons, journal articles are likely to be the major source of information that you include in the Introduction of a research project.

REVISIT AND RESPOND

- What do the number of experiments and sophistication of data analyses suggest about an article? What is Beall's List? When we talk about the publication practices of a journal, what do we mean? Why do reviewers need ethical standards? State the null hypothesis in your own words. Why might replications become more common in the future? What is the file drawer phenomenon?

PHYSICALLY OBTAINING AN ARTICLE: A CLOSER LOOK AT DATABASES

Earlier in the chapter we talked about keywords and narrowing or broadening your search to identify a manageable number of articles to consult. Now we will talk in more depth about electronic resources and about *physically obtaining* those articles.

A lot of browsing is done "online" using electronic resources (E-resources). It is important to know how to obtain the physical copies of the resources about your topic. Your library homepage will probably contain links to a Catalogue (to find books), Electronic Resources such as Databases and Indexes (to find journals), and Online Journals (full text). Databases and indexes are typically used to *locate* an article of interest. Online journals provide articles (although not necessarily for all dates of publication) in downloadable form.

Once you have located an article of interest through a database or index, you want to determine whether the article is immediately downloadable from a journal with online access (from the library's collection of online journals). In databases like PsycINFO, the user enters a keyword and selects several fields ("Select a Field") such as author name, journal where the article appears, publication date, or a combination of these fields to locate a relevant article. The next question is how to obtain that article. This process usually involves your library's electronic journal holdings. For a given article you have located, there is usually an option to check for "full text" (see Figure 2.8).

Some articles are linked directly to the database citation via a linking tool with a symbol that states "PDF full text" (see Figure 2.9). Compare Figures 2.8 and 2.9.

When the PDF Full Text symbol and/or the HTML Full Text symbols are present (see Figure 2.9), just click on one of these links and your article will appear. PDF full text is preferred because the article will have the visual appearance of the actual article (e.g., with the correct page numbers and all figures). The HTML version is computer generated, and not all figures or images may appear; in addition, the formatting is not identical to the actual article, making it difficult to identify original page numbers if you want to quote from the article. If the symbols are not present (see Figure 2.8), you typically click on the

FIGURE 2.8 Screenshot of a Library's Electronic Journal Holdings for a Specific Article With Option to Check for Full Text

3. **Urban design aesthetics**: The evaluative qualities of building exteriors.

Academic Journal

Nasar, Jack L.; Environment and Behavior, Vol 26(3), May, 1994 Special Issue: **Design** review: Public participation in the evaluation of **design**. pp. 377-401. Publisher: Sage Publications; [Journal Article]

Subjects: Aesthetic Preferences; Architecture; Emotional Responses; Evaluation; **Urban** Planning

Times Cited in this Database: (35)

Check for Full Text

Source: PsycINFO®

FIGURE 2.9 Screenshot of a Library's Electronic Journal Holdings for a Specific Article With Option to Download PDF or HTML Full Text

ı. **Impressions** of **psychotherapists' offices.**

Academic Journal

Nasar, Jack L.; Devlin, Ann Sloan; Journal of Counseling Psychology, Vol 58(3), Jul, 2011 pp. 310-320. Publisher: American Psychological Association; [Journal Article]

Subjects: Aesthetic Preferences; Aesthetics; Personalization; **Psychotherapists**; Therapeutic Environment; Adulthood (18 yrs & older); Male; Female

Cited References: (61) Times Cited in this Database: (6)

HTML Full Text   PDF Full Text

Source: PsycINFO®

link that says, "Check for Full text." This link will either provide options for obtaining the article (e.g., "Content is available via the following links" and these will be listed to click on) or you will see a statement something like: "Sorry, no holdings were found for this journal. Please see additional options below for finding this journal." The additional option will typically be requesting the item through **interlibrary loan** (see Figure 2.10). Interlibrary loan is a system that allows library patrons to request library materials not held by their institution. Librarians carefully select the combination of databases they offer (pay for) to give library patrons the greatest coverage, but they can't provide every resource. Interlibrary Loan allows users to obtain needed materials through other libraries.

PsycINFO® Versus PsycARTICLES®

Students may prefer to search for articles using the database **PsycARTICLES®** because *every* article in that database is provided full text. The articles come from journals published by the APA and affiliated publishers. In contrast, articles identified through

Interlibrary loan: system that allows library patrons to request library materials not held by their institution.

PsycARTICLES®: database of articles from the American Psychological Association (APA) and affiliated publishers in which every article is provided full text.

FIGURE 2.10 Screenshot of Interlibrary Loan Request for a Specific Article Not Available at Current Library

Search criteria: Refine or alter criteria

Fisher, Bonnie (05/01/1995). "Fear spots in relation to microlevel physical cues: Exploring the overlooked.". *The journal of research in crime and delinquency (0022-4278)*, 32 (2), p. 214.

Citation: Email ▾ or Export/Save ▾

Sorry, no holdings were found for this journal.

Please see additional options below for finding this journal.

Additional options:
Interlibrary Loan
    Submit a request

Source: PsycINFO®

PsycINFO may provide full text but not necessarily. There is a distinct advantage to PsycINFO, however, because PsycINFO contains abstracts from more than 2,000 journals, many more than provided by PsycARTICLES. By using PsycINFO, you have access to a much greater breadth of information about a particular topic. In other words, potentially having to search a bit longer to obtain a full text version of an article is worth the effort in terms of becoming familiar with the published work on a topic.

REVISIT AND RESPOND

- Explain how you would obtain an article that is not available as full text downloadable. What is the difference between PDF Full Text and HTML Full Text? What is the difference in journal coverage between PsycINFO and PsycARTICLES?

SUMMARY OF THE ARTICLE LOCATOR SEARCH PROCESS

Start with a solid database in your field, such as PsycINFO, locate articles of interest, and THEN see whether those articles are linked directly to full text or available through full text holdings supported by your institution. If not, request the article through your library's version of Interlibrary Loan. Although it may be easier to limit yourself to electronic journal sources to obtain articles directly (i.e., full text downloadable), the shortest path does not necessarily guarantee that you will secure the most important articles.

INTERLIBRARY LOAN (ILL) SYSTEMS AND WORLD CATALOG (WORLDCAT)

You need to be familiar with the manner in which your library obtains materials (typically books and journal articles) that it *neither owns nor to which it has direct access*. As we discussed, these materials can be obtained through some kind of interlibrary loan system. Many libraries offer an interlibrary loan Web interface called ILLiad® to request books and journal articles. You typically need to set up your own ILL (interlibrary loan) account (check with your librarian).

WorldCat (World Catalog) is another useful resource to obtain materials not available in your library. As the name "world" suggests, this database is worldwide; it includes books, monographs, videos, and sound recordings. Most library systems have a link to WorldCat as one of their databases. A book entry in WorldCat will tell you whether your library owns the item, what institutions in your state own it (including public libraries), and who owns the item beyond your state.

WorldCat: worldwide catalog listing books, monographs, videos, and sound recordings; useful for determining what institution owns a resource in order to retrieve it.

REVISIT AND RESPOND

- Explain how you would obtain a book that your library does not own.

> **›› Try This Now**
>
> In WorldCat, search for a book whose title you know and see whether it is in your library's holdings; if not, what library close to you owns the book?

WHAT TO DO WITH YOUR ARTICLES (READ MORE THAN THE ABSTRACT!)

If you develop a research idea by only reading abstracts, the quality of your research project will suffer. A 150–250-word abstract does not provide sufficient detail to make decisions related to your project. You need to read beyond the abstract to determine the paper's true relevance to your idea. You may find it useful to start with the Method and Discussion

FIGURE 2.11   Overview of Connections to Resources Available Through Your Library

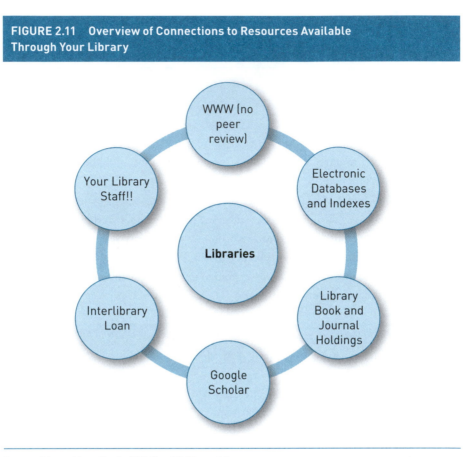

Source: Adapted from Devlin (2006), p. 29, Figure 1.3.

Method: heading in American Psychological Association (APA) research paper in which you present your Participants, Materials/ Measures/ Instruments, and Procedure.

Discussion: title of section in a manuscript when you interpret the results, centered and bolded in American Psychological Association (APA) style.

sections before reading the other sections of the paper. Many of the important details come in the section that describes how the research was done, known as the **Method** section. This section includes the "who" (the participants and their number), the "what" (the measures/equipment), and the "how" (the procedure). You can quickly see the nature and scope of the undertaking and consider its relevance to your circumstances (in terms of participants, measures, and/or equipment). The **Discussion** reports whether the hypotheses were supported, connects the findings to the literature on the topic, acknowledges limitations, and gives some ideas for future directions. The description of the limitations and presentation of future directions both may help shape your research idea.

How many articles do you need to read? There is no firm number, but in reading between 20 and 30 articles, you will become increasingly familiar with the topic and will begin to see the same articles cited again and again. When this happens, you have begun to identify the important publications in the field; these should serve as a foundation for your work.

Many articles you read will follow APA publication style. If that is the case, the articles will be divided into (a) a review of the literature, (b) a method section (with subsections dealing with participants, measures, and procedure), (c) the findings (Results), and (d) the meaning of the work (Discussion).

THE INTRODUCTION

The **introduction** is usually shaped like a funnel, starting out broadly with some general comments about the area of interest, then gradually tapering to focus on particular variables, and finally narrowing to the specific hypotheses, which are usually stated at the end of the introduction (we will cover more aspects of writing in Chapter 11). In the presentation of the literature, which names (key players) and theories appear repeatedly? Are there different "camps" representing conflicting theoretical orientations? Work that is cited repeatedly is sometimes called seminal or keystone. Look out for these studies because they may have historical, methodological, or theoretical importance. Two techniques, **tree backward** and **tree forward** (Martin, 2007, pp. 125–126), help you canvas the literature to make sure you have identified the important work. When you tree backward, you identify a citation in the article you are reading that looks promising (often on the basis of what was said about it in the article), and then go to THAT article to examine its references. You continue to do this, working backward in time from the most recent to the earliest articles. If you *tree forward,* you see which other (more recent) authors have cited the article you are currently reading. To tree forward, you use a database like the Social Sciences Citation Index or the "cited by" functions of PsycINFO or Scopus.

Introduction: part of a manuscript that introduces the topic, reviews relevant literature, and ends with hypotheses.

Tree backward: search technique for working backward through previously published work to obtain resources.

Tree forward: search technique looking forward to see what more recent articles have cited the article of interest.

The Hypotheses

The statement of *hypotheses* (see definition in Chapter 1) typically comes at the end of the introduction. The statement of hypotheses is important; if well stated, with specific predictions, a clear statement of hypotheses makes conducting the analyses straightforward. This sounds easier to do than it is. Even in exploratory correlational research where the investigator wants to look at the relationship of one situation to another, without an intervention, a statement of hypotheses would help guide the research effort. What is it that you really want to know? An interest in type of student housing and sense of community could be turned into an explicit statement with a hypothesis such as:

Students living in triples converted from doubles will report a lower sense of community than will students living in nonconverted doubles.

Participants: section of your Method in which you describe the "who" of your study.

Vulnerable population: population (e.g., children, pregnant women, or prisoners) for whom a full institutional review board (IRB) review is required for research involving these individuals.

Amazon MTurk®: online paid crowdsourcing platform to acquire participants.

Convenience sample: participants gathered through their mere availability and accessibility to the researcher.

Snowball sample: nonprobability sample in which individuals who participate in a study invite others to participate in the study, and they in turn invite still others.

In the Introduction, note which hypotheses have been supported in the literature and where conflicts have occurred because this will highlight areas where work remains to be done (to resolve the conflicts). Other research opportunities are highlighted when authors mention a recent surge in research activity on a given topic after a period without much activity. For example, just a few studies on residence halls were done each year from the late 1960s to the late 1990s, at which time interest in the topic grew (refer to Figure 2.7). Why? Were new residence halls being constructed, which in turn led to the opportunity for field research? Your own experience with student housing would be a good place to start to consider the impact of a variety of student housing arrangements (e.g., campus apartments vs. high-rise residence halls).

THE METHOD SECTION

The *Method* section of articles you read is particularly important because novice research-ers often struggle with the "who" (the participants), the "what" (the measures), and the "how" (the specific steps) in a research project. Following APA style, the Method section is divided into subsections involving participants, materials or measures (also called instru-ments), and procedure. Pay attention to the particular approach that is used in a given area of study. What is the typical approach: Observation? Interviews? Self-report surveys? Is the research correlational (no manipulation of variables), is there experimental manipulation, or a combination? You might try an approach to the research question different from the one typically used.

Participants

One of the biggest challenges is obtaining the "Who" for the study. Often the **partici-pants**, the "who," will be college students, recruited at the researcher's institution (see also Chapter 9 on recruiting participants). In the articles you read, notice whether the partici-pants were college students. Adult volunteers from the community? A special population like residents of an assisted living complex?

Sample size is an important consideration. How many people participated? If partici-pants number more than 100, this might be an issue at small institutions where the par-ticipant pool is limited (see Chapter 9). If a topic requires a specialized population, such as prisoners, this is also a consideration. Certain groups such as prisoners and children are considered **vulnerable populations**. Not only may such populations be difficult to obtain, as in the case of inmates, but also research with vulnerable populations requires special ethics review (see Chapter 4).

How were the participants recruited? Through a participant pool (i.e., usually stu-dents who need to participate in research to fulfill a course requirement)? Were they contacted via e-mail? Direct mailing? Via **AmazonMTurk**® (or Amazon Mechanical Turk), a crowdsourcing platform sponsored by Amazon.com where researchers (requesters) post studies and participants (workers) complete the posted tasks for pay (see Chapter 9)? Were the participants randomly selected within the population or through a **convenience sample**, gathered through their mere availability and accessibility to the researcher (e.g., people who stopped at a research table in the library or student union; the participant pool)? It is worth noting that the participant pool is a convenience sample and is not necessarily representative of the student population. Did the authors use a **snowball sample** (i.e., asking people to participate who in turn recommended other people to participate)? Issues of sampling are covered in Chapter 9.

Materials/Measures/Instruments

Finding appropriate **materials** or **measures** (see Chapter 5 on qualities of measures) is among the biggest challenges for researchers. The first step is identifying what measures might be appropriate. As was true for identifying seminal articles, keep track of the scales and measures used repeatedly in a given area. For example, if you are interested in the topic of self-esteem, you will repeatedly see citations to Morris Rosenberg's Self-Esteem Scale (1965). This scale has a high **internal consistency** (in the neighborhood of .88), which means the items relate to each other (i.e., are measuring the same concept). In addition, there are only 10 items, which is a consideration in terms of the number of items you may ask respondents to complete.

Procedure

What precisely did participants do? The level of detail in this section should enable you to replicate the study or the **procedure**. Consider the time involved in collecting the data—were there individual interviews? Group administration? Online questionnaire administration? Was there equipment? Were there costs involved? (Payment for copyrighted questionnaires? Payment to subjects? Incentives such as a lottery?) In addition to these considerations, are you qualified to administer a given test (usually this applies to clinical measures)? A description of required qualifications is typically stated in the description of the measure. More in-depth coverage of Measures appears in Chapter 5.

THE RESULTS SECTION

Look at the presentation of the **results**; could you understand the statistics? Are sophisticated approaches, such as structural equation modeling, being used in this area of research? Could you see yourself doing statistical analyses of this complexity? Note the structure of the results section. What information is presented first? How are tables and figures used?

Materials: section of the Method in which you describe the "with what" of your study; often called measures, instruments, or apparatus.

Measures: in the Method section where you describe the scales or instruments used.

Internal consistency: statistical measure, usually expressed as Cronbach's alpha, which reflects the degree to which each item of the measure is tapping the construct of interest.

Procedure: section of your Method in which you describe the "how" of your study.

Results: title of the section in a manuscript where the results are presented; in American Psychological Association (APA) style, the word Results is centered and bolded.

THE DISCUSSION SECTION: CONFLICTS AND GAPS

Like the introduction, the Discussion provides direction about research possibilities. The Discussion section is shaped like a triangle, starting narrowly (at the top of the triangle), restating whether the hypotheses were supported. Then it broadens to relate the findings of the research to the work cited in the introduction. The Discussion typically ends with a section on Limitations and Future Directions. If the work is applied, there also may be a specific section called Recommendations.

The Discussion section provides material to consider for research projects. When authors are relating their work to the existing literature, they talk about their findings being consistent (or not) with this literature. If not, then conflict exists. This conflict provides the opportunity to conduct further research to try to resolve the discrepancies. Limitations are a fruitful area to direct future research because the authors point out the shortcomings of their work; you can try to address these shortcomings, such as better measures or a more heterogeneous population. Returning now to an idea from Michael Shermer (1997) in Chapter 1, overreliance on authorities, don't be afraid to criticize research that has been published. Beyond the limitations identified by the authors themselves, you may identify other drawbacks to the work; these provide the opportunity for new research projects.

Future Directions also point to research opportunities. Researchers may not be explicit about the directions the research could take, to protect their own "next steps." At the same time, they may speak in more general terms about possibilities, such as using different age groups or more current measures.

REVIST AND RESPOND

- Explain what information you should keep track of in each of the following sections: Introduction, Method, Results, and Discussion. What are the three sections of the Method? What is the internal consistency of a measure? What is the shape of the Introduction? The Discussion? Why are the Limitations and Future Directions sections important in developing research ideas?

KEEPING TRACK: ILL, MENDELEY, AND REFWORKS

Interlibrary loan (ILL) books must be returned to a lending library within two to three weeks. Your own handwriting may not provide an accurate record of material in these books. Instead, if you are using quotations from books, photocopy the pages from which you are quoting; having these pages will enable you to check the accuracy of the quotations you use.

Mendeley and RefWorks may be useful to the researcher but for different reasons. Mendeley is a free reference manager, and you can easily download and install it on your computer. Returning to our theme of tradition and innovation, Mendeley involves working on "tradition." It is easy to be overwhelmed with articles you have accessed, and unless you print out the articles (which would be expensive), you need a way to retrieve these articles without redoing your database searches. Once you have downloaded a full text article to your desktop, you can add it to your Mendeley library, which you can organize by topic headings. You can then retrieve your articles from your Mendeley reference manager by author name, author keywords, publication, or your own tags. Within Mendeley you can create folders for specific topics, which is especially helpful if you are writing something that covers a range of topics or working on more than one project. If you use quotations in your writing, it is wise to recheck those quotations before submitting a manuscript. Using Mendeley, you easily access the full text paper against which to check the quotation.

> **Mendeley:** free reference manager for organizing and subsequently accessing downloaded articles.

> **» Try This Now**
>
> If you do not have Mendeley on your desktop, consider downloading and installing it.

RefWorks is primarily used by students as a bibliographic management tool. Most students in the social and behavioral sciences will be asked to learn APA style (2010b) for providing citations and references. APA style is challenging to learn because there are many rules that deal with such issues as the use of ampersands, commas, italics, volume numbers, and digital object identifiers. To make it more challenging, in APA style, the format of citations in the text is different from the bibliographic form in the References section. Unlike Mendeley, there is a cost to RefWorks, but institutions typically have purchased a license to the software, and users logged on to the institutional system can use RefWorks "free of charge." In theory, using RefWorks should create error-free bibliographic citations and references. Trying this on the Andrade and Devlin (2015) article, the citation was close but not error-free.

Andrade, C. C., & Devlin, A. S. (2015). Stress reduction in the hospital room: Applying ulrich's theory of supportive design. *Journal of Environmental Psychology, 41,* 125–134. doi:10.1016/j.jenvp.2014.12.001

Can you detect the error? Try this now before reading further.

The "U" in Ulrich (a proper name) was not capitalized in the RefWorks version. In addition, users of APA style need to know the recommended font (Times New Roman) and the recommended font size (12 pt.). The advice in this book is that you learn APA style well enough to detect these kinds of errors.

REASONABLE QUESTIONS AND THE PROBLEM OF THIRD VARIABLES: CLOSING THE RESEARCH GAP

Third variable: variable that influences the relationship between the variables of interest; also called a confounding variable.

Once we have a research question and have run our study, what happens when we ask questions that seem to have a high likelihood of producing strong relationships but do not? The gap between the behaviors of interest may be wide; as a result, other variables or factors that have not been measured "get in the way." These factors are called **third variables**; they have not been assessed (see also Chapters 3 and 6). Third variables are variables the researcher failed to measure that account for the relationship between the variables of interest. If the research gap is wide, there are likely to be several of these third variables. Would you predict a strong relationship between job performance and employee satisfaction? Most of us would because we imagine that people who are satisfied with their jobs are productive. Yet the relationship between performance and satisfaction is relatively small (Iaffaldano & Muchinsky, 1985). Thinking about this relationship more deeply, many factors influence why people are productive in their jobs, not just job satisfaction.

> **»** **Try This Now**
>
> What reasons might people have for being productive at work and for keeping their jobs?

There are many reasons: benefits (including health care); status; no other job prospects; and commuting time. Thus, pressures, concerns, or other unmeasured variables may influence the relationship between job productivity and worker satisfaction. Several explanations exist for any relationship. These other variables are a problem in research. We want to rule out as many of these as we can by taking steps *before* we collect data. We do so by closing the (a) research gap and (b) accounting for background variables (discussed next).

When variables are far apart (e.g., the relationship between parental disciplinary style and student achievement), many other variables may be in play in explaining the outcome of interest (here, academic achievement). You want to limit the number of other variables that may explain the relationship in question, without limiting the research question to the point that it has no **external validity** (see Chapter 3) or applying the results beyond the particular situation examined. In the example of the relationship between parental disciplinary style and student achievement, parents' marital status may connect both of these variables. Divorce may have changed students' educational experience, for example, attending boarding school after a divorce, which may affect both the type and frequency of parental discipline and performance in school. Narrowing the research question to focus on parents' divorce (and timeline) may enable the researcher to predict college achievement better. You might investigate the timing of the divorce as a predictor of academic achievement (e.g., divorces happening within 1 year of matriculation would be associated with lower academic achievement than divorces happening before that time).

External validity: ability to apply the results of research more broadly, that is, beyond the sample used in a particular study. Generalizability is a major emphasis of external validity.

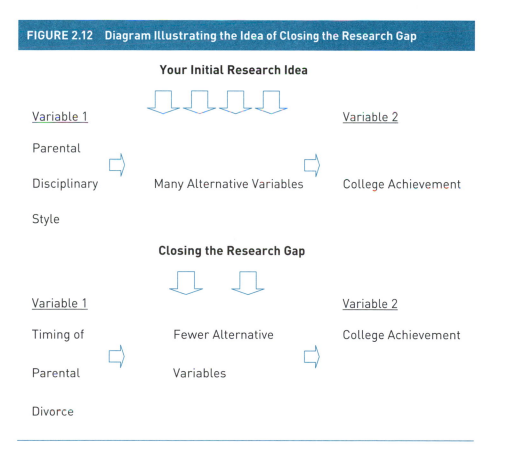

FIGURE 2.12   Diagram Illustrating the Idea of Closing the Research Gap

Your Initial Research Idea

Variable 1

Parental

Disciplinary   Many Alternative Variables   College Achievement

Style

Closing the Research Gap

Variable 1   Variable 2

Timing of   Fewer Alternative   College Achievement

Parental   Variables

Divorce

Demographic variables: background variables (e.g., gender or age) about participants that are used to describe the sample and may be used in analyses in quasi-experimental research.

But in addition to closing the research gap, there may be other relevant variables you need to assess. By including background or **demographic variables** describing the participants (e.g., high school GPA, gender, birth order, or distance of college from hometown), you will reduce the number of relevant unmeasured variables. You cannot include an endless list of demographic questions; be mindful of the "likely suspects." Select those variables from the literature most likely to be relevant (and that you thus need to measure; see Figure 2.12).

REVISIT AND RESPOND

- Explain what a third variable is and why it makes sense to narrow the research gap. What role do demographic variables play in narrowing the research gap? Where should you look to determine which demographic variables to include?

TIME PRESSURE AND TIMELINES

Whatever the length of time you have to complete a research project, start the process by creating a timeline of due dates for components of the project: coming up with ideas, consulting the literature, settling on an approach (research design), identifying and obtaining measures, securing IRB approval, recruiting participants, collecting the data, entering and/or analyzing the data, presenting the results, and explaining the results. As explained earlier in the chapter, the written report (manuscript) includes the Introduction, Method (participants, measures, procedure), Results, and Discussion. Given time pressure, it is a wise idea to write sections along the way, rather than waiting until after you analyze your data.

Divide the semester (12–13 weeks) into weekly segments; then work backward from the final deadline. If your instructor reads drafts, incorporate that into your timeline. Figure 2.13 provides one model to manage the steps in the research process.

You can control your own behavior, but receiving approval from the IRB or feedback on your draft may not happen according to schedule. Manage the time for the activities YOU can control (generating ideas, consulting the literature, writing sections of the manuscript). One other challenge is worth noting. One of the biggest obstacles is obtaining complete measures (with all items and scoring instructions), which is not as straightforward as you might think. We will cover the pitfalls of this task in Chapter 5.

FIGURE 2.13	Steps for Managing the Research Process

Sample Timeline

Week 1	Begin generating ideas
Week 2	Begin to consult the literature; access/order articles and books
Week 3	Settle on an idea and refine it; continue accessing/ordering articles and books; determine your research approach (i.e., correlational vs. experimental)
Week 4	Locate and obtain measures; develop questionnaire either online (e.g., Survey Monkey® or Qualtrics®) or paper version; generate IRB proposal (which includes the full survey with all the measures that will be used in the study; begin draft of Introduction)
Week 5	Submit IRB proposal; continue writing Introduction; write References
Week 6	Receive approval of IRB proposal; revise and resubmit to IRB if necessary
Week 7	Collect data
Week 8	Finish collecting data; write Method section (in past tense)
Week 9	Score, enter, or download data; analyze data
Week 10	Write Results section and begin Discussion
Week 11	Finish Discussion section and produce a draft
Week 12	Submit draft (if professor agrees)
Week 13	Receive draft comments, revise, and submit final paper; present research to peers (e.g., PowerPoint)

Source: Adapted from Devlin, 2006, p. 5.

ACADEMIC FRAUD

Fraud is purposeful deception to achieve some kind of gain, financial or otherwise. When people talk about fraud in research, they generally refer to manipulation of some part of the research endeavor. The University of Virginia has a useful website listing forms of academic fraud. These include plagiarism, multiple submission, false citation, false data, and Internet resources (**http://www.virginia.edu/honor/what-is-academic-fraud-2/**).

Fraud: deception designed to result in personal gain; may take many forms in the research process.

In this book, we focus on aspects of the research process where academic dishonesty may occur. You may be familiar with the phrase "ignorance of the law is no excuse," which essentially means that if you violate standards of conduct, not knowing the "rules" does not excuse the behavior.

We have already discussed examples of fraud in the academic process, most notably, the fabrication of a dataset by a graduate student (see Chapter 1). Why does such behavior occur? There are many reasons why people take these costly shortcuts, among them being extrinsically rather than intrinsically motivated (Davy, Kincaid, Smith, & Trawick, 2007). There is some indication that fraud (data fabrication or falsification) is more prevalent in journals with higher impact factors, suggesting that authors purposely seek to advance their standing with these publications (Steen, 2011a). Research by Steen (2011b) also has suggested that research misconduct is increasing and that journals do not always inform their readership of the reasons for the retraction of papers. More than 30% of the retracted papers unearthed in Steen's analysis were not so identified. Some authors have argued that motivations for power and achievement, labeled *neoliberal values of self-enhancement,* may explain cheating in higher education (Pulfrey & Butera, 2013).

In the work of students in my research methods classes, the incidence of student misconduct has been quite low. When it occurs, it usually involves plagiarism or collaborating on assignments without permission. Fabrication of an entire dataset is at one extreme of academic dishonesty; unintended plagiarism may be at the other. Because plagiarism typically involves the process of writing, the specifics about what it is and how do avoid it are covered in Chapter 11 dealing with writing up and presenting your results.

Summary

At this point, you should have thought of a research idea and examined what has already been done in that area. By now you know the physical holdings and electronic resources your institution's library has, how the interlibrary loan system works (make sure you have created your own account), how to search for journal articles through several different databases, and how to request articles that you cannot immediately download.

An important idea in this chapter is the critical task of narrowing the gap between some variable of interest, such as parental disciplinary style, and its relationship to an outcome, such as college achievement. Your job is to eliminate competing variables by narrowing the research question sufficiently to rule out the most likely alternative explanations for any significant relationship that emerges. You cannot control every variable that may play a role, but you can certainly pose your research question in a way that reduces the likelihood that one of those competing variables provides a better explanation than your candidate.

This chapter presented a timeline that you may find useful in planning the work of the semester. Staying on top of your deadlines will also reduce the likelihood that you will engage in academic dishonesty.

If you have not had time to consider them earlier, here is the list of **REVISIT and RESPOND** questions from this chapter.

- Why might it make sense to think of some ideas before consulting the literature?
- What advantages are there to using your own personal experience to develop research ideas?
- Write down two potential research ideas that come out of your personal experience and two that come from the Internet.
- What is the Library of Congress classification system? What is a keyword?
- What kinds of resources would you expect to find in the Reference section? In what ways can librarians help with your research project?
- What do the number of experiments and sophistication of data analyses suggest about an article? What is Beall's List? When we talk about the publication practices of a journal, what do we mean? Why do reviewers need ethical standards? State the null hypothesis in your own words. Why might replications become more common in the future? What is the file drawer phenomenon?
- Explain how you would obtain an article that is not available as full text downloadable. What is the difference between PDF Full Text and HTML Full Text? What is the difference in journal coverage between PsycINFO and PsycARTICLES?
- Explain how you would obtain a book that your library does not own.
- Explain what information you should keep track of in each of the following sections: Introduction, Method, Results, and Discussion. What are the three sections of the Method? What is the internal consistency of a measure? What is the shape of the Introduction? The Discussion? Why are the Limitations and Future Directions section important to develop research ideas?
- Explain what a third variable is and why it makes sense to narrow the research gap. What role do demographic variables play in narrowing the research gap? Where should you look to determine which demographic variables to include?

BUILD YOUR SKILLS

1. As a first step in writing an introduction, prepare article summaries for 10 relevant articles. Summaries should include:

   (a) The correct bibliographic citation (you could use RefWorks but see also the section in Chapter 11 on APA formatting)

   (b) A sentence describing the topic being investigated

   (c) A brief paragraph summarizing the theory or conceptual reasoning that underlies the research. What population and methods did the authors use? What did the authors demonstrate? What are the important conclusions and implications?

   (d) A sentence describing the findings that are important for your research project. What do the results add to your own approach to your project?

2. As a second step in writing the introduction, prepare a written integration of these 10 articles.

   (a) Try to shape your introduction like a funnel, starting wide and narrowing as you approach your hypotheses (or where your hypotheses will be by the time you submit your IRB proposal!).

   (b) Try to create paragraphs organized around themes; don't simply "stack" the article summaries.

   (c) Re-read the articles you are using to get some idea of how other people write literature reviews. Consider their organizational strategies (Foundation articles? Theory? Methodological approaches? Confounding variables? Anomalous findings?)

   (d) Consider how other researchers explain the manner in which they are building on the previous literature, i.e., taking things further and in new directions.

RESEARCH DESIGN APPROACHES AND ISSUES

An Overview

CHAPTER HIGHLIGHTS

- How research quality affects research answers
- The continuum of certainty: The distinction between correlation and causation
- Characteristics of experimental research
- IVs versus DVs
- Reframing a study: Correlational, to quasi-experimental, to experimental
- Type I versus Type II error
- Relationships among sample size, power, and effect size
- Threats to internal validity (including Campbell & Stanley's 1963 list)
  - Demand characteristics
  - Participant role attitudes
  - Single- and double-blind approaches
  - Pilot studies, cover stories, and manipulation checks
- External validity and ecological validity
- Where research takes place: Laboratory research, field study, field experiment, virtual reality, survey research

OVERVIEW

Experimental design:
research approach with manipulated variables and random assignment.

Quasi-experimental design:
research approach that resembles experimental research but is based on the use of preexisting groups [quasi-independent variables (IVs)].

Internal validity:
extent to which a research design allows you to test the hypothesis adequately.

Type I error:
incorrectly rejecting the null hypothesis when it is true.

Type II error:
failing to reject the null hypothesis when it is false.

This chapter introduces basic concepts about research design and the kinds of research questions that can be answered, depending on your approach. More detailed information about specific designs will come in Chapters 6–8. Fundamental to understanding what research can tell you is the degree of certainty about the results, in particular, the distinction between a study with correlational results and one where causality can be inferred. Moreover, although different research approaches (e.g., **experimental** and **quasi-experimental design**) may use the same statistical analyses, what can be claimed about the results is not the same. In designing a research study, there may be many threats to **internal validity**, that is, whether the design is adequate to answer your research question and evaluate any hypotheses. We will cover those threats to internal validity, talk again about *external validity* (i.e., generalizability or how broadly the findings can be applied; see Chapter 2), and about two kinds of errors: **Type I error** (claiming a result was significant when you should not have done so; also called a "false alarm" or a "false positive") and **Type II error** (not claiming a result as significant when you should have; also called a "miss" or a "false negative"). Aspects of the study that relate to the roles of both the researcher and the participant will be covered, as well as ways to do preliminary testing of your study (pilot studies and manipulation checks). The chapter will briefly describe the different settings in which research takes place, from the laboratory to the field. By the end of the chapter, you should be well versed in the fundamentals of research that apply across different types of research designs.

At the end of this book, Appendix A presents a decision tree to help guide which statistical approach should be used for which kind of research question and Appendix F presents a table of the statistical analyses in terms of the scale types that are used in common research designs. You may find these appendices helpful to consult throughout the book.

RESEARCH QUALITY AFFECTS RESEARCH ANSWERS

Good research involves asking worthwhile questions that combine tradition and innovation, as we saw in Chapter 2. Good research also involves selecting an approach that is appropriate for the question(s) you want to answer. Some research questions can be answered with a high degree of certainty; others cannot. In some instances, we are interested in what might be called exploratory research; we want to gain an understanding of a topic without posing specific hypotheses. Often we use interviews, focus groups, and case studies in such research. These approaches are usually described as qualitative and will be described more fully in Chapter 6.

Whatever your goal and approach, the manner in which you conduct the research affects its quality. Even in exploratory qualitative research where you are trying to get a sense of the issues that matter to people (e.g., reactions to building low-income housing near a neighborhood park), many aspects of your approach, such as the facility where the questions are asked and who is included in the interviews, can affect how people respond. This chapter will emphasize quantitative approaches, but many of the same issues dealing with the internal validity of your research (whether the design enables you to answer the research questions) apply to qualitative research as well.

WHAT RESEARCH CAN TELL YOU: THE CONTINUUM OF CERTAINTY

The degree of control you exercise in conducting your research is usually related to the level of certainty you can have in your results—greater control is related to greater certainty. On one end of the research continuum, we do not manipulate any variable; if we want to quantify people's answers (i.e., quantitative approaches), we typically ask people to answer questions about the topic of interest on a rating scale. For example, we might ask whether there are relationships between the number of times students work out/week, their caloric intake, and their body esteem. Using measures such as rating scales with numerical values, we would be interested in the correlations or associations between variables. Nothing is manipulated. Even in this type of study, there are additional questions we can ask that will increase our confidence in the relationships we see (perhaps we should ask about height and weight, for example, which might affect the relationships).

At the other end of the continuum, we manipulate specific variables, keep everything else the same, and try to infer causality from the study (e.g., randomly assigning students to different workout schedules before measuring their caloric intake and body esteem). You can see that even in this second case, there are still a lot of other "unmeasured" variables (e.g., students' workout schedules prior to the study or whether they are varsity athletes) we would need to assess to be confident that differences in workout schedules caused differences in caloric intake and body esteem.

| Correlation | ⟶ | Causation |

CORRELATION VERSUS CAUSATION

You may have heard the phrase "Correlation is not causation." These two concepts lie at different ends of the spectrum of certainty about relationships. That does not mean that one kind of relationship is always preferable to the other; each is suited to different research questions and situations. Ultimately most researchers seek to understand causes of behavior, it is true, but in some kinds of situations, research that would result in making statements about causality is not possible.

Correlational research: approach to research where no variables are manipulated.

When the research approach is **correlational**, the focus is on the relationships between variables. We change nothing about the situation of interest and simply assess whether relationships exist. We have no evidence that a change in one variable caused a change in the other. Because the variables have not been manipulated, there is no opportunity to assess causality; there is no evidence of influence (that is, one variable cannot be said to affect another). Rather, the concepts of interest are associated or related to one another. When the research approach is **causal**, there is evidence of influence. In this situation, there is an explicit manipulation of (i.e., change to) one or more variables. This change allows us to assess causality.

Causal research: when the research design enables you to test cause-and-effect relationships.

To illustrate the difference, we might first investigate the relationship between students' GPAs and the distance of the college they attend from the students' hometowns. We cannot randomly assign people to a given GPA, nor can we randomly assign them to living in a specific hometown. Students "come that way." We might hypothesize that these variables (GPA and distance of the hometown from the college) co-vary, such that changes in one are associated with changes in the other—for example, that students who have higher GPAs live farther away from their hometown (and those with lower GPAs live closer). In this case, we are predicting a positive relationship (higher GPAs correlate with longer distances), but we cannot infer causality. Why? Because there are many other explanations other than distance for that GPA.

> ## ⏩ Try This Now
>
> List another variable that might be used to help explain this significant relationship between students' GPAs and the distance of the college from their hometowns.

Perhaps you said, "attended boarding school." Perhaps going to boarding school prepares you for attending college a far distance from home, and it is this boarding school preparation, not the distance from home itself, that better explains this relationship with

GPA. The essence of research in which causality can be inferred is control—control over every aspect of the research endeavor that can be controlled. When control is not possible, we have other ways we try to spread out the variability or differences in humans that can interfere with the factors we are studying. For example, when we do a study where people are exposed to different stimuli (e.g., pictures of natural and built environments) to measure environmental preference (i.e., how much they prefer particular environments), we randomly assign the participants to the different pictures (i.e., conditions) to spread out or distribute the variability that exists in the population (our participants). We do this random distribution to try to make sure, for example, that all the Environmental Studies majors don't end up in the condition with pictures of nature! If they did, a higher preference for pictures of the natural environment might be explained by the students' major, not by qualities depicted in the pictures themselves.

When we make a statement about causality, we have to persuade our audience that there are no other likely explanations; we have to rule out what are known as alternative variables represented by unmeasured or *third variables,* which we discussed at the end of Chapter 2. In correlational studies, such variables may lead us to infer incorrectly relationships between our variables of interest when, in fact, it is the third variable at work. There is a wonderful video from Frans de Waal's TED talk on Moral Behavior in Animals that shows what happens when two capuchin monkeys were rewarded unequally for the same "work" and the less-well-rewarded monkey tests out an alternative explanation (**https://www.youtube.com/watch?v=meiU6TxysCg**). One monkey is rewarded with a grape (the preferred food); the other monkey is rewarded with a piece of cucumber for the same task (handing a small stone to the experimenter). When this happens, the monkey that received the cucumber is quite unhappy (throwing the cucumber back at the researcher) and next tests his stone against the side of the cage to make sure that the stone hasn't somehow produced the inequitable result. What this monkey is doing is testing for a third variable, as if to say, "maybe it's the stone that's the problem." Even capuchin monkeys are capable of thinking about alternative explanations!

Combing two previous examples, how might you infer causality in a study involving distance and working out? In the earlier example, we could not randomly assign people to their hometowns, but we might be able to assign first year students randomly to residence halls at different distances from the campus fitness center. Then our research question might be whether living closer to the fitness center has an effect on the number of times a week students go to the center to work out. There are many other variables (representing alternative explanations; see Chapter 2) that we might need to rule out (whether the student is a varsity or club athlete, any health restrictions, athlete status in high school, and so on), but we have manipulated and controlled a variable (distance from the fitness center) and randomly assigned people to the conditions (different residence halls) located at different distances from the fitness center. If there is a result showing that people who live closer to the fitness center work out more times/week than do those who live farther from the fitness center, then we might infer causality related to the variable of distance.

WHY CONDUCT CORRELATIONAL RESEARCH?

You might be asking yourself why people do correlational research if the goal of research is to explain behavior (hence, to determine causality). Correlational research has important purposes. First, it is sometimes used as exploratory research to see whether relationships exist before investing more resources in experimental research. Second, there are many instances in which it is not possible to manipulate variables (such as people's hometowns). Third, it may be unethical to manipulate variables. For example, we could not tell people that a car accident had occurred to a member of their family or that they had failed a final exam to determine their emotional reaction. As we will see in Chapter 4, research on human participants is monitored by review boards to make sure ethical principles are followed.

There are innumerable situations where it is not feasible to manipulate variables. For example, we can't change the condition of the sidewalks in people's neighborhoods to examine the impact of sidewalk upkeep on an activity such as walking. What we would do instead is find neighborhoods (and the people in them) that are alike in as many ways as possible (e.g., health), except for the condition of the sidewalks, and then look at the differences in activity levels across neighborhoods. Again, we would also need to measure background variables such as age and car ownership that could be related to activity levels.

A fourth reason to use correlational research is to study relationships that are naturally occurring. You might assess the relationship between student test scores and involvement in extracurricular activities, without wanting to manipulate either one of those variables. Relatedly, assessing naturally occurring relationships may complement experimental studies conducted in the lab that have been described as artificial.

THE LANGUAGE OF CORRELATION AND CAUSATION

The words you use to describe your research have certain implications. When you use such words as *impact, influence, determine, control, regulate, shape, alter,* or *modify,* you suggest causality. When you use such words as *association, relationship, link,* or *correspondence,* you suggest correlation. In your writing, it is important to use the language that matches the kind of research you have done (see also Chapter 11 on writing up research).

CORRELATIONAL RESEARCH APPROACHES: CORRELATIONAL AND QUASI-EXPERIMENTAL

Correlational research approaches can be divided into two general categories: correlational and quasi-experimental. What the two approaches have in common is that only correlational relationships are involved; that is, no causality can be inferred. What is typically called a correlational approach involves questions about a randomly selected *sample as a whole* in which two or more variables are measured (Category 1 from Figure 2.1); what is called a quasi-experimental approach typically involves questions about differences between *preexisting groups* (Categories 2 and 4 from Figure 2.1).

Although there are groups in quasi-experimental designs, they have not been randomly assigned. Quasi means "resembling." Even though a quasi-experimental design mirrors a **true experimental approach** in some aspects (e.g., asking questions about group differences), it does not include the critical aspect of **random assignment** to condition and the groups preexist (e.g., gender) or can be formed from preexisting situations (e.g., dividing students into those who own cars vs. those who do not based on responses to a questionnaire). Examples of such preexisting groups in quasi-experimental research are gender, class year, marital status, athlete status, coffee drinker or not, or almost anything where the characteristic in question preexisted or was naturally formed.

True experimental approach: research approach in which one or more variables are manipulated and subjects are randomly assigned to condition.

Random assignment: when participants are randomly assigned to the conditions of the study.

HALLMARKS OF TRUE EXPERIMENTAL APPROACHES

In experimental approaches, participants are randomly assigned to conditions in which one or more variables of interest have been manipulated. There is an attempt to control extraneous variables and to measure as many potential third variables as necessary. The outcomes you measure test the effect of these manipulations. As an example, in Devlin et al. (2013), participants (students and adults from the community) viewed one of four photographs of the office of a psychotherapist that varied in the kind of art displayed (Western vs. Multicultural) and the number of art objects on view (1 vs. 6). Participants were randomly assigned

FIGURE 3.1   Four Types of Photographs Displayed in a Psychotherapist's Office

| Western Low | Western High | Multicultural Low | Multicultural High |

Source: Copyright © 2013 by the American Psychological Association. Devlin, Borenstein, Finch, Hassan, Iannotti, & Koufopoulos (2013). Multicultural art in the therapy office: Community and student perceptions of the therapist. *Professional Psychology: Research & Practice, 44*, 168–176. The use of this information does not imply endorsement by the publisher.

to one of the four conditions generated by crossing the two art traditions (Western vs. Multicultural) with the two different numbers of art objects (1 vs. 6) (see Figure 3.1).

Participants answered a series of questions about the characteristics of the therapist whose office they viewed; the office was created for the purposes of the research. The research question was whether the display of art that differed in (a) cultural tradition and (b) number of art objects would impact participants' judgments of the therapist, in particular, his or her openness to multiculturalism. This experimental approach is called a **between subjects design** because the conditions are distributed between (across) participants. In the between subjects approach, each person participates in only one condition. This approach is often used because the researcher is concerned that participating in more than one condition would produce different results than participating in a single condition and that the impact of a given condition could not be isolated. Moreover, the between subjects approach reduces the likelihood that participants will guess the hypothesis of the research. In contrast, in the experimental approach called a **within subjects design**, all participants would have seen all four photographs; that is, they would have been exposed to all of the conditions. Researchers often select a within subjects design when (a) effects of participating in one condition on another are unlikely or (b) there are such effects that carry over and researchers want to study them. Between and within subjects approaches are covered in more depth in Chapters 7 and 8, respectively.

Between subjects design: research in which the conditions of an experiment are distributed across participants such that each participant is in only one condition.

Within subjects design: type of experimental design in which participants are exposed to all of the conditions.

>> **Try This Now**

How does a between subjects design help prevent participants from guessing the research question?

DIFFERENTIATION OF INDEPENDENT AND DEPENDENT VARIABLES

A course in Research Methods exposes you to specific terms that communicate important information. In this chapter, we have already seen important terms, like correlational and quasi-experimental designs. Two critical terms to understand are **independent** and **dependent** variables. Often these are referred to as the IV and DV, respectively. An independent variable is manipulated or varied (like our example of art in the previous section). You could think of this as the variable that is independent or "free to differ." A dependent variable is the outcome of (depends on or is constrained by) exposure to the independent variable. Some researchers look at the independent variable as preceding an effect and, hence, as a cause; the dependent variable reflects the impact of the independent variable and is the outcome or effect.

We also need to identify what is called a **quasi-IV**. You remember that we talked about the difference between quasi-experiments and true experiments (where variables were manipulated and subjects were randomly assigned to condition). Here we will differentiate the parallel terms *quasi-IV* and *"true" IV* (normally just referred to as the *IV*). A quasi-IV is a grouping variable that has not been manipulated (like race or class year). A true IV has been manipulated (like our art example).

As we will see later in this chapter, the statistical analyses for research involving quasi-IVs and IVs are identical; what differs is the language we use to describe the results. When we use quasi-IVs, we use the language of correlation. Thus, if we have sailing team members and nonsailing team members take a cognitive task known as the Mental Rotations Test (MRT; see Vandenberg & Kuse, 1978) and sailing team members score significantly higher than do nonsailing team members on this test, can we state that being a sailing team member caused this higher performance? No. What we can say is that there is a relationship between being a sailing team member and scoring higher on the MRT in comparison to the performance of nonsailing team members.

Independent variable (IV): variable that is manipulated in an experiment.

Dependent variable: variable that reflects the impact of the manipulated or independent variable in research.

Quasi-IV: independent variable (IV) that is naturally occurring (e.g., race and gender) and as a consequence is not assigned at random.

REVISIT AND RESPOND

- Explain how a quasi-IV differs from an IV and the difference in language appropriate to use in a correlational versus an experimental study. Identify the IV (cause) and the DV (effect) in the following statement:

  "The teenager's back was peeling; she must have gotten sunburn."

REFRAMING A RESEARCH IDEA

First come research questions; then come research designs; last come statistical analyses. The manner in which your research question is stated guides the research design. Let's start with a correlational example and transform it into a quasi-experimental and finally an experimental design. This transformation will illustrate that there is usually a way to approximate an experiment based in the real world, even when the specific real-world variables cannot be manipulated.

As we discussed earlier, if you ask a question about the sample as a whole without any manipulation that forms groups, you will have a correlational research design. For example, if you ask whether the number of magazine subscriptions in a home is related to reading scores in fourth graders (see Figure 3.2), you will have a correlational design; the statistics will be Pearson's r.

If you ask a question about group differences, and the groups preexist (like subscribing to print magazines or not), you will have a quasi-experimental design. For example, if you ask whether there are higher fourth-grade reading scores in the homes of people who subscribe to print magazines than in the homes of people who do not, that is a quasi-experimental design (the preexisting groups are composed of people with and without print magazine subscriptions; see Figure 3.3). In that particular situation, if your

FIGURE 3.2 Example of Correlational Research Design

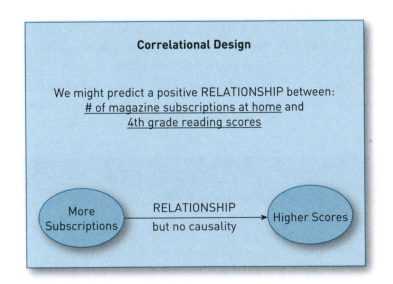

Correlational Design

We might predict a positive RELATIONSHIP between:
# of magazine subscriptions at home and
4th grade reading scores

More Subscriptions → Higher Scores

RELATIONSHIP
but no causality

FIGURE 3.3 Example of Quasi-experimental Research Design

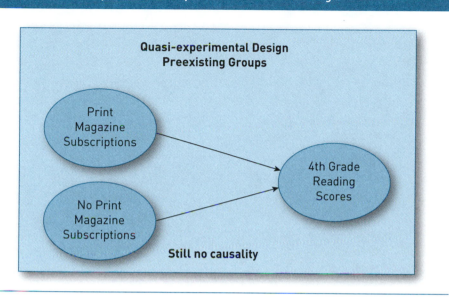

Source: Adapted from Devlin, A. (2006), *Research methods: Planning, conducting, and presenting research.* Belmont, CA.: Wadsworth/Thomson., Figure 2.2.

quasi-independent variable is print magazine subscriptions, which has two levels (yes or no) and your dependent variable is the fourth-grade reading scores of the children from those homes (one DV), your statistical analysis will be an independent samples *t* test. There is still no causality.

If you ask a research question about group differences, and the groups are created through manipulation, you will have an experimental research design. For example, if you create written scenarios (written text describing situations) in which participants are randomly assigned to read a scenario about a home with no (0) magazine subscriptions/month versus a home with 10 magazine subscriptions/month, and you ask participants their estimate of the reading scores of the fourth graders in the home (chosen from a scale of the possible reading scores), that is an experimental design (see Figure 3.4). In this situation, there is one IV (magazine subscriptions) with two levels (0 vs. 10 subscriptions/month) and one DV (the reading score estimate). Again, your statistical analysis will be an independent samples *t* test.

The statistical test in the examples of the quasi-experimental and true experimental designs are the same, but the language you use to describe the results will differ. In the case of the quasi-experimental research, you will use the language of correlation, e.g., probably that subscribing to print magazines is associated with having higher fourth-grade reading scores than is the case in a home where there are no print magazine

FIGURE 3.4 Example of Experimental Research Design

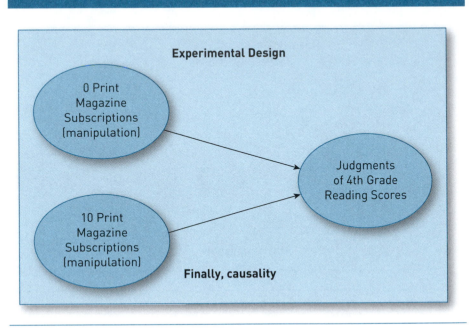

Source: Adapted from Devlin, A. (2006), *Research methods: Planning, conducting, and presenting research.* Belmont, CA.: Wadsworth/Thomson., Figure 2.3.

subscriptions. With this experimental design, you have the language of causality, for example, that reading about a household with 10 magazine subscriptions/month led to judgments of higher reading scores in fourth graders than did reading about a household with no (0) magazine subscription/month.

Appendix A at the end of the book contains a statistical decision tree that you may find helpful when thinking about how to evaluate your research question statistically.

TYPE I VERSUS TYPE II ERROR

Research in the social and behavior sciences typically uses inferential statistics, which means that we use samples to make informed guesses about the characteristics of the population from which the sample is drawn. In other words, we don't know for sure about an answer to a particular outcome because we haven't asked or assessed every person in the population of interest. We have asked what we hope is a representative sample. But we could be wrong because we are using inferences. Type I and Type II errors describe the ways in which we could be wrong. In a Type I error, we claim that we have a significant result when that is not the case. Formally, we reject the null hypothesis (of no difference or relationship between groups) when we should not have done so. In a Type II error, we have missed a finding that is there. Formally, we fail to reject the null hypothesis when there is a difference, that is, when we should have done so.

Figure 3.5 represents the four possible outcomes. We can be correct in two ways: We are correct when we reject the null hypothesis when there is a finding; we are correct when we do not reject the null hypothesis because there is no finding. We can also be incorrect in two ways (our Type I and Type II errors). We are incorrect when we reject the null hypothesis (say there are differences or relationships; a false alarm) when there are none (Type I error). We are also incorrect when we do not reject the null hypothesis and we should have, that is, such differences or relationships are there (Type II error; a miss).

Both Type I and Type II errors should be avoided, but Joseph Simmons, Leif Nelson, and Uri Simonsohn (2011) view Type I as more problematic. Their argument is once these false positives or incorrect statements that a finding exists appear in the literature, they tend to stay there. Such findings can encourage other researchers to investigate the phenomenon further, which may be a waste of resources.

Sources of Type I Error and Remedies

Remember that in inferential statistics, we are estimating likelihoods or probabilities that the data represent the true situation, but we set that likelihood at a given level, called the *alpha level.* By convention, the alpha level is set at .05. What that means is that there are only 5 opportunities in 100 (5 / 100) that we are mistaken in saying that our results are significant when the null hypothesis is true (see also Chapter 2 on this topic).

		Null Is False (there is a difference or relationship)	**Null Is True (there is no difference or relationship)**
FIGURE 3.5 Actual State of Affairs			
Our Action	We reject the null hypothesis	Correct decision	(Type I error)
	We do not reject the null hypothesis	(Type II error)	Correct decision

Bonferroni adjustment: adjustment for Type I error by dividing the alpha level (.05) by the number of statistical tests performed to create a new more stringent alpha level.

Two-tailed significance test: when the critical region for significance is spread across both tails of the distribution.

One-tailed significance test: when the critical region for significance is limited to one tail of the distribution (more lenient than two-tailed tests).

Standard approaches to reduce the likelihood of a Type I error are as follows: adjusting the alpha level; using a two-tailed versus a one-tailed test; and using a **Bonferroni adjustment** for multiple analyses (dividing the alpha level by the number of statistical tests you are performing). In theory, you could set your alpha level at a more stringent level (e.g., .01) to avoid a Type I error, but most researchers do not, fearing that a Type II error will occur.

A second approach is using a two-tailed rather than a one-tailed significance test. Please note that the decision to use a one- versus a two-tailed test is made prior to conducting analyses (and is typically indicated in the hypotheses). The difference between a **two-tailed significance test** and a **one-tailed significance test** deals with how your alpha is distributed. In a two-tailed test, the alpha level (.05) is divided in two (.025), meaning that each tail of the test statistic contains .025 of your alpha. Thus, the two-tailed test is more stringent than a one-tailed test because the critical region for significance is spread across two tails, not just one. A one-tailed test is not adopted in practice unless your hypothesis is stated as uni- rather than as bi-directional. Again, that decision has to be made *prior* to conducting analyses.

Another way in which a Type I error occurs is the use of multiple statistical tests with the same data. This situation may happen in research because there are not enough participants with specific demographic characteristics to run a single analysis. Here's an example. Suppose you want to examine issues involving number of majors (e.g., for students who identified themselves as having one major, two majors, or three majors), class year (first vs. fourth year), and athlete status [varsity athlete (A) or not (NA)] and the dependent variables of interest were GPA and career indecision (see Figure 3.6).

FIGURE 3.6 Example of Using Multiple Statistical Tests With the Same Data

1 Major				2 Majors				3 Majors			
1st		4th		1st		4th		1st		4th	
A	NA	A	NA	A	NA	A	NA	A	NA	A	NA
1	2	3	4	5	6	7	8	9	10	11	12

What this table shows is that we have 12 *cells* (look at the bottom row) to fill with participants with the appropriate characteristics. A minimum number of participants per cell might be 15 individuals. But we don't need just any 15 individuals; each cell must be filled with the 15 who have the required characteristics for that cell. For cell 1, we need 15 students who identify as having one major, are in their first year, and are varsity athletes. Cell 2 is 15 students who identify as having one major, are in their first year, and are not varsity athletes. You can see the difficulty in filling all of the cells with students who have the sought-after characteristics. A single analysis might not be possible. We might have to ignore the athlete status in one analysis and look at class year and number of majors, which is 6 cells (against the DVs, GPA, and career indecision). In another analysis, we might look at number of majors (3) and athlete status (2) against the DVs (6 cells again). In the full analysis, testing all variables at once, you would have 2 (class year) x 2 (athlete status) x 3 (number of majors) = 12 cells. Thus, if we did only 2 of those at a time (and given the selected examples) we would have fewer cells than in the full analysis. In a third analysis, we would look at athlete status (2) and class year (2), which has 4 cells. If we did all of these analyses, we would have run three analyses instead of one. *The likelihood that a Type I error would occur has increased because of these multiple tests.* For that reason, many researchers recommend using a Bonferroni adjustment, which resets the alpha level (more stringently). To use a Bonferroni adjustment, you divide the conventional alpha level (.05) by the number of tests you have run (here 3) to produce a new alpha level—here .017. Now, to consider a finding significant, the result would have to meet the new (more stringent) alpha level. [For those who want to read in more detail about this issue, articles by Banerjee, Chitnis, Jadhav, Bhawalkar, and Chaudhury (2009) and by Bender and Lange (2001) may be helpful.]

REVISIT AND RESPOND

- In your own words, explain the difference between Type I and Type II errors.

TYPE II ERRORS: SAMPLE SIZE, POWER, AND EFFECT SIZE

In a Type II error, we fail to reject the null hypothesis when we should have done so. Often the problem is having too few participants; therefore, having an adequate sample size is the primary way to address this problem. In general, larger sample sizes produce more power (see next section). **Power** is the ability to evaluate your hypothesis adequately. Formally, power is the probability of rejecting H_o (the null hypothesis), assuming H_o is false.

When a study has sufficient power, you can adequately test whether the null hypothesis should be rejected. Without sufficient power, it may not be worthwhile to conduct a study. If findings are nonsignificant, you won't be able to tell whether (a) you missed an effect or (b) no effect exists.

Power: probability of rejecting H_o (the null hypothesis), assuming H_o is false.

There are several reasons why you might not be able to reject the null hypothesis, assuming H_o is false. Your experimental design may be flawed or suffer from other threats to internal validity. Internal validity relates to the extent to which the research design enables you to measure your variables of interest rigorously. All aspects of your research may pose threats to internal validity, such as equipment malfunction, participants who talk during the experiment, or measures with low internal consistency (see Chapters 2 and 5). Low power is another threat to internal validity.

Four factors are generally recognized as impacting the power of the study. In discussing these, David Howell (2013, p. 232) listed (1) the designated alpha level, (2) the true **alternative hypothesis** (essentially how large the difference between H_o and H_1 is), (3) the sample size, and (4) the specific statistical test to be used. In his view, sample size rises to the top as the easiest way to control the power of your study.

Power is associated with effect size (as defined in Chapter 2; Cohen, 1988), which is discussed next. Effect size describes what its label suggests: whether an intervention of interest has an impact or effect. Consider two means of interest (when H_o is true and when H_o is false) and the sampling distribution of the populations from which they were drawn. What is their overlap? If they are far apart and there is little overlap, you have a large effect size; if they are close together and there is a lot of overlap, you have a small effect size. Effect size is indicated by (*d*) and represents the difference between means in standard deviation units. Statistical programs generally have an option for providing estimates of both power and effect size, and authors are often asked to include an estimate of effect size in their manuscripts (Howell, 2013).

In the literature, you will see descriptions of effect sizes as small (.20), medium (.50), and large (.80 and above). Jacob Cohen (1988) is usually the source cited. These three sizes represent different degrees of overlap: 85% (small), 67% (medium), and 53% (large). You can see that these percentages of overlap relate to the idea that there is a lot of overlap when the effect size is small and much less when the effect size is large.

Without doing a power calculation, you can still get some sense of the sample size needed in your topic area (with implications for power) by reading the literature. More participants are needed if the effect size reported in your topic area is small. If no effect size is reported for your area of study, you could make a guess about whether you think it is likely to be small, medium, or large. Without information to the contrary, a conservative estimate (i.e., a small effect size) is probably prudent. Cohen (1988) has published tables that indicate how many participants you will need to detect a difference (i.e., to reject H_o, assuming it is false) for a specific effect size. Power is discussed further in Chapter 7, including the use of an online power calculator.

Alternative hypothesis: hypothesis you have stated will be true if the null hypothesis is rejected.

INTERNAL VALIDITY

The validity of research refers to the degree to which the research evaluates what we claim it does. When we talk about the internal validity of research, we are talking about the degree to which the research was conducted in a manner that allows us to rule out alternative explanations; in other words, we are talking about the quality of the research process. Researchers are always vigilant to the occurrence of what are called **threats to internal validity** (additional types of validity related to measures are discussed in Chapter 5). A well-known list of these threats was produced by the researchers Donald Campbell and Julian Stanley in 1963.

Table 3.1 presents these threats to internal validity discussed by Campbell and Stanley (1963).

Threats to internal validity: factors that undermine the ability of your research to ascertain the influence of an independent variable (IV) on a dependent variable (DV).

TABLE 3.1 ■ Campbell and Stanley's Threats to Internal Validity	
History	Between experimental treatments, something happens to influence the results
Maturation	Capacities of the participants may change as a result of fatigue, illness, age, and hunger, which affect the intervention
Testing	In a situation where there are multiple testing situations, the first test affects how participants respond to subsequent testing
Instrumentation	Changes in equipment and/or observers affect judgments/measurements that are made
Statistical Regression	When participants are selected on the basis of extreme scores (e.g., high or low intelligence), their scores move toward the mean on subsequent testing
Differential Selection	Participants assigned to groups are not equivalent on some important characteristic prior to the intervention
Experimental Mortality	People drop out of studies in a nonequivalent manner (e.g., more older adults than younger adults drop out of the intervention than the control group)
Selection-maturation Interaction	In approaches where you might have quasi-experimental designs with multiple groups (so people are not randomly assigned), some preexisting aspect of the groups might be confounded with the effect of the variable of interest

Source: Adapted from Campbell and Stanley, 1963, p. 5.

History: one of Campbell and Stanley's (1963) threats to internal validity in which something happens between experimental treatments to influence the results.

Maturation: one of Campbell and Stanley's (1963) threats to internal validity in which capacities of the participants may change as a result of fatigue, illness, age, or hunger that affect the intervention.

Testing: one of Campbell and Stanley's (1963) threats to internal validity involving multiple testing situations in which the first test affects how participants respond to subsequent tests.

Solomon four-group design: pretest, posttest research design involving four conditions; takes into account the possible effect of sensitization in responding to the pretest measures.

Let's expand on each one of these threats and identify some others. In truth, some of these threats are beyond your ability to control, but at least you will be aware of them.

History

History is one of those threats you can't control. Events in the world that occur during the course of research (e.g., terrorism or illness) may impact respondents' answers to your surveys or problem-solving skills, as examples. If your sample is large enough, events specific to individuals are likely to be randomly distributed across conditions. In the case of terrorism or some other event that affects the population, you may not be able to tell whether the event interacted with and differentially affected the responses of one group relative to another, especially if the sample size is small.

Maturation

In the case of **maturation**, you have changes to participants that affect their performance. One aspect of maturation you can control is fatigue. If a long battery of measures is administered to participants (for example, of 60 minutes), they may lose interest, and their performance on the later measures would be different than if there were fewer measures. As a researcher, you can pilot test your questionnaire batteries and ask for feedback about fatigue. Solutions might be to administer the questionnaires in two sittings or to reexamine whether all of those surveys are, in fact, essential.

Testing

In **testing**, exposure to one instrument during a pretest or to an assessment that comes between a pretest and a posttest can change people's responses to the posttest. To determine whether this is the case, some researchers use what is known as the **Solomon four-group design** (see Chapter 8), which evaluates what would happen with and without the pretest. This approach is expensive in terms of time and resources because there are four groups to run. Another option is to consider whether the pretest is needed.

Instrumentation

Instrumentation is a threat that is more easily managed, in principle. With regard to instrumentation, for example, the conditions of projecting images for participants to view, being prepared is the best course of action. Knowing how to use all of the equipment is important (e.g., what to do when you get a "no signal" message for LCD projection or what to have participants do when a survey link doesn't load). Routinely checking calibration of equipment is advisable.

Another possible threat to internal validity in the category of instrumentation involves your measures. Make sure you include all of your items, and make sure that your participants have looked at all the pages of the questionnaire, if you are administering a paper version. When administering questionnaires online, it is possible to prompt participants to check that they have answered all of the items they intended to answer; such prompts help cut down on missed items.

Another kind of "instrument" is the researcher. If the researcher is giving task instructions, it is important to have a script to follow to make sure every participant receives the same information. Some researchers record instructions and material delivered in spoken form to ensure that participants hear the same speaking voice, with the same pace.

Another kind of issue involving the researcher is the subjective evaluation of participants' responses. Consider the situation where participants are giving responses to open-ended questions (i.e., questions where participants are free to answer as they wish and do not have preset categories from which to select) and the researcher is categorizing those responses. It is essential that the criteria for each category remain consistent across coders. One way this is accomplished is by creating clear **operational definitions** for each category. Operationally defining a variable is describing it in terms of the processes used to measure or quantify it. Imagine if researchers were categorizing qualities of the hospital environment in terms of Roger Ulrich's (1991) theory of supportive design: positive distraction (PD), social support (SS), and perceived control (PC). If patients mentioned that having access to the Internet improved their experience, we would need an operational definition of each category to place the Internet in one of them. Is the Internet an aspect of positive distraction (something that redirects your attention away from worries and concerns), or is it an aspect of social support (a way to accommodate others or encourage interaction)? Arriving at an operational definition can be challenging.

Statistical Regression

In **statistical regression**, the performance (scores) of participants who are at the extremes on a given measure will move toward the mean on subsequent administrations. In theory, you could address this issue by pretesting participants to avoid those with extreme scores, but if those with extreme scores are a focus of the research (e.g., low and high crossword puzzle–solving skills), then being aware of regression toward the mean is important in evaluating the impact of any intervention.

Differential Selection (Biased Selection of Subjects)

The **biased selection of subjects** is a problem when preexisting characteristics of participants may affect scores on the dependent variable. Imagine we were interested in the effect of exposure to nature on mood, and we unknowingly selected students raised in urban areas, all of whom had been placed in one residence hall where first year students were recruited for the study. In this kind of situation, their upbringing cannot be

Instrumentation: one of Campbell and Stanley's (1963) threats to internal validity in which changes in equipment and/or observers affect judgments/measurements that are made.

Operational definition: describing a variable in terms of the processes used to measure or quantify it.

Statistical regression: one of Campbell and Stanley's (1963) threats to internal validity when participants are selected on the basis of extreme scores (e.g., high or low intelligence) and their scores move toward the mean on subsequent testing.

Differential selection (biased selection of subjects): one of Campbell, and Stanleys (1963) threats to internal validity in which participants assigned to groups are not equivalent on some important characteristic prior to the intervention.

Experimental mortality: one of Campbell and Stanley's (1963) threats to internal validity in which people drop out of studies in a nonequivalent manner (e.g., more older adults than younger adults drop out of the intervention than out of the control group).

separated from exposure to our intervention (e.g., a camping experience in the woods). To avoid this situation, we might do a preevaluation of demographic characteristics (type of upbringing) to avoid this lopsidedness and randomly distribute students with different kinds of upbringing across our conditions.

Experimental Mortality

The term **experimental mortality** signifies not only that people have dropped out but also that participants have dropped out of a study in a nonrandom manner (e.g., more from the control than from the intervention group). That situation creates a problem because those who remain in the study no longer represent our original balance of random assignment to condition. Dropping out of studies commonly occurs in longitudinal research, where participants are followed over long periods of time (see Chapter 8). One well-known exception to longitudinal dropouts is the work involving what are known as Terman's Termites, a group of gifted youngsters followed by the Stanford researcher Lewis Terman for decades (Leslie, 2000).

Selection–maturation interaction: one of Campbell and Stanley's (1963) threats to internal validity in which with quasi-experimental designs with multiple groups, some preexisting aspect of the groups might be confounded with the variable of interest.

Selection–Maturation Interaction

In quasi-experimental research designs where you have not randomly assigned participants to conditions (which is often the case in real-world situations, such as classrooms or company divisions, where you have "naturally assembled collectives;" Campbell & Stanley, 1963, p. 47), some preexisting characteristic of the group may influence the outcome of the experimental manipulation, not the power of the manipulation itself. This is called a **selection–maturation interaction**. The researcher makes every attempt to use equivalent groups, but without the pretesting to guarantee sampling equivalence in the real world, Campbell and Stanley noted, this situation presents a threat to internal validity.

Demand characteristics: "cues available to participants in a study that may enable them to determine the purpose of the study, or what is expected by the researcher" (Corsini, 2002, p. 262).

BEHAVIOR OF THE EXPERIMENTER AND DEMAND CHARACTERISTICS

Continuing with threats to internal validity, one very important threat is the researcher, as was indicated earlier when we talked about instrumentation. The role of the experimenter also fits into a broader category called **demand characteristics.** The label suggests the meaning of the term—something in the research situation demands or shapes our behavior. The formal definition of demand characteristics is "Cues available to participants in a study that may enable them to determine the purpose of the study, or what is expected by the researcher" (Corsini, 2002, p. 262). For the researcher, these cues could come in the attire of the researcher (e.g., a lab coat), the manner of speech, eyegaze, or a host of other qualities. Cues can also come from the physical setting (e.g., size of the room), the other people in the room (e.g., only women), and the status of the researcher (e.g., student vs. professor).

What can be done about demand characteristics? Being aware that such characteristics exist is the first step. Evaluating your behavior and the setting in which the research is to take place is the second step. Changing any problematic aspects of either your behavior or the setting is the third step.

> **>> Try This Now**
>
> Think back to your experience participating in research, and iden-
> tify demand characteristics that existed and how you think they may
> have affected your responses.

BEHAVIOR OF THE PARTICIPANT: ROLE ATTITUDE

Ideally, we would like to have people participate in research who have no preconceived notions of what is going to be asked of them. As we know, we are dealing with humans who have schemas of the way the world works (refer to Chapter 1). Participants may think that certain kinds of behaviors are expected of them because they are in a research laboratory (for example, that it is inappropriate to challenge the experimenter about any aspect of the research). Also, students who have taken no courses in the social sciences differ in their level of naiveté or sophistication (as well as in their skepticism and hypotheses regarding deception) from those who have taken such courses. Students who have taken courses may respond with "insight rather than naiveté" (Adair, 1973, p. 19), which can be a problem for the researcher. John Adair's book *The Human Subject: The Social Psychology of the Psychological Experiment* emphasizes that the research endeavor is a social interaction and that participants are not necessarily passive. Participants may attempt to determine the hypotheses of the study and in doing so threaten the internal validity of the research.

You may not be able to control participants' attitudes, but given Adair's (1973) claim that "The experimenter is half of this social interaction, and his contribution to the data must be assessed or controlled" (p. 65), you can reduce the variability in your own

Single-blind experiment: research design in which participants are unaware of the conditions to which they have been assigned.

Double-blind experiment: research design in which both the participant and the researcher are unaware of the condition to which the participant has been assigned.

Role attitude cues: when participants approach research with a particular attitude, such as cooperativeness; may affect results.

Cooperative attitude: attitude of research participant who tries to help the researcher.

Defensive or apprehensive attitude: attitude of participant who is concerned about performance evaluation.

Negative attitude: attitude of a participant who wants to undermine the research.

behavior. You might consider tape-recording the instructions participants receive or at the very least reading the instructions from a prepared script and having a predetermined protocol for answering questions. In more extreme cases, you may need to resort to a **single-blind** or **double-blind experiment** (discussed later in the chapter).

Based on preexisting ideas of what is expected as a research participant and/or people's general temperament, participants may want to see the researcher (and the research itself) succeed or fail. Adair (1973) provided useful categorizations (called **role attitude cues**) of these preexisting attitudes of participants, which vary from positive to moderately negative. The first attitude is the **cooperative attitude** (pp. 26–28); Adair states that those with cooperative attitudes will approach any experimental situation with that cooperative attitude "where there are no compelling cues to the contrary" (p. 26). To characterize this cooperative attitude, Adair cites the work of Martin Orne (1962), which showed the extent to which participants are willing to go to please the experimenter, including participating in a meaningless task for several hours. The second attitude that Adair presents is the **defensive or apprehensive attitude** (pp. 28–30). Participants with this attitude are often worried their abilities will be measured, given their cultural understanding of what it is that researchers do. Such concerns may lead to attempts to perform even better on the research tasks than otherwise would have been the case. The third role attitude is the **negative attitude** (pp. 30–32). Participants with this attitude may go out of their way to sabotage or otherwise act counter to what they perceive to be the purpose of the experiment. These participants may also simply answer as quickly as possible to exit the situation, taking less time on the research than careful attention would require. Adair cites research that has shown that participants who are participating in research to meet a course requirement are more likely to have a negative attitude than are those who simply volunteer. The social skills of the researcher are important in working to create a positive research experience, whatever the participant's initial motivation. "Subjects should not be treated as inert objects for study. Not only is their awareness of the experiment's purposes a problem, but their attitudes, feelings, and motivations toward research must be considered" (Adair, 1973, p. 32).

SINGLE- AND DOUBLE-BLIND APPROACHES TO RESEARCH

In Chapter 1, we talked in depth about the fact that people's expectations or schemas shape their view of the world. The manner in which researchers approach their research can also shape outcomes. Remember the "Problems in Scientific Thinking" Michael Shermer (1997) listed, including "Theory influences observations" and "The observer changes the observed?" As researchers, we state hypotheses, which we hope will be supported. Our behavior can clearly shape research outcomes, and we must guard against that. Just think back to the selection of stimuli from Amos Tversky and Daniel Kahneman (1973), discussed in Chapter 1, in which the letter K led to support for their hypothesis about the availability heuristic, whereas other researchers have not verified that finding with different letters (Fiedler, 2011).

What steps can we take to make sure we do not influence research outcomes? Among the different approaches people have suggested are using a single-blind or a double-blind approach. In a single-blind approach, participants do not know their research condition. The use of a single-blind approach is common in research. It is the situation in which participants do not know whether they are being given the experimental treatment or a control (placebo). In a double-blind approach, neither participants nor researchers know to which condition the participants have been assigned. The double-blind approach is commonly employed in medical research because the outcomes are important and people's beliefs (both those of the participants and the researchers) may influence the efficacy of the treatment.

COVER STORIES

In a good deal of research, especially research in social psychology, the project would be undermined if participants knew the hypothesis of the study. In that situation, participants might purposely try to provide responses they thought supported or refuted the

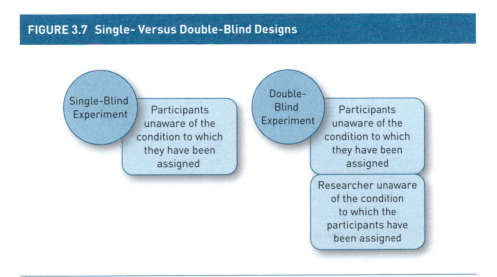

FIGURE 3.7 Single- Versus Double-Blind Designs

Single-Blind Experiment — Participants unaware of the condition to which they have been assigned

Double-Blind Experiment — Participants unaware of the condition to which they have been assigned — Researcher unaware of the condition to which the participants have been assigned

hypothesis. For that reason, researchers are often in the predicament of having to explain why they are asking participants to take part in the research, without "giving away" the real purpose. This situation leads to the need for a **cover story**, that is, a reasonable explanation for the purpose of research that does not reveal the hypothesis.

Chapter 4 on ethical issues covers the difference between passive and active deception. In general, if you are not purposely misstating the reason for the research but are not fully explaining the reason, the approach is considered **passive deception**. If you are purposely misleading participants, this is one reason the research would be considered a case of **active deception**. Frederick Gravetter and Lori-Ann Forzano (2016) provided a nice, simple way of describing the difference: Passive deception is like keeping a secret, and active deception is like telling a lie (p. 112).

In some situations, researchers simply say that the participants are going to take part in a study about attitudes and leave it at that (keeping a secret); this approach is sometimes called incomplete disclosure (see an overview put out by the University of California—Berkeley: **http://cphs.berkeley.edu/deception.pdf**). In other instances, there is no need for a cover story at all. If you were interested in the reactions people have to the design elements in their hospital room, for example, you might directly say that.

There are situations where you might need to have cover stories that involve active deception. Consider the following example. In a research project, the students were interested in what they called the difference between no violence and minor violence (pushing on someone else's arm without much force). Following up on literature they had read about the weapon focus effect and eyewitness testimony (Loftus, Loftus, & Messo, 1987), the students were interested in whether witnessing minor violence would result in lower verbatim recall of a scripted conversation than would witnessing the same conversation without the minor violence.

To conduct the study (St. Pierre & Wong, 2003), the students enlisted the help of two student colleagues (**confederates**) whose task it was to have a mild argument with a slight arm shove (experimental condition) and without the slight arm shove (control condition). Actual participants in this study were the witnesses to this argument and were told by the researcher that they would be filling out some questionnaires. Soon after the student participants and confederates were seated, the researcher told them she needed to leave the room to get some supplies. During her planned absence, the staged encounter took place (with the confederates whose ostensible role was also as participants). After the researcher returned, the actual participants were told to write down, verbatim, the conversation they had just heard. The dependent variable in the study was the number of correctly recalled words (i.e., verbatim recall) from the conversation. The student researchers found a significant effect of the manipulation in that there was significantly lower verbatim recall for the minor than for the no violence condition. This is a situation in which a cover story was necessary to avoid having participants closely attend to the conversation they overheard, which would not occur in a typical setting.

PILOT TESTS AND MANIPULATION CHECKS

If you are doing an experiment and are manipulating one or more variables, you are naturally concerned with whether the manipulation worked, that is, with whether it produced its desired effect. To avoid being disappointed when the null hypothesis cannot be rejected, it is wise first to make sure that the manipulation works (through a **pilot test**). To assess the effectiveness of the intervention in the study itself, you use a **manipulation check** at the end of the study. In a pilot test, you run your study, often with a just a few fellow students, to test your conditions. For example, if you were doing a problem-solving test and your review of the literature had not specified the difficulty or number of items to ask people to solve, you might need to test out your protocol. You would want to make sure that you weren't making it too easy (and hence have a **ceiling effect** where everyone essentially correctly answered all of the items and the scores cluster at the top of the distribution) or conversely making it too hard (and hence have a **floor effect** where essentially everyone answers none or very few of the items and all the scores cluster at the bottom of the distribution).

Related to the pilot test is the notion of a manipulation check. Imagine you were conducting research on the effect of hair color on hirability and you used an application that took a photo and changed the hair color of that person. Apple, Inc. (Cupertino, California) has such an application that a student used in a research project (**https://itunes.apple.com/us/app/hair-color/id485420312?mt=8**). If your hypothesis is that blondes are rated differently than are brunettes or redheads, you need to be sure that people can discern the hair color and pay attention to the hair color they see. If not, your manipulation is unlikely to be effective and you haven't adequately tested your hypothesis. At the end of your study, you would include a question asking the participants to indicate the hair color of the person they rated.

If a manipulation check does not reflect the expected differences between conditions, you have no way of knowing whether the targeted information in your conditions was not attended to by participants when they made their responses or if it was attended to but did not influence respondents significantly differently. One recommendation to avoid this situation is to run a pilot test and analyze the manipulation check question(s) at that

Pilot test: using a small number of participants to test aspects of the research and receive feedback on measures and/or manipulations.

Manipulation check: questions posed in research, typically at the end, to assess whether the participants were aware of the level of the independent variable to which they were assigned.

Ceiling effect: outcome in which scores cluster at the top of the maximum value; creates difficulty in evaluating group differences.

Floor effect: clustering of scores on a measure at the low end of the possible scale values; typically linked to the difficulty of the assessment.

time. If you have already started running the study, you could analyze the manipulation check question(s) fairly early on when about five to seven participants per condition have completed the study. You should be able to get a sense of whether the manipulation check reveals the expected group differences. For example, if you varied hair color in a study of the effects of hair color (blond, brunette) on hirability, your manipulation check question might be, "What was the hair color of the woman in the photo?" If most respondents say something that is on track (e.g., for the brunette condition, acceptable responses might be brown, dark hair, or brunette), you can assume that they perceived the hair color.

SUMMARY OF ADDITIONAL THREATS TO INTERNAL VALIDITY

Campbell and Stanley's (1963) list (history, maturation, testing, instrumentation, statistical regression, differential selection, experimental mortality, selection–maturation interaction):

- Demand characteristics
- Beliefs/attitudes of participants
- Effectiveness of cover story
- Effectiveness of manipulation checks

▶▶ Try This Now

How would you describe **your** role attitude as a participant? Have you tried to guess the hypotheses of experiments in which you have taken part?

REVISIT AND RESPOND

- Of the threats to internal validity listed by Campbell and Stanley (1963), where do you have the most control? The least control? Give an example of a demand characteristic. What are the different role attitudes participants can have, according to Adair (1973)? What is the difference between a cover story and a manipulation check?

EXTERNAL VALIDITY AND ECOLOGICAL VALIDITY

We have spent considerable time talking about internal validity; let's turn our attention outward, to external validity and ecological validity (they are not the same). External validity is the ability to apply the results of research more broadly, that is, beyond the sample used in a particular study. Generalizability is a major emphasis of external validity.

External validity needs to be distinguished from **ecological validity**. In ecological validity, the emphasis is on the degree of verisimilitude (i.e., lifelikeness) of the research to the events and characteristics of real life. The two concepts overlap in that both relate to situations beyond the immediate research setting, but ecological validity specifically emphasizes the realism or degree to which the situation reflects real life, which is not necessarily the case for external validity.

Ecological validity: validity in which the emphasis is on the degree of representativeness of the research to the events and characteristics of real life.

There is tension between external validity and ecological validity in the sense that when you emphasize the discovery of generalizable principles, experimental control is paramount (Banaji & Crowder, 1989). On the other hand, when you emphasize whether a finding occurs in a particular way in the real world, your concern is with natural settings, which typically lend themselves to reduced experimental control (Neisser, 1978). Different methods are typically associated with external and ecological validity. In the case of external validity, laboratory research is emphasized; in the case of ecological validity, field studies are often the focus. These different strategies suggest that a multimethod may be necessary to understand fully a given research topic (Eid & Diener, 2006).

REVISIT AND RESPOND

- Explain the difference between external validity and ecological validity.

WHERE RESEARCH TAKES PLACE

A discussion of external and ecological validity leads naturally to the categories describing where and how research takes place, including laboratory research, field study, field experiment, virtual reality, and survey research. These types of research differ in the degree of control that is possible, on the one hand, and the degree of realism of the situation being investigated, on the other.

Laboratory Research

Laboratory research is defined as research that is conducted in a highly controlled environment, typically with random assignment to condition, to enable the researcher to make causal statements. Such research may, in fact, take place in a laboratory specifically designed for such research, which is more likely to be the case in neuroscience but also occurs in the social and behavioral sciences. A more widely used term to refer to what is meant by laboratory research is experimental research. The essence of this concept is the high degree of control over all variables, including those that are not the focus of manipulation; this degree of control allows the researcher to make inferences about causality.

Field Study

A **field study** is the examination of variables in natural settings without the manipulation of variables. Ann Devlin's (1980) research on housing for older persons would be an example of a field study in which she was still able to look at group differences. No variables were manipulated; nevertheless, she was able to use housing type (high rise vs. garden apartment) and location in the city (three sites) as quasi-independent variables to examine how these variables were related to satisfaction and dissatisfaction with housing among older people.

Field Experiment

Like a field study, a **field experiment** takes place in natural settings. Unlike the field study, a field experiment manipulates variables. Ultimately the field experiment lacks the extent of control available in the lab, but every effort is taken to approximate that control. An example of a field experiment where more control might be possible is research in education settings, where you might have students receive different versions of instructions (by random assignment) to the same exam. You have manipulated a variable (the instructions), but the students in the classroom otherwise are in a setting that is natural and where most aspects of the setting (the instructor, the room, the exam content itself) remain controlled.

Another example of a field experiment in the world beyond the classroom is a study by Wesley Schultz et al. (2016). In this study, the focus was water conservation (in California) and the extent to which that could be influenced (measured by water usage as the dependent variable) by receiving environmental messages (Web-based or postal) in people with different levels of personal norms about conserving water. There were seven conditions in the study with three different kinds of messages that were delivered to residents: (1) descriptive norm—your water use compared with that of similar others in the neighborhood; (2) descriptive norm + injunctive—your water use and neighborhood norms again plus social approval (happy face; below neighborhood norm use of water) or disapproval (sad face; above neighborhood norm use of water) on the feedback; and (3) only information—water conservation tips. The message types were delivered in either of two forms (postal or Web-based); that gives us six conditions so far. One randomized control received no information about the study (the seventh condition). Here participants were clearly in their natural environments, their homes (in San Diego), but there was a fairly elaborate experimental manipulation to investigate how water conservation might be impacted by different kinds of feedback.

Virtual Environments

Virtual environments are typically laboratory environments that combine the control of the experiment with the naturalism of the field. This naturalism is created through virtual means. One definition of a virtual environment is "synthetic sensory information that leads to perceptions of environments and their contexts as if they were not synthetic. An immersive virtual environment (IVE) is one that perceptually surrounds an individual" (Blascovich et al., 2002, p. 105). Virtual environments are used in a range of research topics from clinical psychology (e.g., to deal with phobias) to architecture (e.g., to test wayfinding systems for buildings; see Figure 3.8 from Slone, Burles, Robinson, Levy, & Iaria, 2015). In the research of Edward Slone et al. (2015), the authors hypothesized that the complexity of the floor plan would affect spatial orientation and wayfinding skills. It did. There were more errors, and reaching the target destination took longer when participants were working with the more complex of the two floor plans.

Virtual environments: synthetic environment that combine the control of the laboratory with the naturalism of the field; often use immersive approaches.

FIGURE 3.8 Example of Floor Plans Used in Virtual Environment Research

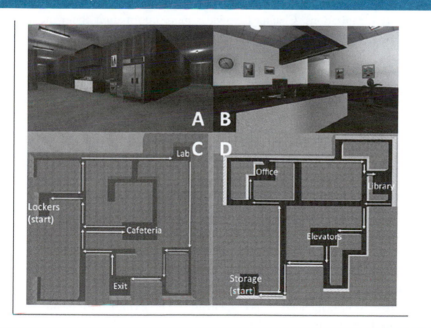

Source: Reprinted with permission from Slone et al., 2015, Figure 1, page 1031.

Survey research: approach to research in which the variables of interest (typically thoughts, feelings, and attitudes) are assessed through a survey.

Survey: series of questions, typically a standardized instrument, that assesses responses to one or more topic.

Survey Research Versus a Survey

An important distinction in terminology contrasts survey research with using a survey instrument as a means to collect information about dependent variables. When you do **survey research**, you are generally doing correlational research in which the variables of interest are captured by questions in a survey. A classic example would be an opinion poll where attitudes, beliefs, and even expected actions (e.g., choice for president) are surveyed. A **survey** is also a label used to describe a standardized instrument that may contain one or more dependent variables. Thus, we have distinguished between a research approach (survey research) and a particular kind of research instrument (a survey).

WHERE QUALITATIVE RESEARCH TAKES PLACE

We began the chapter noting that qualitative approaches to research are often exploratory and seek to understand a particular phenomenon in depth. This research can take place from the lab to the field, but more often, it occurs in the field and in particular within the communities where the research question arose. An example mentioned early in the chapter was exploring reactions to building low-income housing near a neighborhood park. In this situation, the researcher likely would reach out to people who live in the vicinity of the neighborhood park, for example, by contacting neighborhood schools or community organizations. Chapter 6 provides more information about the threats to internal validity that occur even in qualitative research.

Summary

This chapter has provided a general overview of research design as well as of internal and external validity and the components of each. You know the distinction between research where relationships are assessed and research where causal inferences can be drawn. The distinction has been made between IVs and DVs and between true IVs and quasi-IVs. We have seen how a study that started out with a correlational approach can be transformed into one that takes an experimental (causal) approach. In thinking about the number of participants needed for research, you should now be familiar with the concepts of power and effect size, and you should be able to explain the difference between Type I and Type II errors. We have reviewed the classic list of threats to internal validity from Campbell and Stanley (1963) and have expanded that list to include demand characteristics, the beliefs/attitudes of participants, the effectiveness of the cover story, and the effectiveness of manipulation checks. Finally, we have considered the different kinds of locations for research, from the laboratory to the field.

In later chapters, we will examine each of the different research designs (and associated statistics) in more depth.

If you have not had time to consider them earlier, here is the list of **REVISIT and RESPOND** questions from this chapter.

- Explain how a quasi-IV differs from an IV and the difference in language appropriate in a correlational versus an experimental study.
- Identify the IV (cause) and the DV (effect) in the following statement: The teenager's back was peeling; she must have gotten sunburn.
- In your own words, explain the difference between Type I and Type II errors.
- Explain why having sufficient power is important for a study. What are the four factors from Howell (2013) that affect the power of a research design? What is the most common way to increase power? In your own words, describe what an effect size is. How is power related to effect size?
- Of the threats to internal validity listed by Campbell and Stanley (1963), where do you have the most control? The least control? Give an example of a demand characteristic. What are the different role attitudes participants can have, according to Adair (1973)? What is the difference between a cover story and a manipulation check?
- Explain the difference between external validity and ecological validity.

BUILD YOUR SKILLS

Take a correlational research question, e.g., the relationship between preference for the natural environment and mood, and show how you could investigate this as a quasi-experimental study and then as a true experiment.

$SAGE edge™

edge.sagepub.com/devlin

Sharpen your skills with SAGE edge!

SAGE edge for students provides a personalized approach to help you accomplish your coursework goals in an easy-to-use learning environment. You'll find action plans, mobile-friendly eFlashcards, and quizzes, as well as videos, web resources, and links to SAGE journal articles to support and expand on the concepts presented in this chapter.

ETHICS AND THE INSTITUTIONAL REVIEW BOARD (IRB) PROCESS

CHAPTER HIGHLIGHTS

- The need for ethical review: IRBs; purpose and history of ethical oversight
- Nuts and bolts of IRBs: Definitions, membership, and levels
- Components of IRB proposal (esp. informed consent)
- Research with children and alternatives
- Deception and alternatives: Role playing and simulation
- The ethics of subject pool use and alternatives to participation
- Incentives in research
- Advice in preparing your IRB proposal
- IRB training modules: NIH and CITI

OVERVIEW

When thinking about research, one question that arises fairly early is whether there are rules or regulations that govern what you can and cannot study and how you can study it. The answer is "yes." Regulations, starting at the federal level, have been developed to protect people who participate in research (and animals used in research), the researchers

Research:
with respect
to the federal
definition
(45 CFR 46),
involves a
systematic
collection
of data with
the goal of
generalizable
knowledge.

themselves, and the institutions they represent. There are also specific definitions of what constitutes research and what a human subject is. **Research** is essentially a systematic investigation designed to contribute to generalizable knowledge. A human subject is a living individual from whom the researcher gathers information through interaction or intervention or about whom the researcher has access to identifiable private information. Both of these definitions come from the federal regulations known as the **Common Rule** [45 CFR 46.102(d) and (f)], respectively, which is discussed in more detail later in the chapter. Not every study rises to the level of research (e.g., a study on food preferences in a single residence hall might not be designed to contribute to generalizable knowledge), but the ethical treatment of people who participate in studies is an important aspect, despite whether the study is technically "research."

**Common
Rule:** federal
policy adopted
in 1991 that
lists specific
regulations
guiding
research
with human
subjects; also
known as 45
CFR 46 (Code
of Federal
Regulations).

Many students have heard of Stanley Milgram's (1963) research on obedience to authority, either in class or through the 2015 movie about the research (i.e., *The Experimenter*). This research is widely discussed in social science texts and not infrequently leads off the discussion of ethics (e.g., Cozby & Bates, 2014). In the research, participants are deceived, believing they are giving potentially lethal shocks to unseen "learners," who are performing a word association task and are shocked for their incorrect answers. In fact, these learners are confederates, or collaborators of the experimenter, and no such shocks are being administered. Conducted after World War II, the Nazi war crimes were a clear motivation for Milgram's studies; he mentioned them in the introduction to his paper about this research, published in 1963. Milgram questioned the extent to which ordinary people would potentially inflict harm on others when instructed to do so by someone in authority, in this case, an "experimenter."

Deception: in
research when
participants
are not fully
informed of the
purposes and/
or procedures;
receives close
attention in
institutional
review board
(IRB) review.

Milgram's (1963) research raised a host of questions, many of them about **deception** and the extent to which we can ethically mislead people in research. The point of the research was determining the extent to which people follow authority, but concerns were raised about the immediate and long-term effects on the participants, who believed they were inflicting potentially harmful levels of shock. Institutions are sensitive to such issues and have established boards that evaluate the ethical issues raised by research. In considering ethical aspects of research, this chapter will explain why these boards exist and how they work.

> **»** **Try This Now**
>
> Have you ever been deceived by someone you trusted? What were your reactions? How do you think you might feel if you participated in research and found out after the study ended that deception was involved? If you have participated in a study involving deception, what

did the researcher tell you about the need to deceive you? Were you convinced deception was necessary? Ask your instructors about their experiences in research involving deception and their immediate and longer term reactions.

This chapter will explain why we have ethical review boards (typically called *institutional review boards* or *IRBs*) and how to prepare a research proposal to undergo IRB review. Institutions that conduct research with humans and/or animals and receive federal funding to support that research are required to have IRBs to determine that ethical guidelines are being followed. There are separate boards for humans and animals (i.e., infrahuman species). This chapter will concentrate on research with humans. Institutions where there is research on animals have a separate review committee for that research, often called the **Institutional Animal Care and Use Committee (IACUC)**. Whether involving humans or animals, when the research meets ethical guidelines, all parties are protected: the participant/animal, the researcher, and the institution.

The parameters of the research (most importantly the kinds of participants and the degree of risk involved in the research) determine the level of review required. The level of review makes a practical difference for the researcher. Meetings for the highest level of review require all IRB committee members, and those meetings are held infrequently. By learning about the different levels of review, you will be able to gauge how long the review of your proposal is likely to take.

The materials needed to submit a proposal for IRB review are explained, and Appendices B (Informed Consent) and C (Debriefing) at the end of the book provide you with sample documents that are required parts of research. **Informed consent** explains the nature of the research and states participants' rights. By doing so, participants can make fully informed decisions about whether to participate. A **debriefing** or explanation of research document provided at the end of the study explains the specific hypotheses and aims of the study in more detail. If the study involves deception, the debriefing explains why that was necessary. Often institutions provide templates for informed consent and debriefing documents on an institutional website along with other information about the IRB (e.g., committee meeting dates, timelines for review, and application materials).

WHAT IS THE IRB, AND WHY DOES IT EXIST?

Human subjects IRBs are charged with protecting the welfare of individuals who participate in research. An IRB has jurisdiction over the research proposed by any member of

Institutional Animal Care and Use Committee (IACUC): institutional committee that reviews research with animals and their care.

Informed consent: document given to potential research participants that outlines the nature of the research; participants must agree and sign or otherwise provide evidence of consent in order to take part in research.

Debriefing: document given to participants at the conclusion of a research project that explains the hypotheses and rationale for the study.

that institution, and research that involves team members from different institutions may undergo a series of reviews specific to each institution. Thus, despite the federal guidelines, local IRBs may reflect an institutional culture, which often creates both inconsistency in the review process (Schneider, 2015) and complaints from researchers (Cartwright, Hickman, Nelson, & Knafl, 2013).

Belmont Report: federal report issued in 1979 that outlines the principles that guide ethical treatment of research subjects; three major principles are Respect for Persons, Beneficence, and Justice.

Regulations to protect human subjects in research emerged in the mid-twentieth century (Frankl, cited in Williams & Ouren, 1976). Since 1950, several pieces of legislation have targeted protecting the welfare of human subjects (e.g., the National Research Act in 1974) and established commissions to monitor research. One important commission is the National Commission for the Protection of Human Subjects of Biomedical and Behavioral Research (Office for Protection from Research Risks [OPRR], 1993).

Among other duties, this commission was charged with determining the risk–benefit criteria to evaluate research with human subjects (National Research Act, 1974, Section 202. B.2). The commission issued a report in 1979, known as the **Belmont Report** (named after the location where the meetings were held; **http://www.hhs.gov/ohrp/humansubjects/guidance/belmont.html**). The report provided guidelines to help resolve ethical problems in evaluating research with human subjects. The regulations took on more significance when they were codified as **Title 45 Part 46 of the Code of Federal Regulations** by 1981 (Landrum, 1999; Pattullo, 1984). That code will be identified here as 45 CFR 46.

Title 45 Part 46 of the Code of Federal Regulations: federal code that governs the protection of human subjects.

> **» Try This Now**
>
> Do an Internet search for "45 CFR 46," and then bookmark the Health and Humans Services (HHS) site for this part of the Code of Federal Regulations. This is a useful webpage when you have questions about IRB regulations.

In 1991, the federal government took an additional step by adopting what is known as the *Common Rule*, which is the federal policy that protects human subjects. Institutions that receive federal funds for biomedical or behavioral research with human subjects must have an IRB according to law (National Research Act, 1974). The funds need not be for the specific research under review as such funds have been awarded to the institution. In practice, many colleges and universities, despite whether they receive such funds, have established an IRB.

As you might have guessed, there are a number of reasons for having an IRB:

- Protecting the welfare of research participants
- Improving the quality of research proposals
- Addressing liability issues

> **⏩ Try This Now**
>
> Why would it make sense to have an IRB even without federal support for biomedical or behavioral research?

HISTORY OF ETHICAL OVERSIGHT

Nazi biomedical experimentation on concentration camp prisoners during World War II and the judicial hearings of those events by the Nuremberg Military Tribunal led to the creation of the **Nuremberg Code**. These events are often listed as the reason the United States established its own code to protect human subjects. For example, the Belmont Report specifically mentions the Nuremberg War Crimes Trial and subsequent establishment of the Nuremberg code. The substance of the 10 points in the Nuremberg code is as follows (**http://wayback.archive-it.org/4657/20150930181802/http://www.hhs.gov/ohrp/archive/nurcode.html**):

- Voluntary consent is critical
- The results should be beneficial to society and not procurable in any other way
- A knowledge base from animal studies or the literature should suggest that the likely results justify the experiment
- No unnecessary physical or mental suffering or injury is involved
- No research should occur if there is *a priori* knowledge that death or disabling injury may occur
- The degree of risk should never outweigh the importance of what is to be learned
- Every precaution should be taken to prevent even the remote possibility of injury, disability, or death
- Only scientifically qualified individuals should conduct experiments
- Subjects should have the right to stop participating if they have reached a physical or mental state where they judge it impossible to continue
- Scientists must be prepared to stop the research if in their judgment continuing presents the risk of injury, disability, or death to the subject

These stipulations may strike you as emphasizing the risks associated with medical research, but research in the social and behavioral sciences has also raised concerns about the safety and protection of human subjects. For example, the Belmont Report highlights the **Tuskegee syphilis study**:

In this country, in the 1940s, the Tuskegee syphilis study used disadvantaged, rural black men to study the untreated course of a disease that is by no means confined to

Nuremberg Code: ten guidelines for the ethical treatment of human subjects in research that were codified in 1949; emerged out of the Nazi War Crimes Tribunal in Nuremberg.

Tuskegee syphilis study: study of African American men with syphilis that demonstrates violations of ethical principles because the men were left untreated even when a treatment was available; sponsored by the U.S. Public Health Service from 1932 to 1972.

that population. These subjects were deprived of demonstrably effective treatment in order not to interrupt the project, long after such treatment became generally available. (Belmont Report, B.1.3; **http://www.hhs.gov/ohrp/humansubjects/ guidance/belmont.html#xethical**)

This study lasted from 1932 to 1972, although by 1947, penicillin was known to be an effective treatment for syphilis. This research was sponsored by our government (the U.S. Public Health Service), but no formal amends for this unethical undertaking appeared until 1997 when President Bill Clinton offered an apology, calling this episode part of our "shameful past" because the men in the Tuskegee study participated without knowledge and consent. These African American men thought they would receive free medical care when, in fact, the real purpose of their participation was to chart the course of syphilis. Thus, not only did this study violate fundamental principles about informing participants about the nature of the research, but in addition, the undertaking was racist in that the burden of participation fell to one racial group.

Numerous resources exist about the Tuskegee study, including the Centers for Disease Control and Prevention (CDC) website (**http://www.cdc.gov/tuskegee/index.html**), which has links covering the timeline of the study, the Presidential apology, research information, and information about syphilis as a disease. This CDC website also offer links to external websites, such as the National Archives (which has records from the Tuskegee study) and Tuskegee University's own National Center for Bioethics in Research and Health Care (**http://www.tuskegee.edu/about_us/centers_of_excellence/bioethics_center/about_ the_usphs_syphilis_study.aspx**). Other recommended resources include the book *Bad Blood* (Jones, 1981), which traces this research sponsored by the U.S. Public Health Service, and the television movie *Miss Evers' Boys* (Kavanagh & Sargent, 1997), which depicts the (fictitious) experiences of a nurse and four of the participating tenant farmers.

Milgram's Obedience to Authority Study

Another well-known case in the United States that involves ethical issues (and the one mentioned near the beginning of this chapter) is the work of Stanley Milgram (1963) on obedience to authority. Milgram's later research (1974) highlighted the importance of questioning what is ethical research and when deception in research is appropriate (Fisher & Fyrberg, 1994). As many of you may recall from hearing about this study in introductory social science courses, the experiment at Yale University consisted of people in two roles: teachers or learners. In fact, the learners were all confederates in the study, which was stated to be on learning and memory. Only the teachers (adults recruited from the surrounding New Haven, CT, community) were subjects. The basic question in the study was the extent to which people (the teachers) were willing to administer "shocks" to the "learners" when learners answered a question incorrectly. Even after hearing a cry from the learner, more than 80% of the teachers continued administering shocks when a question was incorrectly answered.

Unbeknownst to the teachers, there were no actual shocks, and the learners' cries and protestations to stop were staged. It is unlikely that the identical circumstances of Milgram's (1974) research would receive IRB approval today (Gillespie, 1999), but a modification of Milgram's research, including setting the top "shock" level at 150 volts (in Milgram's original research, it was 450 volts) was approved (Burger, 2009). Readers interested in the safeguards Burger took in this IRB-approved replication are directed to his 2009 article.

Zimbardo's Prison Simulation

Related to the obedience to authority research and receiving renewed public interest is the work of Philip Zimbardo (Haney, Banks, & Zimbardo, 1973) on what is known as the **Stanford prison experiment,** which marked its fortieth anniversary in 2013. Zimbardo cited Milgram's (1963) work on obedience to authority as an influence on the Stanford prison study (Sparkman, 2015). In 2015, a film called *The Stanford Prison Experiment* premiered at the Sundance Film Festival (**http://www.prisonexp.org**). A focus of Zimbardo's research was the extent to which the personality versus the context of the setting and its social roles influenced behavior. The experimenters (Haney et al., 1973) approached this prison research through a simulation, creating a prison in the basement of one of the Stanford University buildings (home of its psychology department), recruiting volunteers for the role of prisoner or guard, screening them for pathology, providing them with role-consistent attire (i.e., uniforms for the guards and prison clothing for the prisoners, but without underclothing), and then watching their behavior unfold. Because some prisoners were judged to have become acutely emotionally agitated, they were released early from the two-week-long simulation. The entire project was halted on Day 6 after Christina Maslach, a newly minted Stanford Ph.D., raised concerns about the emotional suffering exhibited by the "prisoners." Only then did Zimbardo, who was fulfilling two roles, one as researcher and the other as superintendent of the "prison," stop the simulation. Social roles in this physical setting appeared to have had a substantial impact on participants' behavior.

Kennedy Krieger Institute Lead Paint Study

The Milgram (1963) and Zimbardo (1973) research took place decades ago, but a more recent example shows the need for ongoing vigilance to protect human subjects. The research in question involved children in what is often called the **Kennedy Krieger Institute Lead Paint Study**, conducted in Baltimore, Maryland, under the auspices of the Johns Hopkins University (Buchanan & Miller, 2006). Funded by the Environmental Protection Agency, the focus of the Lead-based Paint Abatement and Repair and Maintenance Study was the effectiveness of different steps to rid housing of the toxin lead. Families with children in this study were recruited to live in housing with various levels of lead abatement; thus, some families were enticed to live in housing where lead was present. A justification for exposing children to this potential risk was that these were children who likely already lived in or eventually would live in housing where the children would

Stanford prison experiment: research conducted by Zimbardo and colleagues showing the effect of obedience to authority in a simulated prison environment (Haney, Banks, & Zimbardo, 1973).

Kennedy Krieger Institute Lead Paint Study: research in Baltimore, Maryland, conducted by the Johns Hopkins University and funded by the Environmental Protection Agency (EPA) that exposed some children to lead paint dust.

be exposed to lead. This situation ostensibly existed because of the high percentage of housing stock in Baltimore that contained lead-based paint.

There are many aspects of this study, and rulings were rendered in the trial of *Grimes v Kennedy Krieger Institute* (2001). Children in the study were all low income, some lived in housing where only partial lead abatement was undertaken (hence, exposing the children to risk), and incentives were given to encourage families to participate. This research has been referred to as nontherapeutic in that it offered "no prospect of direct benefit" to the children (Glantz, 2002). Two parents who argued that information about the levels of lead paint dust in their homes was not provided in a timely manner brought lawsuits. The Court of Appeals reversed the original lower court ruling against the plaintiffs (the parents) and stated, "in Maryland, a parent, appropriate relative, or other appropriate surrogate, cannot consent to the participation of a child or other person under legal disability in nontherapeutic research or studies in which there is any risk of injury or damage to the health of the subject" (cited in Glantz, 2002, p. 1071). This ruling should remind you of the safeguards stipulated in the Nuremberg code. In fact, in his article about this case, Leonard Glantz (2002) pointed out that the ruling marked the first time in the U.S. court system that the Nuremberg code had "so explicitly" been adopted "as a source of legally enforceable ethical standards" (p. 1071). Although this research took place well over a decade ago, the Kennedy Krieger Institute is still facing "lead-paint" lawsuits related to the research (Wheeler & Cohn, 2014).

The point demonstrated by just these few examples is that research needs to be reviewed and monitored to ensure that it meets ethical standards.

REVISIT AND RESPOND

- Why do you think an IRB in 2016 would refuse to approve Milgram's (1963) original obedience to authority study? What was ethically questionable about the fact that Zimbardo was serving both as a researcher and as the "superintendent" of the prison in his Stanford prison research (Haney et al., 1973)? In the Kennedy Krieger Institute Lead Paint Study, some of the children were kept at greater risk than others (only partial lead abatement) to further the goals of the study. Which one of the points of the Nuremberg code does this action seem to violate?

Respect for persons: one of the three principles of the Belmont Report that emphasizes people are autonomous agents; specifies the use of informed consent.

The Belmont Report

As introduced earlier, the National Research Act of 1974 led to the creation of a commission that issued what has come to be called the Belmont Report. Published in the Federal Register in 1979, the report is "usually described as an *ethical* statement about research with human subjects" (Maloney, 1984, p. 21). Going beyond the ethical points in the Nuremberg Code, the Belmont Report offers direction in how to protect human subjects, including (Maloney, 1984):

- Assessing risk–benefit criteria
- Creating guidelines for selecting subjects
- Monitoring and evaluating the work of IRBs
- Creating informed consent guidelines for vulnerable populations (children, prisoners, those institutionalized with cognitive impairments)

The Belmont Report is useful to read in its entirety; at the very least, researchers might read Part C: "Applications."

Three ethical principles underlie the Belmont Report: **respect for persons**, **beneficence**, and **justice**. These three core values are reflected in the way we do research (see Figure 4.1).

Respect for persons is the leading principle, which addresses two core ethical guidelines. First, people are to be treated as **autonomous agents**. Autonomous agents are capable of acting independently, i.e., making their own decisions and given the opportunity to do so. Second, when people cannot act as autonomous agents, for example, because of diminished capacity, they are provided with additional protections. How is this principle of respect for persons manifested in research? Through the process of informed consent; the elements of informed consent are covered fully later in the chapter. Informed consent is a document outlining what will happen in the research project and what protections are offered for participants.

The second guiding principle listed is *beneficence*. This word points to the importance of doing good, expressing kindness, and safeguarding well-being. Maloney (1984, p. 34) listed as extensions of this category "1) do not harm and 2) maximize possible benefits and minimize possible harms." In this principle, you can see links to the Nuremberg code. Being able to assess the risks and benefits provided by the research is an aspect of beneficence.

The third principle is *justice*. Stated in the Belmont Report, the essence of this principle is "Who ought to receive the benefits of research and bear its burdens?" Another phrase used in the report framing this principle is "Fairness in distribution." Risks and benefits should be equally distributed across participants. Thinking about the selection of subjects and who takes part in the research is a central task related to the principle of justice.

FIGURE 4.1 Three Ethical Principles That Underlie the Belmont Report

Source: Adapted from Devlin, A. (2006), *Research methods: Planning, conducting, and presenting research.* Belmont, CA.: Wadsworth/Thomson., Figure 5.1.

Beneficence: one of the three principles of the Belmont Report that emphasizes doing no harm (maximizing benefits while minimizing risks).

Justice: one of the three principles of the Belmont Report that emphasizes the fair distribution of risks and rewards of participation.

Autonomous agents: part of Respect for Persons, one of three guiding principles in the Belmont Report, stressing that people need to participate voluntarily in research.

REVISIT AND RESPOND

- Thinking back to the lead paint study, was the principle of justice followed in that research?

THE APA CODE OF ETHICS

American Psychological Association (APA) Code of Ethics: ethical code of conduct guiding the behavior of psychologists; comprises 10 standards.

Before moving on to concrete aspects of ethical research and IRBs, one more ethical code will be described: the *Ethical Principles of Psychologists and Code of Conduct* from the American Psychological Association (2010a), also known as the **American Psychological Association (APA) Code of Ethics**. The APA has published an ethics code since 1953. In the 2010 document, there is a preamble, general principles, and 10 standards. Here we will focus on the standards that pertain to ethical issues in research. As general principles, the code overlaps with the Belmont Report in five principles: Beneficence and Nonmaleficence (do no harm or inflict the least harm); Fidelity and Responsibility (operate within your areas of competence); Integrity; Justice; and Respect for People's Rights and Dignity. Of the standards, Standard 8 (Research and Publication) is the most applicable to issues of ethics in research. Aspects covered in the subsections include informed consent, inducements, deception, debriefing, reporting, and publication credit. The list of items that should be included on an informed consent document is important to read. You could use this list to develop an informed consent document:

- The purpose of the research, expected duration, and procedures
- The right to decline to participate and to withdraw from the research once participation has begun
- The foreseeable consequences of declining or withdrawing
- Reasonably foreseeable factors that may be expected to influence their willingness to participate, such as potential risks, discomfort, or adverse effects
- Any prospective research benefits
- Limits of confidentiality
- Incentives for participation
- Whom to contact for questions about the research and research participants' rights
- Opportunity for the prospective participants to ask questions and receive answers (APA, 2010a, 8.02)

REVISIT AND RESPOND

- What three ethical principles did the Belmont Report establish? What overlap do you see between these three principles and the general principles in the APA Code of Conduct (2010a)? Make a list of the two sets of principles, and show where the overlap is. Why is having an informed consent document a critical part of doing ethical research? Do all three ethical codes (Nuremberg, Belmont, and APA) mention the importance of voluntary consent?

WHAT IS RESEARCH? WHAT ARE HUMAN SUBJECTS?

As mentioned at the beginning of this chapter, there are precise definitions of research and human subjects. Not all data collection is research; not all subjects are humans. We need definitions of these concepts if we are going to understand what IRBs review.

The Common Rule, the federal policy that protects human subjects in research, offers definitions of both "research" and "human subjects." Because not every kind of data gathering qualifies as research, this definition of research is important: "a systematic investigation, including research development, testing and evaluation, designed to develop or contribute to generalizable knowledge" [45 CFR 46.102(d)] (**http://www.hhs.gov/ohrp/humansubjects/guidance/45cfr46.html#46.102**).

REVISIT AND RESPOND

- From this definition, what two critical aspects are required for a study to be considered research?

If you answered "a systematic investigation" and "generalizable knowledge," you are correct. If we want to know what kind of food students prefer for the end of the semester picnic and survey their preferences, is that "research" according to the federal definition? No. We have no interest in generalizable knowledge. What if you wanted students to see how challenging a particular spatial cognition test is? You might give them sample problems to solve and then have them score their responses without handing in their tests. Is generalizable knowledge the goal of this in-class activity? No.

⏩ Try This Now

Imagine you want students to take a spatial cognition test in class and to analyze their data for research purposes with a focus on differences by major. Would that activity require IRB review? What do you think about having students take tests handed out by their instructor (the researcher) during class time?

The answer to the first question is "yes." IRB review would be required because it meets the definition of research (systematic; goal of generalizable knowledge). With regard to using class time for research conducted by the course instructor, IRBs take a dim view of what is called research with such a captive population (Council, Smith, Kaster-Bundgaard, &

Gladue, 1999). Moreover, there is potential coercion involved because the instructor is asking students in the class to participate in the instructor's own research.

Next, we need a definition for human subjects. The definition from the Code of Federal regulations [45 CFR 46.102 (f)] is as follows: "*Human subject* means a living individual about whom an investigator (whether professional or student) conducting research obtains (1) Data through intervention or interaction with the individual, or (2) Identifiable private information."

> **» Try This Now**
>
> Can you think of a source of data that would *not* qualify as involving human subjects?

If you were to use archival data from school records that had no identifiable private information, that approach would not qualify as doing research with human subjects. Nevertheless, if you wanted to link archival data about residence hall vandalism damages to students' evaluations of their residence halls using an instrument like the Sense of Community Index (Chavis, Hogge, McMillan, & Wandersman, 1986), that project would require IRB review. In that case, you are interacting with individuals through a survey.

IRB MEMBERSHIP AND DUTIES

> **» Try This Now**
>
> If you were choosing people to serve on an IRB, what kinds of backgrounds would you want them to have?

The requirements for the IRB include a specific number of people (minimum five) with particular expertise and affiliation. Section 107 of the Code (45 CFR 46) discusses IRB membership in terms of encouraging people that vary in race, gender, and cultural background, as well as in "sensitivity to community attitudes." One member of the committee is to have a scientific and another a nonscientific background. In addition, one member must come from outside the institution and not be an immediate relative of anyone at the institution. If a proposal requires expertise about a specific population (e.g., inmates), a representative of that population or someone experienced in working with that population (e.g., someone who works with community reentry programs for formerly incarcerated individuals) may be invited to attend the meeting to offer an evaluation of the proposal, but that person may not vote.

The fundamental duty of the IRB is the review of research and record keeping documenting that review.

LEVELS OF IRB REVIEW

The federal regulations distinguish levels of review: **exempt**, **expedited**, and **full**.

Exempt

46.101.b (1): "research conducted in established or commonly accepted educational settings, involving normal educational practices; (2) research involving the use of educational tests (cognitive, diagnostic, aptitude, achievement), survey procedures, interview procedures or observation of public behavior *unless* (italics added): (i) information obtained is recorded in such a manner that human subjects can be identified, directly or through identifiers linked to the subjects; and (ii) any disclosure of the human subjects' responses outside the research could reasonably place the subjects at risk of criminal or civil liability or be damaging to the subjects' financial standing, employability, or reputation."

Examples of the exempt category would be the collection of evaluations in a course (an example of normal educational practices) and taking state mastery tests (use of education tests).

For our purposes, an additional important category of exemption is when the research involves "the collection or study of existing data, documents, records, pathological specimens, or diagnostic specimens, if these sources are publicly available or if the information is recorded by the investigator in such a manner that subjects cannot be identified, directly or through identifiers linked to the subjects" [b (4)]. Use of archival data, as mentioned earlier in this chapter, is an important category of exempt research.

It is important to note that whether a proposal qualifies as exempt is determined by the IRB; researchers cannot make that assumption or determination independently. Thus, every proposal must be submitted to the IRB.

Expedited

The next level of review, expedited (46.110), covers most situations that arise in student research proposals (and many faculty proposals as well; **http://www.hhs.gov/ohrp/humansubjects/guidance/45cfr46.html#46.110**). This level of review can be conducted by the IRB chair or by one or more IRB committee members designated by the chair, and the review can generally be completed with a quick turnaround. This subgroup has no authority to disapprove a proposal; the full committee must do that.

Exempt IRB review: type of human subjects institutional review board (IRB) review for research in which there is no more than minimal risk and falling into one of the federally designated exempt from review categories.

Expedited IRB review: type of human subjects institutional review board (IRB) review for research in which there is no more than minimal risk and falling into one of the federally designated expedited review categories.

Full IRB review: required for research that does not meet the guidelines for exempt or expedited institutional review board (IRB) review and/or poses more than minimal risk.

Minimal risk: research is evaluated in terms of whether the probability of discomfort is more than people would encounter in everyday life or in routine psychological or physical evaluations. This level is known as minimal risk.

Office for Human Research Protections (OHRP): federal office that provides oversight for the protection of subjects in human research.

There are several criteria for review under the expedited guidelines. Important concepts to understand are no more than **minimal risk** and vulnerable population (introduced in Chapter 2). The essence of minimal risk is that the activity involved in the research exposes the subject to no greater risk than the person would encounter in everyday situations involving physical and psychological tests [see 46.102(i) for the formal definition]. Vulnerable population is usually defined by the specific categories it contains. Pregnant women, fetuses, neonates, children, those with cognitive impairments, and prisoners are considered vulnerable populations. Those with seen or unseen disabilities also may be considered vulnerable. Depending on the research proposed, some institutions include students and those who are economically disadvantaged as vulnerable. In addition, research involving deception is often excluded from the expedited process, requiring full review (see, for example, the regulations of Florida State University; **http://www .research.fsu.edu/research-offices/human-subjects/**).

On its website, the **Office for Human Research Protections (OHRP)** lists the categories of research that may be appropriate for expedited review. Note that it is the specifics of the research (and not merely the category) that determine the level of review. The concept of minimal risk is one driving factor in determining whether the research qualifies for expedited review. There are nine categories on this list, but of these nine, three are of particular relevance to social and behavioral scientists. The other categories deal more directly with medical procedures (e.g., blood samples, biological specimens, and clinical data such as fMRI) but certainly could be relevant to behavioral neuroscientists. For the social scientists, expedited review might involve (**http://www.hhs.gov/ohrp/policy/expedited98.html**):

- Research involving materials (data, documents, records, or specimens) that have been collected, or will be collected, solely for nonresearch purposes (such as medical treatment or diagnosis)
- Collection of data from voice, video, digital, or image recordings made for research purposes.
- Research on individual or group characteristics or behavior (including, but not limited to, research on perception, cognition, motivation, identity, language, communication, cultural beliefs or practices, and social behavior) or research employing survey, interview, oral history, focus group, program evaluation, human factors evaluation, or quality assurance methodologies

The regulations also remind the reader that some research in these categories may be exempt from review.

Full

Essentially, full review is defined by default. If the research does not qualify for exempt or expedited review, it requires full review. As indicated earlier, projects that involve more than minimal risk and/or vulnerable populations are the usual candidates for full review, but institutions differ in what aspects of a proposal trigger the need for full review.

For the researcher, there are some practical implications of undergoing a full review; the most significant of these is time. Full reviews are typically done monthly; in some locales, these meetings are even less frequent (e.g., quarterly). Often IRBs will post a meeting schedule for the year online to enable researchers to plan their submissions. Typically submissions are done electronically to facilitate distribution of materials to committee members.

REVISIT AND RESPOND

- What makes a project "research" (and, thus, subject to review) in the eyes of the IRB? What kinds of projects qualify as exempt and do not undergo IRB review? What does it mean to say that a proposal involves exposing the participants to more than minimal risk? What is a vulnerable population? Give an example. What is the purpose of having a nonscientist on the IRB committee? An outside member from the community?

COMPONENTS OF THE IRB PROPOSAL

The common elements in an IRB proposal are listed as follows, although each institution may have slightly different requirements. Often the components required for proposal submission are listed on the institution's IRB website:

- **Nature of the project:** Typically this component takes the form of a short literature review where the topic of interest is introduced, relevant literature cited, reasons the proposed research advances knowledge in the area indicated, and possible risks and benefits listed.

- **Description of the participants:** Who will the participants be? Are any minors (younger than 18) involved? Are any other classifications of vulnerable populations involved? Are there inclusion and/or exclusion criteria such as gender, varsity athlete, or class year?

- **Participant recruitment and number:** How will participants be recruited? How many participants are needed? Justification for the number of participants is often required. Will there be incentives (e.g., extra credit or lottery)?

- **Procedure:** What will the participants do (exactly)? Where? When? How long will the study take?

- **Apparatus/Measures:** What apparatus/measures will be used? All *complete* measures (e.g., questionnaires or surveys) must be attached. Information about psychometric properties are typically included (see Chapter 5). Researchers using online survey software should provide the survey link.

Anonymity:
condition of research in which the participant is not known or in which participants' identity cannot be linked to their responses.

Confidentiality:
situation in which the research participant's identity is known and the researcher indicates the extent to which that information will be shared and with whom.

- **Informed consent:** How will informed consent be obtained? If you are asking for a waiver to informed consent, provide your justification. Are participants' responses protected under the condition of **anonymity** (i.e., unlinkable to individuals)? Under the condition of **confidentiality** (i.e., responses are linkable to individuals, but the responses are safeguarded by the researcher)? How will these responses be protected? The informed consent document must be attached.
- **Deception:** Will the study involve any deception? If so, include a justification and an explanation of how debriefing (an explanation of the full purposes of the research) will be handled.
- **Debriefing:** How will participants be debriefed? Attach the debriefing document.
- **Copy of informed consent:** IRB regulations require that researchers provide participants with a copy of the informed consent. The participants sign one copy of the informed consent and return it to the researcher and receive a copy for themselves.

INFORMED CONSENT

Thinking back to the Nuremberg code and the Belmont Report, as well as to the APA Code of Ethics, one critical component common to those ethical guidelines is that research is voluntary and people are autonomous agents. Informed consent is the component of the IRB proposal that addresses that voluntarism. The use of informed consent implies the capacity to consent (or special protection when subjects do not have that capacity), free from coercion. In addition, being fully informed means that you understand the potential risks and benefits involved in the research. The APA guidelines list components of informed consent that must be stated (2010a, 8.02).

Specific Components of Informed Consent

One point made by Norbert Schwarz (1999) is that research engages participants' understanding of the rules of communication (also see Chapter 5 on Measures and Survey Research Tools). In that regard, the informed consent document is "an ongoing, two-way communication process between subjects and the investigator, as well as a specific agreement about the conditions of the research participation" (Sieber, 1992, p. 26). The components that must be covered are presented as a sample informed consent document in Appendix B at the end of this book:

- A statement that the project is research.
- Some statement about the aim or purpose of the research (but see also Chapter 3 regarding demand characteristics).
- The time participating in the study is expected to take.

- A description of what is involved in the research (e.g., filling out four surveys).
- A statement of whether there are any foreseeable risks or discomforts (including physical injury or discomfort; psychological or social discomfort; economic loss; or inconvenience). Often, because none of these is involved, the researcher states: "There are no known risks or discomforts to participating in this research."
- A statement of any benefits to participants that might result. Most of the time, there are no direct benefits and a useful statement is something to the effect that, "While the direct benefits to society are not known, you may learn more about [topic of research] through your participation."
- A statement that explains the extent to which anonymity or confidentiality will be protected. These terms are often used interchangeably. They are different. In a project that claims the data are anonymous, either no identifying information about the individual is collected or, if it is, that information cannot be linked to participants' individual responses. If the data are confidential, the researcher has information that identifies the participant. In the informed consent, the researcher needs to indicate the extent to which confidentiality about that identity is guaranteed and how that will be achieved. Joan Sieber (1992) offered a thorough discussion of these issues.

There are many ways in which breaches of confidentiality can occur, particularly when data are stored electronically. Researchers can protect confidentiality in several ways, for example, using encryption for identifiable data; using subject numbers and not participants' names on survey responses and keeping a separate master code of the names and subject numbers; and making sure informed consent documents are separated from paper survey responses. In addition, if video- or audio-recordings are used, the informed consent must indicate what use will be made of those recordings; how they will be stored and for how long; and the ultimate method of disposal. If video- or audio-recordings are used, the participant should be asked to consent to this in a separate signature block, beyond consenting to the study itself.

Statements Regarding Circumstances When Confidentiality Would Be Broken

The informed consent document is essentially a contract between the individual and the researcher. If the researcher states that confidentiality will be maintained such that only the researcher/research team knows the individual's identity, then that promise should be kept. At the same time, a tension exists between that promise and the duty of the researcher to safeguard the individual/others if the researcher thinks the individual is a danger to him/herself and/or others.

In most research projects, this issue would likely not arise, but there are some instances where precautions need to be taken and the informed consent document modified to state explicitly when confidentiality would be broken (if the data are collected non-anonymously). These instances often involve research on clinical issues. For example, there are some scales (e.g., the Beck Depression Inventory) with questions about suicidal ideation. If an individual responded to such a question suggesting he or she might inflict self-injury, the researcher would need to report this to the appropriate authorities. Institutions usually have a protocol in place about whom to contact in such situations. Recognizing that using the depression inventory opens the possibility of such responses, the informed consent document would include a statement about when confidentiality would be broken and what steps the researcher would then take. Some departments restrict the use of instruments like the Beck Depression Inventory to faculty and to graduate students with appropriate training and supervision. Other departments direct researchers to eliminate the question about suicidal ideation from the inventory. Still others recommend selecting a measure of depression that does not explicitly address suicidal ideation (e.g., CES-D; PHQ-8).

Other Aspects of Informed Consent

We have covered the central aspects of informed consent, those dealing most directly with ethical concerns, but there are additional practical aspects that deserve attention.

CONTACT INFORMATION Some departments recommend that researchers provide their contact information in e-mail form rather than as phone numbers, viewing the e-mail as placing researchers at a lower level of risk for unwanted contact after the research than would a personal phone number. Some researchers prefer the use of a secondary e-mail account limited to use for research. Another option is to list the department office telephone as a point of contact for researchers, if office personnel are willing to handle this task.

SIGNATURE AND WORDING FOR CONSENT At the end of the informed consent document is a section that looks something like this:

> I am 18 years of age or older, have read and understood the explanations and assurances in this document, and voluntarily consent to participate in this research on [indicate topic of research].

Name _____

Signature _____

Date _____

Name and Signature of Person Obtaining Consent _____

You may have noted the stipulation of being 18 years of age or older; this is referred to as the age of majority, which is 18 in most states in the United States. This age stipulation has some very real implications for researchers who are using a participant pool. Some students beginning college are not 18, which is particularly likely to be the case in their first year. If younger than 18, they may not participate in research without parental/guardian consent.

THE LANGUAGE YOU USE Participants need to understand the information in the informed consent. Researchers may lose sight of the technicality of the vocabulary they use. If researchers use a phrase like "health concierge" to describe a study, it would not be surprising to see puzzled expressions! Comprehension is a cognitive process; the length and technicality of informed consent documents may lead to misunderstanding (McEvoy & Keefe, 1999). The Joseph McEvoy and Richard Keefe paper, a useful resource manual about ethics in research, offers wording suggestions about the components of informed consent.

Waiving Informed Consent: When and Why

There may be circumstances where it is not possible and/or desirable to obtain informed consent because of its impact on the validity of the research and/or the safety of participants. The federal regulations cover the circumstances in which researchers may ask for the elements of informed consent to be altered or waived entirely. Moving beyond consideration of research that would be considered exempt, a central issue in determining whether informed consent could be altered or waived is indicated in 46.116.d (1–4). The gist here is that (a) no more than minimal risk is involved, (b) no adverse effects would result from altering or waiving informed consent, (c) there is no practical way to conduct the research otherwise, and (d) after participation, when possible, information about the study is provided to the subject. Examples of situations where the researcher might request a waiver include retrospective analysis of medical chart data (which would have identifying information removed) and naturalistic observation (see Chapter 6) at a low level of risk. At the other end of the risk spectrum are investigations of illegal activities (e.g., banned substance use) or when signing informed consent might place the participant at risk. As an example in the high-risk category, a researcher wanted to interview relatives of individuals who had been incarcerated for opposing the government of a nation (here unspecified). The researcher's IRB agreed that having such signed informed consent documents might put these relatives at risk. In situations such as this, a written document covering the guarantees provided by informed consent could be given to the participant without the requirement of signing it. Ultimately it is up to the local IRB whether the request to waive informed consent is approved.

Obtaining Informed Consent Electronically

A growing trend is delivering questionnaires online (see Chapter 5 for the discussion of online survey software such as **SurveyMonkey®** and Qualtrics®). An approach taken by many researchers is to have a checkbox at the bottom of the page with a statement saying something like, "By checking the box, I acknowledge that I am 18 years of age or older, have read and understood the explanations and assurances in this document, and voluntarily consent to participate in this research." Using the online software, the survey can be constructed in a way (e.g., by using a branching function) that the box must be checked for the survey to advance.

It is important to emphasize that research conducted online would still include informed consent and debriefing documents (see next section). In addition, because there is no way you can control whether a respondent is of legal age to consent, some researchers recommend that you only post materials online that are appropriate for all ages (Buchanan & Williams, 2010). Also, some authorities recommend including a statement on the informed consent about the risks of data breaches that may be involved in collecting data on the Internet. The Society for Science and the Public offers this example:

> *There is always the possibility of tampering from an outside source when using the internet for collecting information. While the confidentiality of your responses will be protected once the data are downloaded from the internet, there is always a possibility of hacking or other security breaches that could threaten the confidentiality of your responses. Please know that you are free to decide not to answer any question.* (**https:// member.societyforscience.org/document.doc?id=752**)

DEBRIEFING

The purpose of debriefing, sometimes called the explanation of research, is to tell participants more about the project, provide follow-up contact information for the researcher, provide contact information (other than the researcher) if there are questions or concerns about the manner in which the research was conducted, list support services (if those are appropriate given the research topic), and provide follow-up resources on the topic (although this last category is not required). Appendix C at the end of this book provides a sample debriefing document. Standard 8 (Research and Publication) of the APA's Code of Ethics (2010a) specifically addresses the debriefing in section 8.08. In telling participants more about the research, you typically talk about why the research is important and what you were trying to test; some researchers explicitly state their hypotheses, being sure to state them without jargon. A good point to remember is that your participants are not experts on the topic. Participants need to be able to understand what you are saying.

As an example, a researcher in behavioral economics might not need to explain "impulse purchasing" but would likely need to tell people the meaning of "the IKEA effect" (where people overvalue something after putting in their own effort; IKEA, Delft, the Netherlands).

The debriefing form lists the contact information for the researcher, which may be in the form of an e-mail (generally preferred) or a phone number. In addition, the debriefing should provide the contact information of an official who is not directly connected to the research, such as the IRB chairperson, another IRB member, or the researcher's department chair. If the participant has a complaint or concern about the research topic and/or the manner in which the research was conducted, that person needs the option to contact someone other than the researcher.

Providing a list of support services is important depending on the nature of the research. For example, if your research is on autobiographical memory and you elicited sad memories from participants, you might provide the contact information for the counseling services at your institution. The point is that any research topic that might be considered upsetting to participants should provide contact information for follow-up services.

Given that much student research is conducted in educational institutions and is viewed as a pedagogical experience, some researchers provide citations to articles or offer links to follow-up reading on the research topic under investigation. The sample debriefing form in Appendix C at the end of the book follows that model.

REVISIT AND RESPOND

- In your own words, explain the difference between anonymity and confidentiality. Under what circumstance(s) would you break confidentiality? What would you say in your informed consent document to alert the participant to that possibility? How do researchers obtain informed consent electronically? Give an example of a circumstance where you would ask to have informed consent waived. What is the purpose of a debriefing document; what issues should be covered?

CHILDREN AS A VULNERABLE POPULATION: IMPLICATIONS FOR RESEARCH

As was discussed earlier in this chapter, research involving vulnerable populations requires full IRB review. We also noted that full IRB meetings may occur infrequently (once/month or less often). Given this infrequency, including vulnerable populations in your research is risky for a single-semester project. As defined earlier, vulnerable populations include prisoners, pregnant women, children, and fetuses (45 CFR 46). Moreover, any given IRB may expand that list to include a variety of other possibilities, such as welfare recipients, those newly immigrated, nursing home patients, or even students!

For researchers, the vulnerable population of greatest interest is often children, defined as younger than the age of majority, which is 18 in most states. Earlier in this chapter we noted that students must be the age of majority to participate in research. If not, they must have parental/guardian consent to do so.

Hurdles in Conducting Research With Children: Gaining Access

There are several hurdles to jump in conducting research with children. Gaining access to children as research participants is a challenge (see also the discussion of barriers in doing ethnographic research in Chapter 6). In the case of research with children, the school system is often the route chosen. If children in a school system will be involved in research, most IRBs require that the research proposal include a letter (or e-mail) of approval from the relevant gatekeepers. These gatekeepers, typically school officials, may include the superintendent of schools, the principal of the particular school in question, and possibly even the classroom teacher(s) involved. Whatever the organization (various kinds of afterschool programs, athletic teams, religious groups), the researcher will be required to provide evidence of endorsement from someone in authority. Receiving such approval is necessary but not sufficient.

Active Consent Versus Passive Consent

The next level of permission involves the child's parent/guardian. For children to participate in research, it almost always requires the **active consent** of the parent/guardian. You may remember going on field trips in school; to do so, your parent/guardian had to "ok" the trip by signing a permission sheet. Providing active consent is essentially the same process. The parent/guardian must "actively" provide this consent (sign a form that is returned to the school or researcher) in which the parent/guardian agrees to his or her child's participation. Federal regulations specify the conditions under which the permission of one parent versus two parents (where possible) is sought [46.408(b)]. Active consent can be distinguished from **passive consent**, in which no form is signed but the parent/guardian does not object to the child's participation in the activity. Without the signed objection, the operating assumption is that the parent/guardian consents. Given the litigious environment in which we live, IRBs seem increasingly unwilling to approve projects that rely on passive consent, although recent evidence suggests that such approvals still occur (Higgerson et al., 2014).

The Child's Assent (Agreement)

The next level of agreement involves the child. It is appropriate to ask children for **assent** (agreement) as soon as they are developmentally able to provide it meaningfully (that is, to understand what is being asked of them so they can make up their minds about

Active consent: consent where the participant or, in the case of children, the parent or guardian, specifically agrees to the research.

Passive consent: situation where agreement to participate (usually of parents/guardians for their child) is assumed in the absence of explicit documentation to the contrary.

Assent: in institutional review board (IRB) research review, children may be asked for their agreement (assent) to participate when developmentally appropriate.

participating). The federal regulations only specify that the assent of the child should be solicited when the child is capable [46.408(a)].

Local IRBs are left to establish the age and form of assent for a specific project (Nelson, 2002). The IRB is only making a judgment about whether children are capable of assent given the scope of a particular project. Children can still refuse, and "the objection of a child of any age is binding, unless the research holds out the prospect of direct benefit that is important to the child and achievable only through the experimental procedures" (Jensen, Fisher, & Hoagwood, 1999, p. 165).

For many conversant with developmental milestones for children, the age of 8–9 marks a developmental period where it may make sense to ask for assent. Using age-appropriate language is essential in communicating what the children are being asked to do. The child's point of view about the research should be considered (Nelson, 2002), from the language used to the research setting, for example, its child-friendliness.

The Office of the Human Research Protection Program at UCLA (**http://ora .research.ucla.edu/OHRPP/Documents/Policy/9/ChildAssent_ParentPerm.pdf**) has a useful website that covers assent, dividing the age ranges into younger than 7, 7–12, and adolescents 13–17. In addition, the document references the federal guidelines that support specific decisions (e.g., when one parent may be sufficient) and covers a variety of other important topics such as how to handle obtaining consent when parents disagree. Relevant federal and state statutes (in this case, for California) related to Human Research Protections are listed, and the site has sample informed consent templates. The website is an extremely useful resource for researchers.

A single semester is only about 13 weeks. In most circumstances in which a research project is a course requirement, successfully completing all of the steps required for doing research with children is risky because of the numbers and levels of gatekeepers. You can control your work habits and task completion, but you can't control how and when other people do their jobs! Carefully consider the limited time frame of a semester before undertaking research with children.

RESEARCH WITH CHILDREN: SECONDARY DATA ANALYSIS

Given the difficulties in gaining permission to conduct research with children, some investigators have made good use of existing datasets that provide archival data about children. This process is called **secondary data analysis**. For example, there is a large dataset known as the Maryland Adolescent Development in Context Study (MADICS), which is a community-based longitudinal study of adolescents and their families. The repository of data, now at the Henry A. Murray Research Archive at Harvard University

Secondary data analysis: analysis using existing datasets with archival data; often used for research with children.

(**http://murray.harvard.edu**), offers information about the normative development of African American adolescents. Such existing datasets offer the opportunity to pose new questions that can be answered through previously collected data (e.g., Fredricks & Eccles, 2006). Jennifer Fredricks and Jacquelynne Eccles looked at whether extracurricular activities were associated with beneficial outcomes (and answered in the affirmative).

REVISIT AND RESPOND

- Give examples of gatekeepers (people who can give permission for research to take place) in a school and for a sports team. Explain the difference between active and passive consent. What does it mean when you ask for the child's assent? About what age do researchers normally consider asking for the child's assent? Explain why active consent of parents/guardians is almost always required with children.

DECEPTION AND ITS ALTERNATIVES

One aspect of research that receives careful attention in the IRB review process is deception. Deception can take a variety of forms. At one end, it is minor, for example, when describing the study in general terms so that participants are not fully informed about the research goals. This form of deception is often called passive deception (as introduced in Chapter 3), which has also been described as deception through omission (Kimmel, Smith, & Klein, 2011). At the other end, deception can take the form of intentionally misleading participants about the goals of the research, giving false feedback about the participant's performance, or using a confederate in the study, among other examples. This kind of deception is typically called active deception (also introduced in Chapter 3), which has also been described as deception by commission (Kimmel et al., 2011).

In some sense, to the extent that hypotheses are not revealed, all research could be said to include deception (Kimmel et al., 2011). Out of the ethical and procedural difficulties involved with deception, alternatives have emerged; these include simulations, approaches to studying real behavior including ethnography and participant observation; and consent to concealment (Sieber, 1992). When participants are told that some information about the study will be withheld until the study's completion, this is called **consent to concealment**. Sieber (1992) raised several questions she hopes researchers will ask before engaging in research involving deception. Of these, the most important may be the following: "Is the study of such overriding importance and so well designed that deception is justified?" (p. 70).

In some cases, the answer to that question may be "yes." An example is a study of real versus imagined gender harassment (Woodzicka & LaFrance, 2001), in which the

Consent to concealment: a type of deception in which consent is obtained when some information is withheld from the participant.

responses of participants in a realistic job interview (for a research assistant position) were compared with those of participants who *imagined* how they would respond to the same set of sexually harassing questions posed by the interviewer. One primary difference was that participants in the real situation reported being afraid, whereas those in the hypothetical situation reported they would feel angry. Moreover, those in the imagined situation (62%) thought they would confront the harasser (the interviewer), whereas none of the women in the real situation did. As Julie Woodzicka and Marianne LaFrance pointed out, "Responses from targets of actual sexual harassment have little in common with responses to imagined sexual harassment" (p. 24), at least on the basis of this study. This study could not have been conducted without the deception necessary to create what the women thought was a real job interview, and it is one situation where we might answer "yes" to Sieber's (1992) criterion of the overriding importance of the study.

Deception: Contribution of the American Psychological Association

As we have seen in this chapter, the APA has its own ethical code (2010a) and addresses the treatment of human subjects in the research process. Every researcher should have a copy of the document, which can be found online (**http://www.apa.org/ethics/code/**) and downloaded in PDF form.

Principle 8.07 of the APA's Ethical Principles (2010a) focuses on the topic of deception. The gist of Principle 8.07 is that the benefits of knowledge gained outweigh the risks of deception; deception should not be used in studies that involve physical or significant emotional pain; an explanation of the deception is provided to participants as soon as possible.

One concern about the use of deception is carryover—that is, how might having experienced deception affect participants' attitudes in subsequent research? The research on the effects of deception is not easily summarized. Some research has suggested participants may grow more suspicious (Orne, 1962; Smith & Richardson, 1983); such reactions have been absent in other reports (e.g., Holmes, 1976a, 1976b). Recent research (Boynton, Portnoy, & Johnson, 2013) has suggested that deceptive information about tasks and false feedback may not necessarily produce mistrust in researchers, but authors of a review of deception in experimental work (Hertwig & Ortmann, 2008a, 2008b) suggested otherwise. Both advocates and detractors of research involving deception can find evidence to support their perspectives.

When students were asked about the role of studies that used deception (Fisher & Fyrberg, 1994), their view was that the benefits of the knowledge to be gained outweighed the costs. Forewarning (i.e., telling people ahead of time that deception was involved) wasn't endorsed because students thought it might lead to differential likelihood to volunteer [see also Campbell and Stanley's (1963) discussion of differential selection in Chapter 3].

In terms of drawbacks, there was some concern that people who had been deceived might be embarrassed when hearing about it during debriefing. Students saw both sides of the ledger, that is, what could be learned from such research but also the potential costs. In the view of Allan Kimmel (2011), "'No deception' is an admirable but unattainable goal" (p. 583) because full disclosure is not reasonable given how that might change participants' responses. Kimmel suggested that researchers use pretesting to determine what levels of deception are truly necessary and pointed to the use of virtual reality as a technology that might help to avoid the use of deception in research.

> **» Try This Now**
>
> Find an article through PsycINFO that involves deception. Think of a way the research could have been accomplished without deception.

Alternatives to Deception: Role Playing and Simulation

Role playing:
playing a role as if you are in the actual situation.

Simulation:
representation, often computer-generated, of a real situation; considered an alternative to deception.

Among the alternatives to deception are **role playing** and **simulation**. In role playing, researchers typically ask participants to behave as if they were actually in a given situation. A simulation is a representation of a real situation; Zimbardo's prison study (Haney et al., 1973; mentioned earlier in the chapter) was a simulation. Today, given technology, simulations are often computer generated (e.g., through virtual reality). On balance, the research has suggested that role playing does not reproduce the same outcomes as emerge under conditions of deception.

A more promising approach is simulation, and immersive reality in particular, which has been embraced by several researchers (e.g., Blascovich et al., 2002; Slater et al., 2006). In 2010, Michaël Dambrun and Elise Vatiné (2010) reexamined Milgram's (1963, 1974) obedience to authority research using an immersive video environment technology. In their approach, participants watched an actor (who had been filmed and faked the behaviors and cries of someone who had been shocked) on a computer screen. Participants knew the "victim" was an actor and the shocks weren't real. The manipulated variables of interest were the visibility of the victim (either seen; or hidden, like Milgram's approach) and the ethnicity of the victim (either French or North African). This immersive approach worked in producing results mirroring Milgram's original research (in the hidden condition). The authors viewed immersive technology as a viable tool for examining "extreme social behaviors" in the absence of deception; this technology further allows the researcher to replicate the research easily (Dambrun & Vatiné, 2010, p. 772). In addition, from the point of view expressed in this book, we might view the approach as one that integrates high ecological validity (the realism) with high generalizability (control).

ETHICS AND STUDENT PARTICIPATION IN RESEARCH: ALTERNATIVES TO THE SUBJECT POOL

Have you ever participated in research as part of a course "requirement," typically through being part of a subject pool? There are established principles specifying the conditions under which students may participate in research. Principle 8.04 of the APA Ethical Principles of Psychologists and Code of Conduct (2010a) has two stipulations in the category of Client/Patient, Student, and Subordinate Research Participants:

(a) When psychologists conduct research with clients/patients, students, or subordinates as participants, psychologists take steps to protect the prospective participants from adverse consequences of declining or withdrawing from participation.

(b) When research participation is a course requirement or an opportunity for extra credit, the prospective participant is given the choice of equitable alternative activities.

With regard to stipulation (a), you can imagine the ethical challenges involved in conducting research with clients or patients. But consider the possible difficulties when faculty members conduct research with participants who may be current or future students. Every effort must be taken to make sure participants feel they can decline to participate or, if they participate, withdraw from the research without penalty.

A second concern is providing alternatives to research in courses where research participation is required. Simply put, participation in research cannot be required. In addition, the only form of extra credit cannot be research participation because that would de facto render it a requirement (and coercive). What are some typical alternatives to research participation?

> **» Try This Now**
>
> If your course requires research participation or offers research participation for extra credit, what alternatives were provided? Compared to participating in research, did the alternative involve equivalent effort?

A common alternative is to have students write a short paper (approximately two pages) summarizing an article related to the research process. In research on alternatives to the course requirement, the most frequently used alternative (for those who had alternatives) was writing a paper, as reported by 62.7% of the respondents (Sieber & Saks, 1989). Some alternatives might be considered inequitable and unattractive. At one liberal arts college, where five hours of research participation are a requirement in a course, the alternative is a 10–15-page research paper focused on the "History of Research Methods in Psychology." The thinking in establishing this alternative was that it should take the student about the same amount of time to write the paper (five hours) as it would to participate in studies that cumulatively took that length of time. When asked if students had selected this alternative, the answer was only 1 student in 16 years! Recommended reading about the ethical issues in using students as research participants is a recent article by Albert Leentjens and James Levenson (2013).

OFFERING INCENTIVES IN RESEARCH: ARE INCENTIVES COERCIVE?

Many different kinds of incentives are used in research, from financial (e.g., cash) to food (e.g., candy and doughnuts) to small tokens (e.g., ballpoint pens). There are no firm ethical guidelines surrounding the use of incentives in research and no mention of it in the Common Rule. IRBs vary in their perspectives on this issue. Like many other aspects of IRB review, there will be local differences.

> **» Try This Now**
>
> Before reading further, what reasons could you cite to allow the use of incentives? To prohibit their use?

In a thoughtful article, Ruth Grant and Jeremy Sugarman (2004) argued that, on balance, incentives do not seem to pose an ethical threat, but they also stated some conditions in which use of incentives would be ethically problematic. Those conditions involve a relationship of dependency with the researcher (e.g., if the researcher is one's course instructor, therapist, or physician), research involving high risk, research involving degrading topics or tasks, and where it takes a large incentive to overcome principled resistance to participating (p. 717). In other words, their view was that it is unethical to use incentives to entice people to participate in research they normally would not consider because of the risks involved. Although they framed their article within the context of medical research, their concerns are applicable to research in the social and behavioral sciences.

In answering the question about whether incentives are coercive, Eleanor Singer and Mick Couper (2008) concluded that offering incentives was not coercive in that participants were not willing to take on higher risks because of the higher incentives available. Their findings mirror previous studies showing the same outcome; that is, that if participants are unwilling to accept a risk at a particular level of incentive, they do not accept that risk if you offer them more.

Often subject pool regulations prohibit the use of incentives within the pool because it sets up a situation of **double-dipping** (e.g., completing a course requirement by choosing to participate in research AND being offered something in addition). Another problem related to use of the subject pool and incentives is that some researchers may have the financial means to offer incentives for participation (e.g., a lottery for a gift card) whereas others do not. In this way, access to the pool is skewed in favor of those who would be able to fund such incentives and creates what might be called an unequal playing field for researchers.

Double-dipping: situation in which you receive benefits from two sources for the effort (e.g., research credit and a gift incentive).

Departments and IRBs may also regulate the use of incentives for research that does not rely on the subject pool. Again, the problem of unequal access to participants because incentives are offered is central. One common policy to regulate incentives is setting a cap on the amount of a gift card or direct payment as a *recruitment strategy*. For example, one department's policy is a limit of a $25 gift card per every 50 participants in a study. Remember that you cannot force people to complete a research project once they start; for that reason, incentives cannot be tied to completion. In other words, incentives should not be viewed as compensation.

When departments and IRBs (usually these policies start at the departmental level) allow incentives, they are more likely to be approved if the research involves aspects that usually discourage participation (i.e., in research where it is difficult to obtain participants). Such aspects might be multiple sessions (e.g., for pre–post studies) or the need for participants to keep a journal or otherwise be involved in more than a single data-gathering session. We will talk more about the strategies involved in recruiting participants and revisit the use of incentives in Chapter 9.

REVISIT AND RESPOND

- Students (and others) cannot be required to participate in research. How does this protection relate to the ethical codes (Nuremberg, Belmont, APA) discussed at the beginning of the chapter? Why must there be equitable alternatives for people who do not want to participate in research as part of a course? Why do departments need guidelines for the use of incentives in research projects (i.e., what might happen without such guidelines)? Why are incentives described as recruitment strategies, not as compensation strategies?

PREPARING AN IRB PROPOSAL

Understanding what the IRB process entails may be part of your course work and perhaps even your major, and it may help prepare you to be a researcher in the future. Carefully following the guidelines for submission will prevent unnecessary delays in processing a proposal; often researchers cut corners in their preparation (Brinthaupt, 2002). Here is advice on preparing a research proposal for IRB review:

1. Plan ahead. IRBs do not meet daily or even weekly. Most post a schedule of meetings online and only meet for proposals that require full review. There is usually a deadline for submitting your proposal in advance of the meeting itself. If you miss the cutoff, you may have to wait another month (or more).

2. Be clear about the deadline for submitting materials, where to send the proposal, and whether you need paper copies (and if so, how many). Most IRB committees now use an electronic submission portal, eliminating the need for paper copies.

3. Understand the levels of IRB review: exempt, expedited, or full (as discussed earlier in this chapter). The speed in processing your proposal relates to the category of review. Plan accordingly.

4. Often institutions have a cover sheet requesting information about the research and the researcher that must accompany the proposal itself. This document typically specifies the material that must be submitted for review. Carefully complete all the sections of this submission form. Your informed consent document and debriefing statements deserve particular care.

5. Complete measures and specifications of your instruments/apparatus must be included. Providing the name of a measure without the items is insufficient. For the IRB to evaluate your proposal, the proposal must be complete. This means

you have to provide all the documents/measures the participants will be asked to complete or experience.

6. If you are a student, make sure that your faculty adviser has reviewed your proposal and signed the form you submit (IRBs want to know that the research has the faculty member's endorsement).

7. For full IRB review, researchers are often asked to attend the meeting in person. As a student, you may be asked to attend that meeting with your faculty adviser. This meeting can be an excellent experience; the feedback from this meeting improves the research project.

8. If your research involves a vulnerable population such as children (as discussed earlier in this chapter), make sure that you have all of the necessary permissions. Written approval from each institutional gatekeeper (e.g., school superintendent and school principal) is typically required when you submit your IRB proposal, as is your plan (and documents) to obtain parental/guardian and child assent if the research is approved.

9. When deception is part of a research project, justify its use in your proposal and explain why alternatives will not suffice.

Beyond the items specified here, Michael Oakes (2002, p. 469) provided a very useful list as you prepare your IRB proposal. In considering the merit of your research, he proposed the following consideration: Would you honestly want "someone you love to participate in your study?"

THE IRB TRAINING MODULES

Researchers are more likely to appreciate their IRB experience if they fully understand the need for such review. To that end, the federal government has developed several useful training modules. These modules cover the history and procedures involved with IRBs. The National Institutes of Health (NIH) Office of Extramural Research offers a course in Protecting Human Research Participants (**https://phrp.nihtraining.com/users/login .php**). This is a free educational module that provides a good overview of the issues with which researchers need to be familiar.

Another alternative is the **Collaborative Institutional Training Initiative (CITI)** offered by the University of Miami (**https://www.citiprogram.org**). This training has been adopted by a range of educational institutions, from major research universities (e.g., Stanford University and the University of Michigan) to small liberal arts colleges

Collaborative Institutional Training Initiative (CITI): online training modules for ethical issues relevant to institutional review board (IRB) review.

(e.g., Bates College and Colorado College). There is a cost for this training, paid either by the institution for an institutional subscription or on an individual learner basis. With either of these modules (NIH or CITI), the training you receive (typically there is a certificate of completion to print out) may enable you to qualify as being "trained" when you go to graduate school or a work environment where research is conducted. Most institutions require that researchers receive IRB training before they submit proposals to the IRB.

Summary

After reading this chapter, you should understand both why we have an IRB review process (that is, the history of ethical concerns often linked to Nazi war crimes) and what that review process entails, including the different levels of IRB review (exempt, expedited, full). You know the technical definitions of "human subject" and "research," both of which have to be met for a project to undergo IRB review. You have seen the overlap between the Nuremberg code, the Belmont Report, and the APA Code of Ethics (2010a). Aspects of the principles of Respect for Persons, Beneficence, and Justice appear in each ethical code. One central component in respect for persons is that individuals are autonomous agents, able to decide whether they want to participate in research after being fully informed. With the sample documents provided in Appendices B and C at the end of this book, you have the knowledge to create your informed consent and debriefing documents. In creating the informed consent document, you have seen the importance of distinguishing between anonymity and confidentiality and the circumstances under which it would be appropriate to break confidentiality. In doing research with vulnerable populations, especially children, issues of consent are critical at the level of (a) any gatekeepers, (b) then parents/guardians, and finally, if developmentally appropriate, (c) the children, who are asked to assent. Another important ethical consideration is whether the research involves deception (especially active), and whether such deception is justified. In addition, the use of incentives is another consideration; understanding that incentives are used to recruit people for research, but not to complete it, is an important distinction. To understand ethical and IRB-related issues better, you can take the federal government training module recommended at the end of this chapter or, if your institution subscribes, the CITI training module.

If you have not had time to consider them earlier, here is the list of **REVISIT and RESPOND** questions from this chapter.

- Why do you think an IRB in 2016 would refuse to approve Milgram's (1963) original obedience to authority study? What was ethically questionable about the fact that Zimbardo was serving both as a researcher and as the "superintendent" of the prison in his Stanford prison research (Haney et al., 1973)? In the Kennedy

Krieger Institute Lead Paint Study, some of the children were kept at greater risk than others (only partial lead abatement) to further the goals of the study. Which one of the points of the Nuremberg code does this action seem to violate?

- Thinking back to the lead paint study, was the principle of Justice followed in that research?

- What three ethical principles did the Belmont Report establish? What overlap do you see between these three principles and the general principles in the APA Code of Conduct (2010a)? Make a list of the two sets of principles and show where the overlap is. Why is having an informed consent document a critical part of doing ethical research? Do all three ethical codes (Nuremberg, Belmont, and APA) mention the importance of voluntary consent?

- From this definition, what two critical aspects are required for a study to be considered research?

- What makes a project "research" (and, thus, subject to review) in the eyes of the IRB? What kinds of projects qualify as exempt and do not undergo IRB review? What does it mean to say that a proposal involves exposing the participants to more than minimal risk? What is a vulnerable population? Give an example. What is the purpose of having a nonscientist on the IRB committee? An outside member from the community?

- In your own words, explain the difference between anonymity and confidentiality. Under what circumstance(s) would you break confidentiality? What would you say in your informed consent document to alert the participant to that possibility? How do researchers obtain informed consent electronically? Give an example of a circumstance where you would ask to have informed consent waived. What is the purpose of a debriefing document; what issues should be covered?

- Give examples of gatekeepers (people who can give permission for research to take place) in a school and for a sports team. Explain the difference between active and passive consent. What does it mean when you ask for the child's assent? About what age do researchers normally consider asking for the child's assent? Explain why active consent of parents/guardians is almost always required with children.

- When you leave out a description of some aspects of the research, this is called _____ deception (fill in the blank). When you purposely mislead participants about some aspects of the research, this is called _____ deception (fill in the blank). What are the potential drawbacks to using deception in terms of participants' attitudes toward subsequent research? Why might immersive virtual reality be a good alternative to using deception, whereas role playing is not? Why could you say that immersive virtual reality combines ecological validity with the potential for generalizability?

- Students (and others) cannot be required to participate in research. How does this protection relate to the ethical codes (Nuremberg, Belmont, APA) discussed at the beginning of the chapter? Why must there be equitable alternatives for people who do not want to participate in research as part of a course? Why do departments need guidelines for the use of incentives in research projects (i.e., what might happen without such guidelines)? Why are incentives described as recruitment strategies, not as compensation strategies?

BUILD YOUR SKILLS

1. Some social and behavioral scientists think IRB review is unnecessary for most research, which involves no more than minimal risk. Using evidence from the chapter, make a case that IRB review is beneficial, even for projects with no more than minimal risk.

2. Identify the informed consent components (discussed earlier in this chapter) in the statements in the sample informed consent document in Appendix B at the end of this book.

3. If you are doing a research project, what level of review (exempt, expedited, or full) is required for your project? Explain your answer.

---

⑤SAGE edge™

edge.sagepub.com/devlin

Sharpen your skills with SAGE edge!

SAGE edge for students provides a personalized approach to help you accomplish your coursework goals in an easy-to-use learning environment. You'll find action plans, mobile-friendly eFlashcards, and quizzes, as well as videos, web resources, and links to SAGE journal articles to support and expand on the concepts presented in this chapter.

MEASURES AND SURVEY RESEARCH TOOLS

CHAPTER HIGHLIGHTS

- Measurement: Ideal versus real
- Measurement scale types
- Identifying measures
  - The literature
  - Databases of tests: PsycTESTS and HaPI
  - Books of measures
  - Department resources and professors
  - Catalogues of measures and fees charged
- Qualities of measures: Reliability and validity
  - Reliability: Test–retest; parallel forms
  - Internal consistency: Split-half; Cronbach's alpha
  - Calculating Cronbach's alpha
  - Validity: Content, face, criterion-related, construct
- Other characteristics of measures
  - Length and difficulty
  - Instructions for scoring
  - Social desirability concerns; measures of social desirability
  - Qualifications for use

- Developing your own measure
- Why develop your own measure?
- Steps in creating your own measure
- Writing items (recommendations from Schwarz, 1999)
- Demographic items and social sensitivity
- Gender, race, ethnicity, income
- Item formatting (number of anchors; odd, even; stem)
- Scale types and flexibility in answering research questions
- Question order
- Online survey software
  - Comparison of features across software programs
  - SurveyMonkey versus Qualtrics
  - Program features
  - Downloading online surveys into SPSS
  - Survey appearance and labeling

OVERVIEW

Validity: extent to which a measure assesses what it is claimed to measure.

Reliability: in statistics, refers to the ability of a measure to produce reproducible outcomes.

Cronbach's alpha: statistical indicator of the internal consistency of a measure.

Finding appropriate scales to use in research can be a challenge. There are challenges both in identifying good scales in the literature and in physically obtaining them. An added pressure is that all measures (in their entirety) must be included in the human subjects institutional review board (IRB) proposal (see Chapter 4), which must be submitted and approved before data collection can begin. For students in a one-semester research methods class, this proposal is typically submitted by midsemester; thus, finding measures for research takes on added pressure.

This chapter covers both identifying good scales and physically obtaining those scales. The chapter explains the different types of scale measurement, the advantages of using measures other people have developed, and the criteria for evaluating the quality of a measure. These criteria include the measure's **validity** (does it measure what it says it measures) and its **reliability** (does it produce the same results over multiple administrations; do all of the items assess the construct in question). Related to reliability, you will learn how to calculate the internal consistency (e.g., **Cronbach's alpha**) for a scale. Cronbach's alpha is a specific measure of internal consistency and reflects the degree to which each item in a scale correlates with each other item on the scale.

Values typically range from 0 to 1 (a negative value is possible but uncommon). The greater the internal consistency of a measure, the greater the extent to which each item is measuring the same **construct**. A construct is an idea or theory whose properties are inferred from some kind of measurement and are not directly observable. Examples of constructs include intelligence, anxiety, self-esteem, and leadership. When you are choosing a measure, the internal consistency is one of the most important characteristics.

The criteria for using a measure may also include the length of the instrument and the difficulty of the items. Cost, copyright, and the requisite level of training to use a measure are other concerns. The chapter will also illustrate the drawbacks to developing your own measures and the kinds of questions (typically demographic or background) that are reasonable to generate yourself. You will not only learn how to locate and obtain measures but also the importance of identifying whether there are subscales and obtaining complete scoring instructions. The chapter will discuss the kinds of scoring issues that sometimes arise (e.g., items that are reverse scored). A resource guide at the end of this book (Appendix D) provides a list of measures commonly used in social science and behavioral neuroscience research.

Construct: idea or theory whose properties are inferred from some kind of measurement and are not directly observable. Examples of constructs include intelligence, anxiety, self-esteem, and leadership.

THE CONCEPT OF MEASUREMENT: IDEAL VERSUS REAL

As we discussed in Chapter 2, when examining the Method section of articles, it is helpful to keep track of the measures used in a particular area of study. Then, as you begin your search for measures, you will have some familiarity with the landscape. Early on in the research process for a semester-length course, you will have to determine your variable(s) of interest, that is, what you are trying to measure (e.g., anxiety and perceived control), and what scales exist for these constructs.

To explain the causes of behavior, researchers need some way to both describe and measure that behavior. In the social and behavioral sciences, we often try to describe and quantify abstract concepts, such as anxiety or sense of community, with scales. True, we may do something far more direct, for example, measure the reaction time to respond to a stimulus on a computer screen. Even then reaction time may be a proxy for some more abstract concept such as speed of perceptual processing.

Any measure you use will fall short in some way. It may not fully capture the essence of the concept you want to measure, or it may include material unrelated to the concept. Consider a concept like managerial competence. Your goal is to come as close as possible to measuring what you and others think managerial competence is (e.g., ability to work with people, delegate tasks, or solve problems), without including extraneous information in your measurement (e.g., attractiveness). You approach this task by identifying an existing measure of that idea, a measure that you find in the literature or one that you create yourself (more on that later). This *measure* of managerial competence is your actual instrument; you give this measure to your participants. The goal is to have maximum overlap between your theoretical concept, here managerial competence, and the actual measure you use, recognizing that the overlap will never be complete.

THE PURPOSE OF MEASURES

By now, you have identified a research question and have developed some preliminary hypotheses. How will you evaluate these hypotheses? What kind of data will you use? You want data that reflect the constructs (e.g., sense of community or managerial competence) central to your research question. As an example, perhaps you are interested in the relationship between the rate and complexity of vocabulary in managers' speech and judgments of managers' competence. You could figure out a way to measure the rate (e.g., number of words/minute) and complexity of vocabulary (e.g., an easy way would be to use the readability statistics in the word processing program). But how are you going to measure the judged competence?

Constructs become more difficult to measure the more abstract they are. When constructs are straightforward, such as rate of speech, the operational definition (as defined in Chapter 3) is easy to specify. When you define the variable by the operations or processes used to measure or quantify it, you have an operational definition. If we were measuring safe driving behavior on a college campus, for example, we might count the number of times drivers come to a complete stop at a particular stop sign. We have quantified the behavior (safe driving) by counting full stops at this designated stop sign. Thus, we have "put into operation" our measures that define safe driving. Some operational definitions seem relatively easy to specify, as this example suggests. Measuring the manager's judged competence is more challenging.

REVISIT AND RESPOND

- What is an operational definition? Give an example. Why is it hard to capture in full the essence of an abstract theoretical concept with a measure? Why is it harder when you measure managerial competence than when you measure rate of speech?

MEASUREMENT SCALE TYPES

In selecting a measure to use, one consideration is the kind of scale type it is. Many researchers emphasize the role of quantifiable (i.e., measured) data, although in Chapter 6, we talk about qualitative approaches where statistical analyses are not the focus. There are four generally accepted types of measurement scales: **nominal**, **ordinal**, **interval**, and **ratio** (Stevens, 1946). Using a particular scale type (e.g., nominal) can restrict the kinds of research questions you can answer and the degree to which you can detect differences in outcomes of interest; thus, knowing about the properties of each scale type is important. Figure 5.1 presents a summary of the characteristics of the four scale types, described in more detail in the next sections.

Nominal Scale Measurement

Nominal measurement scales are scales in which the values reflect no inherent order. These scales are also called **categorical data**, to reflect the fact that the data are assigned to categories. An example of a nominal scale question would be, "Do you own a car?," to which the respondent would reply "yes" or "no." We can count the number of participants in a given category (i.e., how many people said "yes" vs. how many said "no"), but there is no inherent order to the responses ("yes" is not inherently better or higher than "no"). Each answer simply represents a different category on the dimension of car ownership. Categorical data are often seen in research in which open-ended questions are asked. An open-ended question allows the respondent to answer in any way he or she wishes, that is, an **open-ended response**. In a closed-ended question, the respondent selects his or her response from a set of provided options, that is, a **closed-ended response**. Open-ended questions (e.g., "What do you like about your institution?") produce responses that can be put in categories. In response to this question about one's institution, participants may give answers about professors, courses, social life, food, housing, sports, career advising,

Nominal measurement scale: measurement scale (sometimes called categorical) in which there is no inherent order (e.g., questions that can be answered "yes" or "no").

Ordinal measurement scale: type of measurement in which the values are ordered but they are not equally spaced.

Interval measurement scale: type of measurement scale in which the values are ordered and equally spaced throughout; common in social science research.

Ratio measurement scale: scale type with equal intervals and a true zero point.

Categorical data: data in which there is no ordering of values; also called nominal data.

FIGURE 5.1 Characteristics of Four Types of Measurement Scales				
	Nominal	**Ordinal**	**Interval**	**Ratio**
Can be counted	✔	✔	✔	✔
Can be ordered		✔	✔	✔
Known distance between each value			✔	✔
Contains a true zero point				✔

location, library resources, or a host of other possibilities. Notice that one category is not more important or "higher" than another. These responses could be put into separate categories, and a frequency count could be made for each category. Some categories could also be combined; for example, a category could be created for "academics" into which we might put professors, courses, career advising, and library resources. There might be another category for quality of student life, which might include the other aspects (social life, food, housing, sports, and location). Again, there is no inherent ordering of these categories; they are equally valued.

In terms of statistics, categorical data are often analyzed in terms of frequencies (i.e., counts of the number of responses in each category) and their corresponding percentages. Beyond frequency analyses, **chi-square** analyses can be used with categorical data. Chi-square analyses involve dimensions that are nominal (categorical). Often analyses involve a 2 × 2 chi-square (meaning two categories for each dimension), but chi-square analyses are not restricted to just two categories on each dimension. For example, you might ask whether first year students differ from fourth year students in the number of mentions of social life, sports, and courses as sources of satisfaction (see Table 5.1). In this table, one dimension had three categories and the other dimension had two categories (3 × 2). Imagine that you had 500 first year students and 500 fourth year students provide answers to that original open-ended question about what people liked about their institution.

The responses do not need to add up to 500 because participants could mention as many items as they wished and not everyone would mention these particular items. Chi-square analyses are about proportionality, not about the absolute numbers. As you look at these numbers, you can see that there seem to be different proportionalities, especially for courses (fourth year students mention this more often than do first year students) and sports (again, fourth year students mention this more often than do first year students). First year students list social life more often than do fourth year students, but the proportional difference is not as great as in the other categories. If you do the chi-square analysis on these data, there is a significant chi-square $\chi^2 (2, N = 1,764) = 282.92$, $p < .001$, reflecting the fact that the proportions across categories differ. There are online

TABLE 5.1 ■ Comparison of First- and Fourth-Year College Students' Satisfaction With Social Life, Sports, and Courses			
	Social Life	**Sports**	**Courses**
First Year	436	105	76
Fourth Year	336	389	422

calculators to do calculations such as this (e.g., **http://www.socscistatistics.com/tests/ chisquare2/default2.aspx**) without needing to enter the data into a software statistical package such as SPSS Statistics®.

Nominal data are used in what is known as nonparametric statistics. A major difference between **parametric** and **nonparametric statistics** is that nonparametric statistics are viewed as less powerful than are parametric statistics, in that larger sample sizes are needed to achieve the same degree of power that you have with a parametric test (Howell, 2013).

Ordinal Scale Measurement

In ordinal data, there is an "ordering," but there is no knowledge of the distance of one choice in that order from another. What if you were given a list of types of transportation to take in the city: taxi, car, Uber®, bicycle, train, subway, and bus. You were asked to rank order your preference for these transportation modes (1–7) with 1 being first choice to seventh being last choice. Once you had completed that ranking, we have your preferences, but we have no idea how closely preferred these choices are. You might really like car, Uber, and taxi (which you ranked 1, 2, and 3), but you might have very low preference for choices 4–7. We have more information than we do with nominal data (the ordering of your choices) but not all that much more. Among the common statistics used with ranked data are Spearman's rho and Kendall's tau (Howell, 2013). In Spearman's rho, you are calculating the correlation between sets of ranks; in Kendall's tau, the focus is on the inversions in the ranks (e.g., one participant ranks three items: 1—car, 2—Uber, 3—taxi, and another ranks them 1—car, 2—taxi, and 3—Uber). There is an inversion in the second and third ranks for the second participant relative to the first. In both measures (rho and tau), the essence is still a degree of agreement between the participants.

Interval Scale Measurement

Interval scales are the most widely used scale type in the social and behavioral sciences. Interval scale data are also sometimes called **continuous data**. In interval scales, the anchors are assumed to be equally spaced, such that in a 5-point scale, the distance between any two anchors is the same (e.g., 1 to 2 is the same distance as 4 to 5). Interval scales are used in parametric statistics, such as analysis of variance. As mentioned earlier, parametric statistics have some advantages over nonparametric statistics because of their greater power.

One commonly used type of interval scale in the social and behavioral sciences is the **Likert scale.** There's some disagreement about the pronunciation, but it should be pronounced Lick-urt—like licking an ice cream cone (**http://core.ecu.edu/psyc/wuenschk/ StatHelp/Likert.htm**: this link is entertaining reading in that experts talk about what makes something a Likert scale). The Likert scale is a scale in which there are typically five response options or **anchors** that represent degrees of agreement-disagreement to a

Parametric statistics: make assumptions about the population fitting a normal distribution.

Nonparametric statistics: nonparametric statistics make no assumptions about the population fitting a particular normal distribution.

Continuous data: data on an interval scale; often contrasted with categorical data.

Likert scale: frequently used scale type where the anchors are typically five degrees of agreement-disagreement to statements.

Anchors: specific points on a rating scale (each one is a separate anchor).

statement: strongly agree, agree, neither agree/disagree, disagree, and strongly disagree. Each point on a rating scale, not just the extremes, is called an *anchor*. Most researchers treat the Likert scale as interval, but it should be noted that some treat it as ordinal.

Ratio Scale Measurement

A ratio scale has one element missing in an interval scale: a true 0 point. In a ratio scale, 0 represents the absence of a quantity (such as having 0 correct answers on a memory test; other examples include measurements of weight and height; the Kelvin scale for temperature is also a ratio scale). In the social and behavioral sciences, we typically see ratio scales used in performance tasks, such as recognition, recall, or problem-solving tasks. In these instances, performance may be represented as the number of correct answers, which would have the possibility of 0 (none correct).

REVISIT AND RESPOND

- Describe the four different scale types (nominal, ordinal, interval, ratio). Explain the frequent use of interval scale data in the social and behavioral sciences.

SENSITIVITY OF A SCALE AND ANCHOR VALUES

Scale sensitivity: ability of the scale to detect differences.

When people talk about **scale sensitivity**, they usually refer to the idea that the scale is sufficiently fine-grained to detect differences that exist. Figure 5.2 presents an example.

Consider again our earlier example of asking participants to indicate what they like about their institution. If we listed a series of options (courses, sports, food, location) and asked people to use a rating scale with three anchors (1 = not at all; 2 = somewhat; 3 = a lot), we might find little variability in the responses. With just three anchors, there is little room to express a range of opinion. Alternatively, with seven anchors (the second example), a greater range of opinion could be expressed. We would therefore refer to the second option as having greater sensitivity than the first option. When you are selecting measures to use in research, the sensitivity of the measure is one criterion to consider.

FIGURE 5.2 Example of Differences in Sensitivity

	3 Anchors	vs.	7 Anchors	
1		2		3
Not at all		Somewhat		A lot

1	2	3	4	5	6	7
Not at all						A lot

As a general principle, measures that have 5–7 anchors are preferred to those with a smaller or larger number of anchors. With an even number of items (e.g., 4), you will have no neutral point, and having 3 items takes us back to the problem of lack of sensitivity. With 8 anchors, again there is no neutral point, and with 9 anchors, respondents may not be able to make meaningful distinctions with so many choices (Thomas, 2004).

Psychological Meaning of Scale Anchors

An interval scale may incorporate a 0 point, but it is a relative, not an absolute, value. The use and placement of an anchor of 0 in an interval scale also carries with it a psychological meaning that should be considered. In Figure 5.3 illustrating two different 7-point rating scales, the first example has no 0 and the second includes 0 as its lowest scale value.

These two rating scales are arithmetically identical, but would users necessarily interpret them the same way?

FIGURE 5.3 Comparison of Two 7-Point Rating Scales

- Equally spaced intervals (anchors)

  1 2 3 4 5 6 7
  0 1 2 3 4 5 6

Please consider the "psychological" impact of scale ranges that are arithmetically identical, especially when a 0 is included !!

THE PROCESS OF IDENTIFYING MEASURES: THE LITERATURE

With the knowledge of the different scale types (nominal, ordinal, interval, ratio), you are ready to search for a measure. The general search strategies here can be in any domain of social and behavioral science. When you began reading the empirical literature in your topic area, as a way to generate a specific research question, you probably looked at more than 20 articles in that area. As discussed in Chapter 2, those articles are important resources because it makes sense to concentrate first on existing measures, that is, measures other researchers have used. When we talk about measures, we are typically referring to dependent variables (see Chapter 3). If we were to use the word *stimuli,* we would typically be referring to independent variables (see Chapter 3).

Not all disciplines in the social and behavioral sciences use the same words for the section that contains information about the measures. In the discipline of psychology, this section of a journal is called the Method (note that it is singular; as introduced in Chapter 2), and it has three subsections: Participants, Materials (sometimes called Apparatus or Measures or Instruments), and Procedure. The Participants are the "who" of your study; the Materials are the "with what" of your study; the Procedure is the "how" of your study. In other social and behavioral sciences, the terminology is similar, although not identical.

The Measures/Materials/Instruments Section

The Measures/Instruments section is the first place to look to locate a measure for your study. In that section, the author is supposed to provide the name of the measure used, a citation to that source (that is, where the author found that measure), the number of items, a sample item (including the anchors), and the internal consistency or reliability of that measure (or other aspects of what are called the **psychometric properties** of the instrument). Psychometric properties are quantifiable aspects of a measure that indicate its statistical quality. Other information (such as how to score the scale) may or may not be provided. Pay particular attention to measures that are commonly used because that might give you some idea of the endorsement of that scale by researchers. If a scale was only used in one article and that article is not recent (i.e., not within the last 10 years), you might be wise to keep looking.

Psychometric properties: quantifiable aspects of your measure that indicate its statistical qualities.

Given the page restrictions for journal articles, you are unlikely to find all of the items for a measure (unless the measure is very short) in the Measures/Instruments section. You may not even find all of the basic information mentioned in the previous paragraph (e.g., sample items). Authors do not always provide the Cronbach's alpha for a given measure or another indication of the scale's reliability. Without that information, it is hard to determine the quality of the measure.

What is your next step? When describing the measure, the author provided a citation for that measure in the Measures/Instruments section. Your next step is to locate that citation in the References section of the article, and then obtain THAT article (using the tree backward techniques discussed in Chapter 2). You keep repeating that step (that is, backtracking) until one of two things happens at the point when no further sources are listed to examine: You have the full scale or you don't. Through this process of backtracking, you will typically find the article where the scale was introduced and validated. The items for the scale are usually in that article. If not, there may be an author note in the article to contact the corresponding author to obtain the scale. In that case, e-mail the corresponding author to obtain the items. If that person has retired or is otherwise unlocatable, a good strategy is to write an author who has recently used the scale and ask whether that person can send you the items.

PsycTESTS®: American Psychological Association (APA) database of test records that typically provides the test items.

DATABASES OF TESTS (PsycTESTS AND HaPI)

Over the last few years, online databases of measures have become available. The most well known of these is **PsycTESTS®**. A second useful source is the **Health and**

Psychosocial Instruments (HaPI®) database. PsycTESTS, which appeared in 2011, is a database provided through the American Psychological Association (APA) that now contains almost 30,000 records, with coverage beginning in 1910 (to the present). If you look on line at the APA site for this database (**http://www.apa.org/pubs/databases/psyctests/**), it gives you the current count of records available; this count is updated monthly. Typically the actual test or at least sample test items are available, as well as information about the psychometric properties of the test (if those have been published). The database focuses on tests not commercially available, which is an important consideration for researchers (i.e., cost).

This database is very useful. It is possible to use a keyword to search for a test that measures a particular construct. As an example, if we use the keyword "self esteem," it yields 860 results (May 26, 2016). You can sort the results by relevance, oldest, and newest. The default presentation is by relevance. If you took a look at the first measure listed and clicked on the full text symbol, you would see the screenshot in Figure 5.4):

Note that the first page gives you the name of the authors, the number of items (6), and the response format of the items (a Likert scale). You also see the citation for the source of this scale and a section labeled *Permissions.* Pay attention to the permissions to see the requirements for use of this scale. In this instance, you may use it for noncommercial research and educational purposes without contacting the authors. The next page gives you the specific items. Note also that we have seen no mention of the psychometric properties of the scale. But if we go back to the initial listing for this record after we have clicked on the hyperlink for this item ("Self Esteem Measure"), we come to a page called the **detailed record**. On that page is a description, which in this case includes the following at the end of the paragraph:

> The Self-Esteem Measure consists of six items (e.g., "You have a lot of good qualities") analogous to some of the items used in Rosenberg's (1989) scale. Each item is rated on a 5-point scale ranging from 1 (strongly disagree) to 5 (strongly agree). Cronbach's alpha for this measure was .845. (PsycTESTS Database Record (c) 2015 APA, all rights reserved)

The description gives you the Cronbach's alpha. There is no statement about **reverse scoring**. If there were reverse-scored items, this is where you would find out. Usually in cases where there is reverse scoring, some items need to be reverse-scored and others do not. A well-known example is Morris Rosenberg's Self-Esteem Scale (1965); of the 10 items, 5 need to be reverse scored. What this means is that some items are phrased in a way that endorses the construct, in this case, possessing self-esteem, (e.g., high self-esteem; "On the whole I am satisfied with myself"), whereas other statements are phrased in a way that opposes the construct (i.e., low self-esteem; "At times I think I am no good at all"). If the

Health and Psychosocial Instruments (HaPI®): database of instruments that indicates the sources in which a particular instrument is used.

Detailed record: part of the information in PsycTESTS® that may give you psychometric information about a scale.

Reverse scoring: items in a survey stated in a manner that is opposite that of the other items (i.e., stated negatively when the other items are stated positively) and whose anchors need to be reversed.

anchors range from 1 to 4, with a higher number reflecting higher self-esteem, you would need to reverse the numbering (i.e., 4 to 1) for the reverse-scored items. Then, all items are "going in the same direction"; that is, that for all items a high score means the same thing (i.e., endorsement of high self-esteem).

What is the downside to using PsycTESTS? Consider what just happened in Figure 5.4 (Williams & McCarthy, 2014). That scale came first, by relevance, from our key-word search. The original Rosenberg Self-Esteem Scale (RSES; 1965), not modified or

---

FIGURE 5.4 Screenshot of PsycTESTS Result for Self-Esteem Measure Test

Self-Esteem Measure
Version Attached: Full Test

Note: Test name created by PsycTESTS

PsycTESTS Citation:
Williams, M., & McCarthy, B. (2014). Self-Esteem Measure [Database record]. Retrieved from PsycTESTS. doi: http://dx.doi.org/10.1037/t43643-000

Instrument Type:
Rating Scale

Test Format:
This measure comprises six items, each rated on a Likert-type scale ranging from 1 (strongly disagree) to 5 (strongly agree).

Source:
Williams, Monica, & McCarthy, Bill. (2014). Assessing stereotypes of adolescent rape. Journal of Criminal Justice, Vol 42(6), 557-567. doi: 10.1016/j.jcrimjus.2014.09.010, © 2014 by Elsevier. Reproduced by Permission of Elsevier.

Permissions:
Test content may be reproduced and used for non-commercial research and educational purposes without seeking written permission. Distribution must be controlled, meaning only to the participants engaged in the research or enrolled in the educational activity. Any other type of reproduction or distribution of test content is not authorized without written permission from the author and publisher. Always include a credit line that contains the source citation and copyright owner when writing about or using any test.

◢ **PsycTESTS**®

doi: http://dx.doi.org/10.1037/t43643-000

Self-Esteem Measure

Items

    You have a lot of good qualities
    You have a lot to be proud of
    You like yourself just the way you are
    You feel like you are doing everything just about right
    You feel socially accepted
    You feel loved and wanted

Note . Responses are on a 5-point scale (1 = *strongly disagree* ... 5 = *strongly agree*).

translated, is the seventieth entry on this list. PsycTESTS is definitely convenient, and if you can't find a relevant scale in the Measures section of the empirical articles you consulted, PsycTESTS is useful. PsycTESTS is also helpful in seeing whether all items for a given test you want are provided, if they were not available in the literature. The drawback to consulting PsycTESTS *before* consulting the literature is that the most widely used and reliable scale to measure a given construct may not be listed first. Start with the literature.

HaPI (Health and Psychsocial Instruments) is produced by the Behavioral Measurement Database Services (BMDS). A website describing HaPI (**https://www.ebscohost.com/academic/health-and-psychosocial-instruments-hapi**) states that "over 80 unique instruments" are offered within almost 175,000 records (see also **http://bmdshapi.com**). The records are from journals in both the health and psychosocial sciences. Let's do the same keyword search in HaPI as we did in PsycTESTS: *self esteem.* If we use that keyword in our search, the result is 4,301 records (May 26, 2016). But there is redundancy in those records. The number of *unique instruments* offered in the database is far different than the *total number* of records. You can sort by relevance, author, source, date newest, and date oldest. Relevance is the default. The first record that appears is the Rosenberg Self-Esteem Scale (German Version) by Rosenberg [translated by Brauhardt, Rudolph, and Hilbert (2014)]. There is no information about the number of items, item format, or psychometric properties of the scale, although there is a reference to the original Rosenberg (1965) book that introduced and validated the scale. HaPI is useful if you want to see the articles in which a particular scale has appeared, as well as to locate the original source of the scale, but it is not directly useful in providing detailed information about the scale.

BOOKS OF MEASURES

Other useful bibliographic resources (again, after you have consulted the literature) are books of measures. There are books that provide measures and books that critique measures. Offerings include *Encyclopedia of Psychological Assessment* (2 volumes; Fernandez-Ballesteros, 2003), *Measures for Clinical Practice and Research: A Sourcebook* (5th ed.; Corcoran & Fischer, 2013), *Tests Critiques Compendium: Reviews of Major Tests From the Test Critiques Series* (Keyser & Sweetland, 1987), and *Directory of Unpublished Experimental Mental Measures* (Goldman & Mitchell; 9 volumes, 2008 is the most recent). The sourcebook by Kevin Corcoran and Joel Fischer is particularly useful, especially for clinical research. Volume 1 covers couples, families, and children. Volume 2 focuses on adults. In these volumes, the measures are provided as well as the following information for each scale: purpose, authors, description, norms, scoring, reliability, validity, primary reference, and availability. Regarding availability, the usual statement is that the measure may be copied from the volume; if not, the author's contact information (or other avenues for obtaining the article) is provided.

DEPARTMENT RESOURCES AND PROFESSORS

Another source of measures is nearby: your department and its professors. See what measures and equipment your professors have on-hand and/or recommend. Your department may have a file of frequently used scales; these may be available to students with the appropriate training. Typically clinical measures, e.g., the Wexsler Adult Intelligence Scale (WAIS) or projective techniques such as the Rorschach, require specific advanced training (e.g., master's or doctoral level; see also later section in this chapter on Qualifications for Use). In addition, the appendices of honors, master's, and Ph.D. theses in your department will contain complete measures. These are excellent resources.

CATALOGUES OF MEASURES AND FEES CHARGED

Almost without exception, measures offered by test publishing companies cost money. Examples of such companies are Psychological Assessment Resources (PAR), Inc. (**http://www4.parinc.com**), which offers assessments in such areas as achievement, intelligence, neuropsychology, personality, and career development. Consulting Psychologist's Press (**https://www.cpp.com/products/index.aspx**) covers areas in career and organizational development. Among the most well-known of its offerings is the Myers-Briggs® Type Indicator, which is often used in career counseling offices to provide an assessment of personality and help people identify their areas of interest and "types." EdITS (**http://www.edits.net**) has offerings in career counseling and assessment. Although many of the instruments offered through EdITS focus on career counseling, there are some mood assessments [e.g., the Multiple Affect Adjective Checklist-Revised (MAACL-R®)] that are useful for a range of research topics. Western Psychological Services (**http://www.wpspublish.com/app/**) offers assessment instruments in clinical, industrial/organizational, and neuropsychology, among other areas. The Psychological Corporation (**http://www.pearsonclinical.com**) focuses on clinical assessment (e.g., the MMPI®). Finally, Mind Garden (**http://www.mindgarden.com**) has a range of instruments covering leadership, employee burnout, gender roles, and environments. Of the companies offering tests for a fee, Mind Garden might have instruments most likely to be used by student researchers. Among their offerings are the University Residence Environment Scale®, which assesses the social climate of residential groups of students; the Bem Sex Role Inventory®, which is widely used to assess gender role; and the State-Trait Anxiety Inventory for Adults®, which is widely used to assess both state (at the moment) and trait (generalized) anxiety.

What these companies have in common is that they charge fees, although some provide discounts to researchers. Although some tests offered by these companies are available *only* through these companies (many of these tests are clinical instruments that require advanced training in clinical psychology), there are scales available through other routes without charge. As an example, if we take the Bem Sex Role Inventory (BSRI) and check PsycTESTS, we find the test there (all the items) and the Permissions statement says, "May use for Research/Teaching," and no fee is listed. On Mind Garden, the manual for the BSRI is $50; a Remote Online Survey License is $2/participant, with a minimum purchase of 50 (thus, $100). Before assuming that you have to pay for an instrument, a recommended course of action is to check the literature first and then PsycTESTS.

Finally, a word is in order about the availability of tests that you find "online." Doing an online search for a measure (e.g., searching for "*BSRI*") may lead you to a copy of the test. Should you use this measure? There are at least two considerations. First, there is an ethical issue. If the test is one for which particular permissions and/or fees are required, then using a test you found online without paying the fees and having the qualifications for use may be considered unethical. Second, without knowing the items on the original test and their anchors, you can't assume that the test you found is complete and correct.

REVISIT AND RESPOND

- Where should you start your search for a measure? How do PsycTESTS and HaPI differ? What do you learn from reading about the permissions for a scale? What kinds of tests typically have qualifications for use? If a fee is charged for a scale, what other avenues might you pursue before paying the fee?

QUALITIES OF MEASURES: RELIABILITY AND VALIDITY

Among the most important considerations for selecting a scale are its reliability and validity. There are various types of reliability, but the core issue is the consistency of the measure. Consistency can be measured over time (**test–retest reliability**) and can also refer to the degree to which each of the items of the scale is measuring the same construct (called internal consistency, as introduced in Chapter 2, often assessed as Cronbach's alpha). Validity refers to whether the measure assesses what it claims to assess (e.g., does a measure of stress actually assess what people commonly understand stress to be?). We will concentrate on reliability because it is easier for researchers to evaluate this aspect of a measure, although considerations of validity are important as well. We will talk further

Test–retest reliability: form of reliability in which the instrument is given at two points in time and the scores are correlated.

about one form of reliability, inter-rater reliability, when we talk about behavioral observation and content analyses in Chapter 6. Here we will concentrate on the reliability of psychological tests or measures.

Test–Retest Reliability

Test–retest reliability is a measure of the degree to which a test administered at one time (T_1) correlates with that measure at a second time (T_2). Typically, the length of time between administrations is fairly long, which will reduce the likelihood that participants will remember the questions (and their answers). The typical statistical measure of test–retest reliability is Pearson's *r*. An example would be students who took the same test (e.g., a self-esteem scale) at two points in time.

Parallel Forms Reliability (also called Alternate Forms Reliability)

Many people take the SAT® twice to improve their scores. If so, they take a parallel form of the test the second time. Test developers such as the Educational Testing Service are aware that taking the same test twice could artificially inflate students' scores, merely as a function of familiarity with the items. For that reason, test developers continuously create new items (which are included as part of an existing test but do not contribute to a test taker's score). By including such trial items, test developers are assessing the degree to which performance on the old and new items correlate. Test developers need to be sure that the new items are of equivalent difficulty to create a truly parallel form of the test. Therefore, a researcher who is concerned that multiple administrations of a test might affect a participant's scores [think back to Campbell and Stanley's (1963) "Testing" threat to internal validity;, see Chapter 3] mightlook for an instrument with **parallel forms reliability (also called alternate forms reliability)**.

Measures of Internal Consistency: Split-Half Reliability and Cronbach's Alpha

Internal consistency is an important kind of reliability for researchers. Internal consistency reflects the degree to which each item in a scale is measuring the same construct (i.e., the degree to which each item correlates with every other item on the scale). There are two common measures of internal consistency, Cronbach's alpha and **split-half reliability**. Cronbach's alpha is more widely used, but it is worth explaining split-half reliability.

The name "split-half" suggests what happens to calculate this kind of reliability. A test is randomly divided into two halves, and participants take both halves, with the items intermingled, at the same time. Then, the two halves can be separated and a correlation

Parallel forms reliability (also called alternate forms reliability): form of reliability in which equivalent forms of a test are shown to be reliable.

Split-half reliability: one form of reliability of a measure in which the instrument is split into halves and the halves are correlated with each other; sometimes referred to as Spearman-Brown.

can be conducted between the scores on the halves. This approach to assessing the internal consistency of a measure is often used if you want to change the length of a test (lengthen or shorten it). In the Measures/Instruments section of a paper, you may see this kind of reliability referred to as Spearman–Brown's split-half reliability coefficient.

The most widely reported measure of internal consistency is Cronbach's alpha (α). You want the alpha for a measure to be high (.8 or greater; Nunnally, 1978) because the kind of variability you want should come from differences produced by exposure to different conditions, not from variability introduced in scale scores when "poor" test items don't correlate well with other items.

Researchers often accept as a "given" the cutoffs or standards for selecting measures that other researchers attribute to the original source (Lance, Butts, & Michels, 2006). In the case of alpha, the "given" has been .70 or higher, which researchers frequently cite from Jum Nunnally (1978). Charles Lance et al. (2006) revisited Nunnally's (1978) comments and showed that Nunnally said something quite different. First, Nunnally said that there are different standards for different research situations and that the .70 value is only appropriate for "early stages of research on predictor tests or hypothesized measures of a construct" (p. 245). If you are using an established scale for basic research, the .8 level may be acceptable, but Nunnally went on to say that in applied settings where important decisions are being made on the basis of someone's test score, even a value of .9 would be "the minimum that should be tolerated, and a reliability of .95 should be considered a desirable standard" (p. 246). The value of .70 is a long way from .95!

In the Measures/Instruments section of an empirical paper, look for some statement about the internal consistency of a measure and abide by the standards that Nunnally (1978) suggested. You may not always be able to find an appropriate measure that reaches .8 or higher, but that should be a goal. Some commonly used measures have a high Cronbach's alpha. For example, RSES has a reported alpha of .88 (PsycTESTS) and the Frost Indecisiveness Scale, which measures compulsive indecision, has a reported alpha of .9 (PsycTESTS).

THE IMPORTANCE OF COMPUTING YOUR OWN CRONBACH'S ALPHA

As a researcher, the Cronbach's alpha value is one of the important criteria you will use in selecting a measure, but you should also conduct a Cronbach's alpha on your own data and report that in your Results section. You cannot assume that the alpha reported in the literature will be the same for your sample; it may even be higher than the level reported in the literature. It may also be lower, which could be cause for concern. When you calculate the Cronbach's alpha, for example, using SPSS, you will be able to see what the scale value would be if each item on the scale were deleted (see Figure 5.8), and you may be able to improve the Cronbach's alpha.

In SPSS, the steps for calculating a Cronbach's alpha are:

1. Under Analyze from the Menu bar, select "Scale" and choose "Reliability Analysis." An "action box" for Items will open.
2. Move over all of the items you want for the reliability analysis from the variable list to this box (see Figure 5.5).
3. Click open the "Statistics" option and click "Item," "Scale," and "Scale if item deleted" under "Descriptives." Then click "Continue" (see Figure 5.6). In the main analysis box, the default model is Alpha so you don't need to change that. You are ready to click "OK."

In the example here, 10 items from the 39-item Padua Inventory (a scale to measure obsessive-compulsiveness) were used to calculate an alpha from a dataset from Ann

FIGURE 5.5 Screenshot of Reliability Analysis in SPSS

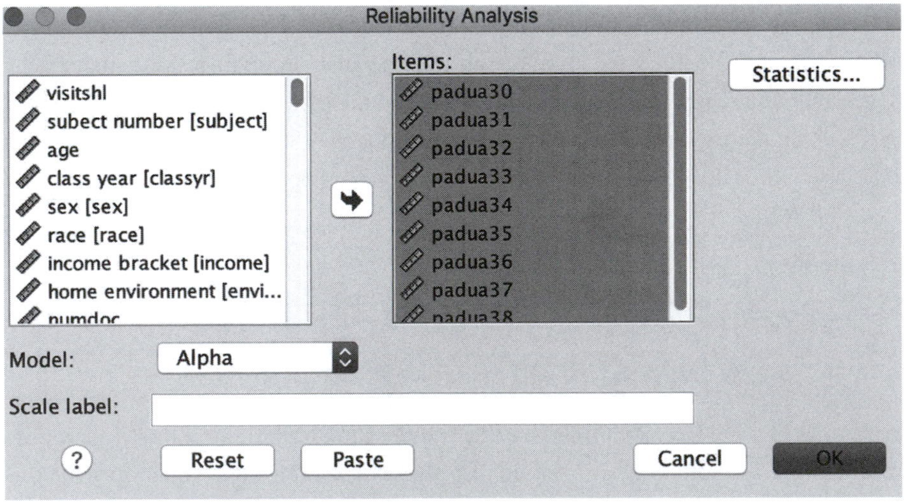

Source: © PsycTESTS, American Psychological Association.

FIGURE 5.6 Screenshot of Reliability Analysis: Statistics Options in SPSS

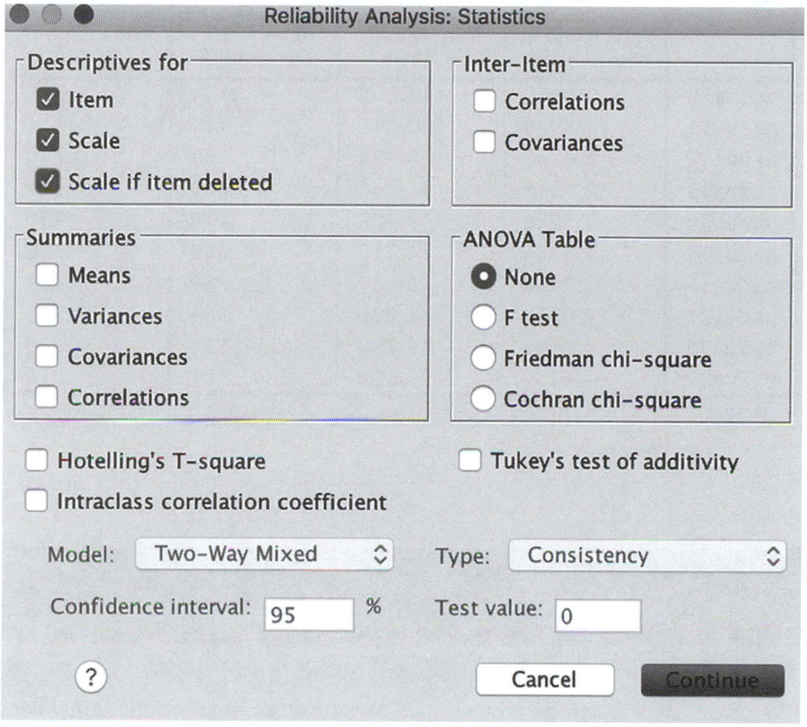

Devlin (2008).[1] We see that the alpha based on these 10 items (Padua 30–Padua 39) is .822 (see Figure 5.7). We also see in Figure 5.8 (labeled "Item-Total Statistics") that the alpha would IMPROVE if we deleted Padua 30. The alpha would be .849 without Padua 30 (see Figure 5.8). What you would do in this instance is go back in to SPSS, take out Padua 30 from your reliability analysis, and rerun the reliability analysis. You would then see whether any other items could be deleted to improve the alpha (in this case, the answer was no).

FIGURE 5.7 Reliability Statistics

Cronbach's Alpha	N of Items
.822	10

---

[1]The alpha for all 39 items in this dataset is .937; for all 39 items, the alpha cannot be improved by deleting any items. In fact, deleting any item would lower that alpha.

Content validity: validity of a measure that focuses on its representativeness from the domain of interest (e.g., a spelling test for fifth graders composed of words selected from books read by fifth graders).

Face validity: type of validity in which the measures subjectively appear to assess what you claim (e.g., a measure of leadership that asks about decisiveness).

Criterion-related validity: degree to which test scores predict the behavior of interest; two types (predictive and concurrent).

Convergent validity: demonstration of agreement between measures hypothesized to be theoretically related; contrasted with divergent validity.

Discriminant validity: situation in which measures hypothesized to be theoretically unrelated are, in fact, unrelated.

FIGURE 5.8 Item-Total Statistics

	Scale Mean if Item Deleted	Scale Variance if Item Deleted	Corrected Item–Total Correlation	Cronbach's Alpha if Item Deleted
padua30	1.8016	11.663	.164	.849
padua31	1.8925	10.641	.424	.817
padua32	2.0165	10.314	.668	.790
padua33	2.0578	11.740	.400	.817
padua34	1.8098	9.608	.728	.780
padua35	1.9834	10.115	.699	.786
padua36	1.7189	8.814	.669	.789
padua37	2.0330	11.222	.564	.805
padua38	1.9669	10.792	.584	.800
padua39	2.1322	12.264	.631	.818

REVISIT AND RESPOND

- Define internal consistency in your own words. Is there one set Cronbach's alpha value for all research purposes? If not, what circumstances require the highest alpha? List the steps you would take to run a reliability analysis on SPSS.

QUALITIES OF MEASURES: VALIDITY

The validity of a scale is its ability to measure what it claims it measures. There are different kinds of validity; some involve numerical calculations, whereas others involve the presentation of a reasoned argument. Here we will cover four categories of validity: **content**, **face**, **criterion-related** (predictive and concurrent), and construct, which includes **convergent** and **discriminant** validity.

Content Validity

Students are well acquainted with the essence of content validity even if they have never used that term. Imagine that you are taking a course in personality theory and are having a test on Monday. As you think about studying for the exam, you want the professor to include material that you actually *covered* in the course (from the text, from lectures), not obscure material in the reading that you didn't cover. Content validity is the idea that the information (here on your test) adequately samples the domain of interest (material covered thus far in your personality course). You can't numerically show that a test has content validity; rather, you present an argument that the test was constructed in a way that it adequately sampled (i.e., included items from) the domain of interest.

> **» Try This Now**
>
> If you were going to construct a test of fifth-grade spelling words with content validity, how would you go about constructing the test?

Face Validity

Face validity refers to the idea that a test "looks like" what it claims to assess. The "looks like" part can refer to the content of the written items, or it may literally refer to how the visual items look (or how the auditory items sound). If you told participants they were going to take a test to assess their ability to identify well-known classical music, participants would expect to hear classical music. If you didn't play classical music, the test would lack face validity.

Why is this important for you as a researcher? If you tell participants they are going to participate in a research project about "X" (e.g., perceived suitability for working in various industries, including technology), and then they fill out measures that have to do with "Y" (e.g., sexism; using the Modern Sexism Scale, because you are really interested in gender discrimination in the tech industry), those measures lack face validity for the problem you identified. The measures don't seem to have anything to do with what you said the study was about. In this situation, that mismatch may increase the demand characteristics in the study (refer to Chapter 3).

Criterion-Related Validity: Predictive and Concurrent

Criterion-related validity answers the question of whether a test predicts an outcome (criterion) of interest. This kind of validity involves a numerical calculation, a correlation, between the test score and the outcome (criterion) score. The difference between the predictive form and the concurrent form is the timing. In **predictive validity**, you are claiming that a measure predicts (forecasts) some outcome of interest that will occur in the future. Thus, the test occurs at one point in time and the outcome at a second point in time. In **concurrent validity**, the correlation between the test and the outcome occurs at the *same point* in time. An example will illustrate the difference. Most students have taken the SAT or ACT® tests, which are often required to apply to college.

Predictive validity: validity in which a measure is shown to forecast (predict) the outcome of interest (the criterion).

Concurrent validity: one of two types of criterion-oriented validity; when the test (the predictor) and the outcome (the criterion) are assessed at the same point in time.

These SAT or ACT scores are supposed to predict first year grade-point average (GPA), and there is even some evidence that the scores correlate well with overall GPA at the end of the fourth year of college (Schmitt et al., 2009). In other words, these tests are claimed to have predictive validity in that students take the tests in high school, yet the tests predict the GPA at the end of the first year of college. How do researchers know these tests have predictive validity? Because they have conducted studies in which there is variability in the test scores (here, SAT or ACT). That is, the researchers have the data for people who have scores that range from the low to the high end of performance, and then they correlate these scores with the first year GPAs of those students. Students with a wide range of such test scores are admitted to college (they have other qualities that influence admission), and this variability provides the opportunity to conduct such predictive validity studies.

In the case of concurrent validity, the test is taken and the outcome (e.g., performance) is measured at the *same point* in time.

> **» Try This Now**
>
> Before reading further, can you think of some drawbacks to concurrent validity, in contrast to predictive validity?

Concurrent validity studies are often used in employment situations where you want to see if a new screening test for applicants predicts job performance. You would thus give the test you were trying out to current employees (incumbents) to see whether the test matched (i.e., correlated with) their current success as employees. A problem with this approach is that there is probably a **restriction of range** with these current employees. The difference between the scores of the high and low performers may not be that large—the score range is restricted (otherwise you probably would have already fired them!). In addition, you would have to assume that the time these incumbents had already spent on the job would not affect performance on your employment screening test. Thus, you would want a test that was not affected by on-the-job experience. Such a test would be better if it measured some reasonably stable indicator, like intelligence. You can see there are quite a few challenges in using measures that are validated concurrently; they are typically viewed as less convincing than are measures that are validated through the predictive approach.

An intriguing example of predictive validity made the national news in 1996 when it was mentioned on *The Tonight Show* and other media outlets. In this instance, an applicant for a position in the New London, Connecticut, Police Department was turned

Restriction of range: when the distribution of scores is not widely dispersed across the range of interest; affects the size of your correlation.

away because he scored "too high" on one of the screening measures, the Wunderlic Personnel test. You can imagine all of the banter around this outcome, such as "Man too smart to be a cop." The police department limited interviews to those who scored from 20 to 27 on the test, and the applicant had a score of 33. Why would the guidelines suggest that someone with a *lower score* would be a better addition to the department than someone with a higher score? The answer comes from the predictive validity studies conducted by the company that produces the test. These studies showed that applicants with the higher scores for police jobs often quit early on after becoming bored with the work. Training these applicants is expensive; thus, municipalities have a rationale for sticking to the predictive cutoffs. The rejected applicant sued but lost his appeal against the city, first in a lower court and then in the 2nd U.S. Circuit Court of Appeals. The court stated that the city's policy was a rational way to select candidates (but also perhaps unwise!) (Larrañeta, 2000).

Construct Validity

Construct validity deals with whether the measure of interest actually assesses what it claims to assess. In a sense this is the essence of validity. How do you demonstrate construct validity? The approach involves creating a logical argument followed by a series of studies. You need to develop what Lee Cronbach and Paul Meehl (1955) called a **nomological network**. Such a network shows a series of lawful relationships, that is, the relationships among observable variables that your theory predicts. You need to situate the construct within a theoretical framework, specify a series of empirical studies that would demonstrate the relationships identified in the theoretical framework, and then conduct these studies. You might go about this by showing that the construct correlates with other measures with which you expect it to be similar to (this is called *convergent validity*) and that it does not correlate highly with measures with which it is hypothesized to be dissimilar (this is called *discriminant validity*). Cronbach and Meehl outlined the process involving this nomological network in an important paper titled "Construct Validity in Psychological Tests" (1955). Cronbach and Meehl didn't offer a diagram of a nomological network in their 1955 paper, but Figure 5.9 shows a hypothetical nomological network. In this example, we want to develop a new (short) test of anxiety. The network shows that we expect particular relationships (positive correlations) between scores on our new test and existing measures of anxiety like the Taylor Manifest Anxiety Scale and the State-Trait Anxiety Inventory (STAI). Furthermore, we hypothesize correlations between scores on our scale and measures of electrodermal activity and heart rate variability (which can detect anxiety). We would not expect our new anxiety measure to correlate highly with a measure of leadership or intelligence, given that anxiety is distinct from these constructs.

Construct validity: degree to which a measure assesses what it is hypothesized to measure; usually documented through a series of studies reflecting a nomological network or series of lawful relationships (Cronbach & Meehl, 1955).

Nomological network: linked to the work of Cronbach and Meehl (1955) concerning the kinds of lawful relationships you would discover to validate a construct.

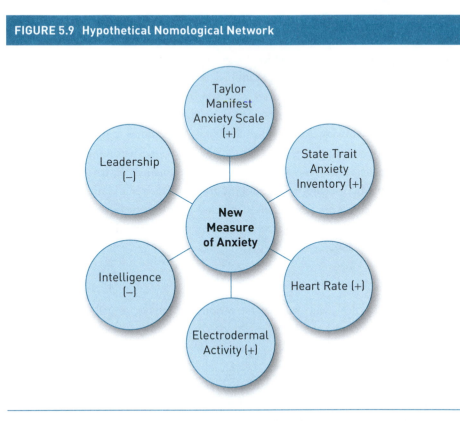

FIGURE 5.9 Hypothetical Nomological Network

LENGTH AND DIFFICULTY OF MEASURES

When selecting measures, the internal consistency will be among the most important criteria you consider. Practical concerns, including the length of the measure and the difficulty of the items, are important as well. When we talked about threats to internal validity (see Chapter 3), one factor on the list from Donald Campbell and Julian Stanley (1963) was Maturation, which could include fatigue. The number of scales you give participants, and the number of items on each scale, should be considered in selecting measures. Your participants are volunteers. How many measures do you plan to use? What is the length of each? Widely used measures vary considerably in length, from the 10-item Rosenberg Self-Esteem Scale (1965) to the NEO-PI-3® (McCrae, Costa, & Martin, 2005), a widely used measure of personality with 240 items and a validity item. The NEO-PI-3 takes about 40 minutes to administer and is typically used by professionals in counseling and education, but it is also used in research.

There is no hard-and-fast rule for the number of items you can expect participants to complete, but if filling out your materials is taking upward of 45 minutes, you might consider eliminating one or more of your measures. How do you know whether your battery of measures takes that long? Pilot testing (see Chapter 3). A set of materials that is lengthy may threaten the internal validity of your study (see Chapter 3).

A related concern is the reading level of the items. Some measures may require a level of reading proficiency that your participants do not possess, although this drawback is unlikely if your participants are college students. Even so, you should be attuned to the possibility that some words will not be understood. For example, one item on the Profile of Mood States is "peeved," a word that not all students may know. Furthermore, you may have participants for whom English is not a first language or individuals with limited education. In the case of the NEO-PI-3, mentioned earlier, the authors reported that some adolescents had difficulty with several items (the test was originally designed for adults). In fact, Robert McCrae et al. (2005) reported that 30 items were replaced because the items were not understood by some adolescent respondents (at least 2% had such difficulty). An example of an old item and the one replacing it are "I am easy-going and lackadaisical" (old item) and "I'm not very ambitious" (replacement) (McCrae et al., 2005, p. 270). The authors reported that the new readability level was grade level 5.3 on the **Flesch–Kincaid scale**. The Flesch–Kincaid reading ease and grade-level scales tell you how difficult it is to understand a passage in English. You can test out this function for your own writing using Microsoft Word® software (this is available under Tools/Spelling and Grammar/Options/Grammar/Show readability statistics).

Flesch–Kincaid scale: provides statistics for the ease of reading of a given passage; available through word processing programs.

INSTRUCTIONS FOR SCORING

After you obtain a measure, you need to know how to score the measure. In some measures, as many as a third of the items may not be included as part of the score (e.g., Bem Sex Role Inventory; Bem, 1974). Many measures include items that are reverse scored (e.g., RSES, 1965; see discussion earlier in the chapter). Reverse-scored items are discussed again in the section on Data Entry in Chapter 10.

NAMES OF MEASURES AND SOCIAL DESIRABILITY CONCERNS

The name of a measure is generally meant to communicate its content. For example, the RSES (1965) is a measure of self-esteem.

> ## ⮞ Try This Now
>
> What problems can you see with telling participants that they are going to take a test that measures self-esteem even if you don't use the full name of the scale?

Scale names or labels may communicate information about the measures that set up unwanted expectancies, that is, demand characteristics. A demand characteristic involves some component of the research process that unintentionally influences the participants' responses (see Chapter 3). You may not want participants to know precisely what you are assessing, a kind of passive deception (see Chapter 4), because it may change the nature of their responses. Often researchers are concerned that respondents will answer in a manner that is more socially desirable (as defined in Chapter 1), which occurs when participants modify their responses to present themselves more favorably. Changing the name of the measure on the survey may eliminate this kind of demand characteristic; another approach is to provide a label without any content (e.g., Scale 1), or no label at all. A measure of managers' competence might become "Managers and Their Work."

Measures of Social Desirability

Most people want to be perceived favorably. We may modify our answers to present ourselves more favorably (e.g., smarter or less biased) than in truth we are. Researchers who administer measures on personal qualities and social issues where social desirability may play a role (e.g., sexual behavior or racism) typically include a measure of social desirability. Such measures allow researchers to assess the degree to which respondents typically answer in a favorable manner. Then, the total score on this measure is used as a control, called a **covariate**, in the analyses. In the case of a social desirability measure, what you are essentially saying (statistically) is that once you have controlled for people's socially desirable responses you can see the "true" relationship between the IV and DV. Using a covariate helps us reduce error variance. Common measures of social desirability

Covariate: variable that can affect the relationship between the dependent variable and the independent variables being assessed.

are the Balanced Inventory of Desirable Responding (BIDR; Paulhus, 1984, 1991) and the Marlowe–Crowne Social Desirability Scale (Crowne & Marlowe, 1960).

Another direction researchers are taking to assess socially desirable responding is using reaction time tests, most notably, the **Implicit Association Test** (**IAT**; Greenwald et al., 2003), which was mentioned in Chapter 1 in the context of dealing with biases when investigating socially sensitive issues. The underlying premise of the IAT is that responding takes time; if some associations come more easily (rapidly) to mind, such as the association of "young people" with "good" rather than of "old people" with "good," the response to the first pairing will be faster. A website has been set up called **Project Implicit** (**https://implicit.harvard.edu/implicit/research/**) for researchers interested in using the IAT. You can contact the research team for help if you are interested in using the IAT in your work. Researchers have used the IAT to tap into implicit attitudes regarding a wide range of social concerns.

Implicit Association Test (IAT): using reaction time, this approach measures respondents' associations between concepts and is considered a way to reduce the social desirability of responses.

Project Implicit: research to assess implicit attitudes

QUALIFICATIONS FOR USE

As already indicated, some measures require specific training and advanced degrees for use. Most of these measures are for clinical and neuropsychological testing, and most of these are only commercially available. If you look at the NEO-PI-3 in the PAR catalogue (**http://www4.parinc.com**), it lists a qualification level, S or B. Those with qualification level S can purchase products listed as A (no qualifications required) and as S ("a degree, certificate, or license to practice in a health care profession or occupation . . . ; plus appropriate training and experience in the ethical administration, scoring, and interpretation of clinical behavioral assessment instruments"). Those with qualification level B can purchase products at levels A, S, and B. For level B, the bar is a four-year degree, a relevant major and additional coursework in measurement theory or related topics, or a license or certificate in the use of psychological tests from an appropriate agency (**http://www4.parinc.com/Supp/Qualifications.aspx**).

If you want to read more about the ethical issues surrounding test use and professional standards, consider the work of Lorraine Eyde (e.g., Eyde, Robertson, & Krug, 2010).

REVISIT AND RESPOND

- What is socially desirable responding? Name two approaches to dealing with this threat to internal validity.

DEVELOPING YOUR OWN INSTRUMENT

The advantages of using existing measures far outweigh the disadvantages. Primary among the positive aspects is that you can select a scale with known reliability and validity. It takes considerable skill and time to develop a scale and to demonstrate its reliability and validity. Given this level of effort, why would researchers develop their own measures? (a) No adequate measure exists to assess a particular construct or to improve significantly on an existing measure (e.g., creating a shorter version or validating the measure in another language); (b) the existing measure costs money; and (c) professional qualifications are required. Here we will concentrate on the fundamental reason for creating a new measure—that no current measure adequately addresses the area of interest.

Developing a New Measure

On occasion, students develop research questions for which they can find no preexisting measure. New forms of social media are developing so rapidly that scales may not exist to assess their effect. For example, a recent student project dealt with Tinder, a program to facilitate social interaction between users who express mutual interest. You "swipe right" if you are endorsing someone whose picture and information appear. At the time the student developed the project, there were few online dating measures specifically targeting the Tinder app, and the student developed three items to supplement a question asking the degree to which someone was likely to "swipe right."

Advice for Writing Items Yourself

Researchers typically write their own demographic or background items assessing participants' characteristics such as age, race, and gender. Among the best guidelines available about writing items is Norbert Schwarz's (1999) article titled "Self-Reports: How the Questions Shape the Answers." Through clear examples, Schwarz showed how question format and response choices affect participants' answers. The complete article by Schwarz is recommended reading. What follows are comments on some of the major points.

How your questions are structured communicates as much information as the content itself, in Schwarz's (1999) view. What respondents understand and you intend may differ unless you are careful. Schwarz explained that respondents are doing their best to interpret what researchers have in mind, given their understanding of the rules of communication, and further that respondents assume that everything that is stated is in some way related to the research goals: "Unfortunately, as researchers we are often not fully aware of the information that our questionnaires—or our experimental procedures . . .—provide, and hence miss the extent to which the questions we ask determine the answers we receive" (p. 103).

A major point is that quite different responses may emerge in an open- versus a closed-ended question approach. In addition, response scales guide participants. In an example of whether people consider themselves successful in life, Schwarz (1999) used a scale from "not at all successful" to "extremely successful." Response anchors go from 0 to 10 in one version and from −5 to +5 in a second version. This numerical distance is the same, in absolute terms. In Version 1, fewer than 15% of the respondents used the anchors in the 0–5 range, whereas in Version 2, the percentage in the −5 to 0 range was 34%. Participants see these scales differently, said Schwarz. The first scale (0 to 10) is considered to be unipolar (varying degrees of one attribute). In contrast, the second scale is viewed as bipolar, with the two ends representing opposites. The psychological meaning of the scales differs: In Version 1, the range from 0 to 5 may indicate not having success to show, that is, nothing above a threshold of 0; in Version 2, the lower 6 points of the scale (−5 to 0) may reflect actual failures, that is, falling below the threshold of 0. This example clearly illustrates the role that scale range, represented by the anchors, can play in shaping our responses (also refer back to Figure 5.2 in this chapter).

Frequency options are another structural aspect to consider. Schwarz (1999) noted that in understanding a scale, people use their knowledge about the world (i.e., their schemas) such as how often events occur (frequently vs. rarely). This point should remind you of the discussion of the availability heuristic and representativeness in Chapter 1. The middle value in a scale is usually interpreted as typical or usual (the average frequency), whereas the anchors at the ends are considered extremes of the available range. If respondents' actual behavior is above that represented by an end anchor (e.g., texting 10 times/day), they may shift their response to align it with the "norm" (as represented in the scale range). This behavior, that is, seeking to conform, is also an aspect of social desirability, discussed earlier in the chapter.

Using an open-ended approach for the response format will help make sure the response options don't have unnecessary weight, in Schwarz's (1999) view. An example would be:

"How many times a day do you text?" _____/times per day.

Specifying the units of measurement (i.e., _____/times per day) for the question is important, he noted, to limit vague answers such as "a lot." The worst choices for frequency alternatives, he stated, involve the quantifiers "sometimes," "often," "frequently," and similar open-to-interpretation options. The meaning of those words depends on the respondent's subjective standard. This variability in interpretation creates a problem for the researcher.

> ### ⟫ Try This Now
>
> In the question "How many times a day do you text?" what assumption about the user's habits is assumed? How could you improve on that question?

Writing Demographic Items and Social Sensitivity

Researchers who are administering a survey typically obtain some background information about their sample, as a way to both characterize the sample and rule out alternative explanations (see Chapter 3). Usually this category of information is called demographics and includes such characteristics as the age, gender, race, educational level, relationship status, and income level of the participant (as defined in Chapter 2). Often, options are listed and instructions to the participant are to "Circle the appropriate response for each item."

With regard to gender, a common method is to print the variable name and the choices as follows:

Gender: M F

> ### ⟫ Try This Now
>
> What problems do you see in giving participants these response options for gender?

Many possibilities for gender extend beyond male and female. Given these possibilities, a recommendation is to let people self-report their gender. Remember that the research experience is an interpersonal one. By providing the opportunity for people to self-report their background characteristics, you show sensitivity to the fact that people define themselves in many different ways. For example, one gender-related term that some individuals now use is "gender fluid." To accommodate all possibilities, when asking about gender the item would look like this:

Gender: _____

In general, obtain the most specific information possible (from the open-ended format), which can later be collapsed into categories if desired. The recommendation is to use the open-ended (i.e., fill in the blank) format for your demographic items. For example, age would look like:

Age: _____

and not as follows, where the participant circles a category:

16–20

21–25

26–30

Use of age spans may obscure group differences *within* a category. The advantage of the open-ended approach is its specificity; you throw away potentially useful information when you start with categories. The disadvantage is the additional effort required if you want to collapse categories, but if you are using online survey software (see later section in this chapter) that is downloadable into a program like SPSS, collapsing data into categories involves just a few steps.

Asking About Race and Ethnicity

For the reasons just discussed about sensitivity and capturing specific information, using open-ended questions to ask about race and ethnicity (they are different) is also recommended. Many researchers see these terms as socially constructed. For some race is defined more in terms of biology, whereas ethnicity is more a reflection of culture, often tied to a geographical region. You may wonder why it is important to ask about these characteristics if your study does not focus on these variables. Asking about these characteristics is important in terms of being able to describe your sample and whether it is representative of the population from which it is drawn. Moreover, in indicating the extent to which research findings are generalizable, it is important to indicate the backgrounds of your participants. As a side note (discussed more in Chapter 11 in the section on use of language), the *Publication Manual of the American Psychological Association* (APA, 2010b) has a very good section on reducing bias (by topic), including gender, sexual orientation, racial and ethnic identity, disabilities, and age.

How will you know whether your sample is representative in terms of characteristics like gender or race? If you are using college students as your participants, you may be able to obtain the percentages for these demographic categories from your registrar, admissions office, office of institutional research, or the institution's website.

Asking About Income

Family income is an item that presents many challenges because participants may not know their household or family income. Moreover, asking people about money is considered an invasive question (i.e., "none-of-your-business"). Don Dillman (Dillman, Smyth, & Christian, 2014), one of the recognized authorities on survey construction, has noted that income is one question that people object to answering. In the experience of many researchers, there are more nonresponses to an item that asks about income than there are to other demographic items.

Some researchers give a list of categories as a way to help situate the range of possibilities for respondents, but this approach has several problems. First, doing so may miss important information *within* categories. Second, it may make people feel uncomfortable because they fit into one extreme (either the low or the high end of the income scale). Third, and related to the first problem of missing information within categories, you may have a ceiling effect, as introduced in Chapter 3. Some respondents may have substantially higher incomes than your scale categories reflect, which may lead to a restricted range at the upper end of the scale. When everyone is at the low end of the income distribution (or fails the test or performs poorly), this is called a floor effect (also introduced in Chapter 3). When income clusters at either end, the restricted range limits the likelihood you will have significant results related to that demographic variable.

Creating Your Own Questions: Item Format

In writing demographic items, the recommendation was to use an open-ended response format whenever possible. If you are developing the measure of a construct, you will likely use response anchors (i.e., decide on the number of anchors for each item and on what the anchors mean). In a scale of precautionary measures (Devlin, 2000), participants were asked to "Rate your likelihood to take these [precautionary] steps on a scale ranging from 1 ('not at all likely to do that') to 5 ('definitely likely to do that')" for each of the 19 behaviors in the precautionary measures scale (e.g., "Avoid areas where few people seem to be"). In line with Schwarz (1999), there are formatting issues to consider, including the number of anchors and the **stem** itself. The stem is the statement or question or prompt to which the respondent replies.

Stem: in a survey, the statement, question, or prompt to which the respondent replies.

As discussed earlier in this chapter in the section on scale sensitivity and anchor values (see Figure 5.2), 5–7 anchors are recommended for surveys. Having too few points (e.g., 3) reduces the variability needed for group differences to emerge. With too many points (e.g., 12), responses become less reliable because people are overloaded with the number of choices.

Odd or Even?

> **›› Try This Now**
>
> Does it matter whether you give respondents an even (six) or an odd (seven) number of anchors?

An odd number of choices (e.g., 7) gives people the opportunity to "be in the middle," that is, to express a neutral position. In the case of six anchors, they must be on one side of the spectrum or the other; if you want their choice to be categorized as positive or negative, for example, or to express clear agreement or disagreement, select an even number of anchors.

The Stem

The stem presents the problem statement or content of the question; it frames the material for respondents. Consider the following options:

(a) **How satisfied do you feel with your institution?**

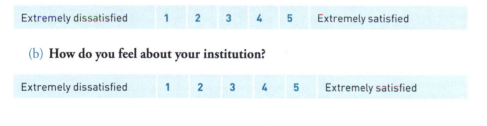

(b) **How do you feel about your institution?**

> **›› Try This Now**
>
> Before reading further, what is the difference between (a) and (b)? What effect do you think each option has on the respondent?

The first example "leads the witness." Because the stem includes "how satisfied do you feel," it suggests that the respondent must possess some degree of satisfaction about the current institution. The second stem does not lead; instead, the anchors provide the context. The first example contains a demand characteristic (discussed in Chapter 3 and earlier in this chapter related to social desirability); reading the stem the participant may think what is necessary is a report of satisfaction [think back to Schwarz's (1999) point that respondents are doing their best to interpret what researchers have in mind]. Also note that the stem is *bolded* and the response options are not. We will talk about the appearance of survey items later in the chapter.

Pilot Testing

Pilot testing questions may increase the internal validity of your research (see Chapter 3). Test them on a small sample of people similar to your participants. Consider their feedback, and revise your items accordingly. Fix problems of misunderstanding, errors pointed out, and any other issues that arise. Because you understand a word in a particular way doesn't mean others will. Include operational definitions of concepts if you want people to respond with the same semantic understanding (think back to the beginning of the chapter where we talked about the difference between the ideal concept and the actual measure).

REVISIT AND RESPOND

- How do the questions shape the answers, according to Schwarz (1999)? Explain why Schwarz recommended using open-ended response formats. How can a researcher demonstrate social sensitivity in the way questions are asked? Why would you choose to use an even number of response anchors? How can the stem of a question "lead the witness"?

SCALE TYPES AND FLEXIBILITY IN ANSWERING RESEARCH QUESTIONS

Earlier in this chapter we discussed the four basic scale types (nominal, ordinal, interval, ratio) and their strengths and weaknesses. You may remember that the interval scale is the most widely used in the social and behavioral sciences. It combines the advantages of parametric statistics with the ability to capture greater sensitivity in the DV than is true for nominal or ordinal scales. When you are writing demographic questions, consider the strengths and weaknesses of these scale types, especially the difference between what you can learn from asking a "yes–no" question versus one that permits a more sensitive measurement. We talked about this sensitivity of a scale and the anchor values in earlier in this chapter (refer to Figure 5.2).

If you are asking a factual question that can only be answered with a "yes" or "no" (e.g., are you enrolled in four courses this semester?), then the nominal scale approach makes sense. Nominal scales are the foundation of **content analysis** (taking open-ended responses and creating categories to capture themes; see Chapter 6) because you are essentially recording whether a participant mentioned a particular category or not (e.g., mentioned courses or not in response to a question about areas of satisfaction with the institution). As soon as you move to questions involving attitudes and perceptions, nominal scale items are less useful because they provide very little information and their range is restricted. Think about asking questions in a way that will involve an interval scale, where a range of responses can be expressed (i.e., the degree of satisfaction with courses at the institution). As we saw earlier in the chapter when talking about scale sensitivity and also about item format, a scale range of 5–7 anchors is generally recommended.

Content analysis: coding scheme based on themes that emerge from qualitative data such as written narratives or newspaper articles; then used for quantitative analyses.

THE ORDER OF QUESTIONS IN A SURVEY

One of the most widely consulted books about survey research is Dillman's book (2000) on mail and Internet surveys. Now in its 4th edition (Dillman et al., 2014), the order of approaches listed in the book's current title reflects the changing landscape of doing survey research: *Internet, Phone, Mail, and Mixed-Mode Surveys: The Tailored Design Method.* Any researcher whose work is primarily survey-based should read this book. For Dillman, a questionnaire is like a conversation; topics that are similar should be grouped together rather than forcing the respondent to revisit a topic area already covered. He recommends starting the questionnaire with questions about the research topic [i.e., what the participant was told in recruitment materials and in the informed consent document (see Chapter 4) was the focus of the research]. Don't start with the demographic items. In practice, demographic items should be the last items before a manipulation check.

Another issue is sensitive items, for example, dealing with experience in therapy or sexual assault. Dillman's advice (Dillman et al., 2014) is to place these items far into the survey and gradually build up to these difficult issues. Such issues are more likely to be answered once the participant has already invested 5–10 minutes responding to other items.

REVISIT AND RESPOND

- List a recommendation from Dillman (Dillman et al., 2014) for the order of items in a survey. Where should demographic items be located in a survey?

ONLINE SURVEY SOFTWARE TOOLS

Online survey software tools such as Survey Monkey® (introduced in Chapter 4) and Qualtrics® (introduced in Chapter 1) enable you to present your survey online for your respondents. This approach has several advantages to both researchers and participants. First, once you create your survey online, it can be sent to anyone, anywhere, with a survey link the program generates for you. The online approach offers a great deal of flexibility (for the researcher and the respondents). In Chapter 9, we will talk in more detail about using AmazonMTurk® (introduced in Chapter 2), which provides an online route to obtain participants through **crowdsourcing**. Crowdsourcing is obtaining something (e.g., ideas) from people online, and one form of crowdsourcing is seeking services. In this case, respondents ("workers") are paid (by the researcher, the "requester") to take the survey. The survey you create through SurveyMonkey or Qualtrics is typically the link that is sent to the "worker" through the AmazonMTurk site.

Crowdsourcing: obtaining ideas or services from a large group of people, typically via the Internet.

Another advantage to online surveys is accuracy. Because respondents are typically responding to set option choices (see Figure 5.10), the approach reduces the likelihood of data entry errors (because some online platforms allow you to download the data directly into statistical software). Third, the approach promotes sustainability because you cut down on the use of paper. Fourth, because some of these programs (e.g., Qualtrics) enable you to download the responses directly into SPSS, this saves time for the researcher (and again cuts down on data entry errors).

What are the disadvantages? First, these programs cost money. The account subscription is usually paid by the institution, but someone has to pay. Second, there is a learning curve to using these programs. Many instructors and students feel that these programs add another significant component to the material that must be covered in a research methods course. Instructors don't always have the time (or the expertise) to cover these survey tools; students may be faced with learning the intricacies of the programs by themselves. Third, when you rely on this approach, some respondents may not have access to computers and the Internet and cannot access your survey. Fourth, the flexibility these programs offer can be a threat to internal validity. If respondents can take the survey (by accessing the link) anytime and anywhere, the circumstances under which this occurs will not be uniform across participants. This variability in procedure is a threat to internal validity. The researcher has no idea whether the respondent was watching television while completing the survey, for example.

To deal with this problem, some departments require students in the participant pool to come to a physical location (where the researcher is present) to access the survey. Usually the researcher has the e-mail address of each respondent, with the link included in the body of the e-mail (in an e-mail draft), and sends that e-mail as soon as the participant appears at the research site. This approach also cuts down on the likelihood that

FIGURE 5.10   Typical Online Survey Option Choices

With respect to the physicians who work in the facility described to you in the previous information, Please answer the following questions:

1. With the schedule of physicians in this hospital, making an appointment to see one of them would be:

1	2	3	4	5	6	7	8	9
Very easy								Very difficult
○	○	○	○	○	○	○	○	○

2. These physicians could be described as:

1	2	3	4	5	6	7	8	9
High achievers								Low achievers
○	○	○	○	○	○	○	○	○

3. Within their profession, these physicians have a:

1	2	3	4	5	6	7	8	9
High rank								Low rank
○	○	○	○	○	○	○	○	○

4. These physicians could be described as:

1	2	3	4	5	6	7	8	9
Competitive								Uncompetitive
○	○	○	○	○	○	○	○	○

respondents will start the survey and stop after a few items; in this case, the demand characteristic created by the presence of the researcher is not such a bad thing!

FEATURES OF ONLINE SURVEY SOFTWARE PROGRAMS

An online article by Michaela Mora from 2013 (http://www.relevantinsights.com/free-online-survey-tools) compares some of the features of several software survey tools: SurveyMonkey, SurveyGizmo®, and QuestionPro®. Figure 5.11 has been created for you summarizing some of the critical information from Mora's article.

FIGURE 5.11 Comparison of Features of Three Software Survey Tools			
General Overview	**Survey Gizmo**	**Survey Monkey**	**Question Pro**
Number of Surveys	Unlimited	Unlimited	Unlimited
Number of Questions	Unlimited	10	12
Number of Responses	50/Month	100/Survey	100/Survey
Multipage Surveys	Yes	Yes	Yes
Account Users	1	1	1
Question Types	8	15	15
Graphic Survey Templates	37	15	18
Real-Time Reporting	Yes	Yes	Yes
Data Exporting	Yes	No	No
Price	Free	Free	Free

Source: © 2016 Qualtrics.

What you should notice is that the price is "free," but that is because these are "limited" versions of the software. If you want more features, you have to pay. Particularly noteworthy is that the "free" version of SurveyMonkey limits you to 10 questions and does not offer data exporting. You need the "Gold" plan (or higher) for that, which costs $300 annually (June 12, 2016; **https://www.surveymonkey.com/pricing/?ut_source=header**).

If we compare the two most widely known survey software programs (SurveyMonkey and Qualtrics), we learn the following (see Figures 5.12 and 5.13):

For SurveyMonkey, if you want randomization (the ability to randomize questions, pages, or conditions across participants), which would be an important tool for research, you need the $300 annual "Gold" package.

Many researchers view Qualtrics as more powerful than SurveyMonkey. For Qualtrics, the "free account" is really a trial version because once you have 100 responses, you need to upgrade to a paid account (see Figure 5.13). For some student research projects, 100 responses may be more than sufficient.

FIGURE 5.12   Overview of SurveyMonkey
SurveyMonkey
Free account
• 10 questions
• 100 responses
• Standard e-mail support
Next level
• $26/month
• Unlimited questions
• 1,000 responses
• Data exporting

Source: Adapted from: Mora, Michaela (Sept. 14, 2013) Three popular online survey tools - What they give for free. http://www.relevantinsights.com/free-online-survey-tools/#sthash.AMHkZoKV.dpbs.

Qualtrics seems to be a more dominant presence in academic research (**http://www.informationweek.com/qualtrics-dominates-academic-survey-research/d/d-id/1110904?**), but SurveyMonkey is also a viable choice for student research. There are

FIGURE 5.13   Overview of Qualtrics
Qualtrics
• Free trial account
• 100 responses, one active survey at a time
• No question limit, 8 question types
• Access to all logic functions and randomization; online reporting
• Full access pricing for academic users typically $500/yr.; 1,000 responses and unlimited surveys; unlimited phone and e-mail support

some more advanced functions that Qualtrics but not SurveyMonkey has, such as the ability to set viewing time for a page, but SurveyMonkey has been expanding its functional capabilities, and the differences between the programs may not be as pronounced as they were.

PROGRAM FEATURES

These programs have many features, such as the preset question types and response options, where you can change both the kind of anchors and the number of anchors for a given question (see Figures 5.14 and 5.15, from a Qualtrics file). You can also include a progress bar, which shows participants how much of the survey they have completed.

FIGURE 5.14 **Screenshot of Preset Question Types and Response Options in Qualtrics**

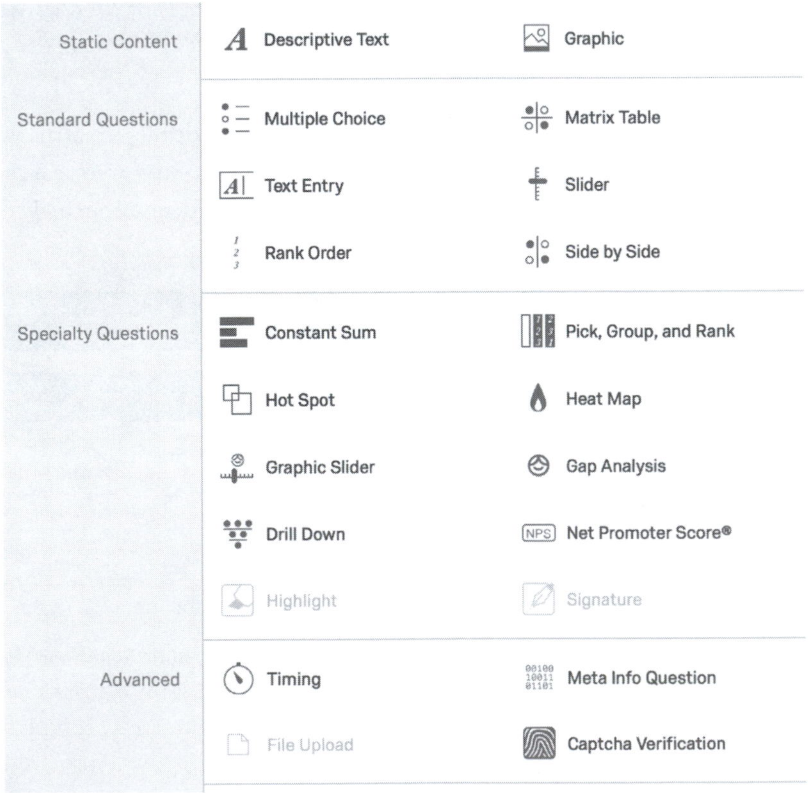

Static Content	*A* Descriptive Text	Graphic
Standard Questions	Multiple Choice	Matrix Table
	Text Entry	Slider
	Rank Order	Side by Side
Specialty Questions	Constant Sum	Pick, Group, and Rank
	Hot Spot	Heat Map
	Graphic Slider	Gap Analysis
	Drill Down	Net Promoter Score®
	Highlight	Signature
Advanced	Timing	Meta Info Question
	File Upload	Captcha Verification

Source: © 2016 Qualtrics.

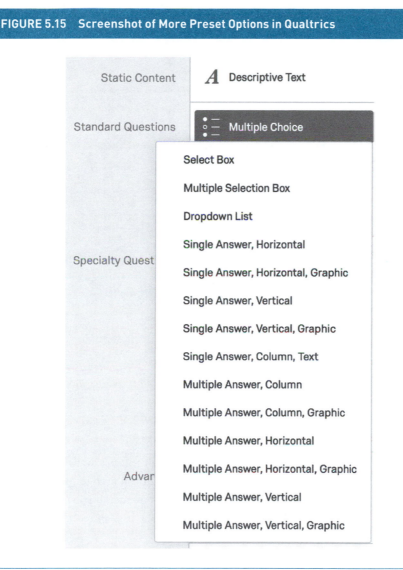

FIGURE 5.15   Screenshot of More Preset Options in Qualtrics

Static Content   *A*   Descriptive Text

Standard Questions   Multiple Choice

Select Box

Multiple Selection Box

Dropdown List

Single Answer, Horizontal

Single Answer, Horizontal, Graphic

Single Answer, Vertical

Single Answer, Vertical, Graphic

Single Answer, Column, Text

Multiple Answer, Column

Multiple Answer, Column, Graphic

Multiple Answer, Horizontal

Multiple Answer, Horizontal, Graphic

Multiple Answer, Vertical

Multiple Answer, Vertical, Graphic

Source: © 2016 Qualtrics.

Again, learning the programs takes time. Figure 5.16 shows part of a Qualtrics survey in which the **randomizer function** is used. This function allows the researcher to randomize the order of presentation of different conditions (contained in separate blocks) across participants. Note that there is an initial Block for Consent, the next Block is for Instructions, then the Condition (here named "nice photo" or "ugly photo") would be shown (note, only the researcher sees that label), followed by a Block with the DVs (74 questions), and ending with a Block that contains the Debriefing.

Randomizer function: feature of some online survey software programs that allows you to distribute conditions and/ or questions randomly across participants.

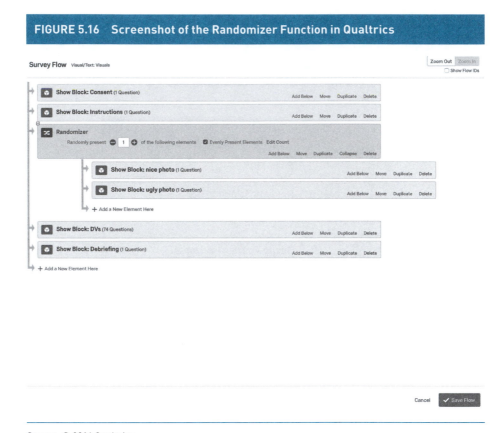

FIGURE 5.16   Screenshot of the Randomizer Function in Qualtrics

Source: © 2016 Qualtrics.

Figure 5.16 is presented as an illustration of the kinds of features available, and it provides a reality check. These programs take time to learn, and you need to spend the time if you plan to be successful using these programs. Also, as a reminder, if you use technology, the links to the surveys may not always work. Prepare a backup plan.

GOOGLE DOCS FORMS

Google Docs® Forms can be used as a platform available to collect data, and it is free. Using Google Docs Forms, you can create a survey and then invite people to participate via e-mail. Their responses are saved automatically using a Google Docs spreadsheet, which in turn can be downloaded to Microsoft Excel® on your desktop. There are many tutorials on the Web that illustrate the steps involved in using this approach. A comparison of Google Docs Forms with SurveyMonkey (prepared by SurveyMonkey, which obviously emphasizes its advantages) can be found at **https://www.surveymonkey.com/ mp/surveymonkey-better-than-google-forms/**.

Google Docs® Forms: feature of Google that enables you to collect survey data; responses are automatically saved to a Google docs spreadsheet.

DOWNLOADING ONLINE SURVEYS INTO SPSS

From the researcher's standpoint, one advantage to using software survey tools is the ability to download the files directly into a statistics program, such as SPSS, or into a spreadsheet, such as Excel. Once the file is downloaded into SPSS, there is usually some additional work to do, particularly to label variables if you did not give them names in your online survey. In addition, although you will be able to identify which participant was in which condition, you still need to create new variables to represent those conditions in SPSS. The example in Figure 5.17 uses Qualtrics.

The far right-hand column in Figure 5.17 shows which participant had which condition, but if you want to run a 2 × 2 analysis (one factor had two levels of photos; the other factor had two levels of text), you need two new columns, one that represents the level of photo the participant saw and the other that represents the level of text the participant saw. It is simple to create those new columns in SPSS; the point is that your work is not necessarily done when you download those responses into SPSS (see also Chapter 10 on Managing Data and Results). Furthermore, you need to have some

FIGURE 5.17 Example of a Qualtrics Survey Downloaded Into SPSS

Q89_1	Q89_2	Q89_3	Q89_4	Q89_5	Q89_6	Q90	Q91	Q93	Q94	Q95	DO_BR_FL_13	
1	1	.	1		.		Connecticut	5	6	.	Good photo/good text	
1	1	.	1	.	.		Pennsylvania	4	8	.	Bad photo/bad text	
1	1	.	1		.		massachusetts	5	4	.	Bad photo/bad text	
.	.	.	.	.	.			.	.	.	Bad photo/good text	
.	.	.	.	.	.			.	.	.	Good photo/good text	
1	1	.	.	.	.		MA	4	6	.	Good photo/bad text	
.	.	.	.	.	.			.	.	.	Bad photo/bad text	
.	.	.	.	.	.			.	.	.	Good photo/good text	
1	1	1	.	.	.		NY	8	1	.	Bad photo/good text	
1	1	.	.	.	.		california	6	8	.	Good photo/good text	
.	.	.	.	.	.			.	.	.	Bad photo/bad text	
1	1	1	1	.	.		New York	1	7	.	Bad photo/bad text	
1	.	.	.	.	.		MA	4	1	.	Bad photo/bad text	
1	1	1	1	.	.		New York	6	8	.	Bad photo/bad text	
.	.	.	.	.	.			.	.	.	Bad photo/bad text	
1	1	1	.	.	.		New Hampshire	3	5	.	Good photo/good text	
.	.	.	.	.	.			.	.	.	Good photo/bad text	
.	.	.	.	.	.			.	.	.	Bad photo/good text	
1	1	.	1	.	.		New Jersey	6	7	.	Good photo/good text	
1	1	1	1	.	.		Ne wYork	9	9	.	Good photo/good text	
1	1	.	1	.	.		New York	2	1	.	Bad photo/good text	
.	.	.	.	.	.			.	.	.	Good photo/good text	

Source: © 2016 Qualtrics.

idea what you are viewing. You can see that the researcher did not label each variable in the Qualtrics survey. Thus, there are a lot of Qs with some numbers after them (e.g., Q93). Without a specific label, you would need to go back to the Qualtrics survey to see what question Q93 is. A better approach would be to take the time to label all of those variables in the original survey. Again, the labeling is seen by the researcher, not by the participant.

On balance, the advantages of being able to download data directly into SPSS probably outweigh the disadvantages, but one more comment is worth considering. Yes, online surveys are increasingly used, but not every participant in every research project will have access to a computer. Even if you are using an online survey, it is good practice to have a paper version available.

SURVEY APPEARANCE

How your survey looks may affect the quality of the data respondents provide. In particular, it is important to think about bolding, numbering, and spacing.

Earlier in the chapter we looked at the difference between question stems and anchors. One of those questions is represented here. You notice that the stem is bolded but the anchors are not.

14. **How do you feel about your institution?**

| Extremely dissatisfied | 1 | 2 | 3 | 4 | 5 | Extremely satisfied |

> **» Try This Now**
>
> Before reading further, what is the purpose of bolding the stem?

Bolding the stem draws attention and separates it from the anchors. Furthermore, in the illustration here, we have added a question number (14). Each question should be numbered, again to draw attention to it. Another issue is the spacing; you should leave enough space between questions to reduce the possibility that respondents will skip over them.

Online survey software spaces the items for you, both vertically on the page and the presentation of the anchors themselves (which can be horizontal or vertical). It is also possible to adjust that spacing to meet your needs. One function of Qualtrics allows researchers to add a prompt that appears if a respondent has skipped one or more items on the page. We cannot force people to answer items (research is voluntary; see Chapter 4 dealing with ethical issues), but we can give them the opportunity to answer an item they may have inadvertently skipped.

Online survey software programs typically have a section where you can make such adjustments to the survey. In Qualtrics, this section is called "Look and Feel." In addition to the adjustments already mentioned, you can determine how many questions per page you want, highlight questions or parts of questions, and add a visual separator between questions. Qualtrics also allows you to have your survey delivered via a smartphone as well as a computer (and will alert you when your survey may not be suitable for smartphone delivery, such as surveys with large graphics).

The care you take in preparing your survey will reflect positively on you and may encourage respondents to take the research project more seriously. This care may also contribute to the internal validity of the study, in that participants may complete more of your questions.

>> **Try This Now**

One feature of Qualtrics is the ability to randomize the presentation of questions on a page and to randomize the distribution of conditions across participants. If you were going to use a paper survey, how would you accomplish those two kinds of randomizations?

REVISIT AND RESPOND

- List two advantages of using online survey software such as Qualtrics and SurveyMonkey. List one disadvantage. What is the advantage of having participants fill out a survey link in your presence rather than simply sending them the link to fill out on their own time? What is the point of "bolding" the stem of a question and labeling each question? Why is it important to label all of your variables in the online survey software? Does the participant see these variable labels? Once you download your data from the online survey software into a statistical program such as SPSS, what else might you need to do if you have different conditions?

Summary

This chapter has given you the tools you need to identify and select existing measures to use in your research. You know the criteria for selection including internal consistency, length, and difficulty. You also know the logical places to look for the measures, including the Measures/Instruments section of empirical journal articles, your department resources, the author of a given scale, PsycTESTS, and test publishers. If the need arises, you can also even create your own scale and calculate its Cronbach's alpha. Furthermore, you know Schwarz's (1999) recommendations for the construction of scale items and response choice formats and can write sound demographic items yourself.

In addition, you should be familiar with some of the most widely used survey software, including Qualtrics and SurveyMonkey, and be able to identify their advantages and disadvantages. Finally, you should recognize that how your survey looks to respondents may very well affect the quality of the data they provide.

In the event that you did not consider them earlier, here are the **REVISIT and RESPOND** prompts that appeared in this chapter.

- What is an operational definition? Give an example. Why is it hard to capture in full the essence of an abstract theoretical concept with a measure? Why is it harder when you measure managerial competence than when you measure rate of speech?
- Describe the four different scale types (nominal, ordinal, interval, ratio). Explain the frequent use of interval scale data in the social and behavioral sciences.
- Where should you start your search for a measure? How do PsycTESTS and HaPI differ? What do you learn from reading about the permissions for a scale? What kinds of tests typically have qualifications for use? If a fee is charged for a scale, what other avenues might you pursue before paying the fee?
- Define internal consistency in your own words. Is there one set Cronbach's alpha value for all research purposes? If not, what circumstances require the highest alpha? List the steps you would take to run a reliability analysis on SPSS.
- Give an example of how you would establish content validity. What does it mean to say a measure has face validity? Why is a measure that has demonstrated predictive validity more powerful than a measure with concurrent validity? In your own words, explain what a nomological network is.
- What is socially desirable responding? Name two approaches to dealing with this threat to internal validity.
- How do the questions shape the answers, according to Schwarz (1999)? Explain why Schwarz recommended using open-ended response formats. How can a

researcher demonstrate social sensitivity in the way questions are asked? Why would you choose to use an even number of response anchors? How can the stem of a question "lead the witness"?

- List a recommendation from Dillman (Dillman et al., 2014) for the order of items in a survey. Where should demographic items be located in a survey?

- List two advantages of using online survey software such as Qualtrics and Survey-Monkey. List one disadvantage. What is the advantage of having participants fill out a survey link in your presence rather than simply sending them the link to fill out on their own time? Why is the point of "bolding" the stem of a question and labeling each question? Why is it important to label all of your variables in the online survey software? Does the participant see these variable labels? Once you download your data from the online survey software into a statistical program such as SPSS, what else might you need to do if you have different conditions?

BUILD YOUR SKILLS

1. Draft your own demographic questions to assess major, geographical upbringing, and political orientation.

2. Sign up for a free trial account of SurveyMonkey or Qualtrics or use Google Doc Forms to create a brief survey to test out the various question types and features.

$SAGE edge™

edge.sagepub.com/devlin

Sharpen your skills with SAGE edge!

SAGE edge for students provides a personalized approach to help you accomplish your coursework goals in an easy-to-use learning environment. You'll find action plans, mobile-friendly eFlashcards, and quizzes, as well as videos, web resources, and links to SAGE journal articles to support and expand on the concepts presented in this chapter.

CORRELATIONAL AND QUALITATIVE RESEARCH

CHAPTER HIGHLIGHTS

- Correlational research: General characteristics
  - ○ Questions about samples as a whole
  - ○ Drawbacks: Third variables and directionality
  - ○ Questions about groups: Quasi-experimental design
  - ○ Statistics for correlational research
- Qualitative research approaches: An overview
  - ○ The concept of reflexivity
  - ○ Resistance to qualitative research in psychology
  - ○ Types of qualitative approaches:
    - *Archival*
    - *Physical traces*
    - *Observation*
    - *Participant and nonparticipant observation*
    - *Ethnography*
    - *Gaining access*
    - *Grounded theory*
    - *Phenomenology*

Focus groups

Interviews: Structured, unstructured, semistructured

Case study

- Where qualitative meets quantitative: Content analysis

OVERVIEW

Qualitative research: in-depth investigation of topics using techniques such as focus groups, interviews, and case studies; emphasis on nonquantitative assessment.

Nonexperimental research: research in which there is no manipulation of variables or random assignment.

This chapter will focus on correlational and **qualitative research**, also referred to as **nonexperimental research**. In surveying research design, Chapter 3 provided an overview of correlational research; this chapter will provide more depth on the topic and will include more information about statistical approaches. More specialized correlational approaches such as time series design and longitudinal research are covered in Chapter 8. The second emphasis of the chapter is qualitative research. Qualitative approaches such as interviews, focus groups, and case studies provide opportunities for in-depth investigation with an emphasis on a nonquantitative approach to understanding behavior.

CORRELATIONAL RESEARCH: GENERAL CHARACTERISTICS

People sometimes equate correlational research with the statistics of correlations (e.g., Pearson's r), but correlational research is an umbrella term that refers to a range of approaches where no variables are manipulated; a range of statistics, not simply Pearson's r, are used. As discussed in Chapter 3, while there is no manipulation of variables or intervention as part of correlational research, internal and external validity are still concerns. Internal validity is the ability of the research design to test the hypotheses adequately. External validity is the ability to apply the research results more broadly. Correlational research can take the form of posing questions about the sample as a whole; it can also take the form of posing questions about differences between preexisting groups (e.g., gender).

QUESTIONS POSED ABOUT THE SAMPLE

There are many instances in which you are interested in the relationships between variables; researchers often use correlational approaches to study variables that are difficult to manipulate. For example, you might be interested in the relationship between gambling (and perhaps more specifically problem gambling) and college student age (18–22), wondering whether older college students are likely to exhibit more problem gambling behaviors because they have more independence from parental supervision than do younger college students. The legal age for gambling varies by state (and type). In Connecticut, you have to be 18 to buy a lottery ticket or wage a parimutuel bet (e.g., for horseracing), but you have to be 21 to gamble in casinos (this requirement is typically linked to drinking age). Some standardized instruments are available to measure gambling behavior. The South Oaks Gambling Screen (SOGS) is one such well-known scale (Lesieur & Blume, 1987). Because college students in southeastern Connecticut have two major casinos (Foxwoods and Mohegan Sun) less than 10 miles apart, a correlational study of gambling behavior and students' age is a workable idea for a research methods project at colleges in southeastern Connecticut to study real-world gambling. True, you could study gambling behavior in the laboratory, but it might have limited ecological validity (refer to Chapter 3). If you want to try to understand whether students who live close to casinos have a gambling problem as measured by their score on the SOGS (which indicates levels of gambling severity) and further whether there is a correlation between student age and score on the SOGS, then a correlational route makes sense.

DRAWBACKS TO CORRELATIONAL APPROACHES

Correlational approaches have advantages, for example, the ability to study naturally occurring behavior, but there are some distinct disadvantages. In addition to the lack of ability to infer causality from using a correlational approach, there are two related issues: third variables and **directionality**. Third variables were introduced in Chapter 2 but are reviewed here because of their importance.

The Third Variable Problem

A third variable is an example of a **confounding variable**, that is, a variable that influences the associations between measured variables of interest leading you to infer incorrectly a relationship between your variables of interest. Continuing the gambling example, imagine there is a significant relationship between students' age and gambling (such that older students participate in more gambling than do younger students). We have a confounding variable in this situation because students' maturational age is associated with their legal age for gambling (21); in other words, there may simply be more gambling among older students because there legally *can* be, not because being older is associated with particular maturational processes that are related to gambling. In this

Directionality: in correlational design, inability to determine the direction of cause and effect.

Confounding variable: extraneous variable that is associated with both the independent and the dependent variable and undermines the researcher's ability to pinpoint causality.

example, we were unable to measure legal gambling behavior in younger students—that is, our unmeasured third variable. To evaluate that issue, we would need to conduct the study in a location in which gambling could legally occur at a younger age (for example, Canada). In other words, we would need to take into account this problematic variable of legal gambling age.

The Problem of Directionality

In experimental research, there is a claim of cause and effect, and typically the independent variable, which is manipulated, is the presumed cause and the dependent variable, the outcome, is the effect. In correlational research, there is no manipulation; hence, there is no effect. In a relationship that appears, we have no way of knowing which direction it flows, that is, which variable is more likely to be a cause or which variable is more likely to be an effect. The following example from Ann Devlin (2006, pp. 50–51) clearly shows this difficulty. My colleague used this example in teaching the relationship of cause and effect to correlation. A graduate student of this professor found a relationship between conflict in a marriage (from questionnaire answers) and aggression of the couple's child documented through playground observations. Three possible causal paths exist for this relationship (see Figure 6.1; from Devlin, 2006, p. 51):

- "**A** (marital conflict) causes stress in the child (or is imitated by the child), **B**.
- Or, a temperamentally difficult child (**B**) causes marital conflict (**A**).
- Or, poverty or another stressor (**C**) causes both **A** and **B**."

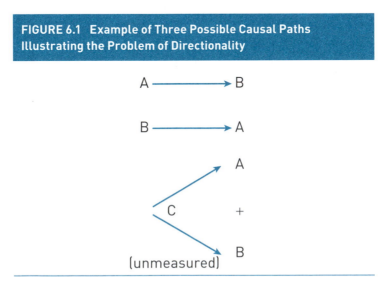

FIGURE 6.1 Example of Three Possible Causal Paths Illustrating the Problem of Directionality

Source: Devlin, A. (2006), Research methods: *Planning, conducting, and presenting research*. Belmont, CA.: Wadsworth/Thomson, Figure 2.4.

Multiple causal explanations are available for a correlation, and the approach cannot tell you which specific cause and effect. When you choose a correlational design, make sure your research question is appropriate. You must manipulate an independent variable to determine cause and effect.

REVISIT AND RESPOND

- Explain the difference between the third variable problem and the directionality problem.

CORRELATIONAL DESIGN: QUASI-EXPERIMENTAL DESIGN (I.E., QUESTIONS ABOUT GROUPS)

If you ask questions about group differences in terms of some relationships of interest but use *preexisting groups* based on demographic characteristics, such as gender, or affiliation, such as being a varsity athlete, you are still using a correlational design. This approach is called quasi-experimental, which was introduced in Chapter 3. The statistics to analyze your data will be identical to those used if you formed the groups of interest through manipulation, but the fact remains that you have no intervention or manipulation; hence, you have no opportunity to assess causality.

Even in a design that has an experimental component (that is, where you manipulated one or more variables), you may include one or more quasi-experimental variables such as gender. Then, when you analyze your results, you can make causal statements related to the manipulated variable but you must use the language of association when you talk about the correlational variable. As an example, imagine you did the study mentioned in Chapter 2 "Perceived Femininity of Women Weightlifters" in which participants are randomly assigned to view a photograph of a woman lifting a 5-lb. (80-oz.) weight or the same woman lifting a 25-lb. (400-oz.) weight. Weight is your experimental variable with two levels, 5 lb. or 25 lb. Participants are asked to judge the sex role characteristics [specifically the femininity and masculinity of the woman lifting the weight, obtained through responses to the Bem Sex Role Inventory (BSRI); see Chapter 5]; those are dependent variables.

At this point, this study qualifies as a true experiment (manipulated variable; random assignment to condition). But imagine that your participants came from a participant pool that included both varsity athletes and students who were not on sports

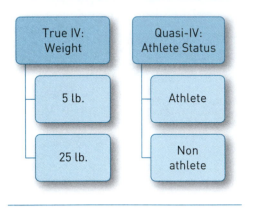

teams and you wanted to take that variable into consideration. If you did so, you would have one true IV (weight lifted) and one quasi-IV (athlete status; see Figure 6.2). Now, we have a study with one true IV and one quasi-IV (the correlational aspect).

Imagine your results showed that judgments of masculinity were significantly higher for the woman lifting the 25-lb. weight than the 5-lb. weight. Also imagine that nonathletes judged the woman to be significantly more masculine, over conditions, than did the athletes. In your Discussion section regarding the effect for weight lifted, you could talk about the picture having affected or influenced people's judgments of masculinity; nevertheless, with regard to the difference between the perceptions of masculinity exhibited by athletes and nonathletes, you would be limited to talking about athlete status as being *associated* with judgments of lower masculinity. Why? In this research you did not randomly assign participants to their status of being athletes or not. Participants arrived with those characteristics.

STATISTICS USED IN CORRELATIONAL DESIGNS

The types of statistics used in correlational designs are linked to whether the research addresses questions about the (a) sample as a whole or (b) groups.

Sample as a Whole

In the case of the sample as a whole, there are two typical approaches: **correlation analysis** and **regression analysis**. Ranked data can also be used to address questions about the sample. Ranked data will be discussed after correlation and regression.

In the case of correlation, you are asking whether two measures given to the participants are statistically correlated to each other. To answer this question, you would typically use **Pearson's *r*.** As an example, let's assume we are interested in the relationship between participants' self-esteem and their attitudes toward disordered eating. We might have given all participants Morris Rosenberg's Self-Esteem Scale (Rosenberg, 1965), a widely used 10-item scale to assess self-esteem and the Eating Attitudes Test (Garner & Garfinkel, 1979), a widely used measure to assess disordered eating; the original version of the scale has 40 items. Using statistical software such as SPSS

Correlation analysis: statistical approach that assesses the relationship between two variables, typically interval scale.

Regression analysis: estimates the ability of a variable (called a predictor) to predict an outcome (called the criterion).

Pearson's *r*: statistical measure of correlation between two variables.

Statistics®, we would correlate the scores on the two measures for the entire sample to produce a Pearson's *r* value, which would indicate the degree of association between the two measures.

If we wanted to see whether scores on the self-esteem scale *predicted* those on the disordered eating scale, we would use regression analysis, in this case, simple regression because we have only one **predictor**, self-esteem. The analysis produces a regression coefficient, *b*. We could also have asked the question the other way around: whether scores on the disordered eating measure predict those on the self-esteem measure; a reasonable theoretical case could be made for either predictor. When we move to multiple regression, we add more predictors (you need at least two for multiple regression) and ask whether each of these variables predicts the outcome (called the **criterion** in both simple and multiple regression) of interest. In addition to the measure of disordered eating, we might have added grade-point average (GPA) and have asked to what extent GPA and self-esteem predict disordered eating, as well as whether one of those predictors is stronger than the other. In multiple regression, researchers often use the **standardized regression weight**, beta (β), because it employs a common unit across measures that have different units (that is, it standardizes them), whereas B, the **unstandardized regression coefficient**, is given in the units associated with that particular measure.

A Word About Nomenclature

In a regression, some researchers use the terms *independent* and *dependent* variables to refer to the *predictor* and *criterion* variables, respectively. The approach here is to use predictor and criterion, the formal terms, because using independent and dependent variables could suggest that manipulation had taken place, when that is not the case in research questions that involve regression.

Ranked Data

Ranked data represent the order in a category, typically in terms of something like preference. Thinking back to scale types in Chapter 5, we differentiated between nominal, ordinal, interval, and ratio scales. Chi-square belongs to the nominal scale type, where there is no inherent order or weight to the categories. When we move to ranks, we are talking about ordinal scale data in which some order to the data exists; that is, something is "higher" or more important or more preferred than something else, but the distance between those ranks is not necessarily equal, which occurs for interval data. Ranked data could be used to reflect the order of preferences for a sample. For example, we might ask students to rank their order of satisfaction with different aspects of college life, from 1 to 5 (choices might be availability of courses, quality of housing, social life, food, and school

Predictor: in regression analysis, the variable being used to predict the criterion (outcome).

Criterion: outcome measure of interest (e.g., in regression analysis).

Standardized regression weight: beta (β) employs a common unit across measures with different units (i.e., it standardizes them).

Unstandardized regression coefficient: coefficient (B) that employs the units associated with the particular measures.

spirit). We could present these ranks as the percentage of people who ranked a given category first through fifth. Ranked data can also be used to examine group differences, which we will discuss shortly.

Nominal Data Distribution: One-Dimensional Chi-Square

Goodness of fit: one-dimensional chi-square that tests the difference between the actual sample and the hypothesized distribution (e.g., 25% of the participants in each class year).

Although encountered less frequently in research, there is also the case of the one-dimensional chi-square, sometimes called the **goodness of fit**. A research question using a goodness-of-fit test is asked in terms of the population as a whole. What if the advertised enrollment for a college is that each class year has the same number of students (e.g., 500), such that you would expect a random sample of the students in your research project to include 25% from each of the four class years. But when you look at your survey respondents, you see that you have 40% from the first year class, 30% from the second year class; 20% from the third year class, and just 10% from the fourth year class. As you might imagine, this distribution differs significantly from the expected distribution of 25% by class year ($p < .001$); in other words, the data are not distributed as your population characteristics predicted. This problem might be the result of recruiting and sampling biases, which we will cover in Chapter 9.

Questions About Nonmanipulated (or Preexisting) Groups

Analysis of variance: statistical test that tests for differences between two or more means.

When we move to answering research questions comparing groups that preexisted, we have moved away from correlation and regression as common statistical approaches (applied to questions about the sample as a whole) and toward analysis of variance and two-dimensional chi-square. Two points are worth remembering here. First, whatever statistical approach you use, for example, **analysis of variance**, a parametric test that evaluates the difference between two or more means, the quasi-experimental data are identical to the data you would have from the same research design with true independent variables. Second, in correlational research that uses preexisting groups or categories, no causality can be inferred and none should be suggested in the language you use.

Questions About Proportionality: Two-Dimensional Chi-Square

Chi-square is often used to look at proportionality of two dimensions (i.e., a 2×2), where both dimensions of the categories are nominal. In general, researchers think of chi-square as answering questions about comparisons between preexisting groups or categories (often these groups are based on demographic characteristics, such as gender, race, and education). For example, you might ask whether the proportion of athletes and nonathletes differs across the categories of majors in the curriculum (science, social

FIGURE 6.3 Example of a 2 × 4 Chi-Square Analysis		
	Athlete n (%)	Nonathlete n (%)
Science	125 (16.4%)	322 (26.0%)
Social Science	436 (57.3%)	450 (36.3%)
Arts	75 (9.9%)	166 (13.4%)
Humanities	125 (16.4%)	300 (24.2%)

science, arts, humanities), which would produce a 2 (athlete status) × 4 (majors in the curriculum) chi-square analysis (see Figure 6.3). There is no manipulation of variables; hence, there is no causality. If we perform the analysis with the data in the table, the result is a significant chi-square: χ^2 (3, $N = 1999$) = 84.45, $p < .001$. We would need to break down the cells further to reach conclusions about the significant differences between specific categories, but it looks as if the proportions are most different in the social science, science, and humanities categories.

Questions About Group Differences in Ranked Data

Ranked data also can be used to express the responses of the sample as a whole, as well as to compare ranks for different groups. Using the earlier example for the whole sample, we might ask first year students and fourth year students to rank their satisfaction with different aspects of college life, from 1 to 5. Our research question is the degree to which the ranked choices of the first and fourth year students are associated. This problem should remind you of correlation; the difference is that here the ranks are based on ordinal data; for Pearson's r, the data are interval. **Spearman's rank order (rho)** would be used for our example; it is the parallel to Pearson's r but now for the nonparametric case (because no assumptions can be made about normal distribution [Howell, 2013]; refer to Chapter 5 of this book for an example comparing group preferences for transportation using ranked data).

REVIST AND RESPOND

- Explain how Spearman's rho, Pearson's r, and chi-square differ. Give an example of a research problem that requires the use of ranked data.

Spearman's rank order (rho): tests association between two ranked variables, or between a ranked variable and a measurement variable; equivalent to a correlation but for a nonparametric situation.

Archival research: research based on existing records such as newspapers, medical records, yearbooks, photographs, or any unpublished or published materials that can be evaluated.

Physical traces: leftover physical elements (e.g., trash) in the environment that can be used as sources of data for research.

Participant observation: type of behavioral observation in which the observer is a member of the group being observed.

Nonparticipant observation: observing participants without taking part in the activities.

Interview: qualitative research approach in which questions are asked of an individual; types are unstructured, semistructured, and structured

Focus groups: form of qualitative research in which people are asked their views on a target issue.

Case study: research approach for in-depth exploration of an event, program, process, or of one or more individuals.

Reflexivity: aspect of qualitative research in which researchers reflect on their experience as part of the research process.

QUALITATIVE RESEARCH

As its label suggests, qualitative research is characterized by a de-emphasis on quantitative analysis (i.e., the reduction of data to numbers), although there may be some quantitative evaluation. Qualitative research takes a variety of forms, but there is an emphasis on understanding behavior as it occurs, without having intervened in the research. In some cases, there are no live participants (e.g., **archival research** and **physical traces**); in other cases, the participants are present but the researcher has varying degrees of involvement (e.g., **participant** and **nonparticipant observation**); in still other cases, there may be a high degree of interaction with participants (e.g., **interviews**, **focus groups**, and **case studies**; see Figure 6.4).

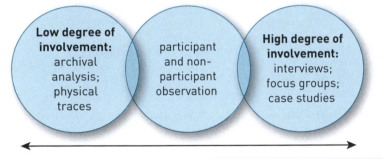

FIGURE 6.4 Overview of Types of Approaches and Degree of Involvement in Qualitative Research

QUALITATIVE RESEARCH AND THE CONCEPT OF REFLEXIVITY

As discussed in Chapter 3, the role of the researcher has to be considered in research, no matter the approach. In qualitative research, an important characteristic of researchers is the concept of **reflexivity**, in which researchers reflect on their experience as part of the research process. For researchers, this concept of reflexivity means reflecting on their role and reactions to the research process. Researchers need to consider their potential for bias given that they may have different status and power than the people in the communities they seek to understand (Nagata, Kohn-Wood, & Suzuki, 2012, p. 261). David Rennie (1999) saw reflexivity as one of the main differentiators of qualitative research from the tradition of **positivism**, where the subjectivity of the experimenter (in theory) is eliminated from the research process. As a philosophical approach, positivism asserts that rational claims about behaviors can be scientifically verified.

ACCEPTANCE OF QUALITATIVE METHODOLOGY IN THE SOCIAL AND BEHAVIORAL SCIENCES

Positivism: philosophical approach to science that stresses information gained through the senses (direct experience).

It is important to consider the standing of qualitative research. Although disciplines such as anthropology place heavy emphasis on qualitative approaches (e.g., ethnographic research), some branches of social science such as psychology have a complex relationship with qualitative research. In the social sciences generally, there is increasing acceptance of qualitative methodology, reflected in the emergence of journals that exclusively publish qualitative research (e.g., *Qualitative Research,* begun in 2000) or publish work that combines quantitative and qualitative methods, called **mixed methods** (e.g., *Journal of Mixed Methods Research,* begun in 2007).

Mixed method: approach to research that typically combines quantitative and qualitative approaches.

At the same time, there has been resistance to embracing qualitative methods in psychology in full. In an article titled "The Qualitative Revolution and Psychology: Science, Politics, and Ethics," Frederick Wertz (2011) explained the history and sources of resistance to accommodating qualitative methodology in psychology. The use of the word "politics" in the subtitle of the article highlights one of those sources. Wertz and others have pointed out that although psychology has a history of qualitative research (think of Sigmund Freud's case histories or Jean Piaget's observations of his children), qualitative methods "have been consistently devalued and marginalized in psychology" (Wertz, 2011, p. 77).

The greater influence, Wertz (2011) explained, is psychology's alignment with the natural sciences and the **hypothetico-deductive method**. The hypothetico-deductive method is commonly called *the scientific method,* in which testable hypotheses are formulated in a way that could be falsifiable. With this alignment with the natural sciences and the scientific method comes funding and power. "The qualitative revolution, inasmuch as it risks transforming psychology's disciplinary identity, threatens the discipline's cultural power and economic well-being" (Wertz, 2011, p. 86). In psychology, to the extent that qualitative methods have become more acceptable and the critiques of positivism more pronounced, this change has been linked to recognition that "the great experiment of applying natural science methods to complex social problems was a failure" (p. 88).

Hypothetico-deductive method: what people refer to as the scientific method in which hypotheses are formulated that can be tested in a potentially falsifiable manner.

The areas in psychology that have been most receptive to qualitative methods are "professional practice, women's issues, and multicultural concerns" according to Wertz

(2011, p. 101), which may reflect the traction of qualitative approaches among people not previously well integrated into the discipline, he argued. Other data reinforce this pattern that qualitative and mixed methods approaches have been more widely adopted in applied domains such as nursing and education than in pure domains (psychology, sociology) and are less likely to appear in what are described as "elite/prestigious" journals (Alise & Teddlie, 2010, p. 121).

Qualitative data are rich; they often provide insights into human behavior that are unavailable when people respond to standardized scales. The increasing use of mixed methods, combining quantitative and qualitative approaches, may create a fuller understanding of the human condition.

REVISIT AND RESPOND

- Why has psychology as a discipline been slow to embrace qualitative methodology?

QUALITATIVE APPROACHES TO RESEARCH

There are a variety of approaches to qualitative research. We will start with those with little involvement of the researcher and move to those where the researcher is deeply involved in the data collection.

Archival Research and Document Analysis

In the examples of correlation considered thus far, researchers are still doing something; that is, they may be administering surveys either to look at relationships within the sample or to look at relationships on the basis of preexisting groups. In these situations, there is still interaction with participants, whether online or in person. In the case of archival research (sometimes called document analysis), there is no interaction with live participants. That is, all data or records have previously created and exist in some kind of accessible format.

Archival material ranges from being open to everyone (e.g., public documents) to being owned by an individual (e.g., private health-care records). You can consider broadly available media such as newspapers or popular media to be a form of archive; you can also think about documents connected to institutions, such as school records that are not linked to specific individuals (e.g., vandalism costs by residence hall), to be archival material. In a third category, the records may be linked to individuals, for example, health data that exist in the form of electronic medical records (EMRs). Archival data that are linked to specific individuals require special permission to use. In the case of electronic medical records, the data need to be what is called **de-identified** such that no distinguishing information about an individual can be associated with the retrieved data. IRB review (see Chapter 4) includes a special question asking whether the data in the study are protected by **Health Insurance Portability and Accountability Act (HIPAA)** laws. If so, special procedures are followed to de-identify the data to gain permission to use it.

There are many other accessible archival sources for students, for example, vandalism records (see Brown & Devlin, 2003). In an intriguing topic, a student examined the newspaper coverage of serial killers that differed by gender. In particular, the student was interested in whether the amount of text, the location of the text (front or interior pages), and the adjectives used to describe the perpetrator and the crime differed by gender. Given search functions for electronic databases, it is possible to conduct these kinds of analyses. Archival sources provide rich information for research, but they vary in their accessibility, from very difficult (e.g., electronic medical records) to very easy (e.g., newspapers).

Physical Traces as Archival Material

Physical traces are a different kind of archival material; they are essentially "leftovers" in the environment, that is, the remains or remnants of behavior that can be physically observed and then analyzed. In his book dealing with environment-behavior research, John Zeisel (1981) devotes an entire chapter to how one might use physical traces in research. Zeisel has training in design as well as sociology, and the book is particularly useful for researchers who come from design backgrounds. Often physical traces can tell us how an environment has been used; for example, trash on the ground outside of a building might indicate an insufficient number of trash containers. Discarded beer cans and bottles under the bushes in a park might tell us something about how the space is being used, especially if these are picked up daily but new ones appear again by morning.

Observational Methods

Observation is a form of data gathering in which the observer(s) collect(s) information through the senses, primarily visual. Auditory information may also be captured and recorded. The term **naturalistic observation** refers to observing individuals in their natural settings, without any kind of intervention or manipulation. The term *naturalistic observation* is sometimes associated with observations in "natural" environments such as animals' natural habitats, but the term also applies more generally, whether one is observing children sharing toys in a preschool, the spatial patterns of people grocery shopping in a supermarket, or the grooming behaviors of chimps.

De-identified data: data in which personally identifying information has been removed; typically involves research with Health Insurance Portability and Accountability Act (HIPAA) data.

Health Insurance Portability and Accountability Act (HIPAA): federal legislation that governs the distribution and safeguarding of healthcare data; pertains to the need to de-identify the data for use in research.

Observation: form of data gathering in which observers collect information through the senses, primarily visual.

Naturalistic observation: observing individuals in their natural settings, without any kind of intervention or manipulation.

Threats to internal validity exist in this mode of data gathering; simply because this approach seems part of our everyday lives does not exempt it from the same general principles that guide all research. First, it is useful to remember what has been suggested about perception: it is a two-way street (Ittelson, 1962). Perception (here observation) is based on stimulus characteristics that are present in what is being observed *and* on the past experience of the observer. We spent a good deal of time in Chapter 1 talking about the ways in which biases of the researcher can interact with the research process. That is especially the case for observation, where the sensory organs of the observer are the primary means of data collection. For that reason, data gathering by observation should be structured and organized, on the one hand, but not disrupt or interfere with the natural flow of behavior in the setting, on the other. In addition, because of the subjective nature of observation, inter-rater reliability (through use of multiple raters) should be established.

HOW TO CAPTURE BEHAVIOR: BEHAVIORAL CATEGORIES

Behavioral categories: categories of behavior, usually predetermined, used to guide the recording of observed behavior.

Behavior coding scheme: approach to observational research in which there is a checklist to code targeted behaviors (e.g., sitting or standing).

Pre–post design: measurement before and after some intervention; can include a control group (preferred) or not (i.e., one group pretest–posttest).

The eye (perceptual system) is not a camera, which is to say that our visual mechanism does not detect every aspect of the scene as a camera would. Even if videotaping is used to record information (more on that shortly), that information too must be rendered useful (categorized) for the purposes of research. Researchers typically use preestablished **behavioral categories**, based on an examination of the literature, to guide their observations. To decide on the final categories, or **behavior coding scheme**, several steps take place.

- First, investigators review the literature to see what categories other researchers interested in the same or a similar topic have used.
- Next, researchers do pilot observations in the setting to see whether these categories from the literature are sufficient.
- If not, new categories are added and some garnered from the literature may be deleted.

As an example, Devlin (1992) used behavioral categories, based on a consultation of the literature and pilot testing, to understand how patients and staff at a state psychiatric hospital spent their time and how much interaction between these two groups there was before and after a renovation of the wards. In a **pre–post design** (i.e., before and after the renovation; see Chapter 8), she was looking at the effect of these physical changes on patient and staff behavior. Table 6.1 shows the behavioral categories for patients that were used in the study.

TABLE 6.1 ■ Behavioral Categories for Patients Used in Devlin (1992)
Sitting
Standing
Lying down
Sleeping
Walking
Smoking
Eating
Playing cards
Watching TV
Writing
Talking to others
Stereotypy

Source: Adapted from Devlin, A. S. (1992). Psychiatric ward renovation: Staff perception and patient behavior. *Environment and Behavior, 24*, 66–84. doi:10.1177/0013916592241003.

Stereotypy is typically defined as a repetitive action and in this study included such activities as rocking, head banging, and tantrum (Devlin, 1992, p. 73). For patients, stereotyping and lying down (defined as "lying down with eyes closed in the sleeping dorm or day hall," p. 73) decreased, whereas television watching and sleeping increased after the renovation. Operational definitions (see Chapters 3 and 5) for all behaviors were developed, even for sleeping. In behavioral observation, it is critical to have such definitions to guide the categorization of behaviors with multiple observers, which are necessary to establish the reliability of the decisions.

Role of the Observer in Recordings

In observational measurement, you have to decide how you are going to record the behavior with the least impact on its natural flow. There are several choices, each with pluses and minuses.

Videotaping

With appropriate institutional review board (IRB) approvals (see Chapter 4), you could videotape the setting of interest. If you install and leave the recording device, you (the researcher) are no longer observable in the setting, which is a benefit. In addition, such recordings can be later viewed by multiple observers, which will help with the process of establishing inter-rater reliability (to be discussed later). On the other hand, you would need to watch all of the videotapes and assign the behaviors to categories, which is a long process. For videotaping, you would still need to make decisions about when, for how long, and from what viewing angle you were going to record the setting.

Concealed Observer

Concealed observer: observing in a setting while concealed; a form of passive deception.

Again with appropriate IRB approvals, you could conceal yourself in a setting to record the behaviors of interest on a coding sheet. Using a **concealed observer** has the advantage of moving directly to behavioral categorization, rather than starting with videotaping, but it is a form of passive deception (as introduced in Chapter 3; see Kimmel, 2001), which may be considered a disadvantage in terms of the IRB review process (see Chapter 4).

Acclimation and Observation

A third approach, and the one used by Devlin (1992) at the state psychiatric hospital, was for observers to spend time in the setting prior to data collection so those being observed (both patients and staff) became used to the presence of the observers. To reduce the possibility that their presence would modify staff and patient behavior, Devlin and a research assistant spent weeks on the hospital ward getting to know the staff and patients prior to the coding. Although they were visible as they coded (they positioned themselves by the nursing station), the pre-familiarization was intended to limit the influence of their presence on the behaviors they observed.

Behavior Recording and Mapping

Often researchers develop their coding schemes and list the behaviors on a sheet of paper, with one sheet used per time period. Observers then place a check by the appropriate category when a behavior occurs. More recently, technology, such as personal digital assistants (PDAs), have been used with the behavioral categories preloaded on the device. For example, Sarkar et al. (2006) used a Palm® PDA with preloaded categories to record the behaviors of 573 preschool children. Today, with advances in technology, applications are available that can be accessed via smartphones, laptops, or tablets. Some options (e.g., Noldus Observer; **http://www.noldus.com/**; **http://www.noldus.com/the-observer-xt/pocket-observer**) have a cost, whereas others (e.g., JWatcher: **http://www.jwatcher .ucla.edu/**; **BORIS**; **http://www.boris.unito.it/**) are open source and free. Whether paper based or technology based, researchers still start with the literature to develop the behavior codes, which Sarkar et al. did as well (p. 408).

The **behavior map** (see Figure 6.5) is a particular kind of recording document in which the variable of interest is the spatial location of the individual. Behavior mapping was combined with the behavior categories in Devlin's (1992) research because she was interested in *where* on the psychiatric unit staff and patients spent their time and whether patients and staff actually interacted in that space. More recent advances in behavior mapping include the development of a tool called DOTT® (**http://www.dotttool.com**). DOTT is an application that integrates behavioral and environmental data about a location, such as a hospital waiting room. People, their behaviors and locations, and environmental characteristics such as lighting and acoustics are recorded on different information layers, which are then integrated. This integration reveals patterns that allow designers to understand better how a facility is being used. As with many aspects of the research process, what was first done manually is now done by technology. Nevertheless, what is to be observed (i.e., the categories) remain the decision of the researcher.

Behavior map: spatial record of the behaviors and location of participants in the setting.

FIGURE 6.5 Example of a Behavior Map

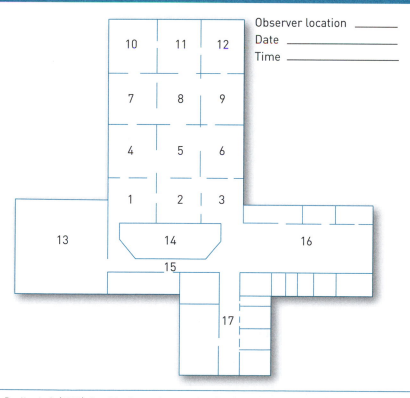

Source: Devlin, A. S. (1992). Psychiatric ward renovation: Staff perception and patient behavior. *Environment and Behavior, 24,* 66–84. doi:10.1177/0013916592241003.

HOW OFTEN AND HOW LONG TO OBSERVE

After deciding on the behavior categories and the means of recording the behavior, you have to decide how frequently to record the behavior and for what duration. Devlin (1992) and a research assistant recorded the behaviors on their paper-coding forms for 1 minute (the duration) at 10-minute intervals an hour at a time, twice a week (the frequency). Behaviors were recorded on a small map that had a superimposed spatial grid (refer to Figure 6.5). Of interest were *where* the behavior occurred, *who* acted (staff or patient), and *what* occurred (e.g., sitting, talking, or playing cards).

Frequency, Duration, and Interval

Frequency analysis: for a dataset, checking the number of times values appear for a given variable.

Frequency: count of the number of times an event or characteristic occurs in a study.

Duration: in behavioral observation, recording how long a behavior lasts

In Devlin's (1992) research, she used **frequency analysis**, which is recording the number of times (i.e., the **frequency**) the behavior occurs in a given period of time (for her it was 1 minute). Other approaches include **duration** (recording how long a particular behavior lasts) and interval, where you segment the observation period into specific intervals and then record whether the behavior occurs during that interval (Jackson, Della-Piana, & Sloane, 1975).

Questions of frequency also apply to the number of times a day, the number of days a week, and the specific days of the week. To make these kinds of decisions, it is useful to spend time in the setting on different days and at different times of the day to get a sense of the variability that occurs. You could imagine that mornings, afternoons, and evenings would all have their own rhythms in different settings, such as cafes, parks, or hospitals.

Dealing With Intricacy and Complexity in Behavior

Although we are talking about nonexperimental approaches, researchers would still like to have some sense of possible causes of behavior that occurs. That goal is very difficult if you look at individual behaviors, focusing on recording a specific behavior (such as sitting) as if it were isolated from a related behavior, such as walking to a destination (before sitting down). Researchers have thus tried to deal with recording sequences of behaviors to understand better possible causal relationships. An example of the important understanding that can be gained from this challenging approach is the work of Jack Wright, Audrey Zakriski, Anselma Hartley, and Harry Parad (2011) dealing with at-risk youth (academic, social, or behavioral problem referrals) who attend a summer residential program. Commenting on gaps in the literature, Wright et al. (2011) noted that "assessment practices rarely include process-oriented, context-sensitive methods, and instead emphasize overall behavior summaries" (p. 215).

In part to address that gap, Zakriski and colleagues (Zakriski, Wright, & Underwood, 2005) looked at contextualized patterns of behavior, that is, behavior in context, not in isolation. Categories were developed to reflect the context in which the behavior occurred (e.g., "adult gave the child a warning," p. 846) as well as the response (e.g., "teased, provoked, or ridiculed, " p. 846). This is an example of researchers who have moved beyond recording an individual category of behavior to also recording the context (precursor) in which that behavior occurs. A much more nuanced understanding of child behavior problems and the situations that provoke negative behavior have been revealed as a result of Zakriski and Wright's research program.

Training for Observation

Training can be extensive when the research demands it. For example, Zakriski et al. (2005) reported that staff training included "group presentations, practice coding of written and role-play vignettes, and individual and group feedback from research staff" (pp. 846–847). Observational research requires multiple observers, and they must be trained because you need to move beyond the subjectivity inherent in a single observer. The (biased) interpretation of a single observer must be countered by using trained multiple observers. When observers (plural) are part of the research process, the researchers need to be given the same operational definitions (often in the form of a coding manual); they need to pilot test the use of the codes; and they then need to compare their categorizations to make sure they are using the codes in the same way. This comparison usually takes the form of an assessment of **inter-rater reliability (IRR)**, discussed in the next section.

REVISIT AND RESPOND

- List three decisions you must make about your procedure before starting your behavioral observations.

CALCULATION OF INTER-RATER RELIABILITY (IRR)

There are three basic approaches to establishing inter-rater reliability or inter-rater agreement, which involves two or more raters or coders: **percent agreement, intraclass correlation (ICC),** and **Cohen's kappa.** Percent agreement is not viewed as a strong approach and is considered inappropriate by some researchers because it does not make a

Inter-rater reliability (IRR): calculation of the extent of agreement between raters.

Percent agreement: degree of agreement between observers, calculated as the number of agreements between observers divided by the number of events observed.

Intraclass correlation (ICC): measures the degree of association between variables that are measured on ordinal, interval, or ratio scales.

Cohen's kappa: measure of inter-rater agreement with nominal data that includes a correction for guessing and, hence, is superior to a calculation based on percent agreement.

correction for chance agreement (Cohen, 1960; Hallgren, 2012). Percent agreement is included here for you to see what it involves and its problems.

Percent agreement is typically used with *nominal* data (e.g., judging that a person smiled or did not smile; in other words, presence or absence of a behavior), although it can be used with the other scale types (ordinal, interval, ratio) under certain circumstances (Hallgren, 2012, p. 4). In a given situation with two choices (e.g., smiled or not), random selection (independent of the true nature of the characteristics) would yield an expected chance agreement of 50% (you have a 50–50 chance of being right). You can see how chance agreement overestimates the true inter-rater reliability. The formula for calculating percent agreement is straightforward:

Total Number of Agreements is divided by the *Total Number of Observations,* and this quotient is *multiplied by 100.* If we have 20 observations and 16 agreements:

$$\frac{16}{20} = .8 \times 100 = 80\%$$

The intraclass coefficient (ICC) measures the degree of association between variables that are measured on ordinal, interval, or ratio scales. Hallgren's tutorial (2012) provided some finer points of consideration for the calculation of ICC, but we focus here on the basic aspects. Hallgren advised that certain basic decisions must be made, among them whether absolute agreement or consistency in the ratings is sought. In other words, do you seek ratings where the numbers assigned by the raters are very close in absolute value, or do you seek ratings in which there is consistency in each rater's assignments, but there might be differences in which end of the scale the raters were using?

Hallgren (2012) provided the example of one rater who operates in the range 1–5 on a rating scale, whereas the other operates between 4 and 8. For this example, Hallgren noted there would be consistency (high degree of agreement) in the ratings if they used similar ranks but a low degree of agreement for the absolute ratings given. Unlike Cohen's kappa, discussed next, ICC reflects the magnitude of the disagreement across raters, not simply the presence or absence of agreement. Although calculation of the ICC measure is beyond the scope of this chapter, you are now aware of this approach.

In Cohen's kappa (Cohen, 1960), we are back to nominal data. Cohen's kappa expresses the degree of agreement for nominal data and includes a correction for chance agreement (an advance over percent agreement). The formula for Cohen's kappa includes a *proportion for actual agreement (P_o)* and a *proportion for chance agreement (P_c).* The formula is:

$$\text{Kappa} = \frac{P_o - P_c}{1 - P_c}$$

Using an example of students who were judged to have smiled or not, we can set up what is called a *confusion matrix* (e.g., Hardin & Shumway, 1997) to help us find the values to plug into the formula for calculating Cohen's kappa (see Figure 6.6).

FIGURE 6.6 Example of a Confusion Matrix

		Observer 1		
		Smile	No Smile	
Observer 2	Smile	7	1	8
	No Smile	3	9	12
		10	10	20

You can see in Figure 6.6 that the agreement is represented both by when each observer said *Smile* (7) and by when each observer said *No Smile* (9); that total agreement is the addition of values along that diagonal: 7 + 9 =16. Then we see that there are two kinds of disagreement: when Observer 1 said *No Smile* and Observer 2 said *Smile* (1) and when Observer 1 said *Smile* and Observer 2 said *No Smile* (3) [1 + 3 = 4]. You can see that row and column totals are produced by adding up the 2 rows (7 + 1 = 8; 3 + 9 = 12) and the 2 columns (7 + 3 =10; 1 + 9 = 10). Percent agreement (P_o) is produced by adding up the proportion of true agreement and then dividing by the total number of observations:

$$\frac{(7+9)}{20} = \frac{16}{20} = .80$$

To calculate the proportion expected by chance (proportion of chance agreement) involves multiplying and then adding the outer and inner row and column totals and dividing that by the square of the total number of observations (here 20^2; Bakeman & Gottman, 1989, pp. 78–80). The math in the example looks like:

$$P_c = \frac{(10 \times 8) + (10 \times 12)}{20^2} = .5$$

Then, plug in these numbers using the original formula:

$$\frac{.8 - .5}{1 - .5} = .6$$

If we go back and compare the value (.6) for Cohen's kappa with the value yielded when we used percent agreement (.8) for the 16 instances of agreement, we can see that Cohen's kappa is stricter in the sense that it adjusts for chance agreement and the resulting degree of agreement is lower.

ACCEPTABLE VALUES FOR INTER-RATER AGREEMENT

It is unlikely that perfect agreement will be found when observers record behaviors. For that reason, we need some guidelines for what are considered acceptable levels of agreement, and steps to take if those levels are not established. Although there are drawbacks to using percent agreement, as we have seen, it is commonly used to report the degree of agreement between coders. With regard to Cohen's kappa, which can have an upward limit of +1.0 and a lower limit of −1.00, Richard Landis and Gary Koch (1977, p. 165) present the following values: < 0 (poor); .00–0.2 (slight agreement); .21–.4 (fair agreement); .41–.60 (moderate agreement); .61–.80 (substantial agreement); and .81–.99 (almost perfect agreement). Some (e.g., McHugh, 2012) have argued that these brackets are too lenient because the "moderate" category could be reached with less than impressive agreement. In our example, we achieved a level of .6 agreement, nearly the lower level for substantial agreement, with 4 out of 20 disagreements.

In terms of an adequate level of percent agreement, there are differences of opinion (Graham, Milanowski, & Miller, 2012), and a useful table in Graham et al. for percentage agreement lists a minimum of 75% and a high level at 90%; for Cohen's kappa, they list the minimum at .61 and a high level at .81; for intraclass correlation, they list the minimum at .8 and high at .9 (see Graham et al., 2012, Table 3, p. 9).

What happens when your level of IRR (whatever your statistical measure) falls below the accepted level? First, finding out about this problem sooner rather than later is advisable. After training, you should run a small pilot study to see the degree of agreement between coders. Observers could jointly participate in several sessions of observation, each recording their data independently, and then run an analysis to calculate the degree of agreement. It is advisable to tape-record these observation sessions to enable you to go back and analyze where the sources of disagreement occurred. By checking on IRR early, you avoid the problem of waiting until the end of the study to see whether you have an acceptable degree of agreement. If the degree of agreement in the pilot study is below the acceptable level, the observers should meet and compare their recorded judgments to see whether they can determine the source of disagreement. The best way to avoid low levels of inter-rater agreement is to construct operational definitions of the target behaviors carefully and provide adequate training.

Training is not a simple process; it is a series of steps that may include first practicing with data similar to your data and then moving to your own data. A particular concern is making sure that the coding is done independently (separately) first to avoid having the judgments made by one coder influence another. Another issue is what is called *coder drift*, in which over time the coding moves away from the original definitions. Any instructor who has graded essay exams may recognize the challenge of making sure the last exams are graded the same as the first! After the coding is finished, the coders meet to see the degree of agreement of their judgments. If there are disagreements, a protocol must be established to resolve these.

REVIST AND RESPOND

- In calculating inter-rater reliability, what advantage does Cohen's kappa have over percent agreement?

PARTICIPANT AND NONPARTICIPANT OBSERVATION AND OVERT/COVERT OBSERVATION

We can distinguish between whether observers take part in the settings where they are observing (participant observation) or do not take part in the settings where they are observing (nonparticipant observation). We can also distinguish whether they observe overtly, that is, in a straightforward manner revealing the purposes of the proposed observations, or covertly. In **covert observation**, the people being observed are not informed about the purpose of the observation (note, this is not the same as concealed observation, discussed earlier in the chapter, in which the observer is hidden from the people being observed). For those interested in a more in-depth discussion of the roles that are possible in field research, Patricia Adler and Peter Adler (1987) have provided a concise book that covers various membership roles, including the researcher as peripheral, active, and complete member. In addition, their book traces the history of approaches to conducting

Covert observation: approach to observation in which the people being observed are not informed about the purpose of the observation.

field research, including the Chicago School (ethnographic fieldwork identified with the work of Park and Burgess), the existential sociologists (with a focus on understanding human existence), and the ethnomethodologists (use of sociological analysis to examine everyday communication and behavior).

A well-known example of a researcher who lived in the settings he studied is Herbert Gans, who was a participant observer and wrote about living in Levittown (Willingboro), New Jersey (Gans, 1969). Another example of research with participant observers is the work of Douglas Frantz and Catherine Collins, who, like Gans, moved to a town shortly after it was occupied. Frantz and Collins wrote about living in Celebration, Florida, the Walt Disney Company–planned community near Disney World (Frantz & Collins, 1999).

In both instances (Frantz & Collins, 1999; Gans, 1969), these observers were participants; their purpose was known to the residents about whom they wrote. Gans and his wife were among the first 25 residents of the community. Because Gans thought that participation restricts the individual to learning about some but not all groups within a community, he selected to "participate only in the life of my own block and as a member of the public at meetings, but that otherwise my role would be that of an observer and informal interviewer" (1969, p. xxiii). He did not reveal that he had moved to Levittown specifically for the purposes of the study but did tell people he was a researcher and that his interest was in how community forms in a place like Levittown.

In the case of Franz and Collins (1999), who were journalists, they wanted to be part of what "seemed like the biggest experiment in social engineering since Levittown" (p. 5). Their approach was "searching for the middle ground between observer and participant" (p. 10), but they were open with other residents about their intention to write a book about their experience living in Celebration.

ETHNOGRAPHY: EXTENDED OBSERVATION

Ethnography: study of people and cultures in a systematic manner.

Ethnography has been defined as "prolonged cultural engagement" (Wendt & Gone, 2012, p. 163) and is included among the qualitative research traditions used for ethnocultural research. Ethnography is "the study of human races and cultures" (of Greek origin; **http://www.merriam-webster.com/dictionary/ethnography**). Another way of viewing ethnography is "examining culture through relationship" (Nagata et al., 2012, p. 11), a statement that captures the essence of ethnographic work. Wertz (2011, p. 82) stated that work in ethnography in the fields of anthropology and sociology has been at the forefront of the "qualitative revolution" and pointed to the work of the

Chicago School of Sociology and the work of anthropologists such as Franz Boas, Robert Bean, Gregory Bateson, and Bronislaw Malinowski as developing the methodology of qualitative fieldwork.

Participant observation is typically the foundation of ethnography. In a chapter in a book on qualitative research methods, Paul Atkinson and Martyn Hammersley (1994) talked about ethnography and participant observation. In their definition of ethnography, they listed the following features and suggested an approach in which most of these features could be considered ethnography:

- "[A] strong emphasis on exploring the nature of particular social phenomena, rather than setting out to test hypotheses about them
- [A] tendency to work primarily with 'unstructured' data, that is, data that have not been coded at the point of data collection in terms of a closed set of analytic categories
- [I]nvestigation of a small number of cases, perhaps just one case, in detail
- [A]nalysis of data that involves explicit interpretation of the meanings and functions of human actions, the product of which mainly takes the form of verbal descriptions and explanations, with quantification and statistical analysis playing a subordinate role at most." (p. 248)

As we have noted before, and reinforced here, Atkinson and Hammersley stated "in a sense *all* social research is a form of participant observation, because we cannot study the social world without being part of it" (p. 249). The examples from Gans (1969) and Franz and Collins (1999), discussed earlier, could be considered ethnographic studies in the sense that they were looking at the culture of the places they inhabited or at "the-way-we-do-things-here."

Students often associate ethnography with cultures very different than their own, but Tony Whitehead (2005) provided a list of the different types of settings that have been the focus of ethnographers. It is presented here in Figure 6.7 to give you some idea of the very wide range of possible settings.

> **⟫ Try This Now**
>
> After reading the list, come up with three additional settings where you think ethnographic research could be conducted.

FIGURE 6.7 List of the Different Settings Ethnographers Study

- Bars
- Churches
- Playgrounds
- Gymnasiums
- Beauty parlors
- Discos
- Farmers markets
- Sports events
- Food activities (dinner, feast)
- Festivals
- Shopping malls
- Jails/prisons

- Parks
- Court rooms
- Family settings
- Hog killings
- Industry or work settings
- Slaughter houses
- School rooms
- Cafeterias
- Swimming pools
- Grocery stores
- Hospitals

- City halls
- Agencies
- Main streets
- Busy neighborhoods
- Town meetings
- Office meetings
- Parties
- Airport/bus terminals
- Barber shops
- Mental institutions
- Ad infinitum

Source: Whitehead, 2005, p. 14.

ISSUES IN ETHNOGRAPHY: GAINING ACCESS

There are several hurdles to jump in doing ethnography, which can be considered a form of fieldwork (Whitehead, 2005). Among the most challenging is gaining access to the population of interest. Martha Feldman, Jeannine Bell, and Michele Berger (2003) commented that access is not achieved at a single point in time for perpetuity; rather, access involves the continuing process of building relationships. Feldman et al. saw access from a "relational perspective" (p. x).

In their useful book about gaining access, Feldman et al. (2003) talked about the tension between the research design (the *who* of your study) and the process of access (the *how* of your study). Often an initial *who* needs to be changed because your initial plans about the *how* of access fail. Each chapter in their book provides suggestions about a particular aspect of gaining access. Doing this kind of fieldwork is challenging, and Feldman et al. reminded us that "Researchers who do fieldwork do not self-select on chutzpah" (p. 33), which reinforces the idea that you have to be persistent and not take it personally when people deny you access.

INITIAL ETHNOGRAPHIC TOURS

Prior to arranging entrance to the setting, researchers may take tours, which have been described as "windshield tours and walking tours" (Whitehead, 2005, p. 14). Whether driving or walking is chosen depends on the size of the community. Whitehead suggested the use of a "Key Community Expert" for these tours (p. 14) to enhance the understanding that can be gained from having someone knowledgeable about the community point out features that people less familiar with the setting might miss.

A useful chart of approaches was provided by Kaur Johl and Sumathi Renganathan (2009, p. 48). Johl and Renganathan listed the stages of preentry, during fieldwork, after fieldwork, and getting back (which means maintaining good rapport for future work) to describe how to gain access to the setting. Although their article was written about fieldwork in general, the guidelines do apply to ethnographic work as a form of fieldwork.

PRESERVING INFORMATION

In his study of Levittown, Gans reported that he "tried not to act like a formal researcher and rarely took notes during the thousands of informal conversational interviews. Instead I memorized the answers, made quick notes as soon as I could, and later wrote the whole interview in my field diary" (1969, p. xxiv). Gans's approach may not work in all situations, and either taking notes or making tape-recordings are alternatives, but each has consequences in terms of the willingness of community members to speak freely. People are more likely to speak freely if they are not being recorded, but this puts great pressure on the researcher to remember the nature of the conversation accurately, and not everyone would be able to memorize the answers, as Gans tried to do. There is a great deal of information to manage. Whitehead (2005) provided a useful contact summary form that would be a guide to preserving information from interaction with members of the community (pp. 26–27).

Triangulation: approach to convergent validity in which the researcher gathers multiple sources of information (e.g., from interviews and observations) to see whether there is a consistent pattern.

Regarding the validity of the information that is obtained, a useful concept is **triangulation.** Triangulation (Stake, 2005) could be thought of as a kind of convergent validity (see Chapter 5) in which the researcher gathers multiple sources of information (e.g., from interviews, observations) to see whether there is a consistent pattern to the narrative. In this way, the meaning of the information may be clarified. Robert Stake pointed out that triangulation will also allow you to appreciate the different realities that may characterize someone's life.

GROUNDED THEORY

Driven by positivism, the hypothetico-deductive method of research involves having a theory, developing hypotheses based on the theory, and then testing these hypotheses. You could refer to this approach as top-down. In contrast, **grounded theory** could be described as primarily bottom-up in the sense that you are starting with observations and crafting a theory or conceptualization out of them. In her chapter on grounded theory, Kathy Charmaz (2003) stated that grounded theory consists of "systematic inductive guidelines for gathering, synthesizing, analysing, and conceptualizing qualitative data to construct theory" (p. 82).

A grounded theory approach may be used because it is too early in the understanding of a given content area to develop testable hypotheses and/or the researcher is interested in processes that are difficult to approach from a strictly quantitative perspective. Charmaz (2003) argued that grounded theory has elements that represent both interpretive and positivistic approaches because it not only contains a focus on how meaning is expressed in people's lives (the interpretive component) but also includes systematic techniques to capture that meaning, which is consistent with positivism. The origins of the grounded theory approach are often attributed to Barney Glaser and Anselm Strauss (1967) in the late 1960s (Charmaz, 2003).

As an example of the use of grounded theory from student research, Noam Waksman (2015) studied heterosexual couples in romantic relationships in which at least one member of the couple was a senior (i.e., was graduating):

> Participants were interviewed separately and asked a protocol of questions regarding their relationships and post-graduate plans. No initial hypotheses were established. Instead, the interviews were transcribed and emergent themes and patterns were identified through a grounded analysis of the interviews. Ultimately, a conceptualization emerged from the previously identified patterns and themes, and the participants were categorized along it. (Waksman, 2015, p. ii)

Waksman (2015) started with an interest in how people in romantic relationships make difficult decisions about their futures when a significant change (i.e., graduation) is imminent. Among his major conceptual interests were identity and life span development, attachment style, gender stereotypes, and sacrifice in relationships. Charmaz, following Herbert Blumer (1969), calls these "sensitizing concepts" (2003, p. 85), which provide a kind of conceptual framework within which to begin the research. She also pointed out that such concepts are a beginning but not an end. As an example, Waksman (2015) used the narratives from his participants to understand better where members of couples

Grounded theory: inductive methodology in which theory emerges out of systematic research (i.e., bottom up).

situated themselves as they faced a decision about the future. He described this process as where each member of the couple put his/her "anchor," either in the relationship or in his/her future career path.

Consistent with a grounded theory approach, Waksman (2015) used coding to organize the data and in turn understand its meaning. Although a full description of the steps in grounded theory is beyond the scope of this chapter, you should have some sense of what might be involved in such an endeavor, understanding that conducting interviews, analyzing transcripts, and coding and recoding data to develop new conceptualizations is a time-consuming process. Interested readers are referred to Charmaz's (2003) chapter for further details.

As a cautionary note, there are financial costs to transcribing recordings if this work is done professionally. Moreover, this process takes time. Some estimates for formal transcription are $1–$1.50 per audio minute. You also need to determine the accuracy rate that is guaranteed by the transcriber and whether there are additional costs related to multiple speakers on the tape, for example. The turnaround time you request will also affect the cost. As another example, one company that has worked for academic clients charges "$110/hour of taped recording transcribed for ONE or TWO voices and reasonably intelligible sound quality" (**http://www.transprof.com/prices-faq/**).

PHENOMENOLOGY

Phenomenology is the "exploration of lived experience or meaning" (Wendt & Gone, 2012, p. 163) and is considered a philosophy associated with Edmund Husserl who worked at the beginning of the twentieth century (Giorgi & Giorgi, 2003). The chapter by Amedeo Giorgi and Barbro Giorgi describes how to use the phenomenological method in social science to study our lived experience: "In general, phenomenological psychological research aims to clarify situations lived through by persons in everyday life" (Giorgi & Giorgi, 2003, p. 26). Like grounded theory methodology, the experience of people is analyzed to look for themes. Unlike grounded theory, these phenomenological themes are then used to understand the whole of the person's experience rather than to develop a theoretical framework (Starks & Brown Trinidad, 2007).

> **Phenomenology:** qualitative approach to investigation that emphasizes consciousness and direct experience.

FOCUS GROUPS

You may be familiar with the term *focus groups,* which are often associated with market research, and you may have participated in one of these groups. Focus groups are a particular kind of interview in which there is "[a] small group selected to discuss a particular topic with the leader keeping the group focused on the particular topic" (Corsini, 2002, p. 384). In her book on focus group discussions, Monique Hennink (2014) listed the following characteristics of focus groups:

- "Focus groups typically consist of 6 to 8 participants, but can be anywhere between 5 and 10 depending on the purpose of the study.
- Participants are preselected and have similar backgrounds or shared experiences related to research issues (e.g., experience of an illness, multiple birth, and so forth).
- The discussion is focused on a specific topic or limited number of issues, to allow sufficient time to discuss each issue in detail.
- The aim is not to reach consensus on the issues discussed, but to uncover a range of perspectives and experiences.
- Discussion between participants is essential to gather the type of data unique to this method of data collection.
- The group is led by a trained moderator who facilitates the discussion to gain breadth and depth from the participants' responses.
- Questions asked by the moderator are carefully designed to stimulate discussion, and moderators are trained to effectively probe group participants to identify a broad range of views.
- A permissive, non-threatening group environment is essential so that participants feel comfortable to share their views without the fear of judgment from others." (pp. 1–2)

An advantage to focus groups over individual interviews is the more efficient use of time without significant loss of the coverage of issues that individual interviews would yield (Hennink, 2014). A further benefit, noted Hennink, is that the interactional nature of the setting leads to content that would not necessarily be revealed in the individual interview format.

Although market researchers were using the focus group tool to investigate brand perception through the mid-1950s, academic researchers did not make the tool part of their arsenal of methods until the 1980s (Hennink, 2014). Sue Wilkinson (2003) traced this rekindling of interest in focus groups to social action research and its use for topics in health psychology such as family planning and sexual attitudes. She also saw the flexibility of the method as a reason it continues to be popular. George Kamberelis and Greg Dimitriadis (2005) traced the use of focus groups for more than a century and included the military, market research, "emancipatory pedagogy," and three waves of feminism (p. 888). **Emancipatory pedagogy** is generally understood to mean freeing both students and teachers from their hierarchical roles and the constraints that mainstream views have on the way they (we) think about society (Nouri & Sajjadi, 2014).

Emancipatory pedagogy: approach to learning that frees students and teachers from hierarchical roles.

Hennink (2014) noted that focus groups can be conducted virtually (e.g., Internet, telephone, or teleconferencing) as well as in person, and Wilkinson (2003) provided a useful series of recommendations about the focus group session itself (e.g., use of name tags, reiteration of the boundaries of anonymity or confidentiality, or ground rules; pp. 193–194). It is worth noting that although the importance of confidentiality may be reiterated, the researcher cannot guarantee that confidentiality will be maintained because the focus group members themselves possess that information. Wilkinson noted that many aspects of research using focus groups are not distinctive (e.g., analysis in terms of themes is not unique to focus groups, as we have seen). Rather, she suggested it is the way the data are collected, in this interactive group form, which is a hallmark of the approach.

Hennink (2014, p. 16) argued that even though focus group discussions are especially useful for exploratory research, they should not be pigeonholed and will work in other research approaches, such as *mixed methods* (which typically combine quantitative and qualitative approaches).

Structure of the Focus Group Process

The process of a focus group has been depicted as an hourglass, opening broadly with introductions and questions about the structure and approach (to provide understanding and establish some rapport), narrowing to the specifics and focused areas for discussion, and then broadening out again to closing questions (Hennink, 2014, p. 51). Hennink provided concrete examples that you could use if you wanted to structure a focus group.

Hennink (2014) also noted that not all topics are appropriate for focus groups and that it is not necessarily the sensitive nature of the topic per se (e.g., sexual encounters) but an emphasis on personal narratives that would make such a topic inappropriate. When a topic is framed in a way that focuses on personal experience, issues of confidentiality in the group occur, and there may be self-censorship, too, such that the group members participate less fully. Hennink (2014) provided a useful (see Table 6.2 of this chapter) checklist for when focus groups versus individual interviews would be appropriate. Another recommended source explaining when focus groups are appropriate is the handbook on focus groups by Richard Krueger and Mary Anne Casey (2009).

>> **Try this Now**

Before looking at the list from Hennink (2014), generate three reasons to use a focus group and three reasons to use individual interviews. Compare your ideas with Hennink's list.

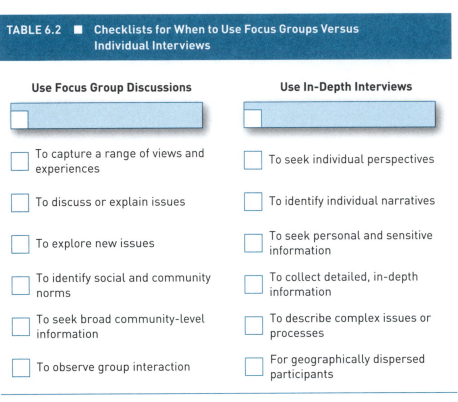

TABLE 6.2 ■ Checklists for When to Use Focus Groups Versus Individual Interviews

Use Focus Group Discussions	Use In-Depth Interviews
☐ To capture a range of views and experiences	☐ To seek individual perspectives
☐ To discuss or explain issues	☐ To identify individual narratives
☐ To explore new issues	☐ To seek personal and sensitive information
☐ To identify social and community norms	☐ To collect detailed, in-depth information
☐ To seek broad community-level information	☐ To describe complex issues or processes
☐ To observe group interaction	☐ For geographically dispersed participants

Source: Hennink, 2014, p. 28. Used with permission.

Structured interview: items prepared in advance and asked in the same way to each person.

Semistructured interview: set of questions or interview guide with room for follow-up and introduction of related topics as appropriate.

Unstructured interview: interview that has a plan, but no specifically devised set of questions in an interview schedule; open-ended questions typically used.

INTERVIEWS: DEGREES OF STRUCTURE

This previous discussion of when to use focus groups versus interviews leads naturally to a discussion of interviews. The essence of the interview is still about exploring meaning, but it is conducted with an individual (Kvale, 1996). Interviews have some of the same advantages as focus groups (rich information), but they have some of the same disadvantages as well (interviews take time and other resources). Researchers have categorized the types of interviews into three domains: **structured**, **semistructured**, and **unstructured** (Gill, Stewart, Treasure, & Chadwick, 2008). These approaches differ in the degree of structure (both of the questions posed and of the response options available). The Robert Wood Johnson Foundation has helpful guidelines on the use of qualitative research that cover structured, semistructured, unstructured, and informal interviews as well as focus groups (**http://www.qualres.org/HomeInte-3595.html**). The foundation's qualitative guide equates the structured interview with self-administered questionnaires (**http://www.qualres.org/HomeStru-3628.html**).

The Structured Interview

In the structured interview, the items are prepared in advance and are asked in the same way, in the same order, for each interviewee, and the response categories are often limited (Fontana & Frey, 2000). The structured questionnaire has been likened to a "verbally administered questionnaire" (Gill et al., 2008, p. 291), in that the questions are preset and there is no follow-up. Many of the recommendations for the order of questions in interviews are the same as what we would give for questionnaires (see Chapter 5). For example, we would recommend placing more sensitive topics farther into the exchange so that rapport has been established before dealing with more difficult issues. Don Dillman's classic book on mail and Internet surveys (2000) is also a good source of information about preparing structured interviews, covering such topics as criteria to consider for the order of the questions, with special emphasis on why the first question must be carefully chosen. If you want people to begin to engage with your survey, the first question, said Dillman, is one that should "apply to everyone," is "easy" to answer, and is "interesting" (p. 92; Dillman, Smyth, & Christian, 2014, p. 230).

The Unstructured Interview

At the opposite end of the spectrum from the structured interview, the data that emerge in the unstructured interview are likely to be described as qualitative in nature (Fontana & Frey, 2000). The researcher has a plan for questions to guide the interview but no specifically developed guide or **interview schedule**, as it is called. The questions are open ended, allowing respondents to answer as they wish, without preset response options. The unstructured interview has a conversational nature but is still recognized as an interview (http://www.qualres.org/HomeUnst-3630.html).

Interview schedule: formal set of questions to be asked in an interview.

The Semistructured Interview

In semistructured interviews, there is a set of questions or interview guide, but there is room for follow-up questions and the initiation of related topics as the interview develops (http://www.qualres.org/HomeSemi-3629.html). The semistructured interview, reported to be the most widely used in health care (Gill et al., 2008), has preidentified categories to investigate, on the one hand, but allows some degree of flexibility for the interviewer for follow-up questions, on the other. In semistructured interviews, you often hear interviewers ask, "Can you tell me a bit more about that?" (Gill et al., 2008, p. 292).

Training for Interviewers

As we have previously seen in this chapter when talking about Zakriski et al.'s (2005) research dealing with observing contextualized patterns of behavior, training was critical to the success of the process (in terms of establishing inter-rater reliability).

The same can be said for training interviewers. In their book on how to minimize interviewer-related error, Floyd Fowler and Thomas Mangione (1990) pointed to the importance of training that involves supervised practice in general interviewing skills (not just reading, lectures, or demonstrations) if interviewers are going to do their job adequately. Training appears to be particularly important for interviewers to feel prepared to deal with the question-and-answer process (i.e., probing) that is typically part of unstructured and semistructured interviewing. As a general rule, Fowler and Mangione suggested training in the two- to four-day range and taping trainees to facilitate feedback on their practice interviews.

The interviewer can be a source of error both in the *how* and in the *who*. Regarding the how, interviewers may not read questions accurately, may miss some of the answers given by respondents, or may differentially (across interviewers) probe with follow-up questions (Fowler & Mangione, 1990). Training may address some of these problems, but training cannot address the *who* of the interviewer, known as **interviewer effects**. Interviewer effects are characteristics of the interviewer (e.g., gender, race, and ethnicity) that may affect the nature and extent of the answers given by respondents. This problem is likely to be the case when sensitive topics such as race are part of the survey and socially desirable responding (see also Chapter 5) might be an issue (Davis, Couper, Janz, Caldwell, & Resnicow, 2010).

Interviewer effects: responses of interviewees that are related to demographic qualities of the interviewer, including race, gender, and ethnicity. These effects are considered a source of error.

This kind of problem can be more easily controlled statistically in large surveys where there are multiple interviewers and a large sample, but it remains a problem in the case of the individual interviewer and presents a threat to the internal validity of the work. There are several excellent books in which interviewing is covered (e.g., see Biemer & Lyberg, 2003; Fowler & Mangione, 1990).

REVISIT AND RESPOND

- Why is the structured interview considered the equivalent of a verbally administered questionnaire? What advantages and disadvantages do you see to the structured interview, the semistructured interview, and the unstructured interview? What are interviewer effects?

RECORDING OR NOT

There are advantages and disadvantages to recording interviews. Recording preserves the record in full and frees the interviewer from note-taking, which may disrupt the flow of the interview, but recording may make interviewees more cautious and less likely to discuss specific topics in full. The more sensitive the topic, the more reticent participants may become.

Regarding the technical issues of recording, it is important to have a "sound check" to make sure you know how to operate your recording equipment and that it is in working order. Recording requires permission beyond standard informed consent (i.e., a separate signature line for consent to record). Furthermore, the informed consent document has to make clear what will be done with the recordings, where they will be stored, how they will be safeguarded, and their ultimate disposition (see Chapter 4).

CASE STUDIES AND CASE HISTORIES

We may think of case studies (as introduced earlier in this chapter) and **case histories** as synonymous terms, but Raymond Corsini (2002) defined a case history as "A record of information relating to a person's medical or psychological condition" (p. 142) and did not provide an entry for "case study." Creswell (2009) stated, "Case studies are a strategy of inquiry in which the researcher explores in depth a program, event, activity, process, or one or more individuals" (p. 13). Thus, Creswell's definition of case study subsumes the narrower definition of case history. Here we will use the term case study. Case studies are considered an **ideographic** approach in that they focus on the individual and individual experiences. Often the ideographic approach is contrasted with the **nomothetic** approach, which emphasizes research with the goal of developing laws of behavior that would apply generally (remember the term *nomological network* in Chapter 5, which was used to describe a set of "lawful" relationships about a construct).

Case studies have a long history in social science, and most students will have read at least one case study in the process of their education. Often case studies are a focus in courses on personality, in which the work of Freud (e.g., *Little Hans* or *Dora: An analysis of a case of hysteria;* Freud, Strachey, Freud, Rothgeb, & Richards, 1953) is highlighted. Steinar Kvale (2003) argued that many aspects of qualitative psychology have been influenced by the psychoanalytical interview, with its roots in Freud's work. Among the examples he cited of such influence are those from Piaget, Theodor Adorno's studies on the authoritarian personality, and Elton Mayo and Fritz Roethlisberger's Hawthorne studies in industrial relations.

Rather than as a therapeutic method, Kvale (2003) saw the psychoanalytical interview as a research method. He listed seven modes of understanding that come out of the psychoanalytical research interview; several of these are widely applicable to social science research: "the individual case study"; "the open mode of interviewing"; "the interpretation of meaning"; "the temporal dimension"; and "the human interaction" (p. 278).

Case history: record of information about a person's medical or psychological history.

Ideographic: research approach that focuses on the individual and individual experiences.

Nomothetic approach: research approach with the goal of developing laws of behavior that would apply generally.

Another area in which case studies have played a central role in qualitative research is in our understanding of the brain. For many years, students have read about the person known in the literature as "H. M.," who suffered from profound anterograde amnesia (difficulty in forming new memories) after undergoing surgery (bilateral medial temporal lobe re-sectioning) for epilepsy (Scoville & Milner, 1957). H. M. was the focus of research by Brenda Milner and was studied for more than five decades; findings from research on H. M.'s capabilities had a profound effect on our understanding of memory systems (Squire, 2009). After his death in 2008, H. M.'s identity was revealed as Henry Gustav Molaison, who lived in Connecticut and had his initial surgery in Hartford. For those interested in reading more about him and some of the controversy that surrounds the data collected on him, a new book has just been published (Dittrich, 2016).

For Stake (2005, p. 443), the case study is a "common way to do qualitative inquiry" that is "neither new nor essentially qualitative." To investigate a case requires that the researcher obtain information about

1. "the nature of the case, particularly its activity and functioning

2. its historical background

3. its physical setting

4. other contexts, such as economic, political, legal, and aesthetic;

5. other cases through which this case is recognized; and

6. those informants through whom the case can be known." (p. 447)

"Place your best intellect into the thick of what is going on" said Stake (2005, p. 449). This comment is a reflection of the importance of *reflexivity*, which we talked about when introducing qualitative research. Misinterpretation of what is going on is a real possibility; researchers have used *triangulation* (mentioned previously in this chapter) to try to reduce that likelihood.

WHERE QUALITATIVE MEETS QUANTITATIVE: CONTENT ANALYSIS

Qualitative approaches may not emphasize a reduction of data to numbers, but they obviously produce information. There are times when researchers may wish to take the narratives, interviews, and other information and organize them into categories as another way of understanding them. Content analysis (as introduced in Chapter 5) is one of these organizational approaches. Content analysis is literally what it sounds like: analyzing content. As an approach, content analysis can be used with any technique that produces "content" to analyze (e.g., interviews, focus groups, and open-ended responses in questionnaires). Content analysis is a systematic analysis of responses, which may be written, spoken, or visual, in terms of categories or themes. In that sense, the approach is reductive and can lead to quantitative analyses if desired. Content analysis has been defined as "[a] systematic, quantitative procedure of analyzing conceptual material (articles, speeches, films) by determining the frequency of specific ideas, concepts, or terms" (Corsini, 2002, p. 215).

Content analysis is often called a qualitative research method (in the sense that it emphasizes open-ended responses), but the data may be subjected to quantitative analysis. In a chapter about focus groups, Wilkinson (2003) pointed out that the categories used in content analysis may be "top-down," that is, from an existing theoretical conceptualization, or "bottom-up," that is, emerging out of the data themselves, in a grounded theory approach (p. 196). Wilkinson also stated that although such categorization has the potential for quantitative analysis, such analysis may not be the primary focus of the research and has the potential to lose some of the rich contextualization of the narratives (see also Wilkinson, 2000, for more discussion of the drawbacks to submitting narrative content to quantitative analysis).

Content analysis may be the sole focus of a project, as might be the case if it emerged from a qualitative study, but content analysis also may be part of a chiefly quantitative study in which a limited number of open-ended questions have been asked. In those situations, it is these responses to open-ended questions that are the focus of content analysis.

The Open-Ended Response

A particular kind of content analysis that research methods students may encounter comes from open-ended questions (see also Chapter 5). Even in a study that is primarily quantitative, such as one where participants fill out a series of scales that are used as dependent variables in analyses, there may be open-ended questions. An example would be a study on student satisfaction among college students in their first year. As a final question, the researcher asks: "What was your most memorable experience during the first year of college?"

Eventually in a content analysis, you may do descriptive analyses (think percentages) or even nonparametric analyses (think chi-squares) using these new categories, but first you have to figure out what to do with the responses. How much people write affects the time it takes to do the content analysis. If you give people a full page for their response, they may write more; if you give them a text box of two lines, they will undoubtedly write less. The response space provided is itself a demand characteristic.

To digest these written responses and do a content analysis, there are a series of recommended steps. First, read through all of the responses, and do this several times. Remember the question, "What was your most memorable experience during the first year of college?" Make some mental notes about the kinds of memorable experiences people mention—did these experiences involve classroom achievements, interpersonal relationships, or sports triumphs? In addition to the specific experience, you might also think about other aspects of the experience that you might want to code, such as emotional tone. Did the experience involve positive or negative emotions?

Next, if each person has only written two lines, it isn't too hard to create a condensed list of responses on separate sheets of paper or in a computer file. That is, you can create a separate document (something like a spreadsheet) with the individual's participant number and then that student's response to the question next to it. It is much easier to think about themes and categories when the responses are more immediately available (that is, you don't have to flip or scan through one response page per participant).

After you have read through these condensed documents several times (three to four), see whether you can create a list of categories that reflects the major topics that came up in students' responses. You want to avoid categories that are too general ("interpersonal event") and those that are too specific ("met someone from Petoskey, Michigan"). You also want the categories to be exhaustive; that is, they should cover all of the responses in some fashion. It would be surprising if you had more than 10 meaningful categories. Even 10 might be too many to achieve a generality-specificity balance. A recommendation would be a maximum of 6–7, remembering that we humans are limited information processors (see Chapter 1). For those specific events mentioned only by one person that don't seem to fit in any of your categories, you can always use the "Other" category designation.

Once you have developed your list of categories, try to develop a brief operational definition (as introduced in Chapter 3) of the category. Why? Because if you are going to reach some conclusions based on these categories, you will need to convince other people of the validity of these categories. You do this through the process of having other people read and categorize the written statements. This process is called developing inter-rater reliability (discussed earlier in this chapter). The judgments about categories need to be independent of the judge; that is, any reasonable person who reads the operational definitions of the categories should reach the same conclusion about which statement belongs in which category. If the categories are too general and a given statement might belong in more than one category, reaching high inter-rater reliability will be a problem (see the section in this chapter called "Acceptable Values for Inter-rater Reliability"). An example of an operational definition for "sports-related memorable event" might be "any mention of an athletic or sports activity (recreational, intramural, JV, or Varsity) in which the person participated."

What if the participant's most memorable event of the first year of college was the following: "Went to the NCAA Women's Basketball Final and watched my team win" (likely to be the case if the student is from UConn). Although this is a sports-related event, the individual in question did not actually *participate* in the athletic event. Hence, with the operational definition we have developed, this particular memorable event would not fit into our sports-related category. This disconnection demonstrates the kind of fine-tuning needed to develop workable categories.

SUMMARY OF STEPS IN A CONTENT ANALYSIS

1. Read through all of the written responses.

2. Create a condensed list of the responses.

3. Create a list of categories (about 6–7).

4. Develop an operational definition for each category.

5. Conduct inter-rater reliability analysis on a sample of participant responses.

Content Categories and Statistics

You may decide to express these qualitative responses in a quantitative form. If so, once you have developed your categories, each category can be represented as an individual variable column. If a given participant mentioned an event in that category, he or she might have a "yes," represented as a "2" for data entry. A lack of a response for a particular category (variable) would be represented as a "no" and probably as a "1" for data entry. Once the categories (variables) are represented as data columns, it is possible to use the variables in statistical analyses. In the most basic form, you could do a frequency analysis to see the percentages of "mentions" for each variable, to determine which category of memorable event for the first year of college was most popular in the sense of being mentioned with the greatest frequency.

You could also ask a question based on group differences. For example, you might ask the question whether students who live on campus and students who live off campus differ in some category of memorable events, such as sports. You could then do a chi-square analysis (both dimensions in this analysis are categorical or nominal variables—on campus vs. off campus; mention of sports vs. no mention of sports) to determine whether the proportions of those who live on campus versus those who live off campus differ with regard to this sports category.

REVISIT AND RESPOND

- What are the advantages and disadvantages of doing a content analysis? Explain how content analysis can be considered both a qualitative and a quantitative approach to research.

COMPUTER-ASSISTED QUALITATIVE DATA ANALYSIS SOFTWARE (CAQDAS)

Software programs have been developed for a range of research approaches, including written text. Rather than have the researcher deal with the wealth of information that grounded theory and phenomenological approaches yield, researchers may turn to software programs to assist with this effort. Note that such programs *assist;* they do not do the conceptual work. To learn more about the specifics of analyzing qualitative data, Carl Auerbach and Louise Silverstein's book *Qualitative Data: An Introduction to Coding and Analysis* (2003) is useful. Qualitative data analysis (QDA) using computer programs such as NVivo® is discussed. Information about this program can be obtained through the distributor's website: **http://www.qsrinternational.com/ products_nvivo.aspx**.

Prior to selecting a particular software program to help with the qualitative analysis, it is wise to read through the literature on your topic and see what software programs other researchers have used, e.g., MAXQDA®.

Software programs for content (and other kinds of) analysis are listed on a useful site (**http://www.sosciso.de/en/software/datenanalyse/qualitativ/**). A site more specifically focused on content analysis is **http://academic.csuohio.edu/neuendorf_ka/ content/**. Jane Fielding, Nigel Fielding, and Graham Hughes (2013) provided an overview of the qualitative data analysis programs that are available for dealing with open-ended question data (OEQ). Their article focuses on OEQ data that may be part of a survey instrument, but remember that studies may include such qualitative data whenever we see examples of text from newspapers, films, social media, visual images, songs, or other sources where language constitutes data.

Fielding et al. (2013) stated that the first step is usually to read through a *single case* (interview); they contrasted this approach with quantitative analysis, which might look at all responses to a *single question* (one variable) first. In qualitative analysis, individual words (keywords) would be the search targets (word frequency) before moving to phrases. In contrast, they pointed out that coding is done by the respondents themselves in survey research through the process of selecting an answer from predetermined categories.

One important function of these **computer-assisted qualitative data analysis software (CAQDAS)** programs is to store a definition of a code, which is then available as needed. Such software programs do not eliminate the role of the researcher; the researcher is actively engaged in deciding what the critical words, and after that the key phrases for searching, will be. The software program doesn't suffer from fatigue or related human errors, but the program would not operate without the judicious and thoughtful preliminary work of the researcher.

Computer-assisted qualitative data analysis software (CAQDAS): software program developed to analyze linguistic responses such as text.

QUALITATIVE RESEARCH AND THE EMOTIONAL SELF: A FINAL CONSIDERATION

An important observation made by Kathleen Gilbert (2001a) is that engaging in qualitative research can be an emotional experience, not only for the participant but also for the researcher and the research team, which may include student research assistants. Many examples in Gilbert's book (2001b) highlighted these issues in the context of research in health-care settings, but the applicability is broader. Emotions may be challenging to deal with. For that reason, there need to be people (e.g., clinicians and counselors) available to help team members work through emotional distress. Gilbert (2001a) also recommended (a) a screening process to look for areas where potential staff members might be vulnerable and (b) an overview that gives applicants a realistic job preview, highlighting both the benefits and the risks of conducting such research.

Summary

This chapter reinforced your knowledge of correlational designs, in particular their purposes, drawbacks, and statistical approaches. Differences between asking questions about the sample as a whole versus focusing on the differences of preexisting groups were explained. The statistics that accompany different kinds of correlational research questions were described. The other emphasis in the chapter was introducing you to the domain of qualitative psychology, from techniques that involve using existing records (i.e., archival) to those that involve face-to-face communication with individual participants (i.e., interviews). As you saw, internal validity is also an issue in qualitative research, and inter-rater reliability is essential when you are organizing and categorizing subjective responses. Techniques for calculating inter-rater reliability were described (percent agreement, intraclass correlation, and Cohen's kappa). Particular emphasis was given to observational research, including creating behavioral categories, preserving the information that is observed, and training observers. In addition, approaches to content analysis were discussed, including steps to conduct a content analysis and the role of computer-assisted qualitative data analysis software (CAQDAS).

If you have not had time to consider them earlier, here is the list of **REVISIT and RESPOND** questions from this chapter.

- Explain the difference between the third variable problem and the directionality problem.
- Explain how Spearman's rho, Pearson's *r*, and chi-square differ. Give an example of a research problem that requires the use of ranked data.
- Why has psychology as a discipline been slow to embrace qualitative methodology?
- List three decisions you must make about your procedure before starting your behavioral observations.
- In calculating inter-rater reliability, what advantage does Cohen's kappa have over percent agreement?
- Why is the structured interview considered the equivalent of a verbally administered questionnaire? What advantages and disadvantages do you see to the structured interview, the semistructured interview, and the unstructured interview? What are interviewer effects?
- What are the advantages and disadvantages of doing a content analysis? Explain how content analysis can be considered both a qualitative and a quantitative approach to research.

BUILD YOUR SKILLS

1. With two other students from class, have one be "observed" while you and the other student function as independent raters (i.e., observers). Ask the person observed to periodically "look puzzled." First, you and the second student must create your operational definition of "looking puzzled." Then, over 10 minutes, every minute, marked when the second hand on a clock reaches 12, you and the other student independently record whether you think the person observed is looking puzzled. After you have these 10 observations, calculate the Cohen's kappa and percent agreement for the behavior. If your inter-rater reliability falls below the accepted levels [.75 for percent agreement and .61 for Cohen's kappa, using Graham et al.'s (2012) standards], meet to discuss why you think you disagreed.

2. Often newspaper articles provide the opportunity for readers to offer comments. With another class member, select a recent newspaper article from your local paper (online) that has at least 30 readers' comments. Then, using the steps in content analysis from this chapter and working together, create the categories (with their operational definitions) into which you then place each of the these comments. If you want more practice in calculating inter-rater reliability, you could each place the comments into the categories separately, and then compare your degree of agreement.

$SAGE edge™

edge.sagepub.com/devlin

Sharpen your skills with SAGE edge!

SAGE edge for students provides a personalized approach to help you accomplish your coursework goals in an easy-to-use learning environment. You'll find action plans, mobile-friendly eFlashcards, and quizzes, as well as videos, web resources, and links to SAGE journal articles to support and expand on the concepts presented in this chapter.

EXPERIMENTAL APPROACHES

Between Subjects Designs

CHAPTER HIGHLIGHTS

- Between subjects design: Overview
  - Advantages, disadvantages
  - Nomenclature
  - Sensitivity of IV and number of levels: Advantages and disadvantages
  - Number of IVs and interaction effects
  - Evaluating interaction effects
- Common types of between subjects designs
  - Randomized groups designs
  - One factor, two levels
  - More than two levels
  - Factorial designs
  - Matched group design
- Multiple comparisons: Planned and unplanned comparisons
- Handling error variance

- Finding and creating IVs
  - Text scenarios, visual images, movie clips, auditory clips
  - Copyright issues
  - Photo release form
- Multiple DVs in research designs
  - MANOVA
- Factor analysis (with example)

OVERVIEW

The focus in this chapter is between subjects design, a kind of experimental design that is the workhorse of social science research. By the end of the chapter, you will understand when to use such designs, how to maximize their potential, and some of the problems associated with these approaches. The chapter will also cover issues related to the number of dependent variables in an analysis to contrast analysis of variance (ANOVA) with multivariate analysis of variance (MANOVA), and it will include a section on factor analysis, which can be particularly useful if you are using items (e.g., visual images) that do not constitute a predetermined scale or measure.

BETWEEN SUBJECTS DESIGNS: WHAT ARE THEY?

A between subjects design (as introduced in Chapter 3) is considered an experimental approach. In a true experiment, a variable is manipulated and participants are randomly assigned to the conditions that are created. Between subjects design, from simple (*t* test) to complex (factorial), distribute or assign the conditions across (between) participants. In between subjects designs, participants in a given condition see, hear, taste, smell, or are otherwise exposed to just *one* of however many conditions there are in the experiment. Between subjects design can be contrasted to another experimental approach, within subjects design (also introduced in Chapter 3 and covered in more detail in Chapter 8) in which participants are typically exposed to *all* of the conditions in the experiment. Between subjects designs can also be contrasted to **mixed designs**, which include both a between subjects component and a within subjects component (also covered in Chapter 8). Between subjects (and within subjects) designs are considered experimental approaches.

Mixed design: design that includes both a within subjects and a between subjects component.

CHARACTERISTICS OF BETWEEN SUBJECTS DESIGNS: ADVANTAGES AND DISADVANTAGES

Between subjects designs are widely used and have certain advantages. The main advantage is that the effect of a particular treatment can be isolated because participants are being exposed to only one condition, and all other (controllable) aspects of the experiment are held constant. The approach also reduces the likelihood that participants will guess the hypothesis of the experiment because they are exposed to only one condition in the study. A third advantage (in comparison with within subjects designs, discussed in Chapter 8) is that there are no **carryover effects**. In a carryover effect, the lingering effect or impact of participating in one condition "carries over" to the experience of participating in another condition. Because participants in between subjects designs are completing only one condition, there is no opportunity for the impact to carryover to another condition.

Nomenclature Surrounding IVs

It might be helpful to talk about the different names that are used to refer to the IV-side of the house. The terms *independent variable* (*IV*), which was defined in Chapter 3; **variable**; **factor**; and **treatment** (used by itself) refer to the independent variable. **Condition**, **level**, and **value** refer to *which version* of the IV or treatment the individual received. The idea of an independent variable is something in a study that is manipulated or specifically altered. Notice the word *variable*. Sometimes researchers simply talk about the number of variables they have by using a shortcut. Another word commonly used to describe the independent variable is *factor*; researchers will often refer to the number of factors they have, especially when talking about a factorial design. *Treatment* is another term used to refer to the independent variable. Thus, these terms all refer to the IV.

In addition, you may hear the term *condition* (as in experimental vs. control condition; or which treatment condition did she receive?). Note that condition refers to WHICH **treatment level** the individual received. In many kinds of experiments, researchers refer to the different *levels* of the IV or levels of treatment. An example would be different dosages (levels) of drugs. When people talk about between subjects research from a statistical perspective, you will often hear them talking about the experimental variable and the *values* of the variable. The variable is the IV, and the values are the levels of that variable. It is easy to misuse these words because of their similarity. To summarize: *IV, factor, treatment,* and *variable* all refer to the independent variable. *Level, condition,* and *value* refer to which version of the treatment or IV the individual received.

Carryover effects: when the impact of one condition extends to subsequent conditions; described as one of the three context effects in within subjects design (Greenwald, 1976).

Variable: term often used to refer to an independent variable (IV).

Factor: another word used to refer to the independent variable; also a dimension that emerges from a factor analysis, a data reduction strategy.

Treatment: another word used for the independent variable (IV).

Condition: in research design, the particular level of a treatment that is used in experimental research (e.g., experimental and control conditions).

Level: term that refers to the specific version of the treatment the participants received (e.g., which dosage of drug). See also *condition* and *value*.

Values: refer to variable or treatment levels; can also refer to numerical values assigned in SPSS Statistics® file.

Treatment level: condition in an experiment; the treatment is defined in terms of its different levels (e.g., experimental and control).

What you want to take away from this discussion of nomenclature is that (a) something is manipulated (the independent variable, variable, factor, or treatment), and that (b) people receive different values, conditions, or levels of what you manipulated. As an example, imagine we are examining the effect of mode of content delivery (Ultra HD Television, HD Television, or streaming on a computer screen) on satisfaction with a lecture. Our independent variable/variable/factor/treatment is mode of delivery, and our three values/levels/conditions are Ultra HD Television, HD Television, and computer. Our DV is satisfaction with the lecture.

REVIST AND RESPOND

- Explain the difference between a treatment and a level. What is another word for treatment? For level?

SENSITIVITY OF IV

Research designs differ in the sensitivity of the information they provide to us. At one end, we have a demonstration, and at the other, we have a range of complex factorial designs, where each factor has many levels. What do we learn as the research designs increase in complexity?

Demonstration: one-level study where the impact of a variable is illustrated but there is no control condition.

At one extreme is a **demonstration**. This is research in which you have one level of a variable; there is no control (which would be considered another level). A demonstration is an illustration of what happens in one situation. True, you can't infer causality without a control, but you may do a demonstration because you want to determine whether an intervention has some noticeable effect (i.e., does anything happen?). You might also want people to describe their reactions to that intervention before adding more levels. Clearly we might learn very little from doing such a demonstration, but many demonstrations, for example, those offered in class to students, operate on the premise that the instructor/researcher is simply illustrating that something can happen. For example, you might show an entertaining video called "The Colour Changing Card Trick" (**https://www.youtube.com/watch?v=v3iPrBrGSJM**) to demonstrate how easy it is to divert people's attention so that they "miss" some of the events taking place. You could ask students to identify (count) the number of "changes" that took place in the video, that is, the dependent variable, or outcome. There is no experiment; no variable is presented in different forms.

You could easily make this an experiment by priming one group with some directions to "attend to the colors" in the video, whereas the control group would see the video without such priming. At that point, we have moved beyond a demonstration. We have a more informative, but still limited, research design. There are two levels of one independent variable (priming for the video or not) and one dependent variable. The appropriate statistical test is an **independent samples *t* test**, an analysis for a situation where there are two levels of the variable and one dependent variable: One group receives the experimental manipulation, and the other is a control group (no treatment).[1] Researchers may also simply use different variations of the manipulation without a true control group. For example, in an experiment discussed in Chapter 6, one group was exposed to a woman holding a 5-lb (80 oz) weight, and the other to a picture of the same woman holding a 25-lb (400 oz) weight. There was no formal control (a woman holding no weight), and one could argue that the experiment would have been improved with a control, but this researcher is still able to answer the question about how people perceive a woman holding either a 5-lb or a 25-lb weight. We have learned more than in a demonstration (e.g., how people perceive a woman holding a 5-lb weight), but we still don't know very much about the minimum and maximum weights that would affect people's judgments of the femininity and masculinity of the weightlifter.

Especially for investigators just beginning research in an area of inquiry, it may be hard to know what range of stimuli to use to measure the effect of interest. That is one reason we talked about manipulation checks in Chapter 3. Researchers need to know whether their manipulation was noticed, that is, if participants paid attention to the stimulus in their condition. Consider the example about exposure to different weights (5 lb or 25 lb) to determine their impact on judged femininity and masculinity. The manipulation check question at the end of the experiment asked what weight the participant saw.

This researcher used two levels of the treatment (5-lb vs. 25-lb weight). What if she wanted to know whether there was a point at which increases in weight produced no further change in judgment? You need a wide enough range of levels (their spacing and number) to reveal the nature of the function (its shape) that links the independent and dependent variables (Corsini, 2002, p. 1020).

> **Independent samples *t* test:** test to determine whether the means of two independent groups differ significantly.

›› Try This Now

How would you increase the sensitivity of this experiment with regard to weight levels? What specific weight levels would you add and why?

---

[1]Note that a control group is the designation for participants who do not receive the intervention or treatment, whereas the term "experimental control" refers to the steps researchers take to reduce threats to internal validity [think back to Campbell and Stanley's (1963) list in Chapter 3].

FIGURE 7.1   Example of a 2 by 5 Design

Athlete	Nonathlete
☐ 5 lbs. (20)	☐ 5 lbs. (20)
☐ 15 lbs. (20)	☐ 15 lbs. (20)
☐ 25 lbs. (20)	☐ 25 lbs. (20)
☐ 35 lbs. (20)	☐ 35 lbs. (20)
☐ 45 lbs. (20)	☐ 45 lbs. (20)

What are the drawbacks to increasing the number of levels in a design? The major drawback is the number of participants such designs require. Although you may see rules of thumb (e.g., that you should have at least 15–20 participants for each level in the design), the number of participants required for each study will differ depending on the power you need to detect whether the null hypothesis should be rejected. Power, in turn, depends on several variables (effect size, sample size, alpha level, and one- vs. two-tailed test; see Chapter 3). A large effect size indicates that the population distributions reflected in the samples have little overlap. In general, in such situations, fewer participants are needed to detect a true difference than when the overlap is greater. For high levels of power, the effect sizes or the samples need to be large (Howell, 2013).

For the moment, let us use a rule of thumb (20 participants per cell) to demonstrate how the complexity of a design affects sample size. Imagine in the study of weights, you used weights at the following levels: 5, 15, 25, 35, and 45 pounds (i.e., five levels; or the metric equivalents of 80, 240, 400, 560, and 720 oz., respectively). At 20 participants per level, that design requires at least 100 participants. What if we also wanted to see whether athletes and nonathletes differed in their judgments of these five conditions, which gives us a 2 (athlete vs. nonathlete) by 5 (levels of weights) design, or a total of 200 participants at a minimum (see Figure 7.1).

Is there enough power in this study; that is, would we be able to detect differences between the different conditions, if they exist? We discussed power in Chapter 3, but it might be helpful to revisit that topic now.

REVISIT AND RESPOND

- Explain the relationship between the sensitivity of the IV and the number of cells required by the design. What are the advantages to having more levels of the IV? Any disadvantages?

MORE ON POWER, SAMPLE SIZE, AND POWER CALCULATIONS

Of the variables that affect power, you can see that sample size gives you the most flexibility, as people are not in the habit of changing either the alpha level of .05, nor can you switch from a two-tailed to a one-tailed test (the use of a one-tailed test has to be stated in your hypotheses), nor can they change the effect size reported in the literature. Recommendations for calculating sample size include performing a power analysis before conducting the study.

The real challenge in determining how many participants you need is obtaining the effect size. David Howell (2013, pp. 234–235) pointed to three routes: (1) existing research, (2) the researcher's decision about the magnitude of difference between μ_1 (the mean under H_0) and μ_2 (the mean under H_1) that would be considered important, and (3) conventions accepted in the literature, such as those by Jacob Cohen (1988; see Chapter 3). In other words, the third route (values from Cohen or others) is used when you have no other way to make an estimate of the parameters you need but is not preferred (Howell, 2013). Howell (2013) mentioned that there are several online software packages (many of them free) for calculating power and pointed to **G*Power** (Faul, Erdfelder, Lang, & Buchner, 2007) as one such option (**http://www.gpower.hhu.de/en.html**). Howell (2013) reminded us that "power = $1-\beta$" (p. 230) and that β is the probability of making a Type II error. Thus, if power is set at .80, the probability is 20% that a Type II error will occur. To decrease that probability, in the same experiment, we would have to increase the number of participants.

As Howell (2013) described, whether you are able to do that depends on the ease/difficulty of obtaining the particular participants you need. College students are easy to obtain, whereas therapy patients might be substantially harder to obtain. Geoffrey Keppel (1982) also provided comments about performing a power analysis; while acknowledging some of the difficulties researchers may encounter when trying to determine power, he underscored the merit of doing so: "An estimate of power, no matter how approximate, gives us some degree of control over type II error" (p. 73). Even though further discussion of power analysis will not be covered in this text, it is important to understand that such analyses can be performed, especially with the help of online calculators. Increasingly, such analyses are expected of researchers. When you cannot reject the null hypothesis in your experiment, a natural question would be whether you had sufficient power to evaluate that hypothesis adequately. A power calculation tells you that, but it should be done *a priori*.

> **G*Power:** free online software that calculates power for a given design.

NUMBER OF IVs AND INTERACTION EFFECTS

Moving beyond one independent variable and its levels, another issue to consider is the *number of independent variables* in the study as a whole. When you have more than one independent variable, there is the possibility of **interaction effects**. An interaction effect

> **Interaction effect:** when the effect of one independent variable (IV) is not the same for all levels of a second IV.

occurs when the effect of an independent variable changes when examined in light of the levels of another variable; that is, the effect of the IV is not the same for all levels of a second variable. Here is an example created using sailors and nonsailors who completed the Mental Rotations Test (MRT; see Vandenberg & Kuse, 1978). We mentioned this test in Chapter 3. In our hypothetical example here, sailing team members and nonsailors completed the test in either timed or untimed conditions, yielding a 2 (sailor vs. nonsailor) by 2 (timing condition) design and analysis (see Figure 7.2). The MRT (1978) has 20 problems, with 2 items per problem, yielding a maximum score of 40 correct answers if each item is counted as "1" with no penalty for guessing. Remember that in this particular example, sailor/nonsailor is a quasi-IV because we haven't randomly assigned people to become sailors or not; timing is a true IV.

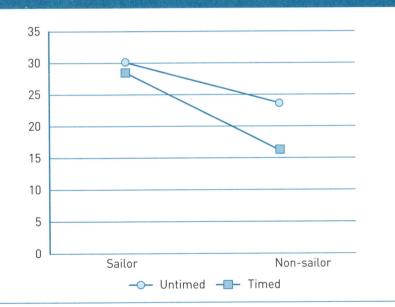

FIGURE 7.2 Example of a 2 by 2 Design With an Interaction

What you see in Figure 7.2 is an interaction effect; sailors perform at about the same level in both the timed and the untimed conditions. Nonsailors, however, do less well in the timed condition. Thus, the effect of timing (one variable) is not the same over each level of the other variable (sailor status). In this example, timing tends to be associated with poorer performance in nonsailors than in sailors presumably because sailing requires practice in mental rotation (making judgments about movements around the race course) under pressure and sailors are better at the task under pressure than are nonsailors.

EVALUATING AN INTERACTION BY HAND

It is possible to evaluate an interaction using SPSS®, which you may have been shown in statistics, but knowing how to evaluate an interaction or **simple effects** "by hand" is useful because it can clarify what is happening from a conceptual point of view and lead to a better grasp of the material. A simple effect is the impact of one of your independent variables limited to one of the levels of your second independent variable. That situation is depicted in Figure 7.2 because timing (one of the independent variables) had an impact on only one of the levels (nonsailors) in the other (quasi) independent variable.

Let's use another hypothetical example. Students were randomly assigned to one of four conditions and were told to imagine living in a residence hall of a particular size: 50, 100, 150, or 200 students (labeled: 1, 2, 3, and 4). In addition, participants were told to imagine they were either first year students or fourth year students. Residence hall and class year were fully crossed in this 4 (residence hall size) by 2 (class status) design, yielding 8 cells. Students then completed a scale that measured whether they thought academic achievement would be fostered in their residence hall. The analysis used class year (first, fourth) and residence hall size (1, 2, 3, and 4) as the IVs and the rating of "Fosters Academic Achievement" as the dependent variable. The analysis showed a significant interaction between class year and residence hall size on that DV. When you think about what your research shows, it is always helpful to look at the means and ask yourself what "story" they tell.

For this example, what story did the means tell? In this case, it might not be easy to see at the outset. We need to evaluate the interaction. The formula for evaluating simple effects involves selecting the two means of interest (you may do this calculation several times with different means of interest), the corresponding ns, and the mean square (MS) error (see Figure 7.3).

The MS error for this analysis was 1.39 (which you would find on your SPSS computer printout), and the degrees of freedom for the comparisons were (1, 719), with a critical value of 3.85 for an alpha of .05 and 6.67 for an alpha of .01. Note that there

Simple effects: way to evaluate the components of an interaction, that is, what is responsible for the interaction.

FIGURE 7.3 Example of Evaluating the Interaction

$$\frac{\left(X_1 + Y_2\right)^2}{\left(\dfrac{1}{n^1} + \dfrac{1}{n^2}\right)\left(MS_{error}\right)} = F \text{ value } (1, \text{omnibus } df)$$

Residence Hall 1 (50)		Residence Hall 2 (100)		Residence Hall 3 (150)		Residence Hall 4 (200)	
1st	4th	1st	4th	1st	4th	1st	4th
n=70	n=119	n=65	n=121	n=51	n=100	n=77	n=132
AA	AA	AA	AA	AA	AA	AA	AA
2.41	3.18	2.81	2.74	2.94	3.28	2.77	3.04

are handy online calculators for the critical values of F (e.g., **http://www.danielsoper .com/statcalc3/calc.aspx?id=4**) if you don't have a textbook with those tables available.

In this situation, as shown in Figure 7.3, you are determining whether students in the first year condition (1st) and students in the fourth year condition (4th) differ by residence hall in the degree to which they think that residence hall fosters academic achievement (AA). For a significant interaction to occur, some pattern has to break down or be inconsistent across residence halls. In other words, if we assume that first year and fourth year students do not differ in their scores on this variable (Academic Achievement: AA) by residence hall, a significant interaction suggests that those scores *do* differ in one or more of the residence halls. To find out where, you need to "do the math."

>> **Try This Now**

Before you look at the calculations here, look at the means again and ask yourself which residence hall you would start with and why. (Hint: If most of the means seem close, look for the situation where they are farther apart.)

TABLE 7.1		
Residence Hall 1	$\dfrac{(3.8-2.41)^2}{(1/119 + 1/70)(1.39)} = 18.79$	
Residence Hall 2	$\dfrac{(2.81-2.74)^2}{(1/65 + 1/121)(1.39)} = 0.15$	
Residence Hall 3	$\dfrac{(3.28-2.94)^2}{(1/100 + 1/51)(1.39)} = 2.81$	
Residence Hall 4	$\dfrac{(3.04-2.77)^2}{(1/132 + 1/77)(1.39)} = 2.55$	

What do these results tell you? You see a pattern that in general, students in the first year and fourth year conditions do not significantly differ in their judgment of the degree to which they think the residence hall they read about fosters academic achievement, but in the Residence Hall 1 condition, they do differ significantly. In the Residence Hall 1 condition, those in the fourth year condition responded that the residence hall promotes academic achievement significantly more so than did those in the first year condition. Imagining themselves as fourth year students in a small residence hall, students may have been more likely to think this condition promoted academic achievement, perhaps relating smaller size with quietness.

Thus far we have talked about the situation where there are two IVs (residence hall size and class status). What happens when we have three? In the research dealing with multicultural art (discussed in Chapter 3), participants viewed one of two kinds of art (Multicultural or Western) that varied in the number of those art objects present (1 vs. 6). In addition, both college students and citizens from the community viewed the photographs. This approach produces a 2 (kind of art; true IV) by 2 (number of art objects; true IV) by 2 (sample type; quasi IV) design, with the possibility of 3 main effects (one each for art, art objects, and sample type); 3 two-way interactions (art × number; art × sample; number × sample); and 1 three-way interaction (art × number × sample)!

You can see how quickly the design becomes complicated. In the study described here, there was a three-way interaction of the culture of the art, number of objects displayed, and the sample, for all four dependent variables in the study (see Devlin et al., 2013, for details). Moving beyond two IVs can potentially create difficult-to-understand interactions for readers. As a result, the conclusions from the research may not have their full impact.

Be aware of what moving beyond two IVs (or quasi-IVs) will mean for statistical analysis and interpretation. In addition, there is another reason to be cautious about moving beyond two IVs; that caution has to do with filling all of the cells that are created by your design. If you are using true IVs, the issue of the number of IVs you have is less challenging than if quasi-IVs are involved. With true IVs, you need more participants if you have more cells, but these participants are "anyone" in terms of randomly assigning them to condition. That is, unless you care about the demographic characteristics of the sample in terms of gender or class year, as examples, you simply randomly assign people to as many cells as you have in your design.

What if you DO care about those background characteristics, for example, in terms of class year (first, second, third, and fourth) and whether people have ever seen a psychotherapist or not? Then, you have the problem of filling the cells with not just anyone but with a sufficient number of people with the needed demographic characteristics. If we go back to our previous example of the multicultural art and include class year and previous experience with therapy or not (and eliminate the student × community sample quasi-IV), we would now have a 2 (art: M:Multicultural or W:Western) × 2 (number of objects; 1 or 6) × 4 (class year; 1, 2, 3, or 4) × 2 (therapy experience; Yes/No) design or 32 cells to fill (see Figure 7.4).

FIGURE 7.4 Example of a 2 by 2 by 4 by 2 Design

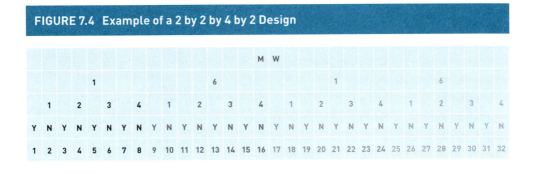

As we discussed in Chapter 3, what typically happens with this kind of design is that you are unable to run a single analysis with all of those cells filled, especially if your access to participants in a participant pool is limited. Many departments limit the number of participants each researcher can use from the pool (see Chapter 9 about obtaining participants). What you would probably end up doing is using the art and number of objects displayed in each analysis but with class year in one analysis and with therapy experience in a second analysis. You would not get to see the interaction of class year and therapy experience with the other conditions, but it would be a reasonable approach to a large design with these sample restrictions. You would also need to perform a Bonferroni adjustment (see Chapter 3; and later in this chapter) to correct for the possibility of Type I error because you performed multiple analyses.

REVISIT AND RESPOND

- What kinds of challenges do you potentially face if you have a design with three IVs?

COMMON TYPES OF BETWEEN SUBJECTS DESIGN

In the next section, when we talk about both the number of IVs and the number of levels of a given IV, we will include the statistics associated with the design. At this stage in our discussion, all of the designs have one dependent variable.

Randomized Groups Design

A common approach to research design involves randomly assigning groups to different levels of one or more independent variables (hence, the label **randomized groups design**). In the sections that follow, the routine statistical test used for a given design is featured to reinforce the link between research design and statistical analysis.

Randomized groups design: randomly assigning groups to different levels of one or more independent variables.

One IV (Factor), Two Levels: Independent Samples *t* Test

As we saw earlier in this chapter when talking about the sensitivity of the IV, one of the simplest research designs involves a single factor with just two levels (and one dependent variable). The associated statistical approach for this situation is an independent samples *t* test. A *t* test is the special case of analysis of variance when you compare only two levels of one IV. The word *independent* in this situation refers to the fact that the groups are randomly assigned to a condition and are not connected to each other. Typically, the levels of the IV are your experimental group and your control group. You are interested in whether the means of the two groups are sufficiently different, leading you to reject the null hypothesis.

Consider an example where an institutional researcher wants to know whether students who were randomly assigned to take a required first year seminar in the first semester had higher first year grade-point averages (GPAs) than students who were randomly assigned to take this required seminar in the second semester. In this situation, you have one IV (required seminar) with two levels (semester taken: first or second) and one dependent variable (first year GPA). An independent samples t test is the statistical analysis to use in this situation.

This design is straightforward and requires fewer participants compared with more complex designs, and the design is appropriate for the research question.

Expanding on the Number of Levels With One Independent Variable

This sections looks at different ways to expand on the number of levels with one independent variable. One-way ANOVA and two-factor designs are two such options. Different ways of presenting the nomenclature are also discussed.

ONE-WAY ANOVA   One way to improve on most designs is to increase the number of levels in your IV. This will provide more information about the IV. Consider the research discussed earlier that involved the weight held by the woman. In that example, we had *five levels of the IV* (weight held): 5, 15, 25, 35, and 45 lbs. (see Figure 7.1). What if we had limited that research to just 5 lbs. and 15 lbs. or 5 lbs. and 45 lbs.? Imagine that there is no additional impact of weight held on judged femininity and masculinity after 25 lbs. If we had used just the 5-lb. and 45-lb. conditions, we would have missed knowing when this plateau occurred.

In this research example with one IV (with five levels) and one DV (here for purposes of the example we will use only judged masculinity of the weight-holder), the appropriate statistical approach here is called a **one-way ANOVA**. The use of the term *one-way* refers to the fact that we have just one IV in this situation (that has at least three levels; with only two levels, it would be a t test). We have only one DV; hence we have *analysis of variance* (ANOVA; as defined in Chapter 6).

TWO-FACTOR DESIGNS   Adding *levels* to an IV increases the complexity and sensitivity of the design, but another way to learn more from a research design is to expand the *number of independent variables.* If we have a second independent variable, not only do we learn whether this factor has an effect on our outcome of interest (our DV), but we also learn whether this variable interacts with our other IV. In other words, having two or more IVs introduces the possibility of interaction effects. A design in which you have more than one IV can be referred to as a **factorial design** (i.e., you have more than one factor).

The advantages to having a two-factor design are the increased information you will have about the variables of interest and the knowledge of significant interaction effects (if they occur). There is greater generalizability of results because you are seeing whether the effect of one variable extends across additional conditions (Howell, 2013).

One-way ANOVA: evaluate through analysis of variance (ANOVA) whether the means of three or more groups (levels of an independent variable (IV)) differ significantly.

Factorial design: design in which there is more than one independent variable (IV).

An additional advantage is that it requires fewer participants to achieve the same degree of power because the effects of one variable are averaged across the effects of the other variable (Howell, 2013).

The disadvantage of this approach is that it still requires more participants than a one-factor design and typically more effort to conduct. Remember that to determine the number of cells you will have in your analysis, you multiply the number of levels in each factor. Thus, in a study about the effect of displaying credentials in a therapist's office, the researchers had a 3 (2, 4, or 9 credentials) by 2 (presence or absence of 2 family photographs) design, yielding 6 cells. They also included a group that saw 0 credentials and no family photographs, adding a seventh group as a control group. In the case of the three levels of credentials (2, 4, 9) and two levels of family photographs (present, absent), these were **fully crossed**, meaning each level in one variable was paired with each level in the other variable once. Howell (2013) defined a factorial design as one in which "all combinations of the levels of the independent variables" are included (p. 412).

> **Fully crossed design:** in a research design when all possible combinations of the levels of the independent variables (IVs) are represented.

A WORD ABOUT NOMENCLATURE   When we had one IV with more than two levels, we called it a *one-way ANOVA* (remember that we are including designs with one DV in this section). That is really the only way to describe it. Nevertheless, with two or more IVs, there are several choices; each of them is acceptable. Using the previously mentioned therapists' credentials (Devlin et al., 2009) for the fully crossed IVs, they had three levels of the credentials condition (2, 4, and 9) and two levels of the family photo condition (present or absent).

There are three possibilities to describe this research design:

- Two-way ANOVA
- Factorial ANOVA
- 3 × 2 ANOVA (or 2 × 3 ANOVA; these are interchangeable)

When you use the label **two-way ANOVA**, you tell your reader you have two factors. When you use the label *factorial ANOVA,* you tell your reader you have at least two factors (but not how many). When you use a label like *3 × 2 ANOVA,* you tell your reader not only how many factors you have but also specifically how many levels each factor has. Thus, if you want to be maximally informative, you would refer to that design as a 3 × 2 ANOVA (or 2 × 3). In addition, some researchers find it helpful to remind readers what the factors are. For that reason, you sometimes see descriptions that follow this format, using our example: a 3 (2, 4, or 9 credentials) × 2 (presence or absence of family photographs) ANOVA (in this case).

> **Two-way ANOVA:** analysis of variance (ANOVA) that has two independent variables (IVs).

MATCHED GROUPS DESIGN

Matched group design: before randomly assigning participants to conditions, you match them on one or more characteristic that you think may affect the dependent variable.

A **matched group design** is like the randomized group design but with a twist. Before randomly assigning the participants to groups, you match them on characteristics you think might have an undue effect on the dependent variable and overshadow any effect of your independent variable. When you have two groups, the matched groups design is called *matched pairs design*. Roger Ulrich's (1984) study comparing the influence of a view to a brick wall versus a stand of deciduous trees for patients after gallbladder surgery is often described as a matched group study. This study was mentioned briefly in Chapter 1.

The patients were matched on a variety of variables thought to influence recovery from surgery, for example, sex, age, whether they smoked, whether they were judged obese, and room/floor level. Was it a true matched study? No. Ulrich's (1984) data were *archival* (see Chapter 6), and the matching that occurred came *after* the fact from identifying appropriate patients in the medical records. Patients were matched on the variables in question, and then the archival data from those matched pairs (one with a view to nature; the "match" with a view to the brick wall) were used in the research. If patients had been matched *before* surgery and then randomly assigned to a view of a brick wall or to nature, we would have a bona fide matched groups study.

REVIST AND RESPOND

- What are the similarities and differences between a randomized groups design and a matched groups design?

MULTIPLE COMPARISONS

Multiple comparisons: situation where you make several comparisons simultaneously to evaluate your hypothesis, leading to the possibility of Type I error.

When a research project involves **multiple comparisons**, for example, three or more levels of an IV, you may encounter the problem of Type I error (see Chapter 3) in that you increase the possibility that you will incorrectly reject the null hypothesis with multiple tests. Using our therapists' credentials example, you have three levels of the credentials IV: People saw 2, 4, or 9 credentials. If you have a main effect for credentials, let's say on the DV therapist's competence, you need to know where the significant differences lie. Therefore, you need to make three comparisons, comparing the means for that DV for 2 versus 4; 2 versus 9; and 4 versus 9.

Howell (2013) has a very good chapter on Multiple Comparisons Among Treatment Means, which includes the various approaches one can take to dealing with the possibility of Type I error. This section will draw from his work. Other recommended readings include Michael Stoline (1981) and James Jaccard, Michael Becker, and Gregory Wood (1984). Howell (2013) explained that the approaches differ in whether they focus on **error rate per comparison (PC)** or **family wise (FW) error rate**. The error rate per comparison (PC) is defined as "the probability of making a Type I error on any given comparison" (p. 371). The FW error rate is the situation where a "set of comparisons among . . . group means" has been run, yielding "a set (often called a *family*) of conclusions" (p. 371). The familywise error rate refers to the probability that the "family of conclusions will contain *at least* one Type I error" (p. 371).

The approach you choose to control for Type I error in the case of multiple comparisons depends on whether you have *a priori* hypotheses. In an earlier version of his text (sixth edition, 2007), Howell provided a table to summarize approaches (see 2007, Table 12.7, p. 375). In a later version of his text, he stated that the distinction between *a priori* and post hoc comparisons is a "fuzzy one," yet he maintained the distinction for the purposes of organization: "In practice, the real distinction seems to come down to the difference between deliberately making a few comparisons that are chosen because of their theoretical or practical nature (and not just because the means looked different) and making comparisons among all possible pairs of means" (2013, p. 372). Some of the approaches in the two categories are used far more than the others; we will concentrate on those.

In the case of *a priori* hypotheses, you have stated which differences you expect to see. These are often called **planned comparisons**. In the case of post hoc analyses, you have made no advance predictions; these are often called **unplanned comparisons**. Given that you have *a priori* hypotheses, you might expect to be looking at only some, not all, of the possible comparisons; hence, the possibility of Type I error should be smaller with planned comparisons than with post hoc (unplanned) analyses, where you might have a larger number of comparisons.

Howell (2013) acknowledged that it is difficult to know which test to select. For one planned comparison, he recommended using the standard *t* test; for a complex comparison, he recommended a linear contrast (p. 398). If you have several planned comparisons and they are not necessarily pairwise, he recommended the multistage Bonferroni *t* because he stated it maximizes power while handling FW error.

When many comparisons are being run in the post hoc situation, Howell recommended Tukey's test or the Ryan Procedure (REGWQ, based on the initials of the originators; Howell, 2007, p. 373), which Howell suggested over the Tukey if you have the Ryan available on your statistics software; if not, the Tukey is adequate. If you are a

Error rate per comparison (PC): in any given comparison, the probability of making a Type I error.

Family wise (FW) error rate: probability of having at least one Type I error in a set of comparisons.

Planned comparisons: you state the differences you expect to see (and hence which comparisons to run) *a priori*.

Unplanned comparisons: you make no advance predictions and run comparisons post hoc, which usually results in a higher probability of Type I error.

researcher who does not have specific hypotheses about the effect of the different levels of your IV, then Tukey is a reasonable choice.

REVISIT AND RESPOND

- What are the differences between planned and unplanned comparisons? In general, which is preferable and why?

HANDLING ERROR VARIANCE

Certain aspects of research are problematic because they decrease the possibility of rejecting the null hypothesis (assuming that it should be rejected). A major source of problems is **error variance**. Error variance is "score variability not systematic or controlled, nor produced by the independent variable" (Corsini, 2002, p. 340). In other words, error variance is unwelcome!

Error variance: variability in the score not produced by the independent variable and not systematic or controlled.

A good deal of the error variability comes from human behavior (trait or state) that interferes with the research manipulation. You can imagine conducting a study on memory in which some participants arrive at the experiment with varying degrees of sleep deprivation and/or caffeine intake. If your sample size is small, these individual differences could profoundly affect the outcome of your experiment despite random assignment to condition. Problems with instrumentation would also affect error variance because the conditions of the experiment are not held constant. In Chapter 3, we talked about the fact that the experiment is a social interaction, and when participants arrive at the research setting, they may come with different attitudes (Adair, 1973). All research includes unwanted sources of error, but you can take steps to minimize error variance.

How to Address Error Variance

In a sense, addressing error variance is another way of talking about minimizing threats to internal validity (see Chapter 3). We can address error variance by increasing experimental control:

- **Random assignment to condition.** Randomly assigning participants to a condition is a fundamental way to try to reduce error variance. By randomly distributing whatever idiosyncrasies participants have that may influence the dependent variable, you are minimizing the chance that those differences will undermine your experiment.

- **Increasing the sensitivity of the independent and dependent variables.** You want to make sure that the levels of the independent variable you have selected will have an effect on the participants, as well as that the measure you have selected to record that effect is sufficiently sensitive to pick up that difference. In the case of the researcher who used 5-lb. and 25-lb. weights to examine their effect on perceived masculinity of the woman holding the weights, she picked weights that were visually distinctive; a 25-lb. weight looks big and heavy, whereas a 5-lb. weight does not. What if she had used 3-lb. and 5-lb. weights?

In the case of the dependent variable, you have to make sure that a scale has validity and reliability (see Chapter 5); if you use an unreliable scale with only a moderate Cronbach's alpha (a measure of whether the items are measuring the same concept), it is possible that the lack of reliability in the scale is contributing to unwanted error.

- **Be consistent.** The concept of consistency simply reminds you that you want to both (a) *treat everyone the same* and (b) *behave and appear the same in all interactions with your participants*—the same level of friendliness, energy, and patience; the same script, the same answers to questions asked, and the same instructions written or spoken; and the same formality of dress and address. Variability in any aspect of the research protocol can introduce unwanted variability into the process.

SUMMARY OF BETWEEN SUBJECTS DESIGN CONSIDERATIONS

Listed below is a summary of aspects of between subjects research designs; these considerations have the potential to affect the internal validity of your project.

Sensitivity (i.e., levels) of the IV

Number of IVs

Number of participants related to complexity of design (i.e., number of cells)

Power and sample size

Interpreting interaction effects

Multiple comparisons and Type I error

Handing error variance

FINDING AND CREATING IVs (SCENARIOS; VISUAL IMAGES; MOVIE CLIPS; AUDITORY CLIPS)

In Chapter 2, we spent time talking about sources of ideas for research projects, starting with the researcher and moving outward to events in the world that capture your attention. Reading the literature about a particular topic shows you what independent variables other researchers have used, the number of levels of those variables, and other aspects of their procedure. There are instances when the materials of other researchers are readily available and appropriate for your use (see Chapter 5 on measures). In other instances you may need to create your own stimulus materials. Often experimenter-created materials such as hypothetical scenarios can be used to study topics in an experimental fashion that would otherwise be impossible either because the manipulation is unethical (e.g., investigating participants' reactions to a fabricated story that a friend was diagnosed with a serious illness) or unfeasible (e.g., your ability to assign students randomly to hometowns).

EXISTING LITERATURE: METHOD SECTION

The Method section in a published paper should be sufficiently detailed to enable you to replicate that study. In practice, this level of detail may not be provided, often because of space limitations in a journal. The good news is that journals available electronically are beginning to use supplemental appendices. Aspects of the article that were too long to provide in the journal pages themselves appear in such appendices. For example, in Ann Devlin and Jack Nasar's (2012) study, the 30 photographs used were made available as online supplemental materials (by permission of the photographer). You may thus be able to find some of the material you need in such online appendices.

When parts of the Method (for IVs, these would be text, visual, or auditory materials) you want to use are not available in the printed article or online, write the corresponding author to see whether you can use the materials. Most authors are responsive to such requests to use their materials. The path to obtain existing materials may have several steps. Important principles here are PLAN IN ADVANCE and LEAVE SUFFICIENT TIME. For more detailed advice about obtaining existing measures, refer to Chapter 5.

Text Scenarios

You may encounter a situation where you have to create or modify the materials yourself. This happens when you pose a research question that has not been asked before (as far as your search of the literature revealed) or when you want to modify existing IVs to change aspects of the research question. Researchers may want to modify an existing scenario in particular ways across conditions. An example would be the use of résumés that differ only in the target variable, such as gender or ethnicity (communicated by the name on the résumé).

One original study that explored the evaluation of gender based on such stimulus materials was done by Philip Goldberg (1968), who gave college women booklets of six different articles; half the women read the articles attributed to Joan McKay, and the other half read the same articles attributed to John McKay. The title of the article "Are Women Prejudiced Against Women?" was answered in the affirmative; the study is cited as "a classic, influential experiment" (Swim, Borgida, Maruyama, & Myers, 1989, p. 409) exploring gender bias. To create the essays that participants read, Goldberg (1968) selected articles from six different publications and edited them for word length. In other words, he had to create the stimulus materials.

If you were updating Goldberg's (1968) study today, you might wonder whether Joan and John are appropriate names to use. Where would you go to find names frequently associated with a particular gender? You might try the Social Security Administration (ssa.gov), which provides a list of the top 1,000 boys' and 1,000 girls' names in the United States for the years 1880 to the previous year; in 2015, Emma was the top girl's name and Noah the top boy's name. You can search nationally or by state.

The Importance of Consistency

When crafting text materials or any kind of stimulus materials yourself, you need to keep consistency in mind. Therefore, everything should be the same EXCEPT for the variables you manipulate. Text length is one obvious parameter to keep the same; another variable to think about are characteristics of what is being manipulated. A student's study illustrates the possibilities for creating your own textual stimulus materials but also some of the decisions you need to make. The student was interested in perceptions of the likelihood of relationship success involving a situation with long-distance dating and the race of the partner (in this case, male). The researcher had a 2 (race: Caucasian, Asian) by 3 (distance: Boston, Chicago, Los Angeles) design in which, across the six scenarios, what varied was the stated race of the male partner and his job location. The student changed one other variable, the *name* of the male partner. In the Caucasian vignettes, his name was Michael Smith; in the Asian vignettes, his name was Hitoshi Yoshida.

> ### ⟫ Try This Now
>
> What was the student's reason for changing the name in the two conditions? What were the benefits and drawbacks to this name change? Could you simply use initials and keep them constant across conditions?

VISUAL IMAGES: MANIPULATING AN IMAGE

Visual images provide an incredibly rich resource for research. With the available image editing software, such as Adobe Photoshop®, you are in a position to take one stimulus and modify it to use in other conditions. Photoshop is not free, but your institution may provide the software to use. Alternatively, you can search the Web for free alternatives to Photoshop (there are several possibilities, such as the GNU Image Manipulation Program or GIMP).

Numerous applications (apps) and websites exist that provide images that are modifiable for a specific purpose, such as "Model My Diet," which could be used to show what an avatar of a man or woman would look like before and after a particular weight loss, or apps available through Apple iTunes® that let people see how they would look with a different hair color or hairstyle. There are other apps where you can see yourself aging, balding, or wearing braces, as just some examples. When using such programs from the Web, you would need to check with the site administrators to see the copyright issues that pertain to using the images in publications.

Finding Images Online

Public domain: material available to the public as a whole and not subject to copyright.

Copyright: when works are legally protected.

There are literally thousands of images online that you might consider using for research purposes, but you need to use images that are in the **public domain**, obtain permission to use an image not in the public domain, and possibly pay to use an image that has a **copyright**. Simply because an image is posted online does not mean you can copy it to use in your research project. A useful set of guidelines covering using images is available from MIT libraries: (**http://libguides.mit.edu/usingimages**). Additional information from the MIT libraries covers finding images that are available for reuse, through a Creative Commons search or a Google Advanced Image Search (**http://libguides .mit.edu/c.php?g=176183&p=1159045**). Consider also looking through the Public Domain Images site (**http://www.public-domain-image.com**).

Repositories of images can be purchased through such sites as Shutterstock.com and iStockphoto.com. If you need professional photographs of particular images, for example, architecture, the cost of use for the photographs taken can be substantial ($100s of dollars per image).

Taking Your Own Photos

There are instances where you cannot manipulate one image on Photoshop to produce the multiple visual stimuli you need, nor can you find public domain photographs on the Web that meet your research requirements (e.g., too many variables other than your manipulated change from photograph to photograph). In that case, you may end up taking your own photographs.

As an example, a student wanted to examine the impact of same-race versus other-race friendships through reactions to photographs of those situations (Chandra, 2015). The student used a social medium (Facebook®) to create a Facebook profile page that varied in the racial composition of the target photograph, which had two conditions. In a between subjects design, one group saw a photograph of the target African American woman with a Caucasian friend; the other photograph showed the same African American woman with an African American friend. The researcher was interested in the effects of these different photographs on participants' judgments of the self-esteem and collective self-esteem of the target woman.

Because the student could not find any Web photographs that fit the research requirements, the student had friends attending another college pose for the two photographs used in the study. What needed to stay constant was everything about the photograph (the lighting, the clothing, the facial expressions, and so on) except for the race of the friend. The photographs the student took were a reasonable approximation to the ideal given unavoidable limitations (e.g., the friends in the different conditions were not physically identical). You can see that such research presents challenges to internal validity. The student also needed to obtain permission of the individuals in the photographs to use the images in research. In such situations, a photo/video release form is required.

Photo/Video Release Form

When you take a photograph or video of someone to use in research, you need that person to sign a release form that indicates how the photograph or video can be used. Duke University provides a nice list of the components needed in such a photo or video release (**https://ors.duke.edu/orsmanual/photograph-and-film-releases**). Figure 7.5 provides an example of a form for photo release, based on the Duke components; the form could easily be modified to cover videos. Here I have structured the form much like an informed consent document, but that is not the only model. Many examples of forms are available if you search online. In addition to the Duke components, some release forms contain a statement that using the photographs involves no financial considerations or remuneration.

Using Friends on Campus or at Work

If you are going to take a photograph to use in research, you need to consider the impact of whether that individual will be known to your sample, which is likely to

FIGURE 7.5 Example of Photo Release Form Based on Suggestions From Duke University

Photo Release Form

Name of Researcher

Name of Institution

Address of Institution

I understand that I am being asked to provide permission for [insert researcher's name] to use photograph(s) taken of me dealing with [describe the material to be released, i.e., the content of the photographs and the date taken, if possible] to be used in research about [insert title or description of the study].

I understand that I have been asked to have my photograph(s) used in the following ways: [insert ways the material would be used, such as 1) being shown to participants in an online experiment; and 2) used in presentations and print and/or electronic publications].

[If the researcher has guaranteed that the individual's name will not be used, include a statement such as] I have been told that my name will not be used in any presentation of my photograph.

I understand that signing this release is voluntary, and that I am not required to do so, even though I gave permission for the photographs to be taken.

I am at least 18 years of age, have read and understand the statements in this document, and voluntarily agree to the release of my photograph(s) for the purposes of the described research.

Printed name _____

Signature _____

Date _____

be the case at small schools. Such familiarity is almost always a problem because it may influence participants' responses and is a confounding variable. For that reason, if you are taking your own photographs of people, you may want to use friends from another campus or your hometown. Again, planning for this event takes time. PLAN AHEAD!

Films

Brief excerpts of films can be used in research under the **Fair Use Doctrine**, a U.S. doctrine that stipulates the conditions under which copyrighted materials may be used without acquiring permission. Researchers have commonly used films to induce a particular mood in participants. For example, Jennifer Spoor and Janice Kelly (2009) used short clips (about 7 minutes) to induce a sad mood using *Sophie's Choice* and *Terms of Endearment* and a happy mood with *Good Morning, Vietnam* and *Ferris Bueller's Day Off.* Neutral mood was established with a clip from *The Mosquito Coast.* Videos in the public domain are available for use when their copyright has not been renewed or they have reached a particular legal age. See **http://www .unc.edu/~unclng/public-d.htm** for a chart of the restrictions. Videos that are posted on YouTube® are not necessarily in the public domain, and the best course of action if you want to use such a video in research is to request permission from the creator.

Fair Use Doctrine: U.S. legal doctrine that enables you to use copyrighted materials under certain circumstances.

Auditory Clips

The same comments about Fair Use apply to auditory material. Auditory material can be used for a variety of purposes in research, from inducing a mood to being the focus of the research itself. For example, exposure to a piano sonata by Wolfgang Amadeus Mozart (KV 488) was claimed to improve performance on spatial tasks (Rauscher, Shaw, & Ky, 1993) and came to be known as "the Mozart effect." This research spawned a proliferation of studies trying to replicate the original findings, but a meta-analysis of almost 40 studies in 2010 showed little support for this phenomenon (Pietschnig, Voracek, & Formann, 2010).

In a creative use of auditory stimuli, a student researcher manipulated the voices heard by participants in four conditions by using GarageBand®, an application from Apple. In this between subjects design, the researcher was interested in judgments of women's authority in the workplace based on hearing variations in pitch and speaking rate. In one feature of GarageBand, you can record a voice and then manipulate aspects of that voice and save it as an mp3 file. In this case, the researcher manipulated the speaking rate (beats per minute) and the vocal pitch (low, high) of the recording, creating a 2 (faster, slower speaking rate) × 2 (low, high pitch) design.

REVISIT AND RESPOND

- What are some of the challenges in creating your own stimuli to use in research? Where can you look for free images to use in research? What is the purpose of a **photo release form**?

MULTIPLE DEPENDENT VARIABLES (DVs) IN A RESEARCH DESIGN

In earlier sections in this chapter, we restricted our discussion to a single dependent variable or outcome in a research design, with associated statistical tests such as *t* test and ANOVA. Although using a single dependent variable is straightforward in terms of design and statistics, it has the disadvantage of putting all of the focus on just one variable (i.e., all your eggs in one basket), which may be a risky approach, especially if you are investigating a new area of research. An alternative approach is including more than one dependent variable.

Here we will talk about having multiple dependent variables and the particular case of conceptually related dependent variables. **Multivariate analysis of variance (MANOVA)** is used in a case where you have conceptually related dependent variables.

One primary advantage of using MANOVA (in contrast to running your analyses for multiple DVs as separate ANOVAs) is to reduce the possibility of Type I error. If your study is one in which you have participants complete several measures that are arguably related to each other, such as a test for locus of control and a test for self-efficacy, you would use MANOVA because these variables are conceptually related. If your DVs were self-esteem and political affiliation, it would be hard to make a case that these variables are conceptually related (unless you had found research in the literature to suggest otherwise). In the case of unrelated DVs, the analyses are run separately for each DV. Another advantage to using MANOVA is that differences might emerge that would not appear with ANOVA, for example, that combinations of responses to DVs may reveal differences between groups that are not apparent when the DVs are considered separately (Tabachnick & Fidell, 1983).

What Does a Significant MANOVA Indicate?

When you have a significant MANOVA result, it means that your dependent variables have formed a significant linear combination for the independent variable in the analysis. What does this show? From a significant finding for ANOVA (one DV), we learn whether the differences between groups on that one DV are likely the result of chance occurrence. If we consider the question of multiple DVs (MANOVA), it is as if we are running these ANOVAs at the same time. The analysis involves not one but *a combination* consisting of these multiple (conceptually related) DVs, and we learn whether groups differing significantly on this combination are, again, likely the result of chance occurrence (Tabachnick, & Fidell, 1983).

If you have more than one IV, you may have significant linear combinations for each IV and possibly for the interactions that are formed. Given that you performed a MANOVA because you argued that your dependent variables were conceptually related, you might expect to see this significant linear combination.

After reporting your significant MANOVA (Wilks's lambda is the multivariate statistic generally recommended; Tabachnick & Fidell, 1983, p. 249), you move on to examine your univariate effects. The ANOVA results will reveal how the levels of the IVs are reflected in the DVs, in terms of differences in means. For example, in the study on the effects of credentials discussed earlier in this chapter, the authors could perform a one-way MANOVA with the levels of credentials as the IV (0, 2, 4, 9) and three conceptually related DVs (Therapist's Qualifications, Friendliness, Energy) to evaluate the hypothesis that displaying more credentials would produce more positive ratings of the therapist. In terms of labeling the specific approach to MANOVA you have, the naming rules are identical in ANOVA and MANOVA (i.e., one-way, two-way/factorial/2 × 3, and so on) because the rules for labeling the IV side of the house are the same.

Mismatch Between MANOVA and ANOVA Findings

What about the mismatch where you do NOT have a significant multivariate effect but you have a significant univariate effect? Barbara Tabachnick and Linda Fidell (1983) commented that the individual univariate *F*s may be more powerful than the multivariate *F* (p. 249). In this case, you might say that something like "*a priori* hypotheses argued for an examination of the univariate findings" and examine them with caution (remember, you need *a priori* hypotheses to do this). Tabachnick and Fidell (1983) were cautious in this situation: "In this case, about the best one can do is report the nonsignificant multivariate *F* but offer the univariate and/or stepdown results as a guide to future research, with tentative interpretation" (p. 250).

Restrictions to Using MANOVA

Are there restrictions to using MANOVA? Yes. One is **multicollinearity**. When multicollinearity occurs, two variables are highly correlated with each other, rendering their unique contribution questionable. In this situation, you would eliminate one of those DVs from the analysis (Tabachnick & Fidell, 1983). As an example, what if a researcher administered the MRT (Vandenberg & Kuse, 1978; with 2 correct items

Multicollinearity: of concern in multivariate analysis when dependent or predictor variables are highly correlated (and in a sense redundant), rendering their unique contribution questionable.

per each of 20 problems) and scored subjects' performances three ways: no correction for guessing, 1 point off for each incorrect item, or the entire problem wrong (2 points off) if *either* item in the problem is incorrect. If the researcher were to perform a MANOVA with these conceptually related DVs, the researcher would have multicollinearity because these three ways of scoring the MRT are correlated above .9 with each other! Obviously there would be no point in including all three methods of scoring with this redundancy. What is the cut-off for judging that multicollinearity has occurred? Although there is no firm rule, many researchers seem to have settled for .70 and above.

Another concern is the presence of outliers, and Tabachnick and Fidell (1983) recommended running tests for outliers in each cell of the design and then that you "*transform or eliminate any significant outliers from MANOVA or MANCOVA analysis*" (p. 232, emphasis in original). An **outlier** is a data point at a distance from another data point that may indicate variability in measurement or experimental error or neither (chance occurrence). We will talk more about outliers in Chapter 10. There are other problems to consider such as unequal sample sizes, missing data, violations of homogeneity of variance, linearity, and small sample sizes, but these are beyond the scope of this chapter. The interested reader is directed to Tabachnick and Fidell (1983 or newer editions) or to Maurice Tatsuoka (1988).

Outlier:
data point at a distance from other data points; may indicate variability in measurement or experimental error or neither (chance occurrence).

REVISIT AND RESPOND

- When is MANOVA the appropriate approach with multiple dependent variables? If MANOVA is not appropriate, what analyses will you do?

FACTOR ANALYSIS: AN OVERVIEW

Factor analysis: data reduction technique that takes items and statistically clusters groups of items to differentiate them maximally.

Factor analysis is considered a data reduction strategy, which can be particularly useful in exploratory research, and it came out of Charles Spearman's work on human abilities (Tatsuoka, 1988). The studies on credentials (Devlin et al., 2009) and multicultural art (Devlin et al., 2013) mentioned in this chapter both used factor analyses to create the therapist-related dependent variables in the studies. Factor analysis can be used with a variety of kinds of stimuli, including written items and images. In addition to learning the steps in doing a factor analysis, it is important to know that such analyses require large samples (>100, with 1,000 considered "excellent"; Tabachnick & Fidell, 1983, p. 379).

The purpose in presenting an overview of factor analysis is to give you some idea how it might be used. An in-depth discussion of the specific steps involved is beyond the scope of this chapter, but after reading this section, you should have some sense of the situations in which the technique is appropriate. Recommended readings include Tabachnick and Fidell's book on multivariate statistics (1983) and Tatsuoka's (1988) book on multivariate analysis.

Speaking about principal components analysis or factor analysis, Tabachnick and Fidell (1983) stated that "the researcher is usually interested in discovering which variables in a data set form coherent subgroups that are relatively independent of one another" (p. 372). Tabachnick and Fidell (1983) and others have distinguished between **exploratory factor analysis (EFA)**, typically used in beginning investigations in a research area, and **confirmatory factor analysis (CFA)**, where CFA is "performed to test hypotheses about the structure of underlying processes" (p. 373). Tabachnick and Fidell emphasized that at the end of the process of factor analysis, the factors that emerge should make sense or hang together, and it is this "interpretability of results" (p. 373) that is as important as the specific procedural steps that have been followed in the computations.

Judging a Book by Its Cover: An Example of Factor Analysis

In Devlin (2008), the author was exploring the effect that medical building facades had on people's judgments of expected quality of care and expected comfort in that setting. She started out by taking pictures of the exteriors of medical buildings in Connecticut, Rhode Island, and Michigan, and she accumulated 34 images. Although she had some general idea about the ways in which these buildings differed (age, size, construction material, style), she wanted participants to make judgments for each building on the dimensions of (a) quality of care and (b) comfort in the environment. But she had far too many ratings to do all of the paired comparisons for 34 buildings, given concerns we have discussed about Type I error earlier in this chapter.

In this situation, given that the facades might differ in some consistent ways, Devlin (2008) decided to use factor analysis. By subjecting the ratings to factor analysis (separately for expected quality of care and comfort in the environment), she was able to reduce the ratings of the 34 images to 3 factors (groupings, clusters) for quality of care and to 4 factors for comfort in the environment. She labeled the quality of care factors: Traditional House Type (14 buildings); Brick Office Type (9 buildings); and Large Medical Type (4 buildings). You will notice that this building total (14 + 9 + 4) is only 27. As part of doing a factor analysis, not all items end up clearly "belonging to" a factor. These items are then eliminated according to specific rules for conducting factor analyses. Figure 7.6 shows images from the study for the three Quality of Care factors.

Exploratory factor analysis (EFA): typically used in the beginning stages of data reduction to uncover the relationships in a set of items.

Confirmatory factor analysis (CFA): used to verify a factor structure in a given set of variables.

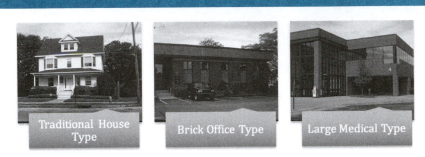

FIGURE 7.6 Example of Three Quality of Care Factors Used in Factor Analysis

Traditional House Type

Brick Office Type

Large Medical Type

Source: Reprinted with permission from Devlin, 2008.

As a technique, factor analysis is attempting to determine which stimuli (facades in this case) are rated in such a way that they cluster together but distinctively from other clusters. Each separate cluster would be a factor. If all facades were rated similarly for quality of care, there would be just one large factor. But you can see from the images that there was variability in the types of buildings and that the participants' ratings reflected those differences; hence, more than one factor emerged.

What can you do with these factors? You could use these factors as dependent variables in an analysis, which is what Devlin (2008) did, looking first at whether the ratings of the factors themselves differed significantly (a within subjects analysis, introduced in Chapter 3 and discussed in more detail in Chapter 8) and then at whether men and women differed in their ratings of the factors (a between subjects analysis). Factor scores to use as dependent variables are created by adding the ratings of the items (here buildings) that load, that is, belong to, a particular factor (according to a series of statistical rules about which items belong to that factor) and then dividing that sum by the number of items (buildings) that belong to a given factor. In her between subjects analysis, Devlin compared how men and women responded to the different factor types and found that men rated the Brick Office Type significantly higher than women did for the variable Quality of Care. Another way of saying that is that women were less impressed with the Brick Office Type!

REVISIT AND RESPOND

- Why is factor analysis described as a data reduction technique? Explain how factors can be used in data analyses.

Summary

This chapter covered important considerations for using between subjects designs, such as sensitivity of the IV, complexity of the design and consequences for sample size, and interaction effects. You saw that as the complexity of the design increased, you need to be concerned about the impact of multiple comparisons. In this chapter, you also learned the importance of nomenclature (names for IVs and levels; names for types of ANOVAs). Another emphasis was techniques for creating your own stimuli, whether text, image, or sound, including attention to copyright issues. We also covered using more than one DV, specifically the conditions for conducting MANOVA. An example of a factor analysis was provided to show how you might use this data reduction technique.

If you have not had time to consider them earlier, here is the list of **REVISIT and RESPOND** questions from this chapter:

- Explain the difference between a treatment and a level. What is another word for treatment? For level?
- Explain the relationship between the sensitivity of the IV and the number of cells required by the design. What are the advantages to having more levels of the IV? Any disadvantages?
- In your own words, explain what an interaction effect is.
- What kinds of challenges do you potentially face if you have a design with three IVs?
- What are the similarities and differences between a randomized groups design and a matched groups design?
- What are the differences between planned and unplanned comparisons? In general, which is preferable and why?
- What are some of the challenges in creating your own stimuli to use in research? Where can you look for free images to use in research? What is the purpose of a photo release form?
- When is MANOVA the appropriate approach with multiple dependent variables? If MANOVA is not appropriate, what analyses will you do?
- Why is factor analysis described as a data reduction technique? Explain how factors can be used in data analyses.

BUILD YOUR SKILLS

1. By this time in the course, if you are doing a research project, you will have decided on a research design and your measures. You should be able to fill out the following Project Update Form with the appropriate information:

Project Update Form

1. Research design (check one):

   Correlational (questions of the sample) _____

   Quasi-experimental (questions about pre-existing groups) _____

   Experimental (manipulation of variables and random assignment) _____

   Other (including combinations of the above; please specify): _____

2. Number of participants you want: _____

3. Source(s) of participants (where you will get them): _____

4. *If correlational* (scales correlated for sample):

   Hypothesis(ses): _____

   Names of scales: _____

5. *If quasi-experimental* (looking at pre-existing group differences [e.g., gender, class year] without random assignment to condition):

   Hypothesis(ses): _____

   Quasi-experimental variable(s)? _____

   Dependent variable scales/measures?: _____

6. If experimental:

   Hypothesis(ses):_____

   True independent variable(s): _____

   How many levels (of each IV) do you have? _____

   Any quasi-experimental variables? _____

   Dependent variable(s): _____

   Dependent variable scale/measures:_____

7. *Other* (if you have selected another research design, explain it here and present your hypotheses, variables, and measures, as appropriate).

2. The study by Goldberg (1968) earlier in this chapter investigated gender bias by changing the names of the authors on identical articles to see whether the name (Joan vs. John) affected judgments about the quality of the articles. It did. Using the format of a résumé, select an independent variable (but not gender) you think could be changed in a résumé to assess other aspects of bias and have at least two levels of the variable (i.e., at least two résumés). Among the possibilities are race, ethnicity, age, national origin, marital status, religion, weight, and income. You may think of others. You can use your own résumé as a starting point or find a résumé online (many websites offer examples). Communicate the essence of the variable without stating it explicitly; otherwise, it would create a demand characteristic. Think of three possible DVs to use to evaluate the impact of the résumé (e.g., perceived competence or likelihood to hire). Are these variables likely to be conceptually related?

---

⑤SAGE edge™

edge.sagepub.com/devlin

Sharpen your skills with SAGE edge!

SAGE edge for students provides a personalized approach to help you accomplish your coursework goals in an easy-to-use learning environment. You'll find action plans, mobile-friendly eFlashcards, and quizzes, as well as videos, web resources, and links to SAGE journal articles to support and expand on the concepts presented in this chapter.

WITHIN, MIXED, PRE–POST EXPERIMENTAL, AND SPECIALIZED CORRELATIONAL DESIGNS

CHAPTER HIGHLIGHTS

- Experimental Approaches
  - Within subjects designs: Overview
  - Practice, sensitization, carryover
  - Participant mortality
  - Kinds of research areas commonly addressed
  - Dealing with carryover
  - Complete counterbalancing, partial counterbalancing, Latin Square
  - Types of within subjects designs
  - Adding complexity through the number and levels of IVs
  - Mixed designs: Description and examples
  - Pre–post: Types
  - Single-group pre–post
  - Experimental-control pre–post
  - Solomon four-group design

Repeated measures: type of research design and analysis in which there are repeated measures for the same people.

Time-series analysis: analysis of data points collected repeatedly over time.

Longitudinal design: research design in which the same participants are followed over a long period of time (e.g., Terman's Termites).

Cross-sectional design: correlational approach, typically when different populations are measured at the same point in time (e.g., first year students and fourth year students).

- Specialized Correlational Designs
  - Time series and interrupted time series
  - Post-occupancy evaluation: Real-world example
  - Nonequivalent control group problems
  - Longitudinal designs: Advantages and disadvantages
  - Cross-sectional designs: Advantages and disadvantages
  - Cohort-sequential designs
  - Multiple method advantages

OVERVIEW

In Chapter 7, we focused on between-subjects designs, an experimental approach in which each participant is exposed to only one condition. A separate chapter was devoted to this topic because it is widely used in social science. It has the advantage of reducing the possibility that participants will detect what is being manipulated and consequently alter their behavior. But there are situations in which you *want* participants exposed to all conditions in a study, that is, for "everyone to see/do everything." This experimental approach is called a *within subjects design* (introduced in Chapter 3; also called **repeated measures)** and has the advantage that participants are their own controls. When participants are their own controls, a large source of error variance, the participant, is minimized. Despite several advantages to this approach, there are disadvantages, such as *carryover effects* (briefly mentioned in Chapter 7). This chapter will cover ways to address some aspects of carryover, for example through *counterbalancing* (that is, balancing out the order in which the conditions are experienced across participants; see Chapter 1). In addition, this chapter will cover *mixed designs* (also briefly mentioned in Chapter 7), an experimental approach that includes both within and between subjects components, as well as another experimental approach: the *pre–post design* (introduced in Chapter 6).

The chapter will conclude with a presentation of more specialized correlational approaches: **time-series analysis, longitudinal, cross-sectional**, and **cohort-sequential**. Longitudinal, cross-sectional, and cohort-sequential designs are sometimes referred to as *developmental designs*. By the end of this chapter, you will have a good sense of when and how these approaches are used in the social and behavioral sciences.

CHARACTERISTICS OF WITHIN SUBJECTS DESIGN: ADVANTAGES AND DISADVANTAGES

A distinct advantage of within subjects designs over between subjects designs is statistical—that a given level of power can be achieved with fewer participants; a within subjects study in which there are 10 participants who participate in two different treatments would require 20 participants if run as a between subjects design. Furthermore, because "treatment differences are not confounded with subject differences" (Greenwald, 1976, p. 315), when subjects serve as their own controls, within subjects designs also reduce the error variance that comes with individual differences in between subjects designs. In fact, some researchers have listed the statistical benefits as the primary advantage of within subjects designs. For example, Geoffrey Keppel (1982) stated that "control of subject heterogeneity—i.e., individual differences" as the primary advantage (p. 369). There also may be savings in time (e.g., related to not having to repeat instructions in the case of humans) and pretraining preparation (e.g., in the case of animals) when using within subjects designs (Keppel, 1982).

In a classic article, Anthony Greenwald (1976) discussed within subjects designs with the title: "Within-Subjects Designs: To Use or Not to Use?" What is helpful about this article is that Greenwald focused more on psychological than on statistical considerations in the choice of research design. In Greenwald's emphasis on psychological effects, he cautioned us that exposure to more than one condition (context) can modify the impact of the treatment; the result of multiple exposure is sometimes called a **range effect** (Poulton, 1973; for interested readers, Poulton's paper contains a table listing a series of range effects found in the literature). Geenwald discussed three categories of **context effects**: Practice, Sensitization, and Carryover (p. 314). Context effects are a much more serious threat to validity in within than in between subjects designs. Nevertheless, a point Greenwald made, following other researchers, is that the use of a between subjects design *does not guarantee* the elimination of context effects. Experience outside the lab (i.e., extra-laboratory experience) could contribute to the contextual experience of the participant, or a context could be established for a particular treatment level that was absent in other treatment levels.

With regard to **practice effects**, sometimes called **transfer effects**, within subjects designs are most suitable for situations when what you want to study *is* the effect of practice (such as studies on learning). But if practice is not a focus, then a within subjects

Cohort-sequential design: research design that combines both cross-sectional and longitudinal components; cohorts are selected at different points in time and followed longitudinally; used to address drawbacks to cross-sectional design.

Range effect: effect of multiple exposures (e.g., in within subjects design).

Context effects: effects of practice, sensitization, and carryover; part of within subjects design when people are exposed to multiple conditions.

Practice effects: one of the three context effects that may operate in within subjects designs.

approach would only make sense with certain modifications. These modifications might include providing the treatments in different orders across participants, or having participants first practice to reach a criterion of mastery, after which additional practice experienced in the treatment levels would not be such a concern.

Sensitization is another potential problem. Greenwald (1976) used the example of a study of illumination on productivity, in which worker productivity is assessed under different lighting levels. The problem is that workers may detect that different lighting levels are being used and thus respond differently than if the worker were exposed to only one lighting level. Suggestions are to alter the treatment levels (here lighting) gradually to avoid detection and/or to vary other aspects of the work environment systematically to avoid the sole focus on the treatment variable (here lighting). Greenwald also noted that sensitization could be useful in studies that looked at the participants' abilities to detect differences, as is likely to be the case in psychophysiological research, which combines a psychological manipulation (independent variable or IV) with a physiological dependent variable (DV; e.g., heart rate or blood pressure).

The Challenges of Carryover

Regarding carryover, you are concerned that the impact of one treatment lingers, or carries over to, subsequent treatments. If we were interested in the effect of doses of caffeine on alertness, you could see that a first administration of caffeine (e.g., one ounce of espresso) would carry over to the next administration (e.g., two ounces of espresso) and likely alter performance on some cognitive measure of alertness (e.g., word recall). Greenwald (1976) noted that carryover effects can sometimes be addressed by separating the administrations in time.

What kind of time separation do you think might be necessary in the example of caffeine intake? One possibility is having participants return on the following day for their second administration of caffeine, an approach that would work if there were no practice effects involved in the cognitive task (we would use a parallel form of the word list) and if you could actually get the participants to return. Student participants recruited from a participant pool do not always return in multiple session projects (see Chapter 9 on obtaining participants). When intercondition carryover occurs (that is, the effects of one administration carryover to the next administration), certain kinds of research topics are more suitable than others. Greenwald noted that in these situations, studies on learning are prominent (p. 318).

A particularly problematic form of carryover is known as "**differential carryover**" (Keppel, 1982, p. 371), which cannot be addressed through counterbalancing, which is having different orders of administration across participants (note, counterbalancing will be discussed in more detail later in the chapter). In differential carryover, the carryover effects vary depending on what has preceded them and on what is being tested in a particular condition. Keppel commented that separating the sessions by time, to allow any impact of the preceding condition to fade, is the best way to deal with these carryover effects. You could see this approach working in the example of different doses of espresso. But as mentioned, when you separate conditions by time to reduce the possible carryover effects, you may lose participants (they don't return).

》 Try This Now

What kinds of conditions can you think of where the exposure is not reversible?

Some treatment effects may not be reversible, such as exposure to a particular kind of therapy intervention. In this case, putting more time between this experience and another condition will not eliminate the effect of that therapy intervention. Thus, not all research is suitable for the within subjects approach.

External Validity in Within Subjects Approaches

In using an example from persuasion research, Greenwald (1976) noted that researchers often use between subjects design to keep communication messages (e.g., from an expert vs. a nonexpert source) separate to assess their independent effects. He argued that in terms of external validity, a within subjects design might be more appropriate because in the real world, we are typically bombarded by competing messages. Thus, the within subjects design should not be rejected out of hand. The choice of research design always returns to the question of what the researcher wants to learn.

Subject Mortality

Subject mortality or *experimental mortality* (when participants drop out; see Chapter 3) is a problem in between subjects designs, particularly if there is differential dropout (more subjects drop out of one or more conditions than the others). In the case of within subjects designs, differential dropout is not a problem (because participants are in all conditions), but there is a problem in that when any participant drops out, you have a loss of power because each participant is in all of those conditions.

Writing in the context of research in behavioral economics, such as willingness to pay studies (studies where participants are asked the maximum amount they are willing to pay for something), Gary Charness, Uri Gneezy, and Michael Kuhn (2012) listed the advantages of within subjects design: eliminating random assignment as a criterion for internal validity, increasing statistical power, and alignment with theory in which humans operate within markets with multiple prices. As disadvantages, they cited "a slew of confounds" that arise from exposing people to more than one treatment. Like Greenwald (1976), they argued that rather than simply accepting this laundry list of positives and negatives, it is always the research question that determines the research design.

Additional concerns about within subjects designs are reminiscent of Donald Campbell and Julian Stanley's (1963) list of threats to internal validity (see Chapter 3), such as maturation, which includes influences like fatigue. You can see that if participants are asked to do a series of trials, they may grow tired, and they may experience a decrease in motivation such that their effort in the later trials is lower than their effort in the initial trials. Changes in the physical environment or instrumentation might also differ across trials, which would introduce error even with the same participants.

REVISIT AND RESPOND

- Describe a statistical advantage to using within subjects design. Explain what practice, sensitization, and carryover mean in the context of within subjects design. Explain why research on learning is well suited for within subjects design.

TYPES OF RESEARCH QUESTIONS MORE COMMONLY ASKED IN WITHIN SUBJECTS DESIGNS

You might be likely to use within subjects design if you were interested in carryover effects, such as studies on learning. Keppel (1982) stated that within subjects designs comprise a large portion of research in behavioral science and are the "obvious choice" if you want to measure changes in behavior related to "learning, transfer of training, forgetting, attitude change" while being "particularly efficient and sensitive," which is contrasted to the parallel between subjects designs (p. 365).

Another use of within subjects design (referred to as repeated measures) is by researchers who study attitudes. These researchers may often use polls that were taken before an expected decision is handed down (e.g., the O. J. Simpson verdict; Nier, Mottola, & Gaertner, 2000) and then compare the before-and-after measures. For example,

Jason Nier et al. assessed racial attitudes one week before and nine weeks after the O. J. Simpson verdict was handed down. In this research, participants' attitudes toward racism (measured using the Modern Racism Scale) were assessed at these three different points in time; time was treated as a repeated measure.

COUNTERBALANCING

One of the biggest challenges in within subjects designs is the problem of carryover effects. If possible (that is, if there are no problems with differential carryover), researchers use various approaches to balance the order in which participants experience the conditions. This approach is called *counterbalancing*.

Complete Counterbalancing

In **complete counterbalancing**, all possible sequences of your treatments are used and the same number of times (often just once). Complete counterbalancing is not a problem if you have few conditions (e.g., five conditions would yield 5 × 4 × 3 × 2 × 1 or 120 orders), but you can see that if you added more conditions or a second variable, complete counterbalancing would require a large number of participants. Note that although the concept of counterbalancing is usually applied to the conditions or treatment levels, it may also apply to the order in which the dependent variables are completed. If you have more than one dependent variable, you might be concerned that answering a particular DV where the content of the questions is pretty transparent might bias answers to subsequent DVs. If you want to guard against the possibility, you would counterbalance the order of administration of the DVs.

Partial Counterbalancing

In **partial counterbalancing**, an approximation to counterbalancing is used but not every possible treatment order. Typically you would use as many random sequences as there were participants available, and you would randomly assign a different sequence to each participant. There are online programs that will create a random order of numbers for you (e.g., **http://www.endmemo.com/math/randomorder.php**).

Latin Square

Latin Square is a particular kind of counterbalancing in which each treatment appears in each row and column one time (i.e., there are as many orders as treatments). Thus, a Latin Square in which there are five treatments can be illustrated as follows (see Figure 8.1).

Complete counter-balancing: counterbalancing in which all possible orders are used.

Partial counter-balancing: presenting some but not all possible sequences of material to control for order effects; typically random orders are used, a different sequence for each participant.

Latin Square: approach to counterbalancing where each treatment appears in each row and each column one time, i.e., where there are as many orders as treatments.

FIGURE 8.1 Example of a Latin Square

	1st	2nd	3rd	4th	5th
1st	A	B	C	D	E
2nd	B	C	D	E	A
3rd	C	D	E	A	B
4th	D	E	A	B	C
5th	E	A	B	C	D

If we focus on treatment A, we can see it appears once in the first, second, third, fourth, and fifth rows and once in the first, second, third, fourth, and fifth columns. The same statement can be made for each of the other treatments (B, C, D, and E).

REVISIT AND RESPOND

- What is the purpose of counterbalancing a design? What are the differences between complete counterbalancing, partial counterbalancing, and Latin Square design? When would you use each of them?

SIMPLE AND COMPLEX WITHIN SUBJECTS DESIGNS

If you think back to the discussion of between subjects designs in Chapter 7, the most basic design was a single variable with two levels. The same is true of the within subjects situation. Consider a within subjects design where you have a single variable (exercise) with two levels (Stairmaster and Rowing Machine). Your DV is satisfaction with exercising. Every participant would complete these two levels (two types of machines) with the DV measured *after use of each kind of machine*. Normally, to guard against order effects, use of the Stairmaster and the Rowing Machine would be counterbalanced, and then the scores by level would be averaged. Some researchers might also make order an IV (discussed later in the section on mixed designs).

ADDING COMPLEXITY TO WITHIN SUBJECTS DESIGNS

You can make your within subjects design more complex in two ways, in the same way you could for between subjects designs. As in the case of between subjects designs, adding complexity will increase what you learn about the subject under investigation. You can add more levels to a single variable or you can add more variables. Let's do both.

Consider two variables (exercise machine, music) where one of those variables (exercise machine) has three levels (Stairmaster, Rowing Machine, Elliptical) and the other has two (classical music, pop music). Remember, every participant needs to do all of these conditions. Assume the dependent variable is satisfaction with exercising. We have the repeated measures of satisfaction with exercising as a function of the two types of variables (exercise machine type, music type). We would thus be able to see which condition(s) produced higher levels of satisfaction with exercising.

Remember that participants would experience all six combinations of these two variables (see Figure 8.2). But the order in which the participants experience these conditions is obviously an issue because there would be carryover effects, such as fatigue. For that reason we would need to have counterbalancing.

FIGURE 8.2 Example of a More Complex Within Subjects Design With Six Combinations of Two Variables

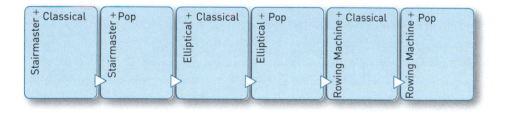

>> **Try This Now**

Based on your understanding of counterbalancing discussed earlier in this chapter, would we be likely to use *complete* counterbalancing?

Complete counterbalancing would require $6 \times 5 \times 4 \times 3 \times 2 \times 1$ (720) participants. No, given the large number of participants this would require, we would probably not use that approach.

> ### ≫ Try This Now
>
> What kind of partial counterbalancing would you recommend?

Even with partial counterbalancing, consider the fatigue that this experiment would produce if run in a single session. For that reason, we might intersperse a week between sessions and have participants use only one type of exercise machine per week.

If you add more variables, you can see how a design would rapidly increase in complexity. Complexity can be considered added to the IV side of the house in the case of analysis of variance (ANOVA; as in the exercise example) and added to the DV side of the house in the case of multivariate ANOVA (MANOVA).

Within Subjects MANOVA

In the case of within subjects MANOVA, the dependent variables that everyone assesses are distinct but conceptually related (refer to Chapter 7). You may have a research project in which you want to know whether the same participants respond to these related measures differently. The appropriate analysis would be a within subjects MANOVA. In Ann Devlin's (2008) study (see Chapter 7), she initially wanted to know whether her participants judged the perceived quality of care to be different as reflected in the photographs of 34 medical buildings. In a within subjects analysis such as this, "everyone rated everything" (the 34 photographs of medical buildings). For this study, the ratings of the 34 buildings were subjected to a factor analysis that yielded the three factors for quality of care (Traditional House Type, Brick Office Type, Large Medical Type; see Figure 7.6). In a within subjects (repeated measures) analysis, Devlin found that the quality of each building type was significantly different from the other two, with the Large Medical Type rated the highest, followed by the Traditional House Type, in turn followed by the Brick Office Type.

MIXED DESIGNS

In a mixed design, the research includes both a within subjects component and a between subjects components. Mixed design should not be confused with mixed methods (i.e., combining quantitative and qualitative approaches; see Chapter 6). A common way in which mixed design is used is when the order of presentation of stimuli is counterbalanced, and then order is evaluated as a between subjects component in an otherwise within subjects design. Marc Berman, John Jonides, and Stephen Kaplan (2008) used a mixed design with counterbalancing as the between subjects IV to investigate exposure to nature versus urban images on attention restoration. Following work in attention restoration theory (Kaplan, 1995), Berman et al. were interested in whether exposure to 50 images of nature (from Nova Scotia) could restore directed attention more effectively than could exposure to 50 images of urban environments (scenes from Detroit, Chicago, and Ann Arbor). Participants either saw nature images Week 1 followed by urban images Week 2 or vice versa. There were no effects of order of presentation, and once that was determined, the authors could combine the results from the two orders.

The results from Berman et al. (2008) found some support for their hypotheses, in that performance on the backward digit span, a test of directed attention, improved after viewing nature, but not urban, images. Notice that not only did they use counterbalancing of the content of the pictures, but they also separated the trials by a week to handle fatigue. Viewing and rating 50 images, plus completing the attention network test (which consists of more than 250 trials) and the backward digit span, as well as a mood assessment, could be exhausting. Separating the picture exposure by a week follows one of the practices recommended to deal with potential carryover effects.

Other ways in which a mixed design is often used is the situation where one variable of interest might have irreversible carryover effects and would need to be approached as a between subjects variable. Consider comparing the use of acupuncture versus spinal adjustment in the presence of different types of music (classical, pop) on pain perception before, during, and after treatment. You could counterbalance the order of presentation of the music across participants, but the clinical intervention (acupuncture or spinal adjustment) would need to be a between subjects variable because either of those clinical treatments might produce irreversible (one hopes positive) changes.

REVISIT AND RESPOND

- List two ways you can add complexity to a within subjects design. What is a mixed design?

PRE–POST DESIGNS: CHARACTERISTICS

Pre–post designs are designs in which you have a measurement, an intervention occurs, and then you repeat the measurement. Pre–post design falls in the category of experimental design, in the view of Campbell and Stanley (1963). There is control over the introduction of the intervention, and you use random assignment to condition (as soon as you move beyond the single-group pre–post design; see next section).

» **Try This Now**

Before reading further, pre–post design should remind you of yet another kind of research approach we have covered (in this chapter). Can you identify it?

Pre–post measures are essentially repeated measures in that you repeat measurements, typically at two points. Like repeated measures, cautions about carryover effects apply, particularly the idea that exposure to the preassessment may in some way change the way participants respond to the intervention.

TYPES OF PRE–POST DESIGNS

Pre–post designs come in a variety of forms, with associated strengths and weaknesses. The following section will cover some of these designs, with associated strengths and weaknesses. The reader wanting a more comprehensive list of pre–post designs is directed to Campbell and Stanley (1963).

Single-Group Pre–Post Design

In this situation, there is no control group, and participants (presumably from your participant pool) complete measures before and after your intervention. The threats to internal validity in this approach are obvious. For that reason, one could argue that there is no point in using a **single-group pre–post design**. In fact, Campbell and Stanley (1963) stated, "such studies have such a total absence of control as to be of almost no scientific value" (p. 6), and they considered this approach a "pre-experimental" design. Campbell and Stanley (1963) represented this design as "O X O" where "O" represents measurement and "X" represents a treatment. That representational system of "X" and "O" is incorporated in Figures 8.3 and 8.4.

Single-group pre–post design: called "pre-experimental" by Campbell and Stanley (1963); measures participants before and after an intervention, without a control group.

Experimental-Control Pre–Post Design

The next step is to add a control group, which would complete the pretest and posttest measures but would have no intervention. This approach is diagrammed in Figure 8.3.

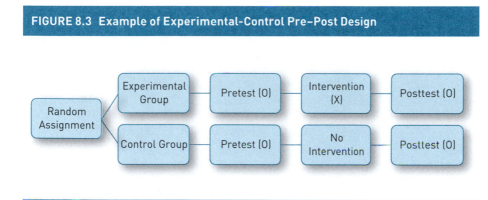

FIGURE 8.3 Example of Experimental-Control Pre–Post Design

> ❯❯ **Try This Now**
>
> Do you see any problems with this approach?

Solomon Four-Group Design

Using a pretest may sensitize participants and change their behavior in a way that it becomes difficult to separate the effects of the intervention from the effects of the pretest plus intervention (that is, the pretest may enhance the effect of the intervention so that you see a difference on the posttest scores, but it would not appear if you simply had the intervention by itself). The solution? The solution is the Solomon four-group design (introduced in Chapter 3), what we might call the gold standard for this kind of research design. This approach was recommended by Campbell and Stanley (1963) in situations where you want to be able to compare the measures before and after the intervention (e.g., SAT scores before and after the experimental group took a practice course).

In Figure 8.4, which diagrams the Solomon four-group design, you can see that the controls represented in Group 3 and Group 4 parallel Group 1 and Group 2, but without the pretest. The Solomon four-group design is expensive. In addition to the number of participants you will need, you also need to administer the pretests in parallel (same timing for Groups 1 and 2) and the posttests in parallel (same timing) for all four groups.

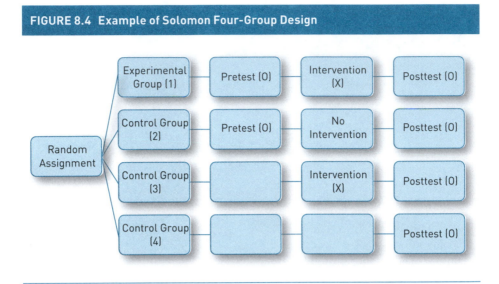

FIGURE 8.4 Example of Solomon Four-Group Design

REVISIT AND RESPOND

- Why would Campbell and Stanley (1963) label the single-group pre–post design a "pre-experimental" design? What are the advantages and disadvantages of the Solomon four-group design?

SPECIALIZED CORRELATIONAL DESIGNS

Up to this point in Chapter 8, we have covered experimental designs (within, mixed, and pre–post). Now we will turn to some specialized correlational designs, many of which emphasize the idea of taking measurements over multiple points in time.

TIME-SERIES AND INTERRUPTED TIME-SERIES DESIGN

In time-series designs, you have many observations on the same variable that are conducted consecutively over a period of time (Shadish, Cook, & Campbell, 2002). Examples of measures would be "a learning curve, accident rates over a number of years, or monthly admission to mental hospitals" (Corsini, 2002, p. 1004). Although there does not seem to be a precise number (it depends on the variability in the data), the sense from reading the literature is that time-series analyses require frequent measurement; William Shadish et al. (2002) pointed to 100 observations (data points) as usually recommended.

Interrupted Time Series

In the interrupted time-series approach, you have measurement before and after "something" occurs, and often that "something" occurs naturally. Such events may be highly visible (e.g., natural disasters such as Hurricane Katrina; social upheaval such as the fall of the Berlin wall; or criminal events such as the Sandy Hook massacre), but the events may also be much less initially noticeable to the general public, such as the elimination of laws prohibiting selling alcohol on Sunday (in some states).

The "interruption" may be unanticipated (in the case of natural disaster) or intentional, such as installing new security cameras to monitor an area in a residence hall where vandalism occurs. Groups that tend to be naturally occurring, such as people who live in a flood plain or tornado alley or in a community where a major crime has occurred, can provide useful opportunities to understand the impact of these changes using interrupted time-series research.

Interrupted time-series analysis is an approach often used by policy makers in a wide range of fields, from health to economics. Consider how many research questions are related to policy changes, from the number of deaths in car accidents before and after seatbelt laws were passed, to graduation rates related to the introduction of school reform such as the No Child Left Behind (NCLB) Act of 2001, to diagnoses of fetal alcohol syndrome before and after warning labels were added to alcoholic beverages.

> **Interrupted time-series analysis:** quantitative research approach in which multiple assessments are made before and after the occurrence of an event (e.g., passing of legislation).

STRENGTHS AND WEAKNESSES OF THIS APPROACH

The strength of a time-series approach is most often the naturally occurring groups, that is, people (and their behaviors) in their natural surroundings outside of the research laboratory. In the case of the interrupted time series, you also can pinpoint the date where the intervention or event occurred. Thus, a strength of this approach is its ecological validity. The weakness of the approach, and it is substantial, is the threat to internal validity created by this approach. Without a control group, how can you attribute any change in the "after" measurements to the event or intervention that has occurred? Many researchers using time-series analyses tend to approach the answer to that question statistically, and the interrupted time-series approach requires a substantial number of data points to meet the requirements of the statistical analysis. What researchers look for is a different slope in the plotted data points after the event when compared to the pre-event slope.

Figure 8.5 presents an interrupted time-series study from the Netherlands in which two events were introduced: (1) guidelines to help general practitioners (GPs) give advice for smoking cessation were introduced in 2007, and (2) complete insurance coverage for those undergoing smoking cessation treatment was introduced in 2011. The researchers visually inspected the time-series plots and used regression analyses that were segmented. They were examining whether there was a significant change in the slope and level of the smoking cessation medications that were prescribed and in the prevalence of smoking in the population (Verbiest et al., 2013).

What you can probably see (and they report) is that there was no significant impact of the introduction of the guidelines for the GPs on the number of dispensed smoking cessation medications. Nevertheless, when the insurance coverage was introduced, there was a drop in prevalence of smoking and an increase in prescriptions written for smoking cessation medications. Then, when the insurance coverage was eliminated, there was a rise in the prevalence of smoking and a drop in smoking medication prescriptions. What you could probably recommend on the basis of this study is the importance of insurance coverage if you want to reduce the prevalence of smoking in that population.

Clearly it is easier to use the interrupted time-series approach if you know when the "event" will occur, but in the case of natural disasters, that is unlikely to be the case.

FIGURE 8.5 Interrupted Time-Series Study on Smoking Prevalence

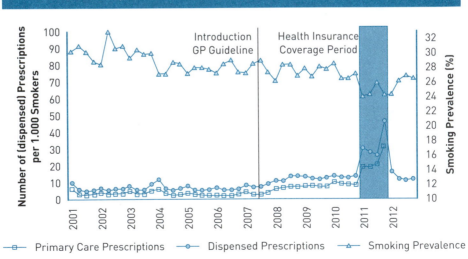

Source: Verbiest et al. (2013). An increase in primary care prescriptions of stop-smoking medication as a result of health insurance coverage in the Netherlands: Population based study. *Addiction, 108*, 2183–2192. doi:10.1111/add.12289 © 2013 Society for the Study of Addiction.

Still, there may be archival data, such as Gallup poll data, that could be used to compare changes in attitudes that can be tracked in relationship to the occurrence of a particular event. In the Marjolein Verbiest et al. (2013) research on smoking prevalence, they used national databases that contained the number of prescriptions written by GPs and the number of prescriptions that were dispensed in outpatient pharmacies. They also had access to the Dutch Continuous Survey of Smoking Habits (DCSSH) that targets individuals at least 15 years of age. What this research example illustrates is that it is possible to do interrupted time-series work if you have the appropriate databases.

WHEN IS THIS APPROACH USED?

The interrupted time-series approach has been tracked in such areas as attorney advertising, consumer product safety, epidemiology, gun control, workplace safety, and television (Shadish et al., 2002). This approach also has been used a good deal by policy makers (e.g., to evaluate the impact of legislation such as seatbelt use). At the same time, the approach probably had the strongest claim to validity in the biological and physical sciences (Campbell & Stanley, 1963), where it was a typical approach to experimentation in the nineteenth century. As Campbell and Stanley pointed out, such use in the physical sciences makes sense; they gave the example of dipping an iron bar in a bath of nitric acid and recording the loss in weight (p. 37). You can be pretty sure that the event (exposure to nitric acid) caused the change in weight in the iron bar. In the social and behavioral sciences, many alternative explanations exist for every behavior that occurs. For that reason, interrupted time-series analysis involves many observations to establish first the stable level of responding before the event and then reveal any change in the slope of responding after the event.

REVISIT AND RESPOND

- What kinds of research questions seem well suited for interrupted times-series design? Why does this approach involve so many points of measurement? Where would you look to find data for this approach?

REAL-WORLD CHALLENGES: POSTOCCUPANCY EVALUATION (POE)

When resources (time and money) permit, architects and designers may conduct what is called a **postoccupancy evaluation (POE)**, essentially determining how a building

Postoccupancy evaluation (POE): analysis often done by architects to evaluate building performance (how it functions); usually only posttest.

performs (i.e., functions) after it is completed (and occupied; e.g., Zimring & Reizenstein, 1980). The POE approach has been applied to renovations as well as new construction. This may sound like the pre–post experimental design, but it is not an experiment (no random assignment). In some situations, what happens would not impress us as research because many POEs take the form of a posttest-only assessment. That is, architects do some kind of assessment of building performance, both for the physical metrics of the building and for the psychological responses of the occupants, after the building is completed.

The research approach may improve if measures are taken both before and after the construction or renovation takes place. For example, there has been considerable interest in the effect of open plan offices (without permanent walls) on the productivity of office workers, and since the open plan was introduced in the late 1960s, comparisons have been made of workers who moved from traditional offices to open plan offices (e.g., Oldham & Brass, 1979). These studies, however, still lack aspects we consider essential to rule out alternative hypotheses: random assignment to condition and a control group.

Nonequivalent Control Group

Nonequivalent control group: in a pre–post design, use of a control group like the intervention group to the extent possible but not randomly assigned.

The approach typified by the POE still lacks a control group. To try to remedy that situation, researchers may try to find what is called a **nonequivalent control group**, that is, people like those undergoing the change but without the intervention. In the case of the office example, you are looking for a group that did not move to a new open plan office but in other ways was like the group that moved. If a company had multiple office locations, it is possible that you might find such a nonequivalent group.

You still lack random assignment to condition, but at least you are trying to look at what happens to similar others not undergoing the change. As you might imagine, finding a reasonable nonequivalent control group is difficult. In the case of the POEs, you are trying to find "equivalent people" in "equivalent buildings" with "equivalent organizational structure" where a renovation has not occurred.

A very real problem for researchers is the challenge of doing high-quality research in *field settings* (see Chapter 3). Architects and designers face this problem whenever they want to evaluate the effect of actual buildings that people occupy using a POE.

REVISIT AND RESPOND

- What is a postoccupancy evaluation (POE)? What is a nonequivalent control group, and why are these hard to find in the real world?

LONGITUDINAL AND CROSS-SECTIONAL DESIGNS

The book has emphasized the idea that the research question directs the research design. Some kinds of research questions/topics are particularly well suited for specific research designs. For example, studies involving learning are a good match for within subjects design, as mentioned earlier in this chapter.

When the topic is development, two approaches are common. These approaches are longitudinal and cross-sectional. In the longitudinal approach, you follow the same people over time. In the cross-sectional approach, different people typically varying in age or some other important characteristic are assessed at the same point in time. As an example of these different approaches, consider college students. Many students undergo transformation during their college experience, perhaps beginning with a lack of clarity about career plans, but graduating with a sense of the career they want to pursue in life. It would be informative to study this transformation, which would be appropriate as a longitudinal project. Unfortunately, this kind of examination is impossible in a single semester. When researchers cannot conduct longitudinal studies but want to contrast individuals who represent different points along a developmental spectrum, they often use a cross-sectional approach.

ADVANTAGES AND DISADVANTAGES OF THE LONGITUDINAL APPROACH

One primary advantage to the longitudinal approach over the cross-sectional approach is that you can be more sure that the changes you see are associated with the maturation of the individuals. One well-known longitudinal study (Wisconsin Longitudinal Study; WLS) involved a random sample of more than 10,000 men and women and one of their randomly selected siblings who graduated from high schools in Wisconsin in 1957 (Herd, Card, & Roan, 2014). This study focused on psychological, sociological, and physical changes over the lives of these individuals. The WLS has been described as "the most comprehensive long-standing cohort study currently in existence" (Herd et al., 2014, p. 36).

Initially the focus of WLS was more on understanding what influenced status attainment (what happens to people) over the course of their lives. As the cohort has aged, there has been more emphasis on health, and recently genetic data (through saliva samples) have been added to the database. These data will allow researchers (Herd et al., 2014) to consider inter-relationships among genes, environment, and behavior. Among the important findings of this study are the negative effects of childhood physical abuse and limited resources on health in later life. Funded by the National Institute on Aging since 1991, the dataset can be downloaded for free (**http://www.ssc.wisc.edu/wlsresearch/**).

Disadvantages to the longitudinal approach are time and money. These are significant challenges. Many researchers do not have the time to invest in longitudinal research. Not only is it expensive in terms of the researcher's time, but it may also affect decisions about the researcher's career if the results of longitudinal studies take years to appear in publications. In addition, longitudinal studies may suffer from experimental mortality in that participants may be unwilling to continue to be "measured" year after year. There are some notable exceptions. In Chapter 3, we talked about Lewis Terman's study of the gifted and talented. This research constitutes a famous exception to the usual pattern of experimental mortality in longitudinal research. Terman's Termites, as Terman's participants came to be called, were initially studied in the 1920s as children but remained in the study over their adult lives (Leslie, 2000; Terman & Oden, 1959). The WLS study also appears to have had high **response rates**, with actual mortality (death) the leading cause of attrition (Herd et al., 2014). In 2014, the response rate (contacted either by phone or mail) was 78%.

> **Response rate:** percentage of people who respond to a survey; usually calculated by the number of people who responded divided by the number invited.

More typical of experimental mortality is a study in which college students, who participated in an outdoor orientation program during first year orientation and those who did not (a nonequivalent control group), were followed over four years. The purpose was to assess the relationship of that initial experience with nature to college adjustment. Participants completed measures before and after the orientation experience, at the end of their first year and at the end of their senior year. Experimental mortality was a reality in the research, and it increased over time. Approximately 47% of the outdoor program group and 46% of the control group did not complete the final surveys (Devlin, 1996).

In addition to the concern with resources and experimental mortality, there are other challenges in longitudinal studies. One of these issues involves measurement [i.e., Campbell & Stanley's (1963) idea of testing; see Chapter 3] in which these repeated measurements may in fact affect responses to what is being measured. Participants may be sensitive to the way they answer questions and may adjust their answers over time to present consistency. At their core, longitudinal designs are correlational, and although they may provide access to understanding that is not available through any other approach, there can be no causal conclusions.

Examples of Research Questions in Longitudinal Designs

Research in developmental psychology depends heavily on the longitudinal approach. In addition to the WLS, other well-known examples of research done with this framework include answering such questions as whether personality traits remain stable over one's

life (e.g., Roberts & DelVecchio, 2000). In an important group of longitudinal studies, Gary Evans and his colleagues have been investigating the effects of poverty-related
stress on children's development (e.g., Doan, Dich, & Evans, 2014; Evans, 2003; Evans &
Cassells, 2014; Evans & Kim, 2012). Participants were recruited from public schools
and cooperative extension programs in upstate New York. An important longitudinal
research question in this research program is the effect of living in poverty on **allostatic
load.** What is allostatic load? We have hormones that mediate our responses to stress, and
although these are adaptive for survival, if they are active over extended periods of time,
they "exact a price" and can negatively affect us; this is known as allostatic load (McEwen,
2000). Many physiological processes are affected, including "cardiovascular, metabolic,
immune, and brain functioning" (Doan et al., 2014, p. 1403).

    As a reminder, longitudinal research is extremely resource intensive. The Doan
et al. (2014) study reported on participants who were collected in three waves, about ages
9, 13, and 17. The study involved both assent (from the youth) and consent (from the
guardians) as well as payment for participation (see Chapter 4 about these ethical issues).
Two researchers independently interviewed the mothers and youth in the participants'
homes. Research of this kind requires commitment, perseverance, and resources.

    Many of the major ongoing longitudinal research programs focus heavily on children
and youth, which makes sense because a primary focus of longitudinal research is the
process of development. The U.S. government sponsors the Early Childhood Longitudinal Study (ECLS) program that investigates children's development, their readiness
for school, and their experience in school (**https://nces.ed.gov/ecls/**). The approach
uses **cohorts** (people having something in common, e.g., age assessed over time) and
follows them from birth to kindergarten (one cohort) and from kindergarten to eighth
grade (a second cohort). Case-level data, with restrictions about sample size reporting
(to make sure individuals can't be identified), are available to qualified researchers,
whose papers must first be evaluated by the National Center for Education Statistics
(NCES) Data Security Office. Data at a higher level of aggregation are available to the
general public in the Data Analysis System (**http://nces.ed.gov/das/**). Fortunately for
researchers, the U.S. government is shouldering some of the cost of creating these valuable databases.

Successful Longitudinal Research: Practical Issues

Just as we saw earlier when talking about gaining entrance to settings in ethnography (see
Chapter 6), similar recommendations regarding successful research programs appear for
longitudinal research. Jennie Grammer, Jennifer Coffman, Peter Ornstein, and Frederick
Morrison (2013), whose work was on children's cognitive development, provided several
recommendations in this regard:

Allostatic load:
with repeated
exposure, the
stress on the
body negatively
affects
physiological
processes.

Cohort: group
of people
that share
a particular
characteristic,
such as age.

a) building and maintaining good relationships with communities of research participants, b) working to develop a skilled staff of researchers, c) conducting child-centered investigations, and d) giving back to the individuals who have participated in your research. (pp. 522–523)

They also reminded us that longitudinal research requires different skill sets. Collecting data is certainly one aspect, but keeping track of all of the data is important as well. In that regard, they suggested that finding and keeping highly trained research assistants is essential.

Grammer et al. (2013) provided practical advice about how to attract people to participate in research, for example, by having a project logo that captures attention and is easy to remember (and could be featured on free t-shirts and tote bags) and refrigerator magnets that have the study's contact information. They also mentioned using social media and having a Web presence.

Other often overlooked advice Grammer et al. (2013) provided (that could apply to many research projects, longitudinal or not) involves making participants comfortable, for example, creating research space that is welcoming, and trying to address the kinds of barriers to participation people face (like babysitters and transportation costs). They recommended offering research sessions at different times of the day and days of the week to accommodate diverse schedules (p. 524). Grammer et al. reminded us about the perils of parking, particularly on college campuses, where it is hard to know where you are allowed to park. As a researcher, you can address this obstacle by providing reserved parking spaces for participants or making sure that parking passes are handed out to participants by campus security when participants arrive on campus.

Similar to the recommendations made in doing ethnographic research (see Chapter 6), "giving back" is an important aspect of longitudinal research and can involve tokens of appreciation such as certificates of participation (Grammer et al., 2013, p. 525).

REVIST AND RESPOND

- What is the chief benefit of longitudinal designs, in your view? What issues prevent researchers from undertaking longitudinal research? As a researcher, what can you do to reduce the likelihood that participants will drop out of a longitudinal study? What specific steps can you take to make participants welcome?

ADVANTAGES AND DISADVANTAGES OF THE CROSS-SECTIONAL APPROACH

The clearest advantage of the cross-sectional approach is savings in time and researcher effort. Cross-sectional research can be described as a quasi-experimental approach because you are focusing on naturally occurring group characteristics (typically age is the focus) that you want to compare at the same point in time. Still, a quasi-experimental approach is fundamentally correlational, as was discussed in Chapter 3. Like longitudinal designs, cross-sectional designs tell us about relationships, not about causality. Furthermore, a significant disadvantage of the cross-sectional approach is the possibility of what are known as generational or **cohort effects**. As noted previously, a cohort is a group of individuals that share something, usually defined in terms of a similar age and set of experiences. An explanation of cohort effects is provided next.

Cohort effects: differences attributable to experiencing a particular generation.

Cohort effects can be thought of as the differences in culture associated with a particular generation. If you were contrasting hand–eye coordination of teenagers with individuals in their 60s, and the sample of participants in their 60s performed significantly worse than did the teenagers, you might associate a decline in hand–eye coordination with the natural aging process. But consider the changes in technology and the time spent with technology that have occurred since the 60-somethings were teenagers, and you can see that something in addition to the natural aging process may explain the hand–eye coordination scores you see. Age and technology are confounded; you cannot separate out the experience of technology from the age group. Teenagers and 60-somethings are not simply different in age; they represent different cohorts for the same developmental span.

COHORT-SEQUENTIAL DESIGN

One way researchers have tried to address the drawbacks to the cross-sectional approach is by using what is called a cohort-sequential design. A cohort-sequential design is one in which there are both cross-sectional and longitudinal components. This approach is an attempt to measure generational effects, if they exist, but it does not eliminate them. As an example, K. J. Van Manen and Susan Whitbourne (1997) were interested in the relationships between psychosocial development and life experiences, for example, that a strong sense of identity would be linked to more career success than would a weaker sense of identity. Cohort 1 began in 1966, and Cohort 2 started 11 years later in 1977. Figure 8.6 depicts the longitudinal aspects (across the horizontal axis) and the cross-sectional aspects (down the vertical axis) of their design. You could think of the

FIGURE 8.6 Longitudinal and Cross-Sectional Aspects of Van Manen and Whitbourne's (1997) Design

Source: Based on data from Van Manen, K., & Whitbourne, S. (1997). Psychosocial development and life experiences in adulthood: A 22-year sequential study. *Psychology and Aging, 12,* 239–246.

longitudinal approach (horizontal) as involving individual cohorts and the cross-sectional approach (vertical) as involving multiple cohorts.

Among their findings, Van Manen and Whitbourne (1997) argued that the distinctiveness of the 1960s seemed to have an effect on men pursuing higher education that was not consistent with the pattern of scores of men in college over the next two decades. Thus, there was something unique about the 1960s, in contrast to the 1970s and the 1980s. Decades have their own culture. They argued that in different time periods (cohorts), different norms may be operating, which in turn will yield different opportunities with regard to socialization. For that reason, among others, research that takes account of differences between cohorts is essential.

REVISIT AND RESPOND

- What is a cohort? Explain how a cohort sequential approach combines aspects of both cross-sectional and longitudinal designs.

ADVANTAGES OF USING MULTIPLE METHODS

This chapter has looked at several different research designs, including within subjects, mixed, pre–post, time series, interrupted time series, longitudinal, cross-sectional, and cohort sequential. Grammer et al. (2013), mentioned earlier in the chapter, saw a value to using numerous approaches, stating that "Each approach—including cross-sectional, longitudinal, experimental, observational, microgenetic, and intervention, and various combinations of these methods—provides a unique perspective on children's changing abilities" (p. 516). An important point made by Grammer et al. is that research designs complement each other. In their work, what they witnessed in the field subsequently led to laboratory experiments, which in turn led to additional observations in the field. Thus, the research process is iterative and may involve feedback as well as feed forward loops. The focus of Grammer et al. was children's cognitive abilities, but the case for the advantages of the multimethod approach can be made in almost every domain of investigation.

As another example, researchers have looked at the impact of the hospital inpatient room design on patients' stress level in a series of studies: one an experimental study (Andrade & Devlin, 2015); one a field study (Devlin, Andrade, & Lima, 2014); and one using qualitative responses from the field study (Devlin, Andrade, & Carvalho, 2016). The experimental study (which was conducted first) tested Roger Ulrich's (1991) theory of supportive design in the laboratory. Then, the field study tested the theory on orthopedic patients in five different hospital units across two countries (the United States and Portugal). The field study confirmed the laboratory findings (meditational analyses showed that perceptions of positive distraction and social support predict patients' stress levels but perceived control does not). The lack of confirmation of the role of perceived control in mediating stress has now led to a study investigating that topic (Andrade & Devlin, 2016). The qualitative study, based on patients' answers to questions about aspects of the environment that influenced their satisfaction with the hospitalization, and whether these aspects were positive or negative, refined our understanding of the role of the hospital's physical environment for well-being. Results also showed that some aspects of concern to patients (e.g., maintenance and functionality) fall outside of Ulrich's theory, suggesting that the theory might need to be expanded. This example illustrates how the use of different methods can confirm findings (e.g., similar outcomes in the laboratory and field studies about positive distraction and social support), lead to further research (e.g., about perceived control), and may uncover information unavailable from a single approach, as the qualitative data suggested.

Summary

Implicit throughout this chapter is the notion that research designs can be complementary and that a multimethod approach may provide the opportunity for triangulation (see Chapter 6), that is, when multiple approaches point to the same outcome, which gives you more confidence in your findings. Just as between and within subjects designs may complement each other, so too can cross-sectional and longitudinal designs, essentially in the form of the cohort sequential approach. When researchers are tackling major issues such as explaining cognitive development, one methodological approach is unlikely to answer all of our questions.

An important series of correlational approaches covered in the chapter are time series and interrupted time series. Interrupted time-series approaches are often not fully covered in undergraduate courses; by providing examples in this chapter, the hope is that you will see how useful this approach can be for particular kinds of questions about populations. Such questions would be difficult to answer in any other way.

We began the chapter with within subjects designs and their advantages and disadvantages. For the right kinds of research questions, especially those where carryover effects ARE the focus, within subjects designs provide a powerful tool.

If you have not had time to consider them earlier, here is the list of **REFLECT and REVIEW** questions from this chapter.

- Describe a statistical advantage to using within subjects design. Explain what practice, sensitization, and carryover mean in the context of within subjects design. Explain why research on learning is well suited for within subjects design.
- What is the purpose of counterbalancing a design? What are the differences between complete counterbalancing, partial counterbalancing, and Latin Square design? When would you use each of them?
- List two ways you can add complexity to a within subjects design. What is a mixed design?
- Why would Campbell and Stanley (1963) label the single-group pre–post design a "pre-experimental" design? What are the advantages and disadvantages of the Solomon four-group design?
- What kinds of research questions seem well suited for interrupted times-series design? Why does this approach involve so many points of measurement? Where would you look to find data for this approach?
- What is a postoccupancy evaluation (POE)? What is a nonequivalent control group, and why are these hard to find in the real world?

- What is the chief benefit of longitudinal designs, in your view? What issues prevent researchers from undertaking longitudinal research? As a researcher, what can you do to reduce the likelihood that participants will drop out of a longitudinal study? What specific steps can you take to make participants welcome?
- What is a cohort? Explain how a cohort sequential approach combines aspects of both cross-sectional and longitudinal designs.

BUILD YOUR SKILLS

Imagine that you wanted to use a one-semester longitudinal study to track the development of team trust in four students working together on a project in a research methods course. How many points in time would you assess team trust? At what specific points in time? Why? How would you prevent experimental mortality? How would you try to reduce the impact of "testing," that is, when administration of measures at Time 1 affects responses to subsequent administrations of the measures? Present an argument that even with these challenges, a longitudinal approach is better than a cross-sectional approach for this research topic.

$SAGE edge™

edge.sagepub.com/devlin

Sharpen your skills with SAGE edge!

SAGE edge for students provides a personalized approach to help you accomplish your coursework goals in an easy-to-use learning environment. You'll find action plans, mobile-friendly eFlashcards, and quizzes, as well as videos, web resources, and links to SAGE journal articles to support and expand on the concepts presented in this chapter.

RECRUITING PARTICIPANTS

CHAPTER HIGHLIGHTS

- Subject pools: Characteristics, software, practical issues
- Recruiting off campus
- Service learning: Benefits; conflicts and multiple relationships
- 12 tips for recruiting in the field (Dustin's Dozen)
- Recruiting online: Social media; adverts and snowballing; ethical concerns
- Types of sampling
- Response issues
- Incentives: Practical considerations
- Amazon Mechanical Turk and online paid panels

OVERVIEW

Far in advance of recruiting participants, researchers confront the challenge of who these people will be and how they will be reached, given that this information is required for institutional review board (IRB) approval. Thinking back to the definition in the Code of Federal regulations (45 CFR 46; see Chapter 4), doing research with human subjects requires IRB review. In this definition, the human subjects are living, and the researcher is interacting or intervening with the individual or obtaining identifiable private information about that person. True, research may involve archival information that does not include identifiable information, but the focus here will be on subjects with whom one plans to interact.

This chapter will emphasize the practical aspects of recruiting participants and cover the most common sources of participants, starting with the "closest link," university subject pools, and ending with the "farthest link," online crowdsourcing platforms like Amazon MTurk® and paid participant panels. Issues in recruiting off campus will be discussed, as will the use of vulnerable populations and the challenges in securing permissions (see also Chapter 4). The use of incentives will be covered, as will the timing of your request over the course of the semester. Concepts in sampling will be introduced and related to internal validity.

WHO PARTICIPATES IN RESEARCH: AN OVERVIEW

Representativeness (sampling):
degree to which a sample reflects the characteristics in the parent population.

When we think about scientific findings regarding human nature, we need to ask ourselves about the participants (people) in that research. In particular, we need to think about how representative they are of the population in question across the demographic categories of interest (e.g., age, gender, education, race, and income). **Representativeness (sampling)** is the degree to which your sample reflects the population as a whole. Much of the information we have about human nature comes from a very limited slice of humanity. This is a problem for science. You may not be able to solve that problem in your research, but at the very least, you need to be aware of the "who" of your research and the "how" of your sampling. Both who participates and how you obtain those individuals may limit your results. Such issues are part of sampling bias, as discussed in this chapter.

Subject pool:
groups of individuals, typically undergraduate students, formed to provide participants for research; also called participant pool.

In research, especially in social science (and psychology in particular), there is a heavy reliance on subject pools for research participants. A **subject pool** is formed of individuals who have agreed to serve as participants for research. In a study titled "The Weirdest People in the World?" Joseph Henrich, Steven Heine, and Ara Norenzayan (2010) talked about the predominance of participants who come from societies that are "Western, Educated, Industrialized, Rich, and Democratic" (hence WEIRD) in research. This paper should be required reading for anyone conducting research with human subjects, particularly studies that rely on subject pools. Henrich et al. argued that it is "Western, and more specifically American, undergraduates who form the bulk of the database in the experimental branches of psychology, cognitive science, and economics, as well as allied fields" (p. 61).

There is increasing recognition that unless we increase the diversity of our samples, we have a skewed picture of human nature. The title of Robert Guthrie's 1976 book *Even the Rat Was White* points to this lack of representativeness in psychology and social science more broadly. Echoing a theme we saw when talking about the value in adding qualitative to our heavily quantitative approaches (see Chapter 6), Paul Rozin (2009) talked about the kinds of research we should be publishing. In such research, there is an emphasis on questions that reflect greater diversity, not only of participants, the focus of this chapter, but also of approaches. Are we making any progress on this front? Although there seems to be an increase in the number of non-U.S. authors publishing in psychology journals and an increase in multiauthor collaborations (Piocuda, Smyers, Knyshev, Harris, & Rai, 2015), Jorge Piocuda et al. did not report whether there was internationalization of the samples in that research. Research from Jeffrey Arnett (2008) showed that for 2007, "in 67% of American studies published in *JPSP,* the samples consisted of undergraduate psychology students" (p. 604). *JPSP,* the *Journal of Personality and Social Psychology,* is one of the premier journals in the discipline.

> **» Try This Now**
>
> What is the potential impact of using WEIRD people, and American undergraduates in particular, on our understanding of human nature? Are there kinds of studies where you think using WEIRD people would be less likely to limit the results?

THE SUBJECT POOL: THE WORKHORSE OF SOCIAL SCIENCE RESEARCH

A good deal of research is done using American undergraduates, and most of these people come from subject pools in psychology. There are two general types of subject pools: unpaid and paid. **Unpaid subject pools** are those typically linked to course participation requirements, where participating in research (or an alternative, see Chapter 4) is a requirement of the course. Unpaid pools may also provide a source of extra credit in a course. It is important to reinforce the fact that participation in such pools is voluntary; we cannot require people to participate in research.

Paid subject pools are typically available at large research universities where faculty research grants fund the pools. Participants may be students, staff, faculty, and even individuals unrelated to the institution; these volunteers are paid to participate in research projects. Such pools may be offered within psychology departments, medical schools, or business schools, as examples.

Unpaid subject pool: group of people who are not paid to participate in research; most commonly a university subject pool.

Paid subject pool: a group of people who are paid to participate in research.

THE DRAWBACKS TO SUBJECT POOLS: CONCERNS ABOUT INTERNAL VALIDITY

As indicated in the research reported by Arnett (2008) and by Henrich et al. (2010), there is a lack of diversity in undergraduate subject pools. Such pools are thus unrepresentative of the public at large. There are other ways in which these pools are unrepresentative. Some of these differences have to do with when people are likely to participate and in what form (in person vs. online).

Across the subject pool, participants differ in ways that may affect the internal validity of the research project. For example, there are differences in extraversion between those who choose to participate in person (higher levels of extraversion) compared to those who select to participate online. Furthermore, those who participate earlier in the semester are likely to be more conscientious and to be women than are those who participate later in the semester (Witt, Donnellan, & Orlando, 2011). Using the NEO-PI-3®, a widely used personality inventory (see Chapter 5), research looking at the timing of participation in the semester showed that higher levels of extraversion and openness were associated with participating later in the semester (Aviv, Zelinski, Rallo, & Larson, 2002). As A. L. Aviv et al. (2002) argued, the differences in personality associated with participating at different times of the semester create confounds and undermine the internal validity of the research unless steps are taken to address these problems.

> **» Try This Now**
>
> Given these differences in personality characteristics and when people decide to participate, what might happen if we run an experiment with sequential conditions, such that all of Condition 1 is run in September and all of Condition 2 is run in November?

As Aviv et al. (2002) discussed, this kind of sequential approach may lead to unrepresentativeness, given that personality may be confounded with time of the semester. Another type of research approach that is problematic is a study that is conducted over a short period of time (e.g., 1–2 weeks). In both of those scenarios (sequential and short time frame), the people who volunteer at an early point in time likely will differ from those who volunteer later in the semester. And these differences may interact with the variable(s) in the study.

How would you change the way the subject pool is managed to eliminate this problem? The solution offered by Aviv et al. (2002) is to eliminate choice. By randomly assigning participants to experiments, these potentially damaging differences in the nonrandom distribution of personality characteristics are eliminated. Aviv et al. stated that there are psychology departments in the United States that assign participants in this manner. It is unclear how common this approach is.

> **» Try This Now**
>
> How does your institution recruit and assign participants for experiments?

LIMITS ON THE NUMBER OF PARTICIPANTS AVAILABLE FROM UNPAID SUBJECT POOLS

Participants are valuable because they are limited in number, typically being generated through course requirements. For that reason, most unpaid subject pools set restrictions on the number of participants any given researcher may acquire through the pool. There is typically a priority system of who has access and in what order. The size of the institution and hence the number of students enrolled has a direct bearing on the number of participants available for research. Research is more difficult to conduct at small institutions because of the limited number of participants available.

REVISIT AND RESPOND

- List two potential threats to the internal validity of a study when you use a subject pool and how researchers have tried to combat these threats.

KEEPING TRACK OF PARTICIPANTS: ONLINE PARTICIPANT MANAGEMENT SYSTEMS

Increasingly institutions are turning to software not only to create studies (e.g., SurveyMonkey® and Qualtrics®) but also to manage recordkeeping between researchers and participants. One of the most widely used cloud-based **participant management systems** is **Sona Systems**® (**https://www.sona-systems.com/default.aspx**), which describes itself as the "global leader in university research software" that "serves the top 50 universities in the US" according to its website.

This kind of software brings researchers and participants together. Researchers and participants create accounts; researchers can post their studies online, and participants can sign up online for these posted studies. Many features help to streamline the research process. Researchers can list criteria for participation (e.g., athlete status, class year, or gender), send reminders, automatically award credit, reserve rooms for running their studies, document no-shows or excused absences, as well as several other conveniences. Participants have a way to document their participation rather than relying on signed informed consent documents, which are easy to misplace.

Participant management system: way to keep track of research participants, commonly now through a software system.

Sona Systems®: online participant management software used to keep track of the involvement of participants in research.

The software is relatively straightforward, and this approach to managing participants is widely accepted. As Sona Systems states on its website, "The days of bulletin boards and sign up sheets are over." As you might expect, there is a fee for such participant management software. For Sona, the price depends on the volume of usage, measured by the number of participant sessions managed in the system.

PRACTICAL ISSUES IN COMMUNICATING ABOUT RECRUITING

Whether you are recruiting from the subject pool or elsewhere (more on that shortly), some aspects to the study affect its success, in terms of both attracting participants and internal validity.

Study Labels

Earlier in the book (see Chapter 3 on demand characteristics and cover stories; see Chapter 5 on scale labels) we discussed the ways in which research is a communication process. What participants see or hear about the research influences their perceptions about what is going to take place. One of these influences is the title of the study.

Consider the following two titles for the same project:

Perceptions of Women in Sports

Perceptions of Femininity and Women's Weightlifting

The research in question (mentioned in Chapters 6 and 7) is assessing how judgments of femininity and masculinity are affected by exposure to women holding barbells of different weights [5 lbs (80 oz) or 25 lbs (400 oz)], but including femininity in the title would likely bias participants. When you advertise your study (whatever the platform), you want to describe the nature of the study in general terms without providing information that discloses the hypotheses. This same caution is in order at the beginning and end of your informed consent where you describe the study (see Appendix B at the end of the book for a sample informed consent document).

Study Length

You recall that one of the elements of informed consent (see Chapter 4) is a statement of how long the research could be expected to take. Normally researchers determine this length by pilot testing or having a friend or colleague complete the study (e.g., fill out the questionnaires) and then use that estimate on the informed consent and in advertising the study. Typically students in a research pool who are participating for course credit are required to fulfill a given number of hours of participation (e.g., five), although some institutions state the requirement in terms of a specific number of studies. Students are astute; if they need to participate in a given number of hours, they often select studies that take more time (up to a point) to reduce the absolute number of studies they need for their course requirement. If your study takes 30 minutes, or 45 minutes, or 60 minutes, it may have more "takers" than if it were only a 15-minute study. The length of the advertised study also plays a role in crowdsourcing platforms like Amazon Mechanical Turk (discussed later in the chapter). If potential workers think that the ratio of pay/length of task is unfavorable (e.g., $0.25 for a 30-minute survey), you may have few participants (called "Workers").

Time of the Semester

The time of the semester you recruit participants can affect who signs up. Women and those who are conscientious are more likely to sign up earlier in the semester (Witt et al., 2011); those who are extraverts and exhibit openness to experience are more likely to sign up later in the semester (Aviv et al., 2002). Beyond these differences, which may affect the internal validity of your study, there is the basic problem of running out of participants in the pool. If you wait until after Thanksgiving or Spring Break to collect your data from the pool, there are likely to be few subject hours left. In addition, you have little time to analyze the data and complete your research paper before the semester ends.

Time of Day and Day of Week

If you are using a subject pool where students have to appear in person to take a study, it makes sense to offer multiple data collection sessions scheduled at different times of the day and throughout the week. Most in-person sessions would be held later in the afternoon (after classes end) when rooms to run research are available. It is important to consider that some participant groups (e.g., athletes) are restricted in their availability. Offering evening as well as afternoon sessions thus makes sense. In addition, think about the days of the week that should produce the greatest level of participation. One recommendation is that you offer sessions Monday–Thursday, with less emphasis on Friday. Some researchers recommend Tuesday–Thursday because students returning to campus after a weekend may not remember a Monday obligation.

Attrition or Experimental Mortality

Attrition, or dropping out (also called experimental mortality, see Chapters 3 and 8), is likely to be a problem in longitudinal research or some within subjects designs where you are worried about carryover effects and want to schedule sessions with time in between. An additional possibility is the case of pre–post research (see Chapter 8 for each of these research designs). In the case of longitudinal research, you are collecting data from the same people, sometimes for years. In the within subjects approach, where carryover effects are a concern, you may want the effect of one treatment level to wear off before assessing the effect of another treatment level (e.g., the effect of different doses of caffeine on memory). In the pre–post approach, you may want to test whether an intervention has an effect extended in time. For that reason, you may schedule a break between data collection sessions and request that people return for a follow-up session on a different day. You cannot require participants to return, nor can you withhold research credit if they don't.

> **》 Try This Now**
>
> What strategies might you employ to encourage people to return for follow-up sessions?

The most effective way to persuade people to return is to explain the importance of their participation and the effect that dropping out would have on the research. Remembering that the research process is one of communication, establishing a connection to your participants by treating them with respect, and thanking them for participating helps to create a positive climate for the research process. This positive climate is easier to establish in person than online, but the same principles of respect and civility hold for online studies.

REVISIT AND RESPOND

- Imagine that you are doing a study on the effect of wearing glasses on perceptions of professionalism in the workplace. Come up with a title that reflects the recommendations for labeling your study (to avoid demand characteristics). When would you schedule your study (day of week, time of day) for maximum representativeness?

RESEARCH ON SENSITIVE TOPICS AND THE ROLE OF THE IRB

Earlier in the book (see Chapter 5) we discussed the order of questions in a survey. Don Dillman et al.'s (Dillman, Smyth, & Christian, 2014) advice was to place sensitive questions as far into the survey as possible so that some level of trust between the participants and the researcher has a chance to be established. A level of trust could come from clear communication, for example, organizing the material by topic and labeling sections numerically. But what about the situation when the research topic itself is sensitive, such as sexual assault or addiction?

> **>> Try This Now**
>
> In your opinion, does the researcher have an obligation to inform participants that the topic may be sensitive? Could warning have an effect on who participates (i.e., the representativeness of the sample)?

Beyond establishing a level of trust, the issue of the sensitivity of the topic is an ethical one. Researchers have an ethical obligation to alert participants to material that may be upsetting, and most researchers endorse alerting participants to that possibility.[1] Heather McCosker, Alan Barnard, and Rod Gerber (2001) pointed out that not only is sensitive research an issue for participants, but also the nature of the information may have an effect on a variety of other groups. It may be relevant to researchers (concerns for safety when interviewing individuals who may be violent), members of ethics committees (who read the proposal), transcribers of information (who read interviews with sensitive material), and even readers of publications that include that material.

RECRUITING OFF CAMPUS

Not every research question can be evaluated using a sample of undergraduate college students, nor do we want to rely on such pools to develop our understanding of human nature (Henrich et al., 2010). One principle to remember is that the nature of the research question influences the selection of the participants; target recruitment for locations where you are likely to find people with the characteristics you seek. If you were interested in organic food, for example, you might go to local farmers' markets (understanding that you need permission to recruit at private venues).

When you move off campus, the difficulty of recruiting participants typically increases substantially. The following sections address how to recruit successfully in the field.

USING YOUR PERSONAL CONNECTIONS

One of the best ways to recruit people off campus is to use your personal connections. These connections can be direct, for example, your membership in an off-campus group (e.g., soccer club or religious organization) or indirect (e.g., knowing someone who is a member of a group, or whose parents or relatives or neighbors belong to a group or

---

[1]There are concerns in the classroom about teaching topics that may include sensitive material; alerting students to this material is referred to as including a *trigger warning* (Flaherty, 2014).

organization). Gaining access to workplace environments for research can also be facilitated through connections, using one's relatives as the primary example. Your institution's career services office may be another good source of contacts. Given the interconnectedness possible through social media, reaching out to friends and acquaintances is easy.

In Ann Devlin et al. (2013), one sample in this study of responses to multicultural art in a therapist's office was a community group. The data collection took place in the large activity space of a community health clinic. The sample was obtained through identifying connections to the community. The director of the health clinic, a spouse of a colleague at the author's institution, not only helped advertise the study in the community but also attended every data collection session to assist with translations (the study was offered in English and Spanish). The sessions were run at lunchtime for convenience; pizza and beverages were provided; and an incentive (a $10 voucher to use at a local grocery store) was offered.

USING YOUR INSTITUTION'S CONNECTIONS

In addition to the personal connections, your institution or place of work may have formal connections to other institutions or facilities. Your school may be part of an athletic conference or a consortium of schools that shares resources; through work you may belong to a larger network of similar job types or categories. Your institution may belong to organizations as well (e.g., National Association of Independent Colleges and Universities or National High School Coaches Association). Doing an Internet search using the term "organizations in higher education" will produce a list of possibilities to investigate; the same approach could be tried with any job category. Another resource from institutions is the alumni network.

BUREAUCRACY

As we discussed in the section on ethnography (see Chapter 6), gaining access is one of the challenges to conducting research in the community. Remember that IRBs (see Chapter 4) will expect verification of permission to gain access to a particular sample.

VULNERABLE POPULATIONS IN THE COMMUNITY

As we saw in Chapter 4, vulnerable populations trigger *Full IRB Review*, the highest level. The vulnerable population most often selected for student research is children, defined as those who have not reached the age of majority. Many layers of permissions are required for vulnerable populations (see Chapter 4 for coverage of permission with children).

When doing research with populations where the state has control, such as inmates in correctional facilities or patients in state psychiatric facilities, the permission, if granted at all, may take as long as a year to secure.

PHYSICAL SECURITY ISSUES IN CONDUCTING RESEARCH OFF CAMPUS

Whether doing research off campus with vulnerable populations or not, security issues for both the participant and the researcher are relevant. Often discussion about security issues focuses on the data itself, especially online data, and how it should be safeguarded (see, for example, Quinn, 2015), but here we will focus on aspects of physical security.

For both the participant and the researcher, one major question is where the research will take place and who else will be there. To enhance security, recommendations are usually to conduct the research in a public place (e.g., a café or a library) unless doing so would put the participant at risk (see Chapter 4). The presence of others may provide security for the participant (strength in numbers) but also for the researcher. If the research deals with sexual assault, addiction, or another topic considered sensitive where the participant might become agitated and/or someone connected to the participant might confront the researcher, having others at the location of the research is advisable. If research is being conducted in a school and having someone else in the room would limit disclosure by the participant or make the participant uncomfortable, a recommendation is to conduct the research in a quiet area but with the door open or ajar. As a researcher, you don't want to be in a potentially compromising situation, which might lead to accusations of misconduct.

An online source of guidelines from the United Kingdom provides helpful advice for the safety of researchers (**http://the-sra.org.uk/wp-content/uploads/safety_code_of_practice.pdf**).

These recommendations include assessing risk in the field (e.g., determining whether public transportation is available); investigating housing and living environments ahead of time (e.g., understanding the layout of dense housing complexes); and telling the interviewee that others know your whereabouts and your schedule. Assessment of risk is particularly important if you are in areas where there is crime, it is the evening, or you are in someone's home.

REVISIT AND RESPOND

- What kinds of connections do you have that would enable you to conduct research with off-campus populations? What steps would you take to safeguard your physical security and the security of your participants? Beyond the steps that are outlined in this chapter, what other ideas do you have about securing your physical safety?

SERVICE LEARNING COURSES AND RECRUITING PARTICIPANTS: OPPORTUNITIES AND COMPLICATIONS

Service learning: academic experiences that integrate course material and work in the field.

Service learning courses are those in which students integrate academic material with internships or volunteer work in the community (and typically receive course credit in the process). This approach is a form of experiential learning where students put into action what they have learned (or are learning) in the classroom.

> **❯❯ Try This Now**
>
> Before reading further, what are the advantages you see to using service learning experiences to collect data? What are the potential drawbacks? [Think back to Zimbardo's (Haney, Banks, & Zimbardo, 1973) double role as researcher and prison superintendent in Chapter 4.]

Conducting research in the setting where you are currently doing an internship or otherwise participating in service learning raises potential ethical conflicts and may be considered exploitative (see the next section on conflicts of interest and multiple relationships). Because doing service learning and conducting research at the same time may create conflicts about motivations and goals, it makes more sense to do research in a service learning setting *after* you have concluded your course work there. If the setting is large enough, another possibility is to do research in another part of the setting where you are not interning (e.g., a different classroom, unit, department, or branch).

Double agent: situation in which you are fulfilling two roles at once and may not be acting solely in the client's/ participant's best interest.

After you conclude your internship, you will likely continue to have access to the setting, but you will no longer be a "**double agent**" (Yanos & Ziedonis, 2006). The idea in being a double agent is that you may not be acting solely in the best interest of your client (here, the people you serve in the service learning environment), if you are also interested in them as research participants. In other words, if you are both an intern and a researcher, you have a potential conflict of interest.

CONFLICTS OF INTEREST AND MULTIPLE RELATIONSHIPS

Participants are not available in unlimited numbers; most subject pools have restrictions to the number of people you can obtain through the pool. Given those pressures, researchers often turn to sources where they have connections, such as clubs, athletic teams, religious groups, and career-related List Serves. When we approach people to whom we have a connection, several ethical issues emerge, especially if there are power differences in the people asking and the people responding. For example, given that one interest area for student research is athletics, you can imagine someone who is a team captain or fourth year student recruiting younger team members as participants.

>> Try This Now

What conflicts of interest might there be when fourth year students or team captains recruit players from their teams to be research participants?

The American Psychological Association (APA) Code of Ethics has a section (2010a, 3.05) dealing with avoiding **multiple relationships**. The gist of this guideline is that if you are in a professional role with a person (e.g., therapist or teacher) you should not enter into another kind of role with that person (e.g., as a researcher collaborator) if the possibility exists that the new relationship might impair your judgment or effectiveness in your professional work as a psychologist. Although we are not assuming the researcher is a psychologist, we are talking about the idea that having multiple relationships with potential participants should raise warning flags. Lynne Roberts and Peter Allen (2015) discussed this issue in the context of research in education and suggest that when one's students are possible participants, such students should be considered a vulnerable population. Imagine the situation where an assistant lacrosse coach, enrolled in an MA program, wants to use members of his or her team as participants in a study of personality, athlete goals and strivings (as reflected in personal narratives), and career objectives. How can the researcher avoid the possibility of coercion in this situation?

Some researchers in this kind of situation have someone else approach the team members; in addition, the guarantee is made that the data will be collected anonymously and that participants' identities will not be known to the researcher. Nevertheless, if there are few players, it is possible that some identifying information may be revealed in the narratives the players produce. Yet another possibility, and one that makes more sense in terms of reducing the possibility of coercion, is to use another team at the institution, or from another institution altogether. It is likely that the research questions are not about a specific team (e.g., lacrosse) but about athletes more generally. For that reason, a substitute team, either at one's institution or at another institution (making use of one's contacts) is a reasonable approach and one that avoids the conflict of interest.

Multiple relationships: described in 3.05 of the American Psychological Association (APA) Code of Ethics (2010a), in which your professional role (e.g., therapist) may be compromised by taking on a second role (e.g., research collaborator) with regard to the same individual.

REVISIT AND RESPOND

- What are the benefits of conducting research at service learning sites? What are the potential drawbacks? What does it mean to be a "double agent" in the context of research? If you want to collect data from a group where you are a member, how can you avoid the possibility of coercion in requesting their participation?

DUSTIN'S DOZEN: TIPS FOR COLLECTING DATA IN THE FIELD

(Quoted or in some sections closely adapted from Devlin, 2006, pp. 141–144.)

We have talked about places one might find participants, such as service learning courses or clubs or other institutions. Next we will talk about recommendations for collecting data in public places such as train stations or plazas. Sarah Ibrahim and Souraya Sidani (2014) categorized strategies into those that are proactive (direct) and reactive (indirect). Proactive approaches include face-to-face encounters at such sites as community centers, health centers, churches, centers for seniors, farmers' markets, and street fairs. I would also add libraries, community parks, and parades (before and after the event). Reactive (indirect) approaches include working through community leaders, snowballing, word of mouth, and media.

The many useful suggestions from a former graduate student, Dustin Wielt, have been complied into a list of do's and don'ts for collecting data in the field. Dustin's MA project was a study of the attributions people made about murderers as a function of the murderer's criminal history, psychiatric history, and social status. Over the two months he collected his data (a sample of more than 300 participants), his major collection point was the local Amtrak train station, but he also collected data in a laundromat. Here are Dustin's recommendations:

1. *Dress decently.* As Dustin said, don't dress like a "bum." If you are a male student, wear a shirt tucked in and a belt. Don't wear a baseball cap facing backward. Basically, if you are negotiating with a business owner about whether you can collect data at his or her establishment, dress appropriately. And dress appropriately when you collect the data, of course!

2. *The inverse correlation.* There seems to be an inverse correlation between the likelihood of gaining permission to collect data at a facility and the size of the bureaucracy. For example, Dustin asked permission of the local Amtrak police and the Amtrak counter personnel for permission to distribute questionnaires at

the local train station. They granted permission, with the caveat that if anyone complained, he would be asked to leave. Then they "shook" on it. This agreement worked very well. But when Dustin pursued gaining permission from the much larger regional train station by calling the number of an Amtrak official there, the response was "no." The higher up you are required to go to get permission (and the less likely you are to do it in person), the less likely it is that the permission will be granted. This same experience was replicated in seeking permission from the local owner of a laundromat ("yes") versus from the manager of a chain of laundromats ("no").

3. *Avoid "No Solicitation" locations.* As a matter of policy, establishments that have "No solicitation" signs posted are less likely to agree to your research.

4. *Carefully select your "first ask" of the day.* As your first "ask" of the day, try to identify someone who seems likely to cooperate with you. As an example, Dustin found that women who were reading books were likely to agree to participate. If they said "yes," the people sitting around them became curious and were more likely to agree. If the first person you ask who is sitting in a group says "no," it is less likely that others will then have the courage to override this social norm and say "yes." Dustin estimated that on average, approximately 60% of those he first asked said "yes" immediately, and if they asked a question about the research, another 10% said "yes."

Although there may be difficulties, the train station turned out to be a good location for data collection. In Dustin's sample, he had an age range of 18–84, and the sample was almost normally distributed. There was also racial and socioeconomic diversity, as well as a fairly good gender split (53% women, 47% men). There may be other ways in which this sample is not representative (people who take trains may be different in certain respects from those who do not), but it is a reasonable place to start.

Although he did not implement it, another strategy Dustin considered was the use of a *confederate* (see Chapter 4) who could be approached first for a given day's data collection session to say "yes," thereby establishing a climate of cooperation. In the two months that Dustin collected data at the train station, he had only two to three people who were asked twice to fill out the questionnaire, so the number of repeats was quite low, and a confederate could be effective in this situation with a high turnover of people.

5. *Personalize your "pitch."* Ask the individual for participation in YOUR project, as opposed to simply asking for participation. It is harder to turn down someone when you are turning down the individual as opposed to a representative of a large organization.

6. *Be mobile.* Rather than putting yourself at a desk or in a stationary position, which strangers may be reluctant to approach, move around the setting. If you are collecting data at a train station, a laundromat, or some other facility, put your questionnaires on a clipboard and approach people for their help. This approach works much more effectively than waiting for people to approach you.

7. *Approach people with a respect for their personal space.* Stand about 5–6 feet away when you first ask people to participate. If they agree to participate, you can move closer to hand them the clipboard. Dustin recommended having about 10 clipboards available (in a backpack or tote) to hand out and then "reloading" them with fresh questionnaires so that materials are always available. He provided pens (which he retrieved) for all participants. He placed the debriefing form, face down, at the end of the questionnaire so that it was immediately available to participants when they finished the questionnaire. Make sure that the informed consent information in the introduction to the study is printed in large enough type so that people can easily read it.

8. *Be ready to assist those with low reading levels.* At the laundromat, Dustin found several people for whom English was a second language or for whom reading at a sixth-grade level was a problem. Although he asked people if they had any questions before they started filling out the questionnaires, on occasion, people asked him for definitions of words (one example is the word "generous"). At this point, he offered to read the questionnaire to this particular individual, and she agreed. Questionnaires can be designed for a minimum reading level, and certain word processing programs have reading-level indicators (refer to explanation in Chapter 5 under "Length and Difficulty of Measures"). You can also pilot your materials by asking several people to read your questions and comment on the appropriateness of the reading level for your target population. Although questionnaires can be designed for a given minimum reading level, it is still the case that the researcher may need to assist participants. When this happens, the researcher then will need to make a decision about the validity of the data (because people's responses may change in a socially desirable direction) and whether these data should be included in the analyses.

9. *Limit the length of your survey.* Dustin estimated that a 10–15-minute questionnaire is the maximum length that will work, especially in places like train stations where people are waiting but may not arrive too much in advance of their trains.

He also said that the day before Thanksgiving was his most successful data collection session, where he collected more than 100 questionnaires as people began their holiday travel. Trains were running 10–15 minutes late all day, so that even those who had planned to arrive just a few minutes before the train's scheduled departure had "time on their hands."

10. *Be sensitive to the day of the week and the time of day.* Dustin found that weekends were better than weekdays for cooperation as weekend travelers were more likely to be traveling for pleasure as opposed to business. Business people traveling on Monday mornings were the least cooperative.

At the laundromat, the best time to approach people was the moment after they had put their clothes in the dryer (rather than when they were folding clothes, for example).

11. *Safeguard your personal information.* Dustin recommended listing the department's phone number rather than your home or dorm number as a contact number on the debriefing sheet. This is a matter of safety. He was once called at 3:30 a.m. by someone who was drunk and disoriented. This person wanted more information about the study but was clearly in need of other kind of assistance. As standard procedure, some IRBs now require that researchers give their e-mail contact, not their phone contact.

12. *Be ready for challenges.* Challenges to research may come in many different guises. Some people may want to engage you in a lengthy conversation, and you may need to extricate yourself and move on. Others may criticize your research because they know something about questionnaire construction or the topic you are studying. The best advice is to remain polite. Reiterate that they are under no obligation to fill out the questionnaire.

IDENTIFYING INFORMATION

In addition to these very good suggestions from Dustin, an additional recommendation is to wear a hangtag with your identifying information, in particular your institutional affiliation. If you are collecting data in the town where your institution is located, this information will be readily recognizable (e.g., your college seal and name) and will help establish your credibility.

OTHER SOURCES OF PARTICIPANTS: THE ONLINE APPROACH

Given the limitations of subject pools and the difficulties associated with recruiting in the community, researchers increasingly seek other sources of participants. These sources include social media, **online crowdsourcing platforms** like Amazon Mechanical Turk, and **paid panels** (although such panels are somewhat expensive). An online crowdsourcing platform provides a way to obtain feedback from people (paid or unpaid) about an idea or topic. A paid panel is a group of individuals with particular characteristics who are paid to provide feedback about a product or topic.

Online crowdsourcing platform: paid or unpaid participants used to obtain feedback online about a topic.

Paid panel: a group of people with identified characteristics (e.g., luxury car owners) that are asked to respond to a survey.

Use of Social Media for Recruiting

Social media provide not only the opportunity for investigating their contents (i.e., studying behavior online) but also tools for recruiting. Among outlets, Facebook® has received the most attention as a recruiting tool. In their recent paper, Michal Kosinski, Sandra Matz, Samuel Gosling, Vesselin Popov, and David Stillwell (2015) outlined the strengths of the tool as well as some of the drawbacks to consider.

Among the problems they cited are the tendency for participants to rush through the survey, the lack of control over the circumstances in which participants complete the survey, the psychological distance between the researcher and the participant because they are not face to face, and the potential difficulties with communication if there are cultural or linguistic differences. Despite these difficulties, Kosinski et al. (2015) presented evidence of the high quality of data obtained using Facebook.

In using Facebook, Kosinski et al. (2015) discussed the merit of different kinds of incentives and discouraged the use of financial incentives. Instead, they said that providing feedback about performance or scores would encourage greater attention to the task and more honest responding in the case of self-report measures. This idea seems especially well suited for the kinds of research on personality they study (e.g., providing feedback about how participants' personality profiles compare with averages). It is unclear how easy it would be to adapt this recommendation for all kinds of studies, but it is worth considering. The basic idea is that people are likely to participate because they will learn something specific about themselves. There are also economic advantages to using this kind of informational feedback (i.e., it's inexpensive).

ONLINE USE OF ADVERTS (ADVERTISEMENTS) VERSUS SNOWBALL SAMPLES

Much of the research discussed in Kosinski et al. (2015) focuses on the use of placing advertisements on Facebook (**adverts**; an informal British term for advertising) to attract participants, but of course, this costs money. Their recommendation is to use adverts for studies focused on difficult-to-reach populations. As an example of difficult-to-reach populations, Kosinski et al. mentioned people who are stigmatized in what is called the "offline world" (p. 545). Research using these social media platforms has its own vocabulary; people choosing to do research on these platforms need to understand the vocabulary as well as the particulars of the technology.

Students and other researchers increasingly use Facebook as a way to post studies, relying primarily on what is known as snowball sampling (as introduced in Chapter 2; additional kinds of sampling are discussed later in the chapter). In snowball sampling, those first asked to participate (usually one's friends) in turn ask THEIR friends, and this process is repeated in a sequence. Kosinski et al. (2015) discussed the disadvantages of snowball sampling in their article (especially concerning representativeness) but concluded that the difficulties can be overcome. Their primary example was a project called "myPersonality" that originally used snowball sampling but ultimately, as a result of its popularity, "went viral," and in four years had more than 6 million participants (p. 544). Importantly, this is not **random sampling**, where each person in the population has an equal chance of being selected. Your friends are probably like you and therefore create an inherent bias in the sample. But Kosinski et al. went on to argue that most samples are not representative anyway (from undergraduate psychology students to Amazon MTurkers) and that Facebook provides a reasonable "high quality" alternative (p. 545) that would minimize the disadvantages of snowball sampling, given the (a) potential size of the sample and (b) diversity of the potential population of Facebook respondents.

Addressing the use of Web-based surveys more broadly, Samuel Gosling, Simine Vazire, Sanjay Srivastava, and Oliver John (2004) dealt with the issue of the validity in such surveys. They reported good news. The samples are diverse, at least to the extent of traditional samples; the samples are not filled with highly maladjusted people; the format of the interaction is not an issue; and the results are not biased by less serious participants

Advert: British term for advertisement; used in relationship to advertisements on Facebook® or other social media.

Random sample: sample in which each person has an equal probability of being chosen.

(e.g., rushing through the surveys) or by the anonymity the Internet provides (e.g., being dishonest in responding). By and large the findings are consistent with the findings from more traditional approaches.

ETHICAL ISSUES IN ONLINE ENVIRONMENTS: THE FACEBOOK EMOTIONAL CONTAGION STUDY

An important point Kosinski et al. (2015) made deals with ethical issues. In their view, there are few if any substantive guidelines for conducting research in online environments such as Facebook. They argued that IRBs (and federal agencies and the APA) need to begin considering what these ethical challenges might be.

Data mining:
examining large datasets to discover patterns.

One issue being discussed is whether using information from Facebook (**data mining**, that is, examining large datasets to discover patterns) qualifies as research with human subjects. Think back to our definition of human subjects at the beginning of this chapter (and see Chapter 4). Lauren Solberg (2010) argued that such information does not qualify as research. In her view acquiring data this way would qualify as using human subjects *only* if we were talking about their private information. In the event that the Department of Health and Human Services (HHS) Office for Human Research Protections (OHRP) and local IRBs determine that such use of Facebook *does* constitute research with human subjects, Solberg recommended that such research be considered exempt or at the most expedited (see Chapter 4). Solberg (2010) is among several researchers worried about what has been called the "mission creep" (p. 335) of IRBs (see, for example, Schneider, 2015), and she hopes that OHRP will help set guidelines to limit what she considers the overreaching of IRBs.

This issue of the degree of privacy of your data posted on social media will continue to receive attention. As an example, the research of Adam Kramer, Jamie Guillory, and Jeffrey Hancock (2014) was recently in the news. Their study involved the manipulation of the News Feed function on Facebook and retrieval of the subsequent postings. This study was a collaboration of researchers at Facebook and Cornell University in which the emotional content of the News Feed function (which is managed by an algorithm set and controlled by Facebook) was modified without users' consent and without IRB review.

Emotional contagion:
convergence of emotions across individuals.

Emotional contagion is the convergence of emotions across individuals. The research showed that emotional contagion might occur in the absence of interpersonal contact. The research question was whether the emotional content expressed via the News Feed would lead people to post content of their own that was emotionally consistent with that posted on the News Feed. The research was not considered to be under the purview of the Cornell IRB because the study was being conducted by Facebook, a company that is not bound by the Code of Federal Regulations regarding IRBs.

There has been considerable discussion about the ethics of this Facebook research (e.g., Meyer, 2014). When establishing a Facebook account, any user agrees to Facebook's data use policy, which allows Facebook to use the information for research, among other purposes. If there had been IRB review, what might the outcome have been?

> ## ⟫ Try This Now
>
> Given what you know about the work of IRBs from Chapter 4 and your own use of Facebook, (a) do you think an IRB review of the Kramer et al. (2014) emotional contagion study was needed? (b) If so, what steps for approval would have been required?

In all likelihood, the outcome would have been a waiver of the requirement for informed consent. Why? In this situation there was no evidence that users' participation on Facebook in this situation involved more risk than they would encounter in everyday life. As this study of emotional contagion shows, the Internet is a brave new world in terms of the privacy of information. Fortunately, researchers are beginning to provide resources to help manage the privacy issues involved with Internet studies. Robert Kraut et al. (2004) provided a very nice flow chart (see Figure 1, p. 110), which may help researchers determine whether informed consent should be obtained and documented in a given Internet study. The authors also gave advice about how to manage debriefing in such studies and discussed the kinds of research unsuited to the Internet.

REVISIT AND RESPOND

- What are some of the major challenges that Kosinski et al. (2015) identified in doing research on Facebook? Why did they discourage using financial incentives? What did they use instead? What is an advert? A snowball sample? What does the research of Gosling et al. (2004) show about the validity of Web-based surveys? What is the "emotional contagion" study, and what ethical issues did it raise?

SAMPLING

The next section will cover different approaches to sampling. The "who" of your participants and the "how" of their recruitment directly impact the generalizability of your results. We want to be able to say that our sample mirrors, or is representative of, the population of interest (e.g., the student body).

Probability and Nonprobability Samples

In our coverage of Internet research, we talked about snowball sampling (see Chapter 2), a procedure for procuring participants that depends on people taking the survey and then typically forwarding the link to others. Who are these people in the snowball sample? When we ask who the participants in the study were, we are concerned with aspects of generalizability. To whom could we extend the findings? The answer to that question depends on the nature of the topic being studied, the people in the sample, and how they were selected.

Nonprobability sample: sample for which you cannot make precise estimates of representativeness (e.g., snowball or convenience).

Two general classifications are sometimes distinguished: **nonprobability sampling** and **probability sampling**. Snowball sampling is a form of nonprobability sampling; we can't make a precise estimate of the representativeness of those in the sample. Probability sampling is the ability to make such precise statements about the representativeness of your sample. As we talked about earlier in the chapter, there is arguably a limited degree of representativeness in the samples used in social science because so many of them rely on undergraduate subject pools. These pools offer nonprobability samples.

Probability sample: sample for which you can make precise estimates of representativeness.

Nonprobability Samples: Snowball Samples and Convenience Samples

In the earlier section dealing with social media such as Facebook, we talked about snowball sampling. You encourage people who have taken your survey to send it to other people they know. These friends in turn ask others, and so on, gathering momentum (the size of the sample grows) like a snowball rolling down the hill. This type of sampling is also called **chain sampling** or **referral sampling**. Convenience samples (as introduced in Chapter 2) are samples that are easily obtainable (e.g., people studying in the library whom you approach about participating in research or the participant pool). Like snowball samples, convenience samples are nonprobability samples. Because convenience samples use those readily available, they often fail to mirror the population of interest. In the case of college students, for example, students enrolled in a particular major, such as psychology, who are part of the participant pool, may not mirror the student population as a whole in class year, gender, race, income, or a host of other ways.

Chain sampling: another name for snowball sampling.

Referral sampling: another name for snowball sampling

REVISIT AND RESPOND

- Using the concept of representativeness, explain why an undergraduate subject pool is a nonprobability sample.

Types of Probability Sampling

In probability sampling, you can make precise estimates of representativeness. There are a variety of types of probability sampling, which will be discussed next. A core characteristic of probability sampling is the concept of representativeness.

RANDOM SAMPLING The essence of random sampling is that every member of the population has an equal chance of being selected. If you randomly sampled students at your institution to acquire your sample, this would mean having access to every name in the population and using a random approach (e.g., picking names at random from the student database) to select the participants. This is an ideal and has been approximated through surveys that use landlines and random digit dialing to reach target participants.

A question you (and others) may ask is what happens to sampling approaches as the use of landlines declines? In research dealing with health, Stephen Blumberg and Julian Luke (2014) stated that a potential for bias exists when surveys rely on landline-based surveys because age groups vary in their reliance on wireless versus landlines. For example, in the 23–29-year-old group, 65.7% live in wireless-only households, in data from the National Health Interview Survey Early Release Program summarized by Blumberg and Luke (**http://www.cdc.gov/nchs/nhis.htm**). Every six months, the National Center for Health Statistics releases data on the use of wireless technology by households in the United States. This source is an important database for those trying to reach survey respondents via landlines or wireless technology and puts the issue of possible bias into perspective.

STRATIFIED RANDOM SAMPLING One potential drawback to random sampling is that your sample might not include members who have a specific demographic characteristic of interest (e.g., a particular income level or a particular race). In **stratified random sampling**, you are typically making an adjustment to the results that would emerge in straightforward random sampling. If you want your sample to reflect specific subgroups within the population (representative of a particular demographic characteristic such as class year), and you want to make sure your final sample captures these characteristics, then you create these subgroups, called **strata**, and sample randomly within those strata. In our example of class year, there would be four strata, one for each of the class years (first year, sophomore, juniors, seniors). To perform stratified random sampling, you would need access to the demographic characteristics of interest, which might be available from an institutional researcher or registrar (in the case of an educational institution), or from city, state, or national databases, depending on the research question.

PROPORTIONATE SAMPLING When you move to **proportionate sampling** or stratification, you take the additional step of making sure that the sample you draw from each

Stratified random sampling: sampling in which the population is divided into subgroups, called strata, and then randomly sampling within those subgroups to ensure a representative sample.

Strata: name for the specific subgroups used in stratified random sampling.

Proportionate sample: individuals in the sample are divided into subgroups, called strata, to reflect some particular characteristic (e.g., race). Sampling in each stratum is done to reflect the proportion of that characteristic in the population as a whole.

strata is proportionate to the percentage of people in that subgroup in the population as a whole. In our example of class year, the class sizes may not be equal for a variety of reasons (e.g., how many were admitted in a given year and how many transferred or dropped out). Using proportionate sampling means that you are less likely to over- or underrepresent the targeted characteristics of those in your strata. You would need access to the same kind of demographic statistics for proportionate sampling as for stratified random sampling.

Systematic sampling: known population (e.g., students listed in their college directory) is systematically sampled (e.g., every fourth name) after a random start.

SYSTEMATIC SAMPLING In **systematic sampling**, where the full population can be identified (like all students who attend a college), every kth element (e.g., tenth student name) after a random start is selected. Researchers sometimes use this approach with a student directory as a way to approximate a random sample. The kth element is known as the sampling interval and can be determined by dividing the population size by the desired sample size. Thus, if we have an institution of 2,000 students and we want a sample of 100 students, we would select every twentieth student after a random start; if we want a sample of 200 students, we would use every tenth student.

Cluster sampling: when a sample of individuals is divided into a naturally occurring group, such as a classroom.

CLUSTER SAMPLING In **cluster sampling**, the sample is divided into clusters, typically based on naturally occurring groups (e.g., classrooms, hospital floors, or neighborhoods), and then a random sample of the clusters is selected. The cluster is the sampling unit, but each individual in a particular cluster is included in the analyses. As an example, you might do a study with classrooms in a school district where you don't have the resources to include every classroom. To obtain some assessment about the performance of children in classrooms across the school district, you would pick a random sample of these classrooms.

REVISIT AND RESPOND

- In general, explain why using probability sampling is preferable to nonprobability sampling. What makes something a random sample? How do stratified random and proportionate sampling differ? In what way is systematic sampling like random sampling? For cluster sampling, what does it mean to say that a cluster is the sampling unit?

NONRESPONSE BIAS AND THREATS TO INTERNAL VALIDITY

In an ideal world, your project would use random sampling and everyone selected would respond and complete the measures in your study. Life is seldom like that (never, in fact). Most of the time, a portion of your sample (more than 50% in many studies where the researcher has no connection to the population) will simply not respond. When you divide the number of people who responded by the number of people invited, this gives you the percentage responding. In reporting response rates, even a simple formula like that (responded/invited) is typically adjusted to account for such things as surveys that were undeliverable. It is important for researchers to be clear about how their response rate is calculated. Otherwise, we have an example of a questionable ethical practice (here, reporting your response rate as higher than it was).

⟫ Try This Now

Have you ever received a survey in the mail or been contacted by telephone and not responded? As you think about your research, what level of responding would be adequate, in your view?

NONRESPONSE AND NONRESPONSE BIAS

Before proceeding, we need to distinguish between **nonresponse** and **nonresponse bias**. Nonresponse rate is simply a numerical statement of the number of people who did not respond. Nonresponse bias occurs when those who do *not* respond are different from those who *do* respond on one or more characteristics that are important to your study.

Does nonresponding automatically create nonresponse bias? No, but there are situations when nonresponding does create bias. Imagine you are looking at the relationship between where someone was raised (rural vs. urban) and the number of walks he or she had taken in the arboretum on campus and other measures of connectedness to nature. When you examine your data, you see that those who did not respond lived farther away from the arboretum than did those who responded to your survey (you could ascertain this through their addresses in the student directory). In this instance, that differential nonresponse does create nonresponse bias because the distance of the residence hall from the arboretum might affect their use of the arboretum.

When you are using a student population, the demographic makeup of the population is probably available to you through the college website (e.g., geographic distribution, gender, and percentage of students on sports teams) or through data available from the institutional researcher. By checking these data, you can see to what extent your sample mirrors the larger population, at least on those characteristics that are known. Whether nonresponse bias is present depends on the centrality of those characteristics to your hypotheses. For those wishing to learn more about estimating nonresponse bias in mail

Nonresponse: a lack of response to a something, typically a survey.

Nonresponse bias: when those who do not respond differ from those who do in terms of characteristics central to your hypothesis.

surveys, a frequently cited article by Scott Armstrong and Terry Overton (1977) is recommended. Of the methods they discussed, comparing your results to known values of the population (such as archival information about the student body) is the easiest approach.

Many of the recommendations in Dillman et al.'s (2014) book deal with achieving the highest return rate on your survey to avoid (a) nonresponse and (b) nonresponse bias. This book is a core resource for survey researchers. Given that nonresponse bias is not that easy to estimate (Wagner, 2010), taking steps to avoid it is important.

REVISIT AND RESPOND

- Why is nonresponse not necessarily nonresponse bias? For basic demographic characteristics of a college sample, where could you find information about the population?

RESPONSE RATES AND REPORTING THEM

What do we know about rates of responding to surveys? One clear message is that return rates are dropping (Baruch, 1999; Wagner, 2010). Pew Research Center data (**http:// www.people-press.org/2012/05/15/assessing-the-representativeness-of-public-opin ion-surveys/**) show that whereas a response rate of 36% was found to their telephone surveys in 1997, that rate had dropped to 9% by 2012.

Yehuda Baruch (1999) distinguished between questionnaires that are returned and questionnaires that are returned and usable. He argued that it is the returned *and* usable return rate that should be reported. Otherwise, researchers are inflating their success.

Mode of Delivery

Another consideration is that response rates differ by mode of delivery, with response rates to online surveys typically lower than those to mail surveys (Tuten, 2010). Nevertheless, the response rates for online surveys may change over time in a given study. In one study (Kongsved, Basnov, Holm-Christensen, & Hjollund, 2007), the superiority of paper-and-pencil surveys was shown in terms of the initial response rate (in contrast to an Internet distribution). After a reminder, however, the completeness with which the questionnaire was filled out was significantly higher for the Internet than for the paper-and-pencil version. Furthermore, the authors argued that as the Internet becomes more familiar to people as a way to respond to questionnaires, it likely will be a more effective mode of delivery than the paper-and-pencil approach.

INCENTIVES: PRACTICAL ISSUES

Given the need to encourage people to respond to surveys or otherwise take part in research, you might ask whether incentives are effective in increasing response rates. The answer is "yes." Chapter 4 covered the ethical aspects of offering incentives, in particular, whether they could be considered coercive. Here the focus is the practical aspects of incentives.

A point made in Chapter 4 is that there are no guidelines at the federal level that prohibit offering incentives. Often the determination of approving incentives is made at the local level in terms of (a) whether they are permitted and, if so, (b) their type and value.

Perspectives on Financial Incentives

There is evidence that small cash incentives work well (Dillman et al., 2014), but incentives may be prohibited by some departments. In a frequently cited meta-analysis on the effectiveness of incentives, Allan Church (1993) reported that initially sending rewards (either monetary, 19.1% return rate above controls; or nonmonetary, 7.9% return rate above controls) significantly increased response rates more than did promising rewards when the survey was returned (called **promised incentives**). The nonmonetary rewards were highly variable, including small tokens (e.g., golf balls), entry into a lottery, or in one study, a turkey! Church recommended against using rewards delayed until survey return (promised incentives) and questioned whether nonmonetary rewards are worth the return on investment, given the greater success with upfront monetary rewards. A 2015 meta-analysis (Mercer, Caporaso, Cantor, & Townsend, 2015) again showed the advantage of **prepaid incentives** in contrast to promised incentives in increasing response rates, particularly for mail surveys.

In the literature on incentives, one theme that has emerged is that lotteries, although often used in online research, may not be particularly effective incentives. In a chapter from a book covering online behavioral research methods (Gosling & Johnson, 2010), Anja Göritz (2010) reflects on the use of incentives. In online research, the most widely used approach is lotteries (also called *sweepstakes* or *prize draws*) perhaps because they are easier to implement than prepaid incentives given the Web modality. At the same time, Göritz stated, "Regarding the type of incentive to be used, lotteries are usually cheap but may be ineffective" (p. 228). She recommended that those with a small research budget "keep the lottery payout to a minimum" (p. 228) presumably because of its limited effectiveness.

Promised incentives: incentives for research promised at survey return.

Prepaid incentives: incentives that are given in advance of participation.

REVISIT AND RESPOND

- In terms of responding to surveys, what do we know about the relative effectiveness of (a) incentives versus no incentives? (b) Monetary versus gift incentives? (c) Prepaid versus promised incentives?

AMAZON MECHANICAL TURK (MTURK): THE WORLD AWAITS

Worker: name given to participant on Amazon Mechanical Turk®.

Human Intelligence Task (HIT): name for a study posted on Amazon Mechanical Turk®.

Requester: name given to person posting research on Amazon Mechanical Turk®.

At the beginning of the chapter, we talked about the use of institutional subject pools, where there may be limits to the number of participants available to any given researcher. Now we will move to the opposite end of the spectrum, online sources of paid participants, limited only by your ability to pay. In particular, we will focus on Amazon Mechanical Turk (introduced in Chapter 2), which provides a market of paid (by you) online workers who are interested in participating in research. **Workers**, as they are known, sign up for a particular **Human Intelligence Task (HIT)**, which you, the **Requester**, post on the Amazon Mechanical Turk website (**https://www.mturk.com/mturk/welcome**) (Figure 9.1 shows the home page if you click on this link. Please note that Amazon often uses uppercase on the site to refer to Workers and the Requester, but we will use lowercase hereafter.)

FIGURE 9.1 Screenshot of Amazon Mechanical Turk Home Page

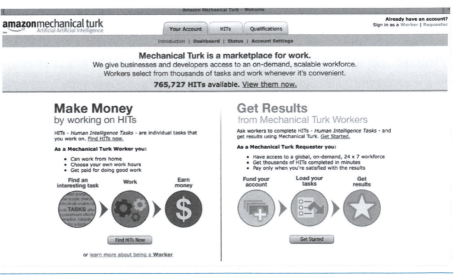

Source: © Amazon.

Amazon Mechanical Turk (AMT or MTurk) was started in 2005 (Bartneck, Duenser, Moltchanova, & Zawieska, 2015). There are other pools of online workers, such as Innocentive, oDesk, or CloudCrowd (Chandler, Mueller, & Paolacci, 2014), but Amazon Mechanical Turk may be the most well known.

As an introduction to what is known about Amazon MTurk, a paper by Garbiele Paolacci and Jesse Chandler (2014) is helpful. They described MTurk as an online labor market, with most participants coming from the United States and India. Summarizing what is known, Paolacci and Chandler stated that workers tend to be "younger (about 30 years old), overeducated, underemployed, less religious, and more liberal than the general population. . . . Within the United States, Asians are overrepresented and Blacks and Hispanics are underrepresented relative to the population as a whole" (p. 185). MTurker workers tend to be more introverted than are college student samples. Furthermore, there is some evidence that there are differences in performance on cognitive tasks, with workers learning less quickly and likely to have more difficulty with complex tasks than is true of college student samples (Paolacci & Chandler, 2014).

As Paolacci and Chandler (2014) pointed out, MTurk is not representative of the general population, but then neither is the undergraduate participant pool. Another issue they raised is that workers want to please researchers; for that reason, social desirability is an issue. One of their recommendations is to use between subjects designs (if appropriate; see Chapter 7) to avoid carryover effects (Paolacci & Chandler, 2014; see Chapter 8). Whether workers understand the task appears to make a difference in the quality of responses (Paolacci & Chandler), so it is a good idea to be very clear in what you are asking in your "HIT." Two other steps you can take to improve the quality of data are (1) thanking workers and (2) clearly explaining the meaning of the task to be completed (Paolacci & Chandler, 2014).

Amazon MTurk (AMT) is a tool undergoing rapid change (Litman, Robinson, & Rosenzweig, 2015). Compensation is now viewed as the primary motivator, in both India and the United States. The workforce of MTurkers is estimated to be on the order of half a million individuals worldwide with an increasingly larger percentage of workers coming from India (Litman et al., 2015). In the work of Leib Litman et al., financial compensation emerged as the primary motivation for completing HITs (more than killing time, having fun, gaining self-knowledge, and doing interesting tasks). Participants from India were more sensitive to the financial compensation issues, whereas U.S. participants produced high-quality data independent of compensation. For participants from India, Litman et al. argued that quality assurance steps are still necessary to assure the level of data is high.

With regard to platforms like MTurk, the rules of the game are changing rapidly. In other words, with regard to the nuts and bolts of use, what is written now likely will be out of date by the time this book is published. For that reason, we concentrate here more on the conceptual issues and general approach rather than on the particulars of setting up a HIT. Nevertheless, to improve understanding of the material that follows, it might be helpful to know a few basics:

- AMT offers internal templates within which to create simple HITs. If you want to conduct more complicated research using a between subjects design and random assignment to condition, your best approach is to create your survey in Qualtrics or SurveyMonkey and embed your survey link in the HIT (see Chapter 5 for coverage of online survey software).
- Most of the workers come from the United States and India. There are more complicated ways to acquire participants with particular characteristics, but in the simplest approach, you can set qualifications within your HIT that specify country of location and the percentage of HIT approvals workers must have.
- Workers are evaluated in terms of whether they finish the HIT and whether you approve their work. You can therefore specify that workers for your study have a particular level of HIT approval rating, such as 95%.
- What you pay workers is a moving target, but you are unlikely to get people to accept your HIT for a study lasting more than 10 minutes if you offer less than $0.50 (and that amount is steadily creeping upward). In research about the characteristics of MTurkers, workers now report that they are attracted to MTurk to earn money.
- If workers do not like your HIT (e.g., think it took longer than you said it would), they may post negative comments about you on MTurk list serves or forums. If you are thin-skinned, this form of data collection may not be for you.
- You will have to provide your social security number to be a requester or a worker (this presumably has to do with issues related to income earned and/or money paid).
- Amazon charges a commission fee.

Online sources of participants are a particularly attractive option for small institutions with limited participant pools, where it would not be uncommon for data collection to spread over two semesters if not into the next year to acquire the needed number of participants for a given study. Dan Johnson and Lauren Borden (2012) agreed with this perspective and saw the use of Amazon Mechanical Turk as a way to overcome the limited participant pools characteristic of small institutions. Their article provides a nice overview to the nuts and bolts of using MTurk. Michael Buhrmester, Tracy Kwang, and Samuel Gosling (2011) also encouraged the use of this tool because it provides a somewhat inexpensive way to access a more diverse pool than in traditional approaches (i.e., subject pools), and the quality of the data is as high (e.g., regarding psychometric standards) as is true of other approaches.

QUESTIONS OF VALIDITY IN USING AMAZON MTURK

A core question for researchers who contemplate using MTurk is the extent to which participants solicited from MTurk are similar to other samples you might use, such as undergraduate subject pools. Chandler et al. (2014) addressed one aspect of this question. Among the concerns are that MTurkers might be non-naïve (that is, they might be knowledgeable about the research task) in a variety of ways. For example, workers might participate in multiple related studies and thus learn something about the tasks and the hypotheses. Forums and list serves exist for MTurkers to share their views of research, particular research projects, and even particular requesters (researchers). This is another way workers might learn about the goals of research.

On the plus side, Chandler et al. (2014) pointed out that the MTurk participant pool is more diverse than you would find in academic participant pools and that the quality of data is as good, sometimes better, than data collected from traditional approaches. The quality of these data has been demonstrated in a variety of research domains (social, clinical, personality, and cognitive).

Chandler et al. (2014) provided several specific ways to decrease duplicate workers (see their article for the programming specifics). Because the sophistication of workers is growing, Chandler et al. recommended avoiding what they call *commonly used experimental procedures* (e.g., the trolley problem, which is used in evaluating moral dilemmas). The trolley problem (there are variations) is a hypothetical ethical dilemma problem involving the participant, who is standing by a lever in the train yard. Pulling the lever can divert the runaway trolley from its current course (which will kill five people if the participant does nothing); if the participant pulls the lever, the trolley will be diverted to a secondary track, where one person tied to that track will then be killed. The participant must decide what to do.

Another recommendation is to use **attention check questions** (questions that assess whether you are reading carefully; a commonly used question is "I am having a heart attack right now"; Chandler et al., 2014; Peer, Vosgerau, & Acquisti, 2014).

Attention check questions: questions inserted in a survey to check whether the respondent is actually reading the items (e.g., "I am having a heart attack right now").

REVIST AND RESPOND

- What is Amazon Mechanical Turk? What do we know about the validity of data collected on AMT and its comparability to data collected through more traditional approaches? Most workers come from which two countries? What is the primary motivation to participate in MTurk studies? Name a step you can take to assure that you will get workers to complete your task ("HIT") with care.

ONLINE PAID PANELS

Online panels consist of individuals who have typically been asked to sign up to participate in research. They may be customers, patients, or people who possess desirable target demographics (e.g., high income or luxury car ownership). These individuals have known demographic characteristics and can be recruited for studies that request those characteristics. There are many companies (e.g., Research Now and Toluna) that conduct research with such panels, which are often used by market research companies. Greenbook (**http://www.greenbook.org**), a guide for companies that want market research, has a list of such panels on its website.

SurveyMonkey and Qualtrics also offer paid panels for conducting research. Qualtrics Panel Services uses the services of other companies, including Research Now, Toluna, GMI, Clearvoice, and SSI (Survey Sampling International), to provide panels to interested customers (in other words, they outsource this). SurveyMonkey has its own panel service called Survey Monkey Audience. Its website lists examples from $1 to $3/response, but it provides the following criteria for determining the price: number of responses, targeting criteria, and survey length. Respondents come from the people who themselves take surveys on Survey-Monkey (**https://www.surveymonkey.com/mp/audience/our-survey-respondents/**).

Using these panels costs money, significantly more than the cost of collecting data on Amazon Mechanical Turk. If your research requires a specific consumer segment (e.g., people interested in installing a high-end sound system in their luxury vehicle), you might expect to pay more than $50/respondent. Some advice for using such panels comes from Ron Sellars, of GreyMatter Research and Consulting, in a blog posting dealing with online panel quality (**http://www.greenbookblog.org/2011/05/31/how-do-you-assure-online-panel-quality/**). If you need participants with targeted demographic characteristics, you might investigate what such panels have to offer, but be prepared to spend money.

REVISIT AND RESPOND

- What are online panels? What kinds of firms use them? Why are such panels expensive? (Think about the cost of finding people with particular characteristics.)

Summary

With the information from this chapter, you have a very good idea of the samples used in research—how representative they are and where we find them. You also know how to look beyond the subject pool to recruit participants in the community or online, and the specific obstacles that may stand in your way, especially concerning vulnerable populations. Definitions of sampling approaches have been discussed, and you know the difference between nonprobability sampling, for example, through snowballing, and probability sampling, including random sampling, stratified random sampling, proportionate sampling, systematic sampling, and cluster sampling. There is a good deal of practical advice in this chapter, from labeling your study to Dustin's Dozen for research in the field. You have the information to make the best use of incentives (what works and what doesn't). Amazon Mechanical Turk has been introduced as an online labor market, and you have a beginning knowledge of how it works and why it is an important source for small departments.

In the event that you did not consider them earlier, here are the **REVISIT and RESPOND** prompts that appeared in this chapter.

- List two potential threats to the internal validity of a study when you use a subject pool and how researchers have tried to combat these threats.
- Imagine that you are doing a study on the effect of wearing glasses on perceptions of professionalism in the workplace. Come up with a title that reflects the recommendations for labeling your study (to avoid demand characteristics). When would you schedule your study (day of week, time of day) for maximum representativeness?
- What kinds of connections do you have that would enable you to conduct research with off-campus populations? What steps would you take to safeguard your physical security and the security of your participants? Beyond the steps that are outlined in this chapter, what other ideas do you have about securing your physical safety?
- What are the benefits of conducting research at service learning sites? What are the potential drawbacks? What does it mean to be a "double agent" in the context of research? If you want to collect data from a group where you are a member, how can you avoid the possibility of coercion in requesting their participation?
- Which of Dustin's recommendations seem to focus on permissions and which on approaches to potential participants? Of Dustin's recommendations, list the five you think are most important and justify your choices. Add a recommendation you think he overlooked.
- What are some of the major challenges that Kosinski et al. (2015) identified in doing research on Facebook? Why did they discourage using financial incentives? What did they use instead? What is an advert? A snowball sample? What does the research of Gosling et al. (2004) show about the validity of Web-based surveys? What is the "emotional contagion" study, and what ethical issues did it raise?
- Using the concept of representativeness, explain why an undergraduate subject pool is a nonprobability sample.

- In general, explain why using probability sampling is preferable to nonprobability sampling. What makes something a random sample? How do stratified random and proportionate sampling differ? In what way is systematic sampling like random sampling? For cluster sampling, what does it mean to say that a cluster is the sampling unit?

- Why is nonresponse not necessarily nonresponse bias? For basic demographic characteristics of a college sample, where could you find information about the population?

- In terms of responding to surveys, what do we know about the relative effectiveness of (a) incentives versus no incentives? (b) Monetary versus gift incentives? (c) Prepaid versus promised incentives?

- What is Amazon Mechanical Turk? What do we know about the validity of data collected on AMT and its comparability to data collected through more traditional approaches? Most workers come from which two countries? What is the primary motivation to participate in MTurk studies? Name a step you can take to assure that you will get workers to complete your task ("HIT") with care.

- What are online panels? What kinds of firms use them? Why are such panels expensive? (Think about the cost of finding people with particular characteristics.)

BUILD YOUR SKILLS

Go online and investigate Amazon Mechanical Turk **(https://www.mturk.com/mturk/ welcome)**. One of the first things you can do is click on the HITS that are available (there are more than 1,000,000). You can search by the reward amount, the time allotted, and several other characteristics. Investigate the range of HITS available to learn more about this paid crowdsourcing platform.

$SAGE edge™

edge.sagepub.com/devlin

Sharpen your skills with SAGE edge!

SAGE edge for students provides a personalized approach to help you accomplish your coursework goals in an easy-to-use learning environment. You'll find action plans, mobile-friendly eFlashcards, and quizzes, as well as videos, web resources, and links to SAGE journal articles to support and expand on the concepts presented in this chapter.

ORGANIZING DATA AND ANALYZING RESULTS

CHAPTER HIGHLIGHTS

- Data files
  - Paper versus electronic surveys
  - Data view, variable view, and coding
  - Reasons for individual item entry
- Missing data: Points of view and choices
- Out-of-range values versus outliers
- Opportunistic biases and "going fishing"
- Significance levels
- Useful commands in SPSS: Compute, Recode, Select Cases
- Evaluating hypotheses
- Making use of free response items

OVERVIEW

Many quotations attribute success to a formula where preparation is 90% and perspiration or luck is the remainder. In truth, only preparation matters in research. Thinking back to our earlier chapters on research design, clearly stating hypotheses that can be evaluated by your research design is a critical step in running analyses. Designing a study that minimizes threats to internal validity is also important if these analyses are to yield significant results. By the time you have collected your data, it is too late to correct mistakes in those arenas. What you can do at this point is make sure you organize and label your data. Doing so will eliminate frustrations that arise when you don't know what a variable represents and what its values mean.

This chapter compares the different steps to perform in data analysis if you start with a paper versus an electronic version of your survey instrument. The chapter has three major foci: steps in (1) organizing the data; (2) considering what adjustments you can make to data that are missing, out of range, or outliers; and (3) analyzing the data. For analyzing your data, common analyses in SPSS Statistics® will be covered, and a summary of commands is presented in Appendix E at the end of the book. Other statistical packages will be briefly described at the end of the chapter, but because SPSS is considered very easy to use, it is emphasized. The particulars of presenting your data (that is, writing about them) will be covered in Chapter 11. Materials related to this chapter are also included as appendices. These include a decision tree to help you select the appropriate statistical analysis (Appendix A) and a summary of scale types and associated statistical analyses used in common research approaches (Appendix F).

PAPER AND ONLINE SURVEYS: AN OVERVIEW

When you use a paper version of a survey, you prepare the document in a word processing program, make copies of the document, and distribute the document to your participants (often in person). Participants provide their responses on these documents. You then take the documents, create a data file (e.g., in SPSS), and then enter the data by hand. When you use an online approach, you use survey software such as SurveyMonkey® or Qualtrics® to create an electronic version of the same questionnaire, and then send your participants a link to this survey. Participants respond to the survey online; responses are then downloadable to a statistical program like SPSS. If you are using a "free" survey software program (one of the "no-extras" packages), remember to check whether data are downloadable into a statistical package (see Chapter 5).

There are few differences between the SPSS file constructed by hand and the one constructed electronically. The major difference is that in the version by hand you create the labeling you need for every variable (and its values) as you enter the data. When data are downloaded into SPSS from an online questionnaire, most variable labels are there in generic form (e.g., "Q35"), but you may need to add specification to the variable labels and values after the fact.

> **» Try This Now**
>
> What advantages do you see to using an online version of your survey?

Among the advantages to the online approach are its portability (the survey can be taken anytime, anywhere), its "reach" (that is, the possibility of sending it to an unlimited number of participants), and the elimination of most data input errors. Given these advantages, why would anyone administer a questionnaire by hand? First, there may be projects where individual administration is required. For example, playing the Operation® board game after exposure to a stressful stimulus would require performance scores to be recorded and entered by hand. Knowing how to create a data file from scratch is therefore important and a fundamental skill every researcher should acquire. Second, thinking back to our discussion of representativeness in Chapter 9, although 87% of the U.S. population has an Internet connection (Pew statistics, **http://www.pew internet.org/2014/02/27/part-1-how-the-internet-has-woven-itself-into-american-life/**), some categories of individuals are less likely to be connected (and, thus, could not easily respond to an online survey).

Internet use is not distributed evenly across the age spectrum, with the lowest percentage of users in the 65 years and older category. Internet use also divides along income levels, with lower use likely if your income is less than $30,000/year, again according to the Pew data. In the Ann Devlin et al. (2013) research dealing with multicultural art in a therapist's office, the community sample completed a paper-and-pencil version of the instrument at a community health center. Using a paper version with the community sample enabled people (a) unfamiliar with computers or (b) without access to the Internet to take part in the study. Furthermore, the on-the-spot availability of versions of the questionnaire in different languages (Spanish and English) was important in terms of being responsive and building trust. The researcher was also present to answer questions.

Another disadvantage to electronic surveys is that you are not there to deal with technology malfunctions (e.g., a link that doesn't work). Other issues that researchers note are the problems with the standardization of administration; you don't know what else people are doing (e.g., talking or listening to music) when completing your online survey. A final consideration is that face-to-face contact, which occurs during the paper administration, may lead to more thoughtful and complete survey responses (see also Chapter 9 for a discussion of these issues) than is true for the online approach.

THE IMPORTANCE OF LABELING

Label everything. You will accomplish this slightly differently depending on your approach (paper vs. electronic), but you want to keep track of (a) the day of administration, (b) the time of administration, (c) the place of administration, and (d) any particularities of administration. If you are conducting a between subjects design, make sure you use some code to keep track of who was in what condition. This differentiation may be straightforward in an electronic version where you have a *randomizer function* (see Chapter 5) to distribute the different conditions across participants (the program keeps track), but if you are exposing participants to different conditions (e.g., by projecting an image on a screen) in a "paper" version, make sure you record which experimental stimulus (image/scenario/text) they saw.

In addition, each survey should be labeled with a participant number (start with 1). If you have paper surveys, write the participant number, the day, the time, the place of administration, and the condition (if applicable) in the same place on each questionnaire (usually the upper right-hand corner). Some researchers recommend that you write the participant number on *each* page of a participant's questionnaire. You would certainly want to do this if you separated the pages (e.g., for doing content analyses of several questions and worked on those pages separately from other parts of the survey).

With regard to the particularities of administration, you might have a journal in which you record the date, time, place, and comments about how the session went. If participants came late, left quickly, were talking or laughing, or otherwise may have influenced others' responses, you want to note that. For example, if one or two people quickly complete the survey and leave, this behavior may prime the remaining individuals to rush through the material as well. Participants may offer observations about the study that are also useful to record and integrate into a Discussion section in your research paper.

If the data are collected online using survey software such as Qualtrics, the day and time of administration and completion time will be recorded automatically. You won't have a sense of any particularities regarding sessions unless people complete their online surveys in your presence.

LABELING IN A DATA FILE AND DECIDING ON A CODING SYSTEM

When you create a data file in SPSS from scratch, you literally have a blank slate (see Figure 10.1). As soon as you start working on your data file, "Save" it with a name that suggests what the file contains (e.g., Research.Methods.Project). Add your new data to this basic file, and save every 10–15 minutes or so. A word of warning: SPSS does not update automatically with regard to analyses and actions you have already taken on your data (e.g., creating a new variable). When you add new data to your file, you will have to (a) check for missing data and potential outliers, (b) recreate your new computed variables, and (c) rerun any previous analyses. *Thus, it makes good sense to wait to run analyses, even preliminary analyses, until you have entered all of the data you will have and made any justifiable adjustments.* An exception to that recommendation might be the case where you want to check on the success of a manipulation check before collecting all of your data.

Notice in Figure 10.1 that you have two ways to view the data, **Data View** and **Variable View** listed at the bottom of the screen. Data View shows you the actual numerical values for the data you enter (in Figure 10.1, we have entered no numbers); Variable View shows you the concept or category (e.g., age, gender, class year, experimental condition, and label for a scale item) to which the numerical value applies. The concept of a variable was discussed in Chapter 7 when we covered nomenclature surrounding independent variables. There, we distinguished between the idea of a *treatment* and a *level.* A treatment is another name for variable; a level is another way of talking about the particular value a variable can take on. When you set up a data file, this distinction between variable and level is critical.

People often think that each value of a variable (for example, each class year, first, second, third, and fourth) has its *own* column in SPSS. No. All values for a given variable will be accommodated by that *one* variable; each variable has its own column.

Data View: in SPSS Statistics®, view of the data by cases (rows) and columns (variables).

Variable View: view in SPSS Statistics® in which the variables and their characteristics (e.g., name, data type, and length) are found.

FIGURE 10.1   Blank Slate to Start SPSS

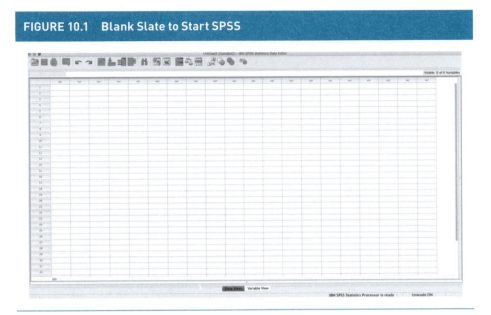

The numbers in that column reflect the values on that variable for each participant. The next section makes explicit this distinction between a variable and the value on that variable.

Deciding on a Coding System

When you create a data file by hand, you are entering numbers; the numbers may have a preexisting meaning, like someone's age (e.g., 19), or the number "3," in the case of a survey item that is to be answered on a scale from 1 to 7. In other cases, you have to assign a number (that stands for its meaning) to each level (value) of a variable, like gender or class year. In other words, if the numerical values are not predetermined, *you* decide on the values you want to use to represent the levels of the variable. In differentiating one class year from another, we need to assign a separate numerical value to each class year. When assigning values, there are a few principles to keep in mind. First, use numbers that seem logical or make sense intuitively. Second, you want to assign consecutive values because this makes conducting analyses easier in SPSS.

> **>> Try This Now**
>
> Using the two principles just stated (logic and consecutive sequence), if you had five class years of students to represent, what numbers would you select?

FIGURE 10.2   Variable View of Subject Number, Age, and Class Year

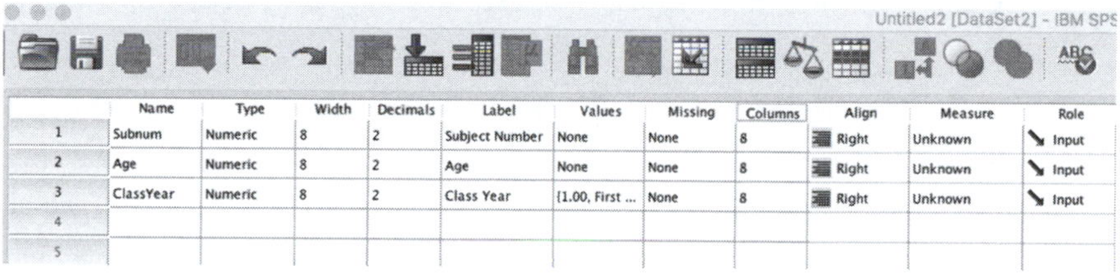

Look at the following example showing the Variable View (Figure 10.2) and the Variable View specifying the values we have assigned for Class year (Figure 10.3).

What you see in Figure 10.2 is the Variable View in which we have typed in the "Name" and "Label" for three variables (Subject Number, Age, and Class Year), and in the case of Class Year, we have specified the values (or levels) for that variable (see Figure 10.3). Please note, the "Name" of a variable must be continuous (ClassYear; no spaces), whereas the "Label" can include spaces ("Class Year"). SPSS no longer limits the number of characters you can have for the variable "Name;" nevertheless, keeping variable names somewhat short helps you quickly locate the variable you seek.

FIGURE 10.3   Variable View Specifying Values for Class Year

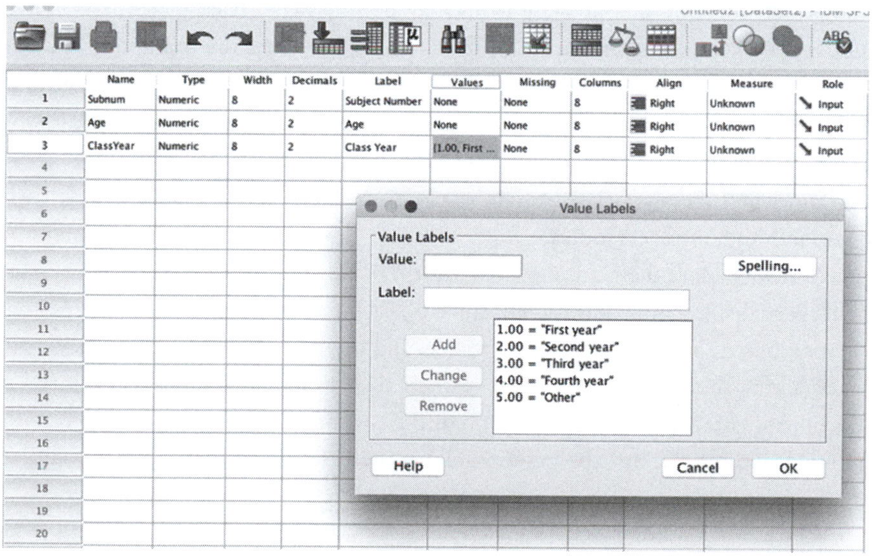

We have specified values (levels by name) for Class Year because the numbers we have used to represent class year (1, 2, 3, 4, and 5) have no meaning in and of themselves. We have to indicate that "1" means "first year," which is a choice we have made. You will use numbers to represent different levels of nominal variables like gender, class year, and your experimental conditions. Numbers also represent the scores on scale items [e.g., 1–4 on the Rosenberg Self-Esteem Scale (1965)]. In the Variable View you have the opportunity to specify those values (refer to Figure 10.3). In the case of Class Year, we have said 1 = first year, 2 = second year, 3 = third year, 4 = fourth year, and 5 = other. There is an intuitive correspondence between the numeral 1 and first year. In deciding on your coding system, it is wise to capitalize on these parallelisms; use commonsense.

> ## ❯❯ Try This Now
>
> Should you take the time to specify the values for *each scale item?*

Yes, up to a point. It is not necessary to label exhaustively for a given scale if each item has the same response options. You need to record or specify the response range for at least one of those scale items (minimum to maximum) and what the values represent. For example, if you have a scale of 40 items, and each item has the same choices of "1 = not at all" to "7 = a lot" (and only anchors 1 and 7 are defined for respondents on the questionnaire itself, refer to Figure 5.2), then specifying the minimum and maximum anchor labels for only one of these items may be sufficient. If each item has *different* response options (refer to Figure 5.10), then you need to enter the minimum and maximum values for *each item* (see Figure 10.4). Thus, for the survey question, "With the schedule of physicians in this hospital, making an appointment with one of them would be," and the response options of "1 = very easy" to "9 = very difficult," you will specify those values and their associated meanings; in doing so, you will remind yourself what the low and high numbers indicate.

Next, if we look at the Data View (Figure 10.5), we see the numbers we have entered for each participant (going horizontally; rows) on each variable (going vertically; columns).

Remember, a column represents a variable, and the level of that variable (the score, if you are talking about interval data) for a particular participant for that variable is entered in the appropriate *cell* (at the intersection of the row and column). Thus, Subject 4 has responded with an "8" for the question about the ease of scheduling an appointment with physicians.

FIGURE 10.4   Specifying Minimum and Maximum Values for a Variable

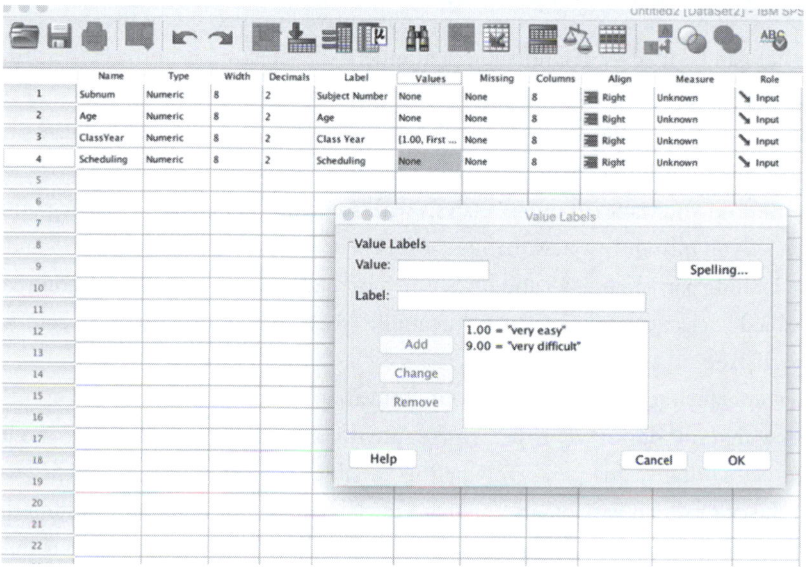

FIGURE 10.5   Data View of Entered Data

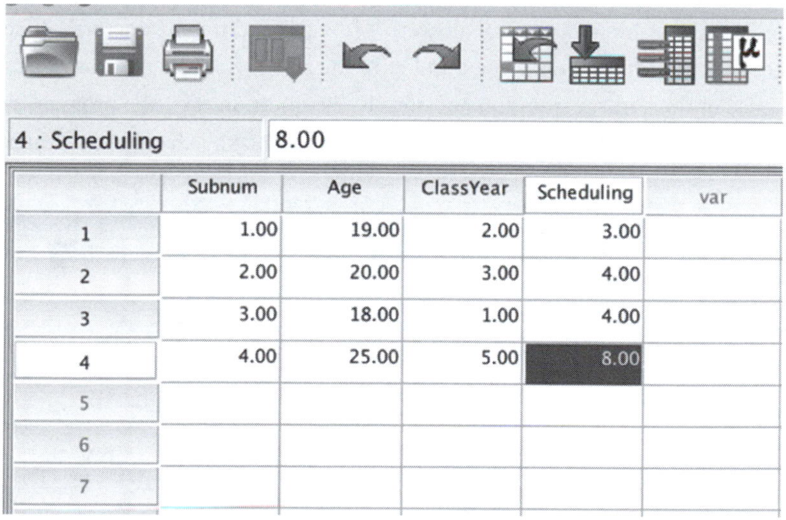

OTHER LABELING RECOMMENDATIONS

As a statistical program, SPSS comes with consecutive numbers along the y-axis (vertical edge) that can be used as default subject numbers. This feature is not sufficient to identify subjects by number. As your first variable, you want to create `subnum` or a similar variable name that indicates subject number. Why? Because then the subject number becomes a manipulable variable (i.e., you can take actions with it). The `subnum` variable is useful if you want to run an analysis with some but not all of the participants. For example, if you introduce a new manipulation check beginning with subject 35 and want to only include participants 35 and higher in your analyses, you would use a command in SPSS called "Select Cases" to restrict the sample (see a later section on SPSS commands) and specify the `subnum` variable.

A second labeling issue involves the kind of variable you have. You notice in the Variable View that one option is "Type." Make sure this is a **numeric data type** if you intend to do any quantitative analyses involving this variable. You can change the Type by clicking on the cell for that variable in Variable View. The default assignment is numeric, but in some software programs where you have used only words (strings) in your question and the response is a text box, the variable might be downloadable as a **string variable type** (see Figure 10.6).

People often wonder why they get an error message when they try to do analyses with one of these string variables. You need to change this variable type to Numeric to do statistical analyses. As an example, you can see for Q88, the variable Type is String, but the question is one that has a numerical answer: "How many different doctors' offices have you visited for care? (please enter the number in the box)." Because there are no numerical response options in the question and simply the question text, the program defaults to String here. To conduct analyses, the variable Type must be changed to Numeric.

Numeric data type: in SPSS Statistics®, a data type that permits numerical analysis.

String variable type: data type in SPSS Statistics® on which no numerical analyses can be performed.

FIGURE 10.6 Example of a String Type Variable

Q80	Numeric	8	0	The next quest...	None	None	5	Right	Scale	Input
Q81	Numeric	8	0	1. Have you ev...	{1, Yes}...	None	5	Right	Scale	Input
Q82	String	2000	0	If yes, please e...	None	None	15	Left	Nominal	Input
Q83.0	Numeric	8	0	2. Have you ev...	{1, Yes}...	None	5	Right	Scale	Input
Q84	String	2000	0	If yes, how old ...	None	None	15	Left	Nominal	Input
Q85	String	2000	0	How many nigh...	None	None	15	Left	Nominal	Input
Q86	Numeric	8	0	3. Is any family...	{1, Yes}...	None	5	Right	Scale	Input
Q87	String	2000	0	If yes, who (ple...	None	None	15	Left	Nominal	Input
Q88	String	2000	0	4. How many di...	None	None	15	Left	Nominal	Input
Q89_1	Numeric	8	0	5. In what type...	None	None	5	Right	Scale	Input
Q89_2	Numeric	8	0	5. In what type...	None	None	5	Right	Scale	Input

FIGURE 10.7	Use of Default Labeling

LABELING ISSUES IN ONLINE SURVEY SOFTWARE

In online survey software programs such as Qualtrics, it is easy to create a survey and distribute it. It is tempting to accept the default labeling of question numbers, for example, Q51, Q53, Q55, Q57, and so on. When you download the data into SPSS (see Figure 10.7), you don't know which question is which.

> **» Try This Now**
>
> What problems might you encounter if you use this default labeling?

As you can see, there is a lot of nontransparent labeling here, that is, a lot of Qs followed by numbers with no hint of the question related to a particular "Q." It is very simple to label a question within your Qualtrics survey; this label will be visible only to you. When you download the data with labels into SPSS, you will know what you have. Figure 10.8 shows the difference between variables with specific labels and without.

ENTERING INDIVIDUAL ITEMS VERSUS ITEM TOTALS

Our dependent variables are often scale totals, for example, the total for the State Trait Anxiety Inventory (STAI) or Morris Rosenberg's Self Esteem Scale (RSES; 1965).

FIGURE 10.8 Partially Labeled Data Visible in SPSS

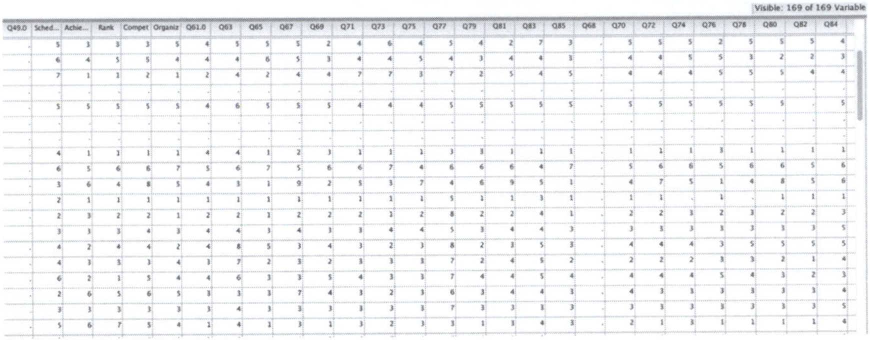

Visible: 169 of 169 Variable

Q49.0	Sched...	Achie...	Rank	Compet	Organiz	Q61.0	Q63	Q65	Q67	Q69	Q71	Q73	Q75	Q77	Q79	Q81	Q83	Q85	Q68	Q70	Q72	Q74	Q76	Q78	Q80	Q82	Q84
.	5	3	3	3	5	4	5	5	5	2	4	6	4	5	4	2	7	3	.	5	5	5	2	5	5	5	4
.	6	4	5	5	4	4	4	6	5	3	4	4	5	4	3	4	4	3	.	4	4	5	5	3	2	2	3
.	7	1	1	2	1	2	4	2	4	4	7	7	3	7	2	5	4	5	.	4	4	4	5	5	5	4	4
.	.	.	.	.	.	.	.	.	.	.	.	.	.	.	.	.	.	.	.	.	.	.	.	.	.	.	.
.	5	5	5	5	5	4	6	5	5	5	4	4	4	5	5	5	5	5	.	5	5	5	5	5	5	.	5
.	.	.	.	.	.	.	.	.	.	.	.	.	.	.	.	.	.	.	.	.	.	.	.	.	.	.	.
.	.	.	.	.	.	.	.	.	.	.	.	.	.	.	.	.	.	.	.	.	.	.	.	.	.	.	.
.	4	1	1	1	1	4	4	1	2	3	1	1	1	3	3	1	1	1	.	1	1	1	3	1	1	1	1
.	6	5	6	6	7	5	6	7	5	6	6	7	4	6	6	6	4	7	.	5	6	6	5	6	6	5	6
.	3	6	4	8	5	4	3	1	9	2	5	3	7	4	6	9	5	1	.	4	7	5	1	4	8	5	6
.	2	1	1	1	1	1	1	1	1	1	1	1	1	5	1	1	3	1	.	1	1	.	1	.	1	1	1
.	2	3	2	2	1	2	2	1	2	2	2	1	2	8	2	2	4	1	.	2	2	3	2	3	2	2	3
.	3	3	3	4	3	4	4	3	4	3	3	4	4	5	3	4	4	3	.	3	3	3	3	3	3	3	5
.	4	2	4	4	2	4	8	5	3	4	3	2	3	8	2	3	5	3	.	4	4	4	3	5	5	5	5
.	4	3	3	3	4	3	7	2	3	2	3	3	3	7	2	4	5	2	.	2	2	2	3	3	2	1	4
.	6	2	1	5	4	4	6	3	3	5	4	3	3	7	4	4	5	4	.	4	4	4	5	4	3	2	3
.	2	6	5	6	5	3	3	3	7	4	3	2	3	6	3	4	4	3	.	4	3	3	3	3	3	3	4
.	3	3	3	3	3	3	4	3	3	3	3	3	3	7	3	3	3	3	.	3	3	3	3	3	3	3	5
.	5	6	7	5	4	1	4	1	3	1	3	2	3	3	1	3	4	3	.	2	1	3	1	1	1	1	4

If you are entering your data by hand and you plan to use the item total as your dependent variable, you might ask why you need to enter the score for each item. In the case of the RSES, there are 10 items; in the case of STAI, there are 20, but many scales have a larger number of items, and entering each score for each participant takes time.

Try This Now

What advantage might there be to entering the score for each item in a scale?

Compute Function: tool in SPSS Statistics® that allows you to create new variables through arithmetic operations.

If you answered, "to calculate the Cronbach's alpha of the measure," you are correct. You may recall we reviewed how to calculate the Cronbach's alpha in Chapter 5 when we discussed the criteria for selecting a measure. Not only do you want to state the Cronbach's alpha in the literature for a given measure, but you also want to report the Cronbach's alpha for *your sample* for that measure. When you download data from a survey software platform like Qualtrics, those individual item scores will already be in the data file, but with a paper version, those data must be entered by hand. Later in this chapter we will review the SPSS commands for various functions, one of which is the **Compute Function**. The Compute Function allows you to compute the total of any number of items; this is the command you would use to calculate the Scale Total *after* determining the Cronbach's alpha for the scale.

BACKING UP DATA

When a hard drive crashes, people learn how important it is to save and back up your data. Don't learn the hard way. Every time you enter a line of data for a participant, save your data. Make sure that you have a backup system such as an external hard drive; Apple's Mac® also has a function called Time Machine. In addition, there are backup systems that are cloud-based. Some institutions provide these (e.g., Crash Pad Cloud) for their users. There are other alternatives, including such cloud-based applications as **Dropbox**®, which is a cloud-based storage system that also facilitates sharing files if you are working on a project. There is a free version (Dropbox Basic) that has 2 GB of storage.

Dropbox®: cloud-based file sharing system.

DEALING WITH MISSING DATA: DIFFERING POINTS OF VIEW

Returning to a theme from earlier in the book, careful research is the best recommendation for increasing the validity of your study. In the case of your dataset, you want to come as close as you can to having a dataset with complete cases (participants answered every question); in other words, you don't want missing data. Good communication skills, both in person and through every written communication to participants, will increase the likelihood of complete cases. Paul Allison (2001) has written a book on dealing with missing data; nevertheless, he stated:

> The only really good solution to the missing data problem is not to have any. So in the design and execution of research projects, it is essential to put great effort into minimizing the occurrence of missing data. Statistical adjustments can never make up for sloppy research. (pp. 2–3)

Researchers take different approaches to dealing with missing data (Pigott, 2001; Schafer & Graham, 2002; Schlomer, Bauman, & Card, 2010). At a minimum, researchers should report the amount, source, and pattern of such missing data (Schlomer et al., 2010). The amount has to do with the proportion of missing data, and there is no agreed upon standard for what an acceptable level is (Schlomer et al., 2010); acceptable proportions range from 5% to 20%. The source of the missing data is either nonresponse (that is, participants leave one or more items blank) or attrition. Attrition is likely to be the case for longitudinal or multiple-session studies. Most students will encounter missing data in the context of nonresponse (i.e., missing responses).

Listwise Deletion and Pairwise Deletion

Listwise deletion: when there are missing data, the elimination of the complete case if any data are missing.

After determining the amount, source, and pattern of missing data (how you determine the pattern of missing data is a topic beyond the scope of this chapter), what next? Some researchers delete a case altogether if any data are missing; this is called **listwise deletion**, complete case analysis, or case deletion; you retain only the complete cases in the dataset (Pigott, 2001; Schafer & Graham, 2002; Schlomer et al., 2010). In other words, your dataset will contain only those participants (cases) where every item was answered. Other researchers include the data of a participant in those analyses where there are complete data for *that particular analysis;* this is called **pairwise deletion** or available case analysis (Pigott, 2001; Schlomer et al., 2010). When the *N*s are different for analyses in a study, pairwise deletion has occurred. For example, a given participant might have answered every item for one scale (dependent variable, DV) but skipped some items on another scale (DV). If you are doing a correlation, for example, SPSS will give the option of specifying listwise or pairwise deletion.

Pairwise deletion: approach to handling missing data in which a participant is dropped on analyses for only the missing variable(s) for that analysis, not altogether.

Imputation

Imputation: process of replacing missing values with substitutes (e.g., sample means).

Still other researchers include the participant in analyses with a limit to the number of permissible missing items (e.g., 1 out of 10 items on the RSES). In this case, the researcher replaces the missing data through a strategy called **imputation**: replacing missing values with substitute values. This commonly used approach has limitations because of distortion (underestimation) of variances and covariances and has been criticized (Schlomer et al., 2010). Some researchers feel that using imputation is like fabricating data. Still, many researchers use this approach. Students should know that there are more advanced techniques (e.g., multiple imputation and maximum likelihood estimation) available for replacing missing data (Pigott, 2001; Schafer & Graham, 2002; Schlomer et al., 2010); you may come across these terms in articles you read. These topics would be covered in more advanced courses in statistics and are beyond the scope of this chapter.

Despite the drawbacks to using sample mean replacement for missing data, we will talk about it further because it could be used if the researcher acknowledges its limitations, specifically that the results could bias an outcome.

REVISIT AND RESPOND

- Thinking back to Chapters 3 and 7 where the topic of power was discussed, remember that losing subjects affects the potential power of your research, that is, your ability to avoid a Type II error. The loss of power is one reason Allison (2001) said, "The only really good solution to the missing data problem is not to have any." But if you do have missing data, what choices do you have to deal with it? In that regard, explain the difference between listwise deletion and pairwise deletion. When you replace data through imputation, what does that mean?

REPLACING MISSING DATA THROUGH SINGLE VALUE IMPUTATION

Our focus here is interval (i.e., continuous) data. There are more advanced approaches to replacing missing values when the data are categorical (see, for example, Allison, 2001), but these are beyond the scope of this chapter. First, let us consider why it makes more sense to replace continuous than categorical data.

>> **Try This Now**

Why might it be a problem to use a sample mean to replace a missing categorical item, such as whether someone is an athlete?

For items that are categorical (e.g., gender, political party, and race), missing data often are not replaced. That is, when a participant has not answered a question that reflects a nominal category, it may make little sense to take an average and substitute the mean value. For example, what if you have five categories of race, represented as numerical values, 1–5, and the mean of your sample for race is 2.4. What race is a 2.4? You can see the difficulty here. But what if you are talking about interval scale (continuous) data, and someone has left a particular item blank, where the question had the response options 1–5. Would a mean of 2.4 be interpretable? Yes.

The question thus becomes whether to substitute missing data and, if so, the limits to such substitution. There are no firm rules. As mentioned earlier, researchers differ in their perspectives on this, just as they do on many issues such as including or excluding extreme values, called *outliers* (as introduced in Chapter 7). What is clear is that if you choose to substitute missing data, you need to explain exactly what you have done. Transparency in all aspects of research is critical.

SOME RECOMMENDATIONS FOR MISSING DATA

If you have sufficient power, you can use listwise deletion (complete case analysis, that is, use only cases that are complete on every measure). A second option, more likely to be used if you have less power, is to use pairwise deletion (use the cases for which you have complete data for a particular analysis). The third, and least desirable option, is to replace the missing values by imputing the sample mean (to achieve complete cases or at least complete cases for as many measures as seems reasonable).

But what is reasonable? When have you replaced too many missing data points? As stated earlier, there is no hard-and-fast rule, and acceptable boundaries range from replacing 5% to 20% of missing data. Given this range, a reasonable recommendation would be to set a limit of no more than 10% of the items missing for a given participant on a given measure. Then, for each missing item, you compute the sample mean (we will cover this SPSS command in a later section) and enter the imputed value in the blank cell for each participant missing a response for that item.

IDENTIFYING MISSING DATA

How do you know which items are missing? In the case of paper surveys, it is obvious. You come across an item with no response. Then, when you enter the data into a data file, you will have an empty cell for that variable for that participant. In the case of data files that are downloaded from online survey software, you can run a *frequency analysis* (as introduced in Chapter 6; see more discussion in the section on SPSS commands later in this chapter) for each relevant variable. That analysis will tell you which variables have missing items and how many data points are missing for each variable. From there, one easy way to proceed is to scan down the column for each variable with missing data and look for the empty cells. Make a note of them (that is, which subjects have missing data on this item), and determine whether the variable is continuous or categorical. If the variable is continuous, replace it with the sample mean if you have made the decision to replace missing data and the participant meets your cutoff for the percentage of missing data allowed. You determine the sample mean by running a **descriptives** analysis in SPSS for each continuous variable (see more discussion in the section on SPSS commands later in this chapter).

HANDLING OUT-OF-RANGE VALUES

In this chapter, **out-of-range values** refer to values that are outside the range specified in your response anchors. This situation will typically occur in data the researcher enters by hand because online response items for scales permit only the choices you have specified, and these are preserved when you download the data into a statistical package such as SPSS.

To discover whether you have any of these out of range values, you would conduct a *frequency analysis* for all of your items. You would do the frequency analysis for both interval and nominal data because here you are looking for the values that are reported. For example, if the response anchors for a given item are 1–7, and the frequency analysis for that item shows an "8," you know that "8" is likely to be a data entry error. In Data View, you can scan down the column for that item and identify the subject with this out-of-range value. Then, you return to your original questionnaire for that subject, locate the item, and see how the participant actually responded (i.e., what value the participant selected).

It is possible to have an out-of-range value in an online questionnaire if the item is fill-in-the-blank (e.g., age) where participants type in their response. If you do frequencies for such open-ended items where a numerical value was supposed to be typed in by the participant, and you see an unlikely response (e.g., "199" for age in a sample of undergraduates), you might reasonably conclude that the person meant to type in something else (e.g., "19"). If you change the number, you would report this "adjustment" in your paper (i.e., changing 199 to 19).

HANDLING OUTLIERS

Outliers are data points that differ significantly from the other data. Such data points can occur for a variety of reasons, and the nature of the outlier determines whether it should be excluded. Outliers generally occur because of variability in the data or from experimental error. In the latter case, you can make a good argument for excluding them. In the former case, excluding the outliers is less clear-cut. Let's take an example. If you use a touchscreen monitor to record the time it takes for people to find a location on an

---

Descriptives: statistical presentation of measures of central tendency and dispersion that characterize a set of data.

Out-of-range values: values not specified in the data (e.g., a value of 8 on a scale range of 1–7).

interactive map displayed on the monitor, and there is an error in the recording mechanism that produces very long times to touch the screen, then you might reasonably exclude those cases (e.g., Devlin & Bernstein, 1997; see discussion of this issue in Devlin, 2006). You might be justified in excluding those cases particularly if you set the exclusion criteria BEFORE you collected your data. If long times to touch the screen could be related to someone's hesitancy to make a decision, and arguably to their confidence, the decision to exclude those data is questionable.

Like detecting the pattern of missing data in your dataset, the statistical approaches for dealing with outliers that occur for a reason *other* than such experimental errors as equipment malfunction are beyond the scope of this chapter. The focus here is to provide some basic sense of what the issues are and specifically to consider the ethical aspects.

REVISIT AND RESPOND

- Explain the difference between data that represent out-of-range values and data that represent outliers.

Outliers and Opportunistic Bias

Opportunistic bias: pursuing data analysis in multiple ways that increases the chances of finding significant results.

One of the major concerns in dealing with outliers is whether the researcher is creating **opportunistic bias** (DeCoster, Sparks, Sparks, Sparks, & Sparks, 2015), that is, creating opportunities to find statistical significance that otherwise would not have been the case. Jamie DeCoster et al.'s (2015) article highlighted the kinds of practices that researchers may follow to improve their chances of finding significance. Such practices involve reporting only the desirable results from a larger set of analyses, changing the statistical approach to achieve greater significance, and adjusting the variable (e.g., using different cut-off points for categorization), among several examples. This article is well worth reading for anyone who wants to conduct research because it reminds us that ethical choices face us in every decision. The flexibility researchers have in deciding how to analyze and report their data has also been described as the "*researcher degrees of freedom*" (Simmons, Nelson, & Simonsohn, 2011, p. 1359, emphasis in the original). Given the scrutiny that social science is undergoing as a result of high-profile cases of fraud in research (think back to the example in Chapter 1), being aware of opportunistic bias should make you more thoughtful about the decisions in your own research.

Regarding outliers, whether such opportunistic bias is present depends on the reason the case is an outlier (and what you do about it). Vic Barnett and Toby Lewis (1994), who were cited in DeCoster et al. (2015), said people agree that genuine errors (such as a computer malfunction) are a reason to exclude outliers. At the same time, when such errors are absent, excluding outliers (the ones that are not the result of experimental error) is not a step to take lightly.

Similar to DeCoster et al. (2015), Joseph Simmons et al. (2011) discussed the self-serving nature of the decisions researchers make, including what to consider an outlier. Simmons et al. made several recommendations for dealing with the flexibility in data collection and analysis that results in false positives (rejecting the null hypothesis when you should not have done so). Regarding eliminating observations (which would include outliers), they stated, "If observations are eliminated, authors must also report what the statistical results are if those observations are included" (p. 1362). The emphasis in their recommendations is for authors to be transparent about what they have done and why. Simmons et al. argued that reviewers (and readers) can then evaluate the extent to which a given finding depends on excluding the data.

As with missing data, there are no hard-and-fast rules for deciding when something is too divergent to be excluded (Zijlstra, Van der Ark, & Sijtsma, 2011). You have to present a rational, defensible argument for what you did and, given the recommendations of Simmons et al. (2011), present the findings when these outliers were *included* as well as when they were *excluded*.

REVIST AND RESPOND

- What is opportunistic bias? How does it apply to the concept of an outlier? Are genuine experimental errors a justifiable reason to exclude outliers? If there is no evidence of genuine error and outliers exist, reporting the results with and without the outliers is recommended. Why is transparency in reporting your data "adjustments" so important?

GOING FISHING AND OTHER DATA DREDGING PRACTICES

We have just discussed opportunistic bias and the questionable decisions researchers sometimes make about handling their data. There are other questionable data handling practices that occur called **going fishing** (also called **data dredging**). In the absence of significant results for the stated hypotheses, researchers sometimes undertake additional analyses as part of data exploration; this has been called "going on a fishing expedition" (Bem, 2004, p. 187). In their discussion of opportunistic bias, DeCoster et al. (2015) focused their comments on tactics that could lead to the discovery of findings related to

Going fishing: term that describes exploring your data post hoc for significant findings.

Data dredging: exploration of large sets of data to discover statistically significant patterns not originally hypothesized.

the *initial hypotheses.* Here we are talking about exploring data in terms of relationships that were *not* originally postulated.

Various names are given to the steps you could take to "go fish." Norbert Kerr (1998) talked about **HARKing**: hypothesizing after the results are known. In his article, Kerr took aim at authors such as Daryl Bem (1987, 2004) who suggested that you write your research paper focused on the results that emerged, not on those that were hypothesized. Kerr defined HARKing as "presenting post hoc hypotheses in a research report as if they were, in fact, a priori hypotheses" (p. 197). The reasons HARKing is a problem in his view are as follows: Type I errors are translated into theory; such hypotheses "fail Popper's criterion of disconfirmability" (p. 205); and an explanation designed to fit post hoc results (accommodation) is less likely to be correct than one based on hypothesizing those results (prediction). Other problems are losing information about the original hypothesis through HARKing; that statistical abuses are promoted (such as the use of one-tailed tests without a priori hypotheses); and communication of an inaccurate model of science that presents a more positive image than is justified (also see Kerr's summary, p. 211). Among the solutions he recommended (in addition to not HARKing) is empirical replication.

In terms of other questionable practices, Uri Simonsohn, Leif Nelson, and Joseph Simmons (2014) talk about **p-hacking** (p. 534), which is when researchers file away the subsets of analyses that have failed to yield significant results. They argued that this practice makes the file drawer phenomenon (see Chapter 2) even more problematic and further inflates the perceived reliability of data that are published—few unsuccessful studies in the drawer may represent many unsuccessful analyses.

HARKing:
hypothesizing after results are known (Kerr, 1998).

p-hacking:
processes such as continuing to test data or conducting post hoc analyses to produce significant results.

REVISIT AND RESPOND

- In your own words, describe "going fishing" and *p*-hacking. How is *p*-hacking related to the file drawer phenomenon? Opportunistic bias deals with adjustments to data in the context of your original hypotheses, whereas HARKing deals with hypothesizing after the results are known. When HARKing occurs, you explore aspects of your data that were not originally hypothesized, and significant findings may emerge. Why does this process communicate a more positive image of science than is justified?

ETHICS, CLEANING UP, AND REPORTING YOUR DATA: FINAL COMMENTS

We have just reviewed a variety of different (potentially questionable) practices that researchers may take involving missing data, outliers, and post hoc hypothesizing. It has always been important to tell readers how you have handled your data. Today, with the levels of fraud in science, it seems even more important to be clear about what changes you have made to your data—the outliers you exclude, the missing data you replace, or even the rounding rules you apply. Joseph Schafer and John Graham (2002) referred to the concept of **coarsened data**, in which various techniques such as rounding, grouping, or censoring (p. 148) reduce the amount of information the data would otherwise provide. The articles we have discussed point to the same fundamental principle: You have an ethical responsibility to report in full and justify what steps you have taken with every aspect of handling your data. As a last comment on this issue, the Center for Open Science (COS) has a statement it advises reviewers to request of authors: "I request that the authors add a statement to the paper confirming whether, for all experiments, they have reported all measures, conditions, data exclusions, and how they determined their sample sizes. The authors should, of course, add any additional text to ensure the statement is accurate" (**https://osf.io/hadz3/**). What this statement underscores is the increasing importance of "open science," to align scientific values with scientific practices.

Coarsened data: idea that data lose some of their specificity (e.g., through rounding).

PRELIMINARY ANALYSES

Before you run any formal analyses to evaluate your hypotheses, you need to finish any required (and justified) changes to the data file: (a) Identify any missing data; (2) determine whether you are going to replace the missing data, which will be a limitation to be discussed in your paper; (3) identify outliers; and (4) determine whether you can justify excluding them on the basis of experimental error. With regard to missing data (see earlier sections), you need to determine whether you are going to use listwise deletion, pairwise deletion, or imputation. In the case of imputation, you need to decide on your decision rules, that is, how much data for a participant can be missed and replaced.

Once these issues have been addressed, you can run preliminary analyses, which typically include means and standard deviations for your continuous variables and frequencies for your categorical variables. Doing these analyses will help you get a feel for your data.

SIGNIFICANCE LEVELS AND p VALUES: WHAT ARE THEY?

As we discussed earlier with regard to Type I error (see Chapter 3), we use inferential statistics to estimate probabilities that our data represent the true situation. We set that estimation at a given level, called the *alpha level* (as introduced in Chapter 2). By convention, the alpha level is set at .05. What that means is that there are only 5 opportunities

Significance level: in research, the probability value indicating the likelihood that the finding occurred by chance, usually set at .05.

in 100 (5 / 100) that we are mistaken in saying that our results are significant when, in fact, the null hypothesis is true. The stated probability is also referred to as the **significance level**. We also call this a p value (see Chapter 2) or a probability value. Students are occasionally confused about the meaning of these probabilities and mistakenly think that a larger value (i.e., a larger number) is better; in this case, it is not. A finding at a value of $p = .01$ is more convincing than a finding of $p = .05$ because the .01 value indicates that our result is likely to be a mistake only 1 time in 100, whereas at .05, that likelihood is 5 times in 100 (i.e., the finding is MORE likely to have occurred by chance at .05 than at .01).

>> Try This Now

Which of the following statements is correct:

1. A finding of $p = .01$ is more significant than a finding of $p = .05$.

2. A finding of $p = .01$ is less likely to have occurred than a finding of $p = .05$.

The second statement is correct. Findings either are or are not significant at the stated alpha level, not more significant at one level than another. Rather than getting caught in the trap of saying a finding is "more significant," simply say, "The finding was significant at the [X] level."

REVISIT AND RESPOND

- What does it mean to say that a finding is significant at the .05 level?

TRANSFORMING AND SELECTING DATA: USEFUL COMMANDS IN SPSS

Because it is hard to remember the commands in SPSS and their purpose, we will next review some of the more useful commands and their steps. In the section that follows, we will focus on commands used to transform or select data. Appendix E at the end of the book lists the common commands used to *analyze* the data (e.g., analysis of variance or ANOVA and correlation).

The Compute Function

The purpose of the Compute Function (as introduced earlier in this chapter) is to create new variables. This is done through arithmetic operations, most commonly, addition. The most common use of the Compute Function is adding up the values of individual scale items to create a scale total. This process is also used to create factor scores by adding up items that loaded on particular dimensions in a factor analysis.

Earlier in the chapter we said that individual scale items need to be entered as separate variables to calculate the Cronbach's alpha for the given scale. After you finish that task, you typically want to use the scale total as one of your DVs. You use the Compute Function to calculate that total.

Compute Function Steps: Look at the menu bar; locate the **Transform** option; when you click on Transform, several options appear in the dropdown list. The first of these is Compute. When you click on Compute, an action box appears (see Figure 10.9).

Transform: function in SPSS Statistics® that allows you to reconfigure data, for example, computing a new variable or recoding a variable.

FIGURE 10.9   Action Box for Compute Function

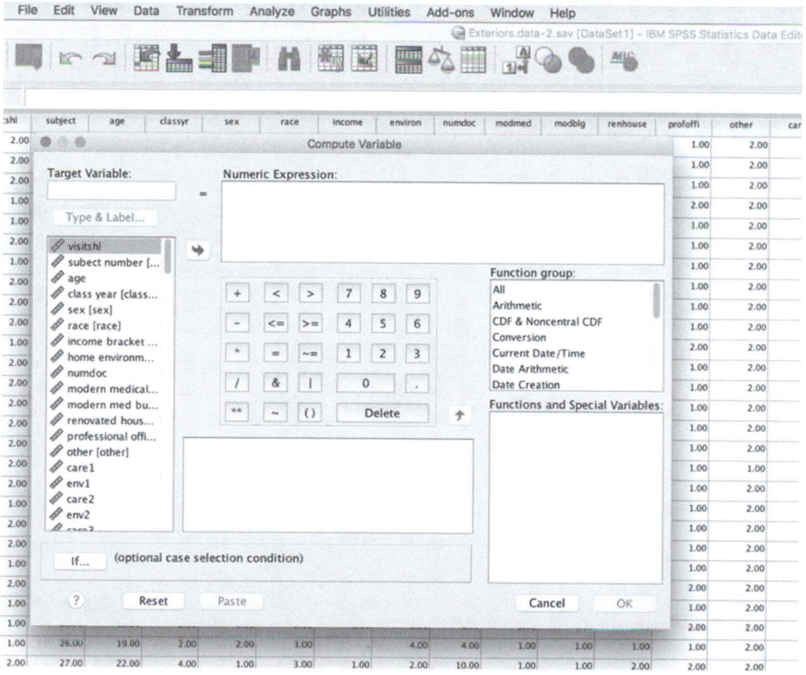

In the upper left, you see an empty box called Target Variable. Here, you will enter the name of the new variable you want to create. Pick a name that is logical. If you are creating a scale total, call it the name of the scale. Our example here involves a measure called the Padua Inventory (a measure of obsessive-compulsiveness); for that reason, a logical name is Padua ScaleTotal (notice there are no spaces between the words). Underneath that box is "Type & Label;" if you click on this, you can provide a name for the variable (here spaces are allowed) "Padua Scale Total" and you can specify the type of variable (e.g., Numeric). Recall we talked about the importance of specifying numeric variables if you are going to perform analyses.

Next, you will move over items from the variable list to the box labeled "Numeric Expression" where you (typically) add the items you need to create your new variables. Note that there are many functions you can perform on your numeric expression (see box under Function group). For the purposes of our example, we are (a) adding and (b) using just three items, called padua1, padua2, and padua3 (from our variable list). Once you are finished, in this case wanting to add up the scores on `padua1`, `padua2`, and `padua3`, you would click "OK" in the lower right-hand corner. Notice that the "OK" is shaded; this indicates that it is available to click (see Figure 10.10).

FIGURE 10.10   Compute Function With Numeric Expression Indicated

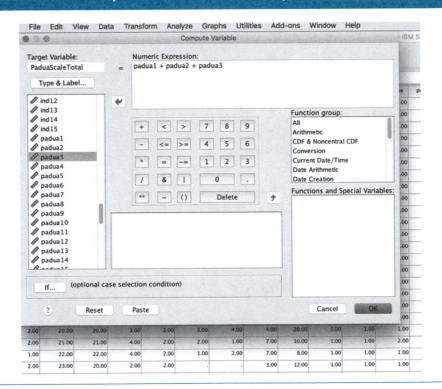

If you look back at Figure 10.9, you see that the "OK" is not highlighted (because there is nothing indicated on which to perform an operation). After you click the highlighted OK button, a new column will appear on the far right end of your data file (see Figure 10.11).

FIGURE 10.11   Data View With New Variable (PaduaScaleTotal)

	caref1.3	caref2.3	caref3.3	ocdlevel	caref4.1	caref4.2	caref4.3	caref4.4	emvf3.1	emvf3.2	emvf3.3	PaduaScale Total	var
00	30.23	30.57	79.25	2.00	32.50	30.25	80.00	28.67	36.17	29.82	54.14	3.00	
00	62.38	58.14	85.50	2.00	64.00	53.88	92.67	42.33	65.83	38.27	54.00	4.00	
00	55.38	54.29	85.00	2.00	53.00	53.75	90.00	66.67	53.33	58.18	78.57	4.00	
00	70.77	65.71	105.00	2.00	73.00	67.50	105.00	76.67	77.50	60.91	77.14	7.00	
00	79.46	70.43	79.25	1.00	79.10	71.13	85.00	73.33	77.75	63.09	88.57	.00	
00	46.38	30.29	77.75	1.00	47.90	30.00	86.00	43.33	65.33	26.36	44.57	1.00	
00	60.85	40.71	77.50	1.00	64.00	37.88	85.00	53.67	58.17	39.00	80.14	1.00	
00	53.00	53.86	60.00	1.00	50.40	53.75	65.00	58.67	41.00	52.45	59.00	.00	
00	59.85	54.00	88.50	2.00	55.10	51.50	95.67	62.00	70.92	40.18	70.14	6.00	
00	85.15	52.71	78.25	2.00	86.60	56.63	74.67	63.00	82.83	54.45	79.14	5.00	
00	76.00	62.86	83.50	1.00	77.50	62.50	91.33	39.33	68.83	36.73	56.71	.00	
00	74.92	35.14	76.00	2.00	69.10	37.00	78.00	56.00	70.58	27.36	78.29	.00	
00	72.00	46.29	85.25	2.00	69.90	49.88	84.00	82.67	69.00	37.82	71.43	9.00	
00	56.92	54.29	82.50	2.00	58.00	55.00	83.33	63.33	45.83	42.73	54.29	3.00	
00	66.00	46.86	73.50	2.00	67.50	45.63	77.33	68.33	70.50	44.27	53.43	4.00	
00	57.92	41.00	68.00	1.00	57.10	44.38	66.00	56.00	54.33	42.45	64.00	1.00	
00	68.85	65.29	72.00	1.00	68.40	66.25	83.33	70.33	57.33	55.56	63.43	1.00	
00	74.54	65.71	85.25	1.00	74.10	67.75	88.00	73.00	75.17	52.55	61.43	1.00	
00	73.15	25.71	85.50	2.00	75.20	28.63	91.33	73.00	68.67	18.00	76.29	5.00	
00	68.23	63.43	79.25	2.00	69.80	60.50	85.67	67.00	74.92	37.55	55.57	9.00	
00	68.62	63.29	80.00	1.00	72.90	62.38	92.67	63.33	69.00	56.91	69.29	1.00	
00	75.85	59.86	94.50	1.00	75.60	61.00	95.33	63.33	77.42	59.45	73.71	3.00	
00	60.46	37.00	92.25	1.00	63.10	33.00	98.67	20.00	64.00	17.27	55.57	.00	

As you see (Figure 10.11), you have created a new variable that is the sum of those three Padua items. Notice that this is a *total*. If we wanted to create a mean of those three items, we would put the items in the Numeric Expression box as before, but this time we would put parentheses around them and then divide that expression by 3 (see Figure 10.12). Notice that we have given this new target variable a different name: `PaduaScaleMean`.

> **» Try This Now**
>
> Why did we need a different variable name?

FIGURE 10.12 PaduaScaleMean **New Target Variable**

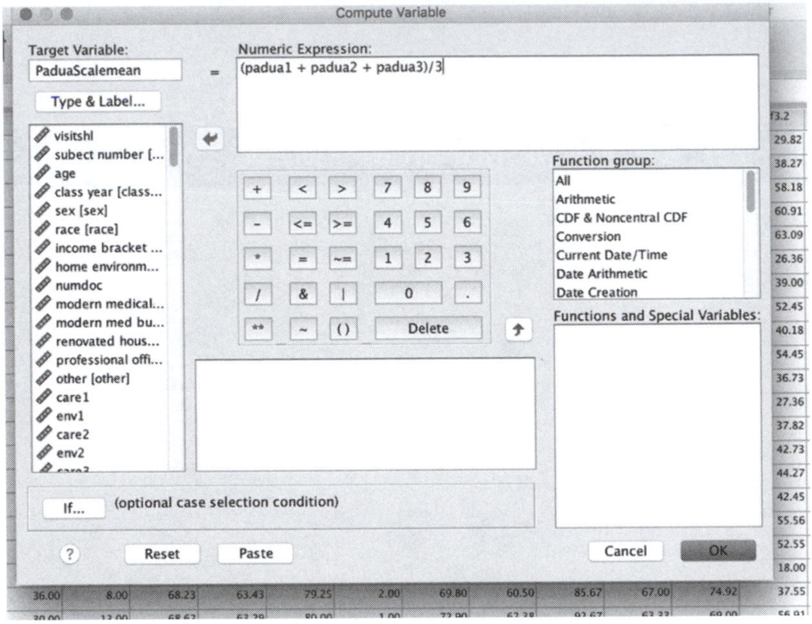

We already had a variable named PaduaScaleTotal and could not reuse it (unless you wanted PaduaScaleMean to replace the variable PaduaScaleTotal). If you attempted to do that, you would get a message on the screen that said "Change Existing Variable?" to make sure that's what you wanted to do. Figure 10.13 shows that after we click "OK" again, we now have a second new variable added on the far right in our data file.

By comparing the two new columns, you can verify for yourself that the scale "mean" is in fact the mean of the total score (left column) for each participant.

Now that you are familiar with the general process, we will not repeat all of the outcomes (i.e., what the far right columns look like) for the next commands we discuss.

Recode into Same Variables and Recode into Different Variables Commands

When you ran some preliminary analyses on your data, you might have noticed some demographic categories with few people in them (for class year, race, religion, housing type, or another variable). In such instances, you might want to collapse or merge categories. Recoding can be used for that purpose. This command might also be useful when you are merging categories for a content analysis. Another use for this function is when you are reverse coding values for a measure.

FIGURE 10.13   Data View Showing `PaduaScaleMean`

	caref4.4	envf3.1	envf3.2	envf3.3	PaduaScaleTotal	PaduaScalemean	var
00	28.67	36.17	29.82	54.14	3.00	1.00	
57	42.33	65.83	38.27	54.00	4.00	1.33	
00	66.67	53.33	58.18	78.57	4.00	1.33	
00	76.67	77.50	60.91	77.14	7.00	2.33	
00	73.33	77.75	63.09	88.57	.00	.00	
00	43.33	65.33	26.36	44.57	1.00	.33	
00	53.67	58.17	39.00	80.14	1.00	.33	
00	58.67	41.00	52.45	59.00	.00	.00	
57	62.00	70.92	40.18	70.14	6.00	2.00	
57	63.00	82.83	54.45	79.14	5.00	1.67	
33	39.33	68.83	36.73	56.71	.00	.00	
00	56.00	70.58	27.36	78.29	.00	.00	
00	82.67	69.00	37.82	71.43	9.00	3.00	
33	63.33	45.83	42.73	54.29	3.00	1.00	
33	68.33	70.50	44.27	53.43	4.00	1.33	
00	56.00	54.33	42.45	64.00	1.00	.33	
33	70.33	57.33	55.56	63.43	1.00	.33	
00	73.00	75.17	52.55	61.43	1.00	.33	
33	73.00	68.67	18.00	76.29	5.00	1.67	
57	67.00	74.92	37.55	55.57	9.00	3.00	
57	63.33	69.00	56.91	69.29	1.00	.33	
33	63.33	77.42	59.45	73.71	3.00	1.00	
57	20.00	64.00	17.27	55.57	.00	.00	
57	56.33	45.12	33.82	67.00	6.00	2.00	
00	44.67	63.03	40.64	46.29	6.00	2.00	
57	51.00	73.42	33.00	75.71	.00	.00	
57	66.33	54.17	44.45	37.43	2.00	.67	
33	33.33	50.67	42.73	51.43	1.00	.33	
33	61.67	73.67	25.45	43.00	.00	.00	
57	80.67	49.33	42.73	84.43	2.00	.67	

Under Transform, there are two related recode commands you might use: **Recode into Same Variables** and **Recode into Different Variables**. These two commands enable you to take an existing variable, change the values on that variable, and replace the original variable (Recode into Same Variables) or create a new variable with your recoding (Recode into Different Variables). At the outset, it is worth noting that some researchers recommend using only Recode into Different Variables. We take that position here.

Recode into Same variables: SPSS Statistics® command in which numerical values are recoded into the existing variable.

Recode into Different Variables: SPSS Statistics® command in which numerical values are recoded into a new variable.

> **Try This Now**
>
> When you take an existing variable and replace it with a new variable (Recode into Same Variables), the old values disappear. Why would some researchers recommend using only Recode into Different Variables?

If you Recode into Different Variables, you retain access to the original variable values if you want to go back and examine or use that original variable in an analysis. If you Recode into Same Variables, those original values are gone from the saved data file.

In the example that follows, we will collapse categories for a Class Year variable and do so using Recode into Different Variables. Recoding into Same Variables follows the same process except that you are not specifying a new variable, just recoding the values in the existing variable.

Imagine you look at your class year data and notice that you have very few "seniors" and "others" relative to the other categories. Depending on your hypotheses, it might make sense to place seniors and others into the same value (category) as juniors. In other words, you are recoding in a way that puts others, seniors, and juniors in the same category; they would all be represented by the same numerical value.

Once you click on *Transform* and then *Recode into Different Variables,* you will want to move the variable `classyr` into the Numeric Variable → Output Box. You will also need to provide a Name and Label for the Output variable (to save screenshots, this has already been done for you; see Figure 10.14). We have named the new variable Class YearRecode and have labeled it `Class Year Recoded`.

You then press "Change" under these labels and the output variable will be specified in the numeric expression box. Next, you need to specify how you want the values recoded. You next click on the box titled "Old and New Values." You also need to check to see what values you originally used (do this in Variable View). For class year in this data file, 5 = other, 4 = senior, 3 = juniors, 2 = sophomores, and 1 = first year students.

FIGURE 10.14   Recode Into Different Variables for Class Year

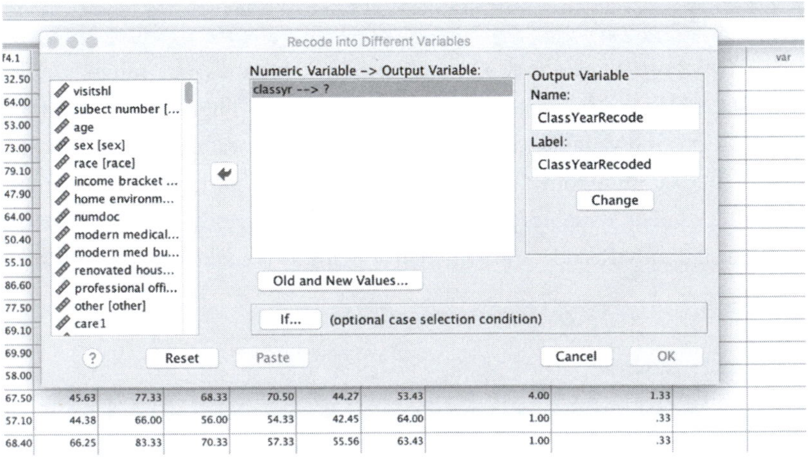

> ## ⟫ Try This Now
>
> How do we transform the "seniors" and "other" classifications into "juniors"?

If you said something to the effect that 5 = 3 and 4 = 3, you are on the right track.

This new variable will have juniors, seniors, and others in one value (3), but you also have to specify the original values you had for sophomores (2s) and first year students (1's). If you don't do this, your new variable will be a column where only 3s are listed; no one else will have a value (they would have empty cells for Class Year for this new variable). Thus, you need to specify the new values for *every* class year (level), even those that don't change (see Figure 10.15). We specify what the old value is (under Old Value), specify what the new value is (under New Value), and then click on "Add" in the Old → New box. Please note that when we click on the last Add (for "1"), we will have specified ALL of the class year values, but our new variable will have only 3s, 2s, and 1s. It is important to remember that all values (even the ones you are not changing) need to be specified for the new variables.

FIGURE 10.15   Changing Old to New Values for Class Year

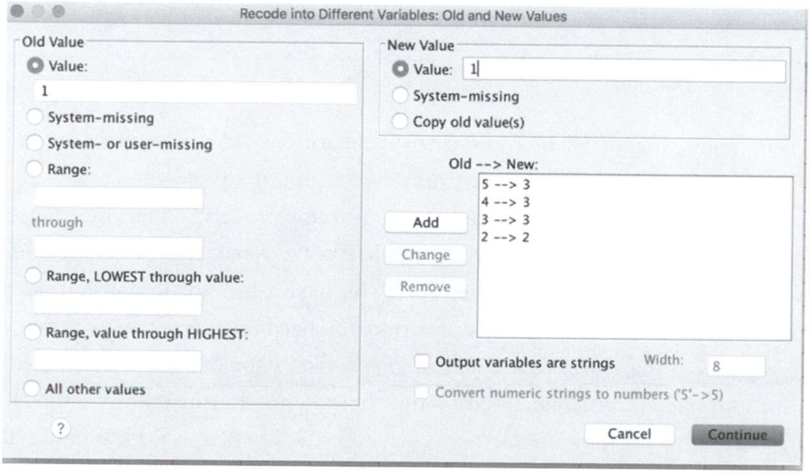

FIGURE 10.16 **Data View Showing New Variable** ClassYearRecode

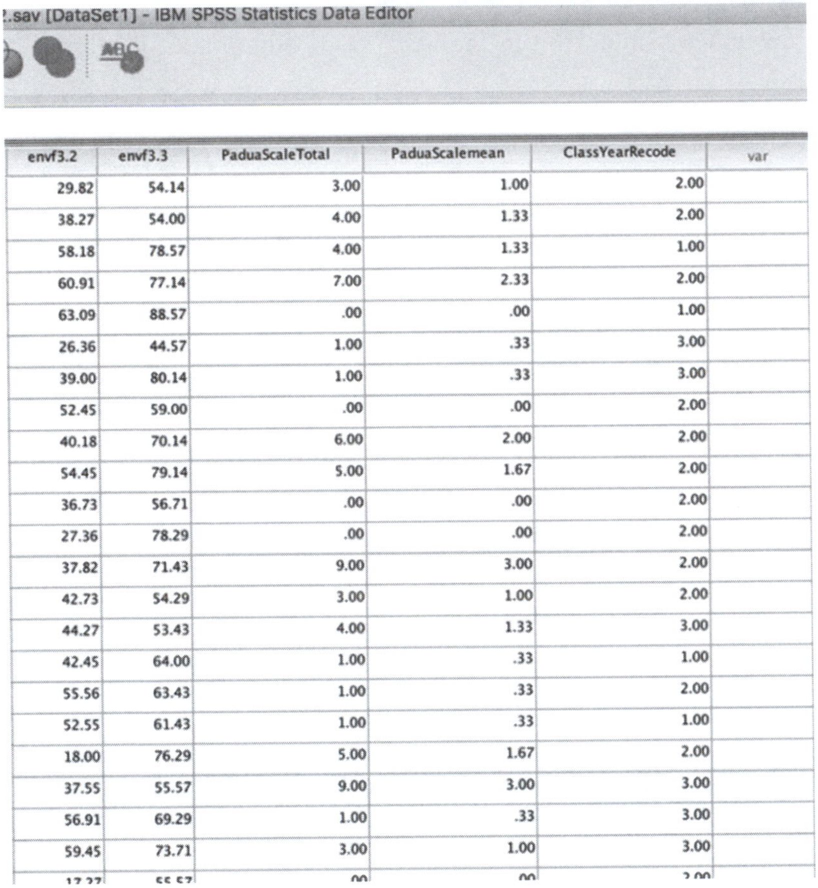

.sav [DataSet1] – IBM SPSS Statistics Data Editor

envf3.2	envf3.3	PaduaScaleTotal	PaduaScalemean	ClassYearRecode	var
29.82	54.14	3.00	1.00	2.00	
38.27	54.00	4.00	1.33	2.00	
58.18	78.57	4.00	1.33	1.00	
60.91	77.14	7.00	2.33	2.00	
63.09	88.57	.00	.00	1.00	
26.36	44.57	1.00	.33	3.00	
39.00	80.14	1.00	.33	3.00	
52.45	59.00	.00	.00	2.00	
40.18	70.14	6.00	2.00	2.00	
54.45	79.14	5.00	1.67	2.00	
36.73	56.71	.00	.00	2.00	
27.36	78.29	.00	.00	2.00	
37.82	71.43	9.00	3.00	2.00	
42.73	54.29	3.00	1.00	2.00	
44.27	53.43	4.00	1.33	3.00	
42.45	64.00	1.00	.33	1.00	
55.56	63.43	1.00	.33	2.00	
52.55	61.43	1.00	.33	1.00	
18.00	76.29	5.00	1.67	2.00	
37.55	55.57	9.00	3.00	3.00	
56.91	69.29	1.00	.33	3.00	
59.45	73.71	3.00	1.00	3.00	
17.27	55.57	.00	.00	2.00	

In Data View, Figure 10.16 shows that you have created a new variable we called ClassYearRecode. As you can see, only 1s, 2s, and 3s are present.

To reverse score scale items, you go through the same process. When you reverse score items, you typically do so because some items in a scale were stated positively and some were stated negatively (refer to Chapter 5). If you have a 5-point response scale, where 1 = strongly agree and 5 = strongly disagree, and you need to reverse score several of your scale items so that the scores reflect statements in the "same direction" (all stated positively, for example), you would reverse score those items. In our example, the changes would be as follows for those items: 5 = 1, 4 = 2, 3 = 3, 2 = 4, 1 = 5. Please note that we have 3 = 3; we do so to make sure people who have 3s appear in the new variable!

Using Recoded Values in Analyses

You need to keep track of items that have been recoded to use them in your analyses. These analyses would typically involve computing Cronbach's alphas and after that creating new variables that reflect scale totals. First, you want to recode any items that need to be reverse scored before computing Cronbach's alphas. If you fail to do that, your Cronbach's alphas might be quite low, which should prompt you to think about what is wrong. Next, you want to make sure you use these new (recoded) variables in your analyses. If you Recode into Different Variables, remember that you still have the original variable for a given item as well as the new (recoded) variable for that *same item* in your variable list. Make sure that in your Cronbach's alpha **reliability analysis**, and subsequently in any new variable you create through the Compute Function, you select the appropriate *recoded variables* to include. For example, the STAI (state version) has 20 items, 10 of which need to be reversed scored. When you run your reliability analysis for this scale and after that create a scale total using the Compute Function, 10 items would be the nonreverse-scored items and 10 would be the newly created reverse-scored variables.

Furthermore, for all scales, make sure you know the theoretical minimum and maximum scores, and make sure you understand what a low score indicates and what a high score indicates.

> **Reliability analysis:** in SPSS Statistics®, refers to the evaluation of data to assess internal consistency, such as Cronbach's alpha.

REVISIT AND RESPOND

- Describe the difference between Recode into Different Variables and Recode into Same Variables. Remember that you can use the Recode Function for collapsing categories and reverse scoring items. Be sure to keep track of the recoded items and use them when you calculate Cronbach's alphas and compute scale totals.

Select Cases Function

On occasion you may want to include some, but not all, of your participants in an analysis, and the **Select Cases Function** allows you to do just that. This possibility might be useful if you want to run an analysis and include only one level of a variable, for example, only women, only sophomores, or only one political category. This function also allows you to combine variable levels, so that you could run an analysis with women, who were sophomores, and who were political Independents. Remember earlier in the chapter when we talked about what to label and the recommendation was to have a separate

> **Select Cases Function:** SPSS Statistics® command in which the analysis is restricted to a subset of the sample (e.g., first year students).

variable for Subject Number? The Select Cases Function is the place where you would be able to make use of the Subject Number variable. You could use Select Cases to restrict the analysis to a subset of subject numbers (participants), for example, subject number 35 and above.

The Select Cases Function is listed under *Data* in the menu bar. The Select Cases Function enables you to restrict an analysis to only those cases you have specified. Once you click on Select Cases, you will see the default screen, which shows that "All" cases are selected. You want to click on the button "If condition is satisfied" (see Figure 10.17) and next on the "If" box beneath it. Once you perform these actions, a screen will appear in which you need to specify the conditions that are to be satisfied.

FIGURE 10.17   Screen Showing Select Cases "If condition" Button

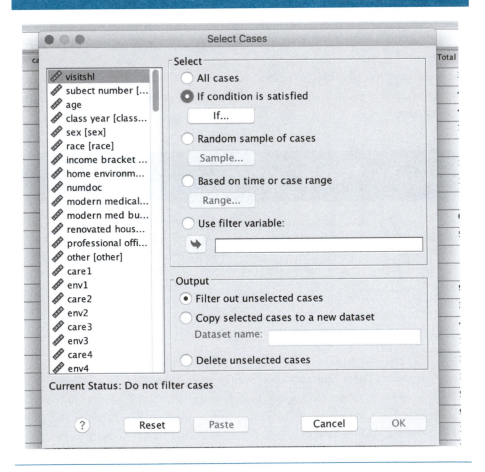

FIGURE 10.18   Screen Showing Empty Select Cases: If Box

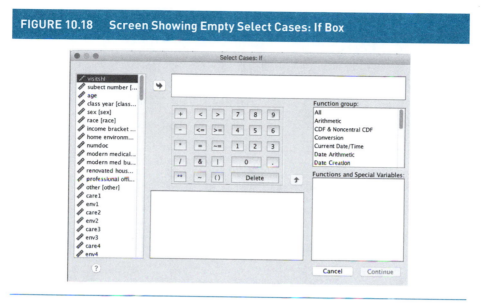

Figure 10.18 shows the screen waiting for you to specify what variable is to be selected or restricted in some way. Next, you move over the target variable (our example here will be Class Year) and specify the value (level) you want to include. In our example, we will use ClassYr = 1 to limit our analysis to first year students (see Figure 10.19).

FIGURE 10.19   Screen Showing Select If "classyr = 1"

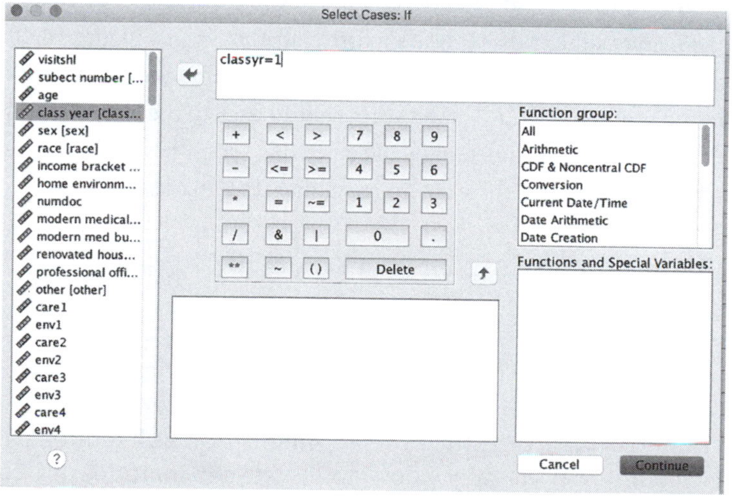

FIGURE 10.20 Screen Illustrating Slash Marks Indicating Excluded Cases

	positive	caref1.3	caref2.3	caref3.3	ocdlevel	caref4.1	caref4.2	caref4.3	caref4.4	envf3.1	envf3.2
1	17.00	30.23	30.57	79.25	2.00	32.50	30.25	80.00	28.67	36.17	29.82
2	14.00	62.38	58.14	85.50	2.00	64.00	53.88	92.67	42.33	65.83	38.27
3	22.00	55.38	54.29	85.00	2.00	53.00	53.75	90.00	66.67	53.33	58.18
4	17.00	70.77	65.71	105.00	2.00	73.00	67.50	105.00	76.67	77.50	60.91
5	20.00	79.46	70.43	79.25	1.00	79.10	71.13	85.00	73.33	77.75	63.09
6	12.00	46.38	30.29	77.75	1.00	47.90	30.00	86.00	43.33	65.33	26.36
7	20.00	60.85	40.71	77.50	1.00	64.00	37.88	85.00	53.67	58.17	39.00
8	24.00	53.00	53.86	60.00	1.00	50.40	53.75	65.00	58.67	41.00	52.45
9	18.00	59.85	54.00	88.50	2.00	55.10	51.50	95.67	62.00	70.92	40.18
10	14.00	85.15	52.71	78.25	2.00	86.60	56.63	74.67	63.00	82.83	54.45
11	20.00	76.00	62.86	83.50	1.00	77.50	62.50	91.33	39.33	68.83	36.73
12	19.00	74.92	35.14	76.00	2.00	69.10	37.00	78.00	56.00	70.58	27.36
13	11.00	72.00	46.29	85.25	2.00	69.90	49.88	84.00	82.67	69.00	37.82
14	24.00	56.92	54.29	82.50	2.00	58.00	55.00	83.33	63.33	45.83	42.73
15	9.00	66.00	46.86	73.50	2.00	67.50	45.63	77.33	68.33	70.50	44.27
16	11.00	57.92	43.00	68.00	1.00	57.10	44.38	66.00	56.00	54.33	42.45
17	14.00	68.85	65.29	72.00	1.00	68.40	66.25	83.33	70.33	57.33	55.56
18	20.00	74.54	65.71	85.25	1.00	74.10	67.75	88.00	73.00	75.17	52.55
19	18.00	73.15	25.71	85.50	2.00	75.20	28.63	91.33	73.00	68.67	18.00
20	8.00	68.23	63.43	79.25	2.00	69.80	60.50	85.67	67.00	74.92	37.55
21	13.00	68.62	63.29	80.00	1.00	72.90	62.38	92.67	63.33	69.00	56.91

4 : envf3.3 — 77.14285714285714

If we click continue, we would next see a screen where we have the opportunity to click "OK." After we do so, and return to our data view, we will see a screen with slash marks through every subject that is NOT a first year student (see Figure 10.20).

From then on, every analysis you run will include *only* first year students. When you are ready to run analyses with "All" cases again, you go back to the Select Cases Function, and click "All" cases. You can determine whether this action has worked by looking at your Data View to make sure there are no remaining slash marks.

> **≫ Try This Now**
>
> When you use the Select Cases Function, you can restrict your analysis to a subset of your sample. Why might this be useful? What steps do you take to return to "all cases" for subsequent analyses? How do you visually know your dataset includes all cases? A subset?

SUMMARY OF DATA ORGANIZATION STEPS

After entering all of your data (give it a file name and save it frequently), take the following steps before running preliminary analyses:

- Run Frequencies on all variables to check for out-of-range values and missing data
- Run Descriptives on continuous variables to check for outliers
- Replace data as appropriate (see recommendations in this chapter)
- Recode any items that require reverse scoring
- Calculate Cronbach's alphas for all scales (make sure you use the correct items if there has been reverse scoring)
- Use the Compute Function to create scale total scores (make sure you use the correct items if there has been reverse scoring)
- In your paper, be sure to explain all of the changes you made to your original data, including steps taken for out-of-range values, missing data, and outliers

EVALUATING YOUR HYPOTHESES: WHERE TO BEGIN

After you have finalized your dataset, doing any replacements that are appropriate (for missing data and/or outliers), you are ready to start your formal analyses. Revisit your hypotheses and conduct your major analyses first; that is, run the analysis that evaluates your hypothesis. In the most parsimonious of experiments, only one analysis may be required, but most researchers end up running several analyses related to their main hypothesis(ses). Appendix A at the end of this book provides a decision tree that may be useful in helping you decide which analysis(ses) to conduct. If your hypotheses are stated clearly, they should "direct" you to the appropriate analysis, but sometimes we need extra guidance. This decision tree is organized into research questions that deal with the sample as a whole versus those that involve questions about group differences. Questions about the sample as a whole may involve reporting descriptive statistics, correlations, and regressions. Research questions about group differences vary in their level of complexity, in terms of both the number and levels of the independent variables and the number of dependent variables. The decision tree is also delineated in terms of the kinds of scale types you have (nominal, ordinal, or interval); the scale type also must be considered to select the appropriate analysis.

As an illustration of an analysis, let's use an example based on the study mentioned several times in this book: the perception of femininity of a woman who lifts weights. This was a between subjects design with the weight held [5 lbs (80 oz) or 25 lbs (400 oz)] as the true independent variable (IV) and the status of the participant (athlete or not) as a quasi-IV. As a DV, the researcher used the Bem Sex Role Inventory to assess the judged femininity of the woman who was pictured lifting the weight.

> ## ⏩ Try This Now
>
> What analysis would you run for this situation? Consult Appendix A at the end of this book if you need a refresher.

This is a situation about group differences (judgments of the woman with the 5-lb vs. the 25-lb weight; athlete vs. nonathlete status of the participant), and there is one DV. In this situation, you would run a factorial ANOVA (which you could call a two-way ANOVA or a 2 × 2 ANOVA if you want more specificity; refer to Chapter 7 on nomenclature). We have two IVs (one is quasi) and one DV.

What happens if none of your hypotheses is supported? If you "go fishing," make sure you clearly present your fishing as *post hoc*. When you go fishing, you are looking at possible relationships in the data that were not specified in your original hypotheses. This activity of fishing has consequences, the most obvious of which is increasing the possibility of Type I error because you are running additional analyses. Often this fishing involves using demographic variables as quasi-IVs.

What if the researcher now used the gender of the respondent as a quasi-IV? The researcher might indeed find an interaction effect with gender and the true IV (5–lb vs. 25-lb weight) in terms of the DV. In this situation, the researcher would need to be clear about exploring relationships that were not initially hypothesized. Unlike Bem (2004), we are not suggesting that you write the article "that makes the most sense now that you have seen the results" (p. 186); rather, the position here is that you write the article based on your original hypotheses and present additional findings as post hoc.

MAKING USE OF FREE RESPONSE ITEMS

As part of going fishing, you may want to make use of free response items, that is, items to open-ended questions. Material in Chapter 6 presented how to handle open-ended responses in terms of content analysis. For that reason, we will only briefly comment on this topic now. Open-ended questions can be a minor or major part of a research project. On the "minor" end of the continuum, participants might be prompted to respond to one or more open-ended questions (e.g., "What aspects of this college do you recommend?). At the "major" end of the spectrum, participants' narratives might be the substance of the study (e.g., Singer, Rexhaj, & Baddeley, 2007). Our example will focus on the "minor" end.

Your goal is to develop categories that reflect the content of the participants' responses, trying to keep the categories mutually exclusive (an item should not be classifiable in more than one category) and at the same level of abstraction. Regarding abstraction, one category (e.g., trees), should not be subsumable within another (e.g., nature). The outcome of content analyses typically are presented as frequencies or used in chi-squares, given their status as nominal data.

ADDITIONAL AIDS: ONLINE CALCULATORS AND WORD CLOUDS

Some aids are available online that can help with additional statistical calculations in the absence of a complete data file. There is also a program that enables you to take qualitative content (i.e., words) and visually express the pattern of response (i.e., frequency).

Sometimes you may want to run statistics for which you have summary numbers without having a complete data file. Often this happens in the case of chi-square, where for example, you may want to compare the percentage of individuals in a given gender or racial category in your sample (to check for representativeness) against statistics you have for the population as a whole (e.g., college enrollment data for those variables). In those cases, you might want to use an online program such as the Easy Chi Square calculator (**http://www.socscistatistics.com/tests/chisquare/default2.aspx**), Social Science Statistics (**http://www.socscistatistics.com/tests/chisquare2/Default2.aspx**), or GraphPad software (**http://graphpad.com/quickcalcs/chisquared1.cfm**).

A far different but equally useful online resource is a program called **Wordle**™ (**http://www.Wordle.net**), which can be used effectively with content analyses. This program takes the text you have and presents it as a cloud of words; words that have greater frequency appear larger. The program enables you to use different fonts, colors, and other stylistic elements to create a visually striking and effective image. This resource is particularly useful for conference presentations (see Chapter 11).

Wordle™: program for generating word clouds from text that show the frequency with which certain words appear; useful in presentations.

OTHER STATISTICAL SOFTWARE

This chapter has emphasized SPSS because it is an easy statistical package to use. But SPSS is also expensive. Other statistical packages are available, some of them free, and your institution may use them. Among the more popular statistical packages are SAS®,

Stata®, R, and MPlus®. Microsoft Excel® is also an option, especially if you have the Data Analysis ToolPak and Solver add-ins. You can run descriptive statistics, regression, *t* test, ANOVA, and correlation, but the Data Analysis ToolPak and Solver add-ins are not available for Mac in all Microsoft Excel versions. An overview is provided at the following URL: **https://support.office.com/en-us/article/Use-the-Analysis-ToolPak-to-perform-complex-data-analysis-f77cbd44-fdce-4c4e-872b-898f4c90c007**.

A good overview of the differences among SPSS, SAS, and Stata is provided on a UCLA website (**http://www.ats.ucla.edu/stat/mult_pkg/compare_packages.htm**).

SAS is described there as having power and programming capacity but with a steep learning curve. Stata is acknowledged to be good with regression, fairly easy to learn, and widely used in econometrics. SPSS is described as more widely used in social science and medicine.

R is an open source programming language (i.e., free), which makes it attractive, but it is a programming language and as such requires a certain amount of effort to master. Patrick Burns (**http://www.burns-stat.com/pages/Tutor/R_relative_statpack.pdf**) provides some comparative comments about the different statistical packages in comparison to R. MPlus, for which there is a cost, seems more appropriate for higher-level analyses because it is particularly good for structural equation modeling and latent variable analysis (**https://www.statmodel.com/glance.shtml**).

Summary

This chapter stressed the importance of organization and "bookkeeping" in terms of labeling your data. A comparison of the advantages and disadvantages of paper versus online surveys was presented, with instructions for labeling in each approach. Time was spent talking about problems with datasets, including missing data and outliers. In dealing with missing data, the listwise, pairwise, and imputation approaches were presented. In the context of missing data and outliers, the concept of opportunistic bias was introduced, which covered the questionable practice of making changes to data to increase the likelihood of finding significant results. Another approach is "going fishing" to find relationships that are post hoc. Throughout this chapter (and this book), the importance of the transparency of what you are doing in your research has been stressed. The chapter concludes with useful commands in SPSS (Compute, Recode, and Select Cases). Appendix E at the end of the book covers the commonly used Analyze functions in SPSS. Appendix A provides a simple decision tree for selecting the appropriate analysis for your research question.

In the event that you did not consider them earlier, here are the **REVISIT and RESPOND** prompts that appeared in this chapter.

- Why is labeling carefully important? What kinds of problems does it avoid? When is it sufficient to label the values on one but not on every item in a scale? Describe two guidelines for labeling variables and specifying values. You can run a _____ test of internal consistency when you enter individual items from a scale.

- Thinking back to Chapters 3 and 7 where the topic of power was discussed, remember that losing subjects affects the potential power of your research, that is, your ability to avoid a Type II error. The loss of power is one reason Allison (2001) said, "The only really good solution to the missing data problem is not to have any." But if you do have missing data, what choices do you have to deal with it? In that regard, explain the difference between listwise deletion and pairwise deletion. When you replace data through imputation, what does that mean?

- Explain the difference between data that represent out-of-range values and data that represent outliers.

- What is opportunistic bias? How does it apply to the concept of an outlier? Are genuine experimental errors a justifiable reason to exclude outliers? If there is no evidence of genuine error and outliers exist, reporting the results with and without the outliers is recommended. Why is transparency in reporting your data "adjustments" so important?

- In your own words, describe "going fishing" and _p_-hacking. How is _p_-hacking related to the file drawer phenomenon? Opportunistic bias deals with adjustments to data in the context of your original hypotheses, whereas HARKing deals with hypothesizing after the results are known. When HARKing occurs, you explore aspects of your data that were not originally hypothesized, and significant findings may emerge. Why does this process communicate a more positive image of science than is justified?

- What does it mean to say that a finding is significant at the .05 level?

- Describe the difference between Recode into Different Variables and Recode into Same Variables. Remember that you can use the Recode Function for collapsing categories and reverse scoring items. Be sure to keep track of the recoded items and use them when you calculate Cronbach's alphas and compute scale totals.

BUILD YOUR SKILLS

1. A drawback to both opportunistic bias and HARKing is that these approaches make the results seem more reliable than they are. When we replicate a study, we repeat it. How is replication an important tool in "setting the record straight" about the results of such studies?

2. Open-ended questions, even short ones (e.g., "Explain what factors influenced your answer"), can be useful in creating a richer picture of participants' reactions than if only close-ended questions (i.e., with choices specified) are used. How do you analyze these open-ended data? How could you use them in your Discussion as examples?

11

WRITING AND PRESENTING YOUR RESEARCH

CHAPTER HIGHLIGHTS

- Writing: One section at a time
- Writing: Avoiding plagiarism
- Sections and formatting
  - Abstract: Content and keywords
  - Title
  - Introduction: First sentences; integration of the literature
  - Method: Participants, measures, procedure
  - Writing about results: Create a story
  - Common statistical measures (what and how to report)
  - Discussion: What to cover (narrow to broad); limitations; nonsignificant results
- General formatting issues in APA style
- Common grammatical mistakes
- Presentation software
- Large print posters
- Recommended reading

OVERVIEW

This chapter combines material about the content of your paper with specific information about formatting style, drawing advice from the American Psychological Association's (APA's) *Publication Manual* (6th edition, 2010b). Material includes creating the title, abstract, and first sentences; integrating the literature; writing a complete and detailed method section; presenting results that "tell a story" (Salovey, 2000); and presenting an argument to support the claims you are making for your data in the Discussion. The most important formatting specifics of APA style are presented (e.g., the formatting of numbers; when et al. can be used), and common grammatical issues are reviewed (e.g., while vs. whereas). In addition, the chapter discusses the problem of plagiarism and how it can be avoided. The chapter ends with recommendations about how to create an effective paper presentation using presentation software (e.g., Microsoft PowerPoint), as well as the challenges of creating large-scale posters.

WRITING: ONE SECTION AT A TIME

The last major step in the research process is writing about your research; thankfully, this process is done in sections, not all at once. If you prepared an institutional review board (IRB) proposal, you had an introduction that included a review of the pertinent literature and your hypotheses, as well as a method section that presented your approach to recruiting participants, the materials to be used in the research, and the procedure you planned to use. Your references were included in the IRB proposal. After you complete your data analyses, you essentially have three components left to write: the Results section, the Discussion, and the Abstract. Even if your course does not require an IRB proposal, there will likely be writing deadlines (e.g., when the Introduction is due) to space out the process of completing your paper.

As you start to complete your paper, look at the 6th edition of the *Publication Manual of the American Psychological Association* (hereafter the *Publication Manual;* 2010b), which lists the components of the research manuscript. In fact, Chapter 2 of the *Publication Manual* is titled: "Manuscript Structure and Content." The major components are as follows: the Abstract, Introduction, Method (Participants, Materials, Procedure), Results, Discussion, and References.

Many research methods instructors have you write your paper in the form of a manuscript submission because you then learn to prepare all the parts of a manuscript. That is the approach taken here. In a manuscript submission, the order of sections at the end of the paper is (1) references, (2) tables, (3) figures, and (4) appendices, although appendices are rarely part of a manuscript submission because of space restrictions in journals. In contrast, student research papers typically have appendices that include the informed consent, debriefing, and materials. In the body of the text, you refer to tables and figures by number (e.g., see Table 1; see Figure 1) and appendices by letter of the alphabet (see Appendix A). In a published manuscript, the tables and figures would be inserted into the text at the point where they were first mentioned.

WRITING: AVOIDING PLAGIARISM

Plagiarism is the use of someone else's work (i.e., text, drawings, designs, or ideas) without giving appropriate credit. Plagiarism can occur in any section of a research report, but it seems more likely to happen when you are summarizing other people's work in an Introduction. It makes good sense to understand plagiarism and how to avoid it. You may remember reading about an example of large-scale fraud (fabrication of data) in Chapter 1 when we discussed having too much reverence for the printed word. Plagiarism is a kind of fraud in that it involves deception intended to provide personal gain.

> **Plagiarism:**
> use of someone else's work (i.e., text, drawings, designs, or ideas) without giving appropriate credit.

Most institutions have tutorials and/or websites for students that define plagiarism and give plenty of examples of what not to do. This book will not duplicate that information but will provide a few guidelines. How can you avoid plagiarism? First, you need to know what issues are involved. There are a variety of problems that lead to plagiarism. These problems include mismanaging your time; careless note-taking, which leads to not crediting sources when using direct quotations; using too many quotations linked together; paraphrasing too closely; and failing to acknowledge the source of your research ideas.

Mismanaging Your Time

One reason that students knowingly plagiarize is that they are backed against a wall with a deadline. When students have not worked steadily on a project over the course of the semester, they run out of time to do their work and rely on the work of others.

REMEDY If you follow the timeline provided in this chapter, it will help you complete your work in a timely manner and avoid the temptation to rely on others' work.

Careless Note-Taking (Not Crediting Sources for Direct Quotes)

Another reason students plagiarize, sometimes unintentionally, is that their notes fail to differentiate between the exact wording in an article and their notes taken *about* that article. Using quotations that don't include quotation marks and don't give credit to the original author is considered plagiarism.

REMEDY Develop a system in your note-taking that differentiates "normal" note-taking from note-taking that includes a quotation. For example, when you write down an exact quote, treat it differently from your normal notes (e.g., highlight it or underline it). Using Mendeley, the free reference manager, you can easily access all of the articles you are using for a paper. Then, when writing the paper, recheck the quotations you have highlighted in your notes and selected for the paper to make sure the quotations are accurate. You need to cite the quotation properly by enclosing it in quotation marks and providing the author, date, and page number (required by APA style). In addition to using Mendeley, you could also make photocopies of the original text of articles from which you think you may be quoting.

Too Many Direct Quotes

Many instructors have seen papers where one quotation after another is presented, often filling pages of the student's report. Linking together a series of quotations to produce a paper or part of a paper may not be judged plagiarism if the author is appropriately acknowledged, but it is problematic (**http://write-site.athabascau.ca/avoiding-plagia rism.php#avoiding**). Why? Because you have essentially duplicated the structure of the author's argument and contributed essentially none of your own ideas.

REMEDY The goal is to understand what an author has said, consider its relevance to the case you are making, and then state that contribution in your own prose. In other words, use direct quotations sparingly. One approach is to use quotations only when the author has said something so eloquently and effectively that it succinctly captures the idea you want to present. Those quotations are rarer than you think!

Rephrasing (Paraphrasing) too Closely

Writers may rearrange the words in a sentence or borrow strings of text and think they have successfully paraphrased an author. In all likelihood, they have not moved far enough away from the original text. Your institution will likely have documents to show how to paraphrase material from a paper successfully. The University of Wisconsin–Madison has a particularly helpful website on this issue: **https://writing.wisc.edu/Handbook/QPA_paraphrase.html**

Failing to Give Adequate Credit for the Source of Your Ideas

Ideas for research come from a variety of places, but not infrequently students get research ideas by looking at the Limitations and Future Directions sections of published manuscripts.

REMEDY If you develop an idea based on limitations or future directions mentioned by an author, be sure to cite that paper when you talk about your research idea in the Introduction.

You might say, "So and so (authors, year) suggested their research could be expanded by using adults older than 50 years of age. The present research seeks to build on that earlier work by including both young adults (25–40) and older adults (50–70)."

» Try This Now

Consult your library's resources and see what guidelines your institution provides for avoiding plagiarism.

THE WRITING ITSELF: CLEAR AND SIMPLE

Particular sources are often cited if you want to read about writing well. These sources include Daryl Bem's "Writing the Empirical Journal Article" (2004). This article should be required reading; in it, Bem covered: "How should you write?" "For whom should you write?" and "The shape of an article." In addition, he addressed strategic topics in each section of the paper (Introduction through Discussion); he also included a section on grammatical errors, sexist language, and a variety of other critical issues. Many recommendations in this chapter are drawn from Bem's article.

This is the same article in which Bem covered "going fishing" in his section "Which article should you write?" (2004). The position here is to write the article that presents your original hypotheses, not, as Bem suggested, the one that "makes the most sense now that you have seen the results" (p. 186). Despite this difference of opinion about the focus of your written article, his other advice is valuable. Another useful resource is Robert Sternberg's edited volume *Guide to Publishing in Psychology Journals* (2000a). This book is helpful whatever your plans for your paper (from meeting a course requirement to publishing the manuscript in any social science journal). There are chapters on each component (e.g., Introduction, Titles, and Abstracts) as well as advice about presenting your research design. The chapter on results by Peter Salovey (2000) is particularly useful.

The writing in scholarly publications should be clear, but that does not mean lifeless. Bem's (2004) article emphasized two principles: clarity and accuracy. Your prose should reflect both. He noted that clarity is supported by "good organization," which the structure of a journal article essentially provides for you. The second aspect of clarity he specified is simple and direct writing; use words that are commonly understood. Related principles we would add are careful selection of words and succinctness. Look for a word that simply and directly expresses your meaning, and remember that multiple adjectives are unnecessary.

> **» Try This Now**
>
> Which of these options would you choose and why?
>
> 1. The finding is important.
>
> 2. The finding is very important.
>
> Option 1 is preferred because the word "important" sufficiently carries the meaning that the finding is consequential; "very" is unnecessary. Writers often pile on modifiers assuming their writing will have greater impact. Careful word choice eliminates the need to "pile on."

THE "SHAPE" OF YOUR PAPER

The *Publication Manual* (2010b) provides the organization of your paper (i.e., the sequence of sections and their contents), but that is not the same as the "shape" of your paper. Bem (2004) suggested that your paper take the shape of an hourglass, starting broadly with the first sentence of your Introduction and gradually narrowing through the Introduction to the statement of your hypotheses. Bem described the Method and Results sections as the "neck" (p. 190) of the hourglass, noting that these are the most specific parts of your paper. These sections are written with the same level of specificity throughout. The Discussion starts more narrowly, tied to the meaning of your results, and then widens to integrate your findings with those in the broader literature. After considering limitations, you conclude with the implications of the research.

THE TITLE OF THE PAPER AND ITS IMPORTANCE

Two overlooked elements at the front end of your paper are the title and abstract. First, let's look at the title. The *Publication Manual* recommends your title be no more than 12 words (2010b, p. 23), reflect the topic and variables studied, and do so with style, if possible. An important aspect of both the title and abstract is that they are used for indexing in databases such as PsycINFO®. Researchers may come across your article by doing a database search based on keywords, and your title and abstract need to contain those keywords. Here is a title that has some style while directly stating the variables under study: "A room with a cue: Personality judgments based on offices and bedrooms" (Gosling, Ko, Mannarelli, & Morris, 2002). You might argue that these authors were squandering their word limit by using a primary and a secondary title, but the interest generated by the play on words more than compensates for the "expense." The subtitle could stand on its own, but this would leave a dull title.

Sternberg (2000b) claimed the reader can answer the question "Are you an interesting thinker or a dull one?" (p. 38) by reading your title and abstract. The title is the first clue. Sternberg suggested you avoid titles that include such words as investigation, study, examination, or experiment, which are often married with a preposition ("on" or "of") (p. 39).

THE ABSTRACT

The abstract describes the essence of your research and determines whether the reader will bother to go further. The title communicates what variables might be involved, but the abstract provides information about the method, results, and implications. In a sense, the abstract is a condensed version of your paper because it contains all of the important elements. The abstract has a body (usually about 150–250 words in length) and usually four to six keywords [the *Publication Manual* (2010b) specifies no limit]. Journals will often specify how many keywords to include. We discussed the function of a keyword (a search term to retrieve information) in Chapter 2. Keywords are critical because those searchable terms are the words researchers enter into search function boxes as they look for articles in an area of interest.

> **» Try This Now**
>
> Based on your current research project, generate four to five keywords that reflect the content of your article.

The length of the abstract is determined by the journal to which an article is submitted, but typical limits range from about 150 to 250 words. There are exceptions, however, and if you plan to submit your manuscript for submission, you should consult the specific requirements for that journal. These requirements are typically listed on the homepage of the journal under "Manuscript Submissions."

REVISIT AND RESPOND

- What components of the title and abstract are indexed to communicate your work? Why qualities should a title have? A title should be no longer than _____ words.

Content of the Abstract

Abstract: short summary (150–250 words) of a research paper that includes a brief overview about the research problem, method, results, and discussion; includes keywords.

The **abstract** has a little bit of everything; that is, the abstract contains a bit of information about the major sections of a research paper. There are different emphases in the abstract depending on the kind of paper you are writing (e.g., empirical, meta-analysis, theory-oriented, or case study); here we will concentrate on the elements for an empirical article, which is the most common. The recommendations in this section come from the *Publication Manual,* specifically Section 2.04 (2010b).

Briefly, you need to state (a) the topic you are studying (e.g., social comparison); (b) characteristics of your participants and their classification; typically number, gender, race or ethnicity, and age (e.g., undergraduates); (c) methodological approach (e.g., correlational, between subjects, case study, and qualitative) and major dependent variables (e.g., Rosenberg Self-Esteem Scale); (d) results; statistical significance, confidence intervals, and effect sizes are typically provided, as appropriate (e.g., first year students engaged in significantly more social comparison than did fourth year students, $p = .032$); and (e) implications or applications.

Formatting the Abstract

The abstract has distinctive formatting: (a) the word "Abstract" is centered unbolded at the top of the page; (b) the text of the abstract starts flush left; (c) the word *Keywords* is italicized, followed by a colon, placed beneath the end of the abstract text, and indented five spaces from the left margin; and (d) the keywords or phrases themselves are not italicized and no period is placed after the last keyword. Here is an example of keyword formatting from Ann Devlin and Jack Nasar (2012):

> *Keywords:* therapists' perceptions, therapists' offices, aesthetics, environmental meaning, person perception

When in doubt about formatting issues, consult the *Publication Manual* (2010b). The sample papers beginning on page 41 (pages 41–59) of the 6th edition provide an excellent visual reference.

THE INTRODUCTION: CONTENT

Think about what you are trying to accomplish in the Introduction. The wide funnel at the beginning presents the general area under investigation. The core or meat of the Introduction reviews the influential research that shaped your perspective and your study. The end of the Introduction shows how you are going to build on this literature you have just reviewed (i.e., the tradition) and how your research will address the problem you introduced earlier to move the field forward (i.e., the innovation; review Chapter 2).

In their chapter on writing the Introduction, Philip Kendall, Jennifer Silk, and Brian Chu (2000) made the point that the literature review in an Introduction is not exhaustive or indiscriminate; rather, the influential studies should be carefully presented. You are summarizing what is known about the problem at the moment, highlighting the literature that has significantly contributed to the current state of knowledge (often these articles are cited frequently in the literature). Regarding setting the stage in the opening paragraph, Kendall et al. listed several strategies: "rhetorical question; everyday experience; analogy/metaphor; striking statistic/fact; historical fact; lack of previous research" (p. 43). You want to draw in your reader; to that end, the first sentence of your Introduction deserves attention.

First Sentences

The first sentence of your paper sets the stage for your reader. Remember Bem's (2004) description that the paper is shaped like an hourglass; the Introduction starts out broadly before narrowing to the specifics of the research. He also stated that, "Whenever possible, try to open with a statement about people (or animals), not psychologists or their research (This rule is almost always violated. Do not use journals as a model here.)" (p. 191).

⏵⏵ Try This Now

Here are first sentences from three published journal articles related to the role of the natural environment in human well-being: How well do they conform to Bem's (2004) and Kendall et al.'s (2000) advice? Which (if any) of the sentences did you like? Why?

"Humans have a deep-seated need for contact with nature, and researchers often explain this need by drawing on biophilia." (Chen, Tu, & Ho, 2013, p. 301)

"Evidence from disciplines including psychiatry, ecology, psychology, environmental planning, medicine, health, leisure and recreation, and exercise science has revealed that physical activity in nature has the potential to provide positive effects on human health beyond physical responses (e.g., Barton & Pretty, 2010; Brymer, 2009a; Kahn et al., 2009; Leather et al., 1998; Li et al., 2013; Maas et al., 2006; Maller et al., 2008; Weber & Anderson, 2010)." (Brymer, Davids, & Mallabon, 2014, p. 189)

"A significant body of literature has supported the intuitive belief that being in natural environments is good for psychological health." (Trigwell, Francis, & Bagot, 2014, p. 241)

Approaches to Integrating the Literature

In moving from your somewhat general opening statement to the specifics of your research, you will present and integrate literature that sets the stage for your work. You are combining tradition and innovation; first tell the reader what has already been done, and then make the case for how your research advances knowledge in the field.

There are several approaches to this process. You could:

- Take an historical perspective that indicates what the foundational articles are and how the topic has been studied since then (e.g., how Lynch's 1960 book *The Image of the City* initiated research on urban environmental perception).
- Organize the material around a theory that is central to their work and address aspects of the theory (e.g., research conducted on the four components of attention restoration theory: being away, fascination, extent, and compatibility; Kaplan, 1995).
- Integrate research from a methodological perspective, indicating the major research design approaches (e.g., correlational, between subjects, within subjects, mixed, longitudinal, cross-sectional, and qualitative) and emphasize the reliability and validity of measures, if that is an issue.
- Contrast consistent findings with those that are anomalous, or point out confounding variables that have created problems in interpretation.

Whatever approach you take (typically people use a combination), most paragraphs will *integrate the contributions of more than one article*. In other words, you want to avoid what is called "stacking abstracts," in which each paragraph briefly discusses only one article, much the way an abstract does. "Stringing together summaries of studies (stacking abstracts) is the hallmark of lazy writing" (Kendall et al., 2000, p. 49). Your goal is integration. You want to present the literature in clusters or packages that reflect one theme or approach mentioned (historical, methodological, and so on). In addition, the length of text you devote to a given article should reflect its importance or weight. You would spend the most time reviewing the contributions of articles that are pivotal to your research.

A good way to learn more about writing an Introduction is careful study of the approaches that other authors take. Spend time examining the way the authors you cite structure their Introductions. Evaluate how well they succeed in clearly laying out their arguments, and adopt the approaches you think are effective. Don't reinvent the wheel.

REVIST AND RESPOND

- How can the quality of your title affect the likelihood that someone will read your paper? What is the function of keywords? A research paper is shaped like an _____. Explain what should be covered in each section (Abstract, Introduction, Method, Results, Discussion). What does it mean when someone says you are "stacking abstracts?" To avoid stacking abstracts, describe three different ways you can organize your literature.

Citing and Quoting From the Literature

When you integrate the literature, you will be citing the work of others. These citations can be placed in open text or within parentheses. The advice from several sources (Bem, 2004; Kendall et al., 2000) is to put most citations within parentheses (a less high-profile position), not in open text. Open-text citations should be saved for research that has great impact or will be a centerpiece for your work. A corollary is to start your sentences with content, not with authors.

❯❯ Try This Now

Consider the difference between the following two choices. Given our previous discussion, which is preferred?

1. Nasar and Devlin (2011) found that personalization and orderliness were positively related to judgments of the therapist's competence.

2. Personalization and orderliness were positively related to judgments of the therapist's competence (Nasar & Devlin, 2011).

Option 2 is preferred. Your review of the literature is not directly about the researchers; it is about the research. For that reason, authors' names are secondary; their placement should reflect that status.

Quoting directly from authors is tempting, but like stacking abstracts, frequent use of direct quotations is a reflection of lazy writing. You want to understand what is written well enough to communicate its meaning in your own words. Most writers recommend that you save direct quotations for statements that substantially contribute to the impact or "quality" of your paper (Kendall et al., 2000, p. 50) and do so succinctly and elegantly. If you judge it necessary to quote, the author(s), year, and page number of the source of the direct quotation must be included, as you see in the example just cited from Kendall et al. In addition, special formatting is necessary if the passage quoted is 40 words or longer; this formatting is known as a block quotation [see Section 6.03, p. 171, *Publication Manual* (2010b)].

Tense

Most sections of the manuscript (Introduction, Method, Results) are written in the past tense, but there are some exceptions. Present tense would be used when you describe the characteristics of measures that exist (that is, their existence continues; e.g., "There are 15 items in this scale"). In the Discussion, the implications of the results and conclusions are stated in the present tense. As an example, in describing the implications of their work on the supportive design of hospital rooms, the authors stated: "Increasing the number of favorable elements in the hospital room is important because there is a relationship between the number of such elements, and satisfaction with the service, choosing the room again, and stress reduction" (Devlin, Andrade, & Lima, 2014, p. 77). This quotation uses present tense (the verb "is") because the implications continue and are not restricted to the outcome of that particular study.

Length of the Introduction

Your instructor will likely specify the length required for your paper. If you were submitting the manuscript for an empirical article, many journals suggest an Introduction of no more than eight to nine pages, double-spaced. Whether for class or journal submission, keep in mind that the Discussion and Introduction should be roughly balanced in length. Most authors have great difficulty achieving that balance, but it deserves attention. Reading a paper of 30 pages of content in which the Discussion is but 2.5 pages is problematic and suggests that the research has little to contribute to the literature. A short Discussion is likely to be the outcome when you have nonsignificant findings.

REVISIT AND RESPOND

- Explain the recommendations for when to quote and how to cite quoted material (i.e., in text vs. parentheses), the use of present versus past tense in the manuscript, the length of the Introduction (for a manuscript submission), and why it may be hard to balance the length of the Introduction and Discussion.

The Introduction and Method: Centering, Bolding, and Page Sequencing

Formatting in APA style takes a bit of time to master. Beginning with the title page, which includes the title, author(s), and affiliation(s), the pages are numbered consecutively beginning with the number 1. For the Introduction, note there is no heading labeled "Introduction" in your manuscript. Rather, the Introduction starts on p. 3 of the manuscript (page 1 is the title page; page 2 is the abstract) with the title repeated at the top of the page (centered, but not bolded). Once you start the Introduction (on p. 3), the sections of the manuscript *continue without page breaks* until you get to the references. The references start on a new page (centered, but not bolded) no matter where the Discussion ends on the previous page. In APA style, the following headings are centered and bolded: Method, Results, and Discussion. The three sections of the method [Participants, Materials (sometimes called Measures, Instruments, or Apparatus], and Procedure are flush left and bolded.

THE METHOD SECTION

The Method section is straightforward and detailed; it focuses on the presentation of facts regarding the "who" (Participants), the "what" (Materials/Measures), and the "how" (Procedure). Present enough information that another researcher could replicate your study. In addition, many researchers include a Research Design statement in the Method section, typically at the beginning.

Like the Introduction, the Method section will be nearly finished when you submit your IRB proposal. What remains is to specify the number of participants. The *Publication Manual* specifies what information should be included in the Method section (2010b, section 2.06), and we will follow those guidelines.

Research Design

In the Method section, you would present your research design, which would come first. In "Writing Effectively About Design," Harry Reis (2000) provided guidance in terms of how to explain your research design, and a chapter by Salovey (2000) "Results That Get Results: Telling a Good Story" also discussed how to write about research design. One of Reis's main points is that the design statement reminds us whether causality can be inferred. Reis thought people write too much in this section. For him, simpler is better. Stick to the point: Be brief, clear, and thorough. The essential components are the design itself; participant assignment; and specification of independent and dependent variables. Also include what environmental controls (e.g., covariates) you used.

Here are statements of simple research designs to illustrate common approaches:

Correlational. The research design was correlational; all participants received three scales; one measuring mood (Profile of Mood States), one measuring self-esteem (Rosenberg Self-esteem Scale), and one measuring academic motivation (Academic Motivation Scale).

Quasi-experimental. The research design was quasi-experimental. The two quasi-independent variables were class year (four levels) and area of campus housing (four levels). All participants completed two conceptually related dependent variables, the Sense of Community Index and the University Residence Environment Scale.

Experimental. The research design was an experimental, between subjects design with one independent variable (accent strength) containing three levels (none, medium, strong). There was one dependent variable (score on a recognition test). Participants were randomly assigned to condition (one of the three levels of accent strength).

On a related note, it makes good sense to state your research design explicitly in your IRB proposal. In addition, it is good practice to include a Results Statement [essentially your approach to testing your hypothesis(ses)]. This additional information about your approach to data analysis serves several purposes. First, it requires that you think through what you are doing and have a specific plan for data analysis. Second, it will help your instructor (or anyone looking at your proposal) catch problems before they are unfixable.

Here are the Results Statements that would accompany each of the previously presented Research Design statements. Note, for the purposes of an IRB proposal, both the Research Design and Results Statements would be in the future tense, which is adopted here.

Correlational. To evaluate the relationships between variables, Pearson's *r* analyses will be conducted.

Quasi-experimental. To evaluate the relationships of class year and area of campus housing to the two conceptually related dependent variables, factorial multivariate analysis of variance (MANOVA) will be conducted followed by Tukey post hoc analyses.

Experimental. To evaluate the impact of accent strength on the recognition score, a one-way ANOVA will be run followed by Tukey post hoc analyses.

Participants

In this section, you present the numbers of individuals involved, by condition, if your approach is experimental or quasi-experimental; their demographic characteristics; and the sampling procedures used. Note that an uppercase *N* is used to describe the whole sample; lowercase *n*s are used to describe the subsamples.

The demographic characteristics (age, gender, race and/or ethnicity) of the sample are typically presented here rather than in the Results section. Present information you have about the ways in which the sample may differ from the target population. For example, if you are using undergraduates from your institution, institutional statistics regarding the percentage by gender, race, and class year may be available, and you can compare your sample to those figures.

If relevant given your design, present information about drop-outs from conditions. Participant drop-out rates and return rates on surveys are often included in the Method section (Bem, 2004).

The sampling procedure may be detailed and should include the source of the participants (e.g., subject pool), any incentives offered (e.g., payment on Amazon MTurk® or lottery for a gift card drawing); and ethical standards (typically that subjects were treated according to ethical guidelines). If you used a convenience or snowball sample, describe the specific approach (e.g., Facebook®). If you recruited people outside the subject pool on or off campus, describe the location, time of day, days of the week, number of people approached, and number who agreed. If you sent out e-mails or letters, describe the sampling approach (see Chapter 9). If a power analysis was used to determine the sample size, explain that as well.

Measures

The typical focus of the Measures section is the scales used, but it may also contain information about the independent variable, for example, the text used in different scenario conditions or the visual images shown to participants. For example, in their Method section, Nasar and Devlin (2011) described the 30 color images used in their multiple-study research on therapists' offices.

If scales are used in your research, they are presented in the Measures section. One way to organize this information is to have a separate paragraph on each scale in which you present the name of the scale (with its citation); the number of items in the scale; the scale range; the scale anchors; whether there are reverse-scored items; and one or two sample items. In addition, the reliability and validity information about the scale should be presented. This information should include the Cronbach's alpha reported in the literature and the Cronbach's alpha achieved in your research. Here is a paragraph (modified from Devlin, Andrade, & Lima, 2014, p. 32) to illustrate these guidelines:

> Perceived stress was measured using the state version of Spielberger's 20-item State Trait Anxiety Inventory (STAI; Spielberger, Gorsuch, & Lushene, 1970), which assesses the level of stress or anxiety one feels at the present moment. Scores range from 20 to 80; higher scores reflect greater anxiety. A sample item is "I am tense," measured from 1 ("not at all") to 4 ("very much

so"). Ten of the items are reverse scored. Cronbach alphas in the literature range from .86-.95; here the Cronbach's alpha was .90) (**http://www.apa .org/pi/about/publications/caregivers/practice-settings/assessment/tools/trait-state.aspx**).

Procedure

The Procedure covers the "how" of your study. If participants were assigned to condition, you would explain how that was accomplished (randomly or otherwise). This section should include the timeframe and place of the research (if done in person); any instructions or guidelines presented to participants; and whether there was automation of any part of the instructions (e.g., tape-recording to standardize administration). Describe whether the study was administered individually or in groups; if groups, report the group size (or range, if the size varied). Report how the study was described in any advertising or the text of communications about the study sent via e-mail or posted on social media.

If equipment was used (e.g., to record vital signs or to project images), present enough detail for someone to replicate your approach, for example, the model number of the equipment; resolution, viewing distance, viewing angle of images; or decibel level of sound recordings.

If data were collected in the field, for example, observationally, describe the approach taken (e.g., participant vs. nonparticipant observation; see Chapter 6). Include steps taken to establish inter-rater reliability, including training.

REVISIT AND RESPOND

- What information about the participants, measures, and procedure should be presented? Why is it necessary to provide so much detail about the who, the what, and the how of your study? Why would you want to present both the Cronbach's alpha in the literature and the Cronbach's alpha from your study? What does a statement of your research design tell the reader?

WRITING ABOUT RESULTS

Students often think that the numbers by themselves tell the story of the findings; as a consequence, they fail to communicate the narrative explaining the results. Salovey's chapter (2000) "Results That Get Results: Telling a Good Story" describes how to tell a story, as the title of his chapter suggests. Results should be presented in the context of what you were measuring in a particular analysis, for example, the difference in judged competence of a therapist whose office displays 0, 2, 4, or 9 credentials. This statement of what you were trying to examine should come prior to the descriptive statistics. In other words, don't assume that the reader will remember your explicit hypotheses. Bem (2004) suggested that the Results should be written at a level above that of an introductory psychology course but one step below the level of the audience that reads the journal where your article might be publishable.

Start with the important findings (tests of your hypotheses) before presenting secondary findings, and explain the outcome of the results before providing the numerical support [Salovey (2000) called this a "Top Down Structure, " pp. 123–125]. Bem (2004, p. 2000) agreed: Present "each result clearly in prose before wading into numbers and statistics."

Using our example, we might report that a therapist whose office displays at least 4 credentials is judged as more competent than one whose office displays either 2 or 0 credentials, but not as more competent than one whose office displays 9 credentials. Then we would present the numerical support for that statement.

The *Publication Manual,* Section 2.07, covers Results (2010b, pp. 32–35), but chapters by Salovey (2000), Bem (2004), and Elena Grigorenko (2000) are more user-friendly for researchers. You have to understand what a result means to write about it; you can't give a result without translating that into English in terms of what the higher and lower values (e.g., *M*s) indicate (Bcm, 2004). Thus, if you are talking about scores on the State Trait Anxiety Inventory, you need to remind the reader that higher scores reflect higher anxiety than do lower scores.

Other good advice from Salovey is to put "as many of the preliminaries" as possible in the Method section (2000, p. 129). In other words, the demographic characteristics, reliability and validity statistics, manipulation check outcomes, and any other supportive material should be presented before the main event, that is, the formal results. Using this strategy, the Results will be about "THE RESULTS." Echoing other writers who offer advice about communicating clearly, Salovey favored using tables and figures for as many findings as possible because the text is more understandable when the flow is not interrupted by the introduction of numbers.

You are not done when you create a table. Salovey (2000) and Bem (2004) agreed that you need to help the reader understand what is in the table, specifically directing the reader to a particular finding there. Using an example from emotional reactions to watching affective films, Bem (2004, p. 200) illustrated such guidance: "As shown in the first column of Table 2 men produce more tears (2.33 cc) than women (1.89 cc)"; "Do not just wave in the general direction of the table and expect the reader to ferret out the information."

A helpful organizational strategy Salovey (2000) recommended is to create parallelism throughout your paper. What he meant is that the order of presentation of ideas should be the same in your Introduction, Method, Results, and Discussion. As an example, if you write about Roger Ulrich's Theory of Supportive Design (1991), which has three components (positive distraction, social support, and perceived control), and you present the background on each component in that order in the Introduction, present the measures for each component in that order in the Method section; then present the Results for each component in that order. Finally, in the Discussion section, interpret the findings in that order as well.

REVISIT AND RESPOND

- Explain what Salovey (2000) meant when he talked about Results that tell a good story. How do you accomplish that? What is the advantage of putting the "preliminaries" (e.g., reliabilities and demographic characteristics) in the Method section? How do you organize your paper to create parallel construction? Why should you present as many findings as possible in tables and figures?

Writing About Results: The Specifics of What to Present

We have already talked about the top-down presentation of results; you start with the major hypotheses first before moving on to any secondary hypotheses. People reading your paper want to know whether your hypotheses were supported. After covering your major outcomes, additional relationships that were discovered (i.e., "fished" for) can be presented, remembering to make clear that these were post hoc analyses.

But how does the result "look?" First, the heading Results is centered and bolded. Table 11.1 presents the information that typically accompanies a reported finding:

TABLE 11.1 ■ Common Statistical Measures: What and How to Report		
Statistical Test	**What to Report**	**How It Looks**
_t_ test	_M_s and _SD_s for each group _t_ value, _df_, _p_ value (equal variances assumed or not assumed, according to outcome of Levene's Test for Equality of Variances)	$t(120) = 0.50, p = .62$
ANOVAs	_M_s and _SD_s and _n_s for each group _F_ value, _df_, _p_ value for each IV and interaction(s) for the outcome measure (DV) If Tukeys or simple effects tests are needed, give the _p_ value for each significant contrast	$F(4, 117) = 0.74, p = .57$

Source: Adapted from Devlin, 2006, Appendix C, pp. 243–244.

Statistical Test	What to Report	How It Looks
MANOVAs	Ms and SDs and ns for each group for each dependent variable	Wilks's Lambda =.87
		$F_{(6, 436)} = 5.36$, $p = .009$; $\eta^2 = .07$
	Wilks's Lambda, F, df, and p and effect size/eta squared for EACH multivariate effect	
	For each IV that was significant from the multivariate level, indicate the F, df, and p and effect size/eta squared for the univariate tests where there were group differences on each Dependent variable	$F_{(2, 220)} = 6.26$, $p = .009$; $\eta^2 = .05$
	If Tukeys or Simple Effects tests are needed, give the p value for each significant contrast	
Correlation	r value, N, and p value	$r_{(43)} = .87$, $p = .001$
Chi Square	Chi-square value, df, N, and p value	$\chi^2 (1, N = 90) = 6.73$, $p = .008$
	Percentages in each cell	
Regression	F, df, p, beta	Example of vocational maturity predicting vocational indecision: $F_{(15, 99)} = 4.63$, $p < .001$, $Beta = -.378$, $p < .001$ (adapted from Mikulinsky, 2002, p. 42)
Multiple Regression	R-square, F, df, p, $Beta$, t, p, and names of variables. Note that some researchers prefer β, the standardized regression coefficient, instead of Beta	Example where career-oriented variables are used as a block in a hierarchical regression to predict vocational indecision:
		R-square = .24, $F_{(3, 135)} = 14.16$, $p < .001$
		$Beta$ t p
		VMS $-.375$ -4.72 $< .001$
		VDE $.011$ $.146$ $< .001$
		CES $-.234$ -3.00 $< .884$
		(adapted from Mikulinsky, 2002, pp. 42–43)

Source: Adapted from Devlin, 2006, pp. 243–244.

Transparency in Reporting

As discussed in Chapter 10, because transparency is such an important issue, researchers need to describe any steps they took to "clean up" the data. Readers who want to learn more about this topic are directed to a chapter by Grigorenko (2000) in Sternberg's volume (2000a). This information about cleaning up data should be presented at the outset of the Results section (some researchers prefer the Method section). Such information should include (if applicable):

- Any adjustments made to the data (for missing data, outliers); the circumstances surrounding those situations (e.g., whether people dropped out and in which conditions and equipment malfunction); and the specific steps taken to address these issues.
- Response rates and how they were calculated.

Text or Table? Not Both

For a given finding, present the information in text or in a table, not both. One rule of thumb is that when you present an outcome with more than two *M*s and *SD*s, or more than three correlations, use a table (see also *Publication Manual,* 2010b, section 4.41). In the case of the *M*s and *SD*s, this means that a *t* test would not require a table but an ANOVA would. Make it easy for your reader to grasp the results. If you present a lot of numerical information in text (e.g., many *M*s and *SD*s), the reader will quickly lose track of what has been presented. A table is an efficient and effective graphical representation of information. If you had a series of *t* tests, these could easily be presented in a table.

Statistical Presentation in APA Style

Learning a language takes some time; many students view APA style as a language. Anyone who is writing papers in APA style needs to have access to a copy of the current *Publication Manual* (6th edition, 2010b). Ideally you would own a copy. Here are some basic formatting requirements for statistical copy in APA style:

- Statistical symbols (e.g., *F, t, p, M,* and *SD*) are presented in italics.
- Means and standard deviations are often presented within parentheses.

Section 4.35 of the *Publication Manual* (2010b) presents the following important guidelines (a cursory look at just a few journal articles will show you these are little known rules):

- When the theoretical value of a finding cannot exceed 1 (for example, *p* or *r*), there is no 0 to the left of the decimal place. Thus, a *p* value of .03 should be presented as .03, not as 0.03.

- Use a 0 as a placeholder to the left of the decimal place for a finding that is less than 1 but theoretically *could* exceed 1 (e.g., *F, M,* and *SD*). Thus, it is informative to put in that 0 for an *M* of 0.36 because it shows the reader that the value *is* that small. A secondary reason is that if you are lining up values in a table, it will help you keep the columns straight.

There is no hard-and-fast rule about the number of decimal places to present; instructors and journals differ on this issue. The recommendation here is two decimal places, with the exception that *p* values may have three decimal places (see Section 4.35 of the *Publication Manual,* 2010b). This approach provides a good deal of information without exceeding what appears to be the restriction of space in journals:

- Give exact *p* values, except when:
- The *p* value is less than .000; report this as *p* < .001. Remember that *p* is a probability and is never 0.
- You have a large table of correlations and exact *p* values will not fit; use a probability note underneath the table (see section 5.16 of the *Publication Manual,* 2010b). Asterisks are used to present the probability values and are typically *p < .05, ** *p* < .01, ***p < .001. The *Publication Manual* recommends that within the same paper, you use the same asterisk denotations.
- Spacing statistical copy. Look at the presentation of the following finding:

$$F(1, 203) = 5.65, p = .002$$

- Note that the left parenthesis "hugs" the statistical symbol. Notice also, however, that there is a space between the degrees of freedom and a space on either side of the equal signs. For spacing, you can consult the *Publication Manual,* 2010b, section 4.46, p. 118; see also the ANOVA example of spacing on p. 127 in the *Publication Manual.*

ROUNDING RULES These rules sometimes generate a lively discussion in classes because it is clear that people have learned different rules. If you think about the following **rounding rules,** you will see that always rounding up (or not) would lead to an overestimation (or underestimation) in your results. For that reason, you need a rule about when to round up.

Rounding occurs because we are limited in the number of decimal places we can present. Assume here that we are limited to two decimal places. There is no dispute that when the third decimal place number is between 6 and 9, we round UP the decimal place to the left. Thus, 2.136 becomes 2.14. When the third decimal number is between

Rounding rules: rules to guide when you round up, when you leave a value as is, and when the digit in question is 5.

1 and 4, we don't round; we just leave the number as is. Thus, 2.134 becomes 2.13. The trouble starts when the third decimal place number is 5.

Here is the rule when the third decimal place number is 5. If the number to the left of the 5 is EVEN, leave it as is: Thus, 2.145 becomes 2.14. When the number to the left of the 5 is ODD, round up: Thus, 2.175 becomes 2.18.

REVISIT AND RESPOND

- Don't forget that *M*s and *SD*s are statistical symbols and should be italicized, along with other statistical symbols. Explain the role of 0 as a placeholder in the presentation of results where the finding can theoretically be greater than 1 and where it cannot. Explain the rounding rules. Explain how to present a result where the printout shows $p = .0000$. What happens if you always round up (or not)? Findings should be presented in the text or in a table but not both. How many results of a particular kind (e.g., correlation, *M*s, and *SD*s) should you have before moving to a table? What is the advantage of presenting findings in a table?

DISCUSSION

Even when researchers have significant results to interpret, the Discussion (as introduced in Chapter 2) can be a challenge to write. There should be some balance in length between the Introduction and the Discussion; often there is not. The challenge is to interpret the results rather than merely to restate them. There is both tradition and innovation in the Discussion. How the results relate to early research (consistently or not) needs to be specified (the tradition). The significance of the results in adding to the literature and pointing toward future research also needs to be articulated (the innovation).

The Discussion (the heading is centered and bolded) can start with a statement of support, partial support, or nonsupport of the hypotheses. Section 2.08 of the *Publication Manual* (2010b) describes the Discussion section as the place to "examine, interpret, and qualify the results and draw inferences and conclusions from them" (p. 35).

As the language of the *Publication Manual* (2010b) suggests, you are interpreting the results, not restating them. The fact that a given difference occurred (e.g., that displaying 4 credentials resulted in higher judgments of a therapist's competence than displaying 2 or 0 credentials, but that having 9 credentials was not a significant improvement in that regard) needs to be *interpreted*. What might this finding suggest? The Discussion section does not typically include the restatement of the results with numbers; for example, instead of re-reporting *M*s and *SD*s, you would say which group(s) were higher than another or others on a particular measure and explain the implications of that difference.

"Each new statement should contribute something new to the reader's understanding of the problem" (Bem, 2004, p. 202).

Remember that the shape of the Discussion starts more narrowly and then widens to integrate the relationship of the findings to existing literature (the bottom of the hourglass). In addition, you want to comment on the generalizability of the findings (i.e., do the results extend to other populations?). Your data need to support the claims you are making about them. This caution is particularly important with regard to the generalizability of your findings. With the number of WEIRD participants (from countries that are Western, educated, industrialized, rich, and democratic; see Chapter 9) in research, extending your findings beyond such limited samples is usually unjustified.

You are presenting the best case you can about the contribution of your data, but there will be critics; every research study has weaknesses. Robert Calfee (2000) suggested that you essentially make a preemptive strike by anticipating what your critics would say about your claims and present an argument to counter them. "Your task is to argue a series of mini-cases, during which your main job is to develop warrants" (p. 137). A **warrant** shows how evidence supports a claim and rules out alternative explanations.

A related aspect of the Discussion is the Limitations section, where you talk about the threats to internal validity and other challenges to the research. Among the possibilities covered in the *Publication Manual* (2010b) are the internal consistency of the measures (their imprecision), threats to Type I error when you run many tests, and small effect sizes. Yes, you need to mention the major limitations. At the same time, Bem advised not to "dwell compulsively on every flaw!" (2004, p. 202). Move beyond the Limitations to end the Discussion with contributions and possible next steps. Bem's advice was to "end with a bang, not a whimper" (p. 203).

Warrant: argument that shows how evidence supports a claim and rules out alternative explanations.

NONSIGNIFICANT RESULTS: WHAT CAN YOU SAY?

What do you say when you have nonsignificant results? These results are referred to as nonsignificant, not insignificant. Note, use of the word "insignificant" would suggest that the results were inconsequential; nonsignificant means that the results did not reach the stated alpha level to reject the null hypothesis.

First, as in the case of significant results, you state your findings. Next, discuss to what extent these findings do or do not fit with the previous literature. Remember that in the Discussion, you typically cite research that you introduced in the Introduction. After that, you can discuss what threats to internal validity may have affected your research, including procedural or other factors, such as low internal consistency of measures. Small sample sizes, which may have led to a Type II error, are often an issue.

If you did any "fishing," and these analyses resulted in significant results, you could next talk about these results. These are post hoc analyses. In such cases, you may be in a position to introduce new literature. Because these findings were not part of your original hypotheses, you did not present the case for this analysis in your Introduction. For example, in the study on perceptions of femininity mentioned earlier in this book, the researcher's original hypotheses were stated in terms of barbell weight (5 lbs or 25 lbs) but not in terms of athlete status or gender. What if we looked for and found results related to gender? If we wanted to discuss these results, we might need to introduce research showing that views of femininity differ across gender.

STATISTICAL VERSUS PRACTICAL SIGNIFICANCE

Statistical significance: when a result reaches the stated alpha level, typically .05.

Practical significance: results that are useful in an applied setting; often results may be statistically significant but not be large enough to have practical import.

There is a difference between the **statistical significance** and **practical significance** of your findings. Statistical significance is a matter of being able to reject the null hypothesis; small group differences and small correlations, for example, can reach statistical significance with sufficiently large sample sizes. A correlation of .25 might be significant at the .05 level, but remember that squaring r gives you the percentage of variability accounted for by knowing that relationship. In this example, r^2 is .06, which may not be useful in a practical sense.

Simply because you have statistical significance does not mean your results are useful in an applied setting. In an experiment where you were measuring reaction times (in msec), a small difference between age groups might be both statistically significant and practically meaningful (e.g., the time to react to a stimulus and press a brake pedal). If the study focused instead on reaction times to selecting an item off a menu, the results might be statistically but not practically meaningful.

REVISIT AND RESPOND

- What similarities and differences are there when writing a Discussion section with significant versus nonsignificant findings? In terms of discussing results from a "fishing expedition," introducing relevant literature in the Discussion is useful, but how much prominence does this material merit, relative to your original hypotheses? What kinds of issues may come up to address in your Limitations section? What is the distinction between statistical and practical significance?

GENERAL FORMATTING ISSUES: MASTERING APA STYLE

In addition to headings, centering, bolding, page numbers, and basic statistical presentation, there are other aspects of basic APA style that are worth memorizing. We list these issues and reference sections here as well as a few of the lesser known rules; knowing these (and using them correctly) will show that you are a master of APA style. Again, looking at the sample papers that begin on page 41 of the *Publication Manual* (2010b) is a good way to locate the answer to a particular formatting question. For each issue discussed here, the relevant section from the *Publication Manual* is noted.

Running Heads and Page Numbers

Running heads are shortened paper titles that appear at the top of each page (see *Publication Manual,* 2010b, section 8.03, p. 229).

Page numbers appear on every page flush right, starting with the title page, and are numbered consecutively.

Typeface and Right Margin

The recommended typeface for APA manuscripts is Times New Roman, in 12 pt. The manuscript should be double-spaced throughout (exceptions would be some parts of tables or figures to enhance readability). Use a ragged right edge (*Publication Manual,* 2010b, section 8.03).

References and Issue Pagination

One of the finer points of creating your references deals with issue **pagination** for a journal. If a journal paginates (i.e., numbers pages) continuously throughout the year, do not include the issue number in the reference material for that article. All APA journals number consecutively through the year; therefore, no issue number is included for citations from APA journals. You can locate the list of APA journals by going to the APA home page, clicking on Publications and Databases, clicking on Journals; then you can browse journals by title and subject (**http://www.apa.org/ pubs/journals/index.aspx**). For non-APA journals, the easiest way to determine whether an issue number is needed (for most it is not) is to go to the home page of the journal in question, click on all issues or previous issues, and then click on the last issue of that year, for example, December 2015, to see the page numbers. If they are "high," you know the journal paginates continuously.

Pagination: how a journal numbers its pages; if consecutively throughout the year, no issue number is needed in the reference.

Rules for et al. in Text

One detail-oriented aspect of citations is when to use the phrase *et al.,* which means "and others." An extremely valuable page to "bookmark" in your *Publication Manual* is Table 6.1 Basic Citation Styles (2010b, p. 177), which covers in-text citations. Among the rules related to et al. worth memorizing are the following:

- If a citation has one or two authors, you always mention those authors.
- If a citation has from three to five authors, you mention all authors the first time you cite the work; on subsequent mentions, you use the et al. format.
- If a citation has six or more authors, you use et al. the first time you cite the work and thereafter.

The Order of Citations Within Parentheses in Text

Not all journals follow APA style, and it is important to learn "the APA way." Some journals order the citations of works in parentheses chronologically; in APA style, the order of those citations is alphabetically by the first author in a reference. A way to remember this rule is that the order of citations in parentheses should follow their order of appearance in the references, which is alphabetical.

> **» Try This Now**
>
> Here is a citation in text:
>   This line of research (Jones, 1996; Camly & Marks, 1985; Benchella, Stephanski, & Zo, 1975) has been productive.
>   Rewrite this citation in the correct order.
>   If your citation now looks like (Benchella, Stepanski, & Zo, 1975; Camily & Marks, 1985; Jones, 1996), you are correct.

Digital Object Identifiers

Digital object identifier (doi): unique code used in references that locates the reference in an electronic database.

A **digital object identifier (doi)** is a unique code used in references that locates the reference in an electronic database. Increasingly, published papers have these codes, and they should be included at the end of the given reference. Here is an example:

Andrade, C., & Devlin, A. S. (2015). Stress reduction in the hospital room: Applying Ulrich's theory of supportive design. *Journal of Environmental Psychology, 41,* 125–134. doi:10.1016/j.jenvp.2014.12.001

Note several things: (a) The doi is lowercase; (b) it is followed by a colon; (c) there is no space between the colon and the numerical identifier; (d) the numerical identifier begins with "10"; and (e) there is no period after the end of the doi (see *Publication Manual,* 2010b, sections 6.31 and 6.32). Usually, the doi can be found on the title page of the journal article itself. This is almost always the case for recent publications (the last 5–10 years) because doi's have been available for more than 15 years. If the doi is not listed, you can (a) look in the database information about that article (e.g., in PsycINFO) or (b) go to the journal home-page, select the publication year, issue, number, and article; the doi is normally listed with the article. In many of these instances, the doi was added long after the article appeared. On occasion, if these approaches fail, you can Google the article and may find the doi listed.

In cases where there is no doi and you found the reference online, give the URL of the home page of the journal at the end of the citation instead of the doi (*Publication Manual,* 2010b, section 7.01, item 3).

Advance Online Publication

Journals are rarely up-to-date with regard to publishing all of the articles accepted, but with the availability of electronic communication, articles waiting in the queue are often published as **Advance online publications** (*Publication Manual,* 2010b, section 7.01, item 5). The complete article is published in this form; what it lacks is the volume and page numbers it will be assigned. The citation style follows the typical format, except that after the name of the journal, ending with a period, you place the words "Advance online publication" followed by the doi. Here is an example:

> Andrade, C. C., Lima, M. L., Devlin, A. S., & Hernandez, B. (2014). Is it the place or the people? Disentangling the effects of hospitals' physical and social environments on well-being. *Environment and Behavior.* Advance online publication. doi:10.1177/0013916514536182

Advance online publication: full text version of the article available electronically in advance of print publication.

PRESENTING NUMBERS: THE SHORT STORY

With regard to presenting numbers as numerals versus words, there are some useful rules to memorize, but many researchers rely on the *Publication Manual* (2010b) for the rest.

Express numbers in words from one to nine, but as a numeral when you reach 10. There are some important exceptions (*Publication Manual,* 2010b, section 4.31):

- All numbers are written as words when they begin a sentence.
- In the abstract, all numbers appear as numerals (even those less than 10), unless they begin a sentence.

COMMON GRAMMATICAL MISTAKES

The *Publication Manual* provides good coverage of grammatical mistakes (2010b, sections 3.18 to 3.23). What is offered here overlaps with the *Publication Manual* to some extent and reflects mistakes commonly found in published research papers, suggesting the need to highlight these overlooked issues.

Data Versus Datum

> **» Try This Now**
>
> Which of the following sentences is correct?
>
> 1. The data were convincing.
>
> 2. The data was convincing.

If you selected 1, you are correct. The word "data" is plural, and it takes a plural verb. You rarely read about a single datum.

Missing Referents

> **» Try This Now**
>
> Read the following sentence and identify the missing referent in the second sentence.

"The randomization feature malfunctioned, and the data from 25 participants had to be deleted. This makes the outcome questionable."

If you said "this," you are correct. We don't know to what "this" refers in the second sentence; hence, we have a missing referent. You have to tell us what problem you identified in the previous sentence that makes the outcome questionable. A reasonable substitute sentence would be: "This large deletion makes the outcome questionable."

- **Comparative language.** When you use a comparative word like "more," "higher," "better," or "lower," you have to indicate the other group involved in the comparison. As an example in a study that compared women and men, the sentence

"Women scored higher on the test" should be "Women scored higher on the test than did men."

- **Attributing agency where there is none.** When you state: "The study aimed to . . . ," you are attributing intentionality to the study. People have agency; studies do not. Simply saying something like "The aim of the study was to. . . ." fixes the problem.

- **Serial comma (also called the Oxford comma).** In a series of three or more items (also true for authors' citations in text), you need a comma before the coordinating conjunction. Here is an example that illustrates the comma use in the iteration of topics and in the citation: "In the related research on neighborhoods, mental health, and transportation (Smith, Jones, & Blanda, 2009), . . ."

- **While versus whereas**. Commonly, when you use "while," you are describing events that occur at the same time: "Nero played the violin while Rome burned." The word "whereas" is best used for contrasts: "The ice hockey players had higher scores on the power lifting test, whereas the long distance runners had higher scores on the endurance test."

- **Since versus because**. These are subordinate conjunctions. The word "since" should be used to indicate the passage of time (i.e., after that time): "Since the crash of 2008, the middle class has not recovered its earning power, which has affected college enrollments." The word "because" provides an explanation: "The scores of seniors were higher than the scores of first year students because the seniors had taken more English courses than had the first year students."

- **Number versus amount.** These words appear frequently in scientific writing; unfortunately, they are often confused.

» Try This Now

Which of these sentences is correct?

1. The amount of participants exceeded 100.

2. The number of participants exceeded 100.

If you chose 2, you are correct. A simple way to remember the difference is to use "number" when you are referring to a countable noun (e.g., dollars or chairs); use "amount" when you are referring to the conglomerate or mass noun (e.g., money or furniture). It is the number of dollars but the amount of money; the number of chairs but the amount of furniture.

A related issue is when to use "fewer" and when to use "less." "Fewer" should be used with countable nouns (fewer dollars and chairs), whereas less should be used with mass nouns (money and furniture). Here is an example combining both: There were fewer dollars available; as a consequence, less furniture was purchased.

> **》 Try this Now**
>
> If you wanted to purchase bottles of water, how would the second part of the sentence read?

Gender Neutral Language

Gender neutral language: using language that does not favor one gender category.

The purpose of using **gender neutral language** is to avoid bias. You run into this difficulty when you use singular nouns that require a pronoun, but what should that pronoun be? The answer is evolving given the categories of gender emerging. To avoid this difficulty, a simple solution is to use plural nouns (e.g., the participants). Another approach is to replace the pronoun with "that person" or "that individual" or a similar phrase. The *Publication Manual* has several suggestions on this topic (see 2010b, sections on Reducing Bias by Topic, pp. 73–77).

Avoid These Phrases

We have mentioned several examples of lazy writing in this chapter. Repeatedly using nonspecific stock phrases also qualifies as lazy writing. Consider the following phrases:

It was found that . . .

Another study showed . . .

In another study . . .

Notice there is not much specificity to these phrases. You want to craft statements that are specifically tied to the research you present. These stock phrases contribute to the tendency to stack abstracts, which was discussed earlier in this chapter, especially when you introduce each new paragraph with one of these phrases. In addition, the statements "It was found that . . ." or "The study found that . . ." can be eliminated. If you have the sentence "The study found that seniors had higher writing scores than did first year students" you can simply say, "Seniors had higher writing scores than did first year students."

Rather than falling into a routine when you make a general statement about a study, say something specific about it. Better yet, make a statement about a pattern of findings. Consider the phrase "Another study found that . . ."; this phrase suggests the study you are about to mention had an outcome similar to a study previously discussed. Given that you apparently want to say something about a pattern of results, you could talk about "consistent findings" and then cite supporting papers in parentheses: "Consistent findings have emerged showing that. . . ."

Pay Attention to Language That Signals Causality Versus Correlation

Remember that certain words, such as "affect," "impact," "determine," and "effect" (both noun and verb) should be used when describing true experiments. If you have correlational research, talk about relationships and associations (see Chapter 3).

REVISIT AND RESPOND

- First impressions make a difference, and correct grammatical usage "counts." Explain the difference in use between *while* versus *whereas; since* versus *because;* and *number* versus *amount*. What is the best way to avoid gender bias in language? What stock phrases should be avoided at the beginning of sentences? What is a missing referent? When you use comparative language (e.g., *higher*), what does your sentence need to include? What does it mean to attribute agency incorrectly in a sentence? What are words that signify causality? Correlation?

CREATING CONFERENCE PRESENTATIONS

Students often present their research in class; in addition, students may have the opportunity to present at conferences in two forms: a paper or a poster session. Whether presenting in class or at a conference, the same recommendations hold.

Paper Session Presentation

In a conference paper session, presenters have a limited amount of time (usually between 10 and 20 minutes) to present their work. Typically, presentation software such as PowerPoint®, Keynote® (for Macs), or **Prezi**® are used. The conference where you present may provide a template for you as illustrated in Figure 11.1.

Prezi®: presentation software known for its ability to move text or visuals easily.

If you can create your own template theme, choose one that does not overwhelm your text or pictures. Some PowerPoint themes look nice in theory, but in practice, there is too much competition for your eye. You want to deliver your content clearly, and a simple, clean template does that (see Figure 11.2).

GUIDELINES FOR FONTS AND ANIMATIONS Paralleling comments made about the clean visual theme, your font should be easy to read. There is an obvious relationship between your font size and the amount of text that will fit on a slide. One recommendation is that fonts should be at least 30 pt. Another is that you should be able to read the slide from

FIGURE 11.1   Title Slide Illustrating Clean Visual Theme

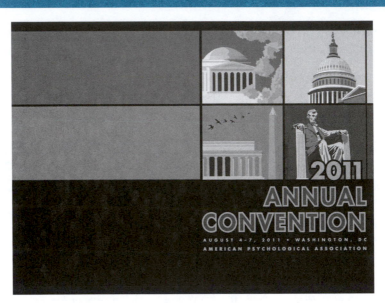

Source: © American Psychologicial Association.

FIGURE 11.2   Title PowerPoint Presentation Slide From APA, 2011

20 feet back. For most conference audiences, use a standard font throughout the presentation (if your audience comes from a design profession, you might consider multiple fonts). Whatever the background of the audience, remember: Readability takes precedence over style.

For presentations, fonts that are *sans serif* such as Arial or Verdana (without the platform or extra strokes, like Garamond, which is used in this chapter) are recommended. Such sans serif fonts reduce clutter when projected on the screen. In addition, avoid "ALL CAPS" because they are hard to read; furthermore, minimize your use of italics (which can also detract from legibility).

The text in your presentation software should reinforce your points, not repeat them verbatim.

Here are additional guidelines:

- Don't read verbatim what is on the slide; your job is to explain, not read.
- Avoid complete sentences; bullet points work well instead.
- Present one big idea on a slide (this can be made through multiple points).

- Six bullet points/slide is plenty; shoot for four.
- Each bullet point should be limited to one line.
- Histograms may be easier to read than line graphs; watch the labeling in the axes. Ask yourself, can people read them from 20 feet back?
- The color combinations make a difference; a white background can wash out in a large lecture hall; slides with a dark background and light-colored text work well.
- Keep animations and transitions to a minimum.

One of the more effective animations is "Appear," which enables you to introduce content (e.g., a bullet point) one point at a time. People can then focus on the story of that bullet point before moving on to the next. Transitions can be distracting unless they are employed judiciously; don't mix different transitions (such as fading) if you use them at all.

It is tempting, especially with presentation software like Prezi, to create a "presentation in motion." This approach may backfire, and the zooming in and out and swirling may confuse rather than clarify. In addition, effectively using software like Prezi takes practice. You need to devote sufficient time to mastering an application before relying on it.

You can use the "presenter version" of the presentation to include data or factual information in the "presenter notes" (using the presenter version takes some practice, too). This information appears to you but not to the audience. Such information would clutter up the slide if included, but incorporating it in your remarks will help you tell the story of your study rather than read off the slide.

GETTING READY TO PRESENT YOUR WORK   Public speaking is a skill; you will improve with practice, but practice is essential. Remember that you are the expert and you have the story to tell; be confident in what you are doing. When you tell a story, you don't need to rely on notes; if your presentation is well prepared (and practiced), the points on the slide will serve as prompts for you. Also remember the time limitation you have. Most people pack more information into the presentation than they can deliver in their allotted time.

Paper sessions typically have a moderator whose job it is to alert you to the time remaining. You may need to adjust what you cover if you have spent too much time on the background of the study. Move quickly through this information to focus more on the *essentials* of the Method, Results, and Discussion. Your paper is the complete version of your work; the presentation is like an executive summary.

PARTS TO THE PRESENTATION   There are some standard slides in a presentation. These include the title slide and an outline slide of what you plan to cover. Sometimes there may be a slide that presents learning objectives (what take-away points you will provide) depending on the audience and the conference. The presentation will mirror your paper:

- Background that motivated the project with a limited number of citations
- Hypotheses

- Essentials of the Method
- Essentials of the Results
- Discussion and Limitations
- Your last slide should have contact information and a logo of your institution.

Poster Presentations

Poster presentations are conference presentations usually held in a large room where you and other people exhibit the essence of research projects in large poster form. Often poster presentations are held in the conference "break room;" between sessions, attendees can grab a cup of coffee and tour the posters at the same time. Typically you stand by your poster and answer questions attendees have about your work (refer to Figure 2.3). The hard part of a poster presentation is not standing there explaining its content. The hard part of the poster presentation is producing the poster!

Conference organizers will usually tell presenters the size of the space available for presenters to exhibit their posters. Often this space is no more than 48" wide × 40" high. Companies offer free downloadable poster templates that you can use as a start for your poster (**http://www.posterpresentations.com/html/free_poster_templates.html**). Another site (**www.posterpresentations.com**) also has free tutorials that will help you work with text, columns, and colors. If you are not provided with size restrictions by the conference organizers, an all-purpose size is 48" wide × 36" high.

To create a poster, you will select a new presentation (in PowerPoint), but go to the "page setup" and select the dimensions (e.g., 48" wide × 36" high); the slides will be sized for "custom." To "work" on your poster, you not only need to see the type, but manage the layout, too.

With regard to printing your poster, most institutions have large-scale printers available. If not, check your local office supply store. Guidelines are also available to explain more of this process if you search online.

SUCCESSFUL POSTERS   Just as with paper presentations using presentation software, a poster will be more successful if it does not say "everything." Use of visual images helps break up "death by text." If your research did not use visual images, you can always insert appropriate clip art. Bullet points are just as successful on a poster as for a PowerPoint paper presentation; decide what take-home messages you want to give your audience, and briefly present these through bullet points on the poster. An example of a "bad scientific poster" and a humorous guide of what "not" to do has been created by Colin Purrington (**http://colinpurrington.com/2012/example-of-bad-scientific-poster/**), in which he lists 20 aspects of why the presented poster is "terrible." There is much to be learned from looking at this example. Purrington also has an informative website that deals with Designing Conference Posters (**http://colinpurrington.com/tips/poster-design**). On this site, he also provides entertaining advice about how to conduct yourself during the poster session (e.g., what to wear).

Poster presenters often make handouts of the slide (poster) or a short version of their research paper to hand attendees; this handout should have the presenter's contact information, which is useful for follow-up questions and networking.

REVISIT AND RESPOND

- Explain why less is more in terms of presentation software and posters. What are the essential slides for a paper presentation? What role do bullet points play? How is giving a presentation like telling a story? What is hard about doing a poster presentation?

Summary

With this final chapter, you have acquired the skills to present not only the content necessary to communicate your research but also the essentials of style that differentiate the novice from the expert. First impressions count; they influence your instructor's evaluation of your work. If you were submitting a manuscript, journal editors quickly decide whether to send out your work for peer review on the basis of content *and* style. How well the manuscript is written and prepared influences their decision. Make sure that someone else reads your work before turning in your paper or submitting your manuscript. Relying on spellcheck is ineffective. Many good writers recommend putting aside your work for a week or more and then returning to polish your prose. One piece of advice is to list your topic sentences to see whether they represent a coherent narrative.

Remember the hourglass shape of the manuscript: starting wide, narrowing through the "neck" of the Method and Results, starting narrowly with the Discussion, and then widening out to your implications for future work. Take seriously the advice to anticipate what your critics (this includes your instructor!) will say and present arguments to address those weaknesses in the work. Finally, look forward to telling the story of your research in successful conference presentations and posters.

In the event that you did not consider them earlier, here are the **REVISIT and RESPOND** prompts that appeared in this chapter:

- What components of the title and abstract are indexed to communicate your work? What qualities should a title have? A title should be no longer than _____ words.
- How can the quality of your title affect the likelihood that someone will read your paper? What is the function of keywords? A research paper is shaped like an _____. Explain what should be covered in each section (Abstract, Introduction, Method, Results, Discussion). What does it mean when someone says you are "stacking abstracts?" To avoid stacking abstracts, describe three different ways you can organize your literature.

- Explain the recommendations for when to quote and how to cite quoted material (i.e., in text vs. parentheses), the use of present versus past tense in the manuscript, the length of the Introduction (for a manuscript submission), and why it may be hard to balance the length of the Introduction and Discussion.

- What information about the participants, measures, and procedure should be presented? Why is it necessary to provide so much detail about the who, the what, and the how of your study? Why would you want to present both the Cronbach's alpha in the literature and the Cronbach's alpha from your study? What does a statement of your research design tell the reader?

- Explain what Salovey (2000) meant when he talked about Results that tell a good story. How do you accomplish that? What is the advantage of putting the "preliminaries" (e.g., reliabilities and demographic characteristics) in the Method section? How do you organize your paper to create parallel construction? Why should you present as many findings as possible in tables and figures?

- Don't forget that Ms and SDs are statistical symbols and should be italicized, along with other statistical symbols. Explain the role of 0 as a placeholder in the presentation of results where the finding can theoretically be greater than 1 and where it cannot. Explain the rounding rules. Explain how to present a result where the printout shows $p = .0000$. What happens if you always round up (or not)? Findings should be presented in the text or in a table but not both. How many results of a particular kind (e.g., correlation, Ms, and SDs) should you have before moving to a table? What is the advantage of presenting findings in a table?

- What similarities and differences are there when writing a Discussion section with significant versus nonsignificant findings? In terms of discussing results from a "fishing expedition," introducing relevant literature in the Discussion is useful, but how much prominence does this material merit, relative to your original hypotheses? What kinds of issues may come up to address in your Limitations section? What is the distinction between statistical and practical significance?

- First impressions make a difference, and correct grammatical usage "counts." Explain the difference in use between *while* versus *whereas; since* versus *because*; and *number* versus *amount*. What is the best way to avoid gender bias in language? What stock phrases should be avoided at the beginning of sentences? What is a missing referent? When you use comparative language (e.g., higher), what does your sentence need to include? What does it mean to attribute agency incorrectly in a sentence? What are words that signify causality? Correlation?

- Explain why less is more in terms of presentation software and posters. What are the essential slides for a paper presentation? What role do bullet points play? How is giving a presentation like telling a story? What is hard about doing a poster presentation?

BUILD YOUR SKILLS

1. Start a new PowerPoint presentation with the 48" × 36" dimensions discussed near the end of this chapter. Then type a sentence or two and select 100% and see how much of the text you can see. Next select 33%. You will see that 33% permits you to monitor what is happening in your columns. A font size of 32 points for the body of the text will work, although the title of the poster may need to be as large as 88 points. Then test out what font size is visible from 20' away. Put from three to eight bullet points on this slide and decide when you reach "death by text."

2. Come up with the title for your paper, following the recommendations (length and "style") in this chapter.

3. What is the first sentence of your Introduction? Does it capture the reader's interest?

Highly Recommended Papers

Throughout this book, comments were made that "this is worth reading" or "everyone should read this paper." Here is a list of papers, monographs, and books that are, in fact, worth reading:

Bem, D. J. (2004). Writing the empirical journal article. In J. M. Darley, M. P. Zanna, & H. L. Roediger, III (Eds.), *The compleat academic: A career guide* (2nd ed., pp. 185–219). Washington, DC: American Psychological Association.

Campbell, D. T., & Stanley, J. C. (1963). *Experimental and quasi-experimental designs for research.* Chicago, IL: Rand McNally.

DeCoster, J., Sparks, E. A., Sparks, J. C., Sparks, G. G., & Sparks, C. W. (2015). Opportunistic biases: Their origins, effects, and an integrated solution. *American Psychologist, 70,* 499–514. doi:10.1037.a0039191

Dillman, D., Smyth, J. D., & Christian, L. M. (2014). *Internet, phone, mail, and mixed-mode surveys: The tailored design method* (4th ed.). New York, NY: Wiley.

Henrich, J., Heine, S. J., & Norenzayan, A. (2010). The weirdest people in the world. *Behavioral and Brain Sciences, 33*(2–3), 61–83. doi:10.1017/S0140525X0999152X

Kerr, N. L. (1998). HARKing: Hypothesizing after the results are known. *Personality and Social Psychology Review, 2,* 196–217. doi:10.1207/s15327957pspr0203_4

Schwarz, N. (1999). Self-reports: How the questions shape the answers. *American Psychologist, 54,* 93–105. doi:10.1037//0003-066X.54.2.93

Simmons, J. P., Nelson, L. D., & Simonsohn, U. (2011). False-positive psychology: Undisclosed flexibility in data collection and analysis allows presenting anything as significant. *Psychological Science, 22,* 1359–1366. doi:10.1177/0956797611417632

Simonsohn, U., Nelson, L. D., & Simmons, J. P. (2014). *P*-curve: A key to the file-drawer. *Journal of Experimental Psychology: General, 143,* 534–547. doi:10.1037/a0033242

Sternberg, R. J. (Ed.). (2000). *Guide to publishing in psychology journals.* New York, NY: Cambridge University Press.

$SAGE edge™

APPENDICES

APPENDIX A

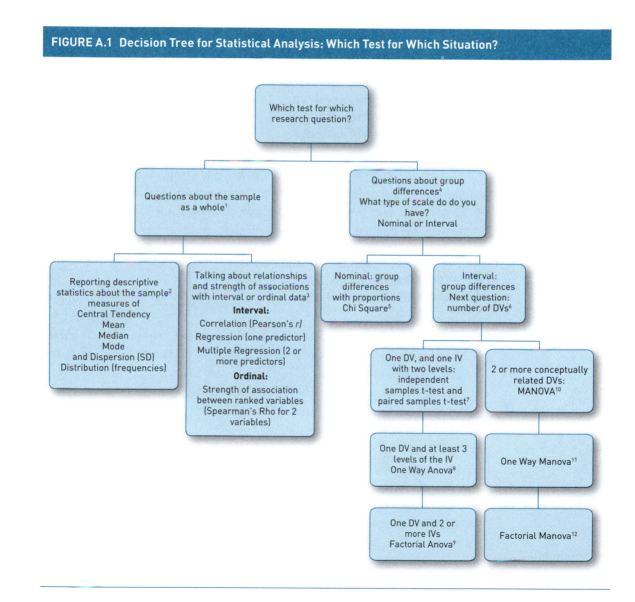

WHICH TEST FOR WHICH RESEARCH QUESTION?

The diagram gives a basic answer to the question "which statistical test should you use for which research question?" There are too many exceptions to cover every possibility, but this diagram gives you some sense of why you would select a given statistic. First, the diagram is organized into questions you would ask about your sample as a whole versus questions that pertain to group differences of interest.

Sample as a whole

[1] WHEN YOU ASK QUESTIONS ABOUT YOUR SAMPLE AS A WHOLE, YOU SEEK TO UNDERSTAND THE CHARACTERISTICS OF THE GROUP

- [2] This could involve asking about measures of central tendency and dispersion, for example, means and standard deviations, on some scales of interest.
- [2] By requesting its frequency, you could also ask about the distribution of some variable, for example, the number of people in each racial category in your sample.

[3] A SECOND CATEGORY OF QUESTION ABOUT THE SAMPLE AS A WHOLE DEALS WITH RELATIONSHIPS AND STRENGTH OF ASSOCIATIONS

- [3] Here you might want to know whether the scores on two measures of interest (e.g., self-esteem and body esteem) are correlated for the sample as a whole. In that case, you would use Pearson's *r*.
- [3] You might ask that question differently if you wanted to know whether body esteem predicts self-esteem (use simple regression).
- [3] If you had a third variable (e.g., life satisfaction), you might be interested in knowing whether self-esteem or body esteem better predicts life satisfaction. Here you would use multiple regression because you have more than one predictor. The scale types for correlation and regression are typically interval.
- [3] If we are interested in knowing the strength of association between ranked variables, for example, the extent to which rankings of three Republican candidates were associated with the rankings of three Democrat candidates in our sample, we would use another statistic, Spearman's Rho (Spearman's rank correlation coefficient), which is for ranked (ordinal) data. This statistic is the equivalent of Pearson's *r* for nonparametric data.

⁴THE SECOND MAJOR CATEGORY OF RESEARCH QUESTIONS IN THE DIAGRAM RELATES TO QUESTIONS ABOUT GROUP DIFFERENCES

One of the first issues to answer is what kind of scale types you are using. There are two common situations: one where only nominal scales are used, and the other in which the dependent variable (DV) is a continuous variable [paired with either a true independent variable (IV) or a quasi-IV]. From a statistical point of view, there is no difference in the tests you would perform with a true independent variable versus a quasi-independent variable. The difference comes when you discuss the causal (true) versus correlational (quasi) nature of the results, as has been mentioned several times in the book.

⁵When you ask questions about *group differences that are represented with nominal data or dimensions,* you use chi-square. An example would be asking the question, "Do athletes and nonathletes differ in car ownership (yes/no)?" Both scales, athlete status and car ownership, are nominal (also called categorical).

⁶When you ask about *group differences using an interval or continuous scale as your DV,* there are a series of increasingly more involved analyses. First we will deal with one dependent variable. It may help to differentiate between what might be called the "IV side of the house" and the "DV side of the house." Here, we are going to *keep the DV set to one* and see what happens on the IV side of the house.

⁷The most basic situation is an independent variable with only two levels and one DV. Here, you would use an *independent samples* t *test.* Do athletes and nonathletes differ on the Rosenberg Self-Esteem Scale? Again, note that the DV is a continuous variable.

⁷A cousin of this analysis is the *paired samples* t *test,* often used in before and after studies. Here, there are again two means of interest, but they typically come from the same people who took a test at Time 1 and again at Time 2 or were exposed to different ways of measuring a variable, such as two ways of measuring stress (a mood scale and an anxiety inventory).

⁸Next, still using one DV, we move to *ONE IV with three or more levels.* This would be called a one-way analysis of variance (ANOVA). The "one" in one-way refers to the number of IVs. For example, we might want to know the level of stress in people who drank one, two, or three cups of espresso. The IV has three levels (each one corresponding to the number of cups of espresso); there is one DV (stress).

⁹Next, still using one DV, we add another IV. *This is called factorial ANOVA,* but there are several ways to label the analysis depending on (a) the number of IVs and (b) the number of levels of each IV. If you have two IVs, you could call this a *two-way ANOVA.* The "two" refers to the number of IVs. If each IV had two levels, you could also call it a *2×2 ANOVA.* If one IV had two levels and the other had three, you could call it a *2×3 ANOVA.* You can see how the labeling changes with the number and levels of IVs involved.

[10]*Multivariate ANOVA (MANOVA)* is used in sitiations where you have *two or more conceptually related DVs.* Thus, if our DVs were measures of body esteem and self-esteem, we would make an argument that these DVs are conceptually related. One major advantage of running a MANOVA is cutting down on Type I error. In a MANOVA, the IV side of the house parallels the labeling for ANOVA. There is no special equivalent of the *t* test; instead, even when we have one IV with just two levels, we would have [11]one-way MANOVA. The use of the term [12]*factorial MANOVA* parallels its use with ANOVA.

APPENDIX B

Sample Informed Consent Document

Study Title: [Insert title, e.g., Spatial Ability and Finding Your Way]

Principal Investigator: [Insert investigator's name, e.g., Professor J. Smith]

[Street address of institution]

[insert investigator's e-mail address]

- You are being invited to participate in [Professor Smith's research about spatial ability and wayfinding.]
- This research will involve [taking a timed test of spatial ability and completing a series of questionnaires.]
- While the direct benefits of this research to society are not known, you may learn more about [your spatial abilities and concerns.]
- This research will take about [30 minutes.]
- No known risks or discomforts are related to participating in this research.
- [Professor Smith] can be contacted at [put e-mail contact here].
- Your participation is voluntary, and you may decline to answer any questions as you see fit.
- You may withdraw from the study without penalty at any time.
- Information you provide will be identified with a code number and NOT your name.
- You may contact the researcher who will answer any questions that you may have about the purposes and procedures of this study.
- This study is not meant to gather information about specific individuals, and your responses will be combined with other participants' data for the purpose of statistical analyses.
- You are being asked to consent to publication of the study results as long as the identity of all participants is protected.
- This research has been approved by the [insert name of institution] Human Subjects Institutional Review Board (IRB). Concerns about any aspect of this study may be addressed to [insert IRB chairperson name and e-mail contact information].

A copy of this informed consent will be given to you.

I am at least 18 years of age, have read these explanations and assurances, and voluntarily consent to participate in this research on [specify topic].

Name of participant (please print)	Signature of participant	Date

Name of person obtaining consent (please print)	Signature	Date

APPENDIX C

Sample Debriefing Statement
(Adapted from Devlin, 2006, Appendix B, p. 241.)

First of all, thank you for participating in this research dealing with [spatial cognition]. In this research, [I am comparing the spatial abilities of people who vary in their experience with wayfinding.] [In addition to Introductory Psychology students at (name of institution), members of the sailing teams at (name of institution), and other schools are filling out these questionnaires. One issue in the literature on spatial cognition is the role that experience may play in developing better spatial abilities. Typically researchers have asked about childhood toy play (e.g., Lincoln logs and building blocks) to estimate exposure to toys that may emphasize spatial ability. To my knowledge, no research has focused on experience with a spatial activity like sailing, and that is the purpose of this research.]

[In addition to sailing experience, this research also assessed the relationship of handedness to spatial ability (left-handed individuals have been reported to possess better spatial abilities than have right-handed individuals).]

If you have any questions or concerns about the manner in which this study was conducted, please contact the IRB chairperson [insert name and e-mail contact of IRB chairperson here].

If you are interested in this topic and want to read the literature in this area, you might enjoy the following articles:

[Gapin, J., & Herzog, T. (2014). Sailing video-imagery: Impacts on imagery ability. *Journal of Imagery Research in Sport and Physical Activity, 9*(1), 13–21. doi:10.1515/jirspa-2012–0002

Reio, T. G., Czarnolewski, M., & Eliot, J. (2004). Handedness and spatial ability: Differential patterns of relationships. *Laterality, 9,* 339–358. doi: 10.1080/13576500342000220]

You may also contact me [Professor Smith] at [e-mail contact] for additional resources.

APPENDIX D

Resource Guide to Commonly
Used Measures

(Adapted and updated from Devlin, 2006, pp. 111–116.)

GENERAL SOURCES OF MEASURES

These directories and source books provide the names of measures and their sources.

Directory of Unpublished Experimental Measures (9 volumes) (Goldman & Mitchell, 2008).

Encyclopedia of Psychological Assessment (Vols. 1 & 2) (Fernandez-Ballesteros, 2003).

Measures for Clinical Practice: A Sourcebook (5th ed.). Vol. 1: Couples, Families, and Children; Vol. 2: Adults (Corcoran & Fischer, 2013).

Practitioner's Guide to Empirically Based Measures of Anxiety (Antony, Orsillo, & Roemer, 2001).

Practitioner's Guide to Empirically Based Measures of Depression (Nezu, Ronan, Meadows, & McClure, 2000).

FEES AND QUALIFICATIONS: GENERAL NOTE

In all instances where there is a statement that fees are charged, you may want to contact the author or publisher to see whether it is possible to use the scale without charge for research. Also, check to make sure that you have the qualifications for use that accompany the description of the test.

PERSONALITY AND CLINICAL PSYCHOLOGY

NEO-PI-3

The NEO-PI-3® (McCrae, Costa, & Martin, 2005) has 240 items and a validity item. Five major domains of personality are measured. This instrument takes about 40 minutes to administer and is typically used by professionals in counseling and education, but it is also used in research. A fee is charged, and it is available from Psychological Assessment Resources, Inc. (PAR); the evaluator must meet American Psychological Association (APA) guidelines.

NEO Five Factory Inventory-3

This is a shortened version of the NEO-PI-3 that consists of 60 items that measure the five domains of adult personality: openness, conscientiousness, extraversion, agreeableness, and neuroticism (McCrae et al., 2005). It is available from Psychological Assessment Resources, Inc. (PAR); the evaluator must meet American Psychological Association (APA) guidelines.

Big Five Inventory (BFI)

The BFI is a standard self-report measure of personality (John, Donahue, & Kentle, 1991) that is free for use for noncommercial research purposes. You can obtain the items for research purposes by following the instructions on the Berkeley Personality Lab website: **https://www.ocf.berkeley.edu/~johnlab/bfi.php**

Rosenberg Self-Esteem Scale (RSES)

The RSES is a widely used 10-item scale measure of self-esteem (Rosenberg, 1965). It is available on PsycTESTS®.

Moos Family Environment Scale (FES)

The FES® measures 10 dimensions of family environments using 90 items (Moos & Moos, 1976. A fee is charged by Mind Garden, Inc.

Beck Depression Inventory®-II

This assesses the level of depression in an individual by using 21 items (Osman et al., 2004). Contact the Beck Institute for Cognitive Behavior Therapy for research-related questions; Qualification level B. (**http://www.beckinstitute.org**). The 21-item categories (but not the response options) are listed on PsycTESTS.

Zuckerman Sensation Seeking Scale, Form V (SSS-V)

The SSS-V assesses the degree to which people seek stimulation (Zuckerman, Eysenck, & Eysenck, 1978). It is available on PsycTESTS.

Multiple Affect Adjective Check List® (MAACL-Revised)

The MAACL-Revised measures anxiety, depression, and hostility by using 132 items. It can be used in terms of today or in general (Zuckerman & Lubin, 1965). A fee is charged by EdITS/Educational and Industrial Testing Service.

The State-Trait Anxiety Inventory®

The STAI is a frequently used measure to assess anxiety in adults by asking 40 questions for both trait and state (Spielberger, Gorsuch, & Lushene, 1970). A fee is charged through Mind Garden, Inc.

Profile of Mood States 2nd Edition™

The POMS uses 65 adjectives to measure dimensions of affect or mood (Heuchert & McNair, n.d.). A fee is charged through MultiHealth Systems (MHS).

Sixteen Personality Factor Questionnaire (16PF™) 5th ed.

This is a comprehensive profile of personality with 16 main scales (Cattell, Cattell, & Cattell, 2002). A fee is charged through Pearson (**http://www.pearsonclinical.com**).

Hassles and Uplifts (HSUP®)

HSUP measures respondents' attitudes about daily situations defined as hassles and uplifts (DeLongis, Coyne, Dakof, Folkman, & Lazarus, 1982). A fee is charged through Mind Garden, Inc.

SOCIAL PSYCHOLOGY

The Bem Sex Role Inventory® (BSRI)

Developed by Sandra Bem (1974), the BSRI is a commonly used measure to assess gender roles. Sixty items (40 scored) assess masculinity, femininity, androgyny, and undifferentiation. Items are available on PsycTESTS. No written permission is necessary if you are using the test for noncommerical research and educational purposes.

Marlowe-Crowne Social Desirability Scale (M-C SDS)

This scale has 33 items commonly used to assess whether participants have a tendency to respond in a socially desirable manner (Crowne & Marlowe, 1960). It is available in the article and on PsycTESTS.

Balanced Inventory of Desirable Responding (BIDR)
Version 6—Form 40

There are two subscales: self-deceptive positivity and impression management. A person who exhibits self-deceptive positivity will give reports that are honest but exaggerated in a positive direction (Paulhus, 1991). Consult the article.

Self-Efficacy Scale

This 30-item measure, with two subscales (general self-efficacy and social self-efficacy), assesses expectations about self-efficacy independent of specific situations. Contact the lead author (Sherer, Maddox, Mercandante, Prentice-Dunn, Jacobs, & Rogers, 1982).

Social Avoidance and Distress Scale (SAD)

The 28-item scale measures anxiety in social situations. It is available in the journal article (Watson & Friend, 1969) and on PsycTESTS.

South Oaks Gambling Screen (SOGS)

The primary use of this 20-item scale is to identify pathological gamblers (Lesieur & Blume, 1987). It is available from the authors; items are in their 1987 article.

Modern Racism Scale

Seven items measure overt racism (McConahay, 1986; McConahay, Hardee, & Batts, 1981. Available from the lead author.

Implicit Association Test (IAT)

A computer-implemented reaction-time test to assess implicit racism and other biases (Greenwald, McGhee, & Schwartz, 1998). Available online at **https://implicit.harvard. edu/implicit/iatdetails.html**

Athletic Identity Measurement Scale (AIMS)

Ten items measure the degree to which an individual possesses an athletic self-concept (Brewer, Van Raalte, & Linder, 1993). Contact the lead author. Only sample items are listed on PsycTESTS.

Kenyon's Attitude Toward Physical Activity Inventory

In a revised version (Mathes & Battista, 1985), nine dimensions of attitudes toward physical activity are assessed. Consult the article.

University Residence Environment Scale (URES®)

Ten dimensions (100 items) are used to assess the social climate of university residence halls (Gerst & Moos, 1972; Smail, DeYoung, & Moos, 1974). A fee is charged through Mind Garden, Inc.

Parental Authority Questionnaire

Sixty-item survey (30 per parent) that measures parental authority from the child's point of view (Buri, 1991). Contact the author.

Core Alcohol and Drug Survey

This 23-item measure assesses alcohol and other drug use and is widely employed in research with college students (Presley, Meilman, & Lyerla, 1994). A fee is charged for survey management, and it is available from the Core Institute.

GENDER AND WOMEN'S ISSUES

Spence and Helmreich Attitude Toward Women (ATW)-Short Version

This 25-item measure assesses individuals' attitudes toward women (Spence, Helmreich, & Stapp, 1973). It is available in the article.

Body Esteem Scale

Twenty-four items assess body esteem (Mendelson & White, 1982); it can be used with children. It is available in the article.

Body Shape Questionnaire (BSQ)

Thirty-four items assess satisfaction with one's body shape (Cooper, Taylor, Cooper, & Fairburn, 1987). Contact the authors.

Eating Disorder Inventory-3® (EDI-3)

Eight subscales, 91 items, can be used to differentiate those with normal dieting behaviors from those with severe disorders (based on original by Garner, Olmstead, & Polivy, 1983). A fee is charged through PAR: Psychological Assessment Resources, Inc.

Eating Attitudes Test (EAT)

This 40-item test is used to assess behaviors indicative of anorexia nervosa (Garner & Garfinkel, 1979). Contact the authors (**http://www.eat-26.com**). Fee is waived.

Eating Attitudes Test (EAT-26)

A shorter version of the 40 item EAT, this 26-item test is used to assess and diagnose eating disorders (Garner, Olmstead, Bohr, & Garfinkel, 1982). Fee is waived and available from **http://www.eat-26.com**

Photographic Figure Rating Scale

Assesses judgments of women's body size attractiveness through rating 10 photographs of women's bodies (Swami, Salem, Furnham, & Tovée, 2008). Items available on PsycTESTS.

Menstrual Joy Questionnaire

This questionnaire (Delaney, Lupton, & Toth, 1987) consists of 10 positive experiences related to menstruation. Contact the authors.

Moos Menstrual Distress Questionnaire (MDQ)

Characteristics of a woman's menstrual cycle are assessed on 8 factors using 47 symptoms (Moos, 1968). Items provided on PsycTESTS. Contact the publisher for permission.

Menstrual Attitude Questionnaire (MAQ)

This questionnaire is divided into five subscales and contains 35 items (Brooks-Gunn & Ruble, 1980). Items available on PsycTESTS.

The Sociocultural Attitudes Towards Appearance Questionnaire (SATAQ)

This 14-item measure assesses familiarity with the ideal of being thin and the degree to which that ideal is endorsed (Heinberg, Thompson, & Stormer, 1995). Contact the authors. The most recent version is the SATAQ-4 with 22 items.

HEALTH PSYCHOLOGY

(Note that many personality scales and scales that measure stress and anxiety are also used in health psychology research.)

Multidimensional Health Locus of Control (MHLC)

The scale contains three dimensions of health behavior that measure the beliefs one has about control of one's health. There are 18 items comprising three subscales (six items each): Internality of Health Locus of Control, Powerful Others Locus of Control, and Chance Locus of Control (Wallston, Wallston, & DeVellis, 1978). The items are available on Psyc-TESTS. See also **http://www.vanderbilt.edu/nursing/kwallston/mhlcforma.htm**

Life Orientation Test (LOT)

The scale measures optimism and outlook (Scheier & Carver, 1985). There are eight scored statements and four filler items. The items are available on PsycTESTS.

Social Readjustment Rating Scale

Measures reactions to life events (Holmes & Rahe, 1967). The 43 items are available on PsycTESTS.

Ways of Coping-Revised

This test is designed to measure the individual differences in the ways people cope with life events (Folkman, Lazarus, Dunkel-Schetter, DeLongis, & Gruen, 1986). There are 51 items (eight different factors identified). The items are available on PsycTESTS.

COPE Inventory

This scale (Carver, Scheier, & Weintraub, 1989) measures the ways in which people respond to stress. A partial list of the items is provided on PsycTESTS. The complete test is available on the lead author's website (**http://www.psy.miami.edu/faculty/ccarver/sclCOPEF.html**).

McGill Pain Questionnaire

The questionnaire (Melzack, 1975) provides sensory, evaluative, and affective measures of subjective pain experience. Consult the journal article.

MEASURES IN BEHAVIORAL NEUROSCIENCE

The following are some commonly used measures in behavioral neuroscience. The best way to learn about these measures is to contact the professor in your department who conducts research in behavioral neuroscience. As is true of research with human participants (see Chapter 4), research with animals must be approved by the official group on your campus that monitors the use of animals in research. This group is often called the Institutional Animal Care and Use Committee (IACUC):

Tail Flick Measure of Pain Sensitivity

Morris Water Maze Test for Spatial Memory

Elevated Plus-Maze Test of Anxiety

Social Interaction Test of Anxiety

Forced Swim Test for Depression

Rotorod Test of Motor Coordination

Radial Arm Maze Test of Spatial Memory

Novel Object Recognition Test of Memory

Conditioned Place Preference Measure of Reward Behavior

Progressive Ratio Operant Conditioning Measure of Reward Behavior

Sucrose Preference Test of Depressive-like Behavior

Open Field Test of Depressive-like Behavior

T-Maze Test of Pharmacologically Induced Obsessive Compulsive-like Behavior

APPENDIX E

Commonly Used Analyze
Functions in SPSS

This appendix contains instructions for using the commonly employed *Analyze* functions in SPSS. A brief description of the purpose of the type of analysis is provided, followed by the steps involved.

First, some general comments. In addition to the primary steps to take in any given analysis, there are usually several associated parameters to specify. These are often found under "Options" and "Statistics." We will specify these additions for each kind of analysis. In this chapter, the use of the symbol " > " indicates to click on the command that follows.

DESCRIPTIVE STATISTICS

Under Descriptive Statistics there are three commonly used functions: Descriptives, Frequencies, and Cross Tabs.

Descriptives provide information such as means and standard deviations about continuous variables. In the example that follows, the variable is numdoc (the number of doctors' offices people have visited):

Descriptive Statistics > Descriptives > Move the items of interest over to the Variables box > Options (select those statistics you want (usually mean, std. deviation, minimum, and maximum) > Continue > OK. Figure E.1 shows the results:

Frequencies are typically used to provide information about categorical (nominal) variables, such as race or gender. You could also use Frequencies to find out how many instances of a given level for a continuous variable you have; for example, for a scale item that ranged from 1 to 5, how many responses were 1s, 2s, 3s, 4s, or 5s.

Descriptive Statistics > Frequencies > Move the variables of interest over to the Variables box > Statistics > click on median and mode > Continue > OK. For our example of Race, the results will show the median, mode, frequencies, and percentages of each value. Also note that the results indicate how many missing cases there are (2; see Figure E.2).

The *Cross Tabs* function enables you to conduct a Chi-Square, the most common choice under Cross Tabs. Chi-square analyses tell you about the proportionality of your data for two variables of interest.

FIGURE E.1 Output for Descriptives Analysis

```
DESCRIPTIVES VARIABLES=numdoc
  /STATISTICS=MEAN STDDEV MIN MAX.
```

➡ **Descriptives**

Descriptive Statistics

	N	Minimum	Maximum	Mean	Std. Deviation
numdoc	122	1.00	100.00	10.0492	10.69321
Valid N (listwise)	122				

FIGURE E.2 Output for Frequencies Analysis

Frequencies

Statistics

race

N	Valid	120
	Missing	2
Median		3.0000
Mode		3.00

race

		Frequency	Percent	Valid Percent	Cumulative Percent
Valid	African American	2	1.6	1.7	1.7
	Asian American	6	4.9	5.0	6.7
	European American	98	80.3	81.7	88.3
	Hispanic American	8	6.6	6.7	95.0
	other	6	4.9	5.0	100.0
	Total	120	98.4	100.0	
Missing	System	2	1.6		
Total		122	100.0		

Descriptive Statistics > Cross Tabs > move over the two nominal variables of interest, one in Row(s), the other in Column(s) > Statistics > Chi Square > Continue > Cells (click on observed and expected counts; click on row, column, and total percentages) > Continue > OK.

For our example of race and class year, the results will show the counts (frequencies) for each level of the two variables and the percentages represented. The statistics are presented in a box labeled "Chi Square Tests." The screen shot shows part of the output (see Figure E.3).

INDEPENDENT SAMPLES *t* TEST

Independent samples *t* tests allow you to compare the means for two independent groups (e.g., experimental and control) on one DV.

Analyze > Compare Means > Independent samples *t*-test > Test variable(s) (put your DVs here; you can run many independent *t*-tests at once) > Grouping variable (this is your IV) > Define groups> Use specified values (e.g., 1, 2) > Continue > OK. Options allow you to set the confidence interval; the default value is 95%, and to decide how you will handle missing data (Listwise or Analysis by Analysis, i.e., Pairwise).

FIGURE E.3 Partial Output for Chi-Square Analysis

		% within race	50.0%	16.7%	19.4%	12.5%	16.7%	19.2%
		% of Total	0.8%	0.8%	15.8%	0.8%	0.8%	19.2%
	senior	Count	1	2	11	0	1	15
		Expected Count	.3	.8	12.3	1.0	.8	15.0
		% within class year	6.7%	13.3%	73.3%	0.0%	6.7%	100.0%
		% within race	50.0%	33.3%	11.2%	0.0%	16.7%	12.5%
		% of Total	0.8%	1.7%	9.2%	0.0%	0.8%	12.5%
	other	Count	0	0	2	0	0	2
		Expected Count	.0	.1	1.6	.1	.1	2.0
		% within class year	0.0%	0.0%	100.0%	0.0%	0.0%	100.0%
		% within race	0.0%	0.0%	2.0%	0.0%	0.0%	1.7%
		% of Total	0.0%	0.0%	1.7%	0.0%	0.0%	1.7%
Total		Count	2	6	98	8	6	120
		Expected Count	2.0	6.0	98.0	8.0	6.0	120.0
		% within class year	1.7%	5.0%	81.7%	6.7%	5.0%	100.0%
		% within race	100.0%	100.0%	100.0%	100.0%	100.0%	100.0%
		% of Total	1.7%	5.0%	81.7%	6.7%	5.0%	100.0%

Chi-Square Tests

	Value	df	Asymptotic Significance (2-sided)
Pearson Chi-Square	20.241[a]	16	.210
Likelihood Ratio	18.558	16	.292
Linear-by-Linear Association	2.899	1	.089
N of Valid Cases	120		

a. 21 cells (84.0%) have expected count less than 5. The minimum expected count is .03.

PAIRED SAMPLES *t* TEST

In a paired samples analysis, you are typically taking the same people and comparing their scores on the same variable at two points in time or comparing the same people on different variables.

Analyze > Compare Means > Paired Samples *t*-test > Highlight and move over the two variables into the paired variables box (you can analyze many pairs at one time) > OK. The Options (confidence interval; missing data) are the same as for independent samples *t* test.

ONE-WAY ANOVA

In One-way ANOVA, you have at least three levels of your IV (and still one DV at a time).

Analyze > Compare Means > Oneway Anova > Dependent List (drag over all of the DVs you want to analyze for a particular IV; you can run many separately at once) > Factor (this is your IV) > Options > Descriptive > Continue; Post hoc > Tukey (the likely choice) > Continue > OK.

FACTORIAL ANOVA

In Factorial ANOVA, you have at least two IVs (still one DV).

Analyze > General Linear Model > Univariate (so you will have 1 DV)

Options > Descriptives (move over the factors into the Display Means for box; click on Descriptive statistics; Estimates of effect size; Observed power) > Continue

Dependent Variable (put in your DV);

Fixed Factor(s); put in the IVs you want for this analysis

Covariate: if you have covariate(s), put them in the covariate box.

Post hoc: if any of your fixed factors has more than two levels, move them over into the Post Hoc Tests for box > Select Tukey (likely choice) > Continue > OK

MANOVA

A MANOVA analysis is appropriate for the situation where you have two or more conceptually related DVs.

Analyze > General linear model > Multivariate

Follow all of the same steps as for factorial ANOVA except that you put in more than one DV.

CORRELATION

In correlational analysis, you are typically testing for the degree of relationship between two continuous variables.

Analyze > Correlate > Bivariate

Move over all variables you wish to correlate into the Variables box

The defaults are Pearson, two-tailed, and flag significant correlations.

SIMPLE REGRESSION

In simple regression, you are interested in the extent to which a given variable (predictor) predicts a specific outcome variable (criterion).

Analyze > Regression > Linear

Move over your criterion variable (here called the dependent variable)

Move over your predictor variable (here called the independent variable) > OK

Statistics > Estimates and Model fit are the defaults; click Confidence intervals (95%).

Leave Model as "Enter;" return it to Enter if it is some other choice (e.g., stepwise).

If you want a histogram, click Plots > DEPENDNT is the default; click on Histogram.

If you want to create a Scatterplot, Click Graphs (at the menu level) > Legacy Dialogs, Scatter/Dot, Simple Scatter, Define: Put your DV (criterion) into the Y-axis box and your IV (predictor) into the X-axis box > OK.

MULTIPLE REGRESSION

Follow the same steps as for Simple Regression except that you will enter more than one predictor variable into the IV box and you will not create a Scatterplot.

RELIABILITY ANALYSIS

As discussed earlier, the Reliability Analysis is most often used when you want to determine the Cronbach's alpha for a particular scale.

Analyze > Scale > Reliability Analysis

Model: default is alpha

Move over all scale items into the Items box

Statistics: click item, scale, scale if item deleted > OK

FACTOR ANALYSIS

In Chapter 5, we briefly discussed how factor analysis could be used, for example, to take a large group of pictures and see what clusters emerge from participants' ratings of those images.

Analyze > Dimension reduction > Factor

Move over variables to be factor analyzed into the Variables box

Extraction > Principal components (likely choice)

Display > Unrotated factor solution; scree plot

Extract–default is Eigenvalues greater than 1 (you can change this later to specify a specific number of factors to extract)

Rotation > Varimax (often selected); display rotated solution > OK

APPENDIX F

Scale Types and Associated Statistical Analyses for Common Research Approaches

(Adapted from Devlin, 2006, p. 63.)

A SUMMARY

Appendix F presents a summary of scale types and associated statistical analyses for common research approaches. Please note that in the case of chi-square, correlation, multiple correlation, and regression, the use of the language of IVs and DVs is not appropriate. The variables in chi-square (in the example, whether people are classified as first year or fourth year students and whether they own a car) are referred to as dimensions. In the case of regression, there are the particular terms predictor (the variable you are using to predict some outcome) and criterion (the outcome you are trying to predict). When we move to t tests, we can appropriately use the classifications of IV and DV.

Test	Data Type	Dimension	Data Type	Dimension
2×2 Chi-Square	Nominal Ex: First year, fourth year students	1 dimension, 2 categories	Nominal Ex: car, no car	1 dimension 2 categories
Correlation Pearson's r	Continuous (interval) Ex: GPA	1	Continuous (interval) Ex: SAT scores	1
Regression	Continuous (interval) Ex: Vocational maturity	1 (predictor variable, X)	Continuous (interval) Ex: Vocational indecision	1 (criterion variable, Y)

Test	Data Type	Dimension	Data Type	Dimension
Multiple Regression	Continuous (interval) Ex: Vocational maturity; self-esteem	2 or more predictor variables, (X1, X2)	Continuous (interval) Ex: Vocational indecision	1 (criterion variable, Y)

Test	IV Data Type	# of IV/ quasi-IVs	DV Data Type	# of DVs
Ind. Samples *t* Test	Nominal Ex: First year students, fourth year students	1 (2 levels)	Continuous (interval) Ex: depression	1
One-way ANOVA	Nominal Ex: urban, suburban, rural upbringing	1 (more than 2 levels; here 3 levels)	Continuous (interval) Ex: Precautionary Measures Scale	1
Factorial ANOVA	Nominal Ex: First, fourth year students; Urban, rural upbringing	2 or more	Continuous (interval) Ex: Precautionary Measures Scale	1
MANOVA	Nominal Ex: urban, rural upbringing	1 or more	Continuous (interval) Ex: Env. Preference Questionnaire (has 7 scales)	2 or more Conceptually related scales

GLOSSARY

Abstract—short summary (150–250 words) of a research paper that includes a brief overview about the research problem, method, results, and discussion; includes keywords.

Active consent—consent where the participant or, in the case of children, the parent or guardian, specifically agrees to the research.

Active deception—situation where there is commission as part of the research, either in the informed consent or in the research procedures themselves, that misleads, provides false feedback, or otherwise misrepresents the research.

Advance online publication—full text version of the article available electronically in advance of print publication.

Advert—British term for advertisement; used in relationship to advertisements on Facebook® or other social media.

Allostatic load—with repeated exposure, the stress on the body negatively affects physiological processes.

Alpha level—probability (usually set at .05) of incorrectly rejecting the null hypothesis.

Alternative hypothesis—hypothesis you have stated will be true if the null hypothesis is rejected.

AmazonMTurk® or Amazon Mechanical Turk—online paid crowdsourcing platform to acquire participants.

American Psychological Association (APA) Code of Ethics—ethical code of conduct guiding the behavior of psychologists; comprises 10 standards.

Analysis of variance—statistical test that tests for differences between two or more means.

Anchors—specific points on a rating scale (each one is a separate anchor).

Anonymity—condition of research in which the participant is not known or in which participants' identity cannot be linked to their responses.

Applied research—research designed to answer practical questions; typically contrasted with basic research.

Archival research—research based on existing records such as newspapers, medical records, yearbooks, photographs, or any unpublished or published materials that can be evaluated.

Assent—in institutional review board (IRB) research review, children may be asked for their agreement (assent) to participate when developmentally appropriate.

Attention check questions—questions inserted in a survey to check whether the respondent is actually reading the items (e.g., "I am having a heart attack right now").

Autonomous agents—part of Respect for Persons, one of three guiding principles in the Belmont Report, stressing that people need to participate voluntarily in research.

Availability—one of the heuristics talked about by Kahneman and Tversky (1972) in which we use examples that easily come to mind.

Basic research—research that focuses on testing fundamental theories or principles, with the goal of generalization.

Beall's List—list evaluating open-access publications in terms of their standards; named after the originator of the list, Jeffrey Beall.

Behavior coding scheme—approach to observational research in which there is a checklist to code targeted behaviors (e.g., sitting or standing).

Behavioral categories—categories of behavior, usually predetermined, used to guide the recording of observed behavior.

Behavior map—spatial record of the behaviors and location of participants in the setting.

Belmont Report—federal report issued in 1979 that outlines the principles that guide ethical treatment of research subjects; three major principles are Respect for Persons, Beneficence, and Justice.

Beneficence—one of the three principles of the Belmont Report that emphasizes doing no harm (maximizing benefits while minimizing risks).

Between subjects design—research in which the conditions of an experiment are distributed across participants such that each participant is in only one condition.

Biased selection of subjects—when preexisting characteristics of participants may affect scores on the dependent variable.

BibMe—free bibliographic tool that automatically fills in the citation information; useful for a variety of citations styles, including American Psychological Association (APA).

Bonferroni adjustment—adjustment for Type I error by dividing the alpha level (.05) by the number of statistical tests performed to create a new more stringent alpha level.

Carryover effects—when the impact of one condition extends to subsequent conditions; described as one of the three context effects in within subjects design (Greenwald, 1976).

Case history—record of information about a person's medical or psychological history.

Case study—research approach for in-depth exploration of an event, program, process, or of one or more individuals.

Categorical data—data in which there is no ordering of values; also called nominal data.

Causal research—when the research design enables you to test cause-and-effect relationships.

Ceiling effect—outcome in which scores cluster at the top of the maximum value; creates difficulty in evaluating group differences.

Chain sampling—another name for snowball sampling.

Chi-square—nonparametric statistical procedure with nominal data to determine whether the distributions of two dimensions differ.

Closed-ended response—approach in which the respondent selects his or her response to a research question from a set of provided options.

Cluster sampling—when a sample of individuals is divided into a naturally occurring group, such as a classroom.

Coarsened data—idea that data lose some of their specificity (e.g., through rounding).

Cohen's kappa—measure of inter-rater agreement with nominal data that includes a correction for guessing and, hence, is superior to a calculation based on percent agreement.

Cohort—group of people that share a particular characteristic, such as age.

Cohort effects—differences attributable to experiencing a particular generation.

Cohort-sequential design—research design that combines both cross-sectional and longitudinal components; cohorts are selected at different points in time and followed longitudinally; used to address drawbacks to cross-sectional design.

Coincidence (gambler's fallacy)—thinking that an event is less likely to occur if it has just occurred or that it is likely to occur if it hasn't occurred for some time (e.g., assuming a slot machine will pay off because it hasn't for the past few hours).

Collaborative Institutional Training Initiative (CITI)—online training modules for ethical issues relevant to institutional review board (IRB) review.

Committee on Publication Ethics (COPE)—sets standards for reviewers who evaluate research.

Common Rule—federal policy adopted in 1991 that lists specific regulations guiding research with human subjects; also known as 45 CFR 46 (Code of Federal Regulations).

Complete counterbalancing—counterbalancing in which all possible orders are used.

Compute Function—tool in SPSS Statistics® that allows you to create new variables through arithmetic operations.

Computer-assisted qualitative data analysis software (CAQDAS)—software program developed to analyze linguistic responses such as text.

Concealed observer—observing in a setting while concealed; a form of passive deception.

Concurrent validity—one of two types of criterion-oriented validity; when the test (the predictor) and the outcome (the criterion) are assessed at the same point in time.

Condition—in research design, the particular level of a treatment that is used in experimental research (e.g., experimental and control conditions).

Confederate—someone who participates in a research project but is actually assisting the experimenter.

Confidence interval—shows range of values that you can be sure contains the population mean a certain percentage of the time (e.g., 95%).

Confidentiality—situation in which the research participant's identity is known and the researcher indicates the extent to which that information will be shared and with whom.

Confirmation bias—tendency to look for information that confirms our hypotheses.

Confirmatory factor analysis (CFA)—used to verify a factor structure in a given set of variables.

Confounding variable—extraneous variable that is associated with both the independent and the dependent variable and undermines the researcher's ability to pinpoint causality.

Consent to concealment—type of deception in which consent is obtained when some information is withheld from the participant.

Construct—idea or theory whose properties are inferred from some kind of measurement and are not directly observable. Examples of constructs include intelligence, anxiety, self-esteem, and leadership.

Construct validity—degree to which a measure assesses what it is hypothesized to measure; usually documented through a series of studies reflecting a nomological network or series of lawful relationships (Cronbach & Meehl, 1955).

Content analysis—coding scheme based on themes that emerge from qualitative data such as written narratives or newspaper articles; then used for quantitative analyses.

Content validity—validity of a measure that focuses on its representativeness from the domain of interest (e.g., a spelling test for fifth graders composed of words selected from books read by fifth graders).

Context effects—effects of practice, sensitization, and carryover; part of within subjects design when people are exposed to multiple conditions.

Continuous data—data on an interval scale; often contrasted with categorical data.

Convenience sample—participants gathered through their mere availability and accessibility to the researcher.

Convergent validity—demonstration of agreement between measures hypothesized to be theoretically related; contrasted with divergent validity.

Cooperative attitude—attitude of research participant who tries to help the researcher.

Copyright—when works are legally protected.

Correlation analysis—statistical approach that assesses the relationship between two variables, typically interval scale.

Correlational research—approach to research where no variables are manipulated.

Counterbalancing—presenting orders of the treatment to control for the influence of extraneous variables in an experiment.

Cover story—explanation about the purpose of research that hides the true nature of the study; used to reduce demand characteristics.

Covariate—variable that can affect the relationship between the dependent variable and the independent variables being assessed.

Covert observation—approach to observation in which the people being observed are not informed about the purpose of the observation.

Criterion—outcome measure of interest (e.g., in regression analysis).

Criterion-related validity—degree to which test scores predict the behavior of interest; two types (predictive and concurrent).

Cronbach's alpha—statistical indicator of the internal consistency of a measure.

Cross-sectional design—correlational approach, typically when different populations are measured at the same point in time (e.g., first year students and fourth year students).

Crowdsourcing—obtaining ideas or services from a large group of people, typically via the Internet.

Data dredging—exploration of large sets of data to discover statistically significant patterns not originally hypothesized.

Data mining—examining large datasets to discover patterns.

Data view—in SPSS Statistics®, view of the data by cases (rows) and columns (variables).

Debriefing—document given to participants at the conclusion of a research project that explains the hypotheses and rationale for the study.

Deception—in research when participants are not fully informed of the purposes and/or procedures; receives close attention in institutional review board (IRB) review.

Defensive or apprehensive attitude—attitude of participant who is concerned about performance evaluation.

De-identified data—data in which personally identifying information has been removed; typically involves research with Health Insurance Portability and Accountability Act (HIPAA) data.

Demand characteristics—"cues available to participants in a study that may enable them to determine the purpose of the study, or what is expected by the researcher" (Corsini, 2002, p. 262).

Demographic variables—background variables (e.g., gender or age) about participants that are used to describe the sample and may be used in analyses in quasi-experimental research.

Demonstration—one-level study where the impact of a variable is illustrated but there is no control condition.

Dependent variable—variable that reflects the impact of the manipulated or independent variable in research.

Descriptives—statistical presentation of measures of central tendency and dispersion that characterize a set of data.

Detailed record—part of the information in PsycTESTS® that may give you psychometric information about a scale.

Differential carryover effects—in within subjects design, when the lingering effects of a treatment are different for one variable than for another; may suggest the need to use a between subjects approach.

Differential selection (biased selection of subjects)—one of Campbell and Stanley's (1963) threats to internal validity in which participants assigned to groups are not equivalent on some important characteristic prior to the intervention.

Digital object identifier (doi)—unique code used in references that locates the reference in an electronic database.

Digital paywall—limits Internet users' access to the publication without a paid subscription.

Directionality—in correlational design, inability to determine the direction of cause and effect.

Discriminant validity—situation in which measures hypothesized to be theoretically unrelated are, in fact, unrelated.

Discussion—title of section in a manuscript when you interpret the results, centered and bolded in American Psychological Association (APA) style.

Double agent—situation in which you are fulfilling two roles at once and may not be acting solely in the client's/participant's best interest.

Double-blind experiment—research design in which both the participant and the researcher are unaware of the condition to which the participant has been assigned.

Double-dipping—situation in which you receive benefits from two sources for the effort (e.g., research credit and a gift incentive).

Dropbox®—cloud-based file sharing system.

Duration—in behavioral observation, recording how long a behavior lasts.

Ecological validity—validity in which the emphasis is on the degree of representativeness of the research to the events and characteristics of real life.

Effect size—quantitative indication of the strength of a particular occurrence.

Electronic database—electronic searchable collection of materials; useful in research.

Emancipatory pedagogy—approach to learning that frees students and teachers from hierarchical roles.

Emotional contagion—convergence of emotions across individuals.

Error rate per comparison (PC)—in any given comparison, the probability of making a Type I error.

Error variance—variability in the score not produced by the independent variable and not systematic or controlled.

Ethnography—study of people and cultures in a systematic manner.

Exempt IRB review—type of human subjects institutional review board (IRB) review for research in which there is no more than minimal risk and falling into one of the federally designated exempt from review categories.

Expedited IRB review—type of human subjects institutional review board (IRB) review for research in which there is no more than minimal risk and falling into one of the federally designated expedited review categories.

Experimental design—research approach with manipulated variables and random assignment.

Experimental mortality—one of Campbell and Stanley's (1963) threats to internal validity in which people drop out of studies in a nonequivalent manner (e.g., more older adults than younger adults drop out of the intervention than out of the control group).

Exploratory factor analysis (EFA)—typically used in the beginning stages of data reduction to uncover the relationships in a set of items.

External validity—ability to apply the results of research more broadly, that is, beyond the sample used in a particular study. Generalizability is a major emphasis of external validity.

Face validity—type of validity in which the measures subjectively appear to assess what you claim (e.g., a measure of leadership that asks about decisiveness).

Factor—another word used to refer to the independent variable; also a dimension that emerges from a factor analysis, a data reduction strategy.

Factor analysis—data reduction technique that takes items and statistically clusters groups of items to differentiate them maximally.

Factorial design—design in which there is more than one independent variable (IV).

Fair Use Doctrine—U.S. legal doctrine that enables you to use copyrighted materials under certain circumstances.

Family wise (FW) error rate—probability of having at least one Type I error in a set of comparisons.

Faulty induction—reasoning from the premises to a conclusion that is not warranted.

Field experiment—research that takes place in natural settings and manipulates variables, unlike a field study.

Field study—examination of variables in natural settings without the manipulation of variables.

File drawer phenomenon or effect—form of publication bias in which research appears more reliable than it is because articles on the topic that have not rejected the null hypothesis have not been published.

Flesch–Kincaid scale—provides statistics for the ease of reading of a given passage; available through word processing programs.

Floor effect—clustering of scores on a measure at the low end of the possible scale values; typically linked to the difficulty of the assessment.

Focus groups—form of qualitative research in which people are asked their views on a target issue.

Fraud—deception designed to result in personal gain; may take many forms in the research process.

Frequency—count of the number of times an event or characteristic occurs in a study.

Frequency analysis—for a dataset, checking the number of times values appear for a given variable.

Full IRB review—required for research that does not meet the guidelines for exempt or expedited institutional review board (IRB) review and/or poses more than minimal risk.

Fully crossed design—in a research design when all possible combinations of the levels of the independent variables (IVs) are represented.

G*Power—free online software that calculates power for a given design.

Gender neutral language—using language that does not favor one gender category.

Going fishing—term that describes exploring your data post hoc for significant findings.

Goodness of fit—one-dimensional chi-square that tests the difference between the actual sample and the hypothesized distribution (e.g., 25% of the participants in each class year).

Google Docs® Forms—feature of Google that enables you to collect survey data; responses are automatically saved to a Google docs spreadsheet.

Google Scholar®—search engine for academic resources.

Grounded theory—inductive methodology in which theory emerges out of systematic research (i.e., bottom up).

HARKing—hypothesizing after results are known (Kerr, 1998).

Hasty generalization—reaching decisions before evidence warrants, or faulty induction.

Health and Psychosocial Instruments (HaPI®)—database of instruments that indicates the sources in which a particular instrument is used.

Health Insurance Portability and Accountability Act (HIPAA)—federal legislation that governs the distribution and safeguarding of healthcare data; pertains to the need to de-identify the data for use in research.

Heuristics—mental shortcuts (e.g., estimations and commonsense) that often guide thinking and problem solving.

Hindsight bias—after an event has occurred, we have the tendency to claim that it could have been easily predicted.

History—one of Campbell and Stanley's (1963) threats to internal validity in which something happens between experimental treatments to influence the results.

Human intelligence task (HIT)—name for a study posted on Amazon Mechanical Turk®.

Human subjects—with regard to the federal definition (45 CFR 46), involves living individuals from whom the researcher obtains data through an interaction or intervention, or about whom the research obtains personally identifiable information.

Hypothesis—"a testable proposition based on theory, stating an expected empirical outcome resulting from specific observable conditions" (Corsini, 2002, p. 463).

Hypothetico-deductive method—what people refer to as the scientific method in which hypotheses are formulated that can be tested in a potentially falsifiable manner.

Ideographic—research approach that focuses on the individual and individual experiences.

Impact factor—number that reflects the average number of times articles from a particular journal have been cited over a particular period of time (e.g., 2 years).

Implicit Association Test (IAT)—using reaction time, this approach measures respondents' associations between concepts and is considered a way to reduce the social desirability of responses.

Imputation—process of replacing missing values with substitutes (e.g., sample means).

Independent samples *t* test—test to determine whether the means of two independent groups differ significantly.

Independent variable (IV)—variable that is manipulated in an experiment.

Informed consent—document given to potential research participants that outlines the nature of the research; participants must agree and sign or otherwise provide evidence of consent in order to take part in research.

Institutional Animal Care and Use Committee (IACUC)—institutional committee that reviews research with animals and their care.

Institutional review board (IRB)—deliberate body that evaluates research with human subjects; required where institutions received federal funds for research.

Instrumentation—one of Campbell and Stanley's (1963) threats to internal validity in which changes in equipment and/or observers affect judgments/measurements that are made.

Interaction effect—when the effect of one independent variable (IV) is not the same for all levels of a second IV.

Interlibrary loan—system that allows library patrons to request library materials not held by their institution.

Internal consistency—statistical measure, usually expressed as Cronbach's alpha, which reflects the degree to which each item of the measure is tapping the construct of interest.

Internal validity—extent to which a research design allows you to test the hypothesis adequately.

Inter-rater reliability (IRR)—calculation of the extent of agreement between raters.

Interrupted time-series analysis—quantitative research approach in which multiple assessments are made before and after the occurrence of an event (e.g., passing of legislation).

Interval—approach in behavioral observation where you segment the observed period into specific intervals and then record whether the target behavior occurred during that interval.

Interval measurement scale—type of measurement scale in which the anchors are equally spaced throughout; common in social science research.

Interview—qualitative research approach in which questions are asked of an individual; types are unstructured, semistructured, and structured.

Interview schedule—formal set of questions to be asked in an interview.

Interviewer effects—responses of interviewees that are related to demographic qualities of the interviewer, including race, gender, and ethnicity. These effects are considered a source of error.

Intraclass correlation (ICC)—measures the degree of association between variables that are measured on ordinal, interval, or ratio scales.

Introduction—part of a manuscript that introduces the topic, reviews relevant literature, and ends with hypotheses.

JSTOR—electronic database that provides access to articles usually 3–5 years (the moving wall) behind the current issue.

Justice—one of the three principles of the Belmont Report that emphasizes the fair distribution of risks and rewards of participation.

Kennedy Krieger Institute Lead Paint Study—research in Baltimore, Maryland, conducted by the Johns Hopkins University and funded by the Environmental Protection Agency (EPA) that exposed some children to lead paint dust.

Keywords—search terms for information retrieval.

Laboratory research—research conducted in a highly controlled environment, typically with random assignment to condition, to enable the researcher to make causal statements.

Latin Square—approach to counterbalancing where each treatment appears in each row and each column one time;, i.e., there are as many orders as treatments.

Law— "a theory accepted as correct, that has no significant rivals in accounting for the facts within its domain" (Corsini, 2002, p. 536).

Level—term that refers to the specific version of the treatment the participants received (e.g., which dosage of drug). See also *condition* and *value*.

LexisNexis—electronic database, which is almost always full text and covers almost 6,000 sources of news, business, legal, medical, and reference publications.

Likert scale—frequently used scale type where the anchors are typically five degrees of agreement-disagreement to statements.

Listwise deletion—when there are missing data, the elimination of the complete case if any data are missing.

Longitudinal design—research design in which the same participants are followed over a long period of time (e.g., Terman's Termites).

Manipulation check—questions posed in research, typically at the end, to assess whether the participants were aware of the level of the independent variable to which they were assigned.

Matched group design—before randomly assigning participants to conditions, you match them on one or more characteristic that you think may affect the dependent variable.

Materials—section of the Method in which you describe the "with what" of your study; often called measures, instruments, or apparatus.

Maturation—one of Campbell and Stanley's (1963) threats to internal validity in which capacities of the participants may change as a result of fatigue, illness, age, or hunger that affect the intervention.

Measures—in the Method section where you describe the scales or instruments used.

Mendeley—free reference manager for organizing and subsequently accessing downloaded articles.

Meta-analysis—meta-analysis is a "study of studies" that uses a statistical approach to synthesize the findings on a particular topic and to report the impact of a given intervention. That impact is reported as an effect size.

Method—heading in American Psychological Association (APA) research paper in which you present your Participants, Materials/Measures/Instruments, and Procedure.

Minimal risk—research is evaluated in terms of whether the probability of discomfort is more than people would encounter in everyday life or in routine psychological or physical evaluations. This level is known as minimal risk.

Mixed design—design that includes both a within subjects and a between subjects component.

Mixed method—approach to research that typically combines quantitative and qualitative approaches.

Multicollinearity—of concern in multivariate analysis when dependent or predictor variables are highly correlated (and in a sense redundant), rendering their unique contribution questionable.

Multiple comparisons—situation where you make several comparisons simultaneously to evaluate your hypothesis, leading to the possibility of Type I error.

Multiple relationships—described in 3.05 of the American Psychological Association (APA) Code of Ethics (2010a), in which your professional role (e.g., therapist) may be compromised by taking on a second role (e.g., research collaborator) with regard to the same individual.

Multivariate analysis of variance (MANOVA)—analysis of variance with two or more conceptually related dependent variables.

Naturalistic observation—observing individuals in their natural settings, without any kind of intervention or manipulation.

Negative attitude—attitude of a participant who wants to undermine the research.

Nominal measurement scale—measurement scale (sometimes called categorical) in which there is no inherent order (e.g., questions that can be answered "yes" or "no").

Nomological network—linked to the work of Cronbach and Meehl (1955) concerning the kinds of lawful relationships you would discover to validate a construct.

Nomothetic approach—research approach with the goal of developing laws of behavior that would apply generally.

Nonexperimental research—research in which there is no manipulation of variables or random assignment.

Nonequivalent control group—in a pre–post design, use of a control group like the intervention group to the extent possible but not randomly assigned.

Nonparametric statistics—nonparametric statistics make no assumptions about the population fitting a particular normal distribution.

Nonparticipant observation—observing participants without taking part in the activities.

Nonprobability sample—sample for which you cannot make precise estimates of representativeness (e.g., snowball or convenience).

Nonresponse—a lack of response to a something, typically a survey.

Nonresponse bias—when those who do not respond differ from those who do in terms of characteristics central to your hypothesis.

Null hypothesis—hypothesis that there are no group differences or relationships between variables.

Null hypothesis significance testing procedure (NHSTP)—using statistical inference, a procedure for evaluating whether the null hypothesis should be rejected.

Numeric data type—in SPSS Statistics®, a data type that permits numerical analysis.

Nuremberg code—ten guidelines for the ethical treatment of human subjects in research that were codified in 1949; emerged out of the Nazi War Crimes Tribunal in Nuremberg.

Observation—form of data gathering in which observers collect information through the senses, primarily visual.

Office for Human Research Protections (OHRP)—federal office that provides oversight for the protection of subjects in human research.

One-tailed significance test—when the critical region for significance is limited to one tail of the distribution (more lenient than two-tailed tests).

One-way ANOVA—evaluate through analysis of variance (ANOVA) whether the means of three or more groups [levels of an independent variable (IV)] differ significantly.

Online crowdsourcing platform—paid or unpaid participants used to obtain feedback online about a topic.

Open-access journals—journals that offer free access to the published articles.

Open-ended responses—qualitative approach that allows the respondent to answer in any way he or she wishes to a research question.

Operational definition—describing a variable in terms of the processes used to measure or quantify it.

Opportunistic bias—pursuing data analysis in multiple ways that increases the chances of finding significant results.

Ordinal measurement scale—type of measurement in which the values are ordered but they are not equally spaced.

Out-of-range values—values not specified in the data (e.g., a value of 8 on a scale range of 1–7).

Outlier—data point at a distance from other data points; may indicate variability in measurement or experimental error or neither (chance occurrence).

Overreliance on authorities—trusting authorities without examining the evidence.

Pagination—how a journal numbers its pages; if consecutively throughout the year, no issue number is needed in the reference.

Paid panel—group of people with identified characteristics (e.g., luxury car owners) that are asked to respond to a survey.

Paid subject pool—group of people who are paid to participate in research.

Pairwise deletion—approach to handling missing data in which a participant is dropped on analyses for only the missing variable(s) for that analysis, not altogether.

Paradigm—in science, an overarching approach to a field of inquiry that frames the questions to be asked and how research is conducted.

Parallel forms reliability (also called alternate forms reliability)—form of reliability in which equivalent forms of a test are shown to be reliable.

Parametric statistics—make assumptions about the population fitting a normal distribution.

Partial counterbalancing—presenting some but not all possible sequences of material to control for order effects; typically random orders are used, a different sequence for each participant.

Participant management system—way to keep track of research participants, commonly now through a software system.

Participants—section of your Method in which you describe the "who" of your study.

Participant observation—type of behavioral observation in which the observer is a member of the group being observed.

Passive consent—situation where agreement to participate (usually of parents/guardians for their child) is assumed in the absence of explicit documentation to the contrary.

Passive deception—form of deception that occurs through omission, rather than through commission; typically involves less than full explanation of the purposes of the research.

Pearson's *r*—statistical measure of correlation between two variables.

Peer review—used in the context of academic work to indicate that a submitted work has been reviewed (usually anonymously) by experts knowledgeable in the field.

Percent agreement—degree of agreement between observers, calculated as the number of agreements between observers divided by the number of events observed.

***p*-hacking**—processes such as continuing to test data or conducting post hoc analyses to produce significant results.

Phenomenology—qualitative approach to investigation that emphasizes consciousness and direct experience.

Photo release form—when signed gives permission for researchers to use such material in research; form specifies the extent of that use.

Physical traces—leftover physical elements (e.g., trash) in the environment that can be used as sources of data for research.

Pilot test—using a small number of participants to test aspects of the research and receive feedback on measures and/or manipulations.

Plagiarism—use of someone else's work (i.e., text, drawings, designs, or ideas) without giving appropriate credit.

Planned comparisons—you state the differences you expect to see (and hence which comparisons to run) *a priori*.

Positivism—philosophical approach to science that stresses information gained through the senses (direct experience).

Postoccupancy evaluation (POE)—analysis often done by architects to evaluate building performance (how it functions); usually only posttest.

Power—probability of rejecting H_o (the null hypothesis), assuming H_o is false.

Practical significance—results that are useful in an applied setting; often results may be statistically significant but not be large enough to have practical import.

Practice effects—one of the three context effects that may operate in within subjects designs.

Pre–post design—measurement before and after some intervention; can include a control group (preferred) or not (i.e., one group pretest–posttest).

Predictive validity—validity in which a measure is shown to forecast (predict) the outcome of interest (the criterion).

Predictor—in regression analysis, the variable being used to predict the criterion (outcome).

Prepaid incentives—incentives that are given in advance of participation.

Prezi®—presentation software known for its ability to move text or visuals easily.

Primary sources—original sources (e.g., data collected for the project or existing sources such as census data) that were created during a particular time period and are used to draw conclusions based on that research.

Probability sample—sample for which you can make precise estimates of representativeness.

Problem-solving inadequacy—when we do not seek to disprove hypotheses, only to confirm them.

Procedure—section of your Method in which you describe the "how" of your study.

Project Implicit—research to assess implicit attitudes.

Project Muse—electronic database of current articles that includes 300 scholarly journals in the social sciences, humanities, and arts.

Promised incentives—incentives for research promised at survey return.

Proportionate sampling—individuals in the sample are divided into subgroups, called strata, to reflect some particular characteristic (e.g., race). Sampling in each stratum is done to reflect the proportion of that characteristic in the population as a whole.

Pseudoscientific thinking—involves reference to a theory or method that is without scientific support.

PsycARTICLES®—database of articles from the American Psychological Association (APA) and affiliated publishers in which every article is provided full text.

Psychometric properties—quantifiable aspects of your measure that indicate its statistical qualities.

PsycINFO®—electronic database of citations and summaries from the American Psychological Association (APA) with almost 4 million records.

PsycTESTS®—American Psychological Association (APA) database of test records that typically provides the test items.

Public domain—material available to the public as a whole and not subject to copyright.

p **value**—probability value based on the characteristics of the observed data used for hypothesis testing.

Qualitative research—in-depth investigation of topics using techniques such as focus groups, interviews, and case studies; emphasis on nonquantitative assessment.

Qualtrics®—online platform for survey research.

Quasi-experimental design—research approach that resembles experimental research but is based on the use of preexisting groups [quasi-independent variables (IVs)].

Quasi-IV—independent variable (IV) that is naturally occurring (e.g., race and gender) and as a consequence is not assigned at random.

Random assignment—when participants are randomly assigned to the conditions of the study.

Randomized groups design—randomly assigning groups to different levels of one or more independent variables.

Randomizer function—feature of some online survey software programs that allows you to distribute conditions and/or questions randomly across participants.

Random sample—sample in which each person has an equal probability of being chosen.

Range effect—effect of multiple exposures (e.g., in within subjects design).

Ratio measurement scale—scale type with equal intervals and a true zero point.

Recode into Different Variables—SPSS Statistics® command in which numerical values are recoded into a new variable.

Recode into Same variables—SPSS Statistics® command in which numerical values are recoded into the existing variable.

Reflexivity—aspect of qualitative research in which researchers reflect on their experience as part of the research process.

RefWorks—bibliographic management tool.

Referral sampling—another name for snowball sampling.

Regression analysis—estimates the ability of a variable (called a predictor) to predict an outcome (called the criterion).

Reliability—in statistics, refers to the ability of a measure to produce reproducible outcomes.

Reliability analysis—in SPSS Statistics®, refers to the evaluation of data to assess internal consistency, such as Cronbach's alpha.

Repeated measures—type of research design and analysis in which there are repeated measures for the same people.

Representativeness (base rate)—one of the heuristics talked about by Kahneman and Tversky

(1972) in which we make decisions based on how representative or characteristic of a particular pattern of events data are (e.g., people think the birth order BGBBGG is more representative of a sequence of births than is BBBGGG).

Representativeness (sampling)—degree to which a sample reflects the characteristics in the parent population.

Reproducibility Project—project in which researchers are trying to reproduce the findings of 100 experimental and correlational articles in psychology.

Requester—name given to person posting research on Amazon Mechanical Turk®.

Research—with respect to the federal definition (45 CFR 46), involves a systematic collection of data with the goal of generalizable knowledge.

Respect for persons—one of the three principles of the Belmont Report that emphasizes people are autonomous agents; specifies the use of informed consent.

Response rate—percentage of people who respond to a survey; usually calculated by the number of people who responded divided by the number invited.

Restriction of range—when the distribution of scores is not widely dispersed across the range of interest; affects the size of your correlation.

Results—title of the section in a manuscript where the results are presented; in American Psychological Association (APA) style, the word Results is centered and bolded.

Reverse scoring—items in a survey stated in a manner that is opposite that of the other items (i.e., stated negatively when the other items are stated positively) and whose anchors need to be reversed.

Review article—provides an overview and brief history of a topic and its challenges.

Role attitude cues—when participants approach research with a particular attitude, such as cooperativeness; may affect results.

Role playing—playing a role as if you are in the actual situation.

Rounding rules—rules to guide when you round up, when you leave a value as is, and when the digit in question is 5.

Scale sensitivity—ability of the scale to detect differences.

Schema—mental representation of a category that can be a role, an object, or an event (e.g., parent, table, or going to the dentist, respectively).

Secondary data analysis—analysis using existing datasets with archival data; often used for research with children.

Secondary sources—sources that analyze or critique the primary sources. Textbooks, magazine articles or blogs summarizing research, systematic review articles, or handbooks on a topic are common secondary sources.

Select Cases Function—SPSS Statistics® command in which the analysis is restricted to a subset of the sample (e.g., first year students).

Selection–maturation interaction—one of Campbell and Stanley's (1963) threats to internal validity in which with quasi-experimental designs with multiple groups, some preexisting aspect of the groups might be confounded with the variable of interest.

Semistructured interview—set of questions or interview guide with room for follow-up and introduction of related topics as appropriate.

Sensitization—"the process of becoming susceptible to a given stimulus" (Corsini, 2002, p. 885). Discussed as one context effect in within subjects design by Greenwald (1976).

Service learning—academic experiences that integrate course material and work in the field.

Significance level—in research, the probability value indicating the likelihood that the finding occurred by chance, usually set at .05.

Simple effects—way to evaluate the components of an interaction, that is, what is responsible for the interaction.

Simulation—representation, often computer-generated, of a real situation; considered an alternative to deception.

Single-blind experiment—research design in which participants are unaware of the conditions to which they have been assigned.

Single-group pre–post design—called "pre-experimental" by Campbell and Stanley (1963);

measures participants before and after an intervention, without a control group.

Snowball sample—nonprobability sample in which individuals who participate in a study invite others to participate in the study, and they in turn invite still others.

Social desirability—responding to experimental stimuli and/or scales in a way that presents the respondent in a positive (socially appropriate) light.

Solomon four-group design—pretest, posttest research design involving four conditions; takes into account the possible effect of sensitization in responding to the pretest measures.

Sona Systems®—online participant management software used to keep track of the involvement of participants in research.

Spearman's rank order (rho)—tests association between two ranked variables, or between a ranked variable and a measurement variable; equivalent to a correlation but for a nonparametric situation.

Split-half reliability—one form of reliability of a measure in which the instrument is split into halves and the halves are correlated with each other; sometimes referred to as Spearman-Brown.

Standardized regression weight—beta (β) employs a common unit across measures with different units (i.e., it standardizes them).

Stanford prison experiment—research conducted by Zimbardo and colleagues showing the effect of obedience to authority in a simulated prison environment (Haney, Banks, & Zimbardo, 1973).

Statistical regression—one of Campbell and Stanley's (1963) threats to internal validity when participants are selected on the basis of extreme scores (e.g., high or low intelligence) and their scores move toward the mean on subsequent testing.

Statistical significance—when a result reaches the stated alpha level, typically .05.

Stem—in a survey, the statement, question, or prompt to which the respondent replies.

Strata—name for the specific subgroups used in stratified random sampling.

Stratified random sampling—sampling in which the population is divided into subgroups, called strata, and then randomly sampling within those subgroups to ensure a representative sample.

String variable type—data type in SPSS Statistics® on which no numerical analyses can be performed.

Structured interview—items prepared in advance and asked in the same way to each person.

Subject pool—groups of individuals, typically undergraduate students, formed to provide participants for research; also called participant pool.

Survey—series of questions, typically a standardized instrument, that assesses responses to one or more topic.

SurveyMonkey®—online platform for survey research.

Survey research—approach to research in which the variables of interest (typically thoughts, feelings, and attitudes) are assessed through a survey.

Systematic sampling—known population (e.g., students listed in their college directory) is systematically sampled (e.g., every fourth name) after a random start.

Testing—one of Campbell and Stanley's (1963) threats to internal validity involving multiple testing situations in which the first test affects how participants respond to subsequent tests.

Test–retest reliability—form of reliability in which the instrument is given at two points in time and the scores are correlated.

Theory—"a body of interrelated principles and hypotheses that explain or predict a group of phenomena and have been largely verified by facts or data" (Corsini, 2002, p. 994).

Third variable—variable that influences the relationship between the variables of interest; also called a confounding variable.

Threats to internal validity—factors that undermine the ability of your research to ascertain the influence of an independent variable (IV) on a dependent variable (DV).

Time-series analysis—analysis of data points collected repeatedly over time.

Title 45 Part 46 of the Code of Federal Regulations—federal code that governs the protection of human subjects.

Transfer effects—when outcomes from one domain affect learning in another domain; sometimes discussed in within subjects designs as practice effects.

Transform—function in SPSS Statistics® that allows you to reconfigure data, for example, computing a new variable or recoding a variable.

Treatment—another word used for the independent variable (IV).

Treatment level—condition in an experiment; the treatment is defined in terms of its different levels (e.g., experimental and control).

Tree backward—search technique for working backward through previously published work to obtain resources.

Tree forward—search technique looking forward to see what more recent articles have cited the article of interest.

Triangulation—approach to convergent validity in which the researcher gathers multiple sources of information (e.g., from interviews and observations) to see whether there is a consistent pattern.

True experimental approach—research approach in which one or more variables are manipulated and subjects are randomly assigned to condition.

Tuskegee syphilis study—study of African American men with syphilis that demonstrates violations of ethical principles because the men were left untreated even when a treatment was available; sponsored by the U.S. Public Health Service from 1932 to 1972.

Two-tailed significance test—when the critical region for significance is spread across both tails of the distribution.

Two-way ANOVA—analysis of variance (ANOVA) that has two independent variables (IVs).

Type I error—incorrectly rejecting the null hypothesis when it is true.

Type II error—failing to reject the null hypothesis when it is false.

Unpaid subject pool—group of people who are not paid to participate in research; most commonly a university subject pool.

Unplanned comparisons—you make no advance predictions and run comparisons post hoc, which usually results in a higher probability of Type I error.

Unstandardized regression coefficient—coefficient (B) that employs the units associated with the particular measures.

Unstructured interview—interview that has a plan, but no specifically devised set of questions in an interview schedule; open-ended questions typically used.

Validity—extent to which a measure assesses what it is claimed to measure.

Values—refer to variable or treatment levels; can also refer to numerical values assigned in SPSS Statistics® file.

Variable—term often used to refer to an independent variable (IV).

Variable View—view in SPSS Statistics® in which the variables and their characteristics (e.g., name, data type, and length) are found.

Virtual environments—synthetic environment that combine the control of the laboratory with the naturalism of the field; often use immersive approaches.

Vulnerable population—population (e.g., children, pregnant women, or prisoners) for whom a full institutional review board (IRB) review is required for research involving these individuals.

Warrant—argument that shows how evidence supports a claim and rules out alternative explanations.

Wason Selection Task—logic problem in which you have to determine which of four two-sided cards need to be turned over to evaluate the stated hypothesis (e.g., if there is a vowel on one side, there is an even number on the other).

Weber–Fechner law—when the magnitude of a physical stimulus is increased/decreased by a constant ratio, people's reactions to it also increase/decrease by equal increments.

Within subjects design—type of experimental design in which participants are exposed to all of the conditions.

Wordle™—program for generating word clouds from text that show the frequency with which certain words appear; useful in presentations.

Worker—name given to participant on Amazon Mechanical Turk®.

WorldCat—worldwide catalog listing books, monographs, videos, and sound recordings; useful for determining what institution owns a resource in order to retrieve it.

REFERENCES

Adair, J. G. (1973). *The human subject: The social psychology of the psychological experiment.* Boston, MA: Little, Brown.

Adler, P. A., & Adler, P. (1987). *Membership roles in field research.* Newbury Park, CA: Sage.

Alise, M. A., & Teddlie, C. (2010). A continuation of the paradigm wars? Prevalence rates of methodological approaches across the social/behavioral sciences. *Journal of Mixed Methods Research, 4,* 103–126. doi:10.1177/1558689809360805

Allison, P. D. (2001). *Missing data.* Thousand Oaks, CA: Sage.

Altbach, P. G., & Rapple, B. (2012, March 8). Anarchy and commercialism. Essay on problems with state of journal publishing. Retrieved from https://www.insidehighered.com/views/2012/03/08/essay-problems-state-journal-publishing

American Press Institute. (2014, March 17). How Americans get their news. Retrieved from http://www.americanpressinstitute.org/publications/reports/survey-research/how-americans-get-news/

American Psychological Association (APA). (2010a). *Ethical principles of psychologists and code of conduct.* Retrieved from http://www.apa.org/ethics/code/

American Psychological Association (APA). (2010b). *Publication manual of the American Psychological Association* (6th ed.).Washington, DC: Author.

American Sociological Association (ASA). (2010). *ASA style guide* (4th ed.). Washington, DC: Author.

Andrade, C. C., & Devlin, A. S. (2015). Stress reduction in the hospital room: Applying Ulrich's theory of supportive design. *Journal of Environmental Psychology, 41,* 125–134. doi:10.1016/j.jenvp.2014.12.001

Andrade, C. C., & Devlin, A. S. (in press). Who wants control in the hospital room? Environmental control, stress, and desirability of control. *Psyecology.*

Antony, M. M., Orsillo, S. M., & Roemer, L. (2001). *Practitioner's guide to empirically based measures of anxiety.* New York, NY: Springer.

Armstrong, J. S., & Overton, T. S. (1977). Estimating nonresponse bias in mail surveys. *Journal of Marketing Research, 14,* 396–402.

Arnett, J. (2008). The neglected 95%. Why American psychology needs to become less American. *American Psychologist, 63,* 602–614. doi:10.1037/0003-066X.63.7.602

Atkinson, P., & Hammersley, M. (1994). Ethnography and participant observation. In N. K. Denzin, & Y. S. Lincoln (Eds.), *Handbook of qualitative research* (pp. 248–261). Thousand Oaks, CA: Sage.

Auerbach, C. F., & Silverstein, L. B. (2003). *Qualitative data: An introduction to coding and analysis.* New York: New York University Press.

Aviv, A. L., Zelenski, J. M., Rallo, L., & Larsen, R. J. (2002). Who comes when: Personality differences in early and later participation in a university subject pool. *Personality and Individual Differences, 33,* 487–496. doi:10.1016/S0191-8869(01)00199-4

Bakeman, R., & Gottman, J. M. (1989). *Observing interaction: An introduction to sequential analysis.* Cambridge, England: Cambridge University Press.

Banaji, M. R., & Crowder, R. G. (1989). The bankruptcy of everyday memory. *American Psychologist, 44,* 1185–1193. doi:10.1037/0003-066X.44.9.1185

Banerjee, A., Chitnis, U. B., Jadhav, S. L., Bhawalkar, J. S., & Chaudhury, S. (2009). Hypothesis testing, type I and type II errors. *Industrial Psychiatry Journal, 18*(2), 127–131. doi:10.4103/0972-6748.62274

Barnett, V., & Lewis, T. (1994). *Outliers in statistical data* (3rd ed.). New York, NY: Wiley.

Bartneck, C., Duenser, A., Motchanova, E., & Zawieska, K. (2015, April 14). Comparing the similarity of responses received from studies in Amazon's Mechanical Turk to studies conducted online and with direct recruitment. *PLoS ONE, 10*(4), 1–23. doi:10.1371/journal.pone.0121595

Baruch, Y. (1999). Response rate in academic studies—A comparative analysis. *Human Relations, 52,* 421–438. doi:10.1177/001872679905200401

Bem, D. J. (1987). Writing the empirical journal article. In M. P. Zanna, & J. M. Darley (Eds.), *The compleat academic: A practical guide for the beginning social scientist* (pp. 171–201). Washington, DC: American Psychological Association.

Bem, D. J. (2004). Writing the empirical journal article. In J. M. Darley, M. P. Zanna, & H. L. Roediger III (Eds.), *The compleat academic: A career guide* (2nd ed., pp. 185–219). Washington, DC: American Psychological Association.

Bem, S. L. (1974). The measurement of psychological androgyny. *Journal of Consulting and Clinical Psychology, 42*, 155–162. doi:10.1037/h0036215

Bender, R., & Lange, S. (2001). Adjusting for multiple testing—When and how? *Journal of Clinical Epidemiology, 54*, 343–349. doi:10.1016/S0895-4356(00)00314-0

Berman, M., Jonides, J., & Kaplan, S. (2008). The cognitive benefits of interacting with nature. *Psychological Science, 19*, 1207–1212. doi:10.1111/j.1467-9280.2008.02225x

Biemer, P. P., & Lyberg, L. E. (2003). *Introduction to survey quality.* Hoboken, NJ: Wiley.

Blascovich, J., Loomis, J., Beall, A. C., Swinth, K. R., Hoyt, C. L., & Bailenson, J. N. (2002). Immersive virtual environment technology as a methodological tool for social psychology. *Psychological Inquiry, 13*, 103–124. doi:10.1207/S15327965PLI1302_01

Blumberg, S. J., & Luke, J. V. (2014, July). Wireless substitution: Early release of estimates from the National Health Interview Survey, July–December 2013. *National Center for Health Statistics.*

Retrieved from http://www.cdc.gov/nchs/nhis.htm

Blumer, H. (1969). *Symbolic interactionism.* Englewood Cliffs, NJ: Prentice Hall.

Boynton, M. H., Portnoy, D. B., & Johnson, B. T. (2013). Exploring the ethics and psychological impact of deception in psychological research. *IRB: Ethics and Human Research, 35*(2), 7–13.

Brauhardt, A., Rudolph, A., & Hilbert, A. (2014). Implicit cognitive processes in binge-eating disorder and obesity. *Journal of Behavior Therapy and Experimental Psychiatry, 45*, 285–290. doi:10.1016/j.jbtep.2014.01.001

Brewer, B. W., Van Raalte, J. L., & Linder, D. E. (1993). Athletic identity: Hercules' muscles or Achilles heel? *International Journal of Sport Psychology, 24*, 237–254.

Brinthaupt, T. M. (2002). Teaching research ethics: Illustrating the nature of the researcher-IRB relationship. *Teaching of Psychology, 29*, 243–245.

Brooks-Gunn, J., & Ruble, D. N. (1980). The menstrual attitude questionnaire. *Psychosomatic Medicine, 42*, 503–512. doi:10.1097/00006842-198009000-00005

Brown, G., & Devlin, A. S. (2003). Vandalism: Environmental and social factors. *Journal of College Student Development, 44*, 502–516. doi:10.1353/csd.2003.0037

Brymer, E., Davids, K., & Mallabon, L. (2014). Understanding the psychological health and well-being benefits of physical activity in nature: An ecological dynamics analysis. *Ecopsychology, 6*, 189–197. doi:10.1089/eco.2013.0110

Buchanan, D. R., & Miller, F. G. (2006). Justice and fairness in the Kennedy Krieger Institute Lead Paint Study: The ethics of public health research on less expensive, less effective interventions. *American Journal of Public Health, 96*, 781–787. doi:10.2105/AJPH.2005.063719

Buchanan, T., & Williams, J. E. (2010). Ethical issues in psychological research on the Internet. In S. D. Gosling, & J. A. Johnson (Eds.), *Advanced methods for conducting online behavioral research* (pp. 255–271). Washington, DC: American Psychological Association.

Buhrmester, M., Kwang, T., & Gosling, S. D. (2011). Amazon's Mechanical Turk: A new source of inexpensive, yet high-quality, data? *Perspectives on Psychological Science, 6*, 3–5. doi:10.1177/1745691610393980

Burger, J. M. (2009). Replicating Milgram: Would people still obey today? *American Psychologist, 64*, 1–11. doi:10.1037/a0010932

Buri, J. R. (1991). Parental Authority Questionnaire. *Journal of Personality Assessment, 57*, 110–119. doi:10.1207/s15327752jpa5701_13

Calfee, R. (2000). What does it all mean? The discussion. In R. J. Sternberg (Ed.), *Guide to publishing in psychology journals* (pp. 133–145). New York, NY: Cambridge University Press.

Calhoun, C. (Ed.) (2002). *Dictionary of the social sciences.* New York, NY: Oxford University Press.

Campbell, D. T., & Stanley, J. C. (1963). *Experimental and quasi-experimental designs for research.* Chicago, IL: Rand McNally.

Cartwright, J. C., Hickman, S. E., Nelson, C. A., & Knafl, K. A. (2013). Investigators' successful strategies for working with institutional review boards. *Research in Nursing & Health, 36,* 478–486. doi:10.1002/nur.21553

Carver, C. S., Scheier, M. F., & Weintraub, J. K. (1989). Assessing coping strategies: A theoretically based approach. *Journal of Personality and Social Psychology, 56,* 267–283.

Cattell, R. B., Cattell, A. K., & Cattell, H. E. P. (2002). *16PF® Fifth Edition.* Retrieved from http://www.pearsonclinical.com/psychology/products/100000483/16pf-fifth-edition.quick.html

Chandler, J., Mueller, P., & Paolacci, G. (2014). Nonnaïveté among Amazon Mechanical Turk workers: Consequences and solutions for behavioral researchers. *Behavioral Research, 46,* 112–130. doi:10.3758/s13428-013-0365-7

Chandra, A. (2015). Facial profiling: Perceptions of Facebook profile picture composition. *Connecticut College Psychology Journal, 27,* 47–65.

Charmaz, K. (2003). Grounded theory. In J. A. Smith (Ed.), *Qualitative psychology: A practical guide to research methods* (pp. 81–110). Thousand Oaks, CA: Sage.

Charness, G., Gneezy, U., & Kuhn, M. A. (2012). Experimental methods: Between-subject and within-subject design. *Journal of Economic Behavior & Organization, 81,* 1–8. doi:10.1016/j.jeb0.2011.08.009

Chavis, D. M., Hogge, J. H., McMillan, D. W., & Wandersman, A. (1986). Sense of community through Brunswik's lens: A first look. *Journal of Community Psychology, 14,* 22–40. doi:10.1002/

1520–6629(198601)14:1<24::AID-JCOP2290140104>3.0.CO;2-P

Chen, H.-M., Tu, H.-M., & Ho, C.-I. (2013). Understanding biophilia leisure as facilitating well-being and the environment: An examination of participants' attitudes toward horticultural activity. *Leisure Sciences: An Interdisciplinary Journal, 35,* 301–319. doi:10.1080/01490400.2013.797323

Church, A. H. (1993). Estimating the effect of incentives on mail survey response rates: A meta-analysis. *Public Opinion Quarterly, 57,* 62–79. doi:10.1086/269355

Cohen, J. (1960). A coefficient of agreement for nominal scales. *Educational and Psychological Measurement, 20,* 37–46. doi:10.1177/001316446002000104

Cohen, J. (1988). *Statistical power analyses for the behavioral sciences* (2nd ed.). New York, NY: Academic Press.

Cooper, P. J., Taylor, M. J., Cooper, Z., & Fairburn, C. G. (1987). The development and validation of the body shape questionnaire. *International Journal of Eating Disorders, 6,* 485–494. doi:10.1002/1098-108X(198707)6:4<485::AID-EAT2260060405>3.0.CO;2-O

Corcoran, K., & Fischer, J. (2013). *Measures for clinical practice and research: A sourcebook* (5th ed., Vols. 1 & 2). New York, NY: Oxford University Press.

Corsini, R. J. (Ed.). (2002). *The dictionary of psychology.* New York, NY: Brunner-Routledge.

Council, J. R., Smith, E. J. H., Kaster-Bundgaard, J., & Gladue, B. A. (1997). Ethical evaluation of hypnosis research: A survey of investigators and their institutional

review boards. *American Journal of Clinical Hypnosis, 39,* 258–265. doi:10.1080/00029157.1997.10403393

Cozby, P., & Bates, S. (2014). *Methods in behavioral research* (12th ed.). New York, NY: McGraw-Hill.

Creswell, J. W. (2009). *Research design: Qualitative, quantitative, and mixed methods approaches.* Thousand Oaks, CA: Sage.

Cronbach, L. J., & Meehl, P. E. (1955). Construct validity in psychological tests. *Psychological Bulletin, 52,* 281–302. doi:10.1037/h0040957

Crowne, D. P., & Marlowe, D. (1960). A new scale of social desirability independent of psychopathology. *Journal of Consulting Psychology, 24,* 349–354. doi:10.1037/h0047358

Dambrun, M., & Vatiné, E. (2010). Reopening the study of extreme social behaviors: Obedience to authority within an immersive video environment. *European Journal of Social Psychology, 40,* 760–773. doi:10.1002/ejsp.646

Damon, W., & Lerner, R. M. (2006). *Handbook of child psychology* (4 vol., 6th ed.). Hoboken, NJ: Wiley.

Davis, R. E., Couper, M. P., Janz, N. K., Caldwell, C. H., & Resnicow, K. (2010). Interviewer effects in public health surveys. *Health Education Research, 25,* 14–26. doi:10.1093/her/cyp046

Davy, J. A., Kincaid, J. F., Smith, K. J., & Trawick, M. A. (2007). An examination of the role of attitudinal characteristics and motivation on the cheating behavior of business students. *Ethics & Behavior, 17,* 281–302. doi:10.1080/10508420701519304

DeCoster, J., Sparks, E. A., Sparks, J. C., Sparks, G. G., & Sparks, C. W. (2015). Opportunistic biases: Their origins, effects, and an integrated solution. *American Psychologist, 70,* 499–514. doi:10.1037.a0039191

Delaney, J., Lupton, M. J., & Toth, E. (1987). *The curse: A cultural history of menstruation.* Urbana: University of Illinois Press.

DeLongis, A., Coyne, J. C., Dakof, G., Folkman, S., & Lazarus, R. S. (1982). Relationship of daily hassles, uplifts, and major life events to health status. *Health Psychology, 1,* 119–136.

Devlin, A. S. (1980). Housing for the elderly: Cognitive considerations. *Environment and Behavior, 12,* 451–466. doi:10.1177/0013916580124003

Devlin, A. S. (1992). Psychiatric ward renovation: Staff perception and patient behavior. *Environment and Behavior, 24,* 66–84. doi:10.1177/0013916592241003

Devlin, A. S. (1996). Survival skills training during freshman orientation: Its role in college adjustment. *Journal of College Student Development, 37,* 324–334.

Devlin, A. S. (2000). City behavior and precautionary measures. *Journal of Applied Social Psychology, 30,* 2158–2171. doi:10.1111/j.1559-1816.2000.tb02430.x

Devlin, A. S. (2006). *Research methods: Planning, conducting, and presenting research.* Belmont, CA.: Wadsworth/Thomson.

Devlin, A. S. (2008). Judging a book by its cover: Medical building facades and judgments of care. *Environment and Behavior, 40,* 307–329. doi:10.1177/0013916507302242

Devlin, A. S., Andrade, C. C., & Carvalho, D. (2016). Qualities of inpatient hospital rooms: Patients' perspectives. *Health Environments Research and Design Journal, 9,* 190–211. doi:10.1177/1937586715607052

Devlin, A. S., Andrade, C. C., & Lima, M. L. (2014). *Hospital rooms and patients' well-being: Exploring modeling variables.* Grant report to the Academy of Architecture for Health Foundation.

Devlin, A. S., & Bernstein, J. (1997). Interactive way-finding: Map style and effectiveness. *Journal of Environmental Psychology, 17,* 99–110. doi:10.1006/jevp.1997.0045

Devlin, A. S., Borenstein, B., Finch, C., Hassan, M., Iannotti, E., & Koufopoulos, J. (2013). Multicultural art in the counseling office: Community and student perceptions of the therapist. *Professional Psychology: Research & Practice, 44,* 168–176. doi:10.1037/a0031925

Devlin, A. S., Donovan, S., Nicolov, A., Nold, O., Packard, A., & Zandan, G. (2009). "Impressive?" Credentials, family photographs, and the perception of therapist qualities. *Journal of Environmental Psychology, 29,* 503–512. doi:10.1016/j.jenvp.2009.08.008

Devlin, A. S., & Nasar, J. L. (2012). Impressions of psychotherapists' offices: Do therapists and clients agree? *Professional Psychology: Research & Practice, 43,* 118–122. doi:10.1037/a0027292

Dillman, D. (2000). *Mail and Internet surveys: The tailored design method.* New York, NY: Wiley.

Dillman, D., Smyth, J. D., & Christian, L. M. (2014). *Internet, phone, mail, and mixed-mode surveys: The tailored design method* (4th ed.). New York, NY: Wiley.

Dittrich, L. (2016). *Patient H. M.: A story of memory, madness, and family secrets.* New York, NY: Random House.

Doan, S. N., Dich, N., & Evans, G. W. (2014). Childhood cumulative risk and later allostatic load: Mediating role of substance use. *Health Psychology, 33,* 1402–1409. doi:10.1037/a0034790

Dreyfus, H. (1972). *What computers still can't do: A critique of artificial reason.* Cambridge, MA: MIT Press.

Dweck, C. (2006). *Mindset: The new psychology of success.* New York, NY: Random House.

Egan, M. (2015, March 9). The Big Bang effect: Computer science stereotypes are getting better, not worse. *Quartz.* Retrieved from http://qz.com/358555/computer-science-stereotypes-are-getting-worse-not-better/

Eid, M., & Diener, E. (2006). Introduction: The need for multimethod measurement in psychology. In M. Eid, & E. Diener (Eds.), *Handbook of multimethod measurement in psychology* (pp. 3–8). Washington, DC: American Psychological Association.

Evans, G. W. (2003). A multimethodological analysis of cumulative risk and allostatic load among rural children. *Developmental Psychology, 39,* 924–933. doi:10.1037/0012-1649.39.5.924

Evans, G. W., & Cassells, R. C. (2014). Childhood poverty, cumulative risk exposure, and mental health in emerging adults. *Clinical Psychological Science, 2,* 287–296. doi:10.1177/2167702613501496

Evans, G. W., & Kim, P. (2012). Childhood poverty and young adults' allostatic load: The mediating role of childhood cumulative risk exposure. *Psychological Science, 23,* 979–983. doi:10.1177/0956797612441218

Eyde, L. D., Robertston, G. J., & Krug, S. E. (2010). *Responsible test use: Case studies for assessing human behavior* (2nd ed.). Washington, DC: American Psychological Association.

Faul, F., Erdfelder, E., Lang, A.-G., & Buchner, A. (2007). G*Power 3: A flexible statistical analysis program for the social, behavioral, and biomedical sciences. *Behavior Research Methods, 41,* 1149–1160. doi:10.3758/BRM.41.4.1149

Feldman, M. S., Bell, J., & Berger, M. T. (2003). *Gaining access: A practical and theoretical guide for qualitative researchers.* New York, NY: Altamira Press.

Fernandez-Ballesteros, R. (2003). *Encyclopedia of psychological assessment* (Vols. 1 & 2). Thousand Oaks, CA: Sage.

Ferraro, F., Pfeffer, J., & Sutton, R. I. (2009). How and why theories matter: A comment on Felin and Foss (2009). *Organization Science, 20,* 669–675. doi:10.1287/orsc.1090.0432

Fiedler, K. (2011). Voodoo correlations are everywhere—Not only in neuroscience. *Perspectives on Psychological Science, 6,* 163–171. doi:10.1177/1745691611400237

Fielding, J., Fielding, N. & Hughes, G. (2013). Opening up open-ended survey data using qualitative software. *Quality & Quantity, 47,* 3261–3276. doi:10.1007/s11135-012-9716-1

Fisher, C. B., & Fyrberg, D. (1994). Participant partners: College

students weigh the costs and benefits of deceptive research. *American Psychologist, 49,* 417–427. doi:10.1037/0003-066X.49.5.417

Flaherty, C. (2014, April 14). Trigger unhappy. *Inside Higher Ed.* Retrieved from https://www.insidehighered.com/news/2014/04/14/oberlin-backs-down-trigger-warnings-professors-who-teach-sensitive-material

Folkman, S., Lazarus, R. S., Dunkel-Schetter, C., DeLongis, A., & Gruen, R. J. (1986). Dynamics of a stressful encounter: Cognitive appraisal, coping, and encounter outcomes. *Journal of Personality and Social Psychology, 50,* 992–1003. doi:10.1037/0022-3514.50.5.992

Fontana, A., & Frey, J. H. (2000). The interview: From structured questions to negotiated text. In N. K. Denzin & Y. S. Lincoln (Eds.), *Handbook of qualitative research* (2nd ed., pp. 645–672). Thousand Oaks, CA: Sage.

Fowler, F. J., & Mangione, T. W. (1990). *Standardized survey interviewing: Minimizing interviewer-related error.* Thousand Oaks, CA: Sage.

Frantz, D., & Collins, C. (1999). *Celebration, U. S. A.: Living in Disney's brave new town.* New York, NY: Henry Holt.

Fredricks, J. A., & Eccles, J. S. (2006). Is extracurricular participation associated with beneficial outcomes? Concurrent and longitudinal relations. *Developmental Psychology, 42,* 698–713. doi:10.1037/0012-1649.42.4.698

Freud, S., Strachey, J., Freud, A., Rothgeb, C. L., & Richards, A. (1953). *The standard edition of the complete psychological works of Sigmund Freud.* London, England: Hogarth Press.

Gallup, A., & Newport, F. (2008). *Gallup Poll cumulative index: Public opinion 1998-2007.* Lanham, MD: Rowman & Littlefield.

Gans, H. (1969). *The Levittowners: Ways of life and politics in a new suburban community.* New York, NY: Vintage.

Garner, D. M., & Garfinkel, P. E. (1979). The Eating Attitudes Test: An index of symptoms of anorexia nervosa. *Psychological Medicine, 9,* 273–279. doi:10.1017/S0033291700030762

Garner, D. M., Olmstead, M. P., Bohr, Y., & Garfinkel, P. E. (1982). The Eating Attitudes Test: Psychometric features and clinical correlates. *Psychological Medicine, 12,* 871–878.

Garner, D. M., Olmstead, M. P., & Polivy, J. (1983). Development and validation of a multidimensional eating disorder inventory for anorexia nervosa and bulimia. *International Journal of Eating Disorders, 2*(2), 15–34.

Gerst, M. S., & Moos, R. H. (1972). Social ecology of university school residences. *Journal of Educational Psychology, 63,* 513–525. doi:10.1037/h0033857

Gibaldi, J. (2009). *MLA handbook for writers of research papers* (7th ed.). New York, NY: Modern Language Association.

Gilbert, K. R. (2001a). Collateral damage? Indirect exposure of staff members to the emotions of qualitative research. In K. R. Gilbert (Ed.), *The emotional nature of qualitative research* (pp. 147–161). New York, NY: CRC Press.

Gilbert, K. R. (2001b). *The emotional nature of qualitative research.* New York, NY: CRC Press.

Gill, P., Stewart, K., Treasure, E., & Chadwick, B. (2008). Methods of data collection in qualitative research: Interviews and focus groups. *British Dental Journal, 204,* 291–295. doi:10.1038/bdj.2008.192

Gillespie, J. F. (1999). The why, what, how, and when of effective faculty use of institutional review boards. In G. Chastain & R. E. Landrum (Eds.), *Protecting human subjects: Departmental subject pools and institutional review boards* (pp. 157–177). Washington, DC: American Psychological Association.

Giorgi, A., & Giorgi, B. (2003). Phenomenology. In J. A. Smith (Ed.), *Qualitative psychology: A practical guide to research methods* (pp. 25–50). Thousand Oaks, CA: Sage.

Glantz, L. (2002). Nontherapeutic research with children: *Grimes v Kennedy Krieger Institute. American Journal of Public Health, 92,* 1070–1073.

Glaser, B. G., & Strauss, A. L. (1967). *The discovery of grounded theory: Strategies for qualitative research.* Chicago, IL: Aldine.

Glass, G. V. (1976). Primary, secondary, and meta-analysis of research. *Educational Researcher, 5*(10), 3–8. doi:10.3102/0013189X005010003

Goldberg, P. (1968). Are women prejudiced against women? *Transaction, 5,* 28–30.

Goldman, B. A., & Mitchell, D. F. (2008). *Directory of unpublished experimental mental measures* (Vol. 9). Washington, DC: American Psychological Association.

Goldstein, E. B. (2010). *Encyclopedia of perception* (Vols. 1 & 2). Thousand Oaks, CA: Sage.

Göritz, A. S. (2010). Using lotteries, loyalty points, and other incentives to increase participant response and completion. In S. D. Gosling & J. A. Johnson (Eds.), *Advanced methods for conducting online behavioral research* (pp. 219–233). Washington, DC: American Psychological Association.

Gosling, S. D., & Johnson, J. A. (Eds.). (2010). *Advanced methods for conducting online behavioral research.* Washington, DC: American Psychological Association.

Gosling, S. D., Ko, S. J., Mannarelli, T., & Morris, M. E. (2002). A room with a cue: Personality judgments based on offices and bedrooms. *Journal of Personality and Social Psychology, 82,* 379–398. doi:10.1037/0022-3514.82.3.379

Gosling, S. D., Vazire, S., Srivastava, S., & John, O. P. (2004). Should we trust Web-based studies? A comparative analysis of six preconceptions about Internet questionnaires. *American Psychologist, 59,* 93–104. doi:10.1037/0003-066X.59.2.93

Graham, M., Milanowski, A., & Miller, J. (2012, February). Measuring and promoting inter-rater agreement of teacher and principal ratings. *Center for Education Compensation Reform.* Retrieved from http://files.eric.ed.gov/fulltext/ED532068.pdf

Grammer, J. K., Coffman, J. L., Ornstein, P. A., & Morrison, P. A. (2013). Change over time: Conducting longitudinal studies of children's cognitive development. *Journal of Cognitive Development, 14,* 515–528. doi:10.1080/15248372.2013.833925

Grant, R. W., & Sugarman, J. (2004). Ethics in human subjects research. Do incentives matter? *Journal of Medicine and Philosophy, 29,* 717–738.

Gravetter, F. J., & Forzano, L.-A. B. (2016). *Research methods for the behavioral sciences* (5th ed.). Stamford, CT: Cengage Learning.

Greenwald, A. G. (1976). Within-subjects design: To use or not to use? *Psychological Bulletin, 83,* 314–320. doi:10.1037/0033-2909.83.2.314

Greenwald, A. G., McGhee, D. E., & Schwartz, J. L. K. (1998). Measuring individual differences in implicit cognition: The implicit association test. *Journal of Personality and Social Psychology, 74,* 1464–1480. doi:10.1037/0022-3514.74.6.1464

Greenwald, A. G., Nosek, B. A., & Banaji, M. R. (2003). Understanding and using the Implicit Association Test. I. An improved scoring algorithm. *Journal of Personality and Social Psychology, 85,* 197–216. doi:10.1037/0022-3514.85.2.197

Grigorenko, E. L. (2000). Doing data analyses and writing up their results: Selected tricks and artifices. In R. J. Sternberg (Ed.), *Guide to publishing in psychology journals* (pp. 98–120). New York, NY: Cambridge University Press.

Grimes v Kennedy Krieger Institute. 366 Md. 29; 782 A.2d 807 (2001).

Groopman, J. (2007). *How doctors think.* Boston, MA: Houghton Mifflin.

Guthrie, R. V. (1976). *Even the rat was white: A historical view of psychology.* New York, NY: Harper & Row.

Hallgren, K. A. (2012). Computing inter-rater reliability for observational data: An overview and tutorial. *Tutorials in Quantitative Methods for Psychology, 8*(1), 23–34.

Haney, C., Banks, W. C., & Zimbardo, P. G. (1973). A study of prisoners and guards in a simulated prison. *Naval Research Review, 30,* 4–17.

Hardin, P. J., & Shumway, J. M. (1997). Statistical significance and normalized confusion matrices. *Photogrammetric Engineering and Remote Sensing, 62,* 735–740.

Hathorn, K., & Nanda, U. (2008). A guide to evidence-based art. Retrieved from https://www.healthdesign.org/sites/default/files/Hathorn_Nanda_Mar08.pdf

Heinberg, L. J., Thompson, J. K., & Stormer, S. (1995). Development and validation of the Sociocultural Attitudes toward Appearance Questionnaire. *International Journal of Eating Disorders, 17,* 81–89.

Hennink, M. M. (2014). *Focus group discussions.* New York, NY: Oxford University Press.

Henrich, J., Heine, S. J., & Norenzayan, A. (2010). The weirdest people in the world. *Behavioral and Brain Sciences, 33*(2–3), 61–83. doi:10.1017/S0140525X0999152X

Herd, P., Carr, D., & Roan, C. (2014). Cohort profile: Wisconsin Longitudinal Study (WLS). *International Journal of Epidemiology, 43,* 34–41. doi:10.1093/ije/dys194

Hertwig, R., & Ortmann, A. (2008a). Deception in experiments: Revisiting the arguments in its defense. *Ethics & Behavior, 18,* 59–92. doi:10.1080/10508420701712990

Hertwig, R., & Ortmann, A. (2008b). Deception in social psychological experiments: Misconceptions and a research agenda. *Social Psychology Quarterly, 71,* 222–227. doi:10.1177/019027250807100304

Heuchert, J., & McNair, D. M. (n.d.). *POMS2®. Profile of Mood States 2nd Edition™.* Retrieved from

http://www.mhs.com/product.aspx?gr=cli&id=overview&prod=poms2

Higgerson, R. A., Olsho, L. E. W., Christie, L.-A. M., Rehder, K., Doksum, K., Gedeit, R., . . . Randolph, A. G. (2014). Variability in IRBs regarding parental acceptance of passive consent. *Pediatrics, 134*(2), 1–8. doi:10.1542/peds.2013-4190

Holmes, D. S. (1976a). Debriefing after psychological experiments: 1. Effectiveness of postdeception dehoaxing. *American Psychologist, 31,* 858–867.

Holmes, D. S. (1976b). Debriefing after psychological experiments: 2. Effectiveness of postdeception desensitizing. *American Psychologist, 31,* 868–875.

Holmes, T. H., & Rahe, R. H. (1967). The Social Readjustment Rating Scale. *Journal of Psychosomatic Research, 11,* 213–218.

Howell, D. C. (2007). *Statistical methods for psychology* (6th ed.). Belmont, CA: Thomson/Wadsworth.

Howell, D. C. (2013). *Statistical methods for psychology* (8th ed.). Belmont, CA: Wadsworth/Cengage Learning.

Howland, J. (2010). How scholarly is Google Scholar? A comparison of Google Scholar to library databases. Retrieved from http://www.jaredhowland.com/presentations/google-scholar-norway/

Iaffaldano, M. T., & Muchinsky, P. M. (1985). Job satisfaction and performance: A meta-analysis. *Psychological Bulletin, 97,* 251–273. doi:10.1037/0033-2909.97.2.251

Ibrahim, S., & Sidani, S. (2014). Strategies to recruit minority persons: A systematic review. *Journal of Immigrant and Minority*

Health, 16, 882–888. doi:10.1007/s10903-013-9783-y

Ittelson, W. H. (1962). Perception and transactional psychology. In S. Koch (Ed.), *Psychology: A study of a science* (Vol. 4, pp. 660–704). New York, NY: McGraw-Hill.

Jaccard, J., Becker, M. A., & Woods, G. (1984). Pairwise multiple comparison procedures: A review. *Psychological Bulletin, 96,* 589–596. doi:10.1037/0033-2909.96.3.589

Jackson, D. A., Della-Piana, G. M., & Sloane, H. N. (1975). *How to establish a behavior observation system.* Englewood Cliffs, NJ: Educational Technology.

Jensen, P. S., Fisher, C. B., & Hoagwood, K. (1999). Special issues in mental health/illness research with children and adolescents. In H. A. Pincus, J. A. Lieberman, & S. Ferris (Eds.), *Ethics in psychiatric research: A resource manual for human subjects protection* (pp. 159–175). Washington, DC: American Psychiatric Association.

Johl, S. K., & Renganathan, S. (2010). Strategies for gaining access in doing fieldwork: Reflection of two researchers. *The Electronic Journal of Business Research Methods, 8,* 42–50.

John, O. P., Donahue, E. M., & Kentle, R. L. (1991). *The Big Five Inventory–Versions 4a and 54.* Berkeley: University of California, Berkeley, Institute of Personality and Social Research.

Johnson, D. R., & Borden, L. A. (2012). Participants at your fingertips: Using Amazon's Mechanical Turk to increase student-faculty collaborative research. *Teaching of Psychology, 39,* 245–251. doi:10.1177/0098628312456615

Jones, J. (1981). *Bad blood*. New York, NY: The Free Press.

Kahneman, D. (1991). Judgment and decision making: A personal view. *Psychological Science, 2*, 142–145. doi:10.1111/j.1467-9280.1991. tb00121.x

Kahneman, D., & Tversky, A. (1972). Subjective probability: A judgment of representativeness. *Cognitive Psychology, 3*, 430–454. doi:10.1016/0010-0285(72)90016-3

Kahneman, D., & Tversky, A. (1973). On the psychology of prediction. *Psychological Review, 80*, 237–251. doi:10.1037/h0034747

Kahneman, D., & Tversky, A. (1979). Prospect theory: An analysis of decisions under risk. *Econometrica, 47*, 23–291. doi:10.2307/1914185

Kamberelis, G., & Dimitriadis, G. (2005). Focus groups: Strategic articulations of pedagogy, politics, and inquiry. In N. K. Denzin & Y. S. Lincoln (Eds.), *The Sage handbook of qualitative research* (3rd ed., pp. 887–907). Thousand Oaks, CA: Sage.

Kaplan, S. (1995). The restorative benefits of nature: Toward an integrative framework. *Environmental Psychology, 15*, 169–182. doi:10.1016/0272-4944(95)90001-2

Kavanagh, D. (Producer), & Sargent, J. (Director). (1997). *Miss Evers' Boys* [Television movie]. USA: HBO NYC Productions.

Kazdin, A. E. (2000). *Encyclopedia of psychology* (Vols. 1–8). Washington, DC: American Psychological Association.

Kendall, P. C., Silk, J. S., & Chu, B. C. (2000). Introducing your research report: Writing the introduction. In R. J. Sternberg (Ed.), *Guide to publishing in psychology journals* pp. (41–57). New York, NY: Cambridge University Press.

Keppel, G. (1982). *Design and analysis: A researcher's handbook* (2nd ed.). Englewood Cliffs, NJ: Prentice-Hall.

Kerr, N. L. (1998). HARKing: Hypothesizing after the results are known. *Personality and Social Psychology Review, 2*, 196–217. doi:10.1207/s15327957pspr0203_4

Keyser, D. J., & Sweetland, R. C. (Eds.). (1987). *Tests critiques compendium: Reviews of major tests from the test critiques series.* Kansas City, MO: Test Corporation of America.

Kimmel, A. J. (2011). Deception in psychological research—a necessary evil? *The Psychologist, 24*, 580–585. Retrieved from https://thepsychologist.bps.org.uk/ volume-24/edition-8/deception-psychological-research-necessary-evil

Kimmel, A. J., Smith, N. C., & Klein, J. G. (2011). Ethical decision making and research deception in the behavioral sciences: An application of social contract theory. *Ethics & Behavior, 21*, 222–251. doi:10.1080/1 0508422.2011.570166

Kluger, J. (2006, November 26). How Americans are living dangerously. *Time Magazine.* http:// content.time.com/time/magazine/ article/0,9171,1562978,00.html

Kongsved, S. M., Basnov, M., Holm-Christensen, K., & Hjollund, N. H. (2007). Response rate and completeness of questionnaires: A randomized study of Internet versus paper-and-pencil versions. *Journal of Medical Internet Research, 9*, 39–48. doi:10.2196/ jmir.9.3.e25

Kosinski, M., Matz, S. C., Gosling, S. D., Popov, V., & Stillwell, D. (2015). Facebook as a research tool for the social sciences: Opportunities, challenges, ethical considerations, and practical guidelines. *American Psychologist, 70*, 543–556. doi:10.1037/a0039210

Kramer, A. D. I., Guillory, J. E., & Hancock, J. T. (2014, June 17). Experimental evidence of massive-scale emotional contagion through social networks. *Proceedings of the National Academy of Sciences, 111*, 8788–8790. doi:10.1073/ pnas.1320040111

Kraut, R., Olson, J., Banaji, M., Bruckman, A., Cohen, J., & Couper, M. (2004). Psychological research online: Report of Board of Scientific Affairs' Advisory Group on the Conduct of Research on the Internet. *American Psychologist, 59*, 105–117. doi:10.1037/0003-066X.59.2.105

Krueger, R. A., & Casey, M. A. (2009). *Focus groups: A practical guide for applied research* (4th ed.). Thousand Oaks, CA: Sage.

Kvale, S. (2003). The psychoanalytical interview as inspiration for qualitative research. In P. M. Camic, J. E. Rhodes, & L. Yardley (Eds.), *Qualitative research in psychology: Expanding perspectives in methodology and design* (pp. 275–297). Washington, DC: American Psychological Association.

LaCour, M., & Green, D. (2014, November 7). When contact changes minds: An experiment on transmission of support for gay equality. *Science, 346*, 1366–1369. doi:10.1126/science.1256151

Lance, C. E., Butts, M. M., & Michels, L. C. (2006). The sources of four commonly reported cutoff criteria: What did they really say? *Organizational Research Methods, 9,* 202–220. doi:10.1177/1094428105284919

Landis, J. R., & Koch, G. G. (1977). The measurement of observer agreement for categorical data. *Biometrics, 33,* 159–174. Retrieved from http://www.jstor.org/stable/2529310

Landrum, R. E. (1999). Introduction. In G. Chastain & R. E. Landrum (Eds.), *Protecting human subjects: Departmental subject pools and institutional review boards* (pp. 3–19). Washington, DC: American Psychological Association.

Larrañeta, I. E. (2000, September 8). Man 'too smart to be cop' loses federal appeal. *The New London Day,* p. C1.

Leentjens, A. F. G., & Levenson, J. L. 2013. Ethical issues concerning the recruitment of university students as research subjects. *Journal of Psychosomatic Research, 75,* 394–398. doi:10.1016/j.jpsychores.2013.03.007

Lesieur, H. R., & Blume, S. B. (1987). The South Oaks Gambling Screen (SOGS): A new instrument for the identification of pathological gamblers. *American Journal of Psychiatry, 144,* 1184–1188.

Leslie, M. (2000, July–August). The vexing legacy of Lewis Terman. *Stanford Alumni Magazine.* Retrieved from https://alumni.stanford.edu/get/page/magazine/article/?article_id=40678

Litman, L., Robinson, J., & Rosenzweig, C. (2015). The relationship between motivation, monetary compensation, and data quality among US- and India-based workers on Mechanical Turk. *Behavioral Research Methods, 47,* 519–528. doi:10.3758/s13428-014-0483-x

Loftus, E. F., Loftus, G. R., & Messo, J. (1987). Some facts about "weapon focus." *Law and Human Behavior, 11,* 55–62. doi:10.1007/BF01044839

Long, L. D., & Kujawa, K. (2015). Is three a crowd? Exploring the development and satisfaction of students in triples. *The Journal of College and University Student Housing, 41*(2), 62–77.

Lynch, K. (1960). *The image of the city.* Cambridge, MA: The MIT Press.

Maloney, D. M. (1984). *Protection of human research subjects: A practical guide to federal laws and regulations.* New York, NY: Plenum Press.

Mann, T. C., & Ferguson, M. (2014). Can we undo our first impressions? The role of reinterpretation in reversing implicit evaluations. *Journal of Personality and Social Psychology, 108,* 823–849. doi:10.1037/pspa0000021

Martin, D. (2007). *Doing psychology experiments* (7th ed.). Boston, MA: Cengage Learning.

Mathes, S., & Battista, R. (1985). College men's and women's motives for participation in physical activity. *Perceptual and Motor Skills, 61,* 719–726. doi:10.2466/pms.1985.61.3.719

McConahay, J. B. (1986). Modern racism, ambivalence, and the Modern Racism Scale. In J. F. Dovidio, & S. L. Gaertner (Eds.), *Prejudice, discrimination, and racism* (pp. 91–125). San Diego, CA: Academic Press.

McConahay, J. B., Hardee, B. B., & Batts, V. (1981). Has racism declined in America? It depends on who is asking and what is asked. *The Journal of Conflict Resolution, 25,* 563–579. doi:10.1177/00220 0278102500401

McCrae, R. R., Costa, P. T., Jr., & Martin, T. A. (2005). The NEO-PI-3: A more readable revised NEO Personality Inventory. *Journal of Personality Assessment, 84,* 261–270. doi:10.1207/s15327752jpa8403_05

McCosker, H., Barnard, A., & Gerber, R. (2001). Undertaking sensitive research: Issues and strategies for meeting the safety needs of all participants. *Forum Qualitative Sozialforschung/Forum: Qualitative Social Research, 2*(1), Art. 22. Retrieved from http://nbn-resolving.de/urn:nbn:de:0114-fqs0101220

McEvoy, J. P., & Keefe, R. S. E. (1999). Informing subjects of risks and benefits. In H. A. Pincus, J. A. Lieberman, & S. Ferris (Eds.), *Ethics in psychiatric research: A resource manual for human subjects protection* (pp. 129–157). Washington, DC: American Psychiatric Association.

McEwen, B. S. (2000). Allostasis and allostatic load: Implications for neuropsychopharmacology. *Neuropsychopharmacology, 22,* 108–124. doi:10.1016/S0893-133X(99)00129-3

McHugh, M. L. (2012). Interrater reliability: The Kappa statistic. *Biochemia Medica, 22,* 276–282.

McIntire, M. E. (2015, June 18). Universities ban smart watches. Wired Campus section. *The Chronicle of Higher Education.* Retrieved from http://chronicle.com/blogs/wiredcampus/universities-ban-smart-watches-during-finals/57003

McQuistion, H. L., Sowers, W. E., Ranz, J. M., & Feldman, J. M. (2012). *Handbook of community psychiatry.* New York: Springer.

Meltzoff, J. (1998). *Critical thinking about research: Psychology and related fields.* Washington,

DC: American Psychological Association.

Melzack, R. (1975). The McGill Pain Questionnaire: Major properties and scoring methods. *Pain, 1,* 277–299. doi:10.1016/0304-3959(75)90044-5

Mendelson, B. K., & White, D. R. (1982). Relation between body-esteem and self-esteem of obese and normal children. *Perceptual and Motor Skills, 54,* 899–905.

Mercer, A., Caporaso, A., Cantor, D., & Townsend, R. (2015). How much gets you how much? Monetary incentives and response rates in household surveys. *Public Opinion Quarterly, 70,* 105–129. doi:10.1093/poq/nfu059

Meyer, M. (2014, June 29). How an IRB could have legitimately approved the Facebook experiment–and why that may be a good thing. *The Faculty Lounge: Conversations about law, culture, and academia.* Retrieved from http://www.thefacultylounge.org/2014/06/how-an-irb-could-have-legitimately-approved-the-facebook-experimentand-why-that-may-be-a-good-thing.html

Mikulinsky, R. (2002). *Vocational indecision in adolescents enrolled in college and secondary school.* Unpublished honors theses. New London, CT: Connecticut College.

Milgram, S. (1963). Behavioral study of obedience. *Journal of Abnormal and Social Psychology, 67,* 371–378. doi:10.1037/h0040525

Milgram, S. (1974). *Obedience to authority: An experimental view.* New York: Harper & Row.

Minsky, M. (1985). *The society of mind.* New York, NY: Simon & Schuster.

Moos, R. H. (1968). The development of a menstrual distress

questionnaire. *Psychosomatic Medicine, 30,* 853–867.

Moos, R. H., & Moos, B. S. (1976). A typology of family social environments. *Family Process, 15,* 357–371. doi:10.1111/j.1545-5300.1976.00357.x

Mora, M. (2013, September 14). Three popular online survey tools–What they give for free. Retrieved from http://www.relevantinsights.com/free-online-survey-tools#sthash.AMHkZoKV.aaqzsRyn.dpbs

Nagata, D. K., Suzuki, L. A., & Kohn-Wood, L. (2012). Qualitative research with ethnocultural populations: Addressing the unique challenges of relationship, role, and context. In D. K. Nagata, L. Kohn-Wood, & L. A. Suzuki (Eds.), *Qualitative strategies for ethnocultural research* (pp. 9–18). Washington, DC: American Psychological Association.

Nasar, J. L., & Devlin, A. S. (2011). Impressions of psychotherapists' offices. *Journal of Counseling Psychology, 58,* 310–320. doi:10.1037/a0023887

Nasar, J. L., & Stamps, A. E., III (2009). Infill McMansions: Style and the psychophysics of size. *Journal of Environmental Psychology, 29,* 110–123. doi:10.1016/j.jenvp.2008.09.003

National Research Act. P.L. 93–348, 42 U.S.C. (1974).

Neisser, U. (1978). Memory: What are the important questions? In M. M. Gruneberg, P. E. Morris, & R. N. Sykes (Eds.), *Practical aspects of memory* (pp. 3–24). London, England: Academic Press.

Nelson, R. M. (2002). Research involving children. In R. J. Amdur & E. A. Bankert (Eds.), *Institutional review board management and*

function (pp. 383–388). Mississauga, Ontario, Canada: Jones and Bartlett.

Nezu, A. M., Ronan, G. F., Meadows, E. A., & McClure, K. S. (2000). *Practitioner's guide to empirically based measures of depression.* New York, NY: Springer.

Nier, J. A., Bajaj, P., McLean, M. C., & Schwartz, E. (2013). Group status, perceptions of agency, and the correspondence bias: Attributional processes in the formation of stereotypes about high and low status groups. *Group Processes & Intergroup Relations, 16,* 476–487. doi:10.1177/1368430212454925

Nier, J. A., Mottola, G. R., & Gaertner, S. L. (2000). The O. J. Simpson verdict as a racially symbolic event: A longitudinal analysis of racial attitude change. *Personality and Social Psychology Bulletin, 26,* 507–516. doi:10.1177/0146167200266009

No Child Left Behind Act (NCLB). P.L. 107–110 (2001).

Nouri, A., & Sajjadi, S. M. (2014). Emancipatory pedagogy in practice: Aims, principles and curriculum orientation. *The International Journal of Critical Pedagogy, 5,* 76–87.

Nunnally, J. C. (1978). *Psychometric theory* (2nd ed.). New York, NY: McGraw-Hill.

Oakes, J. M. (2002). Risks and wrongs in social science research: An evaluator's guide to the IRB. *Evaluation Review, 26,* 443–479. doi:10.1177/019384102236520

Oldham, G. R., & Brass, D. J. (1979). Employee reactions to an open-plan office: A naturally occurring quasi-experiment. *Administrative Science Quarterly, 24,* 267–284. doi:10.2307/2392497

Open Science Collaboration. (2015, August 28). Estimating the reproducibility of psychological science. *Science, 349.* doi:10.1126/science.aac4716

Orne, M. T. (1962). On the social psychology of the psychological experiment: With particular reference of demand characteristics and their implications. *American Psychologist, 17,* 776–783. doi:10.1037/h0043424

Paolacci, G., & Chandler, J. (2014). Inside the Turk: Understanding Mechanical Turk as a participant pool. *Current Directions in Psychological Science, 23,* 184–188. doi:10.1177/0963721414531598

Park, R. E., & Burgess, E. W. (1924). *Introduction to the science of sociology.* Chicago, IL: The University of Chicago Press.

Pattullo, E. L. (1984). Institutional review boards and social research: A disruptive, subjective perspective, retrospective and prospective. In J. E. Sieber (Ed.), *NIH readings on the protection of human subjects in behavioral and social science research* (pp. 10–17). Frederick, MD: University Publications of America.

Paulhus, D. L. (1984). Two component models of socially desirable responding. *Journal of Personality and Social Psychology, 46,* 598–609. doi:10.1037/t08059-000

Paulhus, D. L. (1991). Measurement and control of response bias. In J. P. Robinson, P. R. Shaver, L. S. Wrightsman, & F. M. Andrews (Eds.), *Measures of personality and social psychological attitudes* (pp. 17–59). San Diego, CA: Academic Press.

Peer, E., Vosgerau, J., & Acquisti, A. (2014). Reputation as a sufficient condition for data quality on Amazon Mechanical Turk. Behavior. *Behavior*

Research Methods, 46, 1023–1031. doi:10.3758/s13428-013-0434-y

Pietschnig, J., Voracek, M., & Formann, A. K. (2010). Mozart effect-Shmozart effect: A meta-analysis. *Intelligence, 38,* 314–323. doi:10.1016/j.inte11.2010.03.001

Pigott, T. D. (2001). A review of methods for missing data. *Educational Research and Evaluation, 7,* 353–383. doi:10.1076/edre.7.4.353.8937

Piocuda, J. E., Smyers, J. O., Knyshev, E., Harris, R. J., & Rai, M. (2015). Trends of internationalization and collaboration in U.S. psychology journals, 1950–2010. *Archives of Scientific Psychology, 3,* 82–92. doi:10.1037/arc0000020

Poulton, E. (1973). Unwanted range effects from using with-subjects experimental designs. *Psychological Bulletin, 81,* 201–203. doi:10.1037/h0034731

Presley, C. A., Meilman, P. W., & Lyerla, R. (1994). Development of the Core Alcohol and Drug Survey: Initial findings and future directions. *Journal of American College Health, 42,* 248–255. doi:10.1080/07448481.1994.9936356

Pulfrey, C., & Butera, F. (2013). Why neoliberal values of self-enhancement lead to cheating in higher education: A motivational account. *Psychological Science, 24,* 2153–2162. doi:10.1177/0956797613487221

Quinn, C. R. (2015). General considerations for research with vulnerable populations. *Health & Justice, 3*(1), 1–7. doi:10.1186/s40352-014-0013-z

Rauscher, F. H., Shaw, G. L., & Kay, K. N. (1993). Music and spatial task performance. *Nature, 365,* 311. doi:10.1038/365611a0

Reis, H. T. (2000). Writing effectively about design. In R. J. Sternberg (Ed.), *Guide to publishing in psychology journals* (pp. 81–97). New York, NY: Cambridge University Press.

Remnick, D. (1997, October 20 & 27). The next magic kingdom: Future perfect. *The New Yorker,* 210–224. Retrieved from http://www.newyorker.com/magazine/the-next-magic-kingdom

Rennie, D. L. (1999). Qualitative research: A matter of hermeneutics and the sociology of knowledge. In M. Kopala & L. A. Suzuki (Eds.), *Using qualitative methods in psychology* (pp. 3–13). Thousand Oaks, CA: Sage

Roberts, B. W., & DelVecchio, W. F. (2000). The rank-order consistency of personality traits from childhood to old age: A quantitative review of longitudinal studies. *Psychological Bulletin, 126,* 3–25. doi:10.1037//0033-2909.126.1.3

Roberts, L. D., & Allen, P. J. (2015). Exploring ethical issues associated with using online surveys in educational research. *Educational Research and Evaluation: An International Journal on Theory and Practice, 21*(2), 95–108. doi:10.1080/13803611.2015.1024421

Rosenberg, M. (1965). *Society and the adolescent self-image.* Princeton, NJ: Princeton University Press.

Rosenthal, R. (1979). The "file drawer problem" and tolerance for null results. *Psychological Bulletin, 86,* 638–641. doi:10.1037/0033-2909.86.3.638

Rozin, P. (2009). What kind of empirical research should we publish, fund, and reward? A different perspective. *Perspectives on Psychological Science, 4,* 435–439. doi:10.1111/j.1745-6924.2009.01151.x

Salovey, P. (2000). Results that get results: Telling a good story. In R. J. Sternberg (Ed.), *Guide to publishing in psychology journals* (pp. 121–132). New York, NY: Cambridge University Press.

Sarkar, A., Dutta, A., Dhingra, U., Dinghra, P., Verma, P., Juyal, R., . . . Sazawal, S. (2006). Development and use of behavior and social interaction software installed on Palm handheld for observation of a child's social interactions with the environment. *Behavior Research Methods, 38,* 407–415. doi:10.3758/BF03192794

Schafer, J. L., & Graham, J. W. (2002). Missing data: Our view of the state of the art. *Psychological Methods, 7,* 147–177. doi:10.1037//1082-989X.7.2.147

Scheier, M. F., & Carver, C. S. (1985). Optimism, coping, and health: Assessment and implications of generalized outcome expectancies. *Health Psychology, 4,* 219–247. doi:10.1037/0278-6133.4.3.219

Schlomer, G. L., Bauman, S., & Card, N. A. (2010). Best practices for missing data management in counseling psychology. *Journal of Counseling Psychology, 57,* 1–10. doi:10.1037/a0018082

Schmitt, N., Keeney, J., Oswald, F. L., Pleskac, T. J., Billington, A. Q., Sinha R., & Zorzie, M. (2009). Prediction of 4-year college student performance using cognitive and noncognitive predictors and the impact on demographic status of admitted students. *Journal of Applied Psychology, 94,* 1479–1497. doi:10.1037/a0016810

Schneider, C. E. (2015). *The censor's hand: The misregulation of human-subject research.* Cambridge, MA: MIT Press.

Schultz, P. W., Messina, A., Tronu, G., Limas, E. F., Gupta, R., & Estrada, M. (2016). Personalized normative feedback and the moderating role of personal norms: A field experiment to reduce residential water consumption. *Environment & Behavior, 48,* 686–710. doi:10.1177/0013916514553835

Schwarz, N. (1999). Self-reports: How the questions shape the answers. *American Psychologist, 54,* 93–105. doi:10.1037//0003-066X.54.2.93

Scoville, W. B., & Milner, B. J. (1957). Loss or recent memory after bilateral hippocampal lesions. *Journal of Neurology, Neurosurgery, & Psychiatry, 20,* 11–20. doi:10.1136/jnnp.20.1.11

Sedlmeier, P., Hertwig, R., & Gigerenzer, G. (1998). Are judgments of the positional frequencies of letters systematically biased due to availability? *Journal of Experimental Psychology: Learning, Memory, and Cognition, 24,* 754–770.

Shadish, W. R., Cook, T. D., & Campbell, D. T. (2002). *Experimental and quasi-experimental designs for generalized causal inference.* Boston, MA: Houghton Mifflin.

Sherer, M., Maddox, J. E., Mercandante, B., Prentice-Dunn, S., Jacobs, B., & Rogers, R. W. (1982). The Self-Efficacy Scale: Construction and validation. *Psychological Reports, 51,* 663–671.

Shermer, M. (1997). *Why people believe weird things: Pseudoscience, superstition, and other confusions of our time.* New York, NY: W. H. Freeman.

Sieber, J. E. (1992). *Planning ethically responsible research: A guide for students and internal review boards.* Newbury Park, CA: Sage.

Sieber, J. E., & Saks, M. J. (1989). A census of subject pool characteristics and policies. *American Psychologist, 44,* 1053–1061. doi:10.1037/0003-066X.44.7.1053

Simmons, J. P., Nelson, L. D., & Simonsohn, U. (2011). False-positive psychology: Undisclosed flexibility in data collection and analysis allows presenting anything as significant. *Psychological Science, 22,* 1359–1366. doi:10.1177/0956797611417632

Simonsohn, U., Nelson, L. D., & Simmons, J. P. (2014). *P*-curve: A key to the file-drawer. *Journal of Experimental Psychology: General, 143,* 534–547. doi:10.1037/a0033242

Singer, E., & Couper, M. P. (2008). Do incentives exert undue influence on survey participation? Experimental evidence. *Journal of Empirical Research on Human Research Ethics, 3*(3), 49–56. doi:10.1525/jer.2008.3.3.49

Singer, J., Rexhaj, B., & Baddeley, J. (2007). Older, wiser, and happier? Comparing older adults' and college students' self-defining memories. *Memory, 15,* 886–898. doi:10.1080/09658210701754351

Slater, M., Antley, A., Davison, A., Swapp, D., Guger, C., Barker, C., . . . Sanchez-Vives, M. V. (2006). A virtual reprise of the Stanley Milgram obedience experiments. *PloSONE, 1,* 1–10. doi:10.1371/journal.pone.0000039

Slone, E., Burles, F., Robinson, K., Levy, R. M., & Iaria, G. (2015). Floor plan connectivity influences wayfinding performance in virtual environments. *Environment and Behavior, 47,* 1024–1053. doi:10.1177/0013916514533189

Smail, M. M., DeYoung, A. J., & Moos, R. H. (1974). The University Residence

Environment Scale: A method for describing university student living groups. *Journal of College Student Personnel, 15,* 357–365.

Smith, S. S., & Richardson, D. (1983). Amelioration of deception and harm in psychological research: The important role of debriefing. *Journal of Personality and Social Psychology, 44,* 1075–1082. doi:10.1037/0022-3514.44.5.1075

Solberg, L. (2010). Data mining on Facebook: A free space for researchers or an IRB nightmare? *Journal of Law, Technology, and Policy, 2,* 311–343.

Sparkman, L. (2015, July 17). Philip Zimbardo reflects on "The Stanford Prison Experiment" movie. *The Stanford Daily.* Retrieved from http://www.stanforddaily .com/2015/07/17/philip-zimbardo- reflects-on-the-stanford-prison- experiment-movie/

Spence, J. T., Helmreich, R., & Stapp, J. (1973). A short version of the Attitudes toward Women Scale (AWS). *Journal of the Bulletin of the Psychonomic Society, 2,* 219–220. doi:10.3758/BF03329252

Sperling, G. (1960). The information available in brief visual presentations. *Psychological Monographs: General and Applied, 74*(11), 1–29. doi:10.1037/h0093759

Spielberger, C. D., Gorsuch, R. L., & Lushene, R. E. (1970). *The State-Trait Anxiety Inventory: Test manual.* Palo Alto, CA: Consulting Psychologists Press.

Spoor, J. R., & Kelly, J. R. (2009). Mood congruence in dyads: Effects of valence and leadership. *Social Influence, 4,* 282–297. doi:10.1080/15534510902805366

Squire, L. R. (2009). The legacy of patient H. M. for neuroscience.

Neuron, 61(1), 6–9. doi:10.1016/j. neuron.2008.12.023

St. Pierre, M., & Wong, A. (2003). Accuracy of memory recall for eyewitness events. *Connecticut College Psychology Journal, 15,* 44–49.

Stake, R. E. (2005). Qualitative case studies. In N. K. Denzin & Y. S. Lincoln (Eds.), *The Sage handbook of qualitative research* (3rd ed., pp. 443–466). Thousand Oaks, CA: Sage.

Starks, H., & Brown Trinidad, S. (2007). Choose your method: A comparison of phenomenology, discourse analysis, and grounded theory. *Qualitative Health Research, 17,* 1372–1380. doi:10.1177/1049732307307031

Steen, R. G. (2011a). Retractions in the scientific literature: Do authors deliberately commit research fraud? *Journal of Medical Ethics, 37,* 113–117. doi:10.1136/jme.2010.038125

Steen, R. G. (2011b). Retractions in the scientific literature: Is the incidence of research fraud increasing? *Journal of Medical Ethics, 37,* 249–253. doi:10.1136/ jme.2010.040923

Sternberg, R. J. (1994). *Encyclopedia of human intelligence* (Vols. 1 & 2). New York, NY: Macmillan.

Sternberg, R. J. (Ed.) (2000a). *Guide to publishing in psychology journals.* New York, NY: Cambridge University Press.

Sternberg, R. J. (2000b). Titles and abstracts: They only sound unimportant. In R. J. Sternberg (Ed.), *Guide to publishing in psychology journals* (pp. 37–40). New York, NY: Cambridge University Press.

Stevens, S. S. (1946). On the theory of scales of measurement. *Science,*

103(2684), 677–680. doi:10.1126/ science.103.2684.677

Stoline, M. R. (1981). The status of multiple comparisons: Simultaneous estimation of all pairwise comparisons in one-way ANOVA designs. *The American Statistician, 35,* 134–141. doi:10.2307/268379

Sutton, S., Baum, A., & Johnston, M. (2004). *The SAGE handbook of health psychology.* Thousand Oaks, CA: Sage.

Swami, V., Salem, N., Furnham, A., & Tovée, M. J. (2008). Initial examination of the validity and reliability of the female photo- graphic figure rating scale for body image assessment. *Personality and Individual Differences, 44,* 1752–1761. doi:10.1016/j.paid.2008.02.002

Swim, J. K., Aikin, K. J., Hall, W. S., & Hunter, B. A. (1995). Sexism and racism: Old-fashioned and modern prejudices. *Journal of Personality and Social Psychology, 68,* 199–214. doi:10.1037/0022- 3514.68.2.199

Swim, J. K., Borgida, E., Maruyama, G., & Myers, D. G. (1989). Joan McKay versus John McKay: Do gender stereotypes bias evaluations? *Psychological Bulletin, 105,* 409–429. doi:10.1037/0033- 2909.105.3.409

Tabachnick, B. G., & Fidell, L. S. (1983). *Using multivariate statistics.* New York, NY: Harper & Row.

Tatsuoka, M. M. (1988). *Multivariate analysis: Techniques for educational and psychological research* (2nd ed.). New York, NY: Macmillan.

Terman, L. M., & Oden, M. H. (1959). *The gifted group at mid-life: Thirty- five years' follow-up of the superior child.* Stanford, CA: Stanford University Press.

Thomas, S. J. (2004). *Using Web and paper questionnaires for data-based decision making: From design to interpretation of the results.* Thousand Oaks, CA: Corwin Press.

Trafimow, D., & Marks, M. (2015). Editorial. *Basic and Applied Social Psychology, 37,* 1–2. doi:10.1080/019 73533.2015.1012991

Trigwell, J. L., Francis, A. J. P., & Bagot, K. L. (2014). Nature connectedness and eduaimonic well-being: Spirituality as a potential mediator. *Ecopsychology, 6,* 241–251. doi:10.1089/ ec0.2014.0025

Tuleya, L. G. (2007). *Thesaurus of psychological index terms* (11th ed., revised). Washington, DC: American Psychological Association.

Tuten, T. L. (2010). Conducting online surveys. In S. D. Gosling & J. A. Johnson (Eds.), *Advanced methods for conducting online behavioral research* (pp. 179–192). Washington, DC: American Psychological Association.

Tversky, A., & Kahneman, D. (1971). Belief in the law of small numbers. *Psychological Bulletin, 76,* 105–110. doi:10.1037/h0031322

Tversky, A., & Kahneman, D. (1973). Availability: A heuristic for judging frequency and probability. *Cognitive Psychology, 5,* 207–232. doi:10.1016/0010-0285(73)90033-9

Tversky, A., & Kahneman, D. (1974). Judgment under uncertainty: Heuristics and biases. *Science, 185,* 1124–1131. doi:10.1136/ science.185.4157.1124

Ulrich, R. S. (1984). View through a window may influence recovery from surgery. *Science, 224,* 420–421. Retrieved from http://www.jstor .org/stable/1692984

Ulrich, R. S. (1991). Effects of interior design on wellness: Theory and recent scientific research. *Journal of Health Care Interior Design, 3,* 97–109.

University of Chicago Press. (2010). *The Chicago manual of style* (16th ed.). Chicago, IL: Author.

Vandenberg, S. G., & Kuse, A. R. (1978). Mental rotations, a group test of three-dimensional spatial visualization. *Perceptual and Motor Skills, 47,* 599–604. doi:10.2466/ pms.1978.47.2.599

VandenBos, G. R. (2015). *APA dictionary of psychology* (2nd ed.). Washington, DC: American Psychological Association.

Van Manen, K.-J., & Whitbourne, S. K. (1997). Psychosocial development and life experiences in adulthood: A 22-year sequential study. *Psychology and Aging, 12,* 239–246. doi:10.1037/0882-7974.12.2.239

Verbiest, M. E. A., Chavannes, N. H., Crone, M. R., Nielen, M. M. J., Segaar, D., Korevaar, J. C., & Assendelft, W. J. J. (2013). An increase in primary care prescriptions of stop-smoking medication as a result of health insurance coverage in the Netherlands: Population based study. *Addiction, 108,* 2183–2192. doi:10.1111/add.12289

Vyse, S. (1997). *Believing in magic: The psychology of superstition.* New York, NY: Oxford University Press.

Wagner, T. (2010). The fraction of missing information as a tool for monitoring the quality of survey data. *Public Opinion Quarterly, 74,* 223–243. doi:10.1093/poq/nfq007

Waksman, N. (2015). *Love in the time of graduation: Exploring the identity development of college seniors in romantic relationships* (Unpublished honors thesis). Connecticut College, New London, CT.

Wallston, K. A., Wallston, B. S., & DeVellis, R. (1978). Development of the Multidimensional Health Locus of Control (MHLC) Scales. *Health Education Monographs, 6,* 160–170.

Wason, P. C. (1966). Reasoning. In B. Foss (Ed.), *New horizons in psychology* (pp. 135–151). Harmondsworth, England: Penguin Books.

Wason, P. C. (1968). Reasoning about a rule. *Quarterly Journal of Experimental Psychology, 20,* 273–281. doi:10.1080/14640746808400161

Watson, D., & Friend, R. (1969). Measurement of social-evaluative anxiety. *Journal of Consulting and Clinical Psychology, 33,* 448–457. doi:10.1037/h0027806

Wendt, D. C., & Gone, J. P. (2012). Decolonizing psychological inquiry in American Indian communities: The promise of qualitative methods. In D. K. Nagata, L. Kohn-Wood, & L. A. Suzuki (Eds.), *Qualitative strategies for ethnocultural research* (pp. 161–178). Washington, DC: American Psychological Association.

Wertz, F. J. (2011). The qualitative revolution and psychology: Science, politics, and ethics. *The Humanistic Psychologist, 39,* 77–104. doi:10.1080 /08873267.2011.564531

Wheeler, T. B., & Cohn, M. (2014, June 7). Lead-paint lawsuits dog Kennedy Krieger. Retrieved from http://articles. baltimoresun.com/2014-06-07/ health/bs-hs-lead-lawsuit-new-20140607_1_kennedy-krieger-institute-children-study

Whitehead, T. L. (2005). *Basic classical ethnographic research methods* (Ethnographically informed community and cultural assessment research systems (EICCARS) working paper series). College Park, MD: University of Maryland. Retrieved from http://www.cusag.umd.edu/documents/working papers/classicalethnomethods.pdf

Wilkinson, S. (2000). Women with breast cancer talking causes: Comparing content, biographical and discursive analyses. *Feminism & Psychology, 10,* 431–460. doi:10.1177/0959353500010004003

Wilkinson, S. (2003). Focus groups. In J. A. Smith (Ed.), *Qualitative psychology: A practical guide to research methods* (pp. 184–204). Thousand Oaks, CA: Sage.

Williams, J. G. L., & Ouren, L. H. (1976). Experimenting on humans. *Bulletin of the British Psychological Society, 29,* 334–338.

Williams, M., & McCarthy, B. (2014). *Self-esteem measure* [Database record]. Retrieved from PsycTESTS. doi:10.1037/t43643-000

Witt, E. A., Donnellan, M. B., & Orlando, M. J. (2011). Timing and selection effects within a psychology subject pool: Personality and sex matter. *Personality and Individual Differences, 50,* 355–359. doi:10.1016/j.paid.2010.10.019

Woodzicka, J. A., & LaFrance, M. (2001). Real versus imagined gender harassment. *Journal of Social Issues, 57*(1), 15–30. doi:10.1111/0022-4537.00199

Wright, J. C., Zakriski, A. L., Hartley, A. G., & Parad, H. (2011). Reassessing the assessment of change in at-risk youth: Conflict and coherence in overall versus contextual assessment of behavior. *Journal of the Psychopathology and Behavioral Assessment, 33,* 215–227. doi:10.1007/s10862-011-9233-x

Yanos, P. T., & Ziedonis, D. M. (2006). The patient-oriented clinician-researcher: Advantages and challenges of being a double agent. *Psychiatric Services, 57,* 249–253. doi:10.1176/appi.ps.57.2.249

Zakriski, A. L., Wright, J. C., & Underwood, M. K. (2005). Gender similarities and differences in children's social behavior: Finding personality in contextualized patterns of adaptation. *Journal of*

Personality and Social Psychology, 88, 844–855. doi:10.1037/0022-3514.88.5.844

Zeisel, J. (1981). *Inquiry by design: Tools for environment-behavior research.* Monterey, CA: Brooks/Cole.

Zijlstra, W. P., Van der Ark, L. A., & Sijtsma, K. (2011). Outliers in questionnaire data: Can they be detected and should they be removed? *Journal of Educational and Behavioral Statistics, 36,* 186–212. doi:10.3102/10769986 1036663

Zimring, C., & Reizenstein, J. (1980). Post-occupancy evaluation: An overview. *Environment & Behavior, 12,* 429–250. doi:10.1177/0013916580124002

Zuckerman, M., Eysenck, S. B., & Eysenck, H. J. (1978). Sensation seeking in England and America: Cross-cultural, age, and sex comparisons. *Journal of Consulting and Clinical Psychology, 46,* 139–149. doi:10.1037/0022-006X.46.1.139

Zuckerman, M., & Lubin, B. (1965). *Manual for the multiple affect adjective checklist.* San Diego, CA: Educational and Industrial Testing Service.

NAME INDEX

SUBJECT INDEX